22735

THE BEST IN

THEOLOGY

VOLUME TWO

GENERAL EDITOR
J. I. Packer

EDITOR
Paul Fromer

AREA EDITORS

Old Testament: Bruce Waltke
New Testament: Harold W. Hoehner
Church History: Nathan Hatch
Systematic Theology: David F. Wells
Ethics/Spiritual Life: Klaus Bockmuehl
Pastoral Psychology and Counseling: David G. Benner
Missions: C. Peter Wagner
Homiletics: Haddon W. Robinson
Christian Education: Kenneth O. Gangel

Carol Stream, Illinois

Library
Oakland S.U.M.

22753

THE BEST IN THEOLOGY

Published by Christianity Today, Inc.
Distributed by Word, Inc.

Administrative Editor: Marty L. White
Cover Design: Dwight Walles

All rights reserved. Except for brief quotations in reviews, no part of this book may be reproduced in any form or transmitted in any form or by any means, electronic or mechanical, including photocopy, recording, or any information storage and retrieval system without written permission from the authors.
All articles reprinted by permission.
Library of Congress Catalog Card Number

LC 87-640275

Printed in the United States of America

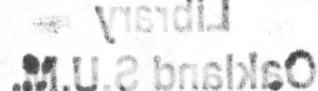
Library
Oakland S.U.M.

CONTENTS

4

Section 3: CHURCH HISTORY

Section 4: SYSTEMATIC THEOLOGY

Section 5: ETHICS/SPIRITUAL LIFE

6

Section 9: PRACTICAL THEOLOGY/CHRISTIAN EDUCATION

EDITOR'S PREFACE

PAUL W. FROMER
Associate Professor of English, Wheaton College
Deputy Editor, CHRISTIANITY TODAY

Picture yourself in a book-lined living room of an evening. The flicker from burning oak logs draws out the carpet's russet tones. Lamplight touches the brooding features of Rembrandt's Aristotle and softens the contours of the sofa and four comfortable chairs drawn up for this night of nights—an evening to be invested in the art of conversation.

You reflect with pleasure on the visitors soon to gather to evaluate new ways to interpret the Bible: Tremper Longman III, from Westminster, an expert on literary approaches; and Donn Morgan, an Episcopalian, who will want to discuss canonical criticism. Craig Blomberg, from Denver Seminary, will have a lot to say on the Synoptics (are Christ's temptation accounts fiction?). And, from the University of Michigan, Gary Herion has been concentrating on ways we read post-industrial times back into OT history with some iffy results.

And you are there with them—Bible open—questioning, comparing, commenting, seeking with them shafts of divine light.

Just such dialogues are a purpose of *The Best in Theology*. No mere fancy, they are a way to view the reading of this volume. Think of yourself as one entering into The Great Conversation, aided by the authors of this year's select articles. They engage thinkers from across the continents and down the ages. With their aid, you enter into discussion with Samuel, Paul, Augustine, Aquinas, Calvin, and with men and women of our century—Christian or not—who have interacted with the world's most absorbing ideas: those that deal with love and hate, God and Satan, worship and self-preoccupation, freedom and slavery, self-discovery and self-rejection, society and the individual, leadership and anarchy.

This book gives one the chance to read, compare, evaluate, and decide about issues not trivial but enduring. The articles printed here were nominated by nine area editors, scholars of proven judgment. They first read widely in their particular field, and then composed a "long list" of articles of merit that covered well the subdivisions of current interest. To the area editors' list the research of the editors made some additions. Editorial give-and-take followed, resulting in a "short list" for each discipline.

Taken together, these short lists contained perhaps fifty pieces. A final editorial judgment was then made, taking into account any recommendations of the area editors, the relative quality of the different articles, the current concerns of the Christian world, the interests of the intended readers, the editorial balance displayed by the total list, and the limits of space.

An area might, in this year's volume, receive more space than it would in another year, because this happens to be its year of gold rather than silver; every area does not produce articles of the same high quality in every year. We do, however, begin with certain space assignments. The fields of OT, NT, church history, systematic theology, and ethics/Christian life are allotted sixty pages each; practical theology, composed of four areas, receives a total of eighty pages. Adjustments are then made according to article strength in each area. Church history articles during 1987, for instance, tending to be highly technical, were less helpful to the nonspecialist, so that area received fewer pages. Ethics/Christian life, on the other hand, was bursting with excellent, applicable articles, so this year it received more pages.

Readers of last year's volume may recall that a 200-page volume was originally projected. So many valuable articles were uncovered, however, and the range of interesting thought in some areas was so great, that we doubled the size of the book to over 400 pages. We have maintained this length, while changing the proportions as appropriate. The thoroughness of the process is seen in the hundreds of hours invested by area editors, and the equivalent of a dozen forty-hour weeks by the editor. The general editor oversaw the process, and made sure it produced the finest selection of articles.

But the resulting selections only start the ball rolling. Consider this scenario: We read an article—perhaps Gary Herion's—suggesting that, contrary to much in-vogue thinking, the prophets had the capacity for independent, creative thought, and were not always mouthpieces for established social groups. Then we begin to question: Are the views of social determinism that are popular among many theologians all that appropriate for understanding, say, Samuel, in a premonarchic, pre-urban society? In fact, what are the values and limits of determinism in describing society today?

Now suppose we turn to a new article and find that we have shifted from certain views in sociology to certain views in literature. Is biblical history better understood by looking at its literary qualities? Where do we draw the line, or is biblical history really historicized fiction?

Immediately the word "interdisciplinary" jumps to mind. Both sociology and literature can help us understand the Bible since the Bible deals with societies, and is itself written down. Articles chosen for *The Best in Theology* help us tap a wide variety of disciplines. Selections report on current thinking, and help us sort out the profitable insights.

Of course, this year's articles deal with many other topics than hermeneutics: One article, for example, concerns the absence of God from our immediate, inner awareness, as Christian psychologists see it (Underwood), and as Christian mystics see it (Feiss). Another studies the giving (versus getting) nature of God (Wright on Phil. 2), and the giving habits of godly men and women based on the will of such a God (Mason on biblical guidelines for aiding the poor).

Other articles explore the conundrums, past and present, of caring for the ill (the entire church history section, dealing with Roman Catholic and Protestant theory and practice). And this leads to the recent, extensive Vatican statement on bioethics, including surrogate fertilization. This in turn spills over into First Amendment effects on religion, and the place of political leverage (Berman). The scientific side of medicine calls up the singularly lucid article (Wood) surveying fifty years of brain research, primarily with epileptics, and the stirring shifts from materialism toward views much more consonant with Christian theology.

Range continues to strengthen the selections in *The Best in Theology*. One woman, a lawyer, is joined by her husband, a pastoral counselor, to write on malpractice suits (Melinda and Thomas Denham). Three articles are by Roman Catholics: Hugh Feiss of Mount Angel Seminary, Marvin O'Connell of the University of Notre Dame, and Pope John Paul II in the "Instruction" on bioethics from the Congregation for the Doctrine of the Faith.

In all, fourteen seminaries, one Christian college, one graduate school, and five universities are represented.

The area editors range from Bruce Waltke at Westminster Theological Seminary, and David Wells at Gordon-Conwell Theological Seminary in the East; to Nathan Hatch at the University of Notre Dame, David Benner at Wheaton College, and Haddon Robinson at Denver Seminary in the Midwest; to Peter Wagner at Fuller Theological Seminary in the West; and from Klaus Bockmuehl at Regent College in Canada; to Harold Hoehner and Kenneth Gangel at Dallas Theological Seminary in Texas. Articles come from two continents, and are written by twenty-three authors.

How were the articles chosen? Bruce Waltke, area editor in OT, again asked editors of about 150 journals of OT and Semitics to nominate their best article of the past year. Peter Wagner, a new area editor, worked with a board of reference of missionaries and missiologists from around the country. Other area editors have been diligently reading widely and have informally consulted colleagues.

In keeping with the worldwide character of the book, we have used the linguistic distinctives and policies of documentation normal to the individual authors. To interpret the characteristic abbreviations for journals in footnotes, please consult the appropriate issue of the journal carrying the article in question. Sometimes the same initials stand for different sources in different journals.

In light of our view of The Great Conversation, no attempt has been made to reconcile the various positions presented. We view all the material as stimulating to the intended readers, and hope for more light than heat as ideas rub against one another.

To help the reader see the larger framework into which the diversity of articles finds a natural home, J. I. Packer has written an introduction integrating theology, spirituality, hermeneutics, and communication under the umbrella of "faith seeking understanding."

The administrative editor, Marty White, typed, proofread, watched over deadlines, and saw to the organizational flow of work, while two editors of CHRISTIANITY TODAY, Terry Muck and Harold Smith, provided valuable advice. Karla Anderson worked with the typesetting, and Carolyn Barry oversaw production. These behind-the-scenes workers have my sincere thanks.

Editing this volume has given me a special opportunity to work with the area editors, whom I consulted at length over a six-month period in determining the emerging character of the volume. Discussions with them on the best articles to choose from among the hundreds published gave opportunity for a good deal of interaction on the nature of the church today, the strengths and weaknesses of evangelicalism, and on the integration of current thought with the history of Christian doctrine. Some are working in areas where little notable material is being published. Others deal with areas that are in tremendous flux, with no fixed pattern emerging. But all have been eager to advise and to work patiently with the materials available.

The church gives little note to its workers in theology—a legacy, no doubt, of the deep suspicion with which scholarship has been regarded by many evangelicals over the past fifty or seventy-five years. This hits hardest at systematic theology, which correlates all other branches. But it also makes more difficult the attempt to study out the new fields—ones with little evangelical base prior to World War II—such as psychology. It is to be hoped that Christ's command to "love the Lord your God with all your . . . mind" will continue to engage the young, who are now preparing in the colleges and seminaries for further service, and are lured by an emphasis on experience shorn from theology that often carries with it little sturdy thought. We need original, God-sensitive thinkers whose minds are tempered in the knowledge of the past. We need bridge builders who can bring the once-for-allness of the gospel to the turbulence of current thought, and claim entire disciplines for the Christ of Scripture.

The area editors are leaders in that exalted task, and deserve special support as they do theology to God's glory.

About the Editor

Paul W. Fromer (B.S., in Chemistry, Syracuse University; graduate work in the Ph.D. program, California Institute of Technology; M.Div., Fuller Theological Seminary; M.A., Wheaton College) is associate professor of English, Wheaton College. He has been deputy editor of CHRISTIANITY TODAY since 1979. He was staff member (1954–57) and area director (1957–60) for InterVarsity

Christian Fellowship in Southern California. He was editor of *His* magazine from 1960 to 1971. His books, co-authored with Margaret Fromer, include one on Colossians, *Putting Christ First* (1986); and *A Woman's Workshop on Philippians* (1982).

INTRODUCTION

J. I. PACKER
General Editor, *The Best in Theology*
Professor of Historical and Systematic Theology
Regent College

I.

"Good reading!" With those words I closed my introduction to the first issue of CHRISTIANITY TODAY's annual, *The Best in Theology*, published at the close of 1986. I expressed that wish with confidence, in light of the quality of the material in the book. The contents of this second volume seem to me to warrant the same wish, expressed perhaps with even greater confidence. Old-time circus ringmasters must have felt good when they knew they had a set of fine acts to introduce, and in the same way I feel good about presenting the selections that our editor and subject editors have come up with. Going through them has been pleasant and profitable to me, and will, I think, be so to many others also.

Who is the ideal reader of these skimmings from the dozens of theological journals and occasional writings that the English-speaking Christian world has produced? He or she is a Christian leader of today or tomorrow—maybe a member of a church's pastoral staff; or a teacher of theology who lacks time to read systematically in all the relevant fields (that's me, folks); or a layperson who periodically gives courses to an adult Sunday school class; or just a thoughtful reader of CHRISTIANITY TODAY who wants to go further into some areas of exploration and debate than CT itself can take them. A book of prayers for schools was published in England under the sassy title *Well, God, Here We Are Again*. Put *Leaders* for *God*, and you would have a good title for this present collection.

What sort of diet is there here for readers to feed on? It is one that is nourishing, balanced, and even of gourmet character. The nourishment is secured by eliminating the unimportant; everything is stimulating and weighty, and items that tackle the trivial and major in minors do not appear. The balance flows from the fact that all the main theological disciplines, theoretical and practical, historical and contemporary, abstract and applied, are represented. The gourmet aspect is a reflection of the discerning palates of the editors, who offer to others only material that they value themselves. No one person could ransack with discrimination all the publications from which these selections come; even a rapid reader with total recall, like C. H. Spurgeon or C. S. Lewis (yes, few know it, but both had this gift) would have found the task too great, for lack of the width of technical learning that sound evaluation requires. So readers owe deep gratitude to our team of experts, each of whom took time and trouble to cream off the best in his own field. In ensuring that only the most relevant and significant material finds its way into this book they have served us all well.

Leaders in ministry are constantly assailed by two temptations. One is to rely on experience for their resources and never to read serious theology at all. The other is to treat the opinions of any professional theologians as definitive, on the grounds that these are the men who know most. Maybe they are, but knowing facts is no guarantee of sound and spiritual judgment. Of one modern pundit it was said, by a godly man I knew, "There must be something wrong with his theology: you can't pray it."

A damaging criticism? Yes, that is the most damaging that could possibly be brought. The pundit in question was formidably learned, but lacked spiritual judgment entirely, and that is a defect readers of theologians must watch out for. Never read theology uncritically! I remember how upset I felt (though I tried not to show it) when an English pastor, wanting to be friendly, told me that he liked my writing because I did his thinking for him. That is the last thing I ever wanted to do, for him or anyone else! The truth is that both temptations ought to be resisted, and the way to resist them is by the discipline of thoughtful reading, letting the experts state their case and then asking oneself whether one agrees, and if so why, and if not why not—in other words, by training and exercising one's own judgment. Older, pre-Dewey pedagogic theory recognized that good judgment, analytical, critical, and applicatory, is of the essence of being educated, and modern psychological theory (not to say, common sense!) sees it as a necessary mark of a mature person; and judgment, like muscle tone, becomes and stays good through steady exercise. One of the purposes of this collection is to further that process.

I called the material "relevant and significant"; what do those words mean? I was using them to mean valuable, in both the short and long term, for the churchly tasks of education, evangelism, nurture, pastoral care, prophetic witness, and visionary leadership, to which officers and functionaries in each congregation are called. These items not only tell us what is being currently discussed in the schools, but they also challenge us to think hard about what we should be saying and doing in our ministry. The idea that what Christian academics are debating is not relevant to the front-line worker is unwarranted in principle and pernicious in practice, since it shields the pastor from challenges to the truth and integrity of what he projects that he needs to face. The goals of academic discussion, however recondite its immediate theme, are always truth and integrity, and when I spoke of the relevance and significance of this material I meant that I saw it as calculated to advance both.

II. UNDERSTANDING

Some years ago I visited a Texas town the London Philharmonic Orchestra was also visiting, and after sitting entranced through as good performances of Weber's *Freischutz* overture, Strauss's *Don Juan*, and Beethoven's *Eroica* as I have ever heard, I was whisked off to a hundred-dollar-a-plate buffet disco that had been laid on to finance the orchestra's visit. There a thrustful rock group (him and her bawling vocals, and them banging drums and electric guitars) provided music that was so loudly amplified you could make known what food you wanted only by pointing to it.

I continue to recall in detail and with delight the taut intensity with which the conductor (Tennstedt) made the British orchestra play its program, but all I can remember of the disco is the awesome noise level, and some of the food, and the grave grin that kept flitting over the face of my friend and host, whose Young Life background has thoroughly prepared him to savor life's unintended humor wherever he finds it.

Applying this, now, to the matter in hand, I want all readers of this book to get from it the sort of absorbed enjoyment that I had from the LPO rather than to be swamped by the articles as I was by the disco. I don't want folk to feel out of their depth, and therefore limit themselves to reading one or two items of immediate interest, and to dismiss the rest as what Winnie-the-Pooh's friend Eeyore called a Confused Noise. So I devote the rest of my introduction to attempting to avert this disaster.

Is there a unifying theme, or focus of concern, that gives a vantage point from which to survey this wide range of material and to see it all as a single whole? Yes, I think so. The unifying theme could be called *understanding*, and the vantage point may be pictured as a mountain rising from a plain—let us call it Mount Wisdom—on which are three adjacent peaks. Two of the peaks are *theology* and *spirituality*, both of which provide a view of all parts of the plain; the third is a broad-topped, boulder-strewn summit, one side of which is called *communication* and the other *hermeneutics*. You have to re-cross this third summit constantly, to and fro, in order to get a synoptic awareness of the total landscape that surrounds you. Let me explain.

Faith seeks understanding: that is the starting-point. A popular evangelistic book for boys in my youth was *The Questions of Jack Wantoknow*; well, every real believer is Jack Wantoknow in person. God made us thinking beings with inquiring minds, and wherever our interest is aroused it is our nature to ask questions of the "what" and "why" and "how" sort. Faith, which is essentially belief expressed in trust, rests on a more-or-less clear perception that what is believed is guaranteed by the authority of God himself, the Creator revealed as Redeemer in the history of Israel, in the person of Jesus Christ, and in the pages of Holy Scripture. Noncognitive analyses of faith that reduce it to a form of the religious feeling or instinct that humans are born with have long been popular, and in some quarters still are. But (as, thank

God, is increasingly being seen) these analyses, though they may work with Christian symbols, actually reduce faith to natural religion and strain all that is distinctively Christian out of it. Christian faith always was a cognitive and volitional response to revelation, grasped as such, and always will be, whatever the more wayward sort of theorists may say.

But now, the point is this: there is no personal faith in God, the God who is Father, Son, and Holy Spirit, without personal interest in God, interest based on perceiving (again, more or less clearly, and sometimes quite smudgily) that we were made to know and love him, and do in fact need him. So if professed Christians fail to ask "what-why-how" questions about God's relation to them and to the rest of his creation, and about behavior that will please and displease him—if, in other words, understanding and gratifying their heavenly Father out of gratitude for grace received is not their continual concern—then something is seriously wrong. Either they are backslidden, their love having grown cold, or they are spiritually stunted, having gone without the spiritual counterpart of food, fresh air, and exercise, or they lack faith despite their profession of it. There is no fourth alternative. For if they were genuine believers, genuinely healthy at heart, they would be seeking understanding all the time.

Naturally, real believers look to their leaders to help them learn about God and godliness, and leaders need resources for the task, just as they do for their own spiritual growth. Where are they to look? The ultimate source is, of course, the Bible itself; but elucidating and applying the Bible, and stockpiling the prudential wisdom that is needed for living out its application in the most fruitful way (the model here is Proverbs), is a corporate enterprise involving the whole church. We are to learn, as we are to live, not as self-sufficient Lone Rangers, but in the give-and-take, to-and-fro, let-us-share of Christian community. That means constantly exchanging ideas and offering hypotheses (educated guesses) for evaluation by others: it means discussion, debate, books, and journals, as means of pursuing the goal of enlarged understanding. *Fides quaerens intellectum*—faith seeking *understanding*—was Anselm's description of his *Proslogion*, in which he formulated his ontological argument for God's existence. All Christian study, however, could truly bear that title.

The quest for understanding never ends, either for the individual Christian or the church. Healthy believers keep learning, gaining greater depth and breadth of understanding than they had, ripening their insight into what they did not know well enough before. The church constantly finds itself facing new questions as it moves through history into new cultural and socio-economic conditions. History neither stands still nor repeats itself, and the church belongs to its flow. However many specific similarities to past situations may appear at any one time, God's people in every generation are traveling a road of which it may be said, as Joshua said to the Israelites preparing to cross Jordan, "You have never been this way before" (Josh. 3:4).

By road and trail one can completely circle round the majestic bulk of Mount Rainier in Washington, though it takes many hours to do; but one can never find a viewing point on the circuit from which one can see the whole mountain from all sides and catch in a single gaze its entire glory. So it is with Scripture in the church: no single generation ever sees all that is in it, and every next generation, viewing it from a different place on the high road of history, sees aspects of its teaching that the previous generation missed. The way Scripture opens up to us depends on the questions we bring to it, or allow it to suggest that we ask, and fresh times raise fresh questions. (This is similar, for instance, to the questions concerning stewardship of the environment, which were forced on Christians two decades ago by man's rape of the Earth, never having been asked before because the need to ask them had not yet arisen.) Under pressure from the new questions, new understanding—that is, enlarged and deepened understanding, at least at the frontiers of thought—has constantly to be sought, and is, in fact, constantly found.

It is as part of this quest for adequate contemporary understanding of God's revelation as it applies to life that the triple focus on theology, spirituality, and hermeneutics fits in.

Theology

Take theology first of these three. The word expresses the thought of discourse about God, as we know, and since the twelfth century it has been used as an umbrella word to cover the whole range of Christian truth and all the disciplines involved in investigating it. (Previously, it had been used to signify the doctrine of God only, and the Western church had used Augustine's terms, *wisdom* and *true philosophy*, as its umbrella words.) In the theological schools of the thirteenth century, linked as they were to the new universities of Europe, much was made of the claim that theology was a science (*scientia*, that is, a field of tested knowledge), and was, in fact, the queen of the sciences, in the sense that all other studies were theology's handmaids, over which she exercised directive control.

Today, no branch of science (natural, historical, or human) accepts any form of theological control; can the claim of queenship be maintained, then, in any form at all? Surely it can, in this sense: that when the sciences have made their "first-order" descriptive statements, giving their account of the matters of fact they have investigated, theology may then enter to make "second-order" interpretative statements, declaring how God stands related to all these facts, and into what frame of his purposes they fit—so far, at least, as the biblical revelation will justify such declarations. (That qualification is important, for often Scripture does not give us much to say about particular scientific facts; theology must practice modesty at all times and not overplay its hand.) Because theology may not dictate methodologies to the sciences nor prescribe the conclusions of any scientific investigations, it has been suggested that rather than "queen," theology should be designated "first lady-in-waiting"! But "queen," understood as pointing to theology's prerogative of relating all the findings of the sciences to God, remains appropriate.

Theology is an activity of thought (theologizing) out of which emerge orthodoxies of belief (Wesley's theology, say, or Barth's, or the "church doctrine" of this or that). Theology's goal is to know and tell the truth, all the truth we have, about God. That truth includes not only the full biblical revelation of God's work, will, and ways, but also the biblical teaching on our communion with God, which is the subject matter of spirituality, and on God's communication with us (mode and content, and their interrelation), which is the theme of hermeneutics. From one standpoint, the second and third of these three items belong to the first; theology, the highest and most dizzy-making peak of Mount Wisdom, is a vantage point giving a view of the other two peaks, as well as of all the country around. From another standpoint, however, spirituality and hermeneutics are studies which, though informed by theology throughout, have their own distinctive angles of vision and interest, as we shall shortly see, and something is lost if they are not treated separately.

The activity of theology is a discharging of four interrelated tasks. *First* comes the receptive task of noting, and with teachable humility embracing, all that God makes known in Scripture about what he has done, is doing, and intends to do, and about the relation in which he stands to everything that the Bible mentions. *Second* is the critical task of relating historic Christian positions and proposals to the biblical witness, both for the interpretative help they give in understanding it and for the corrective adjustment that Scripture may show they need. *Third* is the applicatory task of drawing guidance from the revealed values, plans, and commands of God for the living of contemporary life, along with the parallel exercise of relating revealed truth about the world to what secular philosophy and science say about it. Note that this latter exercise involves much critical cross-questioning ("Does the Bible *really* teach this?" and "Does empirical data *really* warrant that?"), and that no proposed correlations can be more solid than the biblical and philosophico-scientific reasonings that they bring together are in themselves. Then, *fourth* is the communicative task of finding ways to state what has been learned so that it edifies believers, instructs unbelievers, corrects distorted notions, and rebuts anti-Christian arguments. In good theology all four activities find a place.

To illustrate this analysis, consider two of the items in our collection. Bruce Ware's reformulation of divine immutability is exegesis (task one, listening to Scripture) angled to correct both the Thomist idea, largely echoed by Protestant scholastics, that God exists in intrinsic immobility, relating to his world by thought alone, and also the Process view that what we call God grows and develops within what we call his world (task two). Ware clearly wants us to see the Creator's changelessness as undergirding rather than diminishing his religious adequacy and availability, so we may say that

Ware has his eye on tasks three and four also, though limits of space keep him from going very far with them. (But thoughtful readers will be able to work it all out for themselves!) Lawrence Wood's discussion, however, of the way to theologize the results of research into how the human mind correlates with the left and right halves of the brain, is a bold plunge into task three. Starting from the new apparent certainty that the mind is more than a brain state (in other words, my thinking and yours is more than an accidental by-product of electro-chemical happenings in our bodies), Wood asks how the relation of mind to body and of both to God should be conceived. His preference of the Augustinian (neo-Platonist) to the Thomist (Aristotelian) view of the mind-body relation, and of the semi-Pelagian to the Augustinian view of how God the Lord relates to our thinking and choosing, will not carry everyone with it, particularly since no exegetical support is offered on either point. But reflective readers will find that this article, like the other, throws precious light on what it means to be a human individual under God, and that question is right at the heart of the understanding that faith seeks.

Spirituality

The second of Mount Wisdom's three peaks, spirituality, is bracketed with ethics in this book. There is good reason for that. Both fields of study have to do directly with the Christian life, ethics with its moral standards and spirituality with its essential nature as a relationship with God. Each is, from its own point of view, a department of theology, called in its own sphere to fulfill the same fourfold task that was described above as belonging to theology generically. Each, too, has been marked by a variety of emphases and expository traditions within its own history, diverging and converging in ways that constantly fascinate. In relation to the understanding that faith seeks, spirituality is central and focal in a way that ethics is not; the standards are for the furthering of the relationship rather than vice versa. Yet without the righteousness that ethics delineates, one cannot please God, so ethics remains a vital study.

The business of Christian ethics is to fix standards by reference to God's character, creation, and commands, and all its practitioners labor at this task; but they are not at one as to how they use these sources. Strong in both pre- and post-Reformation ethics has been the idea of natural law; that is, a set of values and imperatives rationally discerned by observing and reflecting on the nature of things. In Roman Catholicism, natural law has characteristically been seen as part of the natural theology that is held to provide a framework and foundation, and thus, in effect, a control, for supernatural revelation. Not all accept this theory! Strong as a counter to such thinking has been the categorically biblical elucidation of ethics practiced by the Reformers, the Puritan, Lutheran and Reformed pietists, and Barth, Bonhoeffer, Brunner, Niebuhr, and other neo-orthodox thinkers of this century. Among these latter-day biblicists a further division has appeared between those who equate the command of God with general principles of conduct unshelled from God's directives recorded in Scripture and reapplied to our present-day circumstances, and those like Barth and many self-styled radicals, contextualists, and situationists, who dismiss the idea of general principles and reach their ethical norms in some more roundabout way. Mason's article, however, on poor relief follows the mainstream biblical method, while the notable Instruction on biomedical ethics promulgated by the Pope (who thus for the first time becomes an author in a CT publication) relies largely on tradition, and at one crucial point on the natural law concept of the "proper perfection" of human sexual activity.

Spirituality (also called ascetic, moral, devotional, and mystical theology) embraces all that is involved in mapping, inducing, expressing, diagnosing, deepening, strengthening, and enriching that personal communion with God which we call spiritual life and the New Testament calls eternal life. Often nowadays the term is used in a secular sense, in which it means no more (and no less) than the cultivation and expression of the human spirit in any frame of religion or value whatever. But the proper definition of spirituality and spiritual life is in terms of God's Holy Spirit who quickens our dead souls. There has never been a time when the streams of tradition now called Western Catholic and Eastern Orthodox bypassed spirituality, but strangely and sadly Protestants have neglected this study for nearly three centuries, ever since the great days of Pietism in Europe and New England. Only in our own generation has Protestant technical spirituality wakened up in Rip van Winkle style from its very long sleep; so naturally it lacks as yet the maturity and poise, not to say depth, of its Roman Catholic counterpart. And no one should be surprised to find that Merton, Nouwen, and the medievals have pride of place on the bookshelves of many present-day evangelicals who want to know God better. Nor should it cause surprise if the best material on spirituality in a volume like this turns out to be by Roman Catholics.

What have we here on spirituality? Quite a lot. The treatment of mysticism by Feiss is spirituality; so are the historical studies by O'Connell and Ferngren on living with sickness and ministering to the unwell; so is Underwood's article on our sensations of the presence and absence of God; and the implications for spirituality of the theological and ethical articles already mentioned are large and weighty. Indeed, any theological writing of a catechetical sort, earthing itself in application to life, is from one point of view spirituality. From this standpoint, all the writings of Tertullian, Origen, Athanasius, Augustine, Luther, Wesley, and John Owen are spirituality; so are Calvin's *Institutio*, and the Westminster Confession, and Thomas's *Summa Theologiae*, and even the vast sprawl of Barth's *Dogmatics*. And when someone said to me, "All your books are spirituality really, aren't they?" I had to agree with him, though for twenty-five years I had been writing them without that thought ever occurring to me. Anything written to answer the question How may we live our lives in fellowship with God? will be spirituality, though in order to be that it will have to be theology and ethics too. But the question of fellowship with God really is the second focus of interest in faith's quest for understanding, and wise writers on theology and ethics, not to mention liturgy, missiology, and pastoral themes, will always keep it in view.

Hermeneutics and Communication

I described the third peak of Mount Wisdom as a broad, boulder-strewn summit called *hermeneutics* on one side and *communication* on the other, from no point on which could you see the whole landscape. I was not just being whimsical for the fun of it; that is how faith actually experiences the third focal area in which, naturally and instinctively, it seeks understanding. Here is the experiential analysis.

First, *hermeneutics*. Believers know that their communicator-God addresses his word—that is, his message—to them in the sixty-six books of Holy Scripture, and that the message concerns new life in and through Jesus Christ. Having heard some part of this message already and found fellowship with Christ through it, they now want to receive as much more of it as they can. But the canonical books that comprise the Book in which the message is embodied are products of a series of ancient Near Eastern cultures, not identical with each other, and are all (at surface level, anyhow) very different from the scientific, technological, materialistic, comfort-loving, optimistic, sentimental, urbanized, unstable, post-Christian culture of which today's believers are part. Also, the Book unfolds its theme of humanity in God's hands for weal or woe in a way that fallen minds cannot naturally receive in any form. So to ensure that God's word is heard and not misheard, a threefold discipline must be maintained. Texts must be studied by the historical-critical method, so that we grasp what they meant historically as messages to the humans the writers envisaged as their readers. The principles for doing this constitute *hermeneutics* in the classical (seventeenth-century) sense. Also, the differences between the modern and biblical-period mindsets must be studied in depth, lest applicatory insight into what these messages mean for us becomes derailed through oversights arising from our modern perspective. The habit of doing this constitutes *hermeneutics* in a further contemporary (twentieth-century) sense. Last, constant prayer must be made for spiritual insight in the sense of true realization of God's reality, and of one's own real dependence on him for knowledge, for grace, and indeed for existence itself, and of the specific instruction that he is addressing to one via one's present biblical study. (In hermeneutics it is always specific questions and instructions that call for attention.) The items in this book by Longman, Blomberg, Morgan, Herion, and Wright will all be found to have a place in advancing our hermeneutical endeavors.

Second, *communication*. Believers know themselves to be called to pass on the good news they have received; they are to express their sense of its preciousness not only by praising God for it, but also by proclaiming it to the world. In a hymn written "For the Anniversary Day of One's Conversion," Charles Wesley juxtaposed these well-known verses: "O for a thousand tongues to sing / My great Redeemer's praise; / The glories of my God and King, / The triumphs of his grace!" That is praise; and now—"My gracious Master and my God, / Assist me to proclaim, / And spread through all the earth abroad, / The honors of thy name." But such communication requires hermeneutical skills once more, for the truth must be told in such a way that it can be truly heard and recognized as God's message to those to whom it comes, and not be misunderstood or misapplied. Here the material from White, Long, and Hiebert will bear pondering. Also, since the essence of pastoral care is feeding the flock on the word of God, and the essence of pastoral wisdom must therefore be structuring situations for this purpose, Segler's contribution should be weighed at this point.

May all readers of this collection find that it furthers faith's quest for understanding in their own lives.

Once again: Good reading!

About the General Editor

J. I. Packer (B.A., M.A., D.Phil., Oxford University) is professor of historical and systematic theology, Regent College (Vancouver, B.C., Canada). He was ordained by the Church of England, and now attends Saint John's (Anglican) Church, Shaughnessy, B.C. Many will have read several of his earlier books: *"Fundamentalism" and the Word of God* (1958); *Evangelism and the Sovereignty of God* (1961); and *Knowing God* (1973). A few of his recent books include *Your Father Loves You* (1986); (with Thomas Howard) *Christianity, the True Humanism* (1985); and *Keep in Step with the Spirit* (1984).

OLD TESTAMENT

Bruce Waltke, area editor

OLD TESTAMENT

BRUCE WALTKE
Professor of Old Testament
Westminster Theological Seminary

Introduction

In last year's editorial for the best articles in September 1985 to August 1986 this editor noted the trend for rhetorical and canonical criticisms to replace form and historical criticisms.[1] That trend continues. Thomas G. Long, introducing a collection of five essays aimed to show how theological pre-understandings affect the practice of biblical interpretation for *Theology Today* (1987), noted: "It now appears far more accurate to say that the historical-critical method, which is still very much in business, has been unseated as the only merchant in the central market place. Some point to the emergence of literary approaches to the Bible as evidence of a 'paradigm shift' away from historical and toward poetic approaches to biblical interpretation. Actually there has been a multiplication of 'paradigms' for biblical interpretation. Canonical criticism, structural exegesis, feminist criticism, sociological analysis, rhetorical criticism, and a variety of other approaches present an impressive, but confusing, array of methods and vantage points presently available to the interpreter."[2]

The cutting edge of Old Testament scholarship during this past year addresses the question of the relationship of these new approaches to history. The question of real history must be faced, for as the new editor of *Theology Today*, Craig Dykstra, noted in his editorial, memory is vital to human life. "Without a narrative that sustains us," he wrote, "the world—and we ourselves—are virtually phantom. But the issue is not just whether one has narrative or not. The issue is whether we have one that is true and genuine, one that can sustain us in reality, one that, having been given it and having committed it to memory, frees us from desperately having to continue to make one up."[3] Moreover, the biblical narrative points not only to itself but to actual events. Robert L. Cohn wrote, "Everywhere biblical narrative indicates its intention to be history: the citing of sources, the relentless chronological order, and the oft-repeated command to remember the story and observe the laws all testify to historiographic claim."[4]

In this volume the editor features those articles that pertain to the new critical approaches mentioned by Long, especially those that relate these approaches to the question of history. In addition, he calls the reader's attention to new directions in Old Testament studies and to a few specialized articles he thinks will be of interest to them.

Regarding the new literary criticism that asserts that biblical prose fiction ranges along a spectrum from historicized fiction to fictionalized history, an approach that was given great impetus by Robert Alter's first book in biblical studies, *The Art of Biblical Narrative*, Cohn's article has already been mentioned. Stuart Lasine[5] provokes his readers with a profoundly philosophical and penetrating analysis of the recent trend in literary studies of biblical narrative to establish the meaning and function of indeterminacy in the Bible. Among other things he attacks deconstruction, "a mode of reading texts which subverts the implicit claim of a text to possess adequate grounds, in the system of language it deploys, to establish its structure, unite, and determine meanings." He also argues that "the concept of 'fiction', which posits an unbridgeable gap between textual world and life-world, is incompatible with the genre of Scripture. Tremper Longman III's study of the promise and pitfall of this new literary approach of the study of the Bible is selected here for republication because of its perspicacity, balance, and clarity.[6] Albert Cook,[7] applying the approach to Samuel-Kings, exhibits its promise.

Social criticism, also known as social analysis or social anthropology, oriented to generalizing law-like study of societies and to cross-cultural comparisons, is sometimes pitted against the historical critical approach, but in truth it supplements it. The editor selected, but could not print here, Keith M. Whitelam's essay, "Recreating the History of Israel,"[8] because Whitelam succinctly maps out the contours of this new approach to the Bible and, in addition, calls attention to the new archaeology[9] and the negative consequences of the new shifts in literary studies, structuralism, and canonical criticism to the historical credibility of the final text of the Hebrew Bible. To balance Whitelam's unduly negative evaluation of the biblical text and his overly positive evaluation of social analysis for the writing of the history of Israel, the editor is republishing here Gary A. Herion's penetrating analysis of "the four assumptions that sometimes play powerful roles when social science is used—positivism, reductionism, relativism, and determinism."[10] His critique will be helpful in appraising *Semeia* (an experimental journal for biblical criticism) 37 (1986), entitled "Social Scientific Criticism of the Hebrew Bible and its Social World: The Israelite Monarchy." Chris Hauer, Jr., profitably applies the approach to the rise of the Israelite state.[11]

The best article in rhetorical criticism is that of Wilhelm Wuellner.[12] He sees rhetorical criticism as at a cross-road: "We must choose," he writes, "between two competing versions of rhetorical criticism: the one in which rhetorical criticism is identical with literary criticism, the other in which rhetorical criticism is identical with practical criticism." The former restrains itself to analyzing the text's structure; the latter strives for a "rhetoric reevalued" (B. Vickers), "rhetoric reinvented" (T. Eagleton), or, as Wuellner desires: "a form of *activity* [italics original] inseparable from the wider social relations between writers and readers." He wants rhetorical criticism to take us beyond hermeneutics and structuralism. John Stek, in his literary analysis of Judges 4, presents his readers with a veritable classroom model of "restrained rhetorical criticism" at its best.[13]

Don Morgan makes canonical criticism delightfully palatable in his survey of that approach over the past six years since the publication of Child's seminal work.[14]

John W. Miller[15] effectively critiques the attempt by Phyllis Trible, a leading feminist critic, to demonstrate depatriarchalizing in biblical interpretation.[16] Interestingly, this editor[17] received many affirmative and no negative responses to his one-page essay in the debate on the women's issue.

Marvin E. Tate[18] and R. J. Coggins[19] present immensely useful summaries of the introductions to the Old Testament; unfortunately they have the feel of a survey of the secondary literature, rather than of original works in their own rights. In an essay entitled, "Farewell to JEDP?"[20] the editor of *Expository Times* calls his readers' attention to R. N. Whybray's current attack on the documentary hypothesis and on oral tradition.[21] This editor, independently from Whybray, also concluded that there is little evidence that the Pentateuchal narratives were formed and transmitted orally from ancient times.[22] Alan Millard[23] concludes that the knowledge of writing was widespread in ancient Israel.

Interpretation (July, 1987) offers expositors, who are able to look beyond the questions of authorship, a superb issue on the book of Deuteronomy. The *Concordia Journal*—13/3 (1987)—performs the same service for Esther. C. S. Rodd continues to seek out the best commentaries; this year for Job[24] and Jeremiah.[25] Eugene Merrill presents a very helpful series of articles on the background of Isa. 40—55.[26] Though committed to the unity of Isaiah, Merrill shows how the literary form of 2nd Isaiah would be at home in an exilic setting. F. F. Bruce, self-consciously identifying himself as an evangelical, dates Second Isaiah in the exile.[27] As a follow up to Crenshaw's article, republished in last year's *The Best in Theology*,[28] see now Nili Shupak's article[29] contending that "the first schools in Israel were inspired by an Egyptian prototype and that the Book of Proverbs served as a text in such schools." Gerald Wilson[30] advanced Psalm studies by noting the use of royal psalms at the 'seams' of the Hebrew Psalter.

Menachem Mor and Uriel Rappaport of Haifa University have prepared "A Survey of 25 Years (1960-1985) of Israeli Scholarship on Jewish History in the Temple Period (539 B.C.E.-135 C.E.)" with an extensive bibliography, and Arthur Segal, also of Haifa, carries the exposition of scholarly sources into the field of archaeology. "Together, these articles provide . . . a uniquely comprehensive and analytical view of current research in Israel."[31] Ahlström's[32] review of David Noel Freedman and David Frank Graf (eds.), *Pales-*

tine in Transition: The Emergence of Ancient Israel and Na'aman's[33] review of
Israel in Canaan by Halpern together give the reader another insight in the
impact of social criticism in reconstructing the history of Israel. The theory
that Israel conquered the land ca. 1230 receives a decisive set-back from
David Ussishkin's evidence that Canaanite Lachish did not fall at ca. 1230
B.C. but at 1150 B.C.[34] Since about 100,000 tourists to Jerusalem annually
visit the Garden Tomb, a popular candidate for Jesus' sepulchre, it is of wide
enough interest to mention that Barkay[35] presents convincing evidence that
the tomb was built in the eighth or seventh centuries B.C., was reused in the
Byzantine period, and was not used in the Roman period, the time of Jesus.
William LaSor makes a strong case for baptism by immersion in his study of
Jewish *Miqva'ot*.[36]

In 1981 Kugel[37] rocked the field of Hebrew prosody by jettisoning Bishop
Lowth's universally accepted thesis that the "b verset [Alter's term]" of
parallel lines restates in some way the "a verset" in favor of the thesis that "b"
should be read as a related statement emphasizing "a." In 1985 Alter[38]
adopted Kugel's thesis but tried to distance himself from him. After putting
down Alter's book the editor felt that Alter was guilty of plagiarism. Kugel
now derides Alter for copying him. He entitles his rival's book, *Kugel Slightly
Altered* in his stinging review entitled, "A Feeling of Déjà Lu [sic]"![39] Although
this argument represents the worst in theology, it serves the useful purpose
of making Kugel's radical but right thesis memorable.

In the field of textual criticism Tov, along with others, has been effectively arguing that the goal of textual criticism in some books should not be
to establish one final text but several final texts. He now applies his thesis to
Ezekiel.[40]

Batto offers the reader two brilliant articles on the Ancient Near Eastern
background of the themes, "the sleeping God," a theme that continues into
the New Testament account of Jesus asleep in the boat,[41] and "the covenant
of peace."[42] As an excellent example of exegesis in combination with the
biblical-theological method, the editor recommends the reading of Alex
T. M. Cheung's development of the theme of priesthood.[43] Polkinghorne[44]
brilliantly revives natural theology by revising it not as a demonstrative
discipline but as an insightly inquiry into the nature of the world and not by
looking to particulars in creation but to the root structure of the physical
world. "Its God is not a God of the Gaps, competing with science as the
explanation of events and continually being jostled off the stage of the world
by the advance of knowledge. Rather, God is the Sustainer of the World. . . .
My case for a revived and revised natural theology rests ultimately on the
order of the world." Addinall[45] also commendably brings together natural
and revealed theology.

For an insightful historical development of "scientific creationism" from
a variety of late-nineteenth and early-twentieth-century creationists
through the Scopes trial and the 1960's revival of creationism to the current
spread of strict creationism around the world, see the essay by Ronald L.
Numbers.[46]

Notes

[1] Bruce Waltke, "Old Testament," in *The Best in Theology*, Vol. I (Carol Stream, Ill., [1987]): 27-30.

[2] Thomas G. Long, "Symposium: Committing Hermeneutical Heresy," *Theology Today*, 44/2 (1987): 165-169.

[3] Craig Dykstra, "Editorial: Memory and Truth," *TT*, 44/2 (1987): 163.

[4] Robert L. Cohn, "On the Art of Biblical Narrative," *Biblical Research: Journal of the Chicago Society of Biblical Research*, 31 (1986): 15.

[5] Stuart Lasine, "Indeterminacy and the Bible: A Review of Literary and Anthropological Theories and Their Application to Biblical Texts," *Hebrew Studies*, 27/1 (1986): 48-80.

[6] Tremper Longman, III, "The Literary Approach to the Study of the Old Testament: Promise and Pitfalls," *JETS* 28/4 (December 1985; appeared Sept. 1986): 385-398.

[7] Albert Cook, " 'Fiction' and History in Samuel and Kings," *JSOT* 36 (1986): 27-48.

[8] Keith W. Whitelam, "Recreating the History of Israel," *JSOT*, 35 (1986): 45-70.

[9] Herschel Shanks critiques Dever's new archaeology in "Dever's 'Sermon on the Mound'," *BAR*, 13/2 (1987): 54-57.

[10] Gary A. Herion, "The Impact of Modern and Social Science Assumptions on the Reconstruction of Israelite History," *JSOT*, 34 (1986): 3-33.

[11] Chris Hauer, Jr., "From Alt to Anthropology: The Rise of the Israelite State," *JSOT*, 36 (1986): 3-15.

[12] Wilhelm Wuellner, "Where Is Rhetorical Criticism Taking Us?" *CBQ* 49/3 (1987): 448-463.

[13] John H. Stek, "The Bee and the Mountain Goat: A Literary Reading of Judges 4," in *A Tribute to Gleason Archer: Essays on the Old Testament*, edited by Walter C. Kaiser, Jr. and Ronald F. Youngblood (Chicago: Moody Press, 1986): 53-86.

[14] Donn F. Morgan, "Canon Criticism: Method or Madness?" *ATR* 68/2.

[15] John W. Miller, "Depatriarchalizing God in Biblical Interpretation: A Critique," *CBQ* 48/6 (1986): 609-616.

[16] Phyllis Trible, "Depatriarchalizing in Biblical Interpretation," *JAAR*, 41 (1973): 30-48.

[17] Bruce Waltke, "Shared Leadership or Male Headship?" *CT* (Oct. 3, 1986): 13-I.

[18] Marvin E. Tate, "A Survey of Some Introductions to the Old Testament," *Review and Expositor*, 84 (Spring, 1987): 315-321.

[19] R. J. Coggins, "Recent Continental Old Testament Literature," *Exp Tim*, 97 (1986): 298-301.

[20] *The Expository Times*, 98/10 (1987): 289f.

[21] R. N. Whybray, *The Making of the Pentateuch: A Methodological Study* (JSOT Press [1987]).

[22] Bruce K. Waltke, "Oral Tradition," in *A Tribute to Gleason Archer*, op. cit., 17-34.

[23] Alan R. Millard, "The Question of Israelite Literacy," *Bible Review* (Fall, 1987): 22-31.

[24] C. S. Rodd, "Which Is the Best Commentary on Job?" *Exp Tim* 97 (1986): 356-359.

[25] C. S. Rodd, "Which Is the Best Commentary? VI. Jeremiah," *Exp Tim* 98/6 (1987): 171-174.

[26] Eugene H. Merrill, "The Literary Character of Isaiah 40-55. Part I: Survey of a Century of Studies on Isaiah 40-55," *Bib Sac* 144/573 (1987): 24-43; _____, "Literary Genres in Isaiah 40-55: Part 2 of the Literary Character of Isaiah 40-55," *Bib. Sac* 144/574 (1987): 144-156; _____, "Isaiah 40-55 As Anti-Babylonian Polemic," *Grace Theological Journal*, 8/1 (1987): 3-18.

[27] F. F. Bruce, "My View: Faith vs. Scientific Study of the Bible," *BRev*, 3/2 (1987): 4.

[28] James L. Crenshaw, "Education in Ancient Israel," *JBL*, 104/4 (Dec. 1985): 601-15.

[29] Nili Shupak, "The 'Sitz im Leben' of the Book of Proverbs in the Light of a Comparison of Biblical and Egyptian Wisdom Literature," *RB*, 94/1 (1987): 98-119.

[30] Gerald H. Wilson, "The Use of Royal Psalms at the 'Seams' of the Hebrew Psalter," *JSOT*, 35 (1986): 85-94.

[31] David M. Bossman, ed., "Presenting the Issue: No Time to Hate," *BTB* 16/2 (1986): 46.

[32] G. W. Ahlström, *BO*, 43/86: 177f.

[33] Nadav Na'aman, *JQR*, 75/2 (1987): 158-161.

[34] David Ussishkin, "Lachish: Key to the Israelite Conquest of Canaan," *BAR*, 13/1 (1987): 18-39.

[35] Gabriel Barkay, "The Garden Tomb: Was Jesus Buried Here," *BAR*, 12/2 (1986): 40-57.

[36] William Sanford LaSor: "Discovering What Jewish Miqva'ot Can Tell Us About Christian Baptism" *BAR* 13/1 (1987): 52-59.

[37] James L. Kugel, *The Idea of Biblical Poetry* (New Haven and London, 1981).

[38] Robert Alter, "The Art of Biblical Poetry," (New York: Basic Books, Inc., 1985).

[39] James L. Kugel, "A Feeling of Déjà Lu," *JR*, 67/1 (1987): 66-79.

[40] Emmanuel Tov, "Recensional Differences between the MT and LXX of Ezekiel," *ETL*, 62 (1986): 89-101.

[41] Bernard F. Batto, "The Sleeping God: An Ancient Near Eastern Motif of Divine Sovereignty," *Bib*, 63/2 (1987): 153.

[42] _____, "The Covenant of Peace: A Neglected Ancient Near Eastern Motif," *CBQ*, 49/2 (1987): 187-211.

[43] Alex T. M. Cheung, "The Priest as the Redeemed Man: A Biblical-Theological Study of the Priesthood," *JETS* 29/3 (1986): 265-75.

[44] John C. Polkinghorne, "Creation and Structure of the Physical World," *TT* 44/1 (1987): 53-68.

[45] Peter Addinall, "What Is Meant by a Theology of the OT?" *Exp Tim*, 97 (1986): 332-336.

[46] Ronald L. Numbers, "The Creationists," *Zygon*, 22/2 (1987): 133-164.

About the Area Editor

Bruce Waltke (Th.M., Dallas Theological Seminary; Th.D., Dallas Theological Seminary; Ph.D., Harvard University) is professor of Old Testament at Westminster Theological Seminary. He is affiliated with the Orthodox Presbyterian Church. Until 1985 he was assistant editor of the Expositor's Bible Commentary. He currently serves on the Committee for Bible Translation of the *New International Version of the Holy Bible*. He is a contributor of the notes for the books of Psalms and Proverbs for the forthcoming *New American Standard Study Bible*. His books include *Micah* in the Tyndale Old Testament Commentary series (Leicester: InterVarsity Press, forthcoming); *Intermediate Hebrew Grammar* (Winona Lake: Eisenbrauns, forthcoming); and *Theological Word Book of the Old Testament* (1980).

THE LITERARY APPROACH TO THE STUDY OF THE OLD TESTAMENT: PROMISE AND PITFALLS

TREMPER LONGMAN III
Associate Professor of Old Testament
Westminster Theological Seminary

Article from *Journal of the Evangelical Theological Society*

Many scholars claim that we are undergoing a paradigm shift in interpretive methodology today. The predominant historical paradigm is being replaced by a literary approach to the study of the Bible. Source, form and redaction criticism are assailed as inadequate or even unnecessary tools for the study of the biblical text. As one reads the secondary literature, one feels an almost revolutionary attitude toward traditional modes of studying the Bible—a breaking of the shackles of history and also a feeling of freedom to approach the texts as wholes again rather than a need to divide them up.[1]

On the other hand it is very easy to find words of warning from all sides of the theological spectrum:

> There is something artificial in the idea of "the Bible as literature." Or rather, it can be artificial and contrary to the perception of both most believers and most unbelievers.[2]

> Those who talk of reading the Bible as literature sometimes mean, I think, reading it without attending to the main thing it is about.[3]

> Whoever turns a gospel of Christ into a novel has wounded my heart.[4]

> The persons who enjoy these writings solely because of their literary merit are essentially parasites; and we know that parasites, when they become too numerous, are pests. I could easily fulminate for a whole hour against the men of letters who have gone into ecstasies over "the Bible as literature."[5]

The literary approach to the study of the Bible is both an old and a new phenomenon. It is old in that many ancient examples can be evoked of biblical scholars applying principles from broader literary studies to the study of the Bible. The Church fathers frequently applied to the elucidation of biblical texts tools, concepts and techniques that they had learned in the study of classical literature. To substantiate this claim one might mention

Jerome's scansion of biblical poems into iambic pentameters[6] and Augustine's negative literary evaluation of the biblical texts over against classical literature.[7] However, the literary approach is a new phenomenon in terms of the self-consciousness and rigor with which secular literary theories and methods are being employed toward the understanding of particular biblical texts and toward the justification of broader theories of interpretation. The roots of the resurgence of a literary approach may be found in part in the work of James Muilenburg and Louis Alonso-Schökel in the late 1950s and early 1960s. Muilenburg, for example, advocated an approach to biblical texts that treated them as literary wholes over against the enterprise of form criticism, whose impulse was to dissect the text.[8]

But Muilenburg did not explicitly utilize literary theory in his writings. This is another characteristic of the most recent writings in the area and appears to have been introduced into biblical studies by scholars who were attracted to French structuralism both as a theory of reading and as (and some may feel that this is a contradiction) a way to explicate texts. A large number of studies have appeared bearing titles like "A Structuralist Approach to . . . " and "A Semiotic Approach to . . . ". Recently the word "deconstruction" has appeared in the literature, showing the new influence of Jacques Derrida on biblical interpretation.

But what precisely is the literary approach to the study of the Bible? Many answers have been given, but—put simply—the literary approach as I use the term means to recognize that the Bible displays literary characteristics and thus to treat the Bible as if it were a piece of literature. At this point I am not identifying the Bible as a work of literature. I will discuss this more carefully at a later point in the paper. My comment here is clarified by Northrup Frye, who says that the Bible "is as literary as it can well be without actually being literature."[9] It recognizes that artful verbal expression is frequently encountered in the OT and NT and therefore employs tools and concepts used to study the formal features of literature.[10] It is a method for shedding light on artistic and rhetorical characteristics of the Bible. We will examine in more detail in what way biblical narrative is literary or artistic when we look at the last pitfall of the approach.

We will begin with an examination of the potential pitfalls of a literary approach and then argue for its promise. To avoid anticlimax in the paper I will proceed from pitfalls that are less significant to those that are of the most importance.

1. The first difficulty with the literary approach is that the field of secular theory and the related discipline of linguistics are divided among themselves. There is a great deal of infighting about the basic questions of literature and interpretation. Thus a number of different schools of thought seek domination in the field. The biblical scholar faces a dilemma at this point. Students of the Bible find it difficult enough to keep abreast of their own field

without keeping current with a second one. Of course it is the explosion of information in all disciplines that leads to the narrow focus of modern scholarship. The usual result is that biblical scholars follow one particular school of thought or else one particularly prominent thinker and use that as the guide to a literary approach. Due to a desire to seem current or avant-garde it is commonly the most current theory that is adopted. Of course there is also a lag between biblical studies and the rest of the disciplines. Francis Schaeffer described how this works in general.[11] A new philosophical approach comes on the scene. It influences art, literary theory, sociology, music and then finally biblical studies. In any case this process may be observed here. Deconstruction is a philosophical movement identified most closely with Jacques Derrida, gaining prominence in the late 1960s and early 1970s and just now making an impact on biblical studies.

My point, however, is that the hard-and-fast-school divisions in literary theory are imported into biblical studies with little methodological reflection. Every major movement in literary theory of the past forty years is mirrored in the work of biblical scholars: New Criticism (Weiss, Childs),[12] Frye's archetypal approach to literature (by Frye himself and L. Ryken),[13] phenomenology (Detweiler,[14] Ricoeur), structuralist (Jobling, Polzin, McKnight),[15] Marxist (Gottwald,[16] liberation theologians), feminist (Trible, Reuther, Fiorenza),[17] deconstructionist (Crossan, Miscall).[18]

The task of the apologist is to analyze the deep philosophical roots of each of these schools of thought. This, I believe, needs to be done. As a biblical scholar working on method, however, I can recognize positive (though perhaps distorted) insights that each of these schools provides. I agree with John Barton when he says that "all of the methods . . . have something in them, but none of them is the 'correct' method," and when a few sentences later he states that our methods are best seen as "codifications of intuitions about the text which may occur to intelligent readers."[19]

Among the many positive contributions that may be gleaned from each of these schools of thought I would (and this is just a random list to give examples) include the New Critical insight that we must focus our interpretation on the text rather than on the author's background, the structuralist attention to literary conventions, and feminism's and Marxism's emphasis on the themes of sexual and economic justice in literature. And even deconstructionism against its will can give us an insight into the effect of the fall on language, the schism between signifier and signified.[20]

In each case the secular theory leads to a new imbalance. New Criticism rightly attacked certain forms of appealing to the author's intention for the meaning of a text, but it went too far in restricting the interpreter to the text alone—the text as artifact—leaving both author and reader out of the picture. Marxist and feminist readings (both, by the way, are reader-response theories) distort the text by having their themes be their only interpretive grids. Deconstructionists use their insight into the slippage between sign and object to attack theology or any type of literary communication.

Summarizing the first pitfall: The literary approach easily and often falls into the application of one particular and usually current literary theory to the biblical text. Biblical scholars become structuralists; they become semioticians. The problem is that biblical scholars—except in a very few exceptional cases—cannot maintain expertise in a second field, and therefore they fall prey to the current theoretical fashion.

My response to this is to be eclectic and to "plunder the Egyptians." My basic theoretical beliefs are Christian, and any methodological insights that fundamentally conflict with those convictions must be rejected. But, due to common grace, helpful insights may be gleaned from all fields of scholarship.

2. The second pitfall follows from the first. Literary theory is often obscurantist. Each school of thought develops its own in-language. *Actant, signifie*, narratology, interpretant, *différance*, aporia—these are only a few among the many esoterisms of the field.

An illustration of the type of obscurantism that I am referring to is found in the structuralist analysis of the book of Job by Robert Polzin. Following the method of the famous anthropologist Claude Levi-Strauss, Polzin (after lengthy discussion) concludes by summarizing the message of the book of Job with the following mathematics-like formula: $Fx(a):Fy(b) \doteq Fx(b):Fa-1(y)$.[21]

Now I am arguing not against technical terminology but against glorying in it. When new technical terms are introduced into scholarly discussion they must be carefully defined. This does not happen in most theoretical discussions.

The solution is of course not to throw out the literary approach but to seek clarity of expression. It is interesting to observe that the two books that have had the biggest impact on biblical scholarship in the area of literary approach are Robert Alter's *The Art of Biblical Narrative*[22] and James Kugel's *The Idea of Biblical Poetry*[23] on prose and poetry respectively. Both are low on technical jargon and high in terms of help in the explication of texts.

3. The next danger is that of imposing modern western concepts and categories on ancient Semitic literature. If done, according to some critics of the literary approach, it could lead to a radical distortion of the text. On the surface of it, it looks as if the danger is real. Modern literary theory develops its concepts from its encounter with modern literature. Propp and Greimas developed their theories of the structure of folktales by analyzing Russian stories.[24] This schema has been applied to biblical stories by many, notably by Roland Barthes.[25] Theories of Hebrew metrics are usually based on systems employed in other modern poetic traditions. The oral basis of much of biblical literature is "uncovered" by means of comparisons with classical and Yugoslavian oral literature.[26]

The list could be lengthened considerably. This appears to be an insensitivity toward what Anthony Thiselton calls the two horizons of the act of interpretation.[27] The ancient text comes from a culture far removed in time and space from that of the modern interpreter. This must be taken into account during the act of interpretation, or the exegesis will be distorted by reading modern values and presuppositions into the ancient text.

Kugel is the biggest critic of the literary method from this perspective. He expresses his reservations theoretically in an article entitled "On the Bible and Literary Criticism"[28] and practically in his rightly much-acclaimed *The Idea of Biblical Poetry*. Here he points out (1) that "there is no word for poetry in biblical Hebrew" and thus "to speak of 'poetry' at all in the Bible will be to impose a concept foreign to the biblical world,"[29] and (2) that no single characteristic or group of characteristics is capable of differentiating prose from poetry in the Hebrew Bible. True enough, parallelism occurs in prose and meter does not exist. Thus Kugel avoids the designation "poetry" to describe a distinct genre in the OT, preferring instead to speak of "high style."

While agreeing with Kugel to a large extent, I believe he goes too far in rejecting the generic term "poetry." If one reads a psalm and then reads a chapter of Leviticus, one can see and feel a difference. That difference may be summarized on one level by contrasting the short, terse lines of the psalm with the lengthy lines of Leviticus. There is also a heightening of certain rhetorical devices in the psalm that normally would not be found to the same magnitude in the Leviticus section: parallelism, metaphors, less restriction on the syntax, etc. In this terseness and heightened use of rhetorical devices we see a literary phenomenon related to our own poetry as distinguished from prose. Of course Kugel recognizes most of this, but he still hesitates to call the psalm poetic. His hesitation stems from the fear of distorting biblical materials by imposing foreign literary constructs on them. But on still another level, not discussed by Kugel as far as I can remember, is the relative deviance from common speech in our two passages. Leviticus is closer to common speech patterns than the psalms passage. And if anything characterizes poetry over against prose in any literary tradition, it is that the former is further removed from common, everyday speech than the latter. True, we are still speaking of a relative difference between prose and poetry. I would not in the least deny an element of literary artifice to the prose sections of Scripture. But the difference is substantial enough to be called a generic distinction, and our modern categories of prose and poetry are the closest to the phenomenon we discover in the Bible.

I have struggled with this issue particularly in the area of genre theory. My dissertation was on fifteen Akkadian texts that I described as fictional autobiographies, and since many would not date the beginning of autobiography until Rousseau in the seventeenth century I needed to justify my genre identification.[30] I had to admit that there is not universal generic similarity. New genres develop; old ones die out.[31] In addition, certain cultures utilize some genres and neglect others. For example, in the ancient world there is nothing comparable to the modern novel. In the same way, twentieth-century American literature contains few if any omens. Nevertheless, though a culture-free genre system does not exist, the native literary classification of each culture (or lack of it, as in the case of prose-poetry in Hebrew) need not be adopted (uncritically) in order to identify the genres of that culture.

The separation of etic and emic approaches to literature deals with these cultural determinants in literary classification.[32] The emic seeks native designations and classifications of literature. The advantage of this method is that the researcher gains insight into the native consciousness of a particular text and also the relationship between that text and others bearing the same designation. The etic view of literature imposes a non-native grid or classification scheme on the texts in order to categorize them. While there is always the danger of distorting understanding of the texts by imposing foreign standards on them, it must be pointed out that the Israelite scribes were not concerned with a precise and self-conscious generic classification of their literature. Both were innovations of the Greeks. While the biblical authors identified a few different forms of speech—song (šîr), proverb (māšāl), and so on—and these provide helpful keys to research, they are not systematic or rigorous in their categorization (nor would one expect it of them).

4. The next pitfall is the danger of moving completely away from any concept of authorial intent and determinant meaning of a text. Here we are moving in a very sticky theoretical area. Paradoxically enough, I will later emphasize the other pole—that the literary approach focuses our attention more on the text than on the author during the act of interpretation. I believe that these two poles are harmonizable.

But first let us deal with the danger of moving away completely from any concept of the author in interpretation. If there is anything that unites secular theory since the advent of New Criticism in the middle of this century it is the denial of the author. Traditional criticism invested a lot of stock in the author. S. Bermann describes the attitude of traditional criticism:

> If we read histories, biographies, and Keat's own letters with enough scholarly patience and skill, we could be confident of "getting the poem right," "understanding it," "interpreting its truth."

Thus it is pivotal to know that Keats wrote his sonnet "Bright Star" with its themes of love and death as he was caring for his brother Tom who was dying of tuberculosis (and infecting John) and also that he was sobered by his mortality in his passion for Fanny. "I have two luxuries to brood over in my walks, your Lovliness and the hour of my death, O that I could have possession of them both in the same minute."[33]

We have all heard the arguments against such approaches—and they are powerful. How is it possible to reconstruct an author's intention in a literary work, since he may not even have been conscious of it himself? The poet often is his own worst interpreter. How can we get back into the mind of the poet? This problem is obviously heightened in the study of an ancient text.

It was the New Critics of the 1940s and 1950s who moved away from authorial intent, a view formalized by Wimsatt and Beardsley in their description of the "intentional fallacy" and their concomitant focus on the text alone as verbal icon.[34] The intentional fallacy, as defined by Abrams,

> claimed that whether the author has expressly stated what his intention was in writing a poem, or whether it is merely inferred from what we know about his life and opinions, his intention is irrelevant to the literary critic, because meaning and value reside within the text of the finished, free-standing, and public work of literature itself.[35]

There is here an obvious shift away from the author that continued and heightened as we move from New Criticism to structuralism and to deconstruction. The emphasis has been redirected. Literature is an act of communication that may be described as a dynamic between poet-poem-audience, or between author-text-reader. Attention has been drawn by New Criticism and structuralism primarily to the text, and by reader-response theories (including those of Iser and Fish, feminism and Marxism) to the reader and his constitutive participation in the formation of meaning in the literary act.

There has been one major voice of dissent to this trend. E. D. Hirsch[36] posits an author-centered interpretive method. The goal is to arrive at the author's intent. This, he believes, provides an anchor of determinant meaning in the sea of relativity unleashed by other theories.

I will not comment on this pitfall until later. Let me simply say here that Hirsch provides a needed counterbalance to the trend in secular theory—although he is considered to be something strange by his fellow literary critics.

5. The last pitfall is indeed the one about which I have the most concern. Along with the move away from the author in contemporary theory one can also note the tendency to deny or severely limit any referential function to literature. "The poet affirmeth nothing," states Philip Sidney. Frank Lentricchia follows the history of literary theory for the last forty years along the theme of the denial of any external reference for literature.[37] Literature is not an insight into the world but a limitless semiotic play.

Perhaps this modern tendency goes back to Ferdinand de Saussure's theory of the sign. He argued that a sign is composed of two parts: the signifier and the signified. But there is no natural connection between the two. Rather, the relationship is arbitrary—that is, conventional. One can see this with words. For example, according to Saussure the fact that different languages have different words for "horse" indicates that the relationship is arbitrary and determined by custom. According to Saussure and the semiotic tradition that emanates from his writings, the sign does not point to an object out there in reality. It is not the relationship between a word and a thing. After all, it might point to a nonexistent or metaphorical horse, and thus the sign unites an acoustical image with a concept rather than a word with a thing.[38]

In any case the rupture between the literary and the referential is there in modern literary theory. And, as one might expect, the recognition of the literary characteristics of the Bible has led on the part of some scholars to an equation of the Bible and literature. There follows an acceptance of the view that literary texts do not refer to anything outside of themselves. In particular they do not make reference to history. This leads on the part of some to a complete or substantial denial of an historical approach to the text. Most often this takes the form of a denial or denigration of traditional historical-critical methods. Source and form criticism particularly are attacked. The following quotations may be taken as representative not of all who adopt the literary approach but of some:

> Above all, we must keep in mind that narrative is a *form of representation*. Abraham in Genesis is not a real person any more than the painting of an apple is real fruit.[39]

> Once the unity of the story is experienced, one is able to participate in the world of the story. Although the author of the Gospel of Mark certainly used sources rooted in the historical events surrounding the life of Jesus, the final text is a literary creation with an autonomous integrity, just as Leonardo's portrait of the Mona Lisa exists independently as a vision of life apart from any resemblance or nonresemblance to the person who posed for it or as a play of Shakespeare has integrity apart from reference to the historical character depicted there. Thus, Mark's narrative contains a closed and self-sufficient world with its own integrity. ... When viewed as a literary achievement the statements in Mark's narrative, rather than being a representation of historical events, refer to the people, places, and events *in the story*.[40]

> As long as readers require the gospel to be a window to the ministry of Jesus before they will see truth in it, accepting the gospel will mean believing that the story it tells corresponds exactly to what actually happened during Jesus' ministry. When the gospel is viewed as a mirror, though of course not a mirror in which we see only ourselves, its meaning can be found on this side of it, that is, between text and reader, in the experience of reading the text, and belief in the gospel can mean openness to the ways it calls readers to interact with it, with life, and with their own world.[41]

The last writer further states: "The real issue is whether 'his story' can be true if it is not history."[42] For him the answer is yes.

Similar evaluation may be seen in the hermeneutics of Hans Frei, who feels that the major error in both traditional critical and conservative exegesis is the loss of the understanding that biblical narrative is history-like and not true history with an ostentive, or external, reference.[43] Further, Alter's brilliant analysis of OT narrative is coupled with the assumption that the nature of the narrative is "historicized fiction" or "fictional history."[44]

The result of this approach is a turning away from historical investigation of the text as impossible or irrelevant. The traditional methods of historical criticism are abandoned or radically modified or given secondary consideration. Concern to discover the original *Sitz im Leben* or to discuss the tradition history of a text languishes among this new breed of scholar. This worries traditional critical scholarship, so that we find among recent titles ones like that of Leander Keck: "Will the Historical-Critical Method Survive?"[45] Now to see historical criticism on the brink of destruction is something that is more likely to bring expressions of joy than of terror to the face of most evangelicals. But of course the danger cuts two ways. Both traditional criticism and evangelicalism have a high stake in the question of history.

The danger summarily stated and already illustrated in the quotations above is this. According to Wellek and Warren the distinguishing characteristics of literature are "fictionality," "invention" and "imagination."[46] To identify Genesis as a work of literature pure and simple is to move it out of the realm of history. This seems to be the tendency of some if not much of the literary approach to the study of the OT.

But there is an easy way out of this, hinted at earlier with our citation from Frye. Genesis is not really literature, or at least it is not literature in this sense, or—better—it is more than literature. A second quotation from Frye is relevant here: "The Bible possesses literary qualities but is not itself reducible to a work of literature."[47]

On the one hand, Genesis is not reducible to a work of fiction. On the other hand, we are justified and required to apply a literary approach because it possesses literary qualities. Another distinguishing characteristic of literature is that it is self-consciously structured and expressed. As the Russian formalists put it, language is "foregrounded." There is literary artifice in the parallelism between the first three days of creation and the last three (as framework hypothesis has pointed out—whether this parallelism is mirroring the actual sequence of God's creative acts is a moot point here). There is artifice in the symmetrical structures of the flood story (as pointed out by Wenham) and the Babel story (as pointed out by Fokkelmann)—or, to go a little more afield, the Solomon narrative (as pointed out by Dillard).[48]

The point is that we do not have "objective," "neutral," "unshaped" reporting of events. Of course this is impossible anyway, since there is no such thing as a brute fact (as C. Van Til has argued). An uninterpreted historical report is not even conceivable.

But it must be admitted that Genesis, for example, is not attempting to be as close as possible to a dispassionate reporting of events. Rather, we have proclamation—with the result that the history is shaped to differing degrees. The point is that the biblical narrators are concerned not only to tell us facts but also to guide our perspective of and responses to those events.

So OT prose narrative may be described as selective, structured, emphasized and interpreted stories. The author/narrator controls the way we view the events. Thus plot analysis, narrator studies, character studies, point-of-view analysis, examination of plot retardation devices, etc., may be helpful (though definitely partial) approaches toward the understanding of a text.

The question of historical truth boils down to the question of who ultimately is guiding us in our interpretation of these events. If men alone, then artifice may be deceptive; if God, then it may not. To recognize this is to recognize that a literary analysis of an historical book is not incompatible with a high view of the historicity of the text—even one like my own, which affirms the inerrancy and infallibility of Scripture in the area of history.

Let me insert an aside here. I do not want to give the mistaken impression that I am historicizing all of Scripture at this point. I believe that the generic intention of each book and section of book needs to be analyzed before attributing an historical reference to the book.

From the side of theory, appeal may be made to those who argue that literature is an act of communication between the writer and the reader that functions in more than one way. Besides a poetic function the text may also have a referential function, according to Roman Jakobson's communication model of literary discourse.[49] Of course the poetic function may become so dominant that the referential function ceases to exist, so that truly "the poet affirmeth nothing" to the opposite pole when there is a concerted effort to rid the text of self-referential language (i.e. metaphor)—an impossible goal— like in scientific discourse. I see the biblical text for the most part somewhere in between.

Thus while we must recognize the potential pitfalls of a literary approach we see that they are avoidable. Positively, though, what value is there in a literary approach? Why bother developing such an approach and applying it to the text?

I have already hinted at the answer a number of times: While not to be reduced to literature pure and simple, the Bible is amenable to literary analysis. Indeed, some of the most illuminating work on the Hebrew Bible in the past decade has been from a literary point of view, often done by literary scholars. Biblical scholars do not always make the most sensitive readers, particularly traditional critics. C. S. Lewis states:

> Whatever these men may be as Biblical critics, I distrust them as critics. They seem to me to lack literary judgement, to be imperceptive about the very quality of the texts they are reading. . . . These men ask me to believe they can read between the lines of the old texts; the evidence is their obvious inability to read (in any sense worth discussing) the lines them-

selves. They claim to see fern-seed and can't see an elephant ten yards away in broad daylight.[50]

But in what ways or why is a literary approach beneficial? I would like to list just a few.

1. It assists us in coming to an understanding of the conventions of biblical storytelling. Alter affirms that

> every culture, even every era in a particular culture, develops distinctive and sometimes intricate codes for telling its stories, involving everything from narrative point of view, procedures of description and characterization, the management of dialogue, to the ordering of time and the organization of plot.[51]

The literary text is an act of communication from writer to reader. The text is the message. For it to work—that is, communicate—the sender and receiver have to speak the same language. The writer through the use of conventional forms sends signals to the reader to tell him how he is to take the message. We all know such obvious generic signals as "Once upon a time" and "A novel by . . . ". Poetry is recognizable by all the white space on the page.

A literary approach explores and makes explicit the conventions of biblical literature, to understand what message it intends to carry. To discover that Deuteronomy is in the form of a treaty, that the narrator shapes the reader's response to the characters of a text in different ways, that repetition is not a sign of multiple sources but a literary device, is significant.

Now in ordinary reading much of this happens automatically. We passively let the narrator shape our interpretation of the event he is reporting to us, we make an unconscious genre identification, etc. But when we interpret the text it is important to make these explicit. This is doubly so since the Bible is an ancient text and the conventions employed are often not ones we are used to.

Let me conclude this point with an observation: Much of the Bible is literature in the sense of story. Why is that the case? Why did God not reveal to us his mighty acts in history in the form of a *Cambridge Ancient History*— or, better, why is the Bible not in the form of a systematic theology? The ultimate answer to this is to appeal to God's wisdom, but I still wish to suggest two positive functions of the literary form of the Bible. (1) Defamiliarization and distanciation are concepts discussed by Russian formalists who describe the function of art as "the renewal of perception, the seeing of the world suddenly in a new light, in a new and unforeseen way."[52] To cast truth in the form of a story—to present it in an artistic fashion—leads the reader/hearer to pay closer attention to it, to be shocked to reconsider what might otherwise easily become a truism. A proverb is a good, focused example. Which speaks more powerfully: "Speak righteously" or "The mouth of the righteous flows with wisdom, but the perverted tongue will be cut out" (Prov. 10:31)? Which communicates more vividly: the statement "Love your neighbor as yourself" or the story of the Good Samaritan? (2) Literature appeals to the whole man, it involves our whole being—intellect, will, emotions—to a greater extent than, say, the Westminster Confession.

2. A literary approach draws our attention to whole texts. We have a tendency even as evangelicals to atomize the text, to focus our attention on a word or a few verses. Traditional critical scholarship has the same problem for a different reason: Form and source criticism lead it to disbelieve that the whole text is original. The literary approach asks the question of the force of the whole.

This is why so many evangelical scholars have seen the literary approach as serving an apologetic function. If it can be shown that the Joseph narrative, the flood narrative (Wenham), the rise-of-the-monarchy section (1 Samuel 8-12, Eslinger), the book of Judges (Gooding) all are examples of literary wholes, then cannot we dispense with source criticism?[53]

3. Work in literary criticism helps us to understand the reading process. Our focus must be on the text. But, in the words of Geoffrey Strickland: "All that we say or think about a particular utterance or piece of writing presupposes an assumption on our part, correct or otherwise, concerning the intention of the speaker or writer."[54] However, we must also recognize the role of the reader and his predisposition as he approaches the text. Now I do not want to advocate the view of some reader-response theorists that the reader actually creates the meaning of the text. Rather, the text imposes restrictions on possible interpretations. But the reader's background and his interests will lead him to attend to certain parts of the Bible's message more than other parts and more than other people. It is in this connection that I would want to introduce the relevance of contextualization and multiperspectival approaches to the text. This is also the place to situate the value of what might be called ideological readers even when they are unbalanced. Feminists and liberation theologians read the Bible with focused glasses that often lead to distortion, but they do bring out important issues and themes that other less interested readers miss.

But the point in this section is that reading involves the interaction of the writer with the reader through the text, so that any theory that concentrates on one of the three to the exclusion of the others may be distorted.

More could be said about the promise and benefits of a literary approach. But in the final analysis the proof is in the pudding. Does the approach lead to illuminating exegesis? The answer is "Yes," and it is demonstrated in such insightful analyses as those of R. Alter, D. J. A. Clines, C. Conroy, A. Berlin, R. A. Culpepper, D. Gunn and others.

Already we are all more or less consciously or subconsciously aesthetic critics. The work I am doing is to make it more conscious than subconscious and thereby also make it (I hope) more accurate—that is, more true to the text.

Notes

[1] J. D. Crossan, " 'Ruth Amid the Alien Corn': Perspectives and Methods in Contemporary Biblical Criticism," in *The Biblical Mosaic* (ed. R. Polzin and E. Rothman; Philadelphia: Fortress, 1982) 199; cf. M. Fishbane, "Recent Work on Biblical Narrative," *Prooftexts* 1 (1981) 99.

[2] K. Stendahl, "The Bible as a Classic and the Bible as Holy Scripture," *JBL* 103 (1984) 6.

[3] C. S. Lewis, *Reflections on the Psalms* (Glasgow: Collins, 1961) 10.

[4] Written by the Romantic intellectual J. G. Herder as quoted in F. Kermode, *The Genesis of Secrecy* (Cambridge: Harvard University, 1979) 120.

[5] T. S. Eliot as quoted in J. Barr, "Reading the Bible as Literature," *BJRL* 56 (1973-74) 12.

[6] Discussed in J. Kugel, *The Idea of Biblical Poetry* (New Haven: Yale University, 1981) 152.

[7] Ibid., pp. 159-160.

[8] J. Muilenburg, "Form Criticism and Beyond," *JBL* 88 (1969) 1-18.

[9] N. Frye, *The Great Code* (London: Ark, 1983) 62.

[10] A. Berlin, *Poetics and Interpretation of Biblical Narrative* (Sheffield: Almond, 1983), esp. chap. 4.

[11] F. A. Schaeffer, *The God Who Is There* (Downers Grove: InterVarsity, 1968) 13-84.

[12] M. Weiss, *The Bible from Within: The Method of Total Interpretation* (Jerusalem: Magnes, 1984); on Childs see the comments by J. Barton, *Reading the Old Testament: Method in Biblical Study* (Philadelphia: Westminster, 1984) 140-157.

[13] Frye, *Code*; L. Ryken, *How to Read the Bible as Literature* (Grand Rapids: Zondervan, 1984).

[14] R. Detweiler, *Story, Sign, and Self: Phenomenology and Structuralism as Literary-Critical Methods* (Philadelphia: Fortress, 1978).

[15] D. Jobling, *The Sense of Biblical Narrative: Three Structural Analyses in the Old Testament (1 Samuel 13-31, Numbers 11-12, 1 Kings 17-18)* (JSOTSup 7; Sheffield: Almond, 1978); R. M. Polzin, *Biblical Structuralism: Method and Subjectivity in the Study of Ancient Texts* (Philadelphia/Missoula: Fortress/Scholars, 1977); E. V. McKnight, *Meaning in Texts* (Philadelphia: Fortress, 1978).

[16] N. Gottwald, *The Tribes of Yahweh* (Maryknoll: Orbis, 1979).

[17] See the collected essays in *JSOT* 22 (1982).

[18] J. D. Crossan, *Cliffs of Fall: Paradox and Polyvalence in the Parables of Jesus* (New York: Seabury, 1980); P. D. Miscall, *The Workings of Old Testament Narrative* (Philadelphia/Chico: Fortress/Scholars, 1983).

[19] Barton, *Reading* 5.

[20] M. Edwards, *Towards a Christian Poetics* (London: Macmillan, 1984) 217-237.

[21] Polzin, *Structuralism* 75.

[22] New York: Basic, 1981.

[23] See n. 6.

[24] V. Propp, *Morphology of the Folktale* (Austin: University of Texas, 1968); A. J. Greimas, *Structural Semantics: An Attempt at a Method* (Lincoln: University of Nebraska, 1983).

[25] R. Barthes, "La lutte avec l'ange: analyse textuelle de Genèse 32.23-33," in *Analyse structurale et exégèse biblique*, pp. 27-40.

[26] F. M. Cross, "Prose and Poetry in the Mythic and Epic Texts from Ugarit," *HTR* 67 (1974) 1-15; cf. A. B. Lord, *The Singer of Tales* (Cambridge: Harvard University, 1964).

[27] A. Thiselton, *The Two Horizons: New Testament Hermeneutics and Philosophical Description* (Grand Rapids: Eerdmans, 1980).

[28] *Prooftexts* 1 (1981) 99-104.

[29] Kugel, *Idea* 69.

[30] R. Longman, III, *Fictional Akkadian Autobiography* (forthcoming from Eisenbrauns).

[31] A. Fowler, "The Life and Death of Literary Forms," *New Literary History* 2 (1970/71) 199-216.

[32] K. Pike, *Language in Relation to a Unified Theory of Human Behavior* (The Hague: Mouton, 1967), chap. 2; V. Poythress, "Analysing a Biblical Text: Some Important Linguistic Distinctions," *SJT* 32 (1979) 319-331. The emic/etic distinction was first proposed in linguistics, where it was used to distinguish native understanding of language from modern linguists' analyses. Pike was the first to generalize the distinction into a principle that could be used in the study of any aspect of culture. V. Poythress further refined the concept. For the tendency of taking linguistic categories and applying them to other disciplines see J. Culler, *The Pursuit of Signs* (Ithaca: Cornell University, 1981).

[33] S. Bermann, "Revolution in Literary Criticism," *Princeton Alumni Weekly* (November 21, 1984) 10.

[34] W. K. Wimsatt and M. Beardsley, "The Intentional Fallacy," reprinted in *The Verbal Icon* (The University Press of Kentucky, 1954) 3-18.

[35] M. H. Abrams, *A Glossary of Literary Terms* (4th ed.; New York: Holt, Rinehart and Winston, 1981) 83.

[36] E. D. Hirsch, *Validity in Interpretation* (New Haven: Yale University, 1967); *The Aims of Interpretation* (Chicago: University Press, 1976).

[37] F. Lentricchia, *After the New Criticism* (Chicago: University Press, 1980).

[38] Ibid., p. 118.

[39] Berlin, *Poetics* 13.

[40] D. Rhoads and D. Michie, *Mark as Story: An Introduction to the Narrative of a Gospel* (Philadelphia: Fortress, 1982) 3-4.

[41] R. A. Culpepper, *Anatomy of the Fourth Gospel* (Philadelphia: Fortress, 1983) 236-237.

[42] Ibid.

[43] H. Frei, *The Eclipse of Biblical Narrative* (New Haven: Yale University, 1974).

[44] R. Alter, *The Art of Biblical Narrative.*

[45] An article in *Orientation by Disorientation* (ed. R. A. Spencer; Pittsburgh: Pickwick, 1980) 115-127.

[46] R. Wellek and A. Warren, *Theory of Literature* (New York: Harcourt Brace Jovanovich, 1942) 26.

[47] Frye, *Code* xiv.

[48] G. J. Wenham, "The Coherence of the Flood Narrative," *VT* 28 (1978) 336-348; J. P. Fokkelmann, *Narrative Art in Genesis* (Assen/Amsterdam: van Gorcum, 1978) 11 ff.; R. B. Dillard, "The Literary Structure of the Chronicler's Solomon Narrative," *JSOT* 30 (1984) 85-93.

[49] Cf. N. R. Petersen, *Literary Criticism for New Testament Critics* (Philadelphia: Fortress, 1978) 33ff.

[50] C. S. Lewis, *Fern-Seed and Elephants* (Glasgow; Collins, 1975) 106, 111.

[51] R. Alter, "A Response to Critics," *JSOT* 27 (1983) 113-117.

[52] F. Jameson, *Prison-House of Language* (Princeton: University Press, 1972) 52.

[53] Wenham, "Coherence"; L. Eslinger, "Viewpoints and Point of View in 1 Samuel 8-12," *JSOT* 26 (1983) 61-76; D. W. Gooding, "The Composition of the Book of Judges," *EI* 16 (1982) 70-79.

[54] G. Strickland, *Structuralism or Criticism? Thoughts on How We Read* (Cambridge: University Press, 1981) 36.

THE IMPACT OF MODERN AND SOCIAL SCIENCE ASSUMPTIONS ON THE RECONSTRUCTION OF ISRAELITE HISTORY*

GARY A. HERION
Adjunct Assistant Professor in the Program on Studies in Religion
University of Michigan

Article from *Journal for the Study of the Old Testament*

The past few years have witnessed an increasing interest in using the social sciences to elucidate the history of ancient Israel. This interest is typically expressed in the biblical scholar who re-examines the historical data in terms of particular models or theories borrowed from this or that social science discipline. The results of this cross-disciplinary activity generally have been positive, if for no other reason than because they sensitize biblical historians to the nomothetic aspects (as opposed to the idiographic features) of ancient Israel,[1] and because they force them to confront the social dimension of Israelite religion (see the important statement of Gottwald 1979:8-17).

However, there are also some problems inherent in this cross-disciplinary activity, problems related to what is commonly labelled 'the sociology of knowledge'. Most biblical scholars have become increasingly aware of the subtle ways in which scholars' backgrounds and training, heritage, social-class position and even gender influence their views about ancient Israel. Yet there is at least one other factor that plays a crucial role in shaping the sociology of their knowledge: modernism. This paper will focus on the ways in which scholars' distinctively modern social contexts and experiences of society help to shape the 'pre-understandings' they have about what is generally 'true' of human social life, and about what is particularly 'true' of ancient Israelite society.[2]

This has an important bearing on biblical studies' interest in social science, since in many respects the assumptions of the social sciences and those of the modern social context are similar:

> They came into existence together and are indissolubly interlinked. A critique of social science cannot but be a critique of modern society, and vice versa (Bellah 1981: 8).

These modern assumptions or perspectives that helped to bring the social sciences into existence may be listed as positivism, reductionism, relativism and determinism. By viewing the 'social scientizing' of biblical studies in terms of these four assumptions, this paper will exhibit a superficial dependency upon Robert Bellah's somewhat polemical and oversimplified article 'Biblical Religion and Social Science in the Modern World' (1981). However, it must be pointed out that Bellah's description there of the nature of the social sciences is hardly an accurate portrayal of the current state of social science inquiry since each of these four assumptions has fallen under critical review and has been rejected by large portions of the social science community. Nevertheless, he has identified certain tendencies that come to play powerful roles when students of biblical religion begin utilizing the social sciences (cf. the very useful introduction in Wilson 1984: 1-29).

Modern Assumptions and the Scholarly Perspective

An important part of scholars' modernism is the extent to which they live in a complex society and are thereby thoroughly accustomed to the vital and seemingly natural social roles played by formal institutions. A consequence of this is that sometimes the modern person tends to assume that social organization should typically proceed through such formally organized, collective bodies or institutions (Wirth 1938: 23), taking for granted what economist Kenneth Boulding has called 'the organizational revolution'.[3] Sometimes, however, this can lead even some scholars to assume that formal, organizational or institutional structure is a universal prerequisite in all other societies as well, including ancient Near Eastern and village-based societies. Thus, the experiences of society built into the modern context can sometimes operate to limit the number of understandable options available to historians when they reconstruct the past.[4]

The past eighty years of inquiry into the Hebrew prophets may well be called as illustration. The old nineteenth-century view of the prophet as 'inspired individual' has given over to the twentieth-century view of the prophet as 'organizational spokesman', a view that reached an extreme forty years ago with the thesis that every prophet held an 'office' or was a member of some 'guild' or 'cult association'. The current interest in the prophets' 'support groups' or 'followings' is yet a more recent illustration of how modern, scholarly understandings of 'social organization' can sometimes be confused with distinctively different concepts such as 'political organization' or 'professional organization', all of which are more familiar to the scholar living in the modern world.

As one example of such a modernist view of social organization one may cite Odil Steck's article on 'Theological Streams of Tradition' (1977), noting especially his assumption that the prophetic stream (like the wisdom stream of the royal court and the cultic stream of the temple) must have had some kind of institutional 'centers' associated with formally organized, collective bodies:

Distinctive, long-lasting intellectual movements of this kind are not borne
by individuals but only by groups in which the tradition streams are kept in
flux through transmission, learned discussion, and development of new
witnesses to the tradition. For carrying out their activities and training their
successors these groups need fixed meeting places and durable, more or
less established institutions (pp. 197-98).

Although Steck admits that 'we do not have a concrete historical picture of
these centers of prophetic tradition' (pp. 201-202), this notable lack of evidence does not prompt him to re-evaluate his assumptions or to consider
alternative hypotheses. In fact, his assumptions appear specifically to rule
out other possibilities—e.g. that 'prophetic' traditions may have been nurtured and transmitted outside such institutional settings and without official
maintenance, perhaps being part of the more loosely structured 'cultural
repertoire' of peasant villages. Steck's assumption might be attributed in
part to a modern context that naturally associates religious (and political)
expression with formally organized, institutional settings, groups and activities. Thus, a modern tendency to assume society's prerequisite need for
formal institutions may interfere when reconstructing the tradition-process
behind the Hebrew prophets by limiting scholars' pre-understanding (and
therefore limiting the number of intelligible options available to them).[5]

Social Science Assumptions and the Scholarly Perspective

In order to demonstrate more precisely the variety of ways in which distinctively modern social contexts and experiences can shape one's preunderstandings of what was 'true' (or at least possible) in ancient Israel, one must
examine in more detail the four assumptions that sometimes play powerful
roles when social science is used—positivism, reductionism, relativism and
determinism. It is important to keep in mind that these four basic assumptions are usually interwoven with one another, often making it difficult to
isolate clearly the unadulterated influence of any one of them. Nevertheless,
it is possible to view these four in terms of two pairs of influences: 1. the way
in which positivism and reductionism combine to influence cross-disciplinary methodology; and 2. the way in which relativism and determinism combine to shape a more 'scientific' view of Israelite religion.

Positivism, Reductionism and the Cross-Disciplinary Method
Positivism may be defined broadly as the desire to emulate the empirical
methods of natural science in the quest for knowledge. At best, positivism
encourages methodological and intellectual rigor while stressing the central
role that reason must play in scholarship. However, positivism can sometimes degenerate into a form of 'scientism' in which science is no longer
understood as one form of knowledge but where the nomothetic character of
science comes to be viewed as the only valid terms in which any 'knowledge'

can be achieved (Habermas 1972: 4). In such an intellectual climate, many scholars trained in the more 'subjective' approaches of the humanities (history, theology and philosophy) may come to believe that the 'more objective' social sciences per se can render a more accurate picture of what was 'real' in ancient Israel. Consequently there may arise certain inhibitions about criticizing the more 'prestigious' social sciences.[6]

Ideally, responsible interdisciplinary activity is a two-way street, meaning that the historical and the social scientific approaches to knowledge inevitably affect and alter one another when they are brought together. Most social scientists concede this, viewing the tasks of the social sciences and history (as well as the humanities in general) as being complementary. However, it seems that sometimes in the appeal to the social positivist inclinations may operate in such a way that the interdisciplinary 'two-way street' carries mainly 'one-way traffic' from the social sciences into historical studies, but not vice versa. As a result, biblical studies sometimes witnesses the uncritical (not necessarily inaccurate always, but unquestioning) use of social science models and theories.

It is impossible to appreciate fully this impact of positivism without simultaneously appreciating the impact of reductionism. *Reductionism* generally is the tendency to explain as much of the complex as possible in terms of the simple. This means that if one is to handle complex phenomena, one has little choice but to 'chunk' or abstract similarities, thereby reducing the number of items being considered (Malina 1982: 231-32). Such abstractions of similarities are called 'models' or 'typologies' in the social sciences. While no model has yet been devised that can explain 100 percent of the variance, the study of any real social phenomena would be difficult if not altogether impossible without the aid of models. Yet models or typologies must be used with a conscientious regard for their limitations; the reduction of complexity always entails a certain methodological risk since the line separating the enlightening epitome from the vulgarized distortion can sometimes be very fine.

Since the construction and use of models have been integral parts of the 'social scientizing' of biblical studies, a few remarks about the nature of models seem in order. All societies are alike in some respects, and each differs from others in other respects. Yet some social phenomena have certain features in common enabling us to designate them from a 'type' of phenomenon. This 'type' or 'model' is constructed by assembling and listing only those common features, temporarily ignoring the existing differences, divergences, inconsistencies and irregularities. For this reason it must never be forgotten that a 'type' is not 'real':

> The type is an imagined entity, created only because through it we may hope to understand reality. Its function is to suggest aspects of real societies which deserve further study, and especially to suggest hypotheses as to what, under certain defined conditions, may be generally true about society (Redfield 1947: 295).

Three important points emerge: 1. models are hypothetical entities, not real descriptions; 2. they are to be used to analyze existing data, not to serve as substitutions in the absence of data; and 3. they do not conclude a study or provide definitive answers, but rather they (a) summarize current thought, or they (b) help to raise new questions for study, suggest fresh lines of inquiry, and expose relevant topics for research when used as a basis of comparison with real phenomena. It is suggested here that positivist and reductionist tendencies sometimes combine in such a way that these three important points become lost, and that consequently the application of social science models and theories to biblical studies sometimes lacks proper methodological rigor and balance.

Relativism, Determinism and the Scientific Study of Religion
In focusing on the remaining two assumptions, it should be noted that relativism and determinism have dovetailed to shape an empirical approach to the study of religion that is often associated with the social sciences, and that in this respect they can influence scholarly pre-understandings and reconstructions of ancient Israel. *Relativism* is here defined as the assumption that issues of morality and religion can never be considered truly right or wrong in any 'absolute' sense, but rather that they vary with (or are 'relative' to) persons, societies and cultures. In conjunction with this, *determinism* may be defined as the general tendency to think that human values, choices and actions are caused (or 'determined') by certain variables in the social and cultural environment.[7]

These assumptions can combine to produce a general view of human values that denies the individual any genuine claim to socially autonomous or 'transcendent' beliefs. In this view, it is characteristically assumed that human values—including religious beliefs—are not held independently or actively but rather that they result from socialization. In other words, values are not seen as reflecting any deep-seated, personal belief in anything truly universal; instead, they become indications of one's acquiescence to a particular set of norms prevalent in the immediate social environment. If a person should claim to possess a deep-seated, autonomous belief in certain transcendent 'things', this is typically dismissed as simply an example of the extent to which 'superstructural' social concerns and interests have successfully been internalized by the individual.[8]

This general view of human values is in some respects similar to certain social science theories of religion. From its inception in the French enlightenment, sociology was committed to the positivist view that religion is institutionalized ignorance, a vestige of man's primitive past doomed to disappear in an era of scientific rationalism. This view was laid to rest when Emile Durkheim's celebrated study of totemism (1912) demonstrated that religion often functions in a very sophisticated manner to help control, stabilize and legitimize social systems. Ever since, the social sciences have tended to consider 'religion' primarily as a public, not a private phenomenon, and they have tended to find beneath it particular social control interests, but not more transcendent values or beliefs.

This view of passive man and ideological religion may be associated generally with the rise of modernism and urbanism, wherein 'the juxtaposition of divergent personalities and modes of life tends to produce a relativistic perspective and a sense of toleration of differences which . . . lead toward the secularization of life' (Wirth 1938: 15). The modern, urban context requires religious groups and individuals to interact with others on the basis of some 'relative moral minimum' rather than a 'transcendent moral absolute', compromising internally held values and beliefs for the rational pursuit of shared social, economic and political interests (Lenski 1961: 9; Wirth 1938: 18).

This truism of modern, urban society has been summed up by the theologian Harvey Cox, who notes that 'in the secular city, it is not religion but politics that brings unity and meaning to human life and thought' (1965: 254). There is a two-part corollary to this statement: 1. religion remains meaningful in such an environment only to the extent that it, too, is secularized and 'politicized' (relativism); and 2. when religious views are expressed in this milieu, it is likely that certain (sometimes latent) social, economic or political interests underlie and prompt them (determinism—more specifically, social or economic determinism).

It is interesting to note what might result if this modern truism were read into the ancient past. One might assume a priori that ancient persons were not individuals actively motivated by or autonomously voicing their deep-seated private beliefs and values. Guided by these relativist and determinist assumptions, one might be more inclined to view the ancients as being influenced by and giving expression to the social, economic and political interests of the immediate social group of which they were a part. Consequently, the religious mindset of the ancient Near Easterner could be portrayed as being every bit as secular in its orientation as is the modern mindset.[9] It is important to note that when this happens one is not necessarily rendering a picture of the past that is more accurate (or more erroneous), only one that is more understandable, meaningful or 'relevant' to a modern audience.

Example A: The Impact of These Assumptions
on Reconstructions of the Hebrew Prophets

Robert Wilson's *Prophecy and Society in Ancient Israel* (1980) provides a useful illustration of how these modern, social science assumptions can sometimes play a decisive role in shaping reconstructions of the past. In this important work, Wilson examines the entire range of phenomena associated with Hebrew prophecy in terms of I. M. Lewis's anthropological model of central/peripheral intermediation. In many cases the model clarifies quite clearly certain instances of prophecy recorded in the Hebrew Bible, and if biblical scholars possessed a complete record of all 'prophetic' activity occurring in Palestine during the OT period (including especially the activities of the so-called 'false prophets'), Wilson's study probably would describe very well the aggregate of such activities.[10]

Yet even a brief review of Wilson's study reveals the unmistakable impact that relativism and determinism have had upon his view of prophetic religion, and that positivism and reductionism have had upon his cross-disciplinary method. The issue at hand concerns the extent to which Wilson's reconstruction might have been unduly determined by these assumptions.

The Impact of Relativism and Determinism

At the heart of Wilson's study lies the suggestion that the anthropological model of intermediation provides a close parallel to biblical 'prophecy'. Wilson points out that

> Intermediaries do not operate in a vacuum. They are integral parts of their societies and cannot exist without social guidance and support (p.51).

and that consequently

> [o]n the basis of the comparative evidence, we may expect Israelite society to have been involved in every phase of prophetic activity, from the prophet's 'call' to the delivery of his message (p. 86).

His description of how external group processes shape or determine the content of an intermediary's/prophet's message is quite detailed (pp. 51-62). He notes that the 'candidate is frequently trained at the request of the society and is encouraged in his attempts to bring about the expected intermediation' (p. 53).[11] His study then proceeds to promote the view that every prophet in Israel (writing and nonwriting, 'true' and 'false', cultic and non-cultic, court and noncourt, Yahwist and non-Yahwist) should be approached less as an individual autonomously voicing his inner convictions and more as a group spokesman whose message has been shaped by some external social forces and interests.

By tying the prophet so closely to group processes, Wilson has appreciably limited the range within which one is now permitted to understand the historical nature of the prophet and his message. The religious 'tone' of a prophet's message may now be explained, at best, as indicative of the extent to which he had internalized the interests of his support group or, at worst, as mere ideological 'forms of speech' under which may be found a particular sociopolitical or socioeconomic agenda. In this view, the prophet's autonomy and individuality essentially have been stripped from him: his personal convictions, values and beliefs are either nonexistent (which makes him a hypocrite) or more simply they are reflective of his particular (central or peripheral) group's interests (which makes him a spokesman). The prophet's genuine sense of any 'good' transcending his social group's interests has been effectively denied.

The point here is not to deny that Hebrew prophets could be group spokesmen, even though Wilson's blanket application of this conclusion to every single prophet is arguable (cf. Herion 1982: 245-53). Rather it is to note that Wilson's reconstruction of this ancient Israelite phenomenon amounts to a classic description of modern, urban relativism and social determinism.[12] The diminished capacity of the individual to believe autonomously in absolutes—which is characteristic of the secular, modern world—has been projected on to the world of the ancient Near East. The result is the view that in ancient Israel, as in the modern 'secular city', it was not any socially transcendent religious values or convictions but relative (and partisan) sociopolitical goals or socioeconomic interests that brought unity and meaning to the life and thought of the Hebrew prophet.

The Impact of Positivism and Reductionism
It was noted above that at the heart of Wilson's study lies the assumption that there can be no socially isolated intermediaries. Wilson's reconstruction concludes that in ancient Israel there indeed were no socially isolated prophets. There is a perfect correlation here between assumption and conclusion. The issue is whether there might be something in Wilson's cross-disciplinary methodology that accounts for such neat symmetry.

Perhaps a good place to begin is with the observation that there exists some evidence which could easily be interpreted in such a way as to challenge the validity of the assumption and the accuracy of the conclusion, and thereby to disturb the symmetry of the reconstruction (cf. Heschel 1962, I.3-26, especially pp. 17-19). As one important example one may note Jeremiah's lament to Yahweh: 'I sat alone because your hand was upon me' (15.17). While it would be possible simply to reinterpret this passage (e.g. as a mere figure of speech that should not be taken literally), Wilson ignores it altogether. This is significant because it provides a useful glimpse into how the cross-disciplinary method often operates: data are consistently manipulated to the distinct advantage of the model, although the reverse is never attempted. In order to fit the historical data into the central/peripheral scheme of the model that necessarily ties prophets to support groups, some evidence is omitted (e.g. Jer. 15.17; 1 Kgs. 19.10,14) and a great deal is simply explained away—e.g. Micaiah had a 'weak' support group in 1 Kgs. 22 (p. 211), or Jer. 20.10 refers to the prophet being rejected by 'portions' of his support group (p. 246).

When Wilson does attempt to reinterpret the evidence, this often involves questionable and sweeping re-creations of entire prophetic biographies and careers. In short, the methodological stance toward the historical data seems highly critical (even revisionist at times), while the stance toward the social science model seems credulous. Wilson has permitted the model to interpret the data for him—in fact, he seems improperly to have permitted it to fill in gaps existing in the data—but he has not permitted the data reciprocally to address, much less to challenge the model. This is not an appropriate method for using models since basic to all models is their falsifiability (cf. the critique by Long 1982: 251).

It is here suggested that this methodological oversight may, in part, result from a positivist bias about the supremacy of more 'scientific' approaches to knowledge, a bias that inhibits one from critically reviewing those approaches—e.g. passive acceptance of the more 'scientific' definitions (of religion) or the more 'scientific' models (of intermediation). Another part of the oversight might well be attributed to a reductionism that leads one to confuse a simple, abstract model with an actual description of complex reality. Despite these problems, however, it must be underscored that Wilson has provided biblical scholars with an important aid for the study of the Hebrew prophets. His model of intermediation is an extremely useful one, but not because it necessarily fills in any gaps in data or serves as a possible description of what was 'real' in ancient Israel. It is important because, when used properly and critically, it can point scholars to potentially fruitful areas for further study.

The model performs this service only to the extent that one permits it and the data to go their separate ways. Unfortunately, in the quest for precise and definitive (not to mention publishable) results, many biblical scholars utilizing social science seem reluctant to permit this, perhaps believing incorrectly that unless there is a direct and consistent correlation between model and data their theses were wrong and their research was a waste of time and effort. Thus scholars may be found overlooking data (probably subconsciously) that do not mesh with their models or else straining them in such a way that they do mesh. Yet the point where the social science model and the historical data diverge is precisely the area where further study should be directed. Without the model there could be no such divergence, and without the divergence it would be much more difficult to ascertain what are the truly exceptional (and therefore important) historical features of ancient Israel. Social science models, therefore, have great heuristic value. One must then seek not to gloss over or to downplay the divergences between data and model but rather to recognize them, to underscore them for colleagues, and to invite those colleagues to join in the task of trying to account for the divergences.

Thus, for example, Wilson's study now invites scholars to raise important questions about the nature of a prophet's 'support group'. What does it mean to say that these groups were socially organized, as opposed to being politically, professionally, religiously or culturally organized? What does it mean to say that they were socially *organized*, as opposed simply to 'being present' in society? In what sense did 'support groups' provide the impulse behind a prophet's outspokenness, and in what sense did they coalesce as a response to his message? More fundamentally, however, the divergence between the model of intermediation and the data about Hebrew prophecy suggests that Wilson may have initiated his study with too narrow a concept of 'support group' in mind. In the future, it might be more appropriate (as well as less relativistic and deterministic) to begin more generally with references to a prophet's 'support structure', noting that in some instances this may indeed have been a tangible (central or peripheral) social group, but that in other instances a prophet's 'support structure' may have been something more intangible and internalized such as a cultural heritage or a religious tradition. These things also exist in society, although they do not necessarily manifest themselves as an identifiable, socially organized 'group'.[13] To the extent that cultural and religious values (not just social solidarities) can give an individual both vision and resolve, it seems fair to consider them important potential elements in a prophet's 'support structure'.

Example B: The Impact of These Assumptions on Reconstructions of Premonarchic Israel

Norman Gottwald's Tribes of Yahweh (1979) provides another useful illustration of how modern, social science assumptions can sometimes play a decisive role in shaping reconstructions of the past. In this extensive re-examination of the nature of premonarchic Israel, Gottwald introduces a wealth of social science material presented against the backdrop of the macro-sociological theories of Durkheim, Weber and Marx. The cumulative effect of this is to underscore in a most convincing manner the importance of the social dimension in ancient Israel—more specifically, the relationship between Israelite religion and society.

A brief review of Gottwald's study also reveals the impact that relativism and determinism have had upon his view of premonarchic religion, and that positivism and reductionism have had upon his sociological method. Once again, the issue at hand concerns the extent to which Gottwald's reconstruction might have been unduly determined by these assumptions.

The Impact of Relativism and Determinism

At the core of Gottwald's study lies the assumption that 'only as the full *materiality* of ancient Israel is more securely grasped will we be able to make proper sense of its *spirituality*' (p. xxv). In light of this assumption, it is not surprising that Gottwald tends to locate causality as low as possible on the 'conceptual pyramid of culture',[14] with technological innovations (iron, waterproof plaster, agricultural terracing) providing a new basis for social relations among now-relative equals; and this, in turn, engendering an 'egalitarian' ethic in early Israel that became ideologically enshrined in Yahwist religion (pp. 650-63). Thus, in premonarchic Israel, religion (Yahwism) was essentially a projection of the economic and political interests of the social organization (tribal confederacy).

This hypothesis draws heavily upon relativist and determinist notions about religion, and perhaps nowhere does this surface more clearly than in Gottwald's critique of John Bright and George Mendenhall (pp. 592-602), both of whom generally share his views about the accompanying religious process.

Religion related to society: contra John Bright

According to Gottwald, Bright improperly severs religion from society by claiming that the religion of early Israel was unique and that its socio-political origins, while revolutionary, were not. The issue here seems to be the applicability of relativism—the assumption that religion must necessarily be tied to the social sphere.

Gottwald counters Bright first with a questionable testimony to the uniqueness of Israel's sociopolitical origins,[15] and secondly with an imaginative (and admittedly caricatured) reconstruction of how unexceptional Israel's rituals and beliefs in God must have seemed to Israel's neighbors (pp. 595-96). From this it logically follows that if Israel's religion was unique it was so only because it was tied to its unique sociopolitical existence.

However, this conclusion is sustained only by misconstruing or ignoring Bright's understanding and use of the word 'religion'. One does not have to read much that Bright has written to realize that he characteristically uses the word 'religion' as it is often used in the humanities, to refer to constitutive factors of human cognitive existence. For him, 'religion' is largely synonymous with 'world view' or 'faith'; it is a process whereby people attempt to make sense out of their experiences of existence. It might be fair to say that Bright presumes a 'religion-experience' nexus, with the understanding that many human experiences come from outside the 'conceptual pyramid of culture'—i.e. beyond a given society's range of control. It seems that it is in this 'area beyond' that Bright presumes the existence of a Truly Other, and hence he feels one is justified in talking about a God 'acting' and 'being revealed' in history (i.e. in human experience).

Gottwald, however, characteristically uses the word 'religion' as it is often used in the social sciences, to refer to symbolic elements of human social existence. He tends to presume a 'religion-society' nexus wherein it is proper to speak of religion narrowly in terms of organized 'belief systems' (doctrines) and 'cult practices' (rituals). By imposing this definition on Bright's use of the word 'religion', Gottwald effectively side-steps Bright's claim that the uniqueness of Israel's religion is to be found in its peculiar way of discovering meaning and coherence in human existence (cf. Bright 1972: 140-56), and thus he is able to rule out any possible connection between religion and factors outside the social domain. By substituting his narrow social science definition of religion ('set of beliefs and cult practices', p. 595), he is able to view religion in such a way that it must be linked to the social process. Thus, Gottwald's ability to demonstrate that relativism was as pervasive in ancient Israel as it is in modern society (and as it is in the theories of Durkheim, Weber and Marx) hinges on little more than the way he has chosen to define the word 'religion'.

Religion determined by society: contra George Mendenhall

Having thereby demonstrated the exclusive connection between religion and social processes, Gottwald moves on to address the ways in which one influences the other. His concern here seems to be one of priority: Which came first, the religion or the society? According to Gottwald, Mendenhall improperly derives early Israelite society from its religion instead of vice versa. The issue here, of course, is the applicability of social determinism—the assumption that social processes influence or determine religious ideas and values.

One does not have to read Mendenhall too deeply to appreciate that he characteristically makes two basic connections when he writes about the relationship of religion to social processes. First, like Bright, he uses the word 'religion' in a much broader sense than doctrines and rituals. It may be fair to say that Mendenhall presumes a 'religion-ethical values' nexus (with these values understood to originate in historical experiences). Thus Mendenhall concludes that since human values influence human choices, and since the sum of these choices patterns the character of social relations and structure, then one correctly may assert that 'religion' (i.e. ethical values) shapes society. Second, Mendenhall tends to contrast his 'religion-ethics' nexus with a 'politics-power' nexus, thereby drawing a sharp distinction between ethical values ('religion') and social control interests ('politics'; cf. especially Mendenhall 1975, and 1973: 198ff.).[16]

In his response to this, Gottwald again either misconstrues or ignores how Mendenhall uses the word 'religion', and again substitutes his narrower social science definition (doctrines and rituals). It is at this point that Gottwald introduces the concept of 'politics' in order to demonstrate 'religion's' dependence upon social processes. Moreover, he avoids a precise, analytical, social science definition of the word in order to embrace a more intuitive, Christian, theological view of politics as 'ethics' (p. 601)—the substance of both in early Israel being 'egalitarianism'.[17] This semantic 'twist' serves Gottwald's thesis well since it enables him to co-opt all of Mendenhall's categories by rearranging all the connections. Thus, Mendenhall's 'religion-ethics' and 'politics-power' connections (and all the issues Mendenhall raised through those connections) are replaced with Gottwald's connections of 'religion' to 'cult' and 'ethics' to 'politics'.

By connecting 'ethics' to 'politics', Gottwald has appreciably limited our options in trying to identify the prime factors of causation. First, he can now agree with Mendenhall in the principle that 'ethical values' are the primary determinants, but in practice he can identify these with 'political interests', not with 'religion', and therefore he can locate them lower on the 'conceptual pyramid of culture'. Second, he can agree with Mendenhall that there are certain ways in which 'religion' can be regarded as a cause, but he identifies these with the ways in which the cult provides secondary, ideological legitimation and reinforcement of existing social, political and economic norms (Yahwism as a 'societal "feedback" servomechanism', pp. 642-49). Once again, Gottwald's ability to demonstrate that social determinism was as pervasive in ancient Israel as it is in modern society (or in Durkheim, Weber and Marx) hinges on little more than the way he has chosen to define such key words as 'religion' and 'politics'. The result is an historical reconstruction unable to concede the Israelite peasants' ability to possess any genuine sense of 'good' transcending their own sociopolitical goals and socioeconomic interests.

The point here is not to assert that early Israel was an exceptional time and place wherein self-interest largely disappeared (not even the Bible makes that statement!); nor is it to deny that premonarchic Yahwism may indeed have come to serve as an ideological projection of social, political and economic interests for a majority of Palestinian peasants (although one may debate Gottwald's assertion that this was the unique aspect of Yahwism from its inception). Rather it is to note that Gottwald's reconstruction amounts to a classic description of modern, urban relativism and social determinism. The result is the view that in premonarchic Israel, as in the modern 'secular city' (or in modern radical political movements, whether of the left or the right), it was not any socially transcendent ethical values or convictions but relative political interests and economic goals that brought unity and meaning to premonarchic Yahwism. Gottwald has not necessarily rendered a picture of ancient Israel that is more accurate (or erroneous), only one that is more intelligible, meaningful and 'relevant' to a modern audience whose perspective is similarly imbued with relativist and determinist assumptions.

The Impact of Positivism and Reductionism
In summarizing his critique of Mendenhall, Gottwald offers a statement reflecting the relativism and determinism that inform his assumptions and that are confirmed by his conclusions. Despite this, the following statement will probably strike most modern scholars as self-evidently true:

> Yet to grant that the religion of the state serves the interests of the state, but to deny that the religion of the tribe or of the intertribal confederacy serves the interests of the tribe or intertribal community, is to desert sociological method at a decisive juncture (1979:601).

As with Wilson, there is almost a perfect correlation between Gottwald's assumption that religion serves the interests of the social organization and his conclusion that in premonarchic times Yahwism served the political and economic interests of the Israelite tribal organization. Early Israel obeys all the rules laid out in the macro-sociological theories of Durkheim, Weber and Marx. The issue here is whether there might be something in Gottwald's sociological methodology that accounts for this neat symmetry.

As noted earlier, Gottwald depends heavily upon the macro-sociological theories of Durkheim, Weber and Marx. All 'theories' are somewhat like 'models' in that they often constitute summaries of current (or in these specific cases, nineteenth-century) thought and that they provide heuristic standards against which 'reality' may be measured. Macro-sociological theories in particular exhibit a much higher level of theoretical abstraction than, say, do micro-sociological theories. Like models, theories are hypothetical entities that are falsifiable in the sense that one expects divergences to result when abstract hypotheses and concrete realities are brought together.

Indeed, the past century has witnessed the application of these macro-sociological theories to countless, concrete social phenomena, and consequently professional social scientists (more so than non-social scientists) have become sensitized to the shortcomings and inadequacies of these theories. The nineteenth-century confidence in relativism and determinism that originally helped to fuel these theories (and which still helps to drive Gottwald's study) has noticeably drained away in most social science academies. In fact, almost all social scientists today would not consider themselves 'materialists' but rather 'idealists' in the sense that they see values and beliefs—including economic self-interest—as the chief driving forces in society. Thus, contra Gottwald, one could say that most social scientists themselves have 'deserted sociological method' in that they no longer depend dogmatically upon relativist and determinist (much less materialist) explanations of social phenomena. As a result of a number of related developments within the social sciences, an increasing number of social scientists have become sensitized to the sometimes powerful influences arising outside the 'conceptual pyramid of culture', and have challenged the truism that religion necessarily serves the interests of society.

In the first place, even classical nineteenth-century studies of the different bases of social solidarity (Durkheim 1893) suggest that religion functions quite differently in folk (or tribal) and urban (or state) types of societies. For example, the notion of religion serving the material interests of the social or political organization makes very little sense when applied to the ideal-typical folk society (Redfield 1947). This does not deny that religion functions to sustain society by promoting the solidarity of its members, but it points out that a wide range of possible relations between religion and society may be found beneath such simple truisms as 'religion serves the interests of society', especially when those interests can be so radically different typologically. The truism only serves to obviate further study and to encourage modern and ethnocentric views about religion's 'social utility' (cf. the comments in Malina 1982: 240-41).

Second, several prominent social science theorists from Tönnies (1887) to Parsons (1960) have hinted at the initial autonomy and independence of inner values by basing their respective social typologies (dependent variables) upon underlying typologies of personal values and volitional processes (independent variables). While few have considered such values and processes under the rubric of 'religion', the important works of Weber (1930) and Lenski (1961) have demonstrated that distinctively 'religious' factors can inform these values and processes in profound ways, helping to shape the 'moral ecology' upon which social relations, institutions and organizations are established.[18]

Third, recent sociological inquiry into the nature and origin of human values has demonstrated that values ultimately arise not from social structures/economic interests per se (as social and economic determinists maintain) but rather from human experiences (Rokeach 1979). This insight is significant because it no longer limits one to looking for causation exclusively within the 'conceptual pyramid of culture'. To the extent that social, economic and even technological factors are parts of those experiences, and to the extent that social organizations can control and meaningfully integrate both its constituents and their experiences, they can all determine human values. Causation can indeed exist within the pyramid of culture, and Gottwald has provided a necessary reinforcement of this important point. However, no social system exists that can completely control this process of integration, no matter how 'totalitarian' it strives to be. Therefore, the potential for new values (or for the resurgence of older, dormant values) is forever present, constantly presenting a challenge or even threat to the social organization (cf. Heirich 1976). Thus, to the extent that experiences lie outside the 'cultural domain' and beyond human personal or social control, the resultant values likewise originate outside the human consciousness. No person or society 'plans' what its values will be. This is the significant element of truth underlying Bright's and Mendenhalls' understanding of the potential 'transcendence' of religion.[19]

The above three areas of development within the social sciences reflect if not an abandonment at least a critical revision of nineteenth-century macro-sociology's comfortable dependence upon neat relativist and determinist assumptions. Yet these very important advancements and revisions seem not to have been significantly incorporated into Gottwald's study. While a number of factors may account for this,[20] it seems also that positivism and reductionism may have played decisive roles in bringing about this methodological omission. Positivism may have had a hand to the extent that the more scholars are convinced of the validity of the 'scientific' nature of the theories being used, the less they may be inclined to appreciate their falsifiability. Simultaneously, reductionism may have worked to blur the distinction between abstract theories about general social tendencies and concrete descriptions of actual social realities.[21] Under the influence of these two factors, it is relatively easy to see why one might avoid dealing with those more-recent developments that would only serve to complicate matters further.

The solution to the methodological problems in *The Tribes of Yahweh* seems to be not so much a matter of recognizing the inevitable divergences between social science theories and historical data but rather the demanding task of incorporating the subsequent criticisms, modifications, qualifications and even the affirmations of the basic social science theories being used. Even though Gottwald seems not to have done this, it must be underscored that he has nevertheless introduced into the discussion a very important theoretical framework from which it is possible to explore a whole new range of issues related to early Israel. The theories of Durkheim, Weber and Marx are extremely important ones, but not because they provide a definitive statement about the 'religion-society' nexus in ancient Israel (or anywhere else for that matter). They are important because they continue to raise issues for scholars subsequently to test, and for this reason these theories must be used with respect to the subsequent qualifications that have resulted from those tests.

When viewed in light of these more recent developments in sociology, Gottwald's study now urges biblical scholars to be much more cautious in making sweeping statements about the necessary 'religion-society' nexus in early Israel. There is still much to understand about how religion may have been related to values, and more specifically about how values in ancient Israel were tied to human experiences. It might well be that experiences such as the collapse of Late Bronze Age civilization (1225-1175 BC) loom large in accounting for the expression of certain 'religious' values or concepts in early Israel; perhaps they may even loom larger as 'value determinants' (particularly for the first generation or so) than do particular social structures (such as an 'egalitarian' confederation of tribes).[22] But even if they do not, the narrow view of religion serving the interests of the social structure can no longer be sustained as an unequivocal, 'scientific' truism.

Finally, Gottwald's study also encourages biblical scholars to be more truly interdisciplinary when using the word 'religion'. He is correct in noting that one cannot continue to use the word exclusively in a humanities sense that overlooks the cult and how it comes to function systemically to symbolize and legitimize the social order and its interests. Conversely, it must now also be recognized that one cannot use the word 'religion' in such a restricted social science sense that values become linked narrowly to social interests instead of more properly (and more broadly) to human experiences. Religion is not entirely a subset or an extension of society; it is a subset and an extension of human experience (a part of which is the experience of society). This suggests that in order fully to ascertain the historical nature and impact of religion in early Israel (or among the Hebrew prophets), biblical scholars must utilize an interdisciplinary method wherein they can prevent positivist and reductionist assumptions from leading them to embrace the more 'scientific' theories of religion without first criticizing them or without appreciating that they still remain just theories.

Conclusion

One hopes this focus on *Prophecy and Society in Ancient Israel* and *Tribes of Yahweh* has illustrated that even in the best studies utilizing the social sciences a special set of modern assumptions can come to play a pronounced role in shaping the sociology of knowledge in biblical studies and, therefore, in shaping conclusions about ancient Israel. This paper has not intended to suggest that positivism, reductionism, relativism and determinism are wholly 'bad' influences on scholarship, for they certainly are not. Rather, it has been suggested that these modern assumptions often work to restrict historical reconstruction by imposing limits on the range of understandable options available to historians even prior to an examination of the evidence. Such 'problems' related to the sociology of knowledge can never be eliminated, but at least they can be acknowledged, and at most one can hope that some ways may be found to compensate for their restrictive influences and to broaden the base of scholarly preunderstandings about society.

It is also hoped that this paper will help to stimulate efforts to discover those ways in which biblical scholars can acquire this greater range of options for reconstructing the historical nature of Israelite religion and society. The present writer feels that four such ways of improving cross-disciplinary research seem to follow naturally from everything that has been said above. They are offered here as tentative suggestions to help biblical scholarship more responsibly refine its use of social science models and theories.

First, there seems to be a crucial need for a truly interdisciplinary understanding of what is meant by the words 'religion' and 'religious values' (see above). Distortions seem to result when either the definitions current in the humanities or those current in the social sciences begin to dominate historical reconstructions. This suggests that biblical scholars ought to exercise special care when using models and theories in a 'social-anthropological' perspective. 'Social anthropology' is that branch of the social sciences that seeks the social and political interpretation of essentially non-political, symbolic expressions and activities (cf. Cohen 1969). This discipline can tend to rely heavily upon relativist and determinist assumptions that religious expressions and activities have sociopolitical interpretations. Scholars must first have a reasonable level of certainty that religion indeed has a sociopolitical function in a given historical context before attempting to interpret the nature of that function. Admittedly, this is a somewhat circular approach to the material; nevertheless, this seems preferable to an uncritical positing of sociopolitical functions in areas where such might not exist.

For example, this suggests that for the moment scholars avoid the popular temptation of examining premonarchic Israel and the Hebrew prophets in social-anthropological terms. While these arguably are the most important, unique and interesting aspects of ancient Israel, the social and political realities associated with them are notoriously ill-defined. (In fact, we have seen that both Gottwald and Wilson for the most part had to 'create' these realities.) Perhaps biblical scholars' social-anthropological skills first ought to be sharpened against the wisdom texts of the monarchic period or the pre-exilic psalms (cf. Herion 1982: 110-92) since in both these cases scholars have better (even cross-cultural) control of the data, fairly straight-forward symbolic and/or religious expressions, and a relatively well-defined sociopolitical context within which to place the data.

Second, the need for scholars to expand their pre-understandings beyond their own modern experiences of complex, urban society suggests that scholars need to acquire a more sympathetic awareness of the simple, 'folk' or primitive types of societies that are typologically contrary to modern society. An informed appreciation of these types of societies should help to counterbalance or nullify the influences of modernism (a) by sensitizing biblical scholars to their own modern tempocentrism and urban ethnocentrism, and (b) by enabling them to recognize a conceptual 'continuum' of societal typologies against which specific features of ancient Israel may be viewed.

Third, because historians of ancient Israel cannot observe firsthand the object of their study as can most scientists, they are always searching for possible analogies to ancient Israelite phenomena. Thus, in addition to studying other texts recovered from the ancient Near Eastern (and Mediterranean) world, biblical scholars may look for possible analogies in that specific branch of the social sciences known as cultural anthropology—more specifically, ethnography. Ethnographic studies of Arab peasant village life may be particularly beneficial to those ancient Near Eastern and biblical scholars who have few occasions to travel the backroads of the Middle East. The conservative aspects of village life there may provide revealing glimpses into the ancient past, and it is curious that more biblical scholars have not sought for analogies in this corpus of material. In many pockets of the Middle East, modernism and industrialism have had little impact, and consequently these cultures can still be comparatively close to those of the ancient Near East both geographically and culturally—although due consideration must be given to the historical variables (notably Islam). Ethnographic studies of more recent non-Semitic societies (e.g. medieval European, Latin American, sub-Saharan African, Far Eastern) will probably yield less convincing analogies to ancient Israel since they are so widely separated historically, geographically and culturally.[23] The least convincing analogies of all will probably be those drawn between ancient Israel and the modern, industrial (and post-industrial) West. Thus, to the extent that the specific branch of the social sciences known as sociology derives its models and theories from the study and observation of this type of society, one may seriously question what it has to contribute to our understanding of ancient Israel.

Fourth, biblical scholars need to adopt a more rigorous method of using social science models and theories. Perhaps this means that every social science study of ancient Israel should begin not simply with a description of a particular model or theory but also with a critical evaluation of it, especially noting how subsequent social science study has qualified, modified or revised that model or theory. It follows from this that every social science study of ancient Israel should be committed to pointing out not only the parallels but more importantly the inevitable divergences that will result whenever social science models or theories are brought together with his-torical data. This heuristic value of social science models and theories finally suggests that every social science study of ancient Israel should conclude with a directive for the continued investigation of the phenomenon in ques-tion. In short, those who engage in this cross-disciplinary study should be as committed to pointing out new and often more subtle questions and lines of investigation as they are committed to answering and clarifying the old ones.

Excursus on 'Genre-Confusion'

I hope that the preceding comments will not be construed either as a general assault on interdisciplinary study or as an attack centering on the works of Robert Wilson and Norman Gottwald. Whatever sharpness one may detect in my criticisms of these works is probably due to the uncertainty and frustra-tion I felt when reading *Prophecy and Society* and *Tribes of Yahweh:* I was never sure what I was supposed to read those books 'as'.

I have gradually begun to suspect that one of the casualties of interdisci-plinary study is clarity about 'genre'. For example, I had no doubt that I was supposed to read both these books generally 'as' historiography, but the difficulty I still experienced in trying to determine what the respective auth-ors were intending to accomplish sensitized me to the wide range of sub-genres associated with history-writing. What 'type' of historiography are these books?

For example, all biblical scholars are familiar with academic historiog-raphy. But even within this sub-genre, distinctions must be made between a work that tests an hypothesis and one that more fundamentally proposes a reconstruction of the past. These distinctions easily become confused in an interdisciplinary study when the researcher fails to note the inevitable diver-gences between social science models and theories and the historical data.

This was the confusion I had in reading *Prophecy and Society in Ancient Israel*. Had Wilson looked for and pointed out the divergences then it would have been more obvious that he was testing an hypothesis rather than proposing a (sweeping) reconstruction. I believe this would have made it easier to respond more fairly to his study since I would then have been more sensitive to what he was trying to accomplish.

Also, when an interdisciplinary study fails to include a critique of the social science theories being applied, the careful reader begins to question how 'realistic' is the resulting picture of the past. In fact, the reader may no longer be certain that the writer is primarily motivated by a 'dispassionate', academic quest for the 'reality' of the past in its own terms. This suggests another type of history writing: ideological historiography. Here the past becomes an authoritative vehicle for expressing and legitimizing contemporary concerns (Plumb 1971; B. Lewis 1975). In fact, the use of social science can actually facilitate such history-writing, since social science can also be highly ideological in its own right.[24] When the authority of 'the past' is combined with the authority of 'science'—not to mention the additional sense of authority that in certain religious circles adheres to any statement made about the Bible or ancient Israel—an interdisciplinary study combining history, social science and biblical studies becomes ripe for ideological exploitation. One is no longer certain whether the study is an objectve accounting of the 'real' past or a partisan advocacy of a desirable future. This was the confusion I had in reading *Tribes of Yahweh*. Had Gottwald criticized the nineteenth-century macro-sociological theories he used, the resulting picture of premonarchic Israel would certainly have been more 'realistic' and less 'utopian'; it would then have been more obvious that Gottwald was indeed writing academically about ancient Israel instead of ideologically about (legitimate) contemporary political concerns, and it would have been easier for me to know how to respond to his study.

Hopefully a more rigorous methodological use of social science models and theories will help clear up much of the historiographic 'genre-confusion' that has accompanied the social scientific study of ancient Israel.

Notes

*The author wishes to thank the James A. Gray Endowment, whose post-doctoral fellowship at the University of North Carolina at Chapel Hill provided him with both the opportunity and the resources to prepare this paper. He also wishes particularly to thank University of North Carolina professors Gerhard Lenski (Sociology) and Jack Sasson (Religious Studies) for their very helpful comments and criticisms of earlier drafts of this manuscript. The author assumes full responsibility for all the inadequacies that remain, as well as for all opinions expressed in this paper.

[1] Wilhelm Windelband formulated the classic distinction between the idiographic aims of the historian and the nomothetic objectives of the sciences; the former being a concern for specific

or unique traits while the latter is an interest in observed regularities and explanatory generalizations. Cf. Mandelbaum 1977:4-14.

[2] Cf. Sasson 1981, who provides a succinct statement about the relationship between modernism and the scholar's pre-understandings: 'Thus whenever a scholar compares kingship, democracy, absolutism, etc., in the Ancient Near East and in the OT, his comparison is understood by his audience—and by him, for that matter—not so much because he has recreated the political realities in Israel and in the Ancient Near East, but because he is using currently understood models as frames of reference' (p. 8).

[3] 'The past fifty or a hundred years have seen a remarkable growth in the number, size and power of organizations of many kinds, ranging through all areas of life. . . . Yet this revolution has received little study, and it is not something of which we are particularly conscious. It has crept upon us silently. It is something we accept as "natural" almost without thinking' (Boulding 1953:3-4).

[4] While kinship is the organizational basis of most simple societies, it is rare these days to find it discussed as a significant aspect of Israelite social organization. In part this is the consequence of kinship's close tie a century ago to now-discredited hypotheses about Israel's nomadic origins; in part its neglect may also stem from a belief that its impact on Israelite society was negligible compared to the impact of formally organized institutions (military, priesthood, bureaucracy, etc.), on the assumption that Israel was a relatively complex society like our own. No one can deny that certain segments of Israelite society indeed resemble modern society (cf. Rosenbloom 1972), but other segments undoubtedly were simpler, and functioned as such. The point is: Can we understand these simpler functions? For example, to what extent can we fully appreciate the social function of kinship systems as long as we experience kinship in a modern setting that has translated many of its traditional functions to formal institutional structures (e.g. daycare centers for children, formal schooling for youths, government assistance for impoverished relatives, nursing homes for the elderly)?

[5] We also tend to retroject modern notions of 'authority' into the past where they do not belong (cf. Arendt 1958). While we have a tendency to institutionalize authority and associate it with the political monopoly of force, this is not at all how authority operates in the more folk-like setting of simple societies. Authority there has nothing to do with coercive force, persuasive argumentation or institutional organization. Because it is so prevalent, so absolute and yet so diffuse as to defy anthropological attempts to 'locate' it, authority in these settings is unlike anything with which we 'politicized' moderns are familiar. Perhaps the closest we in biblical studies have come to recognizing this general type of authority in ancient Israel was in our rather imprecise references to the authority of the judges as being 'charismatic'. Initially there was never any doubt that the word 'charismatic' cautioned against any association of authority with institutional organization; similarly it was understood to refer to something quite different than a judge's ability to coerce or persuade others rationally. Subsequently, however, some scholars have begun to coin qualifying terms such as 'institutional charisma' or 'office charisma', which have not necessarily provided a more accurate picture of the judges, only one that is more easily comprehended in modern terms.

[6] As Robert Bellah has noted, what often guarantees the authority and even the power of professional social scientists is 'the theoretical and methodological prestige of social science as science' (1982: 36).

[7] Both relativism and determinism have been subjects of debate within the social sciences, and most social scientists probably would no longer accept our admittedly reductionistic definitions of these two tendencies. However, there are noticeable traces of these tendencies still lingering in the social sciences, and some social scientists still feel compelled to criticize the ways in which these assumptions dominate some social science studies. Cf. Haes 1980 and McGehee 1982.

[8] It is important for biblical scholars to appreciate that social science consensus on these matters has disappeared. There is now significant dissatisfaction within the social sciences over such a one-sided appeal to the passive conception of man as implied in Marxian historical

materialism. Many—even many neo-Marxists—are trying to strike a more reasonable and accurate balance by supplementing it with the view of active, autonomous man implied in Kantian transcendental idealism (Habermas 1971, 1973, 1976; Dawe 1970; Haes 1980).

[9] Given the fact that most 'religious' texts recovered from the ancient Near East originally were public and ideological in nature, this view would not be at all improper when applied to such texts. The question is: Is it proper to extend this view into a generalization about every 'religious' expression originating in the ancient Near East?

[10] In noting that Wilson's thesis may very well describe what was typical of prophetic phenomena, we must remember that it might not apply at all to those prophets who were not typical. Were Amos, Hosea, Micah, Isaiah or Jeremiah 'typical' pre-exilic prophets? If so, why were their words initially remembered, valued and preserved while those of countless others were not? See Heschel 1962, II.252-53, who argues that these individuals represent a type *sui generis*.

[11] Wilson's use of the word 'expected' is quite revealing: the intermediary's/prophet's message can be predicted once we know which group he represents. Wilson's actual method is the reverse of this: since we know the prophet's message from the biblical text, we can predict the group to which he belonged. The potential for circular reasoning here should be obvious.

[12] 'The individual counts for little, but the voice of the representative is heard with a deference roughly proportional to the numbers for whom he speaks.' Interestingly, this statement was not made by Wilson with respect to the ancient Hebrew prophets (although it seems to apply quite well to his thesis); rather it was made by a sociologist with respect to modern, urban society (Wirth 1938: 14).

[13] Jack Sasson has reminded me furthermore that one must be very cautious when undertaking 'scientific' inquiries dependent on evidence found in literacy pieces (e.g. the non-writing prophets who appear in Deuteronomistic literature). One would somehow feel it inappropriate to apply anthropological models to gain scientific information about the 'seers' found in Homer or in the plays of Sophocles.

[14] The anthropological 'pyramidization' of culture conceives of a culture's economic institutions as the base of a conceptual, three-tiered 'pyramid' anchored to the ecosystem by a technology that can exploit and capitalize upon existing resources, both natural and human. Above this economic base is the middle tier representing the social structures that exist to insure orderly (although not necessarily equitable) economic activity—chief among these is the political monopoly of force (i.e. instruments of government). At the peak of the 'pyramid' are the ideological symbols, including religion and morality, which work to provide a sense of legitimacy and stability for everything underneath. Economic determinism conceives of causation as being from the bottom up (materialism), and religion thus comes to be viewed as the ultimate 'effect'. This has reinforced the relativist tendency to view religion as a public phenomenon related to social control interests, not as a private phenomenon related to personal experience.

[15] 'Gottwald claims that there is no parallel for this development in the Middle East, and I cannot suggest one. I am not persuaded, however, that the dynamics of the process by which Israel came in existence are quite as unique as Gottwald sometimes implies' (Lenski 1980: 275). One wonders if an enterprising Egyptologist could argue a 'peasant revolt' hypothesis to describe the First (or Second) Intermediate period at least as plausibly as Gottwald had done for ancient Israel. Perhaps an enterprising Assyriologist could do the same for the end of the Ur III period.

[16] Mendenhall seems to agree with the social sciences (and with Gottwald) that doctrines and rituals play important roles in social control (cf. 1973: 72-73); but for that reason he tends to think of them in terms of political (power) functions, not religious (ethical) ones. To some extent the differences here between Mendenhall and Gottwald are primarily semantic and emphatic. However, there are very sharp confessional differences in their personal evaluations of political power. Mendenhall, apparently employing a Lutheran 'two-kingdom' concept, seems

to concede the necessity of social control interests while secularizing them. Gottwald, apparently employing a Marxist-style liberation theology, seems to regard upper-class power as illegitimate (even 'evil'?) while lower-class power is justified (even 'righteous'?).

[17] One is reminded of theologian Paul Lehmann's definition of politics as 'activity, and reflection on activity, which aims at and analyzes what it takes to make and keep human life human in the world' (1963: 85), or Harvey Cox's statement that politics is what makes human life and thought meaningful (1965: 254), or Miguez Bonino's contention that politics is the outward form of love (1983), or John Howard Yoder's *The Politics of Jesus* (1972), which is really about the ethics of Jesus. Certainly this confusion of 'politics' with 'ethics' is the consequence of commendable efforts to encourage Christians to act out their values rather than passively to pay them lip-service, the use of the word 'politics' underscoring this call to act. But such naive definitions (conveniently?) avoid the ethically troublesome problem of power—i.e. 'playing to win' instead of 'playing with integrity'. No social scientific study of political phenomena can hope to be taken seriously if it refuses to recognize that 'politics' refers to the manipulation of coercive force in an orderly and prescribed manner. It necessarily assumes a highly utilitarian view of humans as manipulable objects. Thus, the paradox of 'politics' in Gottwald's (and the others') ingenuous sense of the word is that at times it must be somewhat de-humanizing, unloving and unethical if it is to promote humanity, love and ethics. Cf. Mendenhall 1973: 196-97.

[18] The very important concept of 'moral ecology' is analogous to the biological concept of 'gene pool'; it refers to the *pre-existing* 'raw material' out of which selections can be made so as to produce a unique and viable social (or biological) organism (cf. Sullivan 1982). The values constituting the 'moral ecology' are not created by the social organization but rather are presupposed by it. To be sure, all social organizations inevitably turn around and actively promote an ideology to bolster those select values upon which its existence absolutely depends; but many values thus remain untouched or unincorporated by the social organization, and are still capable of inspiring individual and mass divergences from the social norm.

[19] This also helps to clarify something that historians take for granted but that social scientists often tend to be confounded by: change.

[20] One factor undoubtedly is the inevitable 'interdisciplinary lag' and 'academic specialization' that make it impossible to keep abreast of developments in other fields. Another factor may be certain personal ideological or partisan political reasons that make these theoretical abstractions attractive and useful in their unrevised, nineteenth-century forms (see excursus).

[21] The temptation to rely heavily upon theories (or upon intuition) is perhaps especially strong for historians of the ancient past who often have very little 'concrete reality' (i.e. data) to begin with. It is perhaps in this light that we should try to understand Gottwald's appeal to 'imagination' in lieu of evidence. Thus we must appreciate that some of his confident remarks about the state of our knowledge (e.g. 'We know very well what these contemporaries noticed in Israel . . . ', 1979: 596) are really highly subjective intuitions. In fact, on a number of occasions Gottwald seems to recommend as proper methodology the reading of such modern intuitions into the ancient past (1979: xxv and 801 n. 644).

[22] We might also apply these insights to Wilson's *Prophecy and Society in Ancient Israel*. It might well be that experiences such as the westward march of the Assyrian army in the second half of the eighth century BC loom large in accounting for the outburst of prophetic activity in Israel at the time. Perhaps such experiences were more significant in stimulating their religious values than were specific central or peripheral support groups.

[23] In utilizing contemporary Third World ethnography, biblical scholars must appreciate that extensive and sometimes intensive colonialism, Protestant and Catholic evangelism, industrialism and more recently Marxism have all helped to modernize and westernize even the peasant villages there. Significantly, the Arab Third World has most successfully resisted these influences, although even that has begun to change in the past twenty years.

[24] Over thirty years ago Reinhold Niebuhr commented that 'While the ideological taint upon all social judgments is most apparent in the practical conflicts of politics, it is equally discern-

ible, upon close scrutiny, in even the most scientific observations of social scientists' (1953:75). Even in America today sociologists are often viewed as progenitors of social vision and political directions (cf. Bellah 1982: 35).

Works Cited

H. Arendt
1958   'What Was Authority?', in *Authority* (Nomos II), ed. C. F. Friedrich; Cambridge, Mass.: Harvard University: 81-112.
R. Bellah
1981   'Biblical Religion and Social Science in the Modern World', *The National Institute for Campus Ministries Journal* 6/3: 8-22.
1982   'Social Science as Practical Reason', *The Hastings Center Report* 12/5:32-39.
J. M. Bonino
1983   *Toward a Christian Political Ethics*, Philadelphia: Fortress.
K. Boulding
1983   *The Organizational Revolution*, New York: Harper and Brothers.
J. Bright
1972   *A History of Israel*, 2nd edn; Philadelphia: Westminster. In the third edition (1981) Bright responds to Gottwald (1979).
A. Cohen
1969   'Political Anthropology: The Analysis of the Symbolism of Power Relations', *Man* 4: 217-35.
H. Cox
1965   *The Secular City: Secularization and Urbanization in Theological Perspective*, New York: Macmillan.
A. Dawe
1970   'The Two Sociologies', *British Journal of Sociology* 21/2: 207-18.
E. Durkheim
1893   *De la division travail social*, Paris: Alcan; 5th edn., 1926. ET *The Division of Labor in Society*, New York: Macmillan, 1933; repr. Glencoe, Ill.: Free Press, 1949.
1912   *Les formes élémentaires de la vie religieuse*, Paris: Alcan.
N. Gottwald
1979   *The Tribes of Yahweh*, Maryknoll, New York: Orbis.
J. Habermas
1971   *Towards a Rational Society*, London: Heinemann.
1972   *Knowledge and Human Interests*, London: Heinemann.
1973   *Theory and Practice*, Boston: Beacon Press.
1976   *Legitimation Crisis*, London: Heinemann.
J. Haes
1980   The Problem of Cultural Relativism, *Sociological Review* 28/4: 717-43.
M. Heirich
1976   'Cultural Breakthroughs', *American Behavioral Scientist* 19/6: 685-702.
G. Herion
1982   *The Social Organization of Tradition in Monarchic Judah*, Ph.D. dissertation, University of Michigan. Ann Arbor: University Microfilms.
A. Heschel
1962   *The Prophets: An Introduction*, I-II, New York: Harper and Row.
P. Lehmann
1963   *Ethics in a Christian Context*, New York: Harper and Row.

G. Lenski
1961   *The Religious Factor*, Garden City, N.Y.: Doubleday and Co.
1980   Review of Gottwald's *Tribes of Yahweh*, *Religious Studies Review* 6/4: 275-78.
B. Long
1982   'The Social World of Ancient Israel', *Interpretation* 37/3: 243-55.
B. Malina
1982   'The Social Sciences and Biblical Interpretation', *Interpretation* 37/3: 229-42.
M. Mendelbaum
1977   *The Anatomy of Historical Knowledge*, Baltimore: Johns Hopkins.
C. McGehee
1982   'Spiritual Values and Sociology: When We Have Debunked Everything, What Then,' *The American Sociologist* 17:40-46.
G. Mendenhall
1973   *The Tenth Generation*, Baltimore: Johns Hopkins.
1975   'The Conflict Between Value Systems and Social Control', in *Unity and Diversity*, ed. H. Goedicke and J. J. M. Roberts; Baltimore: Johns Hopkins, 169-80.
R. Niebuhr
1953   *Christian Realism and Political Problems*, New York: Scribner.
T. Parsons
1960   'Pattern Variables Revisited', *American Sociological Review* 25: 467-83.
R. Redfield
1947   'The Folk Society', *American Journal of Sociology* 52: 293-308.
M. Rokeach
1979   *Understanding Human Values*, New York: Free Press.
J. Rosenbloom
1972   'Social Science Concepts of Modernization and Biblical History', *JAAR* 40: 437-44.
J. Sasson
1981   'On Choosing Models for Recreating Israelite Pre-Monarchic History', *JSOT* 21: 3-24.
O. Steck
1977   'Theological Streams of Tradition', in *Tradition and Theology in the Old Testament*, ed. D. Knight; Philadelphia: Fortress, 183-214.
W. Sullivan
1982   *Reconstructing Public Philosophy*, Berkeley: University of California.
F. Tönnies
1887   *Gemeinschaft und Gesellschaft*, Leipzig: Reisland.
M. Weber
1930   *The Protestant Ethic and the Spirit of Capitalism*, tr. T. Parsons; London: Allen & Unwin.
R. Wilson
1980   *Prophecy and Society in Ancient Israel*, Philadelphia: Fortress.
1984   *Sociological Approaches to the Old Testament*, Philadelphia: Fortress.
L. Wirth
1938   'Urbanism as a Way of Life', *American Journal of Sociology* 44: 1-24.
J. Yoder
1972   *The Politics of Jesus*, Grand Rapids: Eerdmans.

CANON AND CRITICISM: METHOD OR MADNESS?

DONN F. MORGAN
Professor of Old Testament and Dean of Academic Affairs
Church Divinity School of the Pacific

Article from *Anglican Theological Review*

Over the past two decades there has been a growing emphasis on the role and function of canon as an interpretive principle or category for studying the biblical text.[1] This emphasis has had several different foci. Some have spoken of canon as representative of a different level of meaning in the biblical text, a level that has been overlooked or dismissed by modern historical-critical methodologies. Others have seen canon study as a logical and next step to historical-critical methods, taking seriously the results gained therein. And while some view the study of the biblical text from a canonical perspective as a return to methods and perspectives used in a "pre-critical" era, all have recognized the emphases in this area as "new" to twentieth-century interpretation of the biblical text. In addition to the different goals espoused by those who study the canon have come debates over nomenclature. Canonical reading, canonical context, canonical method, canonical process, and canonical criticism are only a few of the many terms used when this new phenomenon is discussed and debated. While the future of canon studies may not be clear, few would disagree with the judgment that canon has been an important locus for discussion of biblical methodology and biblical theology in the recent past.

Despite numerous publications and the intense debate over canon, there is little if any methodological clarity concerning *how* one is to study the Bible canonically. Does the contemporary concern with canon represent a new methodological approach to the biblical text? Should canonical reading or canonical criticism be viewed as a method in the same manner as form criticism or source criticism? If so, what are the primary characteristics of this method? Are there guidelines and controls for such a method? Or is the recent concern with canon simply a plea for another perspective within which to place the tried and true methods of biblical study?

The answers to these questions are not unimportant in light of the current attention given to canon in biblical studies. For teacher and student alike, it is necessary to determine whether this focus is able to generate a new method or rather must be seen as a particular perspective—one which may be interesting and provocative, but which cannot be emulated in any methodologically rigorous manner. The purpose of this essay, then, is to examine the recent efforts advocating the study of the Old Testament as canon and to determine if there is a method to the madness, as some would characterize it, of this particular concern. Much has been written, pro and con, about Childs, Sanders, et al. My concern is not to review the history of canon study or to criticize it. Rather, we must begin to understand how, if at all, to enter into this arena and approach the text with common methodological guidelines. Like other methods, canonical study may not be our cup of tea, but the overriding question is whether it could be if we so wished.[2]

Presuppositions: The Community of Faith

Canon and Community. They go together. Neither truly exists without the other.[3]

Canonical study presupposes that the biblical text has been and continues to be used as Scripture within many different communities of faith. The concept of canon—as rule, as boundary determiner, as authoritative body of text—is not meaningful without such a presupposition. While such an assumption creates as many problems as it solves (e.g., *which* community of faith? *which* canon? *which* order or sequence of texts?), it also highlights certain characteristics of the biblical text that are of special concern and interest. The subject of study will be the canonical text, that is, a text passed down within the community of faith. While it is certainly possible for anyone to choose a final, complete form of the text as the basis for study (e.g., structuralists, literary critics, et al.), there are at least four reasons that seem to be peculiar to this particular endeavor for the canon critic.

First, the canonical text is chosen precisely because it resides within a faith community, because that faith community provides the context for its existence, its *raison d'être*. This context witnesses to the contemporary importance of the literature as canon. The biblical literature itself is the product of such a use and context. The texts, through a variety of means (study, public reading, prayer, etc.), are a part of a dynamic between text and community that characterizes, and to a certain extent sets apart, the particular faith communities that view them as special. Thus to choose to study the Bible as canon is to recognize both its contemporary functions and the genesis of its use and shape within ancient Israel and the early church.

Second, the form of the biblical text is affected by its setting within a community of faith. The student of canonical texts will look for evidence that the text has been shaped and structured because of its setting and function. Perhaps the best and most well-known example of such structuring or shaping is the Torah. Many have argued that the Torah as canon is best explained not primarily in terms of its literary history but rather in light of its use as Scripture within the post-exilic community of faith.[4] Such a shaping is one result of the dynamic relationship presupposed by its communal setting. Moreover, the shaping of the restoration community of Ezra by a Torah of some indefinite nature on the one hand, and the shaping of Torah by the needs of that community on the other, reflect an interrelationship, a process of interpretation, which continues even after the final form of Torah is fixed. Thus one characteristic of the scriptural text or the fixed canon is its multivalence, testified to by the plethora of interpretations, of "torahs," throughout the history of Judaism and Christianity.

Third, the canonical text is chosen because it is authoritative within the communal context. The nature of that authority is to be understood not usually in terms of the text itself but rather in light of particular communities and long traditions that have spelled out the precise characteristics of biblical authority. One danger faced by students of canon is the temptation to read such notions of authority back into the texts, presupposing that such texts have always operated in light of clear, and often contemporary, definitions of biblical authority. Here, however, the very concept of canon as authoritative is anachronistic.[5] It may be better to speak of "emerging canon" or "nascent Scripture" when referring to issues of authority surrounding the final composition of particular biblical texts. The search for the grounds and nature of authority attached to the biblical text will usually bring us much closer to the contemporary faith community than to the "original."

Fourth, the canonical text represents an interaction between particular communities and their times that can be studied historically. Various critical methods that search for and isolate distinct contributions from particular authors and their historical communities can contribute to the picture of a canonical symphonic orchestra within any given text. The emphasis of the canonical critic on the final form of the text within the community will demand that the orchestra play a clearly understood tune with integrity.

Method: Developing a Perspective

> Biblical 'methods' are *theories* rather than methods: theories which result from the formalizing of intelligent intuitions about the meaning of biblical text.[6]

This statement by John Barton appears to be true for canonical study. Childs, Sanders, and others have spent much time discussing the canonical level, function, and context of biblical texts, arguing that there is a meaning at this level that has not been adequately uncovered by other theories and their concomitant methods.[7] The general basis for such a theory is in place if the presupposition about text and community discussed above is accepted.

But, if this theory is to become usable for others, we must attempt to proceed to the next stage: the development of method. Methods have a way of becoming normative in the eyes of their advocates. This is surely the case with canon study, where the normativeness of the canon is often transposed to the method and sometimes to the results produced by such a method. Yet it is important from the outset to recognize that canon study is not intrinsically more important or valuable simply because it chooses to deal with the canonical shape and function of the biblical text.

The first methodological issue raised in a study of the canon is which final text will be chosen. There has been and continues to be much disagreement in this area. With respect to the Old Testament, for example, should the text be the Masoretic text or the Septuagint or . . . ?[8] It does not appear crucial which text is chosen so long as the interpreter is aware of two factors. First, the choice will depend partially upon concerns extrinsic to the text itself (e.g., different canons, particular interests governed by contemporary issues, etc.). Second, the choice needs to recognize a comparative dimension within the study itself. For example, a study of the Hebrew canonical division of the Writings must be aware that an examination of the organization of these books in the Septuagint will yield quite different results. To suggest that *one* text in *one* canon, in any language and at any time, should be the normative text is to deny the multivalent nature of canon as witnessed to by the faith communities in which it, or rather they (i.e., several canons), are found.

The real methodological issue here turns out to be not *which* final text is chosen, but that *a* final, complete text is chosen. The concern is to provide a *holistic* interpretation of the canonical biblical text since that text is functional within the religious community. Thus the heuristic value of canon study is highlighted. If we can find no legitimate grounds to deny any canon as a starting point, then the value of choosing some particular canon must be found in its ability to discern particular patterns, signs, or structures that may be helpful in understanding the scriptural nature of a particular text, usually described in terms of its theological message. Such patterns may not function in the same way in other canons. This latter, seemingly negative or relativizing recognition well may be valuable in a discussion of the overall function of Scripture as witnessed to by many canons.

Another important characteristic of any critical method is its ability to set limits for its application. For example, form criticism identifies and defines the "form" it studies, isolating a text in terms of its beginning and end in relationship to the context in which it is found. Can or does canon study do likewise? To date there have been two basic limits or scopes for the study of canon, ways we might describe as micro- and macro-canonical analysis. Micro-canonical analysis studies a book or perhaps an even smaller unit. *Introduction to the Old Testament as Scripture* by Brevard Childs is the best-known illustration of micro-canonical analysis. One difficulty raised in the study of canon at the level of individual books is our ability to identify canonical shaping and its resultant meaning and to distinguish it from the results gained by redaction criticism.

Macro-canonical analysis may hold more promise for methodological clarity and uniqueness. The focus of such study would be canonical *complexes* of books, such as Torah, "the Twelve," Former Prophets, Megilloth, etc. Included in the study of these complexes might be a consideration of the sequences of books and their variations within particular canonical collections. Surely tradition history and redaction criticism may aid in delineating the overall shape of some of these literary, canonical complexes.[9] Nevertheless, the canon provides the guidelines and rationale for the organization and for the scope of the textual studies. Such analysis would try to locate those needs and concerns within the community of faith which motivated or were reflected by the resultant canonical structures. The "original" reasons for the order of canonical complexes are often difficult to determine and sometimes the result of factors extrinsic to the text itself. Nevertheless, the interpretations of single books, as units within the larger whole, are controlled by an attempt to locate historical motivation or intention within communities that used them.

As an illustration of macro-canonical analysis, we will briefly examine the two different sequences of Ezra-Nehemiah and Chronicles in various canonical collections. The order of the Christian canon today is dependent primarily upon the Septuagint order. That order employs an historical rationale for the sequence, reading Chronicles before Ezra-Nehemiah. To read this sequence is to see Torah as the final word, to see the focus on the prophets in Chronicles completed in the program of restoration narrated in Ezra-Nehemiah. The attendant values and uses of Torah proclaimed therein become the final (at least for this community) way in which the "new" community is to live and make its way in the world. Such a perspective is not incompatible with much of subsequent Judaism and Christianity with a focus on an establishment religion, a religion of the book. In this way of reading, the repetition of the prophecy of Jeremiah at the end of Chronicles and the beginning of Ezra serves as an effective connection between the two works, especially effective when several books interrupt the sequence, as is the case in many canonical collections. It reminds the community of the continuity between the past prophetic word and the new "established" community.

On the other hand, we may read Ezra-Nehemiah first and then Chronicles, a sequence present in the Hebrew Bible. This order is clearly not historical in its rationale. This sequence begins with a strong statement about the priority and place of Torah in the life of the community. Reading Chronicles next, with its heavy emphasis upon David and the prophets, upon a word given but still to be fulfilled, portrays a community which, while it has its priorities straight with Torah at its center, still awaits the completion of God's word, most probably through a messianic figure—a prophet like Moses, a prophet-king like David. Here the repetition or double use of the

Jeremiah prophecy that begins Ezra and concludes Chronicles forms an *inclusio*, not connecting the end of the state of Judah with the beginning of the restoration, but rather envisioning the establishment of the restoration community as the beginning of a fulfillment of the prophetic promise to give "a future and a hope." This future and hope can only be understood in light of a continuity between the Torah of Moses and the kingship of David. Both sequences, both ways of reading, are possible in the canon. Indeed, they are not only possible but present, in the way particular Jewish and Christian communities have understood the relationship between Torah and Prophets, the old and the new, from early period to the contemporary time.

Beginning, then, with a complete text, what does the student of the canon *do*? According to Childs, for example, we should look for "signs" of canonical shaping; that is, we should look for structural indicators that point to and illustrate the use of this literature as Scripture within the community of faith.[10] In this sense the method is literary in nature, for the structural signs are to be found in the text itself. But how will we know a sign when we see it? What controls or guidelines can be provided which will enable several students of canon to recognize the same signs or, at least, to agree that the signs or structures found by others are methodologically legitimate?

Both Childs and Sanders have identified and described these structural signs as characteristics of the canonical text that often go against the expected flow of the text or that go beyond the "original" intention of the authors or redactors involved. Thus the addition of second Isaiah to first Isaiah represents a canonical structure that produces a result different from what either complex of literature intended. Or again, the final oracle of the book of Amos creates an eschatological function for the book quite different from the "original" prophet or prophetic collection, even more open-ended in scope than was intended by the redactor who placed the final oracle in its present position.

What are the methodological guidelines for locating and isolating these canonical signs? It is precisely here that canonical study is dependent upon other critical methodologies. To the extent that these signs are to be found in the peculiar juxtaposition of sources and oracles, the method of redaction criticism is crucial in their identification. To the extent that these signs are to be found in the overall structure of books or sources, the study is really form criticism writ large. Each of these traditional methods does have guidelines, and, it seems, these guidelines or procedures must be used if canonical analysis is to have any precision. At this point the distinction between canonical study and other methods is very difficult to define and maintain. Perhaps one could argue that canonical study is simply the application of traditional methods to a body of literature viewed holistically, presupposing a particular use, function, and context. But it will be up to other disciplines to identify and explicate that use, function, and context. The canonical perspective appears to have the function of reminding the student of the Bible's nature as Scripture and suggesting that one way of recovering it is to be found in a holistic reading.

In summary, canonical study has been seen to owe a great deal to other critical theories used in biblical scholarship. It has historical concerns to the extent that it attempts to anchor its interpretation of canonical form within the history of the faith communities that use it, paying attention whenever possible to the motivations and needs of the communities that understood its message or Scripture in a particular way. When "new" interpretations of the canon occur, canonical criticism comes closer to contemporary structuralist literary criticism, but the use of the more traditional methods to delineate the shape and structure of "books" prevents it from moving into this area of interpretation totally.

There are, unfortunately, few methodological guidelines for a study of canon. One does begin with a final form of the biblical text. One does, with the help of other critical methods and their controls, evaluate the internal structures of particular canonical books. At a further level, utilizing the results of a study of smaller units, the student of canon can engage in a more creative endeavor, exploring the sequences of books and the implications of their juxtaposition, and the relationships between various parts of the canon (e.g., Torah and Prophets). Controls or guidelines for this procedure are hazy, providing both challenge and freedom for the biblical interpreter. Nevertheless, the boundaries of canon and the understanding that results from this interpretation must be placed within a dynamic that sees Scripture and community of faith in a dialogue. This dynamic presses the canonical interpreter to search for parallel or analogous interpretations within the history of biblical interpretation and to anchor the results in the needs of the particular community. The heuristic nature of canon study is highlighted in this endeavor. It is, indeed, the heuristic nature of canon study that may prove most fruitful in the doing of biblical theology from a canonical perspective.

Canon and Biblical Theology

The importance of canon for Old Testament theology is that it establishes a perspective from which the literature was understood by historic Israel. . . . The appeal to the canonical form of the Scriptures at least seeks to establish a common text as the grounds for theological reflection.[11]

The use of canon in biblical theology is a potentially fruitful endeavor for several reasons. Canonical shape is, for most who study it, a theological shape. The canon can serve as a control to define the scope of literature to be examined and as a heuristic device to explore the interrelationships of biblical traditions with a special focus on canonical units. While theological ways of understanding biblical literature are of special concern to canonical critics, the canon is best seen not as a theological principle, but rather as an organizing principle.

Even a brief examination of biblical canons reveals the existence of several divisions and several different interrelationships between the same books. The very existence of different canons suggests the possibility that, at a theological level, there were different ways of understanding, perhaps even prioritizing, the messages contained within the biblical books. One way of using canon in biblical theology would be to explore the messages and interrelationships of Torah, Prophets, Writings, and New Testament (with its own division, analogous to Torah and Prophets, namely Gospels and Epistles). A biblical theology organized in such a way would call for an investigation of the ways canon or Scripture, in particular combinations, is used within the faith community as it attempts to relate its contemporary needs and concerns to different, sometimes conflicting, blocks of authoritative texts. The results of such an analysis would not be normative but paradigmatic in nature, potentially providing some direction for the contemporary faith community as it struggles with the same dynamic, but in far different circumstances.

Thus, for example, the Writings can be seen as a response of the faith community to both Torah and Prophets. In a different vein, one could explore the theological implications for reading Chronicles before rather than after Ezra-Nehemiah, as done above. Again, Torah or Prophets, as canonical divisions, may or may not be important to the New Testament writers, but to view the New Testament, like the Writings, as a response to Torah and Prophets is a potentially fruitful way of constructing a biblical theology.

It can surely be argued that canon, used in this way, sometimes represents an extrinsic hermeneutical datum inserted into biblical theology. This cannot be denied, though it is surely no more extrinsic than *Heilsgeschichte* or covenant. At the present time biblical theologians are searching for a way of understanding and organizing the diversity within the Bible in a way that does justice to all messages and still provides a synthetic means of prioritizing these messages. It is argued here that canon is one option available.

We have been on a search for a method. Or, in Barton's terms, we have attempted to see if methodological guidelines could be developed from a canonical theory of meaning. The fact that such a search was necessary after many years and thousands of pages written on the topic might have forewarned us of our ultimate conclusions.

It has been seen, for example, that canonical study asks some of the same questions as other critical methods, but answers them with a heightened awareness of the particular use of this literature within a special context, the community of faith. Such a context ultimately differentiates canon study from various forms of literary criticism and at the same time demands that it be related to more traditional methods of biblical analysis.

Perhaps the most that can be said about canon study and its distinctive methodological characteristics is that: (1) it is essentially heuristic in nature; (2) it begins analysis at the level of the final canonical text, a book or an even larger literary complex; (3) the scope of its investigations is often, even usually, larger than many traditional methods; (4) its methods of organization and selection are determined by the boundaries and internal sequences of canon, though it is theoretically open to a variety of canons and therefore to a variety of boundaries and sequences.

The "context" suggested for and by canon study is an important, if not new, contribution to contemporary biblical studies. The role of this literature as Scripture and the effects this role may have had on its shaping and reading, though usually determined with other methods, are worthy of investigation. The multivalent character of particular books within the same or different canons is also important to recognize and study. That such a recognition comes from a study of the text's use as normative or authoritative within a community of faith does not make the attempt to study this nature of Scripture any more or less important. Childs is surely right, however, when he maintains this function or level of textual meaning, this perspective, has often been lost sight of in previous critical study. It is ironic, however, that while this is the case, it also appears true that a recovery of that dimension of the text's meaning is dependent upon the very same methods which have obscured it!

Excursus: On Holistic Reading

The church has always read the Bible in pericopes. One can indeed and should read the Bible as a whole but for purposes of worship, liturgy and preaching rather limited passages have been used since ancient times.[12]

There is a serious problem involved with "reading" the biblical text holistically. The problem is peculiar to canonical, versus structuralist, calls to study the text as a whole. It is centered in the community of faith itself. The fact of the matter is that, regardless of how beneficial a holistic reading may be, the evidence suggests that the community of faith rarely if ever "reads" the biblical texts in this way! Rather, the text is studied in snippets by scholars and scribes (for which there is surely biblical precedent and mandate) and, more importantly perhaps, is read to congregations in pericopes or other small divisions through lectionary cycles and other selective processes. Indeed, there are some books or sections of books that are rarely, if ever, read within certain communities. Moreover, the tendency in much contemporary Bible study is to concentrate on particular pericopes, even verses, and not to read and interpret a "book" as a whole. The question then becomes, "On what grounds does one justify a holistic reading, when this type of reading has not occurred in the past and does not occur within contemporary communities that see this literature as Scripture and canon?"

A call for such a reading could, perhaps, be seen as one more means of interpretation offered to the community of faith or to biblical scholarship. But the canonical rationale for *reading* the text in this way rests upon its scriptural function in a community of faith, and that community never, or rarely, reads it in this manner! We have arrived at a fundamental problem that will not be easily resolved. Unless we are willing to separate the function of Scripture from community practice, the holistic reading (and resultant interpretation) of text *must* be related to the life of the community, past and present, in an integral way.

One possible resolution is to suggest that a holistic reading may serve as a control or context for the reading of "parts" or "snippets." That is, the canon provides a mandatory context for understanding smaller sections, indeed it creates the necessity for interrelating the diverse messages *within* particular books as well as relating the books to each other.

There is another implication, more practical in nature, incumbent upon those who would suggest that canon study should address the text holistically. If the results of such a reading are not to be the province of biblical scholarship alone, then some type of education process within the contemporary faith community must be initiated to create the opportunity and possibility for this type of reading to occur. Such a reading and its resultant interpretive effects might or might not provide another means uniting and understanding lectionary pericopes in preaching and Bible study. In any case, if such an interpretive theory of reading is to be consonant with the rationale that brings it into being, then it must also be in dialogue with present practice. The fact that it will *not* necessarily be in dialogue with the practice of the past suggests, as many have noted, that canonical study is in a very real sense a modern phenomenon. The dynamic between text and community unites past and present, but the focus on holistic reading, from this particular perspective, is new.

Notes

[1] The most important proponents of this approach have been Brevard Childs and James Sanders. In addition to many articles, both of these scholars have written important books. See Childs, *Biblical Theology in Crisis* (Philadelphia: Westminster, 1970); *Introduction to the Old Testament as Scripture* (Philadelphia: Fortress, 1979); *The New Testament as Canon: An Introduction* (Philadelphia: Fortress, 1985); and most recently, *Old Testament Theology in a Canonical Context* (Philadelphia: Fortress, 1986). See Sanders, *Torah and Canon* (Philadelphia: Fortress, 1972); and *Canon and Community* (Philadelphia: Fortress, 1984). [See Morgan's review of *Canon and Community* in *ATR* 67 (April 1985): 175f.-Ed.] There have been many responses, positive and negative, to this call for canonical study of the Bible. See especially the series of articles in *Journal for the Study of the Old Testament* 16 (1980): 2-60, and in *Horizons in Biblical Theology* 2 (1980): 113-211. In addition see James Barr, *Holy Scripture: Canon, Authority,*

Criticism (Philadelphia: Westminster, 1983). A very useful discussion of canon study and its pertinence to other biblical methods may be found in John Barton's *Reading the Old Testament* (Philadelphia: Westminster, 1984). [See Morgan's review of Barton in *ATR* 67 (July 1985): 274-76.-Ed.]

[2] Although the subtitle of Sanders's *Canon and Community* is "A Guide to Canonical Criticism," the book shows very little concern with methodological guidelines for the study of canon. In another recent guide to methods of biblical study, *Biblical Exegesis* by John H. Hayes and Carl R. Holladay (Atlanta: John Knox, 1982), canonical criticism and redaction criticism are simply equated with each other (p. 101); yet Childs, Sanders, and others have consistently described their canonical concerns in distinction from, though related to, redaction criticism and other methods. Such confusion and lack of clarity is part of the reason for this essay.

[3] Sanders, *Canon and Community*, xv.

[4] See Sanders, *Torah and Canon*, 1-53; Childs, *Introduction to the Old Testament as Scripture*, 109-35.

[5] See Barr, *Holy Scripture*, 50ff. See also Sanders's recent discussion in his review of Barr in *Journal of Biblical Literature* 104 (1985): 501-2.

[6] Barton, *Reading the Old Testament*, 205.

[7] See Childs's introductions; Sanders, *Canon and Community*; Barton, *Reading the Old Testament*.

[8] See Childs, *Introduction to the Old Testament as Scripture* (pp. 46-106), who argues strongly for a Masoretic text as the basis of canon study of the Old Testament. Many have questioned this stance (e.g., R. Murphy in his response to Childs in *Journal for the Study of the Old Testament* 16 [1980]; 40-44).

[9] See Childs, "The Exegetical Significance of Canon for the Study of the Old Testament," in *Congress Volume: Göttingen 1977*, Supplements to Vetus Testamentum 29 (Leiden: Brill, 1978), 68; Sanders, *Canon and Community*, 21-45.

[10] See, for example, his discussion of canonical shaping, "Exegetical Significance," 70-77.

[11] Ibid., 79.

[12] Barr, *Holy Scripture*, 91. See the comments of Robert Alter (*The Art of Biblical Narrative* [New York: Basic Books, 1981], 11) concerning the same type of "reading" by the Jewish midrashists. Barr argues that the wholeness of Scripture is derived from the theological perspectives and doctrinal stances we bring to the text rather than from a holistic reading of the text itself.

NEW TESTAMENT

Harold W. Hoehner, area editor

NEW TESTAMENT

HAROLD W. HOEHNER
Professor of New Testament Literature and Exegesis
Director of Th.D. Studies
Dallas Theological Seminary

Introduction

The editors of journals in the New Testament field must select not only the best articles but also those representing the field's various divisions. An abundance of articles is available to them not only because of the increase in number and size of the journals, but also because articles accepted for publication may not appear for two years after submission. I have found that, considering the many good articles published in one year, selecting the two or three best is a challenge indeed. The two printed in this volume of *The Best in Theology* are very different in nature.

Once a giant in the field of study has made a case for a particular interpretation, it is often assumed that his particular viewpoint basically settles the issue. In the last century the well-known biblical exegete J. B. Lightfoot discussed two major interpretations of οὐχ ἁρπαγμὸν ἡγήσατο in Philippians 2:6. The first, held by the Latin Fathers, states that Christ, while knowing that he was equal with God and that this equality was not obtained by an act of aggression, nevertheless emptied himself. The second interpretation, held by the Greek Fathers and adopted by Lightfoot, says that Christ did not regard the rank and privilege of his equality with God as something to be clutched and greedily retained, but instead he relinquished them. More recently, with some modifications, R. P. Martin for the most part supports Lightfoot's theory.[1] This interpretation has now been challenged by N. T. Wright, who thinks it has "been in certain respects quite seriously misleading." Building on Hoover[2] and Moule,[3] Wright thinks Philippians 2:6-7 is speaking of Christ's refusal to use for his advantage the glory he had from the beginning, and so could be translated: "who, being in the form of God, did not regard this divine equality as something to be used for his own advantage, but rather emptied himself."

The second article, by Craig Blomberg, is altogether different in scope. It surveys six approaches or disciplines in the study of the Synoptic Gospels. He not only explains the developments of the various studies but also brings one up to date regarding the literature in these approaches. So this article will acquaint the reader briefly and insightfully with what is being presently discussed.

Last year the two articles for the New Testament section of this volume revolved around the role of the Mosaic Law in the New Testament. While scholars continue to discuss this topic, space will not allow writings on this subject to be included. Out of the many that could have been selected two warrant mention. M. A. Seifrid argues that in Luke-Acts, on the one hand, the Law was kept by the Jewish believers after they embraced faith in Christ but, on the other hand, Luke saw the Law not as the dominant force in his ethic.[4] Another article, by John M. G. Barclay, surveys the recent discussion about the Law in Paul's writings.[5]

A fine article not printed here comes from the main paper in the 41st General Meeting of the Society of New Testament Studies: James P. Martin notes that many changes have come in the twentieth century in the areas of physics, cosmology, theology, and biblical hermeneutics. As a result, he believes a basic shift has occurred from a Mechanical (critical) to a Holistic (post-critical) Paradigm. Hermeneutics is the focus of the post-critical or holistic movements whereby there is the practice of participating in the whole (pre- and post-) history of the text and thus structurally it is evolution-ary in reconstructing history.[6]

Notes

[1] Ralph P. Martin, *Carmen Christi: Philippians 2:5-11 in Recent Interpretation and in the Setting of Early Christian Worship* (SNTSMS 4; Cambridge: Cambridge University Press, 1967; rev. ed. with a new preface, Grand Rapids: William B. Eerdmans Publishing Company, 1983).

[2] R. W. Hoover, "The Harpagmos Enigma: A Philological Solution," *HTR* 56 (1971) 95-119.

[3] C. F. D. Moule, "Further Reflexions of Philippians 2:5-11," *Apostolic History and the Gospel: Biblical and Historical Essays Presented to F. F. Bruce on his 60th Birthday* (eds. W. W. Gasque and R. P. Martin; Grand Rapids: William B. Eerdmans Publishing Company, 1970) 264-76.

[4] M. A. Seifrid, "Jesus and the Law in Acts," *JSNT* 30 (1987) 39-57.

[5] John M. G. Barclay, "Paul and the Law: Observations on Some Recent Debates," *Themelios* 12 (September 1986) 5-15.

[6] James P. Martin, "Toward a Post-Critical Paradigm," *NTS* 33 (July 1987) 370-85.

About the Area Editor

Harold W. Hoehner (B.A., Barrington College; Th.M., Th.D., Dallas Theologi-cal Seminary, Ph.D., Cambridge University; post doctoral work at University of Tübingen and Cambridge University), is director of Th.D. studies and also department chairman and professor of New Testament literature and exege-sis, Dallas Theological Seminary. He was ordained in Grace Bible Church. He is on the board of International Council on Biblical Inerrancy. Two of his writings are *Herod Antipas, XVII* of the Society of New Testament Studies Monograph Series (Cambridge, 1972, reprinted by Zondervan, 1980), and *Chronological Aspects of the Life of Christ* (Zondervan, 1977). He has also contributed to various publications including the *Expositor's Bible Com-mentary*, the revised *International Standard Bible Encyclopedia*, and *Oxford Companion to the Bible*.

ἁρπαγμός AND THE MEANING OF PHILIPPIANS 2:5-11

N. T. WRIGHT
University Lecturer in New Testament
Oxford University

Article from *Journal of Theological Studies*

If Christology has been at the heart of much recent New Testament scholarship, Phil. 2:5-11 has often been near the centre of discussion; and in the thick of the fighting one still finds the troublesome word ἁρπαγμός, which plays an obviously crucial, but often baffling, role in the second half of v. 6: ὅς ἐν μορφῇ θεοῦ ὑπάρχων, οὐχ ἁρπαγμὸν ἡγήσατο τὸ εἶναι ἴσα θεῷ. The word is troublesome for more than one reason. Occurring only here in the New Testament, never in the LXX, and only rarely in extra-biblical Greek (with most of the instances being Patristic quotations of, or allusions to, Phil. 2:6 itself), it has proved a sore trail to philologists and lexicographers, and to those who rely on their work. It has been credited with a wide range of meanings and nuances, each of which has given a subtly different twist not only to the clause, but also to the whole passage in which the word stands. These shades of meaning have become so complex, and the shorthand ways of referring to them so involved, that even the task of describing the different senses on offer has become problematic.[1]

It is with this last headache that we must begin, if we are to introduce some order, perhaps even some peace, into the scholarly battlefield. In the first part of this paper, therefore, I shall suggest that two of the classical descriptions of the problem—those of J. B. Lightfoot in the last century and R. P. Martin in this—have been in certain respects quite seriously misleading. This will clear the ground for the second part, in which I shall attempt to line up the problem in a less unsatisfactory way, and to criticize some of the various senses that thus appear. Finally, in the third section, I shall state my own case, building on the work of R. W. Hoover (one of the problems with recent accounts of the state of the question has been that his work, though often cited, has not so often been understood or taken seriously), and showing that, while his arguments tell against the central philological argument advanced by C. F. D. Moule, several of Moule's ancillary points, particularly the theological emphasis he gives to the hymn as a whole, can and should be salvaged, and that the arguments which have been advanced against his theological position can be satisfactorily met.[2]

I

J. B. Lightfoot set out two, and only two, major options for the interpretation of ἁρπαγμός, ascribing the first to the Latin Fathers and the second—which he himself espoused—to the Greek.[3] The first, followed in the Authorized Version (Christ 'thought it not robbery to be equal with God'), takes ἁρπαγμός in the abstract sense of 'an act of aggression'.[4] The result of this meaning for the sentence as a whole is that Christ, knowing himself to be equal with God, knew also that this equality did not constitute—or, perhaps, was not the result of—an act of aggression; i.e. he knew that it was his by right. This has immediate implications for the force of v. 7: even though he knew that equality with God was his by right, he nevertheless emptied himself. . . . In other words, Christ was under no necessity to relinquish his place of divine splendour (v. 6b), but nevertheless did so voluntarily (v. 7a).

Lightfoot argues against this position, and prefers his second category, that of the Greek Fathers. Noting that ἁρπαγμὸν τι ἡγεῖσθαι conforms to a standard Hellenistic idiom (of ἁρπαγμός and similar words used in a double accusative phrase with a verb of thinking, reckoning, etc.), he suggested the meaning of 'a prize', 'a treasure', glossing this with the idea of 'a treasure *to be greedily clutched and ostentatiously displayed*' (p. 132, my italics). This alters the flow of thought from v. 6 through to v. 7. On the Latin view, Christ's being in the form of God and his unchallengeable right to equality with God are two ways of saying the same, or almost the same, thing, and it is in the ἀλλά-clause that the new idea ('nevertheless . . . ') is introduced. For the Greeks—according to Lightfoot—the contrast begins already with οὐχ ἁρπαγμὸν ἡγήσατο, which is seen as in itself 'a statement of his (i.e. Christ's) condescension' (p. 133). This condescension is expressed, according to this view, in the negative form in v. 6b and in the positive in v. 7a. Christ did not do *x*, but he did *y*, its apparent opposite, instead.[5] Lightfoot then understands this in the sense that Christ did not regard the rank and privilege of his equality with God as something to be clung on to greedily, but instead gave them up:[6] and this, he argues, is the correct way to read the verse. Both meanings, he points out, take for granted the divinity of Christ: it is no credit not to cling on to something that does not belong to you. Lightfoot dismisses briefly two other interpretations, those of Chrysostom among the Fathers and Meyer and Alford among his own contemporaries. We will return to these other options later on.

If we are to categorize Lightfoot's two senses, it comes as a shock to realize that both of them fall within the meaning that subsequent debates have attached to the Latin tag *res rapta*. In recent times, as we will shortly see, that phrase has come to designate the view in which Christ possessed equality with God antecedent to the action described in v. 6. For the Latin Fathers, Paul was understood to be denying that Christ regarded his equality with God as something he had obtained by snatching: if we were to give *res rapta* its proper force ('a thing having-been-snatched'), this must be it. Confusion easily arises here, however, because it is the second meaning—that of the Greek Fathers—which is usually today referred to as *res rapta*. In fact, as Moule has pointed out, it should really be *res retinenda*:[7] the point being made is not so much that equality with God had (or had not) been *obtained* by snatching, but that it was (or was not) *clung on to* in a grasping fashion. This meaning, as both Moule and Hoover have pointed out, is simply a philological impossibility. Part of the trouble, as we shall see, is that the phrase *res rapta* has itself become an idiomatic phrase in scholarly jargon. Leaving behind its proper sense of 'something obtained by snatching', it has come to be used, in the debate as to whether or not (in this passage) Christ is said to have possessed equality with God before his human birth, as a shorthand way of indicating the answer that he did. This, as we shall see, has led to further confusions in the modern debate. To summarize, therefore: Lightfoot distinguished two senses as the key clause, that of the Latin Fathers (properly called *res rapta*, in which Christ is said not to have regarded his divine equality as something obtained by snatching, i.e. to have regarded it as being his by eternal right) and that of the Greek Fathers (properly, though not usually, called *res retinenda*, in which Christ is said not to have regarded his divine equality, already possessed, as something greedily to cling on to). Finding the emphasis of the passage to rule out the former, he opted for the latter as the only viable alternative.

R. P. Martin's account of the clause, written nearly a century after Lightfoot's, groups the rival theories under four headings. He begins with (what he calls) the active sense, which he indicates by the translation 'an act of robbery or usurpation'. His three other senses are variations on the passive meaning. The first two he labels, respectively, *res rapta*[8] and *res rapienda*. The latter view, which grew up chiefly in the post-Lightfoot era, holds that ἁρπαγμός must refer to something *not* already possessed, an equality with God which Christ could have grasped but did not. This view has often been linked with the supposition of an implicit contrast with Adam.[9] Martin claims that his final view—the third of the passive senses—combines the *res rapta* and *res rapienda* positions into one.[10] Christ existed eternally in the form of God, but refused to snatch at the further honour of world sovereignty ('being equal with God'), choosing instead to receive it as the result of obedient suffering and death. Martin's classification, then, is as follows:

(*a*) active sense, i.e. *raptus* ('an act of robbery');

(*b*) passive sense (i), i.e. *res retinenda* ('somthing to be clung on to', misleadingly classified as *res rapta* because the *res* in question is already possessed);

(*c*) passive sense (ii), i.e. *res rapienda* ('something to be grasped *de novo*, something, that is, not already possessed');

(*d*) passive sense (iii), i.e. Martin's supposed blend of *res rapta* and *res rapienda*.

There are, however, several signs of confusion in this analysis. We may begin with (*a*). Martin has placed together in this first category—the 'active' sense—at least three quite different solutions, namely those of Ross and Hooke, of Feuillet, and of the Latin Fathers, and has used criticisms proper only to the last as though they applied equally to all three. As we have seen, the active sense of the Latin Fathers is (theologically) identical with *res rapta* properly understood: even though their sense, strictly, is passive, it makes the same theological point, i.e. a comment on the nature of Christ's divine equality.[11] It is against this Latin view, rather than that of Ross, that the criticisms of Lightfoot which Martin echoes make a strong point (see below).[12] Ross's interpretation looks at the *implications which Christ might have drawn* (but did not) from his equality with God: the Latins', at *the means by which Christ might have obtained* that equality. The difference between the two is particularly apparent in the relation of the clause to its neighbours on either side.[13]

Martin's description of the 'passive' meanings is equally confused: Thus:

Under (*b*), we have noted that by *res rapta* he really means *res retinenda*. He is right to cite Lightfoot as a leading representative of this view, but it is odd that he does not mention Lightfoot's reasons for taking this position, namely, the (supposed) meaning of the idiomatic phrase ἁρπαγμὸν τι ἡγεῖσθαι (which Martin associates rather with his final view, the one he himself champions) and the impossibility of the classic Latin position which Lightfoot regarded as the only serious alternative.[14]

Under (*c*), his account of the *res rapienda* view is similarly problematic. J. A. Beet, whom he cites here, did indeed attack Lightfoot, but did so in order to put forward a view very close to that of Ross in 1910 or Moule in 1968.[15] Some others cited here by Martin belong properly in his third category (e.g. E. Stauffer).[16] For definite examples of *res rapienda* we must look elsewhere.[17]

Under (*d*): Martin's 'third possibility' (pp. 143ff.) fares no better at this initial level, i.e. in the analysis of differing views. He has again collected several quite distinct positions as though they were more or less identical. Starting from the idiom mentioned above, and failing to see that Lightfoot and his followers have used this to support *their* sense, he draws in Bonnard, Käsemann, Cerfaux, and Lohmeyer as 'representatives' of this option. But, while Bonnard does, broadly speaking, follow Lohmeyer by taking the phrase to mean that Christ, possessing divine equality, refused to exploit the privileges of this position,[18] Käsemann (followed by Bornkamm) understands it to mean that Christ actually gave them up altogether (Bornkamm goes so far as to refer to Christ's 'giving up of his divinity' or of his 'divine mode of existence').[19] Käsemann's article is in fact a sustained critique of Lohmeyer, whose view is the real basis for Martin's solution (oddly, since Martin agrees with Käsemann in rejecting Lohmeyer's ethicizing interpretation of the hymn as a whole).[20] Cerfaux and Henry, lumped together as taking 'a somewhat similar line' to Käsemann,[21] in fact neither agree with each other nor come anywhere close to Käsemann. Henry[22] ends up supporting Lightfoot's position, using the phrase *res retinenda*. He too sees the possibility of Lohmeyer's line of thought, but rejects it. It is in Lightfoot's sense, not Cerfaux's, that he writes that equality with God 'est le bien, possédé, que le Christ rénonce à exploiter': i.e. he means by this that Christ *did not cling on to* this status, not that he retained it but did not use it for his own advantage. We have to do with 'une chose possédé à laquelle il ne s'accroche pas'. Cerfaux, for his part,[23] understands the verse to refer to a prize already possessed, *not* given up, but not to be used 'orgeuilleusement et comme par bravade', referring to Christ's conduct of his earthly life. In fact, the *only* link between Cerfaux's view and Martin's is that both claim (Cerfaux in fact with more justice than Martin) to avoid the dichotomy between *res rapta* and *res rapienda*. All that Martin means by this is that there is (*a*) a sense in which Christ already possesses 'equality with God' (this is not in fact, as we have seen, the true meaning of *res rapta*) and (*b*) a sense in which he does not snatch at this equality: see below.

None of these writers, then, is making the point to which Martin is leading up, for which Lohmeyer is the real source: that 'the motif of the hymn is the determination of the path Christ chose as the way to his lordship'.[24] His view is that Christ was always in the form of God, but that he did not yet possess equality with God. Refusing to snatch at this higher state, he attained it instead by the path of humble suffering and death. This view, which has found other supporters since Martin wrote,[25] is in fact a new version of the *res rapienda* meaning of ἁρπαγμός.[26] Martin, however, suggests that it includes *res rapta* as well: 'His installation as Kyrios betokens that "equality with God" which He refused to aspire to in His own right. Yet it properly belonged to Him; hence *res rapta* is true equally with *res rapienda*.'[27]

There are, then, several confusions of analysis present here:

First, while it is true that Lohmeyer's meaning does indeed take ἁρπαγμός as *res rapienda*, it cannot be said to mean *res rapta* either in the sense intended by the Latin Fathers (whose question concerned how Christ *came by* his status of equality with God in the past) or in the sense Martin himself uses, which we have characterized as *res retinenda*. Martin's use of *res rapta* as a shorthand expression referring to Christ's pre-existence leads him into further confusion, for instance on p. 152, where he refers to μορφὴ θεοῦ, rather than τὸ εἶναι ἴσα θεῷ, as *res rapta*. This is misleading, to say the least, since μορφὴ θεοῦ is certainly not the object of οὐχ ἁρπαγμὸν ἡγήσατο.[28]

Secondly, Martin seems to take the idea of 'equality with God' in two different senses, first a bad one and then a good one. Christ did not try to acquire a cosmic sovereignty independent of God, but attained at last to a *valid* 'equality' after his suffering and death. It is at this point, rather than in his category of *res rapta*, that Martin introduces the tag *res retinenda*, [29] but by it he means: 'He had the equality with God as His Image, but refused to exploit it to His personal gain.'[30] But this appears to say that Christ was after all equal with God, which cuts against Martin's subsequent exposition of τὸ εἶναι ἴσα θεῷ,[31] and to refuse to exploit something is not the same thing as not to retain it; in fact, it may be held to entail retaining it, since that which one has given up one is no longer in a position to exploit.

Finally, Martin tries to hold his (and Lohmeyer's) view together with the proverbial sense of ἁρπαγμὸν ἡγεῖσθαι τι. But the proverbial sense, properly understood, points (as we shall see) in a quite different direction.

There have, of course, been many other analyses of the different possible meanings, within this passage, of ἁρπαγμός.[32] I have concentrated thus far on Lightfoot and Martin because they have been taken by so many others as standard reference- and starting-points for future work. That work has, however, taken a wide variety of different directions, and it is necessary to take some account of other interpretations before offering my own conclusions.

II

The clearest method of describing the different options for the interpretation of Phil. 2:6b would seem to be to look at the wider unit of meaning as a whole. Strict concentration on grammar can, as we have seen, lead one to hold together things dissimilar, or to put asunder things that should be joined. The key points to ascertain, in order to differentiate beween distinct opinions, are therefore not merely the analysis of ἁρπαγμός itself, but also (a) the rough meaning assigned to ὅς ἐν μορφῇ θεοῦ ὑπάρχων; (b) the meaning of τὸ εἶναι ἴσα θεῷ; and (c) the result of the action referred to by οὐχ ... ἡγήσατο, in terms of its effect on its grammatical object, τὸ εἶναι ἴσα θεῷ. Using these together, we can distinguish at least ten significantly different analyses.[33] In exposition of these points of view, we will allot most space proportionately to those of Moule and Hoover, since they form the basis of the proposal to be advanced in the concluding section. At the same time, it is important to realize that, though Hoover's philological argument is vital to the whole case, the other views are not ruled out because of that alone. Most of them contain internal weaknesses of their own, and it will be helpful to point out some of these as we go along, lest it be thought that the argument hangs by a single thread.

1. Lightfoot, as we saw, began with the observation of the idiomatic phrase ἁρπαγμὸν ἡγεῖσθαι τι, aligned it with other similar phrases employing words like εὕρημα, discovered that the Greek Fathers, using this phrase, seemed to regard οὐχ ἁρπαγμὸν ἡγήσατο as a statement not of Christ's proper majesty but of his condescension, and concluded that it referred to that abandonment of the privileges of equality with God which took place at the incarnation. Lightfoot was careful to point out that this view in no way

undermined a belief in Christ's divinity. On the contrary, it presupposed it, discovering it in the phrase ἐν μορφῇ θεοῦ ὑπάρχων, and suggesting that ἴσα θεῷ, as opposed to ἴσος θεῷ,[34] meant not divinity itself but the privileges of divinity. This view is undeniably attractive, particularly in its smooth transition from v. 6 to v. 7, and can claim considerable support.[35] It is the one Martin calls *res rapta*, though as we have seen it is really *res retinenda*.

2. Despite Lightfoot's carefully nuanced orthodox reading of the clause, the kenotic understanding of Phil. 2 comes very close to his, needing only to make an adjustment in its view of τὸ εἶναι ἴσα θεῷ. If one makes that phrase mean, more or less, 'divinity', the apparent meaning of vv. 6-7 is that the pre-existent, divine Christ abandoned that divinity in becoming man (to receive it back again, presumably, in his exaltation (vv. 9-11). The former popularity of this view, and the arguments which have led most scholars to avoid it, are well known,[36] though the idea recurs in almost casual phrases from time to time.[37]

3(*a*). The solution offered by such German writers as Käsemann and Bornkamm is more or less a variant on the kenotic version of the *res retinenda* view. Understanding Christ's pre-existent state to be that of an equality with God held in virtue of his identity as the divine *Urmensch*, they see this status as being abandoned.[38] This line of thought avoids kenoticism proper at the cost of importing into the hymn the quite alien idea[39] of gnostic speculation.

3(*b*). The position of Oscar Cullmann is really a variant on 3(*a*), though the similarity is obscured because he labels it (rightly) *res rapienda*.[40] He too believes that Paul refers to a heavenly *Urmensch* who becomes man, but instead of seeing his heavenly existence as equality with God (as Käsemann and Bornkamm), he regards that equality as a further stage at which the *Urmensch* refused to grasp, choosing instead to become man.

4. The next solution is the most complicated in its subdivisions. Classifying ἁρπαγμός as *res rapienda*, this view has to address the question: what is it that Christ did not already possess, and at which he refused to snatch? The answers on offer are (*a*) divinity (the classic *res rapienda*);[41] (*b*) the status of 'cosmocrator' (Lohmeyer, Martin: see below); (*c*) divine honours to be enjoyed during the time of incarnation (Feuillet).[42] This is not too different in *meaning* from Lightfoot's sense, but is clearly reached by a different route. Feuillet has, however, drawn back from this position in his most recent writing on the subject,[43] and offers it only as an alternative to Cerfaux's view, which is, as he rightly sees, supported by Hoover's argument (see his summary, pp. 130-2).

A fourth variation (*d*) on *res rapienda* is offered by M. D. Hooker, though she does not label it thus. Emphasizing the implicit contrast between Christ and Adam, she suggests that Christ did not need to snatch (like Adam) at divine equality *because he already possessed it*.[44] There are problems with this view at the level of classification. Hooker follows Carmignac's central point (see below) that the negative οὐχ apparently modifies ἁρπαγμὸν rather than ἡγήσατο (though this does not seem to affect her translation of the passage). And, whereas for Carmignac Christ considered his divine equality a non-usurpation in the sense that he enjoyed divine honour during his earthly life, for Hooker Christ did not regard his divine equality as something he now needed to grasp, because he already possessed it. Carmignac has Christ looking back at an honour he did not grasp in the past; Hooker has him looking forward, realizing he does not need to grasp it in the future. Thus, while this view is classified as *res rapta* by Martin,[45] it is more properly, as we have seen, *res rapienda*. Hooker's view thus straddles different categories.

This of itself is, of course, not an objection. One might say, so much the worse for the categories. But at the part of her argument crucial for our discussion (her analysis of the poem, and her defence of its subtle and rich paraenetic thrust in its present context, are extremely valuable) the argument becomes awkward. To begin with, it is not the case that only with some sort of *res rapienda* view can the contrast between Christ and Adam be maintained, as she suggests (p. 160): Caird fits it nicely into his revival of Lightfoot's position. More importantly, I am not convinced by her suggestion that τὸ εἶναι ἴσα θεῷ can be read as a reference to Gen. 1:26 (pp. 160f.): the asserted equivalence of μορφή and εἰκών in the LXX, upon which this suggestion partly rests, seems to me illusory.[46] Nor do I think it necessary for her main points of interpretation to be sustained (that Paul is deliberately contrasting Christ and Adam, and that 'his very action in becoming what we are is a demonstration of what he eternally is' [p. 164]) that one should rely, as she seems to on p. 161, on the Rabbinic tradition that saw Adam as already possessing the thing at which, in Gen. 3:5, 22, he grasped. This is scarcely the most natural way to read the combination of Gen. 1:26 and 3:5ff. Finally, although Hooker's point (pp. 162f.) about the irony of ὁμοίωμα and σχῆμα is well taken, it seems odd to describe the pre-incarnate Christ as 'the true Man' (p. 163), 'the one who is truly what Man is meant to be', unless one wishes, as Hooker does not, to join Käsemann and Cullmann. Hooker's main points, as I shall show, may be retained in a scheme which eliminates these problems.

Since Martin's view has gained considerable currency,[47] it is important to point out its inherent weaknesses, in addition to those of its categorization which we noted earlier. First, it cannot (as Martin thinks) claim support from the idiom as analysed by Hoover.[48] Secondly, it drives a sharp wedge between ὅς ἐν μορφῇ θεοῦ ὑπάρχων and τὸ εἶναι ἴσα θεῷ, which does violence both to the regular usage of the articular infinitive (see below) and to the sense of the passage, as is apparent from Martin's confusion as to whether the μορφὴ θεοῦ is given up or not. Thirdly, the idea of Christ's equality with God meaning the status of 'cosmocrator' is inherently unclear. (*a*) What does this status consist in if it is so different from his being in the form of God (in the fully divine sense Martin intends)? (*b*) Why should τὸ εἶναι ἴσα θεῷ mean 'cosmocrator' in this different sense? (c) Why should world lordship be a thing to which Christ should not aspire? and (d) Why is he then entitled to it because of suffering and death? Fourthly, in what way is this view 'soteriological' rather than 'ontological'? Martin, claiming this, nevertheless indicates that the point of the status ἴσα θεῷ would be that it *was* in a particular relation—specifically, independence—to God the Father (p. 152). Fifthly, the parallel between Adam and Christ is hard to see: at no point is the contrast clear between what Adam did and what Christ refused to do.[49] Finally, the emphasis of the hymn is thrown in what, as we will argue, is quite the wrong direction. (a) It fits (as Martin recognizes) very badly in the paraenetic context; (b) the second member of the contrast (οὐχ ἁρπαγμὸν ἡγήσατο . . . being the first) is delayed for an intolerably long time, only appearing in v. 8. It is much more natural to see the second member in ἀλλὰ ἑαυτὸν ἐκένωσεν.

5. The next view is that of the Latin Fathers.[50] They (with exceptions, of course) understood our clause as a statement not of condescension, but of majesty: Christ did not regard his equality with God as a usurpation. Though this view is quite clear in itself, its categorization (is the sense active or passive?) is not: some have seen it as giving ἁρπαγμός an active and abstract sense ('an act of aggression'), but others have taken it as *res rapta* (passive and concrete: Christ did not regard his equality with God as *having been obtained by* usurpation).[51] This view falls, either way, by its own weight: Lightfoot's critique remains very damaging. The natural phrase to follow v. 6, if taken in the Latin sense, is ἀλλὰ φύσει (he considered his equality with God to be not a matter of usurpation but something he had by nature).[52] If Paul had wanted to say that Christ's divine equality was his by right, there would surely have been simpler ways of doing so than our present sentence.

A variation on the Latin view is provided by J. Carmignac, who argues that the position of the negative (with the noun, not the verb) indicates that the sentence refers to the *earthly* Christ regarding his divine glory as being his by right.[53] This, however, places an impossible strain on the rest of the sentence, which then has to read: 'who, during his earthly life, regarded equality with God as being his by right; nevertheless, he *had* emptied himself, and *had* taken on the form of a servant, and *had* been born in the likeness of men . . .' (then back to the ordinary aorist again) 'and he humbled himself . . .'.

6. The account of our passage given by K. Barth in the *Church Dogmatics* cannot be fitted into any other category.[54] In one sense it looks like the *res rapta* of the Latin Fathers, in another like Lightfoot's *res retinenda*. Even if it combined those two, that would make it a new variant: but in each part it is subtly different. The crucial passage reads:

The *kenosis* consists in a renunciation of His being in the form of God alone . . . He did not treat His form in the likeness of God . . . as a robber does his booty. He was not bound by it like someone bound by his possessions . . . He

did not treat it as His one and only and exclusive possibility . . . It was not to
him an inalienable necessity to exist only in that form of God . . . only to be
the eternal Word and not flesh . . .

Strictly speaking, this treats ἁρπαγμός as *res rapta*, something that has been
seized, emphasizing (unlike the Latin Fathers' version of *res rapta*) the
attitude towards one's booty rather than the question of whether or not it
actually is booty at all. Christ, according to Barth, does not regard his
equality with God in the manner of a robber gloating greedily over his hoard.
Then, whereas the Latin Fathers took the clause as a second assertion (after
ὅς ἐν μορφῇ θεοῦ ὑπάρχων) of Christ's divine status, Barth interprets the *res
rapta* idea in the sense of *res retinenda*, with the help of the word 'only':
Christ's existence *only* in the form of God was 'given up' in favour of the new
state of being *both* in the form of God *and* in the form of a servant. But, while
Barth's insistence on the continuing divinity of the man Christ Jesus is (I
believe) healthy, it may be doubted whether this ingenious interpretation is
not over-subtle, and particularly whether it does justice to ἐκένωσεν to see it
as not so much (within the image being used) as Christ emptying himself of
anything but rather as adding to himself something new.

7(*a*). Several scholars have attempted to read v. 6 as a reference not to
Christ's pre-existence but to his (perfect) human life. Thus, for instance, J.
Murphy-O'Connor sees τὸ εἶναι ἴσα θεῷ not as the possession of divine
nature, but as the 'right to be *treated* as if he were god', and says that the force
of this clause is that Christ did not regard this right 'as something to be used
to his own advantage'.[55] It was a right 'of which he was free to dispose'. He
had this right not because he actually was God but because he was a sinless
human being (an idea also invoked by Dunn at this point in the argument).[56]
This kind of view has become popular recently, and it is therefore necessary
to point out some of its inherent weaknesses.[57] Murphy-O'Connor seems
unclear as to just what the phrase in question means: he leans towards
Hoover in the idea of 'using something to one's own advantage', but asserts—
in the teeth of Hoover's conclusions—that 'linguistic evidence unclouded by
presuppositions weighs the balance of probability decisively in favour of *res
retienda*' [*sic*] (pp. 38f.). The idea that Christ, as a mere man, could ever have
had the 'right to be treated as if he were god' is hardly a notion which a Jew
could grasp without asking at once whether, in that case, this man had in
some sense *always* been God.[58] Again, this interpretation reads a great deal
into the phrase τὸ εἶναι ἴσα θεῷ: it has to mean not only 'being treated as if he
were God' but also *the right to be* treated thus: and it is never clear whether
this right is simply not made use of, or whether it is not claimed at all, or
whether it is possessed originally and then given up. Finally, Murphy-O'Connor's view in effect omits v. 7, the stage of Christ's becoming human: his own
summary of his position (p. 40) jumps, revealingly, straight from v. 6 to v. 8.[59]

Two other variations on this theme may be noted more briefly.

7(*b*). J. A. T. Robinson attempted to use Moule's arguments (see below) to support the idea that τὸ εἶναι ἴσα θεῷ referred to the exalted state of the truly human man, given up when Jesus embraced the vocation of suffering and death. This appears to combine the grammatical analysis of ἡγήσατο as *raptus* (active and abstract, meaning 'self-assertion') with the theological understanding of the clause as *res retinenda*, a thing to be retained.[60]

7(c). P. Trudinger and D. W. B. Robinson both attempted to use the arguments of L. L. Hammerich (see below) to suggest the meaning that Jesus refused to use his equality with God as a way of escape from his vocation to suffering.[61] None of these views has received subsequent support. There are, it appears, several different ways of making the subject of ἡγήσατο the human Jesus, some of which imply his pre-existent divinity[62] and some of which do not: but all raise more problems than they solve. G. B. Caird, in commenting on a draft of this paper, wrote that the real difficulty with any 'human Jesus' view of the phrase 'is that it abandons any attempt to take the clauses in chronological, or even logical, order'. This is similar to our point made above in relation to Carmignac.

8. A quite different twist was given to the modern debate when C. F. D. Moule published his article in the first F. F. Bruce *Festschrift*.[63] He argued strongly that ἁρπαγμός is not to be confused with ἅρπαγμα: the -μος ending signifies the action of the verb, the -μα ending its results.[64] This forces him to set on one side the solution of Lightfoot and (since he apparently accepts Lightfoot's understanding of them) the Greek Fathers also, and to support the active, abstract sense of 'snatching', 'grasping': 'he did not regard equality with God as *consisting in* snatching' (p. 266, Moule's italics).

There are more writers on Moule's side than one might realize at first sight. At the beginning of the century not only J. Ross, but also J. A. Beet and, following Ross, W. Warren[65] took this position, for substantially similar reasons to Moule. They had been preceded by the great commentators Meyer and Alford, and have been followed recently not only by Moule but also by J. M. Furness and S. H. Hooke.[66] It is harder to assess the position of B. Reicke,[67] since he seems to combine three separate and perhaps ultimately incompatible views. His main emphasis is close to Moule's:

> Jésus-Christ, . . . ne considerait pas son égalité avec Dieu comme une occasion de commettre rapine, de tirer des choses à soi avec violence. (p. 209)

But he then [68] regards this as a description of the *human* Christ, and proceeds (p. 210) to move towards a position somewhat like Lohmeyer's. Finally, F. E. Vokes[69] having (like Moule) argued strongly for the strictly abstract meaning of ἁρπαγμός (though he acknowledges on p. 672 that, according to the grammarians, the word can, in fact, 'take on a concrete sense'), follows Ross (and F. C. Baur) in understanding the passage to mean that 'Jesus did not make his being on an equality with God a means for self-aggrandisement, for seizing wealth or booty for himself'.[70]

Some recent writers have referred approvingly to Moule's argument without seeming to know what to do with it, leaving it in the end on one side.[71] Others have argued against it, but few of the arguments are cogent: I shall reply to the major ones when expounding my own position shortly, since several of Moule's points are contained within my own.

9. It is necessary to mention here a distinct sense which has frequently been confused with Moule's, namely, that of the Danish philologist L. L. Hammerich.[72] He agrees with Moule that the word is abstract ('*raptus*'), referring to the action of the verb, but then takes it in a passive sense, meaning 'rapture' in the sense of being caught up to heaven, as in a vision. For an ordinary mortal, experiencing the life of heaven *would* be such a 'rapture', but for the pre-existent Christ it was not: it was his normal state. This gives to the sentence the meaning that, for Jesus (who was in the form of God), 'the being equal with God was no *rapture*, no ἁρπαγμός; it was his by nature'. Hammerich then says that, in the incarnation, Christ voluntarily 'gave up his nature, his being with God, and debased himself'. Hammerich's position is thus on the one hand similar in theological meaning to that of the Latin Fathers, while on the other hand it becomes almost kenotic in its results: he gave up his nature. This view (unlike Moule's) has not commended itself to subsequent scholars.

10. Like Lightfoot and Jaeger, R. W. Hoover begins from a study of the Greek idiom which appears to be employed in our clause.[73] Unlike them, he argues not for the sense of 'regard something as a prize (sc. to be clutched on to)', i.e. *res retinenda*, but for the sense of 'regard something as a thing to be taken advantage of'. Though the idiom is parallel in *form* to that which employs ἕρμαιον and εὕρημα, it is not identical in *meaning*. Whereas ἕρμαιον/εὕρημα means 'to prize something as an unexpected windfall', ἁρπαγμὸν ἡγεῖσθαι τι means 'to regard as something to be taken advantage of' or 'to regard as something to be used for one's own advantage'.[74] However, ἁρπαγμός and ἅρπαγμα do both appear in virtually interchangeable contexts *within this idiom*, both taking on a special sense not identical to their usual one.[75] Despite the impression given by many scholars who have referred to his work, Hoover argues specifically that, *within the context of this idiom*, ἁρπαγμός cannot mean either *res rapienda* or *res retinenda*: the former is ruled out because the object under consideration is always something already possessed, the latter because that meaning would make no sense in the non-biblical examples Hoover has collected. *Res rapta* is likewise ruled out by the idiomatic sense: and, though Hoover does not refer to the line of thought now represented by Moule, an insistence on the abstract (and, for Moule, active) sense of ἁρπαγμός is not warranted. The idiom refers, Hoover argues, not to the act of acquiring something (whether before the time envisaged, i.e. *res rapta*, or after, i.e. *res rapienda*), nor to the act of clinging on to it in a grasping way. It refers to the attitude one will take towards something which is in one's possession and grasp already, and which will remain there.

If Hoover is right (and, though his conclusions have often been mis-understood, no one has ventured to challenge him on philological grounds), the views of all the other scholars we have reviewed for the sake of clarity in the current debate are undercut at a stroke. This apparently sweeping judgement may be reinforced by two considerations. First, many of the theories discussed already possess, as we have seen, serious internal weaknesses of their own, which prompt us in any case to look elsewhere. Secondly, Hoover's theory is capable of making excellent theological sense, as we will presently show, and of including within itself many of the strong points of the other theories.

It should be clear that, though Hoover's analysis of the idiom clashes at a formal and philological level with that of Moule, the overall sense achieved by both scholars is similar. For both, the action or attitude envisaged in the clause is not the grasping of, or clinging on to, equality with God, but the attitude—of advantage-taking, of 'getting', of behaving like an oriental des-pot—*based on* that equality. For both, ultimately, the word is abstract and active with a *future* connotation (what one will, or might, do on the basis of something), as opposed to the Latin Fathers' *rapina*, which was abstract and active with a *past* connotation (what one might be supposed to have done). The Latin understanding could, as we saw, equally well be presented as concrete (*res rapta*) and passive, since the thing one might be supposed to have grasped was the τι in question, in this case τὸ εἶναι ἴσα θεῷ. But for Moule and Hoover the 'grasping' or 'advantage-taking' does not *aim at* τὸ εἶναι ἴσα θεῷ: it *begins from* it. Nevertheless, in English at least it is just as easy, and not damaging to the meaning, to turn the phrase around and express the same idea in concrete and passive terms: 'he did not regard his equality with God *as something to be used for his own advantage*'.[76] If Hoover is right, a native speaker of Hellenistic Greek, faced with that English sentence, would very likely, and quite correctly, render it into idiomatic Greek in the very words of Phil. 2:6. And because of this closeness of actual signifi-cance, it is not difficult to see how in fact ἁρπαγμός and ἅρπαγμα could, *precisely within this idiom*, be so nearly interchangeable in meaning.[77] The word, in one and the same sentence, could, depending on how one might choose to look at it, be *either* abstract *or* concrete without a change in the actual meaning of the larger, total sense-unit. And that meaning, putting together Moule's theology and Hoover's philology, is 'Christ did not consider his equality with God as something to take advantage of . . .'.

A further incidental advantage of this theory may be noted here. The proposal of J. Carmignac, discussed earlier, hinged on the fact that in Greek the negative adverb οὐ/οὐχ normally precedes immediately the verb it modi-fies, so that for it to precede instead a noun, as here, suggests that it is the noun *rather than the verb* which is negated. But if, as Hoover has so strongly argued, the phrase ἁρπαγμὸν ἡγεῖσθαι τι *as a whole* forms a recognizable idiom, then the natural place for the negative adverb to come is before the phrase as a whole: which is exactly what we find. It is as though, in English, the phrase were hyphenated: 'he did not consider-it-something-to-take-advantage-of'.

It is probably in this category, if anywhere, that the conclusions of W. Foerster should be placed.[78] He is certainly not to be dismissed as though he were 'taking the phrase as a complete proverb which has no Christological value, except perhaps an incidental one'.[79] The proverbial meaning—a contrast between what one might expect someone to do and what Christ actually did—is in fact quite close to Hoover's sense: 'Jesus did not regard equality with God as a gain to be utilized.'[80] Foerster is, however, quite vague in his exposition of this idea and its alternatives, only giving three possible senses and dismissing the active sense[81] with the objection, noted already, about the lack of an object.

Further support for this position has come from L. Cerfaux and—in his most recent writing on the subject—A. Feuillet. The latter, faced with Hoover's evidence, finds his solution attractive, though he does not (as we saw earlier) abandon entirely his previous position. Instead, he leaves the two as alternatives: 'Le Christ . . . n'avait pas régardé comme un bien précieux à saisir d'être traité sur la terre à l'égal de Dieu' (i.e. res rapienda), 'ou encore comme un avantage à exploiter d'être par nature égal à Dieu.'[82] Despite the formal differences occasioned by Cerfaux's reading of ἁρπαγμός in a passive sense ('Le butin . . . c'est plutot un objet possédé'), his overall understanding of the line of thought corresponds closely to that of Hoover. Christ did not regard his equality with God as something to be exploited for his own gain.[83]

This position has considerable strength, more than its proponents have usually realized. Many advantages of other positions can be retained within it. Before proceeding to demonstrate these, however, it may be helpful to set out in tabular form the ten senses now outlined. The columns show, respectively, the rough meaning attached to μορφή,[84] the meaning given to τὸ εἶναι ἴσα θεῷ (in particular whether or not this is significantly different from μορφὴ θεοῦ), the result of the action of ἡγήσατο in terms of its effect on τὸ εἶναι ἴσα θεῷ, and the grammatical description, and the sense, of ἁρπαγμός itself. The final column gives, merely for ease of reference, a (or the) representative of the view in question, or a label by which it is well known.

It is interesting to note at this point the way in which the modern English translations have tried to come to terms with the problem. Most opt for ambiguity between res retinenda and res rapienda: thus RSV 'did not count equality with God a thing to be grasped', and similarly NASV, NIV. The Authorized Version adopted the Latin view ('thought it not robbery to be equal with God'), J. B. Phillips expressed Lightfoot's position unambiguously ('did not cling to his prerogatives as God's equal'), and the Good News Bible, equally clearly, opted for Martin's, confusions and all ('did not think that by force he should try to become equal with God. Instead, of his own free will he gave it all up'). The NEB and JB retain ambiguity with the help of marginal alternatives. Thus NEB text has *res rapienda* ('did not think to snatch at equality with God'), while the margin suggests *res retinenda* ('did not prize his equality with God'). The Jerusalem Bible glosses its text ('did not cling to his equality with God'—clearly *res retinenda*) with a note explaining that Christ did not regard this equality (further explained as divine honours and prerogatives) as something to grasp (*rapienda?*) or hold on to. None, so far as I have seen, has attempted to express either Moule's or Hoover's understanding. The last section of this paper will suggest some reasons why such a task should be attempted.

III

We may begin with Hoover's strongest point. The idiom here used clearly assumes that the object in question—in this case equality with God—is already possessed. One cannot decide to take advantage of something one does not already have. If, therefore, there is to be any ultimate distinction of meaning between Christ's being in the form of God and Christ possessing τὸ εἶναι ἴσα θεῷ, such a distinction does not, at least, involve seeing either phrase as referring to something less than divinity and/or the honours pertaining to that state. Both expressions mark out Christ Jesus, in his pre-existent state, as one who is indeed, and fully, *capax humanitatis*, but at the same time different from all other human beings in his nature and origin.[85]

A further reason, not usually noticed, for taking τὸ εἶναι ἴσα θεῷ in close connection with ὅς ἐν μορφῇ θεοῦ ὑπάρχων is the regular usage of the articular infinitive (here, τὸ εἶναι) to refer 'to something previously mentioned or otherwise well known'.[86] Among over a dozen possible examples are Rom. 7:18 (τὸ γὰρ θέλειν παράκειταί μοι, τὸ δὲ κατεργάζεσθαι τὸ καλὸν οὔ, where both infinitives refer to the immediately preceding discussion) and 2 Cor. 7:11 (τὸ κατὰ θεὸν λυπηθῆναι, 'this (just mentioned) godly grief'). We should therefore expect that τὸ εἶναι κτλ in our present passage would refer back, epexegetically, to ὅς ἐν μορφῇ θεοῦ ὑπάρχων, and might even suggest the stronger translation 'this divine equality'.

The sense of οὐχ ἁρπαγμὸν ἡγήσατο will then be that Christ, in contrast to what one might have expected (this is the force of Foerster's point), refused to take advantage of his position. This is not (as, for instance, in Feuillet's view) a matter of not adopting, in his incarnate existence, a life-style of divine splendour, whatever that might mean in practice. The emphasis of v. 7 shows that the refusal described by οὐχ ἁρπαγμὸν ἡγήσατο was a refusal to use for his own advantage the glory which he had from the beginning. The all-important difference in meaning between this view and the standard *retinenda* approaches is that *nothing described by either* ἐν μορφῇ θεοῦ ὑπάρχων *or by* τὸ εἶναι ἴσα θεῷ *is given up*: rather, it is reinterpreted, understood in a manner in striking contrast to what one might have expect-

μορφή	τὸ εἶναι ἴσα θεῷ	Meaning of οὐχ . . . ἡγήσατο . . .	Analysis of ἁρπαγμός	Representative or label
1. divine	divine prerogatives	abandoned	idiom: understood as 'prize', i.e. *res retinenda*	Lightfoot
2. divine	divinity itself	abandoned	passive and concrete: *res retinenda*, though often called *res rapta*	Kenotic
3. pre-existent *Urmensch*	(*a*) divine state already possessed	abandoned	passive and concrete: *res retinenda*, often called *res rapta*	Käsemann
	(*b*) divine state *not* already possessed	not snatched at	passive, concrete: *res rapienda*	Cullmann
4. (*a*) not yet divine	divine equality	not snatched at	passive, concrete: *res rapienda*	Kennedy
(*b*) divine, but not yet cosmocrator	cosmocrator, independent of the Father	not snatched at	passive, concrete: *res rapienda* (wrongly described as idiomatic and as combining *res rapta* and *res rapienda*)	Lohmeyer, Martin
(*c*) divine	divine honours enjoyed during incarnation	not snatched at	passive, concrete: *res rapienda*	Feuillet
(*d*) divine	divine likeness (like Adam's)	not needing to be snatched (because already possessed)	passive, concrete: *res rapienda*	Hooker

5. divine	divine equality (c) divine equality *during incarnation*	(a) not obtained by snatching (b) not equivalent to robbery regarded as not being an act of usurpation	passive, concrete: *res rapta* active, abstract: *raptus* active, abstract: *raptus/ rapina*	Latin Fathers (taken two different ways) Carmignac
6. divine	divine equality (and that alone)	not regarded as having been stolen and therefore as not being something to cling on to	passive, concrete: *res rapta/res rapienda*	Barth
7. human	(a) the right to be treated as divine (b) divine equality *qua* truly human being (c) divine equality	not claimed/clung to not meaning self-assertion not regarded as entitling Jesus to Ascension/ last-minute deliverance from cross	passive, concrete: *res retinenda*, but some hints of *rapienda* too active, abstract: *raptus*, but hints of *retinenda* too passive, abstract: *raptus*	Murphy-O'Connor J. A. T. Robinson Trudinger/ D. W. B. Robinson
8. divine	divine equality	not regarded as meaning 'snatching'	active, abstract: *raptus*	Moule
9. divine	divine equality	not regarded as a heavenly 'rapture', i.e. it was his by right (yet he gave it up)	passive, abstract: *raptus* with hints of *retinenda* too	Hammerich
10. divine	divine equality, already possessed	not regarded as something to be taken advantage of	idiomatic usage, with sense determined by whole phrase	Hoover

ed. Over against the standard picture of oriental despots, who understood their position as something to be used for their own advantage, Jesus understood his position to *mean* self-negation, the vocation described in vv. 7-8. In Moule's phrase, divine equality does not mean 'getting' but 'giving': it is properly expressed in self-giving love. We could then translate vv. 6f.: 'who, being in the form of God, did not regard this divine equality as something to be used for his own advantage, but rather emptied himself . . . '.[87]

If we apply this understanding of vv. 6f. to the passage as a whole, a new coherence results. The pre-existent son regarded equality with God not as excusing him from the task of (redemptive) suffering and death, but actually as uniquely qualifying him for that vocation. It is here, not in the views of Käsemann or Martin, that the real underlying soteriology of the 'hymn' is to be found.[88] As in Rom. 5:6ff., the death of Jesus is understood as the appropriate revelation, in action, of the love of God himself (compare too 2 Cor. 5:19). ἐκένωσεν does not refer to the loss of divine attributes, but—in good Pauline fashion[89]—to making something powerless, emptying it of apparent significance. The real humiliation of the incarnation and the cross is that one who was himself God, and who never during the whole process stopped being God, could embrace such a vocation. The real theological emphasis of the hymn, therefore, is not simply a new view of Jesus. It is a new understanding of God. Against the age-old attempts of human beings to make God in their own (arrogant, self-glorifying) image, Calvary reveals the truth about what it meant to be God. Underneath this is the conclusion, all-important in present Christological debate: incarnation and even crucifixion are to be seen as *appropriate* vehicles for the dynamic self-revelation of God.

This view is strengthened by five considerations. First, it explains the relation of vv. 9-11 and vv. 6-8 in a much more satisfying way than the other views. The force of the διό at the start of v. 9 is 'and *that* is why . . . '. The exaltation of the crucified one is not to a nature or rank which only then became appropriate for him. Nor is it a reward for a difficult task well done. Nor is it the climax merely of a passage *per ardua ad astra*. It is the affirmation, by God the Father, that the incarnation and death of Jesus really was the revelation of the divine love in action.[90] In giving to Jesus the title κύριος,[91] and in granting him to share that glory which, according to Isa. 45:23 (quoted in 2:10), no one other than Israel's God is allowed to share, God the Father is as it were endorsing that interpretation of divine equality which, according to v. 6, the Son adopted. The connection between the two parts of the hymn works better, it may be claimed, on this view than on any other.[92]

Secondly, therefore, the whole hymn (and not merely vv. 6-8) fits very well into the paraenetic context both of vv. 1-5 and (though this is not so often discussed) of vv. 12ff. Käsemann may have been right to reject Lohmeyer's comparatively shallow ethicizing of the passage. But this should not prevent a very thorough integration of the hymn into its context in Philippians. The verbal links (e.g. ταπεινοφροσύνη, ἡγούμενοι in v. 3: ὑπηκούσατε,

v. 12: see too μέχρι θανάτου, v. 30) are undergirded by a common *theme*. 'If you are really in Christ, indwelt by the Spirit, inspired by the divine love, prove it by acting this way, the way of divine self-abnegation' (vv. 1-4): 'be obedient, don't grumble—God is at work in you, so behave as his children in the world' (vv. 12-16). If we read the hymn as I have suggested the paraenetic significance does not stop with v. 8, as Martin suggests,[93] but continues all through. God himself recognizes and endorses self-abnegation as the proper expression of divine character. This removes any doubt in the Philippians' mind as to the nature of the behaviour to which they are urged in vv. 1-5. It is not merely the imitation of Christ: it is the outworking of the life of the Spirit of God. Though the word ἀγάπη is not used in the hymn itself (as it is in vv. 1-2), vv. 6-8 might almost serve as a definition of what it means in practice—and vv. 9-11 would then affirm that this love is none other than the love of God himself, at work supremely in Christ and now also, by his Spirit, in his people. The implication is clear: as God endorsed Jesus' interpretation of what equality with God meant in practice, so he will recognize self-giving love in his people as the true mark of the life of the Spirit.

Thirdly, the frequently observed parallel between 2:6ff. and 3:4ff.[94] works very well on this understanding. Moule (pp. 247f.) is anxious that the parallel would only hold if, as Paul had flung away what formerly seemed precious to him, receiving in exchange something else, so Christ had 'deemed equality with God sheer loss' and had abandoned it. I suggest, however, that in 3:4ff. Paul is first outlining the privileged status he enjoyed (and continued, in some senses to enjoy) as a member of Israel, the people of God, and then showing that, because of Christ, this membership had to be regarded as something not to be taken advantage of. He did not give up his membership: he understood it in a new way. This clearly fits into the context of 3:2-3, in which Paul transfers attributes of Israel to the church in Christ. Belonging to God's people did not, he now realized, mean a privileged status, outward symbols of superiority, an elevated moral stature in the world. It meant dying and rising with the Messiah. In hoping for vindication at the resurrection (3:11) Paul is voicing what for him, as an erstwhile Pharisee, was the hope of God's people. So Christ, as himself the true Jew, had led the way for this interpretation of what it meant to be the people of God.

Fourthly, although the parallel between Christ and Adam in the poem has often been thought to necessitate the *res rapienda* view, and although Dunn makes it the basis of his particular interpretation, so that opponents of either of these ideas have often felt compelled to deny the presence of Adam-imagery here, it is not only possible but helpful, within the scheme I am suggesting, to see a characteristically cryptic reference to Adam. Fuller discussion of this point may be found in my article on Paul's Adam-Christology.[95] Adam, in arrogance, thought to become like God: Christ, in humility, became man. The contrast is exact, and coheres thoroughly with, e.g. Rom. 5:12-21.

Fifthly, though the majority of the Patristic references to Phil. 2 do not help very much in elucidating our phrase, there are one or two passages which, it may be claimed, fit very well into the case for which I have argued. Most of the Latin Fathers, as we saw, and among the Greeks Chrysostom in particular, were so concerned to combat Arianism that they read the clause not as a statement of condescension but as an affirmation of rightful divinity.[96] To this extent Lightfoot's analysis is correct: the earlier, and linguistically closer, Patristic evidence is in favour of reading the clause as (part of) a statement of Christ's humility. But beyond that most of the references pose the same problem as our text itself. Lightfoot is right in what he denies—that the Greek Fathers supported the Latin view—but wrong in what he affirms (the *retinenda* view). This does not mean, as Moule suggests (p. 268), that the Greek Fathers have led us up the garden path: merely that we have read them wrongly, which is all too easy to do since, with most of the references being themselves allusions to our passage, we have no external standard from which to get our bearings.

There are, however, just a few passages which lend support to our position. In Eusebius' *Historia Ecclesiae* 5. 2. 2 the writer quotes from the letter circulated by the churches in Lyons and Vienne, and describes how the martyrs, despite their sufferings, would neither proclaim themselves as martyrs nor allow others to address them as such. This, says the document, is evidence of their imitation of Christ, with a reference to Phil. 2:6. It is easy to see how Hoover's sense will work here: the martyrs did not regard their sufferings as something to take advantage of. Eusebius clearly regards them as martyrs anyway: there is no question of their refusing to grasp at a glory they did not possess, or of actually giving up one they did. They continued to be Christlike martyrs, and *as evidence of that* did not use the fact as something to take advantage of.[97] In a subsequent passage (8. 12. 1), in which Phil. 2:6 is not quoted but may well be in mind, Eusebius describes the martyrs of Antioch who, to avoid torture, committed suicide, τὸν θάνατον ἅρπαγμα θέμενοι τῆς τῶν δυσσεβῶν μοχθηρίας. This *could* be read as *res rapienda*. But Hoover's understanding seems to me more probable. The martyrs knew that they were going to die anyway. But, instead of regarding that death as something to be feared or shunned, they regarded it as something to be taken advantage of, to the extent that they were prepared to anticipate their execution by committing suicide, thus using the death they were going to die anyway as an opportunity for stealing a march on their persecutors. The other relevant texts from Eusebius are adequately discussed by Hoover. The disputed passage from Cyril of Alexandria's comment on the angels' visit to Lot (*De Ador.* i. 25) also supports his view[98] and actually makes Moule's philological position very difficult. In the vital passage οὐχ ἁρπαγμὸν τὴν παραίτησιν ὡς ἐξ ἀδρανοῦς καὶ ὑδαρεστέρας ἐποιεῖτο φρενός, the meaning cannot be—as it would have to be if Moule were correct—that Lot did not regard the angels' refusal[99] as *meaning* advantage-taking, as though it (i.e.

the refusal) had come from a feeble and vacillating mind. The sense must be that Lot renewed his invitation because, unlike someone with a feeble and vacillating mind, he did not regard their refusal as something to take advantage of.

Various elements in the position I am advocating have been subject to various criticisms which must now be answered by way of conclusion. Lightfoot regarded the view of Meyer and Alford, which is similar to that of Moule, as 'somewhat strained', but this subjective judgement was really part of his overall view of the meaning of the idiomatic phrase—which, as we have seen, has to be modified in the light of Hoover's arguments. Foerster and Martin[100] argue that Moule's meaning is impossible because, if the word had an active sense, it should have an object. But, as Moule replies, this simply misses the point. An abstract noun like 'snatching', 'grasping', or 'getting' does not need an object: it refers, intransitively, to a particular way of life, namely, that which characterized pagan rulers, and indeed pagan gods and goddesses such as the Philippians might have worshipped in their pre-Christian days.[101] Martin's more recent objection[102] confirms the impression that he has not understood Moule's point, but is merely treating his view as if it were (a) dependent on that of Hammerich and (b) subject to the weaknesses of the old Latin view (with which he confused Ross's position in *Carmen Christi:* see above). Moule's interpretation—and, *mutatis mutandis,* mine—does not lose the mutual tension between vv. 6 and 7, as Martin claims. Verse 6 says that Christ did not regard his status in one way: v. 7 says that he took the opposite way instead. It is of course true that to say 'he did not regard x as y' could be stated in the form 'he regarded x as *not-y*', and *not-y* would then become an anticipation, albeit in negative terms, of the next clause, which states how he acted on that basis. But this is a mere verbal trick, which does not alter the tension or the sequential progress of the hymn. The fact that v. 6 states a *thought*, and v. 7 an *action*, is itself evidence of this. Martin's restatement of his own position ('v. 6b . . . states what Christ might have done, i.e. seized equality with God; only in v. 7 does it say what he chose to do, i.e. give himself') is in fact an overstatement. Verse 6b does not simply 'state what Christ might have done': it says that he did not do it. Allowing for this, Martin's way of formulating the passage to demonstrate its tension and movement could very easily be reworded into Moule's view, or mine, with the tension perfectly well maintained: Christ might have regarded his equality with God as meaning snatching (or, as something to take advantage of), but on the contrary he chose (to regard it as meaning) the way of self-giving, and, further, to act on that understanding.[103]

Nor are the weaknesses in his view which Moule himself disarmingly suggests as damaging as they might seem. We have already seen that the Greek Fathers' use may not be as far from his as it would appear from Lightfoot's reading of them. Nor, as we have seen, is the parallel between 2:5-11 and 3:2-11 lost (Moule, p. 274): it is in fact enhanced. Finally, Moule feels as a weakness the fact that vv. 7-8 appear now to indicate not a descent from 'equality with God', but the true expression of that equality—which looks odd in that it destroys the apparent pattern of 'descent and ascent' (p. 273).[104] Moule's own answer to this is that we are in the presence of irony: '*essentially*, that humiliation *was* itself exaltation' (p. 274, Moule's italics). But this is surely unnecessary. To read ἁρπαγμός as he has done does not *identify* the humiliation of Bethlehem and Calvary with the exaltation either of the pre-existent glory or the post-Easter triumph. There is still a real 'humiliation' followed by a real 'exaltation', and to use the latter word to describe the former event, while obliquely making an important theological point, may in fact obscure the real issue. Better, perhaps, to say that the *via crucis* of 2:6-8, consisting as it does in a real change of state, a real humilia-tion, for the pre-existent one, is—admittedly only to the hindsight of faith— the full revelation of what it meant, in practice, to be equal with God. The one who was eternally 'equal with God' expressed that equality precisely in the sequence of events referred to in vv. 6-8.[105]

These answers strengthen further the already impressive argument for the underlying theological emphasis of Moule's view. When that view has undergone the adjustments necessitated by the arguments of Hoover, these strengths remain in the view I have advocated. The thrust of the passage in itself is that the one who, before becoming human, possessed divine equality did not regard that status as something to take advantage of, but instead interpreted it as a vocation to obedient humiliation and death; and that God the Father acknowledged this interpretation as the true one by exalting him to share his own divine glory. In its wider context, this means that the passage is well able to fulfil the role which, prima facie, it has in Paul's developing argument, namely, that of the example which Christians are to imitate.[106] God acknowledged Christ's self-emptying as the true expression of divine equality: and he will acknowledge Christian self-abnegation (2:1-4, 12-18) in the same way (3:2ff., especially 3:11, 21).

Finally, if there is a conclusion to be drawn from this study in the realm of the linguistic background of the hymn, it is that whoever wrote v. 6 was using a precisely nuanced idiom in a characteristically Hellenistic way. This does not *prove* that the passage was originally composed in Greek, but it makes it very easy to imagine that it was.[107] In particular, it fits its present context so well that it is very hard to see it in any way as a detached, or even detachable, hymn about Christ.[108] The hymn (particularly v. 6, the special object of this study) belongs exactly where it now is. It is of course possible that Paul, realizing that it was going to be appropriate to quote the hymn (assuming that there was one) worded 2:1-5 accordingly, and then continued to echo the same themes later on in the letter. But if someone were to take it upon himself to argue, on the basis of my conclusions, that the 'hymn' was origi-nally written by Paul himself precisely in order to give Christological and above all theological underpinning to the rest of Philippians, especially chaps. 2 and 3, I for one should find it hard to produce convincing counter-arguments.[109]

Notes

[1] One possibility, that of textual emendation, is rightly ruled out altogether by the great majority of scholars, e.g. R. P. Martin, *Carmen Christi: Philippians ii: 5-11 in Recent Interpretation and in the Setting of Early Christian Worship*, SNTSMS 4 (Cambridge, 1967) (2nd edn., with new preface pp. xi-xxxix, Eerdmans, Grand Rapids, 1983), p. 153 (this work is cited hereafter by author's name only).

[2] See R. W. Hoover, 'The Harpagmos Enigma: A Philological Solution', *HTR* lvi (1971), 95-119; C. F. D. Moule, 'Further Reflexions on Philippians 2:5-11', in *Apostolic History and the Gospel: Biblical and Historical Essays presented to F. F. Bruce on his 60th Birthday*, ed. W. W. Gasque and R. P. Martin (Exeter, 1970), pp. 264-76: both cited hereafter by author's name only.

[3] J. B. Lightfoot, *St. Paul's Epistle to the Philippians* (London, 1868), pp. 109ff., 131-5 (the pagination is only slightly different in the other editions sometimes cited). In a note on pp. 135f. Lightfoot mentions, and rejects, another option which we will discuss later.

[4] See Moule, p. 271 n. 1.

[5] See Lightfoot, p. 134.

[6] Lightfoot distinguishes carefully between ἴσος θεῷ and ἴσα θεῷ: 'the former refers rather to the *person*, the latter to the *attributes*' (p. 110, Lightfoot's italics).

[7] Moule, p. 267.

[8] By which he really means *res retinenda*: on p. 138 he describes *res rapta* as 'a shorthand expression for the sense of ἁρπαγμός as a prize which, already in the possession of the owner, is held on to'.

[9] See Martin, pp. 139-43.

[10] pp. 148-53. He describes this as the 'more popular sense' (p. 144).

[11] It is in this category, not that of Ross and Hooke, that we should place the comment of W. Barclay, 'Great Themes of the New Testament, I: Phil. 2: 1-11', *Exp.T.* lxx (1958), 40-4, here as 42, cited by Martin, p. 136 n. 1.

[12] Though the other criticism urged by Martin, p. 136, citing Lightfoot and Gifford, is odd: in what way is this position 'incompatible with the validity of the Lord's claim to be on an equality with God'? No objection like this appears in Lightfoot: nor in the 1897 edition of E. H. Gifford, *The Incarnation: A Study of Philippians II: 5-11* (New York (Martin refers to the 1911 edition, not available to me)). Martin does not mention Lightfoot's first, and major, objection, which concerns the *non sequitur* between the Latin view and the exhortation to humility.

[13] So already J. M. Furness, *Exp.T.* lxix (1957-8), 93f.: D. R. Griffiths, in ibid. 237-9. For Feuillet's view see below (Moule, p. 271, already saw that Feuillet did not belong with the others in Martin's first category): Martin has, perhaps, been misled by Feuillet's note (*RB* li (1942), 62) that he is treating ἁρπαγμός as 'substantif actif'.

[14] This confusion was pointed out by T. F. Glasson in *NTS* xxi (1974-5), 135ff.

[15] See J. A. Beet, in *Expositor* (3rd series, vol. 5, 1887), pp. 115-25, *Exp.T.* iii (1891-2), 307-8, and *Exp.T.* vi (1894), 526-8. Beet was followed by F. G. Cholmondeley, *Exp.T.* vii (1895-6), 47-8.

[16] *New Testament Theology*, ET (London, 1955), pp. 117ff., 283f.

[17] See, for instance, H. A. A. Kennedy, in *The Expositor's Greek Testament*, ed. W. Robertson Nicoll (London, 1912), vol. 3, pp. 436f.; J. A. Bengel, *Gnomon Novi Testamenti* (Williams and Norgate edn., London and Edinburgh, 1862), p. 723; F. P. Badham, in *Exp.T.* xix (1907-8), 331-3; C. A. A. Scott, *Footnotes to St. Paul* (Cambridge, 1935), p. 192; F. W. Beare, *A Commentary on the Epistle to the Philippians* (London, 1959), pp. 79-81.

[18] P. Bonnard, *L'Epître aux Philippiens* (Neuchâtel and Paris, 1950), p. 43.

[19] G. Bornkamm, *Early Christian Experience*, ET (London, 1969), pp. 113, 114.

[20] E. Käsemann, 'A Critical Analysis of Philippians 2:5-11', in *Journal for Theology and Church*, vol. 5 (entitled *God and Christ: Existence and Province*), ed. R. W. Funk (Tübingen/New York, 1968), pp. 45-88: German original in *Z.Th.K.* xlvii (1950), 313-60, and in Käsemann's *Exegetische Versuche und Besinnungen*, Bd. 1 (Göttingen, 1960), 51-95. The reason why Martin draws Käsemann into this category is simply that he wants to use his 'functional', as opposed to 'ontological', reading of τὸ εἶναι ἴσα θεῷ (pp. 151f.).

[21] Martin, pp. 146.

[22] P. Henry, 'Kénose' in the Supplément to the *Dictionnaire de la Bible* (Paris, 1950), cols. 7-161: here at col. 27.

[23] L. Cerfaux, *Le Christ dans la Théologie de Saint Paul* (Paris, 1954), p. 290.

[24] p. 147.

[25] e.g. J. L. Houlden, *Paul's Letters from Prison* (Harmondsworth, 1970), pp. 74f.: J. G. Gibbs, *Creation and Redemption: A Study in Pauline Theology* (Leiden, 1971), p. 83.

[26] So, rightly, Hoover (p. 101). Hoover accuses Martin of 'philological obfuscation' on the grounds (*inter alia*) that he makes ἁρπαγμός carry both active and passive senses at the same time. But this may not be strictly the case. By *res rapta* Martin does not really mean to refer to the active sense (even if, strictly speaking, he should). What he is advocating is actually a combination of *res retinenda* and *res rapienda*.

[27] The final example of a combination of *res rapta* and *res rapienda* is that of C. K. Barrett, in *From First Adam to Last: A Study in Pauline Theology* (London, 1962), pp. 69ff. (see Martin, p. 149 n. 3). Barrett is the only writer, in fact, who actually achieves this combination without collapsing *res rapta* into *res rapienda*: but he does so at the cost of an extremely split Christology, in which, as Man, Christ did not possess the equality with God which he *did* possess as God's eternal Son. Barrett may well be right in seeing that some of the confusion in the passage is caused by Paul's squeezing a contrast between Christ and Adam into the argument: but (*a*) describing how he does this as a combining *res rapta* and *res rapienda*, though ingenious, may not be the most helpful analysis (see below); and (*b*) Barrett is not at all making the same point as Lohmeyer or Martin.

[28] That this is indeed Martin's view is confirmed by the preface to the new edition, where he says (p. xxiii) that 'the soteriological drama moves forward from the station the pre-existent one held as ἐν μορφῇ θεοῦ ὑπάρχων to His decision not to use such a platform as a means of snatching a prize (τὸ εἶναι ἴσα θεῷ), but chose rather to divest Himself of that advantage and take the μορφὴ δούλου as an act of voluntary humiliation. This (*a*) makes the mistake noted, of regarding 'being in the form of God' as the object of the verb, and (*b*) thus misuses Hoover's analysis of the key term, with which he professes to agree—although Hoover in fact pointed out the impossibility of the position Martin still advocates. See too Martin's Tyndale Commentary on Philippians (*The Epistle of Paul to the Philippians: An Introduction and Commentary* (London, 1959)), pp. 98f. A similar confusion appears in E. Schillebeeckx, *Christ: The Christian Experience in the Modern World*, ET (London, 1980), p. 170.

[29] Leading I. H. Marshall ('The Christ-Hymn in Philippians 2:5-11', *Tyndale Bulletin* xix (1968), 104-27, at p. 109) to think that this was Martin's own preferred label for his view.

[30] p. 149.

[31] Martin, pp. 151f.: see his Tyndale Commentary, pp. 96f.

[32] See, e.g., A. Feuillet, *Christologie Paulinienne et Tradition Biblique* (Paris, 1972), pp. 113ff.; G. B. Caird, *Paul's Letters From Prison* (New Clarendon Bible) (London, 1976), pp. 120f.

[33] For ease of reference, these are set out in tabular form in the article.

[34] See n. 6 above.

[35] e.g. Henry (above, n. 22); F. Prat, *The Theology of St. Paul*, ET (London, 1926), vol. 1, p. 319; Caird, *Letters from Prison* pp. 120f.; G. R. Beasley-Murray, in *Peake's Commentary on the Bible*, ed. M. Black and H. H. Rowley (London, 1962), pp. 986f.; O. Hofius, *Der Christushymnus Philipper ii. 6-11*, WUNT 17 (Tübingen, 1976), p. 103 (his translation of the hymn); and perhaps M. R. Vincent, *A Critical and Exegetical Commentary on the Epistles to the Philippians and to Philemon* (ICC) (Edinburgh, 1897), pp. 57ff.: though Vincent is not entirely clear on the matter. L. Bouyer takes a similar view (in *Mélanges Jules Lebreton, 1: RSR* xxxix (1951-2), 281-8), empha-

sizing the parallel with Adam. Recently B. Demarest has supported Lightfoot's position with the claim that it is 'dynamic and ontological' whereas Moule's scheme is 'purely static or ethical' ('Process Theology and the Incarnation', in *Pauline Studies: Essays Presented to F. F. Bruce on his 70th Birthday*, ed. D. A. Hagner and M. J. Harris (Exeter/Grand Rapids, 1980), pp. 122-42, here at p. 141 n. 54).

[36] See Martin, p. 169; Henry, op. cit.; Prat, *Theology* 1.319f.; K. Barth, *Church Dogmatics* 4. 1. 182f. (Edinburgh, 1956); E. R. Fairweather, 'Appended Note: The "Kenotic" Christology', in F. W. Beare, op. cit., pp. 159-74.

[37] e.g., Bornkamm (above, n. 19); Martin, pp. 138f. n. 4. J. G. Gibbs attempts to revive the kenotic view (see, in addition to the work mentioned in n. 25 above, his 'The Relation Between Creation and Redemption according to Phil. ii. 5-11', *Nov.T.* xii (1970), 270-83). But the strong point of his argument (the 'dynamic movement of God in Christ', p. 279) does not, in fact, support '*kenosis*' proper, but can be seen equally well in several other solutions, including our own (see below).

[38] So too J. Jervell, *Imago Dei: Gen. i. 26f. im Spätjudentum, in der Gnosis und in den Paulinischen Briefen* (FRLANT 76) (Göttingen, 1960), pp. 229f.; J. Gnilka, *Der Philipperbrief* (Freiburg/Basel/Wien, 1968), pp. 116f.

[39] So, rightly, D. Georgi, 'Der vorpaulinische Hymnus Phil. ii. 6-11', in *Zeit und Geschichte* (R. Bultmann *Festschrift*), ed. E. Dinkler (Tübingen, 1964), pp. 263-93; L. Hurtado, 'Jesus as Lordly Example in Philippians 2:5-11', in *From Jesus to Paul: Studies in Honour of Francis Wright Beare*, ed. P. Richardson and J. C. Hurd (Waterloo, Ontario, 1984), pp. 113-26, at pp. 116ff.; and others listed in Martin, pp. xixf.

[40] O. Cullmann, *The Christology of the New Testament*, ET (London, 2nd edn., 1963), pp. 177f.

[41] See Martin, pp. 139ff., and above n. 17. Prat (*Theology* 1.317f.) regards this view as Arian and therefore impossible. See further the revival of this position—almost as if it were a new thing!—by J. Harvey, in *Exp.T.* lxxvi (1964-5), 337ff. Harvey is answered by D. F. Hudson, in *Exp.T.* lxxvii (1965-6), 29.

[42] A. Feuillet, 'L'Homme-Dieu Considéré dans sa condition Terrestre de Serviteur et de Rédempteur', *RB* li (1942) (= *Vivre et Penser* 2), 58-79. See also his further study, 'L'Hymne Christologique de l'épître aux Philippiens (ii. 6-11)', *RB* lxxii (1965), 352-80, 481-507, at pp. 366f. See too P. Lamarche, 'L'Hymne de l'Epître aux Philippiens et la Kénose du Christ', in *L'Homme Devant Dieu: Mélanges offerts au Père Henri de Lubac*, vol. 1: Exégèses et Patristique (1963), pp. 147-58.

[43] *Christologie Paulinienne* (above, n. 32), pp. 112-32.

[44] M. D. Hooker, 'Philippians 2:6-11' in *Jesus und Paulus. Festschrift für Werner Georg Kümmel zum 70 Geburtstag*, ed. E. E. Ellis and E.Grässer (Göttingen, 1975), pp. 151-64.

[45] p. 138 n. 2: he gives no examples of scholars who hold it.

[46] See p. 160 n. 14. Only once, in Dan. (LXX) 3:19, does μορφή translate *tselem*, which the LXX translates with εἰκών in Gen. 1:26 and in several other instances.

[47] See above, n. 25: and cf. P. Grelot, 'La valeur de οὐχ . . . ἀλλά . . . dans Philippiens ii. 6-7', *Biblica* liv (1973), 25-42, at pp. 41f. Glasson (above, n. 14) noting Martin's appeal to the idiomatic sense, wrongly assumes that Martin is thereby following Lightfoot. See too J. Coppens, 'Une nouvelle Structuration de l'Hymne Christologique de l'Epître aux Philippiens', *Eph. Théol. Louv.* xliii (1967), 197-202, here at p. 199. Compare Coppen's earlier article against the kenotic theory, in ibid. xli (1965), 147-50. See too J. Gewiess, 'Der Philipperbriefstelle ii. 6b', in *Neotestament-liche Aufsätze* (J. Schmid *Festschrift*), ed. J. Blinzler (Regensburg, 1963), pp. 69-85). Gewiess's view is summarized, and criticized on the basis of the idiomatic sense, by Gnilka (above, n. 38), pp. 115ff.

[48] See above. If μορφὴ θεοῦ really were the object of οὐχ ἁρπαγμὸν ἡγήσατο, as Martin seems to think, a new sort of kenoticism would result, and it is clear that Martin does not want that either. The ambiguity still remains in Martin's New Century Bible, *Philippians* (London, 1976), p. 98: 'what he might have seized, he relinquished.' That which one might seize, one does not already possess: that which one does not possess, one cannot relinquish. See Marshall (above, n. 29), p. 126.

[49] *Pace* Houlden (above, n. 25), p. 75. Was Adam grasping at world sovereignty?

[50] See the very full details in Henry, op. cit. (above, n. 22). Other examples of this view are W. Barclay (above, n. 11) and H. Schumacher, *Christus in seiner Präexistenz und Kenose nach Phil. 2:5-8*, 2 vols. (Pontifical Biblical Institute, Rome, 1914 and 1921).

[51] So Moule, p. 271 n. 1. Moule suggests *res rapienda*, something 'requiring to be snatched', as another possibility: but this view (listed above as no. 4(*d*)) is surely not that of the Latin Fathers.

[52] See the *sed natura* of Augustine and Anselm of Canterbury, noted in Carmignac (see below, next note), pp. 146, 147, etc.

[53] J. Carmignac, 'L'Importance de la place d'une négation: ΟΥΧ ᾽ΑΡΠΑΓΜΟΝ ᾽ΗΓΗΣΑΤΟ (Philippiens II.6)', *NTS* xviii (1971-2), 131-61. Carmignac's view was anticipated in its essentials by J. S. F. Chamberlain ('The Kenosis', *Exp.T.* iv (1892-3), 189-90), who, beginning from J. A. Beet's articles (n. 15 above), argued, without apparently realizing that this is what he was doing, for this variant on the Latin view. Carmignac has been subjected to damaging criticism from P. Grelot (above, n. 47) and A. Feuillet (above, n. 32, pp. 119-22).

[54] *Church Dogmatics* iv. 1. 180: see too Barth's *Erklärung des Philipperbriefes* (Zürich, 1947), pp. 59f. (ET, pp. 60ff.).

[55] 'Christological Anthropology in Phil. II: 6-11', *RB* lxxxiii (1976), 25-50, here at p. 39 (his italics).

[56] Murphy-O'Connor, p. 40; J. D. G. Dunn, *Christology in the Making: An Inquiry into the Origins of the Doctrine of the Incarnation* (London, 1980), pp. 120f.

[57] See, for example, the criticisms of G. Howard, 'Phil. 2:6-11 and the Human Christ', *CBQ* xl (1978), 368-87, at pp. 371f.

[58] See, on this point, the articles of R. Bauckham, 'The Worship of Jesus in Apocalyptic Christianity', *NTS* xxvii (1980-1), 322-41, especially pp. 333ff., and R. T. France, 'The Worship of Jesus: A Neglected Factor in Christological Debate?' in *Christ the Lord: Studies in Christology Presented to Donald Guthrie*, ed. H. H. Rowdon (Leicester, 1982), pp. 17-36.

[59] His exposition of vv. 7-8 (pp. 42-5) is very unsatisfactory, leaning heavily on the hypothesis (criticized by Howard) of a derivation from wisdom speculation. Howard's own position, however (n. 57 above, at p. 377), fares little better: like Murphy-O'Connor he quotes Hoover approvingly while in fact tacitly disagreeing with one of his main conclusions.

[60] J. A. T. Robinson, *The Human Face of God* (London, 1973), pp. 162ff.

[61] P. Trudinger, 'ἁρπαγμός and the Christological Significance of the Ascension', *Exp.T.* lxxix (1967-8), 279; D. W. B. Robinson, 'ἁρπαγμός: The Deliverance that Jesus Refused?', *Exp.T.* lxxx (1968-9), 253ff. These senses thus take ἁρπαγμός as *raptus*, abstract and passive: 'a being snatched away'. The word *raptus* is of course ambiguous, admitting of both active (= *rapina*) and passive senses.

[62] E.g. Carmignac, Feuillet (at least in his earlier view). As Howard points out (p. 378 n. 29), Feuillet took this position in order to avoid apparent kenoticism.

[63] Moule, as above, n. 2.

[64] But what would the 'result' be in this case? See F. E. Vokes' discussion in his article ἁρπαγμός in Philippians 2:5-11', in *Studia Evangelica*, vol. 2, ed. F. L. Cross (= *TU* lxxxvii) (Berlin, 1964), 670-5, here at p. 673.

[65] J. Ross, ' Ἁρπαγμός (Philippians ii. 6)', *JTS* x (1909), 573f.; J. A. Beet (above, n. 15); W. Warren, 'On ἑαυτὸν ἐκένωσεν, Phil. ii. 7', *JTS* (1911), 461-3.

[66] H. A. W. Meyer, *Critical and Exegetical Handbook to the Epistles to the Philippians and Colossians, and to Philemon*, ET (New York, 1885), pp. 68ff.; H. Alford, *The Greek Testament . . .* (London, Oxford, and Cambridge, 1865), pp. 166f.; J. M. Furness, *Exp.T.* lxix (1957-8), 93-4 (simply a restatement of the position of Ross and Warren); S. H. Hooke, *Alpha and Omega: A Study in the Pattern of Revelation* (London, 1961), pp. 257ff. See too the theological position of M. D. Hooker, op. cit., p. 164, though she does not analyse the phrase grammatically in the same way as these writers. D. R. Griffiths, writing after Furness (*Exp.T.* lxix (1957-8), 237-9), misunderstands the position, and aligns it with the *res rapienda* view of Kennedy, Michael (in the Moffatt Commentary), and A. M. Hunter. D. F. Hudson, referring (presumably) to Furness's

article, also adopts the same view as Moule, in opposition to the *res rapienda* view of J. Harvey (n. 41 above).

[67] B. Reicke, 'Unité Chrétienne et Diaconie: Phil. 2:1-11', in *Neotestamentica et Patristica* (Cullmann *Festschrift*) (Leiden, 1962), pp. 203-12.

[68] Like Chamberlain (above, n. 53).

[69] Above, n. 64.

[70] Moule (p. 275) objects that Vokes then slips back into regarding ἁϱπαγμός as a concrete noun (a 'means of self-aggrandisement', Vokes, pp. 674f. (not 624 as in Moule)): but this is surely a linguistic optical illusion. There is hardly any distinction in meaning between 'he did not think that his status *meant* "snatching" ' and 'he did not regard his status *as an occasion for* "snatching" '. The parallel phrases offered by Reicke, p. 209 (e.g. Jas. 1:2), show that this sort of meaning is quite possible.

[71] e.g., Dunn, *Christology*, pp. 116, 313 n. 93; Caird, loc. cit.

[72] 'An Ancient Misunderstanding (Phil. 2:6 "robbery")', *Historisk-filosophiske Meddeleser udgivet af Det Kangelige Danske Videnskabernes Selskab*, Bind 41 nr. 4 (Copenhagen, 1966). Hammerich's views are summarized (and his name misspelt) in *Exp.T.* lxxviii (1967), 193-4.

[73] Hoover (as above, n. 2). The seminal article of W. W. Jaeger ('Eine stilgeschichtliche Studie zum Philipperbrief') may be found in *Hermes* 1 (1915), 537-53.

[74] Hoover, pp. 102-6, including a discussion of an apparent exception in Isodore of Pelusium, *Ep.* iv. 22. Hoover's evidence runs counter to Lightfoot's interpretation of the same passages (Hoover, pp. 108f. n. 20), and to W. F. Arndt and F. W. Gingrich, *A Greek-English Lexicon of the New Testament and Other Early Christian Literature*, 2nd edn., revised and augmented by F. W. Gingrich and F. W. Danker (from W. Bauer's 5th edn. of 1958) (Chicago, n.d.), col. 108.

[75] Details in Hoover, pp. 102ff.

[76] See the comments of F. E. Vokes (above, n. 64, at p. 672), referring to some similar abstract nouns which take on a concrete sense.

[77] For other similar pairs which come to be more or less interchangeable, see e.g. Lightfoot, p. 109, etc.

[78] In *TDNT* i. 472ff.

[79] Martin, p. 153.

[80] Foerster, p. 474.

[81] For which he cites (p. 474 n. 7) Ewald, Schmidt, and G. Kittel.

[82] Feuillet, *Christologie* (above, n. 32), p. 132. This latter idea, as he rightly sees, is not far from that of Cerfaux, who (after only a brief review of the debate, and with no reference to others who take this view) writes that Christ's equality with God is 'un objet possédé sans doute justement mais dont il ne faut pas user orgueilleusement et comme par bravade'. *Christ* (above, n. 23), p. 290.

[83] J. F. Collange, *L'Epître de Saint Paul aux Philippiens* (Neuchâtel, 1973), p. 90, comes close to this without seeing that it is substantially the same theological position as that of Furness and Vokes, which he had earlier rejected. H. Ridderbos (*Paul: An Outline of his Theology*, ET (Grand Rapids, 1975)), pp. 74f., expounds a position apparently similar to Hoover's when he writes: 'Christ did not regard this equality, in which he already shared, as a privilege that had come to him for his own advantage, on the ground of which he could have refused the way of self-emptying and humiliation.' But Ridderbos misleadingly classifies this view as *res rapta*.

[84] There is no space here to go into the details of debate about this word. For our purposes it is sufficient to note (*a*) whether or not it is taken as in some sense a predication of divinity and (*b*) whether or not it is more or less parallel in meaning to τὸ εἶναι ἴσα θεῷ.

[85] Hoover's study does not of itself rule out the possibility that τὸ εἶναι ἴσα θεῷ (and, *a fortiori*, ἐν μοϱφῇ θεοῦ ὑπάϱχων) could be taken in a strictly humanitarian sense: it only affirms that this equality is already possessed. But we have already argued, on other grounds, against the humanitarian interpretation. The true humanity of Christ, in its differences—precisely in being the genuine, uncorrupted article!—from all other examples of humanity, is perhaps the point of the irony noted by Hooker (above, n. 44, pp. 163f.) in the words ὁμοίωμα and σχῆμα.

[86] R. W. Funk, tr. and ed., *A Greek Grammar of the New Testament and Other Early Christian Literature* (revised and translated from Blass-Debrunner) (Chicago, 1973), p. 205.

[87] Professor Moule points out to me that ὑπάρχων can then be understood not as concessive but as causative—'precisely because he was . . . he recognised what it meant'. This potential ambiguity is not without parallel in Paul: see, e.g., Rom. 9:22 (θέλων). The causative sense is, if my whole argument is correct, clearly the one required. George Caird, commenting on a draft of this paper, suggested the following: 'he was in the form of God, and did not regard his equality with God . . . but rather . . . '. Some biblical and historical examples of the sort of behaviour contrasted here, by implication, with that of Jesus are suggested by F. G. Cholmondeley, in *Exp.T.* vii (1895-6), 47-8. Perhaps the most suggestive passage would be 1 Kings 3:4-15, 28 (not mentioned by Cholmondeley).

[88] See the valid criticism of Martin by I. H. Marshall (above, n. 29), pp. 124f., and the warning against trying to force soteriology on to a passage which is about something else, in L. W. Hurtado, op. cit. (above, n. 39), pp. 123f.

[89] See Hooker (above, n. 44), p. 152, citing, e.g. Rom. 4:14; 1 Cor. 1:17; 9:15; 2 Cor. 9:3.

[90] See Hurtado, op. cit, pp. 124f.

[91] Against, e.g. Moule, p. 270.

[92] There is certainly no need to split the hymn up as Jervell does (above, n. 38). We may note at this point that, though our view of the passage does not require that the prefix ὑπερ- in the verb ὑπερύψωσεν (v. 9) should be taken to indicate Jesus' exaltation to a higher glory than that which he possessed at the beginning, and while it is quite likely that the prefix should not, in fact, be pressed in this way, our understanding of the passage makes available a possible sense of further exaltation, which is not the same as that suggested by Martin (pp. 240ff.) and others. In his exaltation Christ does not merely return to a state of glory corresponding to that of his pre-existence, but is now exalted as *man*, God's intended ruler of the world. Here again the *appropriateness* of the incarnation is underlined.

[93] See Marshall's criticisms (above, n. 29, pp. 117ff.), and similarly G. N. Stanton, *Jesus of Nazareth in New Testament Preaching* (SNTSNS 27) (Cambridge, 1974), pp. 101f.; E. Larsson, *Christus als Vorbild* (Uppsala, 1962), pp. 230ff. Larsson rightly compares Rom. 15:1-7 (p. 234); see also Hoover, p. 118.

[94] Those who have noted the parallel include Käsemann, Bultmann, and Hooker.

[95] 'Adam in Pauline Christology', in *SBL 1983 Seminar Papers*, ed. K. H. Richards (Chico, California, 1983), pp. 359-89, here at 373ff. See too Martin, p. xxi.

[96] See the surveys, already noted, by Henry (above, n. 22); Feuillet, *Christologie* (above, n. 32), pp. 113ff.; P. Grelot, 'La traduction et l'interprétation de *Ph*. 2, 6-7: Quelques Eléments d'enquête Patristique', *Nouv.Rév.Theol.* (1971), pp. 897-922, 1009-26; Geweiss, op. cit. (above, n. 47), pp. 75-81. Compare also Lightfoot's account (pp. 134f.) of Chrysostom's position.

[97] So W. Foerster, οὐχ ἁρπαγμὸν ἡγήσατο bei den griechischen Kirchenvätern', *ZNW* xxix (1930), 115-28; Hoover, pp. 108f.; Martin, p. 146; Feuillet, *Christologie*, p. 130.

[98] See Hoover, pp. 110f.

[99] Martin (p. 144) is clearly wrong to understand παραιτήσις here as 'demand'.

[100] Following H. A. A. Kennedy (above, n. 17), pp. 436f. For Foerster see n. 78 above.

[101] See an alternative counter-argument in Beet, *Expositor* (1887), p. 122.

[102] In his New Century Commentary, pp. 96f., and his new introduction to *Carmen Christi*, pp. xxiif.

[103] See Moule's parody, p. 269.

[104] This point is seized on by T. Nagata, quoted by Martin, loc. cit., who contrasts the 'static' nature of Moule's scheme with the 'sequential' progress of the hymn. But this, as we have seen, is to misunderstand the real nature of Moule's view.

[105] Martin (p. xxiii) claims, following Nagata, that the οὐχ . . . ἀλλὰ . . . sequence 'militates against seeing two sides to Christ's being equal with God as if they were complementary'. But this is nothing like what Moule is saying.

[106] See now L. Hurtado, op. cit. (n. 39 above).

[107] See R. Deichgräber, *Gotteshymnus und Christushymnus in der frühen Christenheit* (Göttingen, 1967), p. 129. Of course, a hymn's being composed in Greek does not necessarily indicate that it expresses a 'Hellensitic' theology—whatever that might mean—as opposed to any other sort.

[108] It is not, despite the common assumption to the contrary, a hymn *to* Christ (see, e.g. Martin, pp. 1ff.: so, rightly, Deichgräber, pp. 118f.).

[109] Among many writers who have stood against the tide on this question see J. M. Furness, 'The Authorship of Philippians ii: 6-11', *Exp.T.* lxx (1959-60), 240-3, and 'Behind the Philippian Hymn', *Exp.T.* lxxix (1967-8), 178-82; and George B. Caird, 'The Development of the Doctrine of Christ in the New Testament', in N. Pittenger (ed.), *Christ for Us Today* (London, 1968), pp. 66-80, at pp. 66f.

SYNOPTIC STUDIES:
SOME RECENT METHODOLOGICAL DEVELOPMENTS
AND DEBATES

CRAIG L. BLOMBERG
Assistant Professor of New Testament
Denver Seminary

Article from *Themelios*

New Testament scholarship continues to overwhelm the student who would keep abreast of its developments, as it deluges him with massive quantities of literature and a bewildering array of methods and tools. Nowhere is this problem so pressing as in the study of the synoptic gospels. This article surveys six popular but often misunderstood modern methodologies and a sampling of the most significant, recent literature in each area.[1] The order of presentation follows roughly the chronological order of the rise and/or popularity of the six disciplines.

1. Source Criticism

As recently as 1964, Stephen Neill could write that the synoptic problem was one of the few settled issues of New Testament scholarship.[2] The two-document hypothesis, in which Matthew and Luke independently drew on Mark and Q as their primary sources, commanded virtually unanimous support. B. H. Streeter's more ambitious four-document hypothesis, which added M and L as hypothetical sources for Matthew's and Luke's peculiar material,[3] was less widely held but still considered quite plausible. In that same year, however, William Farmer issued a major challenge to the critical consensus with his detailed attempt to revive the Griesbach hypothesis (named after its stalwart, late eighteenth-century advocate), in which Matthew is seen as the earliest gospel writer, Luke as directly dependent on him, and Mark as the abridger or conflater of the two.[4] Farmer's work gained only a minimal following until the second half of the 1970s, but since then supporters have been emerging from the woodwork in droves, even if they still represent only a vocal minority of scholars worldwide.[5]

Several international colloquia have helped to fuel the recent resurgence of interest in the Griesbach hypothesis.[6] New synopses, in which the gospel parallels are aligned differently from the traditional left-to-right, Matthew-Mark-Luke arrangement, will further this interest,[7] as opponents of the two-document hypothesis argue that readers become unjustifiably prejudiced when they always follow synopses which use Mark as their guide for pericope division and which sandwich the Lucan and Matthean parallels on either side of him.[8] The growing concern to reopen an investigation once thought closed has encouraged others to propose a whole host of different hypotheses, invoking concepts popular a century ago, including proto-gospels,[9] an overarching, primitive *Ur*-gospel,[10] Aramaic gospels later translated into Greek,[11] variants caused by oral tradition,[12] and greater degrees of literary independence.[13] Most of these gain few adherents apart from the students of their creators, but they point to an important insight. The solution to the synoptic problem, by virtue of the complexity of the data and the complexity of the factors involved in the production of any first-century religious or historical documents, is almost certainly very intricate itself, and as a result may well be irrecoverable in many details. Nevertheless, it may still be possible to answer the three main questions to which Streeter's classic theory offered affirmative replies: Did Matthew and Luke use Mark? Did Matthew and Luke use an independent source Q? Are M and L plausible hypotheses?

The cases for and against both Marcan priority and the Q hypothesis are ably laid out in the anthology of classic articles edited by Arthur Bellinzoni.[14] Recent studies increasingly admit that Matthew's use of Mark is not as easily demonstrated as Luke's use of Mark, but this does not necessarily advance the cause of Griesbach; it more naturally suggests the rehabilitation or modification of Augustine's much older view, in which the order of the synoptics matches their order in the canon. The Griesbachians, admittedly, have scored several points; it is now more widely conceded that the argument from order (Matthew and Luke only rarely deviating from Mark in the same way at the same time) could fit in with several different models of synoptic interrelationships,[15] but the view which sees Mark as last has yet to come up with a convincing reason for his omission of all the so-called Q material. Attempts have been made to explain why, on this view, Mark alternated between Matthew and Luke for that material which he did include,[16] but the theological and stylistic features invoked are much more general and less clearly present than the redaction-critical tendencies definable via the two-document hypothesis. Moreover, the type of conflationary process involved—omission of large sections coupled with expansion of detail in passages included—stands on its head the traditional processes of literary abridgment known in antiquity.[17] And attempts to argue that Mark's roughness of style and grammar and potentially misleading historical and theological statements point to his distance from the gospel tradition rather than to his priority[18] make little sense. If Mark did not have Matthew and Luke in front of him, one could plausibly argue this way, but granted a literary interrelationship only a hack writer would replace his otherwise coherent sources with such infelicities.

Significantly, few detailed exegetical or theological studies of major sections of the synoptics have adopted Matthean and/or Lukan priority; it is easier to point out flaws in alternative theories than to make these ones work in practice. Even a sizeable majority of studies of individual passages continue to find Marcan priority generally adequate. Those which dissent usually point out primitive features in Matthew rather than in Luke.[19] This, coupled with some renewed recognition of the *prima facie* reliability of the ancient patristic testimony, especially that of Papias,[20] may suggest a two-stage composition of the gospel of Matthew, or even of Mark, allowing for cross-fertilization of the two traditions at various stages of the gospels' development.[21] If Marcan priority needs to be modified, cross-fertilization is a more promising model to consider than conflation.

Evidence for Q has always been more ambiguous than that which favours Marcan priority. Much recent literature has been conveniently summarized in brief by H. Bigg and in detail by F. Neirynck.[22] Those who would dispense with Q overwhelmingly favour Luke's use of Matthew rather than vice versa, since primitivity is over-all more defensible for Matthew than for Luke. But attempts to explain Luke's rationale in cutting up Matthew's coherent, extended accounts of Jesus' discourses (Mt. 5-7, 10, 13, 18, 23-25) fail miserably. No one has expended as much energy at this task as has Michael Goulder, but with each successive publication he rejects his previous theories in favour of new ones, and most rest on the flimsiest of evidence, so that it is difficult to take them too seriously.[23] On the other hand, noteworthy progress has been made in identifying consistent theological and stylistic features of Q, as traditionally understood, and of proposing plausible, if not demonstrable, *Sitze im Leben* for its formation.[24] It is quite possible that one needs to think of Q in terms of multiple recensions, multiple documents, or the confluence of oral and written traditions, but on the whole Q remains preferable to its competitors.

Even before the reopening of the synoptic problem, M and L remained the shakiest building blocks in the Streeterian edifice. It is almost certainly unreasonable to expect them to be coherent, unified documents, as if Matthew and Luke got all of their information from written sources, and then only from three. Still, meticulous studies of the distinctive language of the peculiarly Lucan material and of the extra-biblical parallels to the peculiarly Matthean material suggest that these two evangelists did rely on some kind of early source material, whether written or oral, for their distinctive elements. Stephen Farris, for example, applies detailed linguistic criteria to argue that Luke 1-2 largely comprise 'translation Greek' (from a Semitic source) different from that which characterizes Luke's writing elsewhere.[25] I have suggested reasons for perceiving a parable source on which Luke drew for much of his central section (9:51-18:14).[26] Most convincingly of all, Richard Bauckham discerns the use of the traditions behind Matthew's special material by Ignatius and other extra-biblical writers, and concludes that

since the Apostolic Fathers knew non-Markan traditions in oral form, it is inconceivable that Matthew and Luke should not have done. Christian

literature outside the Synoptic Gospels provides so much evidence of independent, varying forms of Synoptic material that the *probability* is in favour
of more, not fewer, Synoptic sources.[27]

Clearly the field is wide open for much further study in synoptic source
criticism, even if a modified form of Streeter's approach still remains most
likely.

2. Form criticism

The long overdue replacement for Rudolf Bultmann's famous text, *The History of the Synoptic Tradition*,[28] may have at last appeared, at least in programmatic form, in Klaus Berger's *Formgeschichte des Neuen Testaments*.[29]
Berger attempts to classify not just the synoptic but all the NT materials
according to form, eschewing prejudicial labels such as myth and legend, as
well as remote history-of-religions 'parallels', in favour of categories based
strictly on generic and rhetorical features common to the biblical texts and
other Greek literature of their day. His system of classification is also much
more detailed, utilizing post-Bultmannian research to enunciate and sub-
divide the three main rhetorical divisions of deliberative, epideictic and
juridical texts. In an age when many critics have abandoned form-critical
questions in favour of one or more of those discussed in the rest of this
article, Berger has shown that there is much interpretive benefit to be gained
from the careful analysis of a pericope's form.

Wisely, Berger avoids the pitfalls of so many earlier form-critics by not
attempting to trace the tradition-history of each form or passage. He readily
admits that the two tasks, though related, are separable, and that there is
good reason to believe in at least a generally conservative tradition behind
the transmission of the Jesus-material. The only criterion of authenticity
which he will admit is that of '*wirkungsgeschichtlichen Plausibilität*'[30] (the
plausibility of historical results), that is, that which makes the subsequent
history of the early church understandable. It is of course this issue of
historicity and criteria for authenticity which has exercised so many of the
critics of form criticism.[31] The arguments supporting the trustworthiness of
the gospel tradition continue to be rehearsed, along with the weaknesses of
the critical reconstructions of its tradition history.[32] A few find those weaknesses so severe that they either abandon form criticism altogether or deny
that a period of oral transmission of the tradition ever existed.[33] The 'guarded
tradition' hypothesis of Riesenfeld and Gerhardsson, which proposed that
Jesus taught his disciples in rabbinic fashion to memorize many of his
teachings and narratives of his deeds, which were in turn carefully passed
along to specifically designated tradents in the early Christian community,
remains more defensible.[34] But the value of the rabbinic analogy is somewhat diminished due to its reliance on anachronistic, post-AD 70 parallels
and to its failure to account for Jesus' uniqueness and for the differences
which still remain among the synoptic parallels.[35]

Two lines of research have quite recently broken this stalemate. On the one hand, a trio of German Ph.D. theses have investigated the nature of pre-70 Jewish and Christian oral tradition and discovered that the Riesenfeld-Gerhardsson model suffers neither from anachronism nor from a failure to acknowledge Jesus' distinctiveness. P. G. Müller examines ancient oral tradition in the light of modern speech-act theory, A. F. Zimmermann studies the role of the *didaskalos* or 'teacher' in the early church, and Rainer Riesner surveys the role of memorization in almost every form of ancient education, beginning with the most elementary levels.[36] As a result, all three agree that it is virtually inconceivable that Jesus would not have taught his disciples to learn large bodies of material by heart.

By far the most significant of these three theses is Riesner's. In addition to demonstrating the rote nature of elementary education required of all first-century Jewish boys, Riesner provides five other key reasons why the teaching of and about Jesus would most likely have been preserved quite carefully. (1) Jesus followed the practice of Old Testament prophets by proclaiming the Word of the Lord with the kind of authority that would have commanded respect and concern to safeguard that which was perceived as revelation from God. (2) Jesus' presentation of himself as Messiah, even if in a sometimes veiled way, would reinforce his followers' concern to preserve his words, since one fairly consistent feature in an otherwise diverse body of first-century expectations was that the Messiah would be a teacher of wisdom. (3) The gospels depict Jesus as just such a teacher of wisdom and phrase over 90 percent of his sayings in forms which would have been easy to remember, using figures and styles of speech much like those found in Hebrew poetry. (4) There are numerous hints and a few concrete examples in the gospels of Jesus commanding the twelve to 'learn' specific lessons and to transmit what they learned to others, even before the end of his earthly ministry. (5) Almost all teachers in the Jewish and Graeco-Roman worlds of that day gathered disciples around them in order to perpetuate their teachings and lifestyle, so however different Jesus was from his contemporaries in other ways, he probably resembled them in this respect.

On the other hand, studies of oral tradition in a variety of modern, pre-literary cultures suggest that memorization in the ancient world did not always mean what it does today. For example, A. B. Lord's pioneering study of a quarter-century ago, only recently noticed by more than a handful of biblical scholars, described certain illiterate Yugoslavian folk singers who had 'memorized' epic narratives of up to 100,000 words in length. The plot, the characters, all the main events and the vast majority of the details stayed the same every time they retold or sang the stories. Members of the community were sufficiently familiar with them to correct the singer if he erred in any significant way. Yet anywhere from 10 percent to 40 percent of the precise wording could vary from one performance to the next, quite comparable to the variation found in the synoptic gospels.[37] Lord himself suggests that this model of flexibility in wording, order, inclusion and omission of material may account for many of the variations among synoptic parallels.[38]

Werner Kelber has followed Lord further, noting his disjunction between the fluidity of oral tradition and the fixity of written tradition, and hence rejecting the applicability of the model of 'passive transmission' to the gospels as they now exist, since they clearly drew on written sources.[39] But Kelber overlooks the fact that oral traditions often continued and remained authoritative long after written accounts were produced. Lord specifically cautions that 'the use of writing in setting down oral texts does not *per se* have any effect on oral tradition'.[40] It is only when a community accepts a given written text as normative to the exclusion of all other versions that the oral-written disjunction comes into play. It is not clear that such an acceptance of the gospels as canonical predates the mid-second century. Nevertheless, several of Kelber's emphases about the active involvement of those who handed down the Jesus-tradition, selecting what seemed to them appropriate for a given audience under given social circumstances, may well account for some of the differences among the synoptic parallels.

3. Redaction criticism

Undoubtedly the most thriving discipline in recent years, redaction criticism picks up where form criticism and the study of the transmission of the tradition leave off. It is here that a majority of the differences among gospel parallels is most successfully accounted for. No doubt because they perceive their discipline as neither any more in its infancy nor yet on the wane, current redaction critics write less self-reflectively about their method and busy themselves more with simply analyzing the gospel texts than do practitioners of any of the other criticisms surveyed here.[41]

At the same time, important issues of definition and method require further clarification. Some extreme conservatives, mostly in North America, have rejected redaction criticism outright, often because they believe it necessarily requires an abandonment of belief in the full historicity of the gospels.[42] Such a misunderstanding stems in part from the widespread circulation of introductory texts like that of Norman Perrin, who articulated in great detail a radically sceptical position reflecting the opposite extreme of the theological spectrum.[43] On the other hand, the definition of Richard Soulen's handbook is more widely representative: redaction criticism 'seeks to lay bare the theological perspectives of a biblical writer by analyzing the editorial (redactional) and compositional techniques and interpretations employed by him in shaping and framing the written and/or oral traditions at hand (see Luke 1:1-4)'.[44] The church throughout its history has investigated these questions, even if not under the banner of current terminology or with as much critical introspection.[45] For example, the major evangelical commentaries on the synoptics by D. A. Carson, W. L. Lane and I. H. Marshall all employ redaction criticism to various degrees to yield crucial theological insight into the distinctive emphases of the three gospels without necessarily abandoning belief in their historicity.

Nevertheless, quite often redaction critics still seem needlessly sceptical of the historicity of a given portion of the gospels. This scepticism could be ameliorated if certain common but unwarranted presuppositions not inherent in redaction criticism itself were laid aside. These vitiating presuppositions are not all as well-known as the problems often attaching to form criticism, so they merit brief cataloguing here.[47] (1) Some have assumed that an author's perspective emerges only from a study of how he has edited his sources rather than from a holistic analysis of everything he includes in his work. The former often seems implied, for example in J. A. Fitzmyer's exhaustive commentary on Luke, while the latter, by way of contrast, is the explicit presupposition of C. H. Talbert's more programmatic work on the same gospel.[48] (2) Many commentators treat virtually every pair of passages with any similarity as variants of one original saying or event in Jesus' life. This leads to drastic conclusions about the freedom with which a given evangelist rewrote his sources and overlooks the possibility of apparent parallels not being genuine ones.[49] (3) Drawing conclusions about the nature of the communities which the gospel writers were addressing is a much more subjective process than many critics admit. Meeting a pressing need in his audience is not the only reason an author includes material in his work![50] (4) Many redaction-critical studies build on the unnecessarily sceptical assumptions of more radical form criticism and ignore the positive results noted above. The two most detailed commentaries on Mark currently available, by R. Pesch and J. Gnilka, exemplify a trend to assign material to a pre-Marcan stage of the tradition without seeming willing to consider that it might also be authentic.[51] While it does not immediately follow that traditional material is historical, the probability of its reliability is at least enhanced.

(5) Some bypass the problem of redaction criticism's labeling certain passages as unhistorical by arguing that the gospel material need not be authentic to be authoritative. This view dominates that branch of redaction criticism known as canon criticism, but is not limited to it, and has infected certain evangelical circles as well.[52] Though well-intentioned, this approach makes Christian belief unfalsifiable and therefore unjustifiable. Had the first Christians adopted it, they would have had no rationale for excluding portions of the apocryphal gospels from the canon. (6) Minor grammatical and syntactical differences between parallels are sometimes invested with deep theological significance when they may only reflect the stylistic preferences of their authors. This is more a problem for specialized studies which have smaller databases with which to work, as for example in the books on the parables by C. E. Carlston and J. Drury.[53] (7) Dictional analysis, the study of the characteristic *versus* the unusual vocabulary of a given evangelist, invariably over-estimates the amount of material which can confidently be identified as redactional or tradition on linguistic and statistical grounds alone.[54] (8) Finally, and most significantly, redaction critics astonishingly continue to equate 'redactional' or 'theological' with 'unhistorical' almost by defini-

tion, despite widespread protests against this practice. As already observed, it is quite likely that the gospel writers had access to much information about the life and teaching of Jesus besides their primary written sources.

Despite these eight excesses, redaction criticism remains a valuable tool. Its abuse can be avoided, and, when stripped of the excess baggage it tends to attract, it offers insights into the emphases of the evangelists which make the differences among the gospels more understandable. At times, it can even help clear up knotty problems of harmonization when more traditional methods prove unconvincing.[55]

4. Midrash criticism

Are the gospels midrashic? The answer to this question, which has stirred up much recent controversy, depends largely on one's definition of the term. Midrash, from the Hebrew for 'interpretation', can refer to a wide variety of texts of passages. One fundamental distinction separates midrash as a genre off from midrash as one or more methods of interpretation. As a genre, midrash refers to types of exposition of the Hebrew Scriptures. These divide into three major categories: (a) the targums, (b) the more elaborate 'rewritten Scriptures' such as Josephus' *Jewish Antiquities* or pseudo-Philo's *Biblical Antiquities,* and (c) the earliest Jewish commentaries beginning in the rabbinic period.[56] As methods of interpreting Scripture, midrash usually encompasses one or more of the ancient lists of hermeneutical rules handed down by the rabbis.[57]

Midrashic methods of interpretation undeniably appear in the gospels, including well-known techniques such as *qal-wa-homer,* arguing from the lesser to the greater (*e.g.* Mt. 7:11), as well as less familiar forms such as the proem or homily called *yelammedenu rabbenu* ('let our master teach us'). The latter involves a dialogue with a question, two or more scriptural quotations or allusions, exposition by means of catchwords or parables, and a concluding allusion to one or more of the initial quotations. This form of interpretation can bring order and unity, for example to the cryptic dialogue in which the parable of the Good Samaritan is embedded (Lk. 10:25-37).[58]

More controversial are those instances where midrash is invoked to explain seemingly illegitimate New Testament exegesis of the Old. A classic example from the gospels arises in Matthew 2:15, quoting Hosea 11:1: 'Out of Egypt I called my son.' Matthew appears to have turned a straightforward historical statement about the exodus into a prophecy of Jesus' flight from Herod. Less conservative scholars may simply argue that the evangelist was creating a typical midrashic play on words, somewhat arbitrarily reading a meaning which the word 'son' can have elsewhere in the OT (*i.e.* Messiah) into a passage where it clearly refers to Israel, even though modern expositors recognize the invalidity of such hermeneutics.[59] More conservative scholars often adopt a similar explanation, but combine it with a belief that the NT writers, because they were inspired, could employ methods which would be inadmissible for any other exegete.[60]

The latter view, though, much like the approach of canon criticism noted earlier, could theoretically be employed to justify any exegesis of Scripture, however fanciful, so long as it was performed by an inspired author. There are numerous other possible explanations for the unusual uses of the OT by the NT that should be tested first before recourse be made to anything so drastic. Some of these include use of a different text-type (non-Masoretic Hebrew, LXX, targums), especially where there is reason to believe the Masoretic text may not be the most reliable;[61] use of a later text-type current in the first century, when the point the writer is making does not depend on the distinctive form of that variant text;[62] typological exegesis (probably the best explanation of Mt. 2:15);[63] use of the word 'fulfil' (*plēroō*) with a broader semantic range than is normal in English;[64] insufficient appreciation of the full meaning of an OT text in its larger context;[65] and possibly even *sensus plenior.*[66]

The other storm-centre of recent midrash criticism revolves around the issue of whether or not an entire main section of the gospels or even a whole gospel is midrashic in genre. Thus Luke has been seen as following a sequence of parallels in the book of Deuteronomy for the outline of his central section, or a series of texts from Kings and Chronicles in the earlier chapters.[67] Even more ambitious is Robert Gundry's notion that Matthew is a midrash on Mark and Q, fictitiously embellishing his two sources with unhistorical material which his audience would have recognized as such due to its peculiar nature.[68]

Here at least two points need to be distinguished. First, to refer to any of these portions of the gospels as midrash is to use the term more broadly than the ancient Jews would have permitted. Strictly speaking, midrash as a genre is limited to obvious paraphrases, elaborations or interpretations of specific OT texts, not just possible, vague parallels which only a minority of commentators perceive.[69] The modern use of the term midrash to refer to fictitious events set in the era of the gospel writer (*i.e.* portions of the life of Jesus) also stands on its head the typical Jewish usage, in which midrashic writings largely left contemporary events untampered with (not least because they were more easily investigated) but altered the interpretation of the OT narratives and prophecies to make them match current events more closely.[70] Second, regardless of the terminology, it is not clear that most of the authors of these hypotheses have created convincing cases; several thoroughgoing critiques are readily available.[71] Nevertheless, midrash criticism may have occasionally unearthed OT backgrounds for certain individual passages in the gospels,[72] and Gundry's type of hypothesis should at least alert exegetes to an often-overlooked principle: the superficial appearance of the text as a historical narrative offers no guarantee that the author of that narrative was employing an entirely historical genre. Only a detailed study of the text and a wide diversity of possible parallels in other literature of its time can prove decisive.

5. Social-scientific methods
Dissatisfaction with the limitations of the various branches of historical and literary criticism already discussed is leading growing numbers of biblical critics to experiment with methods borrowed from the social sciences. The synoptics, usually in conjunction with larger portions of Scripture, have thus been interpreted through the grids of modern economic,[73] psychological[74] and anthropological theories.[75] By far the most plentiful, however, are sociological studies of the rise of Christianity.[76] These range from fairly traditional studies of the historical beginnings of the Jesus-movement, which merely seek to highlight its social nature in contrast to modern Western Christianity's overemphasis on individualism, all the way to fairly radical revisionist portraits of Jesus and his disciples as wandering, homeless charismatics.[77]

All of these studies provide fresh perspectives on largely overlooked dimensions of the background and meaning of various gospel texts. Equally often, however, the methods employed mask important presuppositions which lead to a reductionistic analysis of the biblical material. One of the most common of these is the antisupernaturalism inherent in much modern social science, but there are important exceptions. Howard C. Kee and Gerd Theissen, for example, have both eschewed the historical questions about 'what happened' in connection with Jesus' miracles in order to concentrate on the functional questions of how these synoptic narratives affected their first audiences and the communities which came to believe in them.[78] The results of such studies may in some cases make the historicity of the miracle stories more defensible; in others they may render such questions irrelevant or suggest that the gospel writers were not intending to write history at all at certain points.[79] Ironically, E. M. Yamauchi points out that even as biblical scholars are at last learning about modern developments in the social sciences, many sociologists are regaining an appreciation for the need to ask the historical questions and are toning down the more radical theories which the New Testament critics are embracing.[80]

6. Other literary criticisms
Other scholars who have been dissatisfied with the questions and answers supplied by the more traditional historical-critical methods have advocated the introduction, and in some cases the substitution, of purely literary-critical issues and tools. In many North American universities one can almost speak of a complete paradigm shift from interest in the gospels as historical documents to interest in them as literary narratives.[81] In the 1960s and '70s this shift often began via a focus on structuralism, broadly defined as a formalist preoccupation with the text apart from questions of historical background, context, or authorial intent. In some instances the rise of 'Bible as literature' courses led to the analysis of scriptural 'surface structures'— identifying the roles of a story's main characters, the plot, tone, theme,

motifs—in short the standard type of criticism long since applied to fictitious literature such as novels or short stories. Major works of this kind of 'narrative criticism' applied to the gospels are now at last becoming popular, usually without involving any necessary presumptions for or against historicity. Thus, for example, J. D. Kingsbury distinguishes between the fully developed 'round' characters of Jesus and the disciples in Matthew and the monolithic, 'flat' characters of the Jewish leaders and the crowds in order to highlight the role of conflict in the developing story-line of this gospel.[82] Leland Ryken is one of the few evangelicals who has written extensively on the Bible as literature; and his work deserves far more attention than it has received. No interpreter of the parables, for example, can afford to ignore his refutation of the traditional parable-allegory disjunction.[83]

One specialized branch of formalist literary analysis is rhetorical criticism, in which no one has excelled as much as George Kennedy. Kennedy's most recent work, for example, includes an analysis of the Sermon on the Mount which perceives in it a logical structure which closely follows the rules for ancient deliberative rhetoric. Knowing that his views fly fully in the face of the critical consensus, Kennedy considers in the light of the practices of ancient rhetoricians that this carefully knit unity might well represent an abbreviated form of a single, original discourse which Jesus spoke, perhaps more than once in varying forms (thus accounting for Luke's Sermon on the Plain):

> Matthew's version might thus represent what was remembered from several occasions and not what Jesus said verbatim at any one delivery, but in the same sense it could represent a relatively full version of what he was remembered as saying at one period of his ministry.[84]

The term structuralism itself is usually reserved for a more esoteric form of study of the 'deep structures' of a text—the underlying and more fundamental features which allegedly form the basis of all narratives, for example, the functions, motives and interaction among the main characters and objectives in a narrative and, most notably, the types of oppositions and resolutions that develop as the text unfolds.[85] Not too long ago many initiates into this kind of structuralism were heralding it as the only valid tool for literary analysis, and promoting it as an ideology inherently bound up with dialectic philosophy, determinism and atheism.[86] But while much methodological discussion arose, and numerous sample texts were studied, most notably Jesus' parables, few concrete exegetical insights arose that could not have been gained by other means and by employing more familiar terminology. As a result its popularity has waned. Where it is still promoted, it is usually put forward as one method among several,[87] and attention has turned somewhat away from the gospels to the writings of Paul, perhaps in hopes of still proving it valuable. Nevertheless one may read with profit Sandra Perpich's largely successful, though obtusely worded, attempt to combine the techniques of structuralism with the best of another nearly defunct movement, the 'new hermeneutic', in exegeting the parable of the Good Samaritan.[88]

Most gospel scholars who keep up with the new literary criticisms, however, have all but abandoned structuralism in favour of the so-called poststructuralist movements. In the last few years a torrent of poststructuralist studies of the gospels has been unleashed and there are no signs of its diminution. Poststructuralism gathers together a loosely connected collection of methods which usually share at least one common belief: the meaning of a text resides neither in the author's intention (as in traditional historical and literary criticism) nor in the text studied autonomously (as in formalism and structuralism) but in the mind of the reader or, most commonly, in the product of the interaction of the text and the reader.[89]

The most avant-garde and abstruse form of poststructuralism calls itself 'deconstruction' and endorses the process of 'generating conflicting meanings from the same text, and playing those meanings against each other'[90] to show how all language ultimately self-destructs or contradicts itself. Its ideological ancestor is a Nietzschean nihilism and its most prolific contemporary spokesman, the French philosopher Jacques Derrida.[91] J. D. Crossan illustrates a kind of deconstruction applied to the gospels when he argues that, although they highlight Jesus' teaching in parables about God, they advocate belief in Jesus as the 'Parable of God'—God's own self-communication. The texts actually undermine the perspectives they assert.[92] Or again, with the parable of the prodigal son, Crossan discovers an allegory about interpretations of the world. The father stands for reality, the older brother for realism in interpretation, and the prodigal for the one who abandons the search for realism. Thus the inversion of the two sons' roles at the end of the parable proves that 'he who finds the meaning loses it, and he who loses it finds it'.[93]

Less esoteric and more widespread is the practice of reader-response criticism, which seeks to assess the meaning of a text for a reader at various states of the reading process. Instead of focusing only on the text as a whole, it stresses how the reader's perception of meaning changes depending on the amount of a text he has read, and depending on the nature of the sequence of that text's episodes.[94] Robert Fowler, for example, suggests that Mark has created the story of the feeding of the 5,000 (Mk. 6:30-44) on the model of the feeding of the 4,000 (Mk. 8:1-10), and arranged the two accounts in his gospel into a sequence which would highlight the irony of the disciples' failure to understand how Jesus could provide food for the multitudes (Mk. 8:4).[95] Frank Kermode proves less restrained in his reader-response interpretation of the secrecy motif in Mark's gospel. Taking Mark 4:11-12 at face value as a statement of its author's desire to hide the true meaning of the parables, Kermode extrapolates to construct a paradigm for the meaning of the entire gospel which the reader is free to create for himself and which Kermode accomplishes by a sort of 'free-association' with literary parallels as far removed from the world of the gospels as James Joyce's *Ulysses*.[96]

Consistent poststructuralism of course leads to solipsism: one can affirm no objective meaning for one's own work while denying it to everyone else. For Derrida this is no problem: he does not write as if he wishes to be understood! But the majority of less extreme reader-oriented interpreters sooner or later betray this inconsistency. The most helpful are those who eschew both the intentionalist and the affective fallacies but offer a more holistic model, seeking the locus of meaning in a text, but with special attention to the clues that the author has left in the text which disclose his intentions or purposes and which reveal the types of audiences or readers to whom the text was addressed.[97] Anthony Thiselton goes one step further and combines the insights of reader-response criticism with the philosophical school known as 'speech-act theory'. Thus instead of talking about what the text meant *versus* what it means, or about meaning *versus* significance, Thiselton prefers to distinguish the unchanging cognitive truth claim of a passage with the variable action which it generates or accomplishes through its articulation. The reader therefore both does and does not create the meaning of a text, depending on which dimension of meaning is involved. The polyvalent nature of the parables, not surprisingly, has left them as prime candidates for many of the first forays of gospel critics into post-structuralism.[98]

7. Conclusion

Every one of the six disciplines surveyed offers rich rewards for those who will take the time to master them and patiently sift the wheat from the chaff. Each has at times wrongly been put forward as the single most important approach to gospel studies, and all have gained a certain measure of disrepute because of invalid presuppositions, inconsistent applications, or spurious conclusions which can obscure their value. Modern critics must be eclectics, however, drawing widely from wherever historical and exegetical insight may be gained, but scrupulously avoiding too fond an attachment to the latest scholarly fashion. If there is one lesson to be learned from recent criticism, it is that today's assured results do not remain assured for very long, and that specific methods stay in fashion scarcely longer than styles of clothing. But the perplexed student of the gospels profits as little from ignoring all the recent developments of scholarship as from appearing in public in obviously outmoded dress. Successful interaction with the modern world, whether in society or academia, requires awareness of the latest trends and a willingness both to reject that which is bad and to cling fast to that which is good (*cf.* Rom. 12:9).

Notes

[1] It should be emphasized that this article is necessarily selective in its coverage of synoptic studies. The focus of the article is on literary and historical questions rather than, for example,

on questions of theology and application, important though these are. For another recent 'state of the art' report, focusing solely on questions of prolegomena, source and form criticism, see E. Earle Ellis, 'Gospels Criticism', in *Das Evangelium und die Evangelien,* ed. Peter Stuhlmacher (Tübingen: Mohr, 1983), pp. 27-54.

[2] Stephen Neill, *The Interpretation of the New Testament 1861-1961* (Oxford and New York: Oxford University, 1964), p. 339.

[3] B. H. Streeter, *The Four Gospels: A Study of Origins* (London: Macmillan, 1924; New York: Macmillan, 1925).

[4] William R. Farmer, *The Synoptic Problem* (New York and London: Macmillan, 1964).

[5] Most notably Bernard Orchard, *Matthew, Luke, and Mark* (Manchester, Koinonia, 1976); T. R. W. Longstaff, *Evidence of Conflation in Mark?* (Missoula: Scholars, 1977); H. H. Stoldt, *History and Criticism of the Marcan Hypothesis* (Edinburgh: T. & T. Clark; Macon: Mercer, 1980).

[6] William O. Walker, Jr. (ed.), *The Relationships among the Gospels* (San Antonio: Trinity University, 1978); Bernard Orchard and T. R. W. Longstaff (eds), *J. J. Griesbach: Synoptic and Text-Critical Studies 1776-1976* (Cambridge: University Press, 1978); William R. Farmer (ed.), *New Synoptic Studies* (Macon: Mercer, 1983); C. M. Tuckett (ed.), *Synoptic Studies* (Sheffield: JSOT, 1984).

[7] Bernard Orchard, *A Synopsis of the Four Gospels* (Mercer: Macon, 1982; Edinburgh: T. & T. Clark, 1983); Robert W. Funk, *New Gospel Parallels* (Philadelphia: Fortress, 1985).

[8] Bernard Orchard, 'Are All Gospel Synopses Biased?', *TZ* 34 (1978), pp. 149-162; David L. Dungan, 'Theory of Synopsis Construction', *Bib.* 61 (1980), pp. 305-329.

[9] *E.g.* Robert C. Newman, 'The Synoptic Problem: A Proposal for Handling Both Internal and External Evidence', *WTJ* 43 (1980), pp. 132-151; Malcolm Lowe and David Flusser, 'Evidence Corroborating a Modified Proto-Matthean Synoptic Theory', *NTS* 30 (1984), pp. 25-47.

[10] A possible but not necessary implication of David Wenham's provocative reconstruction of a source for Jesus' eschatological discourse which is longer than any of the current synoptic forms and which contains almost all of what they do (*The Rediscovery of Jesus' Eschatological Discourse* [Sheffield: JSOT, 1984]). *Cf.*, more generally, Philippe Rolland, 'Les Evangiles des premières communautés chrétiennes', *RB* 90 (1983), pp. 161-201.

[11] Esp. Frank Zimmermann, *The Aramaic Origin of the Four Gospels* (New York: KTAV, 1979).

[12] Esp. Rudolf Laufen, *Die Doppelüberlieferungen der Logienquelle und des Markusevangeliums* (Bonn: P. Hanstein, 1980); *cf.* more briefly, following targumic analogies, Bruce Chilton, 'Targumic Transmission and Dominical Tradition', in *Gospel Perspectives*, vol. 1, ed. R. T. France and David Wenham (Sheffield: JSOT, 1980), pp. 21-45; and *idem*, 'A Comparative Study of Synoptic Development: The Dispute between Cain and Abel in the Palestinian Targums and the Beelzebul Controversy in the Gospels', *JBL* 101 (1982), pp. 553-562.

[13] *E.g.* J. M. Rist, *On the Independence of Matthew and Mark* (Cambridge: University Press, 1978); Charles H. Dyer, 'Do the Synoptics Depend on Each Other?', *BSac* 138 (1981), pp. 230-245.

[14] Arthur J. Bellinzoni, Jr. (ed.), assisted by Joseph B. Tyson and William O. Walker, Jr., *The Two-Source Hypothesis: A Critical Appraisal* (Macon: Mercer, 1985).

[15] *Cf.* Malcolm Lowe, 'The Demise of Arguments from Order for Markan Priority', *NovT* 24 (1982), pp. 27-36; and C. M. Tuckett, 'Arguments from Order: Definition and Evaluation', in *Synoptic Studies*, pp. 197-219.

[16] *E.g.* W. R. Farmer, 'Modern Developments of Griesbach's Hypothesis', *NTS* 23 (1977), pp. 283-284; T. R. W. Longstaff, 'Crisis and Christology: The Theology of Mark', in *New Synoptic Studies*, pp. 373-392; D. L. Dungan, 'The Purpose and Provenance of the Gospel of Mark according to the Two-Gospel (Owen-Griesbach) Hypothesis', in *ibid.*, pp. 411-440.

[17] C. M. Tuckett, *The Revival of the Griesbach Hypothesis* (Cambridge: University Press, 1983), pp. 41-51; and, as demonstrated even by the most detailed study on behalf of the conflation theory, Longstaff, *Evidence of Conflation*, pp. 10-42. Roland M. Frye, 'The Synoptic Problem and Analogies in Other Literature', in *The Relationships among the Gospels*, p. 285, finds partial parallels to this phenomenon in medieval western Europe but cites no evidence that such procedures existed in the first-century world of the NT.

[18] *E.g.* Pierson Parker, 'The Posteriority of Mark', in *New Synoptic Studies*, pp. 67-142; William

R. Farmer, *Jesus and the Gospel* (Philadelphia: Fortress, 1982), pp. 111-134.

[19] *E.g.* Lamar Cope, 'The Argument Revolves: The Pivotal Evidence for Markan Priority is Reversing Itself', in *New Synoptic Studies*, pp. 143-159; Philip Sigal, 'Aspects of Mark Pointing to Matthean Priority', in *ibid.*, pp. 185-208.

[20] *E.g.* A. C. Perumalil, 'Are Not Papias and Irenaeus Competent to Report on the Gospels?', *ExpT* 91 (1980), pp. 332-337; R. Glover, 'Patristic Quotations and Gospel Sources', *NTS* 31 (1985), pp. 234-268; Anthony Meredith, 'The Evidence of Papias for the Priority of Matthew', in *Synoptic Studies*, pp. 187-196.

[21] See esp. Robert H. Gundry, *Matthew: A Commentary on His Literary and Theological Art* (Grand Rapids: Eerdmans, 1982), pp. 609-622, a position somewhat in tension with, but more promising than, the midrashic interpretation (see below) which informs the bulk of his commentary.

[22] Howard Bigg, 'The Q Debate since 1955', *Themelios* 6.2 (1981), pp. 18-28; F. Neirynck, 'Recent Developments in the Study of Q', in *Logia*, ed. J. Delobel (Leuven: University Press, 1982), pp. 29-75.

[23] *Cf. e.g.* M. D. Goulder, 'The Chiastic Structure of the Lucan Journey', *TU* 87 (1964), pp. 195-202; *idem, The Evangelists' Calendar* (London: SPCK, 1978), esp. pp. 95-101, 146-155; *idem,* 'The Order of a Crank', in *Synoptic Studies*, pp. 111-130. The only one of these studies which is defended in detail is the second one; for a thoroughgoing refutation of it see Leon Morris, 'The Gospels and the Jewish Lectionaries', in *Gospel Perspectives*, vol. 3, ed. R. T. France and David Wenham (1983), pp. 129-156; and Craig L. Blomberg, 'Midrash, Chiasmus, and the Outline of Luke's Central Section', in *ibid.*, esp. pp. 229-233.

[24] In addition to the research surveyed in the articles noted above (n. 22), see esp. Arland D. Jacobson, 'The Literary Unity of Q', *JBL* 101 (1982), pp. 365-389; John S. Kloppenborg, 'Tradition and Redaction in the Synoptic Sayings Source', *CBQ* 46 (1984), pp. 34-62; R. Hodgson, 'On the Gattung of Q: A Dialogue with James M. Robinson', *Bib* 66 (1985), pp. 73-95.

[25] Stephen C. Farris, *The Hymns of Luke's Infancy Narratives* (Sheffield: JSOT, 1985); but note the cautions in my review of this book in a forthcoming issue of *EQ*.

[26] Blomberg, 'Luke's Central Section', pp. 233-247.

[27] Richard Bauckham, 'The Study of Gospel Traditions Outside the Canonical Gospels: Problems and Prospects', in *Gospel Perspectives*, vol. 5, ed. David Wenham (1985), p. 377; refining the work of J. Smit Sibinga, 'Ignatius and Matthew', *NovT* 8 (1966), pp. 263-283.

[28] Oxford: Blackwell; New York: Harper & Row, 1963 (German orig. 1921).

[29] Heidelberg: Quelle und Meyer, 1984.

[30] *Ibid.*, p. 15.

[31] For an important methodological analysis, see Robert H. Stein, 'The Criteria for Authenticity', in *Gospel Perspectives*, vol. 1, pp. 225-263 (but see n. 52 below). *Cf.* also Stewart C. Goetz and Craig L. Blomberg, 'The Burden of Proof', *JSNT* 11 (1981), pp. 39-63.

[32] Among the more recent and less well-known are René Latourelle, *Finding Jesus through the Gospels* (New York: Alba, 1979), pp. 143-198, an unfortunately poor translation of a much better French original; Hugo Staudinger, *The Trustworthiness of the Gospels* (Edinburgh: Handsel, 1981), esp. pp. 1-33; and Wolfgang Schadewalt, 'Die Zuverlassigkeit der synoptischen Tradition', *ThBeitr* 13 (1982), pp. 201-223.

[33] Thus, respectively, Erhardt Güttgemanns, *Candid Questions concerning Gospel Form Criticism* (Pittsburgh: Pickwick, 1979); and Walter Schmithals, 'Kritik der Formkritic', *ZTK* 77 (1980), pp. 149-185.

[34] See originally, Harold Riesenfeld, 'The Gospel Tradition and Its Beginnings', *TU* 73 (1959), pp. 43-65; and Birger Gerhardsson, *Memory and Manuscript* (Lund: Gleerup, 1961). Gerhardsson has replied to his critics on numerous occasions; see esp. *The Origins of the Gospel Traditions* (London: SCM; Philadelphia: Fortress, 1979).

[35] For a critique of and survey of reaction to this 'Scandinavian school', see Peter H. Davids, 'The Gospels and Jewish Tradition: Twenty Years after Gerhardsson', in *Gospel Perspectives*, vol. 1, pp. 75-99.

[36] P. G. Müller, *Der Traditionsprozess im Neuen Testament* (Freiburg: Herder, 1982); A. F.

Zimmermann, *Die urchristlichen Lehrer* (Tübingen: Mohr, 1984); Rainer Riesner, *Jesus als Lehrer* (Tübingen: Mohr, 1981).

[37] Albert B. Lord, *The Singer of Tales* (Cambridge, MA: Harvard, 1960). *Cf.* the studies of native African oral tradition by Jan Vansina, *Oral Tradition: A Study of Historical Methodology* (London: Routledge & Kegan Paul; Chicago: Aldine, 1965).

[38] Albert B. Lord, 'The Gospels as Oral Traditional Literature', in *The Relationships among the Gospels*, pp. 33-91.

[39] Werner Kelber, *The Oral and the Written Gospel* (Philadelphia: Fortress, 1983), drawing heavily on the work of Walter J. Ong. Ong's work is nicely summarized in his *Orality and Literacy* (London and New York: Methuen, 1982).

[40] Lord, *Singer of Tales*, p. 128.

[41] Current research into the theologies of the individual evangelists is thoroughly surveyed in *Aufstieg und Niedergang der römischen Welt*, ed. W. Hasse and H. Temporini, series 2, vol. 25.3 (Berlin and New York: de Gruyter, 1985), pp. 1889-1951, 1969-2035, 2258-2328. A forthcoming issue of *Themelios* will also be surveying this research, so attention here is restricted to questions of method.

[42] The debate is well chronicled in D. L. Turner, 'Evangelicals, Redaction Criticism and the Current Inerrancy Crisis', *Grace Theological Journal* 4 (1983), pp. 263-288; and *idem*, 'Evangelicals, Redaction Criticism and Inerrancy: The Debate Continues', *GTJ* 5 (1984), pp. 37-45.

[43] Norman Perrin, *What is Redaction Criticism?* (Philadelphia: Fortress, 1969; London: SPCK, 1970).

[44] Richard N. Soulen, *Handbook of Biblical Criticism* (Guildford: Lutterworth; Richmond: John Knox, 1977), p. 142.

[45] Moisés Silva, 'Ned B. Stonehouse and Redaction Criticism', *WTJ* 40 (1977-8), pp. 77-88, 281-303, for example, demonstrates how a prominent American evangelical scholar in the 1940s anticipated the questions of German scholarship of a decade later and had already dealt with them in a constructive but conservative fashion. Had his work been given more notice by both fundamentalists and radicals, some of the polarization of more recent years might have been reduced.

[46] D. A. Carson, 'Matthew', in *The Expositor's Bible Commentary*, ed. Frank E. Gaebelein, vol. 8 (Grand Rapids: Zondervan, 1984), pp. 1-599; William L. Lane, *The Gospel according to Mark* (Grand Rapids: Eerdmans, 1974; London: Marshall, Morgan & Scott, 1975); I. Howard Marshall, *The Gospel of Luke* (Exeter: Paternoster; Grand Rapids: Eerdmans, 1978).

[47] For a more thorough critique see esp. D. A. Carson, 'Redaction Criticism: On the Legitimacy and Illegitimacy of a Literary Tool', in *Scripture and Truth*, ed. D. A. Carson and John D. Woodbridge (Grand Rapids: Zondervan; Leicester: IVP, 1983), pp. 119-142.

[48] Joseph A. Fitzmyer, *The Gospel according to Luke*, 2 vols. (Garden City: Doubleday, 1981-5); Charles H. Talbert, *Reading Luke: A Literary and Theological Commentary on the Third Gospel* (New York: Crossroad, 1982).

[49] The most extreme example is Gundry, *Matthew*, but *cf.* also Francis W. Beare, *The Gospel according to Matthew* (Oxford: Blackwell; San Francisco: Harper & Row, 1981). Of course conservatives have often overestimated the number of problems that can be resolved by appealing to the repetition of sayings or events in Jesus' life. For one small sample set of passages, I have proposed a mediating and more objective approach; see Craig L. Blomberg, 'When Is a Parallel Really a Parallel? A Test Case: The Lucan Parables?', *WTJ* 46 (1984), pp. 78-103.

[50] Among the more balanced recent assessments of the purposes of Matthew, Mark and Luke and the needs of the communities to which they wrote are G. N. Stanton, 'The Gospel of Matthew and Judaism', *BJRL* 66 (1984), pp. 264-284; Ernest Best, *Mark: The Gospel as Story* (Edinburgh: T. & T. Clark, 1983), pp. 21-36; Robert Maddox, *The Purpose of Luke-Acts* (Edinburgh: T. & T. Clark, 1982); though none of these is willing to accept the traditional authors and dates for the synoptics.

[51] Rudolf Pesch, *Das Markusevangelium*, 2 vols. (Freiburg: Herder, 1976-7); Joachim Gnilka,

Das Evangelium nach Markus, 2 vols. (Neukirchen-Vluyn: Neukirchener; Zurich: Benziger, 1978-9).

[52] From the perspective of canon criticism, see esp. Brevard Childs, *The New Testament Canon: An Introduction* (Philadelphia: Westminster; London: SCM, 1984); from an evangelical perspective, *cf.* Stein, ' "Criteria" for Authenticity', p. 229.

[53] Charles E. Carlston, *The Parables of the Triple Tradition* (Philadelphia: Fortress, 1975); and John Drury, *The Parables in the Gospels* (London: SPCK, 1985).

[54] *E.g.* Joachim Jeremias, *Die Sprache des Lukasevangeliums* (Göttingen: Vandenhoeck & Ruprecht, 1980); E. J. Pryke, *Redactional Style in the Marcan Gospel* (Cambridge: University Press, 1978); and Gundry, *Matthew*. More briefly, *cf.* even Bruce D. Chilton, 'An Evangelical and Critical Approach to the Sayings of Jesus', *Themelios* 3.3 (1978), pp. 78-85.

[55] For examples, see Craig L. Blomberg, 'The Legitimacy and Limits of Harmonization', in *Hermeneutics, Authority, and Canon*, ed. D. A. Carson and John D. Woodbridge (Grand Rapids: Zondervan; Leicester: IVP, 1986), pp. 139-174.

[56] R. T. France, 'Jewish Historiography, Midrash, and the Gospels', in *Gospel Perspectives*, vol. 3, pp. 99-127. *Cf.* Douglas J. Moo, *The Old Testament in the Gospel Passion Narratives* (Sheffield: Almond, 1983), pp. 5-78.

[57] *Cf.* Richard N. Longenecker, *Biblical Exegesis in the Apostolic Period* (Grand Rapids: Eerdmans, 1975), pp. 19-50: with Jacob Neusner, *Midrash in Context* (Philadelphia: Fortress, 1983).

[58] E. E. Elis, 'How the New Testament Uses the Old', in *New Testament Interpretation*, ed. I. Howard Marshall (Exeter: Paternoster; Grand Rapids: Eerdmans, 1977), pp. 205-206.

[59] A remarkably comprehensive catalogue of allegedly midrashic uses of the OT in the NT, including this one, appears in Alejandro Diez-Macho, 'Derás y exégesis del Nuevo Testamento', *Sefarad* 35 (1975), pp. 37-89.

[60] *E.g.* Richard N. Longenecker, 'Can We Reproduce the Exegesis of the New Testament?', *TynB* 21 (1970), pp. 3-38.

[61] See esp. Moisés Silva, 'The New Testament Use of the Old Testament: Text Form and Authority', in *Scripture and Truth*, pp. 147-165.

[62] See esp. Darrell L. Bock, *Proclamation from Prophecy and Pattern: Lucan Old Testament Christology* (Sheffield: JSOT, 1986).

[63] On typology, *cf.* Leonhard Goppelt, *Typos* (Grand Rapids: Eerdmans, 1982); and Richard M. Davidson, *Typology in Scripture* (Berrien Springs, MI: Andrews University, 1981).

[64] Editor's note to R. Schippers, 'πληρόω', in *NIDNTT*, vol. 1, p. 737. *Cf.* Brevard S. Childs, 'Prophecy and Fulfillment', *Int* 12 (1958), p. 267.

[65] The hallmark of Walter C. Kaiser, Jr., *The Uses of the Old Testament in the New* (Chicago: Moody, 1985), pp. 51-52, but he appeals to this type of explanation too often and too monolithically.

[66] See esp. Douglas J. Moo, 'The Problem of *Sensus Plenior*', in *Hermeneutics, Authority, and Canon*, pp. 179-211; most defences of this theory are less nuanced or convincing.

[67] On the former, originally C. F. Evans, 'The Central Section of St. Luke's Gospel', in *Studies in the Gospels*, ed. D. E. Nineham (Oxford: Blackwell, 1955), pp. 37-53; and more recently elaborated in John Drury, *Tradition and Design in Luke's Gospel* (London: Darton, Longman & Todd, 1976); on the latter, *cf.* L. T. Brodie, 'A New Temple and a New Law: The Unity and Chronicler-Based Nature of Luke 1:1 - 4:22a', *JSNT* 5 (1979), pp. 21-45; *idem*, 'Towards Unraveling Luke's Use of the Old Testament: Luke 7:11-17 as an *Imitatio* of 1 Kings 17:17-24', *NTS* 32 (1986), pp. 247-267.

[68] In addition to his commentary (see n. 21), *cf.* his four short clarificatory articles in debating Norman L. Geisler and Douglas J. Moo in *JETS* 26 (1983), pp. 41-56, 71-86, 95-100, 109-115, and his reply to Julius Scott in 'On Interpreting Matthew's Editorial Comments', *WTJ* 47 (1985), pp. 319-328.

[69] See esp. Gary G. Porton, 'Midrash: Palestinian Jews and the Hebrew Bible in the Greco-Roman Period', in *Aufstieg und Niedergang*, series 2, vol. 19.2 (1979), pp. 103-138; *idem, Understanding Rabbinic Midrash* (Hoboken, NJ: KTAV, 1985); and Renée Bloch, 'Midrash', in

Approaches to Ancient Judaism: Theory and Practice, ed. William S. Green (Missoula: Scholars, 1978), pp. 29-50.

[70] F. F. Bruce, 'Biblical Exposition at Qumran', in *Gospel Perspectives*, vol. 3, p. 87. Cf. F. G. Downing, 'Redaction Criticism: Josephus' *Antiquities* and the Synoptic Gospels (I)', *JSNT* 8 (1980), pp. 46-65; and Richard Bauckham, 'The Liber Antiquitatum Biblicarum of Pseudo-Philo and the Gospels as "Midrash" ', in *Gospel Perspectives*, vol. 3, pp. 33-76.

[71] *E.g.* Philip S. Alexander, 'Midrash and the Gospels', in *Synoptic Studies*, pp. 1-18; Philip B. Payne, 'Midrash and History in the Gospels with Special Reference to R. H. Gundry's *Matthew* in *Gospel Perspectives*, vol. 3, pp. 177-215.

[72] Here no one has been as prolific as J. D. M. Derrett (*Law in the New Testament* [London: Darton, Longman & Todd, 1970]; *Studies in the New Testament*, 4 vols. [Leiden: Brill, 1977-86]); while a number of his proposals rely on very tenuous suggestions concerning OT background to the NT, several others are reasonable and may shed light on some of the more puzzling teachings of Jesus.

[73] Most celebrated is Fernando Belo, *A Materialist Reading of the Gospel of Mark* (Maryknoll: Orbis, 1981); revised and popularized by Michel Clévenot, *Materialist Approaches to the Bible* (Maryknoll: Orbis, 1985).

[74] See esp. Northrop Frye, *The Great Code: The Bible and Literature* (New York: Harcourt, Brace, Jovanovich, 1981; London: Routledge & Kegan Paul, 1982); Wayne G. Rollins, *Jung and the Bible* (Atlanta: John Knox, 1983).

[75] Esp. Bruce J. Malina, *The New Testament World: Insights from Cultural Anthropology* (Atlanta: John Knox, 1981; London: SCM, 1983).

[76] Well surveyed by Derek Tidball, *An Introduction to the Sociology of the New Testament* (Exeter: Paternoster, 1983 [= *The Social Context of the New Testament: A Sociological Analysis* (Grand Rapids: Zondervan, 1984)]); and E. M. Yamauchi, 'Sociology, Scripture and the Supernatural', *JETS* 27 (1984), pp. 169-192.

[77] See *e.g.*, respectively, Gerhard Lohfink, *Jesus and Community: The Social Dimension of Christian Faith* (Philadelphia: Fortress; New York: Paulist, 1984); and Gerd Theissen, *The First Followers of Jesus* (London: SCM [= *Sociology of Early Palestinian Christianity* (Philadelphia: Fortress)], 1978).

[78] Howard C. Kee, *Miracle in the Early Christian World* (New Haven and London: Yale, 1983); Gerd Theissen, *The Miracle Stories of the Early Christian Tradition* (Edinburgh: T. & T. Clark; Philadelphia: Fortress, 1983).

[79] For elaboration, see Craig L. Blomberg, 'New Testament Miracles and Higher Criticism: Climbing Up the Slippery Slope', *JETS* 27 (1984), esp. pp. 434-436.

[80] Yamauchi, 'Sociology', p. 188.

[81] For overviews of these movements, see esp. Norman Petersen, *Literary Criticism for New Testament Critics* (Philadelphia: Fortress, 1978); and E. V. McKnight, *The Bible and the Reader* (Philadelphia: Fortress, 1985).

[82] Jack D. Kingsbury, *Matthew as Story* (Philadelphia: Fortress, 1986). For works of a similar genre, see R. A. Edwards, *Matthew's Story of Jesus* (Philadelphia: Fortress, 1985); David Rhoads and Donald Michie, *Mark as Story* (Philadelphia: Fortress, 1982); Best, *Mark: The Gospel as Story*.

[83] Leland Ryken, *How to Read the Bible as Literature* (Grand Rapids: Zondervan, 1984), pp. 199-203. Over-all this book is a reworking and simplification of *idem, The Literature of the Bible* (Grand Rapids: Zondervan, 1974).

[84] George A. Kennedy, *New Testament Interpretation through Rhetorical Criticism* (Chapel Hill, NC: University of North Carolina, 1984), p. 68.

[85] See esp. Daniel Patte, *What is Structural Exegesis?* (Philadelphia: Fortress, 1976). Cf., more briefly, Carl Armerding, 'Structural Analysis', *Themelios* 4.3 (1979), pp. 96-104; and A. C. Thiselton, 'Structuralism and Biblical Studies: Method or Ideology?', *ExpT* 89 (1978), pp. 329-335.

[86] As pointed out by Robert Detweiler, 'After the New Criticism: Contemporary Methods of Literary Interpretation', in *Orientation by Disorientation*, ed. Richard A. Spencer (Pittsburgh:

Pickwick, 1980), p. 13. *Cf.* Vern Poythress, 'Philosophical Roots of Phenomenological and Structuralist Literary Criticism', *WTJ* 41 (1978), p. 166.

[87] See esp. Raymond F. Collins, *Introduction to the New Testament* (Garden City: Doubleday; London: SCM, 1983), pp. 231-271; Elizabeth S. Malbon, 'Structuralism, Hermeneutics, and Contextual Meaning', *JAAR* 51 (1983), pp. 207-230; Brian Kovacs (ed.), 'A Joint Paper by the Members of the Structuralism and Exegesis SBL Seminar', in *SBL 1982 Seminar Papers*, ed. Kent H. Richards (Chico: Scholars, 1982), pp. 251-270.

[88] Sandra W. Perpich, *A Hermeneutic Critique of Structuralist Exegesis, with Special Reference to Luke 10:29-37* (Lanham, MD: University Press of America, 1984).

[89] James L. Resseguie, 'Reader-Response Criticism and the Synoptic Gospels', *JAAR* 52 (1984), p. 322. *CF.* D. S. Greenwood, 'Poststructuralism and Biblical Studies: Frank Kermode's *The Genesis of Secrecy*', in *Gospel Perspectives*, vol. 3, pp. 263-288.

[90] T. K. Seung, *Structuralism and Hermeneutics* (New York: Columbia University, 1982), p. 271. As with structuralism, simple introductions are hard to find, and the nature of the movements being described has much to do with this. But two valiant attempts are Jonathan Culler, *On Deconstruction: Theory and Criticism after Structuralism* (Ithaca: Cornell; London: Routledge & Kegan Paul, 1983); and Christopher Norris, *Deconstruction: Theory and Practice* (London and New York: Methuen, 1982).

[91] For a sampling of Derrida's own writing, along with sympathetic critiques and applications to NT texts, see the entire issue of *Semeia* 23 (1982).

[92] J. D. Crossan, *The Dark Interval* (Niles, IL and Harlow: Argus Communications, 1975).

[93] *Idem, Cliffs of Fall: Paradox and Polyvalence in the Parables of Jesus* (New York: Seabury, 1980), p. 101. For a survey and critique of Crossan's works, see Frank B. Brown and Elizabeth S. Malbon, 'Parables as a *Via Negativa*: A Critical Review of the Work of John Dominic Crossan', *JR* 64 (1984), pp. 530-538.

[94] At length, *cf.* Stanley Fish, *Is There a Text in This Class?* (Cambridge, MA and London: Harvard, 1980); more briefly, Robert M. Fowler, 'Who Is "The Reader" in Reader-Response Criticism?', *Semeia* 31 (1985), pp. 5-23.

[95] *Idem, Loaves and Fishes* (Chico: Scholars, 1980).

[96] Frank Kermode, *The Genesis of Secrecy* (Cambridge, MA and London: Harvard, 1979). The gospel of Mark has so far proved most conducive to reader-response criticism, with its abrupt transitions, apparent doublets, intercalations and uncertain ending.

[97] See esp. Norman R. Petersen, 'The Reader in the Gospel', *Neotestamentica* 18 (1984), pp. 38-51; H. Frankemölle, 'Kommunikatives Handeln in Gleichnissen Jesu', *NTS* 28 (1982), pp. 61-90.

[98] Anthony C. Thiselton, 'Reader-Response Hermeneutics, Action Models, and the Parables of Jesus', in *The Responsibility of Hermeneutics*, with Roger Lundin and Clarence Walhout (Exeter: Paternoster; Grand Rapids: Eerdmans, 1985), pp. 79-113.

CHURCH HISTORY

Nathan Hatch, area editor

CHURCH HISTORY

NATHAN HATCH
Associate Dean, College of Arts and Letters
University of Notre Dame

Introduction

Among contemporary issues facing modern Christians, none are more problematic and complex than those related to medical issues of life, death, and health. The Christian church needs all the leverage it can muster to gain theological perspective on perennial issues such as sickness, healing, sexuality, mental illness; and more pressing and controversial ones such as abortion, and euthanasia. 1986 saw the publication of a book of historical essays that illuminate the history of health and medicine within the major Judeo-Christian tradition, *Caring and Curing: Health and Medicine in the Western Religious Traditions*, ed. Ronald L. Numbers and Darrel W. Amundsen (New York: Macmillan, 1986). Written in nontechnical language by church historians and historians of medicine, this book provides a historical narrative analyzing how each of twenty traditions understood the nature of issues such as well-being, sexuality, passages, morality, dignity, madness, healing, caring, suffering, and death. The book represents a major research effort of The Park Ridge Center, an ecumenical institute dedicated to the study of health, faith, and ethics, which is sponsored by the Lutheran General Health Care System, Park Ridge, Illinois.

While a number of these essays are superb, two in particular stand out as useful for the purpose of this volume: Marvin R. O'Connell's "The Roman Catholic Tradition Since 1545" and Gary B. Ferngren's "The Evangelical-Fundamentalist Tradition." Marvin O'Connell's essay, covering a sweep of four centuries, from the Council of Trent to the Second Vatican Council, is a masterful analysis of the essential spirit and orientation of traditional Catholicism towards issues of sickness and health. O'Connell is superb in showing the framework in which Catholics produced a well-developed ethical system, in how these standards operated on a popular level, and in distinguishing Catholic approaches from Protestant ones. In addition to addressing the history of specifically medical issues, this essay is an excellent primer on the sacramental system of traditional Catholicism.

Gary B. Ferngren's essay "The Evangelical-Fundamentalist Tradition" focuses on attitudes and practices of evangelicals in the twentieth century. He emphasizes the pluralism of the movement on issues such as divine healing—from the supportive stance of A. B. Simpson and A. J. Gordon to the deep suspicioning of faith healing by B. B. Warfield and most dispensationalists. Ferngren also underscores the rapid changes in recent times in evangelical attitudes towards psychology and the recent attempts to begin to think seriously about a number of issues in medical ethics. Both of these essays provide superb historical grounding for ministers, psychologists, and physicians who wrestle with the complexity of these issues today.

About the Area Editor

Nathan Hatch (M.A. and Ph.D., Washington University, St. Louis, Mo.) is associate dean, College of Arts and Letters, University of Notre Dame. He is affiliated with the Christian Reformed Church. Books include *The Sacred Cause of Liberty* (1977) and, co-authored with Mark Noll, *The Bible in America* (1981).

THE EVANGELICAL-FUNDAMENTALIST TRADITION

GARY B. FERNGREN
Professor of History, Oregon State University

From Chapter 18 in the book
*Caring and Curing: Health and Medicine
in the Western Religious Traditions*

The evangelical tradition has tended until quite recently to view personal well-being almost exclusively in spiritual terms. In reply to the query "What constitutes well-being?" most evangelicals would instinctively have agreed that the well-being of humans in every aspect of their personalities is dependent on their enjoying communion and fellowship with God. The historic stress of evangelicalism on the total depravity of human beings and their need of a Savior has led perhaps inevitably to this perspective. The essence of evangelical religion has traditionally been its emphasis on the necessity of a radical conversion that marks a sharp break from a previous life of sin and a reordering of one's post-conversion life in conformity with biblical standards. Evangelicals have regarded conversion and sanctification as the twin pillars upon which the Christian life is built, as even a cursory perusal of the devotional literature produced by evangelical writers of the past will reveal. Typical is G. W. E. Russell, who wrote of his Victorian upbringing:

> My home was intensely Evangelical and I lived from my earliest days in an atmosphere where the salvation of the individual soul was the supreme and constant concern of life. . . . May my lot be with those evangelical saints from whom I first learned that, in the supreme work of salvation, no human being and no created thing can interfere between the soul and the Creator. Happy is the man whose religious life has been built on the impregnable rock of that belief.[1]

Health and Healing

It is safe to say that concerns of health and healing have not been central to the evangelical-fundamentalist tradition, although they have on occasion been prominent issues in theology or practice. One looks in vain, for example, in *The Fundamentals* for any mention of the subject. In their concern for the defense of Protestant orthodoxy, fundamentalists were too busy fighting other battles to devote much attention to health-related matters. The larger evangelical tradition historically has either reflected the emphases of Protestantism in general or else accommodated itself to the prevailing views of contemporary culture. One cannot, moreover, easily delineate fundamentalist from mainstream evangelical attitudes to health and healing. Both share a common set of core beliefs, but exhibit considerable variation regarding those matters (like healing) not regarded as essential. Evangelicalism and fundamentalism have always been democratic movements. As a result, their theology has usually been popular rather than academic. (*The Fundamentals* and the widely used *Scofield Reference Bible* are good examples.) The Protestant doctrine of the priesthood of the believer has produced much diversity of belief in secondary and tertiary matters. The encouragement of individual Bible study, the predominance of congregational polity, and the lack of concern for (or distrust of) ecclesiastical authority and tradition have contributed to this diversity. Perhaps the public prominence that the leaders of evangelicalism and fundamentalism have enjoyed both within and outside these movements has tended to obscure the pluralism that has always existed in them. One can speak of common themes and underlying assumptions, but it is difficult to make neat distinctions between the two groups.

Traditionally, evangelical attitudes toward health have been ambivalent. At the root of these attitudes is the evangelical emphasis on sanctification, the process by which the Christian life is inwardly transformed in the direction of holiness and godly living. On the one hand, evangelical piety has emphasized that the body is the temple of the Holy Spirit and therefore is to be kept from those habits and vices that would prevent it from glorifying God. On the other hand, evangelicals have usually considered the body of secondary importance in the Christian life, and they have shown little desire (perhaps out of a Protestant aversion to monastic practices) to mortify the body for the sake of the soul, encouraging rather an asceticism of the mind and will.[2] Evangelicals have not ordinarily practiced fasting as a spiritual discipline and vegetarianism has never been a feature of evangelicalism.[3] Warnings against gluttony were (and still are) notable chiefly for their absence.

Two historical influences, however, have shaped evangelical attitudes toward health and its maintenance. The first is the idea of separation from the world, introduced into evangelicalism from pietism through Methodism. Evangelicals sought to promote sanctification by proscribing the use of such addictive substances as tobacco and alcohol. Because such proscription was a feature of Wesleyan practice and later of the Finney revivals and their successors, it became an integral part of the evangelical ethic. Evangelicals gave widespread support to the temperance movement in the nineteenth century, though they were divided on the question of whether temperance called for total abstinence from alcoholic beverages.[4] The influence of the temperance movement declined dramatically in this century after the repeal of the Eighteenth Amendment in 1932, but the evangelical ethic that gave rise to it remains. There has never existed a uniform belief among evangelicals that the use of either tobacco or alcoholic beverages is wrong. Rather, disapproval of them has generally varied according to regional, ethnic, and denominational lines. Nevertheless, their use is still regarded with disfavor among large segments of the evangelical community, particularly among those of Wesleyan or Baptist heritage (but less among those of Presbyterian or Reformed backgrounds). For the former, temperance has become virtually synonymous with total abstinence, which they defended partly on the ground that the Christian's body is the temple of the Holy Spirit, and partly because certain practices were deemed "worldly" owing to their frequent association with the evils that were thought to accompany them. The same arguments have been applied even more strongly to the use of addictive drugs by evangelicals, who have argued that the only acceptable Christian attitude toward them is one not merely of total avoidance, but of the strongest possible condemnation.[5] While most fundamentalists remain strong in their requirement of total abstinence from alcohol, in the 1970s some mainstream evangelicals quietly dropped their insistence that total abstinence is the only consistent evangelical stance. This softening attitude is probably to be explained in part by the accommodation of many evangelicals to modern American culture and the ensuing loss of some traditional distinctives, and in part by the perceived lack of direct biblical support for total abstinence.[6]

A second historical influence that has shaped evangelical thinking about health is the attitude toward faith healing that grew out of the debate over the subject in evangelical circles in the late nineteenth century. No issue related to illness and health has occasioned more discussion in evangelical churches than the matter of faith healing. There was in American Protestantism generally a dramatic surge of interest in religious healing in the nineteenth century. Among those who sought to reclaim for the church the ministry of healing that they believed played a significant role in apostolic times were several evangelicals, the most notable of whom were A. B. Simpson (1844-1919), founder of the Christian and Missionary Alliance, and A. J. Gordon (1836-1895), a nationally prominent Baptist minister in Boston.[7] Both men came to believe in faith healing after they themselves experienced personal healing. Simpson came under the influence of Dr. Charles Cullis, a former Boston physician who maintained an influential ministry of religious healing, and Simpson's belief in faith healing was partly responsible for his decision to leave the Presbyterian ministry for an independent one.[8]

Both Simpson and Gordon came from a Calvinistic tradition that looked with suspicion on any apparent manifestations of modern miraculous healing. The question of the cessation of miracles was much debated by evangelical theologians in the nineteenth century. The traditional Protestant position, since the time of the Reformation, was that miracles had ceased at the end of the apostolic age, and this long remained the view of most Protestants.[9] As late as 1948 the evangelical theologian E. J. Carnell wrote that "the doctrine that miracles no longer occur is one of those fundamental canons which separate Protestantism from Roman Catholicism."[10] The well-known evangelical scholar J. Gresham Machen reflected the same view in distinguishing between miracles, which have ceased, and healing in answer to prayer, which he desribed as "a very wonderful work of God, but it is not a miracle."[11] In *The Ministry of Healing* (1882) Gordon, appealing to Christ's commands to his disciples to heal (for example, in such passages as Mark 16:15-18) and to Christian belief in the unchanging nature of God and His world, argued that miraculous healing was a privilege of Christians of all ages and therefore ought to enjoy a permanent place in the ministry of the church. Gordon's book balanced an emphasis on God's willingness to heal (he cited many examples from the history of the church) with a recognition that God is sovereign in matters of healing. He warned against making healing an end in itself and deprecated fanaticism in the matter.[12]

In *The Gospel of Healing* (1877), Simpson went much farther than Gordon. He argued that sickness, like sin, was caused by Satan and therefore contrary to God's will; Christ came into the world to save human beings both from sin and from the consequences of sin, which included sickness and pain. In his atonement Christ bore both sin and sickness. Hence the Christian could claim divine healing apart from physicians and medicine because it was always God's will to heal.[13] Later in his ministry, Simpson gave less prominence to faith healing and refused to support the healing campaigns that were held in America by the Australian faith healer John Alexander Dowie, thus earning the enmity of the latter.[14]

While faith healing continued to have some evangelical adherents after the turn of the century, it declined appreciably in reaction to the prominence that it came to have in Pentecostal churches. Evangelicals objected to the insistence of Pentecostals that speaking in tongues was normative Christian experience and they were embarrassed by what they regarded as their fanaticism. Pentecostalism came under increasing attack by evangelicals, including Simpson, whom Pentecostals had initially regarded as an ally. A colleague of Simpson's, asked to investigate the new movement, reported: "I am not able to approve the movement, though I am willing to concede that there is probably something of God in it somewhere."[15] By the 1920s, fundamentalists had largely repudiated Pentecostalism.[16]

Faith healing, as championed by Gordon and Simpson, received much criticism from traditional evangelicals. One of the best of the polemical works written against it was *Counterfeit Miracles*, by the redoubtable Princeton theologian Benjamin B. Warfield (1851-1921). Published in 1918, after the heyday of evangelical faith healing, it did more than any other work to influence subsequent evangelical thinking regarding the theology and practice of faith healing. It represented a powerful restatement of the traditional Protestant view that the age of miracles has passed. Warfield's title indicated the position that he took with regard to contemporary claims of miraculous healing. He argued that the function of miracles was to accompany and validate divine revelation and to authenticate a messenger of God.

Miracles do not appear on the pages of Scripture vagrantly, here, there and elsewhere indifferently, without assignable reason. They belong to revelation periods, and appear only when God is speaking to His people through accredited messengers declaring His gracious purposes. Their abundant display in the Apostolic Church is the mark of the richness of the Apostolic age in revelation; and when this revelation period closed, the period of miracle-working had passed by also, as a mere matter of course.[17]

God's special revelation of himself was complete and contained in the biblical record; it remained only to be spread throughout the world. Of course, every age witnessed apparent manifestations of miraculous phenomena, but they could not be accepted as genuine because they did not authenticate new revelation. Warfield examined in successive chapters the "apostolic gifts" associated with Edward Irving (1792-1834), Christian Science, and Protestant faith healing. He suggested that faith healings of all types were susceptible to natural rather than supernatural explanations (for example, hysteria, credulity, superstition, or exaggeration) and they cured only functional disorders and not organic diseases. He distinguished, however, between divine healing, which he accepted as a continuing phenomenon, and miraculous healing, which ceased after the apostolic age.

First of all, as regards the *status quaestionis*, let it be remembered that the question is not: (1) whether God is an answerer of prayer; nor (2) whether in answer to prayer, He heals the sick; nor (3) whether His action in healing the sick is a supernatural act; nor (4) whether the supernaturalness of the act may be so apparent as to demonstrate God's activity in it to all right-thinking minds conversant with the facts. All this we believe. The question at issue is distinctly whether God has pledged Himself to heal the sick miraculously, on the call of His children—that is to say without means—any means—and apart from means, and above means; and this so ordinarily that Christian people may be encouraged, if not required, to discard all means as either unnecessary or even a mark of lack of faith and sinful distrust, and to depend on God alone for the healing of all their sicknesses. This is the issue, even conservatively stated.[18]

Warfield's work was reprinted several times and was widely used in the fundamentalist polemic against Pentecostalism. Nevertheless, many evangelicals were hesitant to accept his premise that miracles had ceased absolutely. While conceding a special role for miracles in authenticating biblical revelation, they wished to leave open the possibility that God still intervened miraculously, particularly in view of the increasingly anti-supernatural emphasis of theological liberalism. Many had heard missionaries describe cases of miraculous healing, and some had observed what they regarded as miraculous healing in their own lives or in the lives of acquaintances. Yet at the same time they vigorously rejected both the claims of Pentecostal faith healers and the theology that lay behind it. Henry W. Frost, in his book *Miraculous Healing* (1931), took a position not far from Warfield's in his criticism of the theology and claims of faith healers, but he was more positive in his conviction of God's continuing willingness on occasion to heal miraculously.[19] In general, evangelical writers from Warfield to the present have stressed God's sovereignty in choosing to heal. They have believed that divine healing is possible, but the exception rather than the rule.

Evangelicals have sometimes cited James 5:13-15, which advises calling the elders of the church to pray for and anoint the sick, as a basis for divine healing. The difficulty has been to understand precisely what the passage teaches. Evangelicals have generally accepted one of three interpretations: that the passage speaks of an apostolic rite that ceased with the passing of the age of miracles;[20] that it speaks of spiritual (not physical) healing;[21] that it offers a supernatural means of recovery to those within the church who are anointed with oil and prayed over.[22] Many evangelical churches have embraced the third view and practiced the rite of anointing the sick. However, evangelical scholars have not agreed on whether the oil was meant to be symbolic of the anointing of the Holy Spirit or representative of a medicinal agent. Gordon believed that it was symbolic of the spiritual unction of the Holy Spirit.[23] Warfield agreed that oil might be symbolic of the power of the Holy Spirit, but favored the view that it referred to a medicinal agent, and that the rite involved asking God effectively to use available medicinal means to restore health.[24] The question was thus whether James advised seeking healing apart from the use of means or through means employed with God's blessing. Because evangelicals have not for the most part rejected the use of medicine, the rite has often been used as a last resort after medicine has failed. But the emphasis has usually been on the effectiveness of corporate prayer rather than on the unction, because evangelicals have rejected any idea of sacramental efficacy.

As the ministry of healing advocated by Gordon and Simpson was taken over and increased by Pentecostals, it declined in evangelical churches. Fundamentalism came to be deeply influenced by dispensationalist theology, which held that speaking in tongues and other miraculous gifts had ceased with the age of the apostles. Fundamentalist ministers often refused to have fellowship with Pentecostals because the latter held views that they regarded as unscriptural and unbalanced. Evangelicals were extremely distrustful of faith healers and usually condemned their ministries. An exception was Kathryn Kuhlman, a charismatic evangelist whose ministry of healing attracted favorable comment from some evangelicals.[25]

One finds little denigration of physicians in evangelical literature; in fact, physicians have generally enjoyed high esteem in evangelical churches.[26] Nor is there evidence that evangelicals or fundamentalists have been more prone than the general population to rely on unorthodox or "fringe" cures (for example, Laetrile to treat cancer). There is little indication of tension between evangelical theory and orthodox medicine. Most evangelicals (including fundamentalists) gratefully accept medicine today, as they have in the past, as God's normal provision for healing. But they believe that he sometimes heals apart from means (when they are lacking or fail) by divine intervention, particularly in direct answer to prayer. One often finds the word *miraculous* used in the writings of twentieth-century evangelicals and fundamentalists (especially in popular works) to describe what nineteenth-century writers would have called "special providences." But whether they call the healing a "miracle" or a "special providence" is perhaps a merely semantic distinction.

In the 1970s there was a resurgence of attempts in some mainstream evangelical circles to restore a healing ministry.[27] The movement reflected charismatic or Pentecostal influences, although somewhat modified to suit evangelical theology. Thus far its influence has been very limited, and it is likely to remain so given the traditional evangelical opposition to an emphasis on faith healing.

Suffering, Mental Health, and Humanitarianism

Closely related to the place of divine healing in the church was the theological understanding of the meaning of sickness and suffering in the world, for the Christian in particular. In opposition to the theology of faith healing, which stressed both the connection between sickness and individual sin and God's desire always to heal sickness, most evangelical theologians continued to maintain the traditional view of orthodox Protestantism that there was a place for sickness and suffering in the life of the Christian.[28] Their arguments were maintained in a considerable body of literature directed in the late nineteenth and early twentieth centuries against the views of men like Simpson and Gordon and in the twentieth century against Pentecostal faith healers.[29] According to this position, sickness resulted directly from the entrance of sin into the world and thus originated in the Fall. Death (both physical and spiritual) and disease were imposed by God on all human beings as a penalty for Adam's sin. As a result of God's curse on a sinful world, all persons could expect to experience illness, suffering, sorrow, guilt, and death. Certain diseases and physical disabilities (for example, venereal disease and cirrhosis of the liver) were linked directly to sin or moral failing, but they were attributed to the sufferer's failure to recognize that disobedience to God's moral law sometimes had physical consequences.

Against the view that it was not God's will that his children suffer from pain or disease and that the power manifested in Christ's miracles was available for healing today, traditional evangelicals argued that in his miracles of healing, exorcism, and raising from the dead, Jesus provided merely a foretaste of a fully redeemed world that still awaited fulfillment. Sin was not yet abolished, nor were disease and death yet banished. Although redeemed, God's people would never experience perfection either in the spiritual or physical realm in this world. They lived in two spheres, experiencing all the manifestations of a fallen world, yet at the same time undergoing the redemption that was being accomplished in their own lives and in God's world. They groaned while awaiting the redemption of the body and the destruction of that final enemy, death. Hence, they argued, Christians should not expect, while living in a sinful world, to be free from the curse of sickness and pain.

In contrast to Simpson and later Pentecostals, who believed that sickness was always caused by Satan and never came from God, their evangelical opponents maintained that although Satan was the author of sin, God had ordained sickness, disease, and death as penalties for sin. They pointed out that God was pictured in the Old Testament as smiting individuals and nations with disease. They acknowledged that Scripture also spoke of Satan's being responsible for both sickness and sin as he waged continual warfare against God's kingdom, but they believed that God permitted Satan to engage in activity only within certain limits, which included the spread of sickness and pain. However, God worked to bring good out of the suffering produced by Satan so that his will (not Satan's) was accomplished. Thus behind Satan's activity was a sovereign God effecting his purposes in the world.

In particular, the traditional theologians emphasized that there was no necessary correlation between godliness and health and that sickness and pain had beneficial spiritual effects in God's economy. The proponents of the theology of faith healing believed not only that sickness resulted from the sinful nature of all human beings, but that it was a consequence of a lack of faith or a particular sin in the life of an individual. Traditional evangelicals replied that both Scripture and experience contradicted such a view; simple observation showed that many godly individuals suffered severe affliction and pain, while the wicked all too frequently enjoyed good health and prosperity. These evangelicals argued that individual suffering was not a matter of merit in which God dispensed punishment as retribution for sin. The English Baptist Charles Spurgeon (1834-1892) asserted that it was well that God did not proportion suffering according to righteousness and wickedness, for he would then encourage an insufferable self-righteousness instead of humble dependence on him.[30] "We deny utterly," wrote the Princeton theologian A. A. Hodge (1823-1886), "that in the case of Christians, whose sins are pardoned for Christ's sake, sickness is any part of the punishment of sin."[31] Christ bore the punishment of sin on the cross; thus evangelicals seldom viewed suffering as a sign of God's anger or displeasure.

What, then, was the purpose of illness and suffering in the life of an evangelical Christian? Evangelical theologians replied that suffering was the fatherly chastisement of God, a mark of his love and concern for one's spiritual well-being, not of his anger. They rejected the idea that illness was an unmixed evil, that it was always or even usually caused by a particular sin, that it indicated God's displeasure or was contrary to his will, and that he willed in every case that sickness be healed. They pointed out that the New Testament promised suffering and tribulation for Christians as a mark of discipleship and that it indicated that God's chastisement was a sign of his favor.

Many of the older writers spoke of the benefits of sickness. "I see in it," wrote the evangelical Anglican bishop J. C. Ryle (1816-1900),

> a useful provision to check the ravages of sin and the devil among men's souls. If man had never sinned I should have been at a loss to discern the benefit of sickness. But since sin is in the world, I can see that sickness is a good. It is a blessing quite as much as a curse. It is a rough schoolmaster, I grant. But it is a real friend to man's soul.[32]

Among its benefits Ryle mentioned the following: A sickness helped to remind human beings of death; it made them think seriously of God; it softened their hearts; it leveled and humbled them; it tried the nature of their religion.[33] Other writers did not hesitate to affirm that God might will sickness in the life of a Christian in order to draw that person to himself or to bring about patience or an attitude of sympathy with the suffering.[34] And finally, evangelical writers argued that suffering prepared Christians for heaven by purifying them and fitting them to meet their Savior, who suffered for their sins. Evangelicals admitted that much suffering could not be explained by the need for chastisement, but they believed that it was sometimes necessary to admit that God is sovereign, to place one's confidence in him, and to seek grace to live with one's questions unanswered. This was not, of course, a strictly evangelical view; one finds it in many of the older Protestant spiritual writers.[35] Although there have been variations in the traditional evangelical view of suffering, it has remained remarkably unchanged in the evangelical and fundamentalist polemic against faith healing since its classic formulation in the nineteenth century.[36]

Until a century ago, pastors routinely dealt with many problems that are now referred to psychiatrists or psychologists.[37] Evangelical views of mental health and disease reflected the older Protestant explanations, which recognized melancholy as a serious disorder that greatly affected the spiritual life, and older treatments of spiritual experience discussed melancholy at length.[38] The older evangelical literature attributed mental illness essentially to three causes: sin, organic disorder, and demonic possession. Evangelicals believed that much mental and emotional suffering was due to sin or moral failings and that therapy should consist primarily of confession and forgiveness. Before the twentieth century, evangelicals, reflecting contemporary medical views, also attributed some forms of melancholy and insanity to lesions of the brain, chemical imbalance, or temperament.[39] They explained at least some mental illness as being the result of demonic possession. Missionaries added credence to the belief that demon-possession was not limited to biblical times by their reports of demonic activity. A work that had great influence in this regard was John L. Nevius' *Demon Possession and Allied Themes* (1892), which described Nevius' experience as a missionary doctor in China.[40] While in much of Protestantism natural and psychological explanations have replaced belief in demonic etiology of mental illness, fundamentalism has produced in this century an enormous literature that testifies to the continuing belief in demonic activity. For example, many evangelicals and fundamentalists ascribed to satanic activity the revival of interest in the occult in the 1970s.[41] Many evangelical theologians and professionally trained psychologists have accepted possession as an authentic phenomenon.[42] They believed that its symptoms differed from those of mental illness and required specifically spiritual therapy, such as prayer or exorcism.

Evangelicals greeted with distrust or hostility the new disciplines of psychiatry and psychology, which gained influence early in the twentieth century. They believed that psychologists were attempting to provide scientific answers to spiritual problems and that psychological theories of religious behavior were invariably reductionist. Doubtless, too, many evangelicals saw in the new psychology speculation that ran counter both to common sense and to their Baconian preference for facts over theories. Evangelicals used similar criticism against Darwinism and higher criticism of the Bible, which they regarded as unscientific and based on unsupported hypotheses.[43] Sigmund Freud, the founder of modern psychoanalysis, came under special attack because of his perceived obsession with sexuality and hostility to religion.[44] While evangelicals and fundamentalists have generally looked with favor on the medical profession and have not insisted on securing medical care from members of their own religious community, treatment of mental and emotional illness has proven to be an exception to this rule. Evangelicals have tended to avoid psychiatric treatment except by evangelical therapists. They feared that the treatment arising out of the perceived anti-Christian presuppositions of modern psychology would be inimical to an evangelical faith.

In the 1950s a few evangelicals, like Henry Brandt and Clyde Narramore, began to adopt in a guarded way psychological perspectives on emotional and mental problems. A trickle of books by evangelical psychologists turned into a stream in the 1960s and a flood in the 1970s, indicating a radical change in evangelical attitudes to psychology.[45] This new emphasis in evangelicalism, which employed psychological techniques without accepting their secular theoretical basis, avoided a confrontation with traditional doctrines. By wedding psychological techniques to conservative theology, evangelical psychologists seemed to make established doctrines more relevant to everyday life, and this might explain why evangelicals responded so readily to their methods. In adopting a problem-centered view of the Christian life (as many did), evangelicals probably reflected the spirit of their age more than they realized. Great numbers of popular books, aimed at an evangelical-fundamentalist audience, have appeared on the market in recent years, dealing with marriage, sexuality, self-fulfillment, depression, loneliness, worry, and peace of mind. Most in some way have combined biblical teaching with insights taken from modern psychology. Films, radio programs, seminars, and conferences on these subjects have become enormously popular. Over fifteen million people have viewed a film series (*Focus on the Family*) by an evangelical child psychologist, James Dobson, who deals with the problems that face the modern Christian family. In many churches, films and panel discussions on problem-oriented themes have replaced preaching in Sunday evening services. Laymen expect evangelical pastors to spend an increasing amount of their time in personal counseling, and the 1970s have witnessed the rapid growth of Christian counseling centers staffed by evangelical psychologists. Seminaries have developed programs and degrees in Christian counseling. At least two evangelical institutions offer Ph.D.s in psychology: Rosemead Graduate School of Psychology, now affiliated with Biola University; and Fuller Theological Seminary's Graduate School of Psychology. Both programs are approved by the American Psychological Association. Their curricula differ from secular ones in their attempt to integrate biblical and theological components into psychological theory and training.

In spite of the marked change in evangelical attitudes toward psychology, there remains a great diversity of approaches. Some evangelical counselors have attempted to integrate the work of secular psychologists with evangelical theology.[46] Others, like Jay Adams, whose self-styled "nouthetic" approach to counseling is popular with many evangelical pastors, have rejected deterministic psychology and the disease model of mental and emotional illness for a moral and biblical one.[47] Still others have attacked modern psychology as dangerous and unbiblical.[48] While evangelicals and fundamentalists have increasingly sought professional help from pastors and Christian counselors for personal problems, many remain reluctant to consult secular psychiatrists and psychologists. Moreover, evangelicals, who are anxious to stress moral responsibility for individual behavior, have resisted modern attempts to define deviant behavior patterns in secular, nonjudgmental ways. Hence they tend to regard alcoholism, for example, as the result of sin rather than as an illness.

Until the modern "psychological revolution" began to influence evangelicalism in the 1950s, evangelicals typically placed little importance on "healthy-mindedness," as psychologists defined the term. "Fundamentally and finally," wrote Vernon Grounds, a well-known Baptist theologian, representing a traditional evangelical view, "Christianity is not concerned about the individual's emotional welfare any more than it is concerned about his physical condition. Fundamentally and finally, Christianity is concerned about the individual's relationship to God."[49] Evangelicals have traditionally emphasized the need for communion with God over a well-adjusted personality and they have placed a higher priority on spiritual than on psychological well-being. "It is infinitely better," wrote Grounds, "to be a neurotic saint than a healthyminded sinner."[50]

Evangelicals regarded mental (like physical) illness as a possible means of bringing the sufferer into closer communion with God and therefore as being sometimes spiritually beneficial. They did not consider health—whether mental or physical—as a sign of God's pleasure, or as a goal of the Christian life. Was it then to be valued and nurtured? Yes, like all God's gifts it was to be accepted with thanksgiving. It was not an ultimate good, or an end in itself, but rather a means to an end, to serve and glorify God and to enjoy fellowship with him. Many evangelicals today would agree at least in theory with the traditional view, but so great has been the emphasis in recent years on the ability of the gospel to solve all personal and interpersonal problems and to bring about personal satisfaction that for many evangelicals the traditional view has probably lost much of its force.[51] The importance given by the television evangelist Robert Schuller and others to self-esteem and the Christian's need of a positive self-image have provoked vigorous debate in evangelical circles over whether the new emphasis represents a necessary corrective to the theology of the Protestant Reformation or a serious departure from it.[52] While evangelical opinion has been divided, it appears that many evangelicals (and virtually all fundamentalists) have been uneasy with this novel concern, which suggests that traditional views still retain a strong hold on much of the evangelical constituency.[53]

Another contemporary movement to which evangelicals have only begun to respond is holistic (or wholistic or whole-person) medicine. The attempt to humanize health-care by restoring an ecological and pastoral approach has attracted some attention among evangelical professionals.[54] It has been featured most prominently in the emphasis given to the theme by a few well-known evangelicals such as Ruth Carter Stapleton.[55] While the subject has enjoyed a vogue in the 1980s, some evangelicals have expressed concern over the influence that eastern mysticism and occultic, humanistic, and syncretistic elements have had within the holistic healing movement, and Stapleton herself (who died in 1983) remains controversial among evangelicals.[56]

Evangelicalism has historically had a strong philanthropic and humanitarian component, though it is one that has produced some tension within the movement. Many of the well-known humanitarian efforts of the nineteenth century stemmed from evangelical influences in both Britain and America, and they created a tradition of voluntary charitable activity that is still active today.[57] Evangelicals undertook philanthropic work in part out of obedience to Christ's command to clothe the naked, feed the hungry, and visit the ill and imprisoned, and in part as a preliminary step to evangelism. Perhaps the chief motive for humanitarian work was evangelistic; but a concern for human souls often led to a desire to relieve the suffering and poverty of those to whom evangelicals ministered. This compassion resulted in work on behalf of prisoners, prostitutes, deprived children, and the poor generally. It also provided a stimulus to active campaigning for humanitarian legislation, particularly in England, where evangelicals like William Wilberforce (1759-1833) and the Earl of Shaftesbury (1801-1885) led movements for factory and prison reform and the abolition of the slave trade.[58] But they preferred where possible to deal with social problems by voluntary charity, believing that aid by the state could never duplicate the compassion and concern for individuals and their souls that motivated philanthropy.

Medical missions did not begin to play an important role in evangelical missionary activity until the second half of the nineteenth century.[59] One estimate put the number of European medical missionaries in 1852 at a mere thirteen. Most missionary societies initially feared that medical work might interfere with the primary goal of missions, the salvation of souls. This attitude gradually underwent reevaluation and evangelical societies came to recognize medicine as a desirable and even necessary part of missionary activity. At first, evangelicals thought its use to be mainly strategic, a means of gaining a hearing for Christianity in areas where missionary work did not find ready acceptance. Evangelicals were much concerned, however, that medicine be auxiliary to evangelism, which they still regarded as paramount. This attitude gave way by the end of the century to the view that the alleviation of human suffering was a Christian duty, which reflected the compassion that Christ demonstrated when he healed the sick. Evangelicals came to view medical missionary endeavors as a practical manifestation of the gospel, undertaken in obedience to Christ's commands, and not merely a means of aiding in the conversion of souls. As a result, by 1900 the number of medical missionaries had risen to 650, many of whom represented evangelical missionary societies.

Evangelicals and fundamentalists have founded few hospitals or healing institutions in the twentieth century. There are several reasons for this. The social concern of nineteenth-century evangelicalism was a casualty of the fundamentalist-modernist controversy. Evangelicals abandoned it at least in part because of fundamentalist opposition to the Social Gospel, advocated by many theological liberals, which evangelicals regarded as emphasizing social action at the expense of proclaiming salvation. Moreover, fundamentalist institutions tended to be decentralized, with the local congregation serving as the focus of the movement, a factor that discouraged the establishment of hospitals. Many evangelicals adopted the "faith missions" approach that relied on God to supply funds, a method pioneered by George Mueller (1805-1898) in his orphanage in Bristol, England, that was not, however, very practicable in the maintenance of hospitals. The belief among fundamentalists in the imminency of Christ's return perhaps also militated against the founding of permanent philanthropic institutions. The fundamentalists' concern with personal salvation led them rather to involvement in such enterprises as slum missions, where philanthropy was closely tied to evangelism.[60]

Passages and Biomedical Issues

Evangelicals have always thought themselves to be, like John Wesley, *homines unius libri* ("people of one book"). They have held that the Bible is fully inspired and authoritative in all its parts. They have considered it alone sufficient to provide the basis of theology and ethics, and they have deemed no position acceptable that does not have the support of Scripture.[61] Thus their procedure in determining matters of faith and practice has been to assemble the relevant data of Scripture in order to reach a conclusion that reflected the truth of God's Word.[62] They fully recognized that allowances had to be made for temporal or cultural differences, but believed that the biblical record, properly interpreted in the plain sense intended by its writers, could provide not merely guidance, but normative teaching on specific questions.[63] Not only evangelicals but orthodox Christians of most Protestant communions held this view until about a century ago.

We may consider the subject of human sexuality as typical of this approach to ethical questions. Evangelical views on the subject were not markedly different from those of Protestantism generally.[64] Evangelicals assumed that there existed a unity in the biblical ethic in spite of differences of time or culture.[65] As part of the creation ordinances (mandates given by God at creation), God had established marriage as the normal sexual relationship between man and woman. He intended that the relationship be monogamous, and within it that sex provide both companionship and the means of procreation. The Fall affected every aspect of human nature, including the sexual function. But, according to evangelical thought, the entry of sin into the world and the frequent perversion of sex did not abrogate the original intention of God. Sexual practices that fell below God's intended standard (for example, divorce, concubinage, polygamy) he sometimes tolerated, while those that were directly contrary to it (for example, adultery, fornication, homosexuality, lesbianism, bestiality) he explicitly condemned in all periods.[66] Among Protestants generally, the traditional consensus that this pattern represented the teaching of Scripture and therefore the normative pattern of human sexuality has broken down since the 1960s. Evangelicals, however, have vigorously opposed situational ethics.[67] Moreover, a recent survey found that evangelicals ranked highest among the religious groups surveyed in their opposition to homosexuality, pre- and extra-marital relations, divorce, and abortion.[68] There have been recently a few challenges to the nearly unanimous moral consensus that has characterized evangelicals and fundamentalists.[69] But as long as they view Scripture as normative, it is unlikely that most evangelicals will abandon traditional views.

There have always been a number of issues in ethics (for example, abortion, contraception, euthanasia), however, that did not admit of easy solutions because Scripture did not clearly address them. In cases such as these, evangelicals drew inferences from general principles or passing biblical references. While traditional attitudes usually prevailed, there was not (nor is there now) unanimity of opinion. Evangelicals, like Protestants generally, in the nineteenth century accepted the traditional view that artificial birth-control was immoral. As contraceptive information came to be propagated, evangelicals, thinking that it would encourage vice and immorality, joined in organizing leagues for the suppression of contraceptives. Traditional attitudes, based on the assumption that birth control was contrary to Scripture (Gen. 38:8-10 was often cited), persisted well into the twentieth century.[70] Yet as evangelicals examined Scripture closely, the presumed objections to contraception no longer seemed compelling.[71] Undoubtedly the Protestant view, dating from the Reformation, that intercourse exists for conjugal pleasure as well as for procreation made it easier for evangelicals than for Catholics to accept birth control.[72]

The question of abortion presented another morally complex issue. Evangelicals, like most other Protestants, accepted the pre-Reformation view that abortion was homicide. They supported their position by citing passages in Scripture (for example, Jer. 1:5, Ps. 139:15-16, Lk. 1:41) that seemed to teach that the fetus was a personal being endued with an immortal soul. Some evangelicals were willing to permit an abortion when the life of the mother was endangered, on the ground that an actual life is of greater value than a potential one. Once this view was accepted, it was possible to argue that there were other (though perhaps rare) cases in which abortion was justified. Thus evangelicals (and Protestants generally) could take a slightly more lenient position than Roman Catholics, though, in fact, many and perhaps most agreed essentially with the traditional view.[73]

As the demand for more liberal abortion laws grew in the 1960s, evangelicals had to define their view more precisely than before. The modern debate over abortion has tended to harden positions, and many evangelicals and fundamentalists have come to consider all abortions wrong. They have been, in fact, in the forefront of opposition to the liberalization of abortion laws, and on few social issues is there so much unanimity among them. A recent poll showed that 95.3 percent of evangelicals opposed abortion (except when the mother's life was in danger), a higher proportion than even Catholics (of whom 90.5 percent were opposed).[74] A film series, *Whatever Happened to the Human Race?*, which featured two well-known evangelicals, Dr. C. Everett Koop (who later became Surgeon General of the United States) and theologian Francis Schaeffer, speaking against abortion and euthanasia enjoyed much success among evangelical audiences.[75] Behind evangelical opposition to abortion has been the belief that the fetus is a potential human being created in the image of God, not merely expendable tissue.

An examination of evangelical views on contraception and abortion reveals an important point: There has been no single evangelical position regarding a number of ethical issues. One has seldom been able to look to official pronouncements of evangelical bodies for guidance. Evangelical and fundamentalist denominations have been reluctant to issue social pronouncements or to speak for their churches. John Eighmy's observation regarding the Southern Baptists that "their conservative theology, religious individualism, and congregational government continue to restrict progressive expression" could be applied to virtually every evangelical denomination.[76] Evangelicals, moreover, have generally refused to be bound by ecclesiastical tradition or reason. On any issue under discussion they have been accustomed to ask, "What does the Bible teach?" On some issues the rejoinder has been either that Scripture did not speak directly to the matter or that its teaching was not clear. Hence on a number of ethical issues a variety of interpretations has been possible.

Evangelicals (like those of other religious traditions) have only recently begun to think seriously about a number of issues in medical ethics (for example, artificial insemination, genetic engineering, in vitro fertilization).[77] But as a group they have tended not to be particularly concerned with issues raised by modern medical technology. They have been more concerned about matters of personal morality (for example, abortion and homosexuality) and these issues have occupied their attention largely to the exclusion of broader issues that they have regarded as peripheral to traditional evangelical concerns. Moreover, the theological conservatism and biblicism of evangelicals and fundamentalists have given them a reluctance to abandon traditional interpretations of Scripture or conservative positions generally, in spite of their formal refusal to recognize the authority of ecclesiastical tradition.

In the eighteenth and nineteenth centuries, frequent reflection on death was characteristic of evangelical religion. Evangelicals viewed life on earth as a vale of tears through which the Christian passed as a preparation for eternal life. Evangelicals regarded the destiny of the soul as being of supreme importance. In evangelical homes, parents taught their children from a young age to think of eternity and they regularly warned them that there was a hell to be shunned and heaven to be gained.[78] Victorian evangelicals brought their children to the deathbeds of family members in order to impress upon them the frailty of life and the necessity of being prepared to meet death.[79] Among many evangelicals, particularly in America, this concern with death gave way to an expectation that the imminent return of Christ might usher Christians into his presence without death. The change in attitude resulted from the widespread growth of premillennialism in evangelical circles in the last third of the nineteenth century. A large proportion of evangelicals (and later fundamentalists) came to believe that they were living in the last days and that signs pointed to the imminent return of Christ to establish his millennial kingdom. This view, called premillennialism, became one of the most significant doctrines of the fundamentalist movement, and many fundamentalists firmly believed (as many continue to believe) that they would see Christ's return in their lifetime.[80] Since about 1960, premillennialism has declined somewhat in its influence within mainstream evangelicalism, although it still retains a strong influence in fundamentalist circles. Evangelical literature today places less stress on "the Blessed Hope" (Christ's Second Coming) than it did a generation ago. The attention given to the joys of heaven and the terrors of hell has declined as well, probably reflecting a greater interest among evangelicals in this world. Instead, contemporary evangelical magazines regularly feature articles, differing little from those produced within other branches of Christianity, on understanding the process of grief or aiding in the emotional adjustment of both the dying and the bereaved.[81]

In caring for the dying pastorally, evangelicals have above all been concerned that those facing death settle the matter of the state of their souls. John Wesley made it a routine part of his busy ministry to visit prisoners condemned to the gallows in order to give spiritual counsel, and evangelical clergy have frequently undertaken a similar ministry to those facing death in institutions. Evangelicals have taken seriously the biblical dictum that "it is appointed unto men once to die, but after this the judgment"—hence their urgency in pressing the question of salvation on those facing death. Since the spread of theological liberalism in the twentieth century, there has been a marked difference between the pastoral concerns of evangelicals, whose theology centers on the question "Is your soul right with God?"; and the concerns of Christians who espouse a theology of universalism, which holds that all persons will be saved. To those of evangelical conviction, all lesser matters have faded in importance when a soul hung in the balance.

Among evangelicals and fundamentalists, assurance of personal salvation has brought to the dying both comfort for the present and hope for the future. Their belief in God's sovereignty has given them confidence that he controls every aspect of life and death and that nothing happens by chance. In this spirit, the well-known evangelical author Joseph Bayly wrote:

> Shortly after our five-year-old died of leukemia, someone asked me how I'd feel if a cure for leukemia were then discovered. My answer was that I'd be thankful, but it would be irrelevant to the death of my son. God determined to take him to His home at the age of five; the means was incidental.[82]

A firm belief in the existence of heaven and hell rather than a vague idea of a future life has strengthened this confidence. Evangelical piety, reflected in popular gospel songs of the late nineteenth and early twentieth centuries (for example, "Face to Face," "When We All Get to Heaven," "When the Roll Is Called Up Yonder"), has centered on the theme of the glorious future that awaits believers with their Savior in heaven.[83] The promise of the resurrection of the body has encouraged those whose bodies were wracked with pain, while those experiencing grief looked forward to a future in which there would be no sorrow. And the greatest of all hopes has been in a future life in which the last enemy, death, will be vanquished. In the face of death, generations of evangelical Christians have found consolation in these beliefs. Because they have held that God alone ought to control human destiny, they have opposed both suicide and active (but not necessarily passive) euthanasia.[84]

In its approach to death, as in its approach to health, sickness, and healing, evangelicalism in its various manifestations has traditionally shown its primary concern to be with salvation and the Christian life in a personal, individualistic manner. Basic to this outlook has been a vital religious experience, a simple but profound faith that Jesus Christ gives meaning to every aspect of life. This attitude is succinctly expressed in the words of the Heidelberg Catechism of 1563, with which evangelicals and fundamentalists, in spite of many differences of style and emphasis, would probably have given warm assent:

> What is thy only comfort in life and death? That I with a body and soul, both in life and death, am not my own, but belong unto my faithful Saviour Jesus Christ; who, with his precious blood, hath fully satisfied for all my sins, and delivered me from all the power of the devil; and so preserves me that without the will of my heavenly Father, not a hair can fall from my head; yea, that all things must be subservient to my salvation, and therefore by his Holy Spirit, he also assures me of eternal life, and makes me sincerely willing and ready, henceforth, to live unto him.[85]

Notes

[1] Quoted in Ian C. Bradley, *The Call to Seriousness: The Evangelical Impact on the Victorians* (New York, 1976), p. 193.

[2] For an evangelical view of asceticism, see Bernard L. Ramm, *The Right, the Good, and the Happy* (Waco, TX, 1971), pp. 57-59. A similar view is expressed by J. A. Ziesler, *Christian Asceticism* (Grand Rapids, MI, 1973), pp. 99-118.

[3] For modern evangelical attempts to introduce fasting as a spiritual discipline, see David R. Smith, *Fasting: A Neglected Discipline* (Fort Washington, PA, 1969); and Richard J. Foster, *Celebration of Discipline: The Path to Spiritual Growth* (San Francisco, 1978), pp. 41-53.

[4] On the evangelical influence on the temperance movement in the nineteenth century, see Frank Thistlethwaite, "The Anglo-American World of Humanitarian Endeavor," in *Ante-Bellum Reform*, ed. David Brion Davis (New York, 1967), pp. 75-77. On revivalism and temperance, see Whitney R. Cross, *The Burned-Over District: The Social and Intellectual History of Enthusiastic Religion in Western New York, 1800-1850* (New York, 1965), pp. 211-217.

[5] See, e.g., Ramm, *The Right*, pp. 103-109.

[6] For evangelical concern about this new attitude, see Jerry G. Dunn (with Bernard Palmer), *What Will You Have to Drink? The New Christian Password* (Beaverlodge, Alberta, 1980).

[7] See Donald Dayton, "The Rise of the Evangelical Healing Movement in Nineteenth Century

America," *Pneuma* 4 (1982): 1-18. On A. J. Gordon, see also Ernest B. Gordon, *Adoniram Judson Gordon: A Biography* (London, n.d.), pp. 333-335, 144-148.

[8] See A. W. Tozer, *Wingspread* (Harrisburg, PA, 1943), pp. 75-88.

[9] For the early Protestant view, see Keith Thomas, *Religion and the Decline of Magic* (New York, 1971), pp. 124-125. For the nineteenth century, see the comments of A. J. Gordon, *The Ministry of Healing* (Harrisburg, PA, n.d.), p. 1.

[10] Quoted in Colin Brown, *Miracles and the Critical Mind* (Grand Rapids, MI, 1984), p. 203.

[11] J. Gresham Machen, *The Christian View of Man* (1937, reprinted London, 1965), pp. 111-112.

[12] See Gordon, *The Ministry of Healing*, pp. 209-223.

[13] A. B. Simpson, *The Gospel of Healing*, rev. ed. (Harrisburg, PA, n.d.), esp. pp. 65-68.

[14] See Tozer, *Wingspread*, pp. 134-135.

[15] Ibid., pp. 132-133.

[16] Marsden, *Fundamentalism*, pp. 93-94.

[17] B. B. Warfield, *Counterfeit Miracles* (1918, reprinted London, 1972), pp. 25-26.

[18] Ibid., pp. 192-193.

[19] Henry W. Frost, *Miraculous Healing* (1931, reprinted Grand Rapids, MI, 1979), esp. pp. 113-125.

[20] See R. V. G. Tasker, *The General Epistle of James*, Tyndale New Testament Commentaries (Grand Rapids, MI, 1977), pp. 130-132.

[21] This is not a widely held view; but see C. E. Putnam, *Modern Religio-Healing: Man's Theories or God's Word?* (Chicago, 1924), pp. 139-149.

[22] See, e.g., Gordon, *Healing* pp. 31-38; and J. Sidlow Baxter, *The Divine Healing of the Body* (Grand Rapids, MI, 1979), pp. 160-171.

[23] Gordon, *Healing*, pp. 31-32.

[24] Warfield, *Counterfeit Miracles*, pp. 171-173.

[25] See, e.g., Baxter, *The Divine Healing of the Body*, pp. 272-277. The well-known British minister and physician, D. Martyn Lloyd-Jones, is more cautious in his assessment of Kuhlman; see *The Supernatural in Medicine* (London, 1971), pp. 3-4, 21.

[26] See, e.g., Frost, *Miraculous Healing*, pp. 75-76, in defense of physicians against their denigration by certain faith healers.

[27] See Charles E. Hummel, *Fire in the Fireplace* (Downers Grove, IL, 1978), pp. 207-223; and Hummel, *Healing* (Downers Grove, IL, 1982). For an account of a rediscovery of healing associated with a course offered by Fuller Seminary, see the composite work *Signs & Wonders Today* (Wheaton, IL, 1983).

[28] For an example of a theology of faith healing, see, e.g., Simpson *The Gospel of Healing*, pp. 76-86.

[29] Against the evangelical healing movement in the nineteenth century, see, e.g., "Prayer and the Prayer-Cure," in A. A. Hodge, *Popular Lectures on Theological Themes* (Philadelphia, 1887), pp. 94-116, esp. pp. 107ff. Against Pentecostal faith healers, see, e.g., Putnam, *Modern Religio-Healing*, pp. 74-154.

[30] "Accidents, not Punishments" (a sermon delivered on September 8, 1861), in C. H. Spurgeon, *Metropolitan Tabernacle Pulpit*, 63 vols. (London, 1855-1917), 7:484. On Spurgeon's attitude to healing, see Russell H. Conwell, *Life of Charles Haddon Spurgeon: The World's Great Preacher* (Philadelphia [?], 1892), pp. 172-186.

[31] Hodge, "Prayer and the Prayer-Cure," p. 109.

[32] "Sickness," in J. C. Ryle, *Practical Religion* (1879, reprinted Cambridge, England, 1969), p. 238.

[33] Ibid., pp. 238-241.

[34] See, e.g., Edward M. Merrins, "Gifts of Healing," *Bibliotheca Sacra* 66 (1909): 408-410.

[35] See, e.g., "Advantages of Sickness," in Jeremy Taylor, *The Rule and Exercises of Holy Dying* (1651, reprinted Philadelphia, 1846), pp. 79-92.

[36] A popular contemporary restatement of the traditional evangelical view of suffering is found in Joni Eareckson and Steve Estes, *A Step Further* (Grand Rapids, MI, 1978), esp. pp. 115-

185, which discusses the theology of suffering in the context of Eareckson's experience as a quadriplegic.

[37] See Michael MacDonald, "Religion, Social Change, and Psychological Healing in England, 1600-1800," in *The Church and Healing*, ed. W. J. Sheils (Oxford, 1982), pp. 101-125.

[38] See, e.g., Archibald Alexander, *Thoughts on Religious Experience* (1844, reprinted Edinburgh, 1967), pp. 32-50. For a modern evangelical discussion, see John White, *The Masks of Melancholy: A Christian Physician Looks at Depression & Suicide* (Downers Grove, IL, 1982). A popular evangelical treatment of the subject, written from a pastoral and biblical perspective, is D. Martyn Lloyd-Jones, *Spiritual Depression: Its Causes and Cure* (Grand Rapids, MI, 1965).

[39] On physiological and moral causes of insanity, see Alexander, *Thoughts on Religious Experience*, pp. 48-49.

[40] See Frederick S. Leahy, *Satan Cast Out* (Edinburgh, 1975), pp. 124-127. A popular modern work that describes purported demonic activity in Borneo is Robert Peterson, *Roaring Lion* (London, 1968).

[41] Leahy, *Satan Cast Out*, pp. 152-159. See also Kurt Koch, *Christian Counseling and the Occult* (Grand Rapids, MI, 1965); and John Warwick Montgomery, *Principalities and Powers* (Minneapolis, 1973).

[42] See, e.g., White, *The Masks of Melancholy*, pp. 21-39.

[43] On evangelicalism's appeal to common sense and Baconian science, see Marsden, *Fundamentalism and American Culture*, pp. 55-62, 212-221.

[44] Typical is Philip E. Hughes, *Christian Ethics in Secular Society* (Grand Rapids, MI, 1983), pp. 81-89, 91.

[45] See Hunter, *American Evangelicalism*, pp. 91-99.

[46] See, e.g., Gary R. Collins, *The Rebuilding of Psychology: An Integration of Psychology and Christianity* (Wheaton, IL, 1977); and H. Newton Malony, ed., *Wholeness and Holiness: Readings in the Psychology/Theology of Mental Health* (Grand Rapids, MI, 1983).

[47] See Jay E. Adams, *Competent to Counsel* (Phillipsburg, NJ, 1970).

[48] See, e.g., Paul C. Vitz, *Psychology as Religion: The Cult of Self-Worship* (Grand Rapids, MI, 1977); and William Kirk Kilpatrick, *Psychological Seduction: The Failure of Modern Psychology* (Nashville, 1983).

[49] Vernon Grounds, *Emotional Problems and the Gospel* (Grand Rapids, MI, 1976), pp. 109-110.

[50] Ibid., p. 110. Contrast William James' description of "The Religion of Healthy-Mindedness" in *The Varieties of Religous Experience* (1902, reprinted New York, 1929), pp. 77-124.

[51] See Hunter, *American Evangelicalism*, pp. 98-99.

[52] See Robert H. Schuller, *Self-Esteem: The New Reformation* (Waco, TX, 1982), For an evaluation of Schuller, see "Hard Questions for Robert Schuller about Sin and Self-esteem," *Christianity Today* 28 (August 10, 1984): 14-20 and Kenneth Kantzer with Paul W. Fromer, "A Theologian Looks at Schuller," ibid., pp. 22-24.

[53] See, e.g., Paul Brownback, *The Danger of Self-Love* (Chicago, 1982); and the strong attack on Schuller's theology by John MacArthur, "Questions for Robert Schuller," *Moody Monthly* 83 (May 1983): 6-10.

[54] See David E. Allen, Lewis P. Bird, and Robert Herrmann, eds., *Whole-Person Medicine: An International Symposium* (Downers Grove, IL, 1980).

[55] See Ruth Carter Stapleton, *The Gift of Inner Healing* (Waco, TX, 1976).

[56] See, e.g., the special issue of the SCP [Spiritual Counterfeits Project] *Journal* 2 (August 1978) devoted to a critical examination of the holistic health movement. On Ruth Carter Stapleton, see Brooks Alexander, "Holistic Health from the Inside," ibid., pp. 14-15.

[57] See Bradley, *The Call to Seriousness*, pp. 119-134.

[58] On evangelical social reform, see Earle E. Cairns, *Saints and Society* (Chicago, 1960); Timothy L. Smith, *Revivalism and Social Reform* (New York, 1957); Donald W. Dayton, *Discovering an Evangelical Heritage* (New York, 1976); W. David Lewis, "The Reformer as Conservative: Protestant Counter-Subversion in the Early Republic," in *The Development of an American Culture*, eds. Stanley Coben and Lorman Ratner (Englewood Cliffs, NJ, 1970), pp. 64-91.

[59] See C. Peter Williams, "Healing and Evangelism: The Place of Medicine in Later Victorian Protestant Missionary Thinking," in *The Church and Healing*, pp. 271-285; and A. F. Walls, " 'The Heavey Artillery of the Missionary Army': The Domestic Importance of the Nineteenth-Century Medical Missionary," ibid., pp. 287-297.

[60] See Timothy P. Weber, *Living in the Shadow of the Second Coming* (New York, 1979), pp. 82-104.

[61] See Timothy P. Weber, "The Two-Edged Sword: The Fundamentalist Use of the Bible," in *The Bible in America: Essays in Cultural History*, eds. Nathan O. Hatch and Mark A. Noll (New York, 1982), pp. 101-120.

[62] For a typical example of this approach to a particular issue, see John Murray, *Divorce* (Philadelphia, 1961).

[63] See George M. Marsden, "Everyone One's Own Interpreter? The Bible, Science, and Authority in Mid-Nineteenth-Century America," in Hatch and Noll, *The Bible in America*, pp. 80-81.

[64] See, e.g., Otto A. Piper, *The Biblical View of Sex and Marriage*, rev. ed. (New York, 1960).

[65] A good example of this approach is John Murray, *Principles of Conduct: Aspects of Biblical Ethics* (London, 1957), esp. pp. 7-9.

[66] Ibid., pp. 45-81. See also Hughes, *Christian Ethics*, pp. 149-181. For an older statement of the traditional evangelical view, see Charles Hodge, *Systematic Theology*, 3 vols. (1872-73, reprinted Grand Rapids, MI, 1977), 3:368-421.

[67] See, e.g., Norman L. Geisler, *Ethics: Alternatives and Issues* (Grand Rapids, MI, 1971), pp. 60-77; and Hughes, *Christian Ethics*, pp. 70-79.

[68] See Hunter, *American Evangelicalism*, pp. 85-86.

[69] See Letha Scanzoni and Virginia Ramey Mollenkott, *Is the Homosexual My Neighbor? Another Christian View* (San Francisco, 1978), which argues for an evangelical acceptance of homosexual behavior. For a restatement of the traditional view, see Richard F. Lovelace, *Homosexuality and the Church* (Old Tappan, NJ, 1978).

[70] See Lloyd A. Kalland, "Views and Positions of the Christian Church—An Historical Review," in *Birth Control and the Christian*, eds. Walter O. Spitzer and Carlyle L. Saylor (Wheaton, IL, 1969), pp. 448-454.

[71] For a list of European and American churches that have taken a positive stance toward birth control, see ibid., p. 459. A good discussion of the arguments on both sides of the issue is found in Geisler, *Ethics*, pp. 211-218.

[72] On the Protestant, and particularly Puritan, emphasis on companionability in marriage, see Roland H. Bainton, *Sex, Love and Marriage: A Christian Survey* (Glasgow, 1958), pp. 99-111; and Lawrence Stone, *The Family, Sex, and Marriage in England, 1500-1800* (New York, 1977), pp. 135-142. Evangelical (and most Protestant) discussions of birth control emphasize the importance of sex as a contributing factor to marital companionship; see, e.g., M. O. Vincent, "Moral Considerations in Contraception," in Spitzer and Saylor, *Birth Control and the Christian*, pp. 247-255; and Geisler, *Ethics*, p. 201. There has recently been a spate of books written by evangelical and fundamentalist authors on the "recreational" aspect of sex within marriage; see, e.g., Tim and Beverly LaHaye, *The Act of Marriage: The Beauty of Sexual Love* (Grand Rapids, MI, 1976).

[73] Most discussions of abortion from an evangelical point of view consider abortion to be justifiable on some grounds; see, e.g., Geisler, *Ethics*, pp. 218-223; Hughes, *Christian Ethics*, p. 179; and "A Protestant Affirmation on the Control of Human Reproduction," in Spitzer and Saylor, *Birth Control and the Christian*, p. xxv.

[74] See Hunter, *American Evangelicalism*, p. 85.

[75] See Francis A. Schaeffer and C. Everett Koop, *Whatever Happened to the Human Race?* (Old Tappan, NJ, 1979).

[76] See John Lee Eighmy, *Churches in Cultural Captivity: A History of the Social Attitudes of Southern Baptists* (Knoxville, TN, 1972), p. 199.

[77] On genetic engineering, see Hughes, *Christian Ethics*, pp. 133-147. On artificial insemination, see ibid., pp. 228-230. Sterilization, genetic engineering, and artificial insemination are also discussed in several essays in Spitzer and Saylor, *Birth Control and the Christian*. A number

of bioethical issues (e.g., organ transplants, sterilization, artificial insemination) are treated in individual articles in Carl F. H. Henry, ed., *Baker's Dictionary of Christian Ethics* (Grand Rapids, MI, 1973).

[78] See Stone, *The Family, Sex and Marriage*, pp. 251-253.

[79] See Bradley, *The Call to Seriousness*, pp. 187-188.

[80] See Timothy P. Weber, *Living in the Shadow*, pp. 43-64.

[81] See, e.g., Joseph Bayly, *The Last Thing We Talk About,* rev. ed. (Grand Rapids, MI, 1973); Bayly, "The Suffering of Children," *Christian Medical Society Journal* 12, 1 (1981): 2-7; Haddon W. Robinson, *Grief* (Grand Rapids, MI, 1976); Donald Howard, *Christians Grieve Too* (Edinburgh, 1979).

[82] Bayly, *The Last Thing We Talk About*, p. 24.

[83] See Bradley, *The Call to Seriousness*, p. 192.

[84] On suicide, see Geisler, *Ethics*, pp. 236-240; and Henri Blocher, *Suicide*, trans. Roger Van Dyk (Downers Grove, IL, 1972). On euthansia, see Geisler, *Ethics*, pp. 231-236; and Hughes, *Christian Ethics*, pp. 125-133.

[85] *The Psalter: With Doctrinal Standards, Liturgy, Church Order, and Added Chorale Section*, rev. ed. (Grand Rapids, Mi, 1947), p. 1 at the rear of the volume.

THE ROMAN CATHOLIC TRADITION SINCE 1545

MARVIN R. O'CONNELL
Professor of History, University of Notre Dame

From Chapter 4 in the book:
*Caring and Curing: Health and Medicine
in the Western Religious Traditions*

One of the landmark events in the long and tumultuous history of Roman Catholicism was the general council that met intermittently at the northern Italian town of Trent between 1545 and 1563. The crisis that prompted Pope Paul III to convoke the first session of this assembly (1545-1547) and his immediate successors to reconvene it twice (1551-1552 and 1562-1563) was so serious that it appeared to have brought the Latin church and western Christendom to the verge of dissolution. There was, first of all, the devastating success of the Protestant Reformation which had spread with remarkable speed across northern Europe so that in less than thirty years new and thriving ecclesiastical organizations had sprung up in Germany, Switzerland, England, and the countries of Scandinavia. Everywhere the church, which had long claimed to define itself by its universality, seemed to be crumbling beneath the assault of a different gospel preached with unprecedented vigor and excitement. Noblemen in Poland and Hungary, academics in France, artisans and entrepreneurs in the Netherlands, even learned and distinguished friars in Italy—none of them was left untouched by the zeal and forceful personalities of the reformers and by the attractiveness of their ideas.[1]

The desperate problem that Protestantism posed for the Roman Church was greatly compounded by its own internal disarray. The cry for reform of abuses had been loud and persistent for a century before Martin Luther posted his *Ninety-five Theses* upon the door of the castle-church in Wittenberg (1517). Indeed, local initiatives in Italy, the Netherlands, and elsewhere had demonstrated that much correction could be achieved thanks to the efforts of a particular preacher or religious institute. Luther himself had begun his career as a representative of an older German reform tradition which, up to his time, had not found it necessary to separate itself from the larger ecclesiastical system. The state of the church, it could be argued, was far better in 1517 than it had been in 1417. But revolutions are often the product of rising expectations, and the very success of reform in certain localities served to underscore the continuing pervasive decay and to contribute to the impatience of Christian men and women with the apparent reluctance of the church as a whole to put right the abuses that disfigured it. A venal, slothful, and ignorant clergy; a laity shot-through with superstition; colossal financial chicanery from indulgence-hawkers to corrupt officials of the Roman curia who routinely sold benefices and dispensations; an administrative chaos which made it virtually impossible to fix responsibility for the abuses and hence to apply the practical means to root them out; popes who were hedonists and simoniacs like Alexander VI (d. 1503) or warriors like Julius II (d. 1513) or dilettantes like Leo X (d. 1521)—all these were commonplace in Christian Europe at the moment the Protestant Reformation began. "According to the testimony of those who were then alive," wrote the Jesuit theologian Robert Bellarmine (1542-1621) nearly a century later, "there was an almost entire abandonment of equity in ecclesiastical judgments; in morals no discipline, in sacred literature no erudition, in divine things no reverence. Religion was almost extinct."[2]

Inevitably the doctrinal challenge to the Roman church merged with the universal revulsion at the abuses, with the result that from the beginning the word *reformation* possessed a certain ambiguity. For many—certainly for the great Protestant leaders like Luther and John Calvin—it meant primarily a reform of doctrine and the pastoral consequences that would necessarily follow. They pointed to the undeniable decay of ecclesiastical institutions as evidence, if not proof, that the synthesis of Catholic teaching that had emerged out of the middle ages was, at least, a distortion of divine revelation. Because the popes, they argued, taught false doctrines—particularly with regard to justification, merit, free will, and the value of human works—the church over which the popes presided had predictably suffered a moral and disciplinary collapse. Teach the truth as revealed in the Bible, the argument ran in effect, and the church will become what God intended it to be, the unspotted bride of Christ.[3]

But this causal link did not recommend itself to everyone. Indeed, it might be said that the fathers—that is, the bishops and the generals of religious orders who enjoyed the conciliar franchise—assembled at the Council of Trent precisely in order to deny it. Not that they denied the abuses. A curial commission nine years earlier had urged upon Paul III the most sweeping internal reforms and had beseeched the pope "to restore the name of Christ, forgotten by the people and by us, the clergy, to our hearts and to our works; to heal our ailments; to bring back the flock of Christ into the one fold; to remove us from the wrath of God and punishment earned by our deserts, which now threatens our very lives."[4] Such lamentations and beatings of the collective breast were typical and worked themselves with startling candor into the council's early debates. "We ourselves," cried Reginald Cardinal Pole (1500-1558), one of the council's presiding officers, at the session of 7 January 1546, "we ourselves are largely responsible for the misfortunes which have befallen us, for the rise of heresy, and the collapse of Christian morality, because we have failed to cultivate the field which was entrusted to us. We are like salt which has lost its savor. Unless we do penance, God will not speak to us."[5]

But to admit the widespread existence of the abuses, to assume the blame for them, even to recognize that "heresy" was nurtured by them, was not the same as assigning false doctrines as their cause. For the fathers of Trent and their Catholic contemporaries the abuses had flourished despite the teaching of the Roman Church, not because of it. For them "reformation" meant purging a system that was fundamentally sound but that had fallen victim over the past several centuries to human frailty and vice. What the Protestants had proposed, controversialist Thomas Stapleton (1535-1598) argued a few years after the Council of Trent, was

> not a reformation but a transformation. If they had not snatched away the substance of the Catholic faith, abolished the Christian sacrifice, denied the sacraments and altogether confused and upset due order and polity; had they instead proposed to criticize and correct the abuses and superstitions which had sprung up in various places on account of the crass negligence of certain pastors, then the church of God would neither have called into question their zeal nor repudiated their counsel.[6]

The Council of Trent set for itself, therefore, two tasks. It aimed first to reassert in clear and unequivocal fashion what it conceived to be the true, traditionally received understanding of divine revelation; or, to put the same thing negatively, to refute the doctrinal innovations of the Protestant reformers. "For they are preaching a gospel other than the one we have received," wrote Stapleton. "It is not really a gospel at all, because it perverts the only true gospel of Jesus Christ. And so with reason the whole church of God says to them, 'Anathema.' "[7] At the same time the council determined to eliminate the financial, administrative, and pedagogical abuses that had led to the corruption of the clergy and the paganization of the laity, without, however, radically altering the ecclesiastical system in place. This two-fold purpose was reflected even in the procedure the council followed, in which both sets of problems were treated simultaneously: Dogmatic issues raised by the Protestants were considered one day, so to speak, and the correction of internal abuses the next.[8]

It would be hard to overemphasize the importance of the Council of Trent. The mind-set of modern Roman Catholicism was framed by its decrees and by the theologies based upon those decrees. Indeed, the very phrase *Roman Catholicism*, with its intrinsic semantic contradiction, could come to have meaning as a sectarian term in distinction to, say, Lutheranism or Calvinism only after Trent managed to stop the hemorrhaging within the older Christian body and to provide it with the tools of survival. To be sure, a stern price had to be paid for the success achieved by the fathers at Trent, a success that was in any event bound to be limited. All hope for the reunion of western Christendom faded when the Protestants were confronted by the conciliar decisions on justification, revelation, and the sacraments. The imposition by the council of a sharply rigorous discipline, however necessary it may have been, underscored the Roman Church's new and unfamiliar role as one Christian denomination competing among many others. Competitiveness bred exclusivity. It led inevitably to the development of a kind of siege mentality and just as inevitably to an increasing centralization of decision making with the pope and his curia, not only because the fathers of the council made the popes the special guardians of its testament, but also because a militant and embattled organization demanded for its existence—so it seemed—a unified command.

Catholicism has continued to claim to be the church of the apostles, but since the sixteenth century it has also been the "tridentine" church, the church reconstructed at Trent. In every phase of modern Catholic life, including that of the treatment of the sick, the teaching and the ideals enunciated at Trent have provided, until very recently, the ultimate norm of belief and practice. This is not to say that all Catholics in all places at all times agreed as to the interpretation of that teaching or even fully understood it, or that they consistently lived up to those ideals. But the stubborn application of the same measure to the activities of the largest single community of Christian believers, spread to every corner of the world over a span of four centuries, was itself enormously significant.

Trent, the Sacramental Principle, and Extreme
Unction: The Anointing of the Dying

What little the fathers of the Council of Trent had to say explicitly about illness and its relief was confined to its statement about the sacrament of extreme unction. The brief decree, dated 25 November 1551, took up only a couple of pages of print. It was assertive rather than argumentative. Significantly, it followed directly upon the much longer decree on the sacrament of penance, because extreme unction was regarded by ancient tradition "as the completion not only of penance but also of the whole Christian life, which ought to be a continual penance." The ambiguity in the use of the word *penance* was accompanied by an obscurity as to the precise situation in which the sacrament was to be received. "This anointing is to be applied to the sick, but especially to those who are in such danger as to appear to be at the end of life, which is why it is also called the sacrament of the dying."[9] *The Catechism of the Council of Trent*, a manual of instruction for the use of parish priests issued just after the council, observed that extreme unction had been called in antiquity "the sacrament of the anointing of the sick," but it predictably followed the conciliar decree in restricting administration "to those only whose malady is such as to excite apprehension of approaching death."[10] Thus it would seem that the sacrament was to be administered only when medical authorities, echoing the Epistle of James, should advise "bringing in the priests of the church."[11]

Both the decree of Trent and the *Catechism* insisted that the primary object of extreme unction was the spiritual, not the physical, well-being of the afflicted person. The council employed familiar scholastic terminology:

> The thing signified [in the sacrament] is the grace of the Holy Ghost whose anointing takes away the sins if there be any still to be expiated, and also the remains of sin, and strengthens the soul of the sick person by exciting in him great confidence in the divine mercy, supported by which the sick person bears more easily the miseries and pains of his illness and resists more easily the temptations of the devil.

Yet, once having established this point, the council added with more solemnity than precision: "At times, when expedient for the welfare of the soul, [extreme unction] restores bodily health."[12] The *Catechism* elaborated only by pointing a cautionary finger: "If in our days the sick obtain [recovery of physical health] less frequently, this is to be attributed, not to any defect in the sacrament, but rather to the weaker faith of a great part of those who are anointed with the sacred oil or by whom it is administered."[13]

Extreme unction, therefore, as the council defined it, shared in the sacramental principle, in an incarnational theology that stressed divine immanence in the human situation and was thus in marked contrast to that keystone of all classical Protestant teaching, the notion of the transcendence of God.[14] This was a crucial difference that cut across all issues, including that of health care. It manifested itself, to be sure, in ways that could be expressed propositionally. Trent thus differed from the Protestant reformers in seeing original sin as debilitating rather than as radically destructive. It differed from them also in relating grace to human merit and striving. The council proclaimed the essential freedom of the human will. But these were hardly more than abstract corollaries of its central vision of God as somehow fleshly, of its conviction that the very reality of God had been so closely mingled with the human that that reality could be captured in ritual and symbol, particularly in the seven sacraments and most particularly in the Eucharist. And such ritual, by conciliar definition, combined as necessary constituents the grossly material—a bit of bread, wine, water, oil—and the purified intention of the believer.

The spiritual system that emerged out of Trent was thus relatively optimistic, sensual, and anthropomorphic. It quite explicitly contradicted the evangel of the Protestant reformers by enhancing the value of good works and of human endeavor by describing grace as a phenomenon that could wax or wane, that could be gained and lost and regained again.[15] At the center of the panoply of good works, the council placed the seven sacraments, which produced their graceful results not so much by the inner and unseen dispositions of minister and recipient as by the proper application of form—for example, Christ's words at the last supper—to matter—bread and wine. So the Council gave its blessing to an older formulary; the sacraments, it said, performed *ex opere operato* (by virtue of their own inner coherence).

Trent in one sense taught an apotheosis of the material, the palpable, and the limited. Thus it defined the church not as an invisible congregation of the elect, but as the corporate body of all the baptized, which necessarily included the morally halt and lame. And what of the physically halt and lame? It stood to reason that if Christ could be brought down upon an altar in the shape of bread by the mumbled Latin of an insignificant and no doubt sinful priest, there should be available to the faithful similar if less noble rituals for a body suffering from one or another of the multitude of afflictions to which flesh is heir.

This conviction took root in the Catholic consciousness not so much because of the short and rather laconic conciliar decree on extreme unction as because of the overall consistency of the tridentine testament. So long as an infant science did not seriously dispute that all of nature was an intimate coupling of the material and spiritual—a view as old as Aristotle and the stuff of poets no less than of philosophers—it did not seem at all unlikely to the tridentine Catholic that an interventionist God should choose to intervene in behalf of his sick children by way of ritual and physical symbol.[16]

The Protestant Reformation with its emphasis upon transcendence was a radical effort to spiritualize the Christian vocation. The Council of Trent rejected this view in the name of a revelation that it construed to mean that the physical *qua* physical possesses an instrumental sacredness. The sacramental principle was wider than the seven sacraments. That there was great risk here of keeping open the door to those superstitious practices that had so outraged the reformers, the conciliar fathers were fully aware. Their awareness expressed itself in the legislation of internal reform they passed, which to a great extent was designed to provide well-ordered ecclesial life at the grass-roots level—witness the enormous attention paid at Trent to the education and demeanor of the parochial clergy. Many of the highly legalistic decisions of the Roman congregations over the next four centuries might be interpreted as responding to the same concern.

But, even so, there existed within the tridentine synthesis an intrinsic tension between the carefully nuanced conciliar and (subsequent) papal teaching and the popular reception and understanding of that teaching. This was a scandal to John Henry Newman (1801-1890), who complained some years before he became a Catholic that Roman officials had routinely failed to place "a practical restraint upon the *natural* tendency of their system."[17] Here was a shrewd observation. There did indeed lie at the heart of post-Reformation Catholicism a "natural tendency" to blur the distinction between genuinely religious activity and superstition—so much so that authority was often reluctant to insist upon the distinction in individual cases. *Tolerari potest* (let the practice be allowed) was not infrequently the decision handed down by a bemused diocesan chancery or Roman congregation. Given Trent's principles, there appears to have been little chance of avoiding the problem; the physical cries out for quantification, ritual invites repetition, and the use of symbols degenerates all too easily into magic. Trent tried to walk a fine line between the spiritualism of its sectarian opponents and an age-old paganism which deified the powers of nature. The Roman Catholic attitude toward illness and its treatment reflected this bold attempt at balance.

The Sacerdotal Mission

There existed within the Roman Catholic community a remarkable consistency in thought and action during the four centuries between the Council of Trent and the second Council of the Vatican (1962-1965). It is permissible, therefore, to make certain generalizations about the tridentine church that might be hazardous if applied to Catholicism before 1545 or since 1965. Attitudes, for example, toward sickness and death, toward sexual morality, and toward the relationship between cultic practice and healing did not differ markedly between, say, the late sixteenth and early twentieth centuries. This is not to say that such attitudes did not have deep medieval or even ancient roots, nor that there were not significant differences in detail in the application of tridentine principles from locality to locality or from group to group. Even so, the fathers of Trent did manage to establish a system with massive staying-power, not least perhaps because, with the emphasis they placed upon divine immanence and sacramentality, they proposed a doctrine and a spirituality that readily recommended themselves to the bulk of the Catholic people. Thus, when the development of scientific medicine in the nineteenth century posed new ethical questions, the Catholic response was a sophistication and elaboration of tridentine teaching, not a repudiation of it.

One safe generalization is that Trent, by insisting upon interlocking sacramentality with all phases of the Christian life, sharply intensified the clericalization of the Roman church. The necessity of a duly ordained priest to perform the sacred rituals was central to the functioning of the tridentine system. Nothing the council did was to be of more importance to the future of Catholicism than its delineation of the ideal priest. He was to be well if narrowly educated, decently but not extravagantly supported, wedded to his parish, subject to his bishop, sober, unworldly, and sustained in his vocation by the regular prayer of the breviary. He was still viewed as a member of a distinct caste—a world away in this regard, at least theoretically, from the Protestant preacher—but he was to see the justification of his status in sacramental service to those less spiritually endowed than he. In order to attain so far as was possible the realization of this ideal, the fathers of Trent

set out in detail the regulations of clerical residence, the financial arrangements, the type of professional training—in new institutions called seminaries—out of which was to emerge this dominant father-figure of tridentine
Catholicism.[18]

Despite Trent's explicit injunction, however, a system of seminaries
developed only slowly and unevenly. Pius IV (d. 1565) tried to set a good
example by establishing the Collegio Romano within months of the closure
of the council.[19] His nephew, Charles Borromeo (1538-1584), Archibishop of
Milan, set up three seminaries in his vast diocese, and the Primate of Portugal
opened one in 1565. The newly founded (1540) Society of Jesus was active
and effective in this task of clerical education, especially in Italy and Poland.
But there was no seminary in Ireland, thanks to English conquest and penal
laws, until the end of the eighteenth century. The seminary at Eichstadt
(1564) stood in lonely eminence among the great sees of the Holy Roman
Empire until Münster (1610) and Prague (1630) finally followed suit. There is
some irony in the fact that the seminary model eventually adopted everywhere else came from France, where the government, jealous as usual of its
prerogatives, never allowed the formal promulgation of the disciplinary
decrees of the Council of Trent. Despite this typically gallican prohibition,
Jacques Olier (1608-1657) and his colleagues at St. Sulpice in Paris worked
out in detail the curriculum, spirituality, and life-style that were almost to
define the training of the parish clergy until the eve of the second Vatican
Council.[20]

It need hardly be said that Trent's priestly ideal, like all other ideals, was
never entirely realized and that indeed the breaching of it was common
enough testimony to human frailty and to the limits of the best-laid plans.
Nevertheless, the fact remains that under the tridentine dispensation the
sluggard and the reprobate could no longer expect ecclesiastical prefer-
ment. Gradually, as the turmoil and violence of the wars of religion (1559-
1648) subsided, the seminary-educated priests became the norm, with the
result that every village in those parts of Europe still in communion with
Rome had its own representative of the Council of Trent. In that rural,
parochial, largely illiterate world—in that "universe of Peasants"[21] that
Europe and Europe's dependencies continued to be until the mid-nineteenth
century, when technology finally began to break down the walls of separation which had from time immemorial divided one little region from
another—the parish priest was uniquely important. He might have been a
brilliant or a dull man, personally effective or ineffective; he might have been
liked or disliked or, sometimes, hated. He was never ignored. He and his
confreres, imbued with a stern self-confidence which was another tridentine
characteristic, believed that they played by right the essential role in daily
Catholic life and were, besides, the lynch-pins of society, because without
them the parishes—the elemental social units—would not exist. Their people did not dispute them on this point nor did their bitterest enemies. For

instance, the persecution of English Catholics during the reign of Elizabeth I (1558-1603) concentrated on destroying the priests trained in the semi-naries-in-exile on the continent, on the assumption that once the priesthood was eliminated, the Catholic church as a viable entity would wither away. The queen's policy in this regard was eminently successful.[22]

The attitude of the parish priest, therefore, toward wellness and illness, caring and curing, and the rites of passage, although by no means the only factor, was crucially important in framing tridentine Catholicism's response to matters related to health care. And special emphasis needs to be given to the fact that the parish priest was both a preacher and a confessor to a degree uncommon among his pre-Reformation counterparts, who had offered mass, baptized, and witnessed marriages but who had been most of the time too ill-trained to impart any kind of formal instruction to the faithful. Increasingly during the years after Trent the parish priest—a regular and sustained pres-ence in the local community, unlike the medieval friar who had performed these functions before, if indeed they had been performed at all—made his influence felt from the pulpit and through the grill of the confessional.[23]

In some places he made his presence felt in the direct practice of medi-cine. It is difficult to be precise as to where or when this so-called *medicina clericalis* was carried on, because strictly speaking it was against the canon law and therefore its practitioners tended to remain discreetly quiet about it. Trent had explicitly, if obliquely, confirmed earlier legislation on the subject by forbidding clerics to engage in any "secular" profession. Clerical medi-cine lingered on nevertheless, particularly in remote locations where a physician was not available and where the parish priest was virtually the only educated person in the area. There was, to be sure, an older tradition which linked religion and medicine to the extent that in the early middle ages almost all European medical practitioners were monks. But the legists of the thirteenth century had condemned this link, and chiefly for two reasons: first, because increasingly clerics had taken to the study and practice of medicine as a way of making money instead of as a way of performing gratis a work of Christian mercy in the relief of human suffering; second, because the skills available to the practitioner were so limited that many a patient died as a direct result of his ministrations, especially if a surgical procedure were involved. The law clearly reflected a fear that *medicina clericalis* could arouse widespread hatred against the clerical estate.[24]

There is enough evidence to suggest, however, that even centuries later, in tridentine times, clerics were still practicing some forms of medicine. In 1626, for example, the Congregation for the Propagation of the Faith (the Vatican bureau in charge of the missions) forbade priests in Bulgaria to "dispense medicines—and in particular laxatives—to the sick, whether they be of the Faith or not." But seven years later the same congregation granted permission to an English Jesuit (who had been trained as a physician before entering the society) to practice medicine on the mission, so long as such activity was not his principal occupation and so long as he took no money for it. In 1641 an even broader mandate was given to the missionaries, who were allowed to practice medicine as a means of aiding in the conversion of unbelievers, provided that they were "truly learned in the profession," that they performed no surgery, that they worked without compensation, and that there were no other doctors available.[25]

This last proviso touched upon a condition as common in parts of Europe as in the mission lands, and it led to a practical softening of the law's rigor, so much so that by the eighteenth century *medicina clericalis* was experiencing a kind of revival. Much of what the parish priest did for his people in this regard might be categorized as simple procedures in first aid. But not infrequently medical practice was carried much farther. For instance, a manual appeared in Italy in 1745 (and went into numerous print-ings) that instructed the parish priest on how to treat illnesses associated with childbirth and even on how to perform a cesarean section when necessary.[26]

Despite the survival of clerical medicine—abetted to some extent by Enlightenment intellectuals who praised it as the one useful service per-formed by an otherwise parasitic profession—the pastor's chief role in the drama of health care had to do with his task as sanctifier and spiritual teacher of his people. He had little enough to say about wellness as such, except that it was a gift of God, as fleeting as one of Shakespeare's seven ages of man, and as tenuous as the next pestilence or accident could make it. Here, he said continually, we have no lasting city, here we have no abiding stay. "Remem-ber, man," he intoned each year at the beginning of Lent as he rubbed ashes upon the foreheads of his parishioners, "remember that thou art dust, and to dust thou shalt return." Pain is our lot in this valley of tears, for we are the banished children of Eve, the victims of our own sins and of all sin, redeemed by the suffering of Calvary and promised the robust health of a resurrected body only after we have endured a crucifixion of our own. Tridentine Catholi-cism was not a religion of social amelioration or of humanitarian concerns; it was as relentlessly other-worldly as its Calvinist rival.

The parish priest, therefore, had a great deal more to say about the other side of the coin, illness and its concomitant suffering. On this subject there was basic consistency throughout the tridentine period, with the tone set more by spiritual writers than by academic theologians. So Robert Bellar-mine, the most distinguished of the thinkers to emerge during the era imme-diately after the council, expressed his conviction that human pain was a sharing in Christ's redemptive pain more eloquently and with far wider influence in a popular tract than he did in his massive formal tomes.[27] Francis de Sales (1567-1622), an even more influential teacher than Bellarmine, stated (1609) in his typically succinct manner the conventional wisdom: "We must accept the sickness that God wishes, in the place he wishes, among the Persons he wishes, and with the inconveniences he wishes."[28] Such views as these the parish priest was invited to ponder and to transmit to his people. Suffering was a *sine qua non* condition of sanctity; this was a dictum that tridentine Catholicism took for granted. Suffering was always judged as edificatory and expiatory if it were accepted in the right spirit. The Council of Trent had stubbornly reasserted the notion of the *temporal* punishment due to sin, punishment to be inflicted in time, either in this world or in purgatory. Clearly, pain and illness were part of the purging process—a kind of good work—through which believers had to pass before they could experience the blessed vision of peace. To suffer, therefore, was to embark upon "the royal road of the holy cross," and those who suffered most were deemed to be the holiest of all.[29]

Prudential limits, however, were placed upon this principle. The church militant admitted of many levels of spiritual capacity. Not everyone could raise pain to the level of ecstasy. Francis of Assisi (1182-1226), who had borne upon his body the very wounds of Jesus, could be admired by all but imitated by only a small elite. The parish priest urged acts of self-denial upon his people, especially during the formal penitential seasons preceding Christmas and Easter, during the "ember days" which marked the beginning of the four seasons, on the vigils of great feasts, and on every Friday. But his ordinary message to the men and women in the pews in front of him was a plea to accept humbly the physical pain which was all too familiar a part of their lives, and of his. One might well argue that stigmatics like Francis of Assisi could have been more easily venerated, and understood, in an age when childbirth, stone, amputation, toothache, and all other conceivable ills had to be endured with only minimal medical aid and with anesthetic which at best could only dull the agony. Sunday after Sunday, in any event, the people were likely to hear their parish priest invoke some variation on the Pauline theme that it was their vocation "to make up what is lacking in the sufferings of Christ," but to do so according to the spiritual rank with which God had endowed them.[30] The discipline of knotted thongs, the bed of boards, and the hairshirt were reserved for the privileged few, and for them only under the strict supervision of a director.[31]

Not many of these clerics who did most to fashion the Catholic consciousness after the Council of Trent entered into the theologians' arcane discussions of how God permitted rather than caused sickness and pain, nor could they explain precisely what responsibility the devil had for human suffering. Formal exorcism was an exotic art, understood by few,[32] but demons were very real persons, their chief "a raging lion, seeking some one to devour,"[33] and it was a boldly enlightened priest indeed who discouraged his people from sprinklings of holy water or wearing of amulets designed to ward off that Satan who, in far-off days, had covered Job's body with boils and had flung him upon a dung heap. Priests and people were likely moreover to ascribe a specific suffering to a specific moral lapse, their own or others', a habit they maintained in the face of official ecclesiastical and theological disapproval. A particularly baneful result of this mentality was the savage persecution of those "witches" popularly believed to be in league with the devil—although of course such persecution was by no means a uniquely Catholic phenomenon.[34]

On another level—one upon which he may have felt surer of himself—the parish priest after the Council of Trent had to deal with problems related to health care from the point of view of moral obligation, and he had to begin with himself. He knew from his seminary training that he was bound under the penalty of grave sin to minister to the seriously sick and particularly to the dying among his parishioners, no matter what the inconvenience or even danger to himself. Ordinarily such ministry included a triad of sacraments: confession, anointing, and Viaticum (the Eucharist, that is, defined as food providing strength for the journey from one stage of life to the next). If the patient were unconscious, then the first and third of these ritual acts were necessarily omitted. The anointing could proceed in any case, and the priest was instructed by his rubrical books that he must be properly vested (wearing a stole, the sign of sacerdotal office), that he take care to join the form of the sacrament (the words, said in Latin: "Through this holy anointing, and through his most loving mercy, may the Lord forgive whatever you have done wrong" by the misuse of the senses) with the matter (the physical application of the oil specially blessed for the purpose by a bishop), and that he anoint the eyes, ears, nostrils, mouth, hands, and feet, six separate rites, each symbolizing the purgation of one of the senses that may have led the dying person into sin during his or her lifetime.[35] The priest could not evade his duty of ministration even at the risk of being infected himself. He could, however, take what the theological manuals called "prudent" precautions; a patient with a very infectious disease might be anointed on one organ only, or, if he had just confessed, the administration of extreme unction might be omitted altogether.[36]

It is worth noting that through these elaborate rules the sacramental system manifested itself as a great chain of being, for the sake of which the rubrical and casuistical demands were made. The tridentine Catholic firmly, if obscurely, believed that this particular dying person, by the eternal decision in the mind of God, was to be saved by the grace conferred by this particular administration of the sacrament, which God also foresaw would be administered at the risk of the life of this particular priest.

Those in the parish who were sick or wounded or simply so aged as to be in the danger of death could receive the sacrament. If the patient recovered and then fell ill once more, he could be anointed again any number of times. Those who were judged incapable of committing sin—small children, the permanently insane—were incapable of receiving extreme unction; the rule of thumb was that those who had no need of the sacrament of penance had no need either of the last anointing which, the Council of Trent had taught, was at root an extension of the church's penitential mission.[37] The deaf, dumb, and blind, by contrast, could be anointed because they may have been guilty of interior sins of thought or desire. A soldier on the field of battle, a felon about to be executed, or a traveller soon to embark upon a dangerous journey could not receive the sacrament, because the proximity of death in none of these cases stemmed from a present bodily infirmity. Opinions differed as to whether women in labor could be anointed; some parish priests did so on the ground that such a woman was genuinely ill, while others refrained, arguing that childbirth was simply the performance of a natural function. Pregnancy was never considered sufficient cause for administration of the sacrament.[38]

The appearance at the cottage door of the priest with a stole around his neck and a vial of holy oil in his hand often occasioned wails of grief from the sick person's friends and relatives, who saw this visitation as a sign that death would inevitably follow. Some even maintained that the administration of the "last sacraments" did the patients serious harm by convincing them they had no hope of recovery. So the parish priest had to remind his people regularly that to refuse the church's final ministrations was itself a mortal sin. Resistance, although it may have been widespread, was mostly impulsive and fleeting. In an age when life was usually "nasty, brutish and short," and when, among Catholic peoples, the sacramental principle loomed so large, the last rites enjoyed a status that no transitory emotions could dislodge.[39] Peter Canisius (1521-1597), the Jesuit writer whose celebrated *Catechism* went into 200 editions and was translated into twelve languages during his lifetime, probably expressed the settled view of most tridentine Catholics:

> Whereupon albeit the health of the body be not restored to the sick (for often we see the patient to die after the unction received), still in this sacrament there is special grace given most constantly to suffer the violence and trouble of sickness to the end, and afterward more patiently to receive death itself; and this it is that God has promised by his apostle: the prayer of faith will save the sick, and our Lord will ease him, and if he be in sins they shall be forgiven him.[40]

In the pulpit and the confessional the parish priest explained wellness, considered as a good in itself, under the rubric of the commandment "Thou shalt not kill." This was an imperative that applied first of all to oneself; direct suicide as well as any form of euthanasia was dimissed as out of hand. The doctrine, however, was not without nuance; exceptional circumstances or the promotion of a greater good might on occasion necessitate a person taking action that would bring about his or her death. It was not deemed suicide, for example, if a soldier remained at a dangerous post even though he would be killed as a result, nor if a virgin, to preserve her chastity, were "to embrace even certain danger of death," so great a good was her "integrity." The distinction between killing oneself and accepting the *certain* danger of death may not always have been clear in practice, but the moralists from whom the parish priests learned their lessons were perfectly straightforward and unequivocal that nobody was obliged to exercise extraordinary means merely to stay alive: "The ill can be excused who, a little before death, out of humility or to give good example, seek to be gathered into the earth, because they do not thereby intend to shorten life."[41]

The requirement to preserve one's life naturally extended to one's health. The parish priest was concerned, however, to point out that maintenance of health had primarily an instrumental function; one must keep oneself strong, not for the sheer animal joy of it, but in order to do one's duty in justice and charity and to take upon oneself the acts of physical self-denial recommended, indeed mandated, by the church. The body was the temple of the Holy Spirit and thus had to be cherished and cared for. Self-mutilation of any kind was sternly forbidden, unless amputation of a limb was called for in order to save one's life. In such an instance the good of the whole prevailed over the survival of the infected part. "Those Parents sin grievously who have their sons castrated in order to enhance their singing, even if the boys consent." (There was little dissent from this judgment except, significantly, in Italy where one seventeenth-century moralist argued that castrati contributed to the common good, because, thanks to them, "the divine praises [were] sung more sweetly in churches.")[42]

Over time the body would gradually decay, or in the twinkling of an eye it would be destroyed. How or when or even why was a decision locked in the mind of God, and it was a feckless enterprise to rail against that unalterable decision. One Catholic preacher, in 1618, chided his congregation for its lack of Christian patience: "Those that are sick afflict themselves that they cannot be well in health. And those that are well do run into disorders as though they hastened to be sick. If anything be amiss, instead of seeking a remedy by patience, they are more angry and make it worse."[43]

Tridentine Catholics were instructed to seek other, more mundane remedies as well. Indeed, they were told that they could be guilty of serious sin if they failed to follow the "informed opinions" of their physician, even to the point of taking prescribed medicines. The doctor, for his part, approached the confessional aware that his profession imposed upon him a long list of possible moral violations. Did he try to treat a serious illness without sufficient skill, or neglect to engage in "special study" when a certain case required it? Did he substitute eccentric forms of treatment, without the support of substantial medical opinion, when more conventional procedures were available? Did he carelessly absent himself when his patient was in danger, or, if justifiably absent, did he prevent other doctors from treating the patient? Did he persuade his patient to indulge in any act "contrary to God's honor or command, for example, pollution, incantation, superstition?" Did he without due cause excuse his patient from the church's law of fasting? Did he see to it that a patient gravely ill saw his confessor? Did he charge too much for his services? Did he fail to treat a poor person in danger of death because he would not be paid? If a surgeon, did he cause an abortion, or did he, more broadly, refuse to take advice in difficult operations?[44]

A physician was admonished to ask himself such questions when he examined his conscience, and indeed some of these queries might have been addressed to him in the confessional box. He would not, however, presuming he was a married man, be asked everything about his sexual life. Confessors were repeatedly warned to use "the maximum circumspection" (the words of Charles Borromeo) in interrogating penitents about sexual matters.[45] Alphonsus Liguori (1696-1787) summed up the mature tridentine consensus in this way: "Ordinarily speaking, the confessor is not bound nor is it fitting for him to inquire about sins of the married in respect to the marital debt, except that, as modestly as he can, he may ask wives if they have rendered it, for example by asking them if they have obeyed their husbands in everything. About other things let him be silent unless asked."[46] The prudence thus recommended to the confessor—and to the preacher as well—represented a considerable shift from pre-tridentine practice.[47] The severe Augustinian tradition, which had a sexual as well as a broader doctrinal context and which was so easily identified in the Catholic mind with Luther and Calvin, survived after Trent only among those latter-day Augustinians, the Jansenists. This was no doubt a significant and influential survival, one more testimony to Augustine's persuasive genius; but it was never more than a minority position among tridentine Catholics at large and its impact lessened drastically once the great school of seventeenth-century French Jansenists had passed away.

Augustine (354-430) had taught that sexual intercourse even within marriage was permissible only with explicit procreative intent (a far different proposition from the one that was to daunt Catholics in the twentieth century, that every act of sexual intercourse *had to be open* to procreative possibility). To be sure, the tridentine church continued to denounce abortion as murder, extramarital sex as lechery, and masturbation as self-indulgence which could cause serious bodily defects like blindness. (Nocturnal, and hence involuntary, emission was, by contrast, described as conducive to "physical health.")[48] But the *Catechism of the Council of Trent* explained the causes of marriage in a manner to dismay Augustinian rigorists of whatever denomination: "First of all, nature itself by an instinct implanted in both sexes impels them to such companionship, and this is further encouraged by the hope of mutual assistance in bearing more easily the discomforts of life and the infirmities of old age. A second reason for marriage is the desire of a family."[49]

Such a doctrine of the primacy of mutual solace was in accord with the radical optimism of tridentine Catholicism. This is not to say that the procreative element was eliminated or even denigrated in the church's official teaching. It did mean, however, that intercourse between married persons was morally licit for some reasons—the fostering of love, physical health, even venereal pleasure which otherwise might be sought in an adulterous union—other than procreation. It also opened the door a crack to the permissibility of birth control. The understanding, in any case, of the phrase *marital debt* underwent a change of some magnitude. The manuals of moral theology that the parish priest consulted spoke often of the economic burdens large numbers of children imposed upon families, especially among the poor. Little if anything was said about the effect upon the health of a woman subjected to frequent pregnancies, perhaps because women neither had nor thought they ought to have an organized voice to raise such an issue. The only permissible way to limit the number of conceptions was by abstinence, and here at least a woman might be able under certain economic circumstances to refrain on occasion from paying the marital debt. So, at any rate, some theologians argued. But although they wrestled manfully with the problem, they could not find a universally acceptable solution that was also consistent with traditional norms of sexual morality. The law of nature demanded that the act of intercourse be complete and integral. The sin of Onan, who spilled his seed on the ground, was fiercely condemned in the Bible.[50] Moralists wrote, moreoever, in and for a society in which great ignorance of physiology, especially female physiology, prevailed. What sort of noncoital intimacy was licit for married couples? Withdrawal of the penis followed by ejaculation *(coitus interruptus)* was clearly wrong, the moralists said. They were not quite sure about a withdrawal not followed by ejaculation *(amplexus reservatus)*; some of them hedged by suggesting that this practice might be venially, not mortally, sinful. Did touches and kisses that might—very likely would—result in orgasm provide a morally allowable alternative? Little wonder that in this jungle the confessor was urged to tread warily and not to ask too many questions.[51]

There were other reasons, besides the absence of a feminist lobby, that the issue of birth control, muddled as it was in its details, remained quiescent within the Roman Church until nearly the end of the tridentine era. Infant mortality was high and population pressure virtually non-existent. (An exception perhaps was Ireland, but the famine crisis there in the 1840s led to later marriage and vast emigration rather than to any coherent policy of restricting conceptions.) An overwhelmingly rural culture continued to put a premium on offspring who could take their places within the farm economy; children, to use the biblical image, were like arrows in the quiver, like olive plants around the table. Contraceptive methods were crude, often ineffective, often the "poisonous potions" that women sometimes took in order to abort and which therefore were identified officially and popularly as homicidal. The condom appeared in the middle of the seventeenth century, but it was expensive and from a moral point of view represented simply another version of *coitus interruptus*. Finally, it is surely safe to say that the issue was not faced squarely, because those who framed the official position—the bishops who taught it authoritatively, the theologians who interpreted it, and the parish priests who transmitted it to the married people under their direct charge—were all without exception celibate males and therefore did not encounter the problem in their day-to-day—or perhaps one should say their night-to-night—lives.

It would be easy to conclude that because the Catholic clergy were not allowed to enjoy sexual pleasure they made it their business to restrict as much as they could the enjoyment of their lay co-religionists. Such a conclusion, however, would leave out of account the fact that sexual teaching and practice among tridentine Catholics did not differ markedly from what prevailed in the Christian world at large. Contraception was frowned upon by most major denominations until well into the twentieth century. Before that no Catholic spokesman, not even the most dour Jansenist, could outdo the bleak attitude toward all things sexual routinely voiced by Puritan preachers in New England—happily married and well-adjusted men, one might suppose, with squads of dutiful children around them. Lack of sensitivity toward the sexual wants and needs of women was certainly not a Catholic preserve. Queen Victoria (1819-1901) was not a Catholic, but her abhorrence of the marriage bed—even though she shared it with a man she deeply loved—represented a long tradition and provided a pattern for generations of respectable, white, Anglo-Saxon, Protestant women.[52] Not before the triumph of secularism in the twentieth century was sexuality as such discovered to be a major health concern. Sexual "compatibility," understood in its emotional implications, would have seemed an effete concept to earlier times. Passion was a matter of animal vigor, particularly of masculine vigor. It is said that the young Louis XIV (1638-1715), when the urge was upon him, would go to his queen's boudoir; if she were indisposed for some reason, he, perfect gentleman that he prided himself upon being, would not disturb her, but instead would satisfy himself with the nearest available lady-in-waiting. The anecdote may not be true, but it is not without its point even so; the double standard, so pervasive at all levels of society, took it for granted that the only health issue involved in sexuality was the assuaging of the physical needs of a king or, indeed, of any normal male.

In theory, both Protestant and Catholic catechesis would have condemned the king's conduct as adultery. But there was a difference. Louis as a Catholic would go to confession (although in fact he seldom did so before old age) and, if he were genuinely sorry and resolutely determined not to repeat the misdeed, have the sin forgiven. The availability of the sacrament of penance—and not just to repair sexual transgressions—could conceivably cut two ways, and it probably did. Protestant critics of the sacramental system pointed to it as a source of the loose morals they discerned in Catholic countries like Italy and Spain; easy "forgiveness," they said, was an invitation to habitual vice. Tridentine Catholics responded that theirs was not a religion of instant and complete conversion, that the necessity imposed upon them as confessing their sins was itself a kind of deterrence as well as an occasion for nurturing within themselves sound dispositions of contrition and amendment. Evidence could no doubt be brought forward to support either position, although it might be harder to demonstrate that one nation was less sinful than another; that the moral tone of Georgian England, for example, was loftier than that of Leopoldine Austria. In any event, when it came to dealing with sexual questions within the tridentine church the parish priest, as always, acted as the agent between the official teachers and the men and women in the pews. And more often than not he developed a salty wisdom. One veteran pastor, who in his village church had heard thousands of confessions and, *ipso facto*, almost that many stories of sexual misconduct, counselled his younger brethren to be surprised at nothing they heard and to take into account that most of the people they served lived close to the stock.

The Popular Response

They were people of the earth, earthy. The large majority of tridentine Catholics, until well past 1900, wrenched their sustenance directly from the reluctant soil. Whether they lived in Catholicism's European heartland, or had emigrated to other temperate areas like Argentina, Australia, or the United States, or were indigenous populations in tropical places like the Philippines or Uganda, converted by missionaries active since the sixteenth century, they dwelt in a world in which staying alive from day to day was a constant struggle, a world of uncertainty and pain. They stood in awe of a powerful nature which appeared to them, as it had to their ancestors back through countless centuries, to combine hostility with caprice. Some years, to be sure, were fatter than others; some land was more fertile, some climates more benign. Through the cycles of inflation and depression some did better than others. But overall, theirs was a life of chronic shortage; overall, they endured inadequate diet, poor housing, and bad sanitation.[53] They suffered more and died sooner than it is possible for their descendants, who stand beyond the door of modernization opened by science and technology, ever fully to appreciate.

They were not, of course, without their joys, not strangers to merriment, festivals, and fresh wine. They had their moments of triumph and serene satisfaction. The frugality which was their ordinary lot made their feasts all the dearer to them. They were neither stuffed nor hollow men, although their eyes often glittered with hunger. The very severity of their existence lent zest and excitement to their lives, in contrast, perhaps to the blandness of a consumerist and hedonist society, built upon the predictability of central heating, the contraceptive pill, and the welfare state. Whether they were "happier" than their descendants or not is a question no mere historian dares ask.

The genius of the tridentine system, but its danger also, was its capacity to mesh its doctrine and practice, based upon the principle of divine immanence, with the acquired habits of country people. Even the dullest peasant could understand the soothing and curative property of oil, the nutritive value of bread, and the cleansing effect of water. The church provided blessings and a sacramental context for all the important human moments from the womb to the deathbed. Formal rites marked the merging of one season into the next. Blessings were furnished for crops, catches of fish, domestic animals, and farm implements. Special saints' day observances focused upon promoting the physical well-being of a particular parish or region. In times of pestilence, the local church often organized processions, mobs of frightened penitents in effect, to implore God to forgive the sinfulness which was conceived to be the cause of the calamity; this common and popular practice, when it defied, as it often did, official rules of quarantine, brought with it a confrontation between church and state.[54]

Beneath this institutionalized framework, and to some degree mingling with it, there existed a vast underworld of cultic activities which had their beginning long before Trent—in many instances indeed long before the advent of Christianity—and which breathed the immemorial rhythms of the countryside as much as they did any religious sensibility. It was to be expected in an age of primitive and sometimes fraudulent medical care, if any care at all was available, that many such activities should be oriented toward warding off or curing disease. As late as the 1770s a Bavarian priest attracted a tremendous following when he proclaimed that illness was a result of demonic possession and should be treated therefore by exorcists rather than doctors. Thousands waited upon his ministrations, and although his movement died with him, the popular conviction that he had been a legitimate healer remained. Not without reason was it said that some islands in the Caribbean became, after the arrival of the Europeans and the subsequent introduction of African slaves, one hundred percent Catholic as well as one hundred percent voodoo. Confessors despaired of persuading Italian women not to mark their bodies with texts from the Bible in order to keep themselves healthy. In eastern France pilgrimages to a wooded shrine, where mothers sought relief for their sick children from a saint who also happened to have been a dog, continued into the latter part of the nineteenth century. In southern Germany a book appeared in 1771 (and promptly went into ten editions) that prescribed as treatment for a sick (and therefore bewitched) cow a dose of blessed salt or bread and forced inhalation of smoke from a fire of blessed sulphur or palm branches. Young men who succeeded in leaping unscathed across a bonfire lit on the vigil of the feast of St. John the Baptist (June 24) were guaranteed good health through the following year. Seers and wizards could be found trudging along every road, ready to cure sprains, burns, or scrofula by a combination of ancient herbal remedies and pseudo-Christian incantations. One French peasant treated rheumatism by applying the bodies of boiled cats to the painful joints, all the while mumbling a set of paters and aves. Prayer to St. Apolline, who had been martyred by having her teeth torn out, together with signs of the cross traced on the sore jaw, was the sure way to get rid of toothache. A pilgrim who had gone to the shrine of St. Hubert in the Ardennes could cure rabies by using a key obtained there combined with certain prayers and sacred gestures. At the end of the seventeenth century, Naples was reputed to have eleven miracle-working statues of the Virgin Mary.[55]

The survival of so much superstition among the masses of tridentine Catholics appears, at first glance, to have confirmed the strictures of Protestant polemicists upon the intrinsically idolatrous character of Catholicism. The truth, however, is considerably more complicated. Certainly the melding into bizarre combinations of crude rural nostrums with pagan ritual and Christian symbol (or vice versa) was commonplace, no less in Catholic Europe than in the mission lands, and it persists to this day. The fact is that tridentine Catholicism, imbued with the principle of immanence, was peculiarly vulnerable to popular cults that involved distorted sacramental acts. The difference between the institutional church—which recommended veneration of relics, blessings for animals, and rogation-day processions to seek divine aid for the bounty of the seasons, to say nothing of the formal ritual grounded in oil and bread—and a populace that invoked age-old rites and incantations, more or less Christianized, to ward off evil was a difference of *degree*, not of a kind. The parish priest, fresh from a tridentine seminary, might disapprove of what he conceived to be the excesses of his people in, say, mixing herbal potions with prayers to the Virgin or seeking cures from a wandering seer with talismans pinned to his hat. But the sin lay in exaggeration, overindulgence, and extravagance, not in the use of physical things for sacred purposes. Neither the priest nor his hierarchical superiors were prepared to deny the reality of an interventionist God who sanctified the Christian people through ritual observance, who, within the confines of the village church, worked the physical miracle of changing bread into Christ's body every morning. And, in any case, how far removed was the average parish priest, despite his time in the seminary, from the tribal instincts of the people from whom he had been taken and to whom he had now returned?[56]

He often found himself hard put to rein in the enthusiasms of his people, especially because he was not totally out of sympathy with those enthusiasms. He faced a dilemma. On the one hand, he risked the outbreak of anticlericalism within the parish if he resisted too forcefully the importunities of his people to grant his official sanction to their enterprises; on the other, he risked the wrath of his relatively sophisticated bishop—particularly from the eighteenth century onward—if he encouraged or winked at the lighting of bonfires on St. John's eve. Most of the time he evaded as best he could the unpleasant choices and hoped no one would ask him how the relief offered to the sick by extreme unction differed from boiled cats applied to rheumatic joints.

To understand the ambivalence tridentine Catholicism experienced in this regard, one must very often remind oneself of the commitment made at Trent to the instrumental function of physical things in the process of justification. The great breach within western Christendom at the time of the Reformation turned indeed upon differing opinions about the value of "faith" and "works" to the Christian man or woman seeking salvation. "Works," so said the fathers of Trent, played an integral part of that process, and they included in the meaning of the word the intrinsic soundness of the material. Matter participated in the divine. Material things therefore were genuine conduits of grace and capable of sharing in the supernatural order. The primacy belonged not to the word alone, but to the Word made flesh. Here was a difference in kind that separated Protestant from Catholic, an irreconcilable difference that no amount of effort has ever managed to solve. The trouble on the Catholic side was that Trent could not, simply by denouncing it, eliminate the manipulative interpretation of its doctrine. Unlettered people stubbornly held to the view that sacramental action had to be automatic in its results, a species of magic. Perhaps it was too much to ask a person writhing in pain that he remember that all ritual acts were at root not demands, not bargains, but petitions.

A solution of sorts to this problem was worked out during the last phase of the tridentine epoch, from the mid-nineteenth century to the mid-twentieth. It did not stem from a flagging of interest among Catholics in extra-medical treatment of sickness. Indeed, it is ironic that the great flowering of pilgrimage devotion should have occurred just at the moment when scientific medicine was embarking upon its dramatic advancement. What led to the solution was the curious combination of two typically modern developments. First was the swift and unprecedented growth of centralization within the Catholic church. The arm of Rome had never been so long as it was during (and since) the pontificate of Pius IX (1846-1878). The relative independence of diocese and parish, at least on a day-to-day basis, was virtually swept away during the eras of the French Revolution and Napoleon. The papal bureaucracy, of which the bishops increasingly became mere agents, kept a stern eye upon the exuberances of local piety.[57] Simultaneously, new modes of mass communication and transport made it easy for people to learn about and travel to glamorous centers of devotion which they quickly came to esteem more than the humdrum ones closer to home.

The miraculous shrines of La Salette and Lourdes (in France), of St. Ann de Beaupré (Canada), of Knock (Ireland), of the Virgin of Guadalupe (Mexico), and of Fatima (Portugal), their walls festooned with the crutches of the cured, have all been preempted by the institutional church. The hierarchy has taken great care to avoid what might be called a peasant reputation from attaching itself, for example, to the healing capacity of the waters of the fountain at Lourdes, where of the thousands of pilgrims who have claimed healing, only sixty-four have been "certified" by ecclesiastical authority. No doubt this exercise of control has helped the church maintain its hold upon at least a portion of its people—during the early 1980s three million pilgrims visited Lourdes each year—culturally uprooted by industrialization and prone to alienation from religion by the whole complexus of modernity.[58] But it has also managed thereby to minimize the tridentine dilemma by insisting upon the petitionary character of these devotions and by formally granting the distinction between public and private revelation: Even the most fervent devotee of the cult of Lourdes must admit that no Catholic is bound to believe that Bernadette Soubirous really saw a lady in a dump outside that Hautes-Pyréneés town in 1858 or that the waters of her fountain have cured anybody of anything.

But in the end all cures fail; the most skilled physician gives way at last to the power of death, and even God does not intervene forever. Bernadette Soubirous, who never washed in the waters she had discovered, died after hideous suffering of bone cancer at the age of thirty-five (1879), and the funeral mass was chanted over her wasted body, as it was over countless other tridentine Catholics less brave and holy than she. It was a somber affair, this rite of farewell, filled with stern reminders that "while we lament the departure of our sister, thy servant, out of this life, we know that we are most certainly to follow her." The amount of pomp depended often upon the social standing of the deceased; a rich man might be buried with a solemn high mass—a priest, assisted by a deacon and a subdeacon—or, in Poland, with three masses going on simultaneously. Nothing was more bleak than a pauper's funeral, no one more abject than he who had no money to leave behind him for masses to be offered for his swift deliverance from purgatory. The village church was in any case suffused in gloom, the priest dressed in black vestments, the hymns sung without accompaniment. The theme was not so much the resurrection as the judgment. *Dies irae, dies illa*, the choir sang: "O day of wrath, that dreadful day. Deliver me, O Lord, from everlasting death on that day of terror, when the heavens and the earth will be shaken, as thou comest to judge the world by fire."

Yet tridentine Catholics did their best to believe what they recited each Sunday in the creed, that they belonged to the communion of saints, that life for them was destined not to be taken away, but only changed. So however sad or fearful they may have felt, they listened with bounding hope to one of the most beautiful of the Gregorian chants, sung as the corpse was carried slowly out of the church to the cemetery: "May the angels take thee into paradise; may the martyrs come to welcome thee on thy way, and lead thee into the holy city, Jerusalem. May the choir of angels welcome thee, and with Lazarus who once was poor may thou have everlasting rest."[59]

Caring and Curing

One of the most striking features of Martin Luther's preaching was the insistence that the loftiest Christian "calling" was to be lived out in the world, not within the confines of a remote monastery or convent.[60] This represented not only a repudiation of Luther's own monastic background, but also of the whole notion of a hierarchically structured spiritual experience to which the church gave witness. The old tradition was that certain individuals were called by God to live in a "higher" state than their fellows, to be guided by the evangelical counsels over and above the observance of the commandments required for everybody, to withdraw from the world and its concerns and its pomps, and to formalize all this by taking upon themselves (as parish priests did not do) the vows of poverty, chastity, and obedience. Predictably, the Fathers of Trent rejected Luther's egalitarianism and maintained that the so-called religious orders of monks, nuns, and friars, although in some instances in need of internal reform, did in fact enjoy a higher than ordinary calling and were essential to the full flowering of the church's life.

Among the evangelical counsels were the admonitions to "visit the sick" and to "bury the dead."[61] It was natural that such works of charity, to the extent that they took on an organized form, should have come to be associated with religious whose vocation demanded a more elevated level of response to cries of distress than that of the average Christian. Thus the *medicina clericalis* that flourished during the early middle ages simply meant the free medical care offered by monks to their tenants and to others living in the neighborhood of their monasteries. Various orders of men dedicated themselves to alleviating, as far as they could, the sufferings of galley slaves, lepers, Christians captured by Moslem pirates, or even foot-sore travellers. Some brothers practiced in-home nursing, others maintained pesthouses in the towns. The Alexian Brothers began their corporate existence in the Netherlands and Rhenish Germany as buriers of victims of the plague and evolved into an order that specialized in operating insane asylums and, in nineteenth-century England at least, hospices for alcoholic priests.[62]

Trent, the council of "good works," supported these endeavors and others like them. But there remained much more sickness and misery than it was possible to deal with. That is why the intervention of Vincent de Paul in the seventeenth century was of such monumental importance.

Vincent de Paul (1580-1660) did more than any other individual to rationalize and institutionalize Catholicism's commitment to caring for the sick. Through his various foundations, and particularly through the Sisters of Charity (whom he recruited indifferently among ladies of the highest rank and among pink-cheeked country girls), he brought intense, organized charitable activity to the Paris slums and to blighted country districts. The precedent had been set for a system that was destined to be imitated everywhere and to affect profoundly the tridentine church as well as society at large. And a revolutionary precedent it was, because prior to the time of the Sisters of Charity, nuns were invariably cloistered, always prohibited from working in the world. Vincent de Paul and his colleagues opened a huge reservoir of feminine energy and talent, all the more so because the older orders of women tended to expand into activist roles, and the scores of orders founded after de Paul's death followed with few exceptions the Vincentian model. But it was the Sisters of Charity themselves who provided in their garb a universal symbol of gentle healing.

> There was no idea of giving them a special habit. Like women of the people they were dressed in a simple drab-colored dress, with their hair stuffed into a cap. In the course of time this dress developed. A coif was allowed to those sisters who found too great discomfort in the exposure of their faces to the cold air; then, for uniformity, the coif became obligatory for all. It was made originally of unstiffened white linen and hung down over the shoulders on either side of the face. Then the two side pieces were slightly raised; to keep them in position they were starched. Finally, with this stiffening the two sides were made to project like wings. The Sisters of Charity thus have wings to fly to the help of the sick and the poor. In this way there gradually developed that religious habit which is known the world over as the emblem of French charity.[63]

By the eve of the Revolution (1789), there were 426 houses of the Sisters of Charity in France alone.[64] A few years later the order was introduced by Elizabeth Ann Seton into the United States, where it operated under diocesan rather than more centralized management.[65] This administrative detail mattered little; what counted was that new orders continued to spring up under the same inspiration, even if the women who joined them did not wear the fabled winged coif. Simple black and white was the garb of the Dominican Sisters of the Sick-Poor, founded by Nathaniel Hawthorne's daughter Rose, a convert to Catholicism, while in Brittany in the 1840s. The Little Sisters of the Poor wore black and brown when they started their worldwide apostolate to the aged.[66] One order of nuns dedicated itself exclusively to caring for patients terminally ill with cancer, that they might die in dignity.

The first nursing sisters were not nurses in the modern professional sense of the term. They "visited" the sick, by which they meant they brought their concern and willingness to alleviate what sufferings they could by keeping the patient clean, decently fed, and as physically comfortable as possible. But at the same time they were beginning the evolutionary process that led by the early twentieth century to the thousands of hospitals, dispensaries, and asylums all over the world where scientific medicine was practiced with nursing nuns as full partners in the enterprise. The most spectacular example was the association of Dr. William J. and Dr. Charles H. Mayo with the Franciscan nuns of Rochester, Minnesota. On 1 November 1887, the doors of St. Mary's Hospital were opened for the first time, with a staff of five nursing sisters under the direction of the Mayo brothers. The nuns, by scrimping and saving, had raised all the money themselves and thus took the initial step leading to the development of one of the greatest medical complexes of all time. They opened a nursing school as well and even enrolled in it themselves in order to refine their skills. The Doctors Mayo (who were not Catholics) took a dim view of this latter idea. "Dr. Charlie and I," Dr. Will observed, "had always done our surgical work with the sisters' help, and we were much concerned as to whether any one could be taught, even by the sisters themselves, to perform the duties of the nurse as well as they. We had absolute confidence, then as now, in this group of women who have no thought outside their duty to the sick."[67]

The achievement at Rochester was in many ways typical of tridentine Catholicism in its American manifestation. The church in the United States, which produced few remarkable thinkers or artists, continued well into the twentieth century to depend upon European models for ideas and ideals. But at the same time, American Catholics revealed a striking ability to institutionalize and organize, and, most visible of all, to express their ethos in brick and mortar. Poor immigrants and their children built great churches and a vast system of schools. They raised unprecedented amounts of money to take on an enterprise so colossal in scale that nothing like it had been seen by any Catholic community anywhere in the world at any time. When the fathers gathered for the second Council of the Vatican—at the end of the tridentine era—there were in operation 950 Catholic hospitals in the United States, with a bed capacity of 156,000, serving sixteen million patients a year. Nearly all of these were the work of religious orders of women, as were the 376 homes for the aged and the 337 nursing schools.[68] A peculiarly American drive to excel, combined with a predictable tridentine exclusivity, led to the foundation of medical schools under Catholic auspices, to the formation of associations of Catholic doctors and nurses, and the provision of learned journals for them to read.

But even thus professionalized, the sisters and their institutions of healing clearly gave priority to cure of soul over cure of body. They acted out of no mere humanitarian impulse, but out of the conviction that performing the corporal works of mercy was a primary means of securing salvation for those who performed them, as well as an occasion of supernatural grace to those for whom they were performed. These were "good works" in the tridentine sense, sacramental as well as ameliorative.

The same point of view suffused that other great tridentine movement, the missions outside Europe.[69] From the century of the Reformation onward the Roman church, to misappropriate George Canning's famous aphorism, "called the new world into existence to redress the balance of the old." Even before the first session of the Council of Trent, missionaries were following the footsteps of explorers and conquerors into Asia and the Americas. They were predominantly members of religious orders of men, chiefly Franciscan friars and Jesuits. (Religious women did not come to the missions in any numbers before the mid-nineteenth century.) Medical activities were always considered part of the missioners' apostolate, but curing illness was never their first objective. They used medical skills as an entree so that their spiritual message would be listened to. Those skills, while perhaps not significant in an absolute sense, were nevertheless impressive to a backward clientele, and they did in fact relieve much suffering.

The last phase of European colonialist expansion, that into Africa in the latter part of the nineteenth century, coincided with rapid advances in scientific medicine, and the medical component of Catholic missionary activity predictably displayed from that time on a new sophistication.[70] Even so, the old priorities did not change. (Twenty years ago I knew an aged nun, retired in Ireland, who had served around the turn of the century as a nurse in a hospital in Nigeria; her greatest boast was that she had baptized fifteen hundred dying infants who, she said proudly, were now in heaven praying for her.) The tridentine church was remarkably consistent in resisting the allure of humanitarian theory, so that its last great spokesman, Pope Pius XII (1939-1958), could write more than four hundred years after the missionary movement had begun: "We wish to pay the highest tribute to the care taken of the sick [in] hospitals, leprosaria, dispensaries, homes for the aged and for new mothers, and orphanages. Such works of charity are undoubtedly of the highest efficacy in preparing the souls of non-Christians and in drawing them to the faith and to the practice of Christianity."[71]

Tridentine Ethics

Out of the Council of Trent and tridentine theology came a strong confirmation of the ancient *jus naturale*, the natural law, which was less the Pauline "law written in men's hearts"[72] and more the expression of the classical view of nature as essentially changeless reality. "Human nature" is understandable, not so much through historical processes as through the constant functioning of the various human faculties. The concept of God's sovereignty was thus adhered to by attributing to every human act a goal or purpose in harmony with God's own intention and revealed by the very "nature" of the act. So, for example, sexual intercourse was clearly (physically) designed to produce offspring, and therefore any attempt to frustrate that object (except by a periodic abstinence which took advantage of the "natural" rhythms of a woman's reproductive system) was unnatural and wrong.

This static view of natural law had immense consequences not only for tridentine Catholicism's judgments about sexual morality, but also for its attitude toward the whole field of medical ethics.[73] Masturbation and homosexual activity (as distinguished from homosexual orientation) were always and under all circumstances sinful, because they involved the obvious misuses of human organs. But what about medical procedures—amputation, for example, or the administration of mood-altering drugs—which just as obviously interfered with the discernibly ordinary course of nature? What about the prolongation of life beyond what nature apparently intended? And, the largest question of all, how did the tridentine Catholic square the advances of medical science with his or her notion of the redemptive character of pain?

The answers to these and related questions were determined—the word is not too strong—by the application of the theory of natural law. So long, for instance, as anesthetic did not permanently impair the proper functions of the human body, its use was deemed permissible. "Ordinary" means must be employed to sustain life, "extraordinary" ones need not be. As for amputations, a corollary of the natural law, the so-called "principle of totality," could be invoked whereby the destruction of a particular limb was permitted for the sake of preserving the "natural" body as a whole.

Roman Catholic medical and sexual ethics adhered consistently to the natural-law model from the Council of Trent to the 1960s. There were, however, considerable differences in the application of principles between pre-industrial and industrial societies. The rapid development of a sophisticated, scientific medicine from the middle of the nineteenth century, and the discovery of cheap and virtually fool-proof methods of contraception in the middle of the twentieth, put an enormous strain on the conceptual system— or at least on the consensus about it—and eventually broke it apart. But before that, the application was relatively simple, because the societal conditions were relatively simple. The questions raised by the primitive medical ethics of Paul Zacchia (1621) and Michael Boudewyns (1666) form a curious hodgepodge by contemporary standards: Is a doctor permitted to pray for illness in order that he will have patients? May a magistrate allow a Jew to practice medicine in his jurisdiction? May a doctor ever prescribe masturbation?[74] The eighteenth and early nineteenth centuries witness no significant advance over such preoccupations. The *medicina clericalis* that survived into the nineteenth century was much less concerned with adumbrating the moral norms for medical practice—they seemed clear enough—than with instructing the parish clergy in fundamental skills to serve people in rural areas who were more often than not without the regular services of a physician. The genre, its name changed to *pastoral medicine*, has not been unknown in the twentieth century, when it has tended to concentrate on psychological matters rather than anatomical. A harbinger of the future has been the relatively recent emphasis Catholic thinkers have given to a theology that questions the notion of body as instrument and instead stresses physical and emotional wellness as an essential aspect of the redemptive process. "Holiness is Wholeness," was Joseph Goldbrunner's celebrated expression of this view.

A not unrelated phenomenon was the willingness of Catholics to adopt twentieth-century categories with regard to mental illness; even to embrace, albeit gingerly, at least some of the principles put forward by the likes of Freud and Jung. The analogy between sacramental confession and psychotherapy was often pointed out, and Catholics, once confident enough to reject what they conceived to be the overstated sexual component of Freudianism, appeared to have no fear of terms like *ego*, *id*, and *unconscious*. But the tridentine church until its very last days remained faithful in this regard to its clerical ethos: The key question raised during the 1950s, in Germany first and then elsewhere, was how the parish priest might contribute to the spiritual well-being of his people by a proper and faith-informed application to the insights of psychology—application to himself no less than to those with whom he had professional dealings.[75]

The rapid advance of scientific medicine gave rise to a Roman Catholic medical ethics as such; to an avalanche of works in all languages, all departing sharply from the concerns of pastoral medicine and all, until very recently, representing the natural-law tradition.[76] The moral theologians in this area have been extremely sophisticated, and they have not feared to tread into questions involving highly complex therapeutic procedures. They have carried with them, until very recently, their natural-law baggage, and at the risk of oversimplifying, it might be said that they have approached every problem of medical morals from the vantage point of the principle of double effect.

This notion, also called the indirect voluntary, was developed during the period immediately after the Council of Trent and received definitive expression from Jean Jury in the mid-nineteenth century.[77] The principle has been succinctly stated by Gerald Kelly:

> The principle of double effect, as the name itself implies, supposes that an action produces two effects. One of these effects is something good which may be legitimately intended; the other is an evil which may not be intended. . . . An action is permitted, in accordance with the principle, if these conditions are fulfilled: 1) the action considered by itself and independently of its effects must not be morally evil; 2) the evil effect must not be the means of producing the good effect; 3) the evil effect is sincerely not intended but merely tolerated; 4) there must be a proportionate reason for performing the action in spite of its evil consequences.[78]

This principle appeared to Catholic moralists as widely applicable in medical matters, because every treatment, every act of surgery or dispensation of drugs, was seen to be in one way or another an intervention in the "natural" functioning of the human person. So even when in a particular case the four conditions of double effect did not fully apply, the assumptions on which it rested remained at the top of the mind of the Catholic ethicist.

Perhaps the most common example of the double effect in recent times has had to do with instances of surgical sterilization. A cancerous uterus may be removed because the act itself falls under the principle of totality (as described earlier), because the evil effect (loss of fertility) does not cause the good effect (removal of a tumor), because (presumably) the woman does not desire the evil effect, and, finally, because the woman's health is a proportionate price to pay for her henceforth sterile condition. Conversely, if a woman's heart condition would make childbirth mortally dangerous for her, a hysterectomy would *not* be justified by double effect, because the good effect (health) would be *caused* by the bad effect (loss of fertility).

Much of Catholic medical ethics over the last generation or so has dealt with biosexual matters. The natural-law position has been advocated with force and, until recently, with virtual unanimity by the church's hierarchy, especially by the prolific Pope Pius XII (d. 1958); supported, again until recently, by most theologians and spiritual writers. Contraception provided the dramatic and controversial instance of this teaching, but it should be borne in mind that what appeared at issue was the conviction that the precepts of the natural law formed a seamless robe; if one of them were ripped away, the whole fabric would unravel. If contraception were allowed, it would mean that no rational opposition could be mounted to abortion, homosexual activity, or even bestiality, artificial insemination, genetic engineering, or indeed a host of medical procedures within the capacity of doctors and hospitals. The static concept of *nature* had to be *consistently* applied, or it fell away to nothing. The papal magisterium, grown so powerful since Trent, maintained its consistency, and when Pope Paul VI issued his encyclical *Humanae Vitae* (1968) confirming the ban on artificial contraception, he provoked the most severe crisis of authority within the church since the Reformation.[79] Just as the genius of the natural law tradition informed all Roman Catholic thinking about ethics in medicine and about the mysteries of birth and sexuality, so the collapse of it promises to dominate discussions and decisions for the unforseeable future.[80]

Since Vatican II

That future is now twenty years old, and, besides the virtual disappearance of the formerly confident arguments based upon the ethics of the natural law, there are plenty of signs that Roman Catholics have indeed entered a new era in their corporate history and have left the tridentine days behind. The liturgy, the common prayer of ordinary people, has been drastically altered. Fish on Friday is only a memory. The sacramental principle itself has come under review by hard-eyed German, Dutch, and Peruvian theologians. Penance has given way to the sacrament of reconciliation, and the old confessional box gathers dust. Extreme unction is now called the anointing of the sick. The funeral mass has become a joyous proclamation of the resurrection rather than a somber reminder of the day of judgment—the vestments all white, the pascal candle glittering at the head of the casket, and the choir singing "Alleluia" rather than "Dies irae." Who, in the western world at least, has gained an indulgence lately?—the issue that ignited the tragic quarrel of the sixteenth century.

The time of Catholic exclusivity has passed away. No more are there flourishing associations of Catholic doctors or Catholic nurses, no more journals strictly for Catholic health practitioners. Catholic hospitals now depend upon public monies and are hardly distinguishable from those operated under Protestant or secular auspices. The nursing sister is a rarity now, and Viaticum is dispensed not by a priest garbed in full regimentals accompanied by bell and candles, but by a member of the ecumenical ministry team who casually carries the Host round the hospital corridors in his (or her) pocket.

The second Council of the Vatican (1962-1965) formally repudiated none of the decisions reached at Trent and indeed claimed many of those decisions as its own. Nevertheless, it did express itself in personalist and historical categories considerably different from the scholastic and legalistic modes of thinking familiar to the sixteenth century. Since the council adjourned, sharp divisions have arisen among Catholic thinkers, and indeed among the Catholic populace at large, as to whether the teaching of Vatican II represents an organic development of the teaching of Trent (as Trent, it would be argued, grew out of soil prepared at Lateran IV in the thirteenth century or even at Nicea in the fourth); or whether Vatican II, particularly its "spirit" or its "thrust," marks a severe break with the past and a radically new orientation of the church, making it more directly relevant to the problems and opportunities of the modern world. The quarrels on this point continue; any description therefore of a contemporary "Catholic position" with regard to health care or anything else remains, within certain broad parameters, necessarily tentative.

There has been a wrenching character to all of these developments, at least for those Catholics born and raised under the tridentine dispensation. Their gravest obligation has become not to romanticize, and therefore trivialize, the church of their youth and, even as they hold fast to the timeless values of their faith, not to indulge in feckless nostalgia which in fact demeans the accomplishments of their forebears. *Ecclesia semper reformanda est;* the church *always* has to be reformed. No believer need fear genuine reform, nor legitimate change. Indeed, "in a higher world it is otherwise; but here below to live is to change, and to be perfect is to have changed often."[81]

Notes

[1] Hubert Jedin, *Geschichte des Konzils von Trient*, 5 vols. in 4 (Freiburg, 1951-1975). First two vols. trans. by Ernest Graf (St. Louis, 1949; London, 1961).

[2] Robert Bellarmine, *Opera*, 7 vols. (Cologne, 1617-1620), 6:206.

[3] See Theodore Casteel, "Calvin and Trent: Calvin's Reaction to the Council of Trent in the Context of his Conciliar Thought," *Harvard Theological Review* 63 (1970): 91-117.

[4] Vincent Schweitzer, ed., *Concilii Tridentini Tractatuum Collectio*, 12 vols. (Freiburg, 1965-1980), 12:134-144.

[5] Quoted by Jedin, *Trent* (Eng. trans.), 2:26.

[6] Thomas Stapleton, *Speculum pravitatis haerecticae* (Douay, 1580), in *Opera Omnia*, 4 vols. (Paris, 1620), 2:394.

[7] See Marvin R. O'Connell, *Thomas Stapleton and the Counter Reformation* (New Haven, CT, 1964), pp. 65-67.

[8] Philip Hughes, *The Church in Crisis* (Garden City, NY, 1961), pp. 309-313.

[9] Henry Denzinger, *Enchiridion Symbolorum Definitionum et Declarationum de rebus Fidei et Morum*, 28th ed. (Freiburg, 1952), pp. 321-323.

[10] *Catechism of the Council of Trent for Parish Priests*, trans. John A. McHugh and Charles J. Callan (New York, 1954), pp. 307-311.

[11] Epistle of James 5:14-15.

[12] Denzinger, *Enchiridion*, p. 322.

[13] *Catechism*, p. 315.

[14] Guy E. Swanson, *Religion and Regime* (Ann Arbor, MI, 1967), esp. pp. 3-43. For sharply dissenting views, see the symposium published in *The Journal of Interdisciplinary History*, 1 (1971), 381-446.

[15] H. Outram Evennett, *The Spirit of the Counter-Reformation* (Cambridge, 1968), pp. 43-66.

[16] C. S. Lewis, *English Literature in the Sixteenth Century Excluding Drama* (Oxford, 1964), esp. pp. 3-9.

[17] John Henry Newman, *Tract Seventy-one* (London, 1839), p. 17. Emphasis added.

[18] See Marvin R. O'Connell, *The Counter Reformation, 1559-1610* (New York, 1974), p. 102.

[19] Ludwig von Pastor, *The History of the Popes*, 40 vols., trans. Ernest Graf et al. (London, 1891-1952), 16:85-89.

[20] See Pierre Pourrat, *Father Olier, Founder of St. Sulpice*, trans. W. S. Reilly (Baltimore, 1932).

[21] Fernand Braudel, *Le Méditerranée et le monde méditerranéen à l'époque de Philippe II*, 2 vols. (Paris, 1966), 1:387, 379.

[22] Philip Hughes, *The Reformation in England*, 3 vols. (New York, 1951-1954), 3:335-373.

[23] Compare Thomas N. Tentler, *Sin and Confession on the Eve of the Reformation* (Princeton, 1977), pp. 95-104.

[24] Ellsworth Kneal, *Medical Practice by the Clergy* (Rome, 1967), pp. 23-39.

[25] Quoted in ibid., pp. 52-57.

[26] Francis Cangiamila, *Embryologia Sacra* (Ieper, 1745).

[27] *The Arte of Dyeing* (London, 1621).

[28] Francis de Sales, *Introduction to the Devout Life*, trans. John K. Ryan (New York, 1950), p. 83.

[29] Henry Boudon (1624-1702), *Le Chemin royal de la sainte croix*, in *Les grands auteurs spirituels* (Montreal, 1945), pp. 20-23.

[30] *Colossians* 1:24.

[31] John Vianney (Curé of Ars), *Sermons for the Sundays and Feasts of the Year* (New York, 1901), pp. 56-66. (Originally preached in the 1850s).

[32] Owen Chadwick, *The Popes and European Revolution* (Oxford, 1981), p. 6.

[33] First Epistle of Peter 5:8-9.

[34] Among the multitude of studies, see the perceptive piece by Lawrence Stone, "The Disenchantment of the World," *New York Review of Books*, 17 (December 2, 1971):17ff.

[35] *Collectio Rituum* (Milwaukee, WI, 1964), pp. 280-283.

[36] Hermann Buzembaum, *Medulla Theologiae Moralis* (Rome, 1844), pp. 583-589 (Original printing 1648).

[37] Denzinger, *Enchiridion*, p. 321.

[38] Charles Billuart, *Summa Summae S. Thomae, vel Compendium Theologiae*, 3 vols. (Venice, 1787), 3:319-320 (Original printing 1754).

[39] In the famous phrase of Thomas Hobbes (1588-1679), *Leviathan* (London, 1651).

[40] Peter Canisius, *Ane Catechisme* (Paris, 1588), fol. 102-104.

[41] Buzembaum, *Medulla*, pp. 172-174.

[42] Thomas Tamburnini (1591-1675), quoted in John Noonan, *Contraception* (Cambridge, MA, 1965), p. 407.

[43] Thomas Doughty, *The Practice How to Finde Ease* (Douay, 1618), fol. 122f.

[44] Buzembaum, *Medulla*, pp. 390ff.

[45] The Archbishop of Mechlin [Engelbert Sterckx], ed., *Instructiones SS. Caroli Barromaei [et al.] de recta Administratione Sacramenti Poenitentiae* (Mechlin, 1850), pp. 25-28.

[46] Quoted in Noonan, *Contraception*, p. 449.

[47] See Tentler, *Sin and Confession*, pp. 162-232.

[48] Jerome Noldin, *De Sexto Praecepto*, 2nd ed. (Oeniponte, 1900), pp. 28ff.

[49] *Catechism*, pp. 343ff.

[50] *Genesis* 38:9-10. The sin of Onan was not simply masturbation, but rather his refusal to raise up children for his deceased brother.

[51] See Noonan, *Contraception*, pp. 368-403.

[52] Elizabeth Longford, *Queen Victoria* (New York, 1966), p. 270.

[53] Fernand Braudel, *The Structures of Every Day Life*, trans. Sian Reynolds (New York, 1981), pp. 187ff.

[54] Carlo M. Cipolla, *Faith, Reason and the Plague in Seventeenth Century Tuscany* (Ithaca, NY, 1979), esp. pp. 50ff.

[55] See Chadwick, *Popes*, pp. 3-47; Jean-Claude Schmitt, *The Holy Greyhound* (Cambridge, 1983), pp. 171-178; Thomas A. Kselman, *Miracles and Prophecies in Nineteenth Century France* (New Brunswick, NJ, 1983), pp. 12-36; and Alain Molinier, "Curés et parpoissiens de la contre-réforme," in Jean Delumeau, ed., *Historire vécue de peuple chrétien*, 2 vols. (Paris, 1979), 2:67-91.

[56] S. J. Connolly, *Priests and People in Pre-famine Ireland, 1780-1845* (New York, 1982), pp. 74-134.

[57] See Marvin R. O'Connell, "Ultramontanism and Dupanloup: The Compromise of 1865," *Church History*, 53 (June 1984):200-217.

[58] See Kselman, *Miracles*, esp. pp. 141-188.

[59] *Collectio Rituum*, pp. 375-405.

[60] Max Weber, *The Protestant Ethic and the Spirit of Capitalism*, trans. Talcott Parsons (New York, 1958), pp. 79ff.

[61] For the "corporal works of Mercy," see *A Catechism of Christian Doctrine*, revised ed. of the *Baltimore Catechism* (Paterson, NJ, 1949), pp. 152-154.

[62] Christopher J. Kauffman, *Tamers of Death* (New York, 1976), esp. pp. 199-210.

[63] Jean Calvet, *Vincent de Paul*, trans. Lancelot C. Sheppard (New York, 1951), p. 111.

[64] Mrs. Jameson, *Sisters of Charity, Catholic and Protestant, and the Communion of Labor* (Boston, 1857), p. 66.

[65] Joseph B. Code, "Bishop John Hughes and the Sisters of Charity," (Louvain, 1949), pp. 1-48.

[66] *Heroines of Charity* (New York, 1860), pp. 225-260.

[67] Helen Clapesattle, *The Doctors Mayo* (Minneapolis, 1941), pp. 242-267, 499.

[68] *The Catholic Directory* (New York, 1964), Statistical recapitulation.

[69] Georges Goyau, *L'eglise en marche: études d'histoire missionaire*, 5 vols. (Paris, 1928-1936).

[70] See Joseph Mullin, *The Catholic Church in Modern Africa* (London, 1965).

[71] *Evangelii Peaecones*, June 2, 1951, in *The Papal Encyclicals, 1939-1958*, ed. Claudia Carlen (New York, 1981), pp. 196-197.

[72] *Romans* 2:15.

[73] See David F. Kelly, *The Emergence of Roman Catholic Medical Ethics in North America* (New York, 1979), esp. pp. 149ff. and 244ff.

[74] Paul Zacchia, *Quaestiones medico-legales*, new ed. (Lyons, 1701); and Michael Boudewyns, *Ventilabrum medico theologicum* (Antwerp, 1666).

[75] Joseph Goldbrunner, *Holiness is Wholeness and Other Essays*, trans. Stanley Godman (Notre Dame, IN, 1964), esp. pp. 3-29; and *Cure of Mind and Cure of Soul* (New York, 1958), pp. 12ff.

[76] See the bibliography in Kelly, *Medical Ethics*, pp. 460-511.

[77] J. Ghoos, "L'Acte á double effect: étude de théologie positive," *Ephemerides Theologiae Lovanienses* 27 (1951): 30-52.

[78] Gerald Kelly, *Medico-moral Problems* (St. Louis, 1958), pp. 12f.

[79] Text of *Humanae Vitae*, July 25, 1968, in *The Papal Encyclicals*, ed. Carlen, pp. 223-236.

[80] Daniel Callahan, ed., *The Catholic Case for Contraception* (London, 1969), esp. pp. 67-70.

[81] John Henry Newman, *An Essay on the Development of Christian Doctrine*, 7th ed. (London, 1890), p. 40.

SYSTEMATIC THEOLOGY

David F. Wells, area editor

SYSTEMATIC THEOLOGY

DAVID F. WELLS
Andrew Mutch Professor of Historical and Systematic Theology
Gordon-Conwell Theological Seminary

Introduction

It is ironic that in many underdeveloped nations the blind forces of nature are personalized, while in the developed countries—especially in the West—the whole of nature is stripped of any spiritual dimension and reduced to a bare mechanism. Who, one wonders, is more "developed" in their attitude toward nature? To be sure, animism in the underdeveloped countries has created a pall of needless fear; the human cost it has exacted has been very high. Yet it would be foolish to imagine that the effect of our secularism has been benign. It has, in fact, reduced the cosmos to nothing more than reactions, chemical and otherwise, reactions that occur in a moral vacuum. Life is chemistry without meaning, action without responsibility.

This itself is ironic, for is it not true that science and technology were born from the womb of Christian faith? Why, then, is the child destroying the parent?

The answers to these questions carry with them the answers to so many of the other conundrums about modernity. It is certainly pertinent to ask, for example, why the scientific enterprise arose in the West rather than the East. And the answer, in so far as guesses can be legitimately hazarded, is that in the West the conceptual conditions existed for such work whereas this was not true of the East. What were these? First, science must assume that the world is real and objective. Second, it must assume that the world functions in ways that are uniform and predictable. The first assumption is secured by the doctrine of creation and the second by the doctrine of providence.[1] Science and technology, then, were originally partners—even children—of Christian faith, but both in the post-Enlightenment world have become parasites. They have lived off their host by borrowing the needed assumptions about the world, but both, at the same time, have sought to destroy their host by denying that there is any reality other than the natural. Scientists, of course, are not alone in this. This mindset is common to our whole secular culture. It is part and parcel of our industrial, urban society. It is what we encounter every day in the millions of words and images that envelop us from T.V., billboards, and magazines.

Some of the results of this thinking would be humorous if they were not so destructive. Consider the following perspectives which have even been known to appear side by side in the same journal. On the one hand, the human being is reduced, in behavioristic contexts, to nothing more than chemical reactions and electrical impulses; in short, we are machines. On the other hand, since the 1950s, the interest in creating artificial intelligence has been growing.[2] We want to make computers that can think. So, people are machines and machines are people!

Given the naturalistic bias of modern science, the pioneering work reported in the first essay on brain research is quite remarkable. It is remarkable because it is not only good science, but *as science* it is recognizing that there is within the natural phenomena a spiritual dimension without which those phenomena cannot be fully understood. This spiritual dimension is not always interpreted in Christian ways, but the biblical perspective is, at least, an option. Such new directions in the sciences are a positive spur to fresh theological thinking. And on the theological side, T. F. Torrance is probably correct in saying that there is now greater freedom for such an undertaking because "the ground has been cleared in the most remarkable way of the old dualist and atomistic modes of thought that have plagued theology for centuries."[3]

The first selection, Lawrence Wood's essay on the new brain research, has been made for two reasons. First, it has highlighted a type of science that is exploring the interplay between natural and spiritual phenomena. Second, it has related this work to the Christian understanding of how mind and body relate to one another. As such, it exemplifies the fruitful relation between science and theology which, in this area at least, has the promise of pushing both beyond former confines and doing so in concert with one another.

The question posed by Wood's essay is whether there is a difference between mind and brain. Are thinking and acting the result exclusively of electrical discharges and therefore explicable in purely naturalistic ways, or is there an operating agent distinct from the brain, which nevertheless works with and through the brain? This type of question would hardly have been entertained in the scientific community until relatively recently. But in the 1960s unexpected discoveries were made as a result of experimental treatments of severe epilepsy. The treatment involved slicing the brain in two in the hope that the half in which the epilepsy was located would be better controlled by the half that was disengaged. The treatment worked. But in the process, neurosurgeons discovered that the brain's functioning was significantly different from what they had thought, and their discoveries have opened up the possibility that there is a reality other than the electro-chemical which is involved in knowing and volition. Wood's essay is a painstaking, thorough piece of research which is quite technical in nature. For these reasons readers might be tempted to look for something that can be read with greater ease and in half the time. That would be a mistake! This essay has opened up these new developments in an exceptional way and we need to be cognizant of them.

The second essay, by Bruce Ware, is looking at an old problem, although without saying so too loudly he is doing so with one eye on contemporary developments. The problem is how and in what ways we can say God does not change if, in fact, he enters into relationship with a world that is ever changing, ever in ebb and flow. Ware rejects the trendy process theology that argues that God partly does and partly does not change in his being, that he is both created and creator, that he is independent of the world and yet dependent on it because its unfolding, of which he is a part, is also the means of his own development. Instead, Ware distinguishes between God's *character*, which does not change, and his *relationships*, which do.

From another point of view, Ware is also exploring the relationship between the immanence and the transcendence of God. Although his discussion is angled in terms of the question of immutability, his essay does make some obvious connections with Wood's essay. For in both cases—albeit for different reasons—we are led to think about the fact that "God is not far from each of us. For in him we live and move and have our being" (Acts 17:27b-28a).

Notes

[1] This is the thesis of R. Hoykaas, *Religion and the Rise of Modern Science* (Edinburgh; Scottish Academic Press, 1972); see also his *Philosophia Libera: Christian Faith and the Freedom of Science* (London; Tyndale Press, 1957). This position was argued earlier by M. B. Foster, "The Christian Doctrine of Creation and the Rise of Modern Science," *Mind*, 43 (1934), 446-68. It is generally sustained in the works of T. F. Torrance, specifically *Theological Science* (New York; Oxford University Press, 1969); *Transformation and Convergence in the Frame of Knowledge: Explorations in the Interrelations of Scientific and Theological Enterprise* (Grand Rapids; Eerdmans Publishing Co., 1986); and *Reality and Scientific Theology* (Edinburgh; Scottish Academic Press, 1985).

[2] This development is documented in Edward Feigenbaum and Arron Barr, eds., *The Handbook of Artificial Intelligence* (3 vols.; Stanford; Heuristech Press, 1981). For different perspectives, see H. Dreyfus, *What Computers Can't Do: A Critique of Artificial Reason* (New York; Harper and Row, 1972); Donald Mackay, *Brains, Machines, and Persons* (Grand Rapids; Eerdmans Publishing Co., 1980).

[3] T. F. Torrance, *The Ground and Grammar of Theology* (Charlottesville; University of Virginia Press, 1980), 178.

About the Area Editor

David Wells (B.D., London University, England; M.Th., Trinity Evangelical Divinity School; Ph.D., University of Manchester, England) is Andrew Mutch professor of historical and systematic theology at Gordon-Conwell Theological Seminary. Born in what is now Zimbabwe, he studied initially at University of Cape Town, where he became a Christian. He is a member of the Lausanne Committee for World Evangelization, and also serves on its theology working group.

He was general editor and part author of *Eerdmans Handbook to Christianity in America* (1983) and *Reformed Theology in America: A History of Its Modern Development* (1985). His recent books include *God the Evangelist: The Role of the Holy Spirit in Bringing Men and Women to Faith* (1987); *The Person of Christ: A Biblical and Historical Analysis of the Incarnation* (1984).

RECENT BRAIN RESEARCH
AND THE MIND-BODY DILEMMA

LAURENCE W. WOOD
Professor of Systematic Theology
Asbury Theological Seminary

Article from *The Asbury Theological Journal*

One of the most debated issues in the history of Western philosophy is the connection between the body and the mind—is there really a difference between the mind (thinking) and the brain (physical activity)?

This debate was formally initiated with Plato's dialogues, especially with the *Phaedo* and the *Timaeus*. Plato (428-348 B.C.) was the first writer to define a human being as a thinking, rational, intelligent soul whose personal existence survived beyond the death of the body (*Timaeus* 30b).[1] Plato was the first writer to make a philosophical distinction between the material world and the immaterial "world beyond" (*Republic* X.614b, c). Plato was the first writer to use the cosmological argument as a proof for God's existence (*Timaeus* 28b, c, 46d, e). Plato was the first writer to identify the "brain" as containing an immortal, rational soul (*Timaeus* 73c, d), thus making it the "head" and "lord" of the body (*Timaeus* 44d). Plato was the first writer to intend a scientific description (*Timaeus* 27a, b) of the way the mind interacts with the brain and the rest of the body (*Timaeus* 73c, d, e, 74a, b).

Scientific thought has come a long way since the early attempts of the ancient Greeks to account for the nature of the universe and its significance for human values. Reading through Plato's primitive anatomical description of the human body illustrates how far advanced our scientific knowledge is today.

Our philosophical progress is not so striking, however. The same themes Plato was the first to explore by means of careful reasoning are still being debated today. One theme is the immortality of the mind. Another issue is whether or not the mind can causally act on the brain and influence behavior (*Phaedrus* 245e). Both of these themes will be addressed in some detail.

Our present purpose is to examine the activity of the knowing mind as it interprets and perceives the world. Plato was the first to discuss this theme in an explicit manner. He metaphorically likens the mind to a charioteer driving a team of winged horses who have fallen from their heavenly heights into the particularity of a physical body (*Phaedrus* 245). One horse is deaf, impulsive, non-rational, symbolizing emotion, passion, desires, divine madness gone wild (*Phaedrus* 253e). The other horse symbolizes hearing and understanding, modesty, temperance, and rational will (*Phaedrus* 253d). The charioteer symbolizes reason and wisdom.

The task of the charioteer is to redirect the *irrational* madness of the unruly horse into a *divine* and appropriate kind of emotion and religious fervor. Only when the impulsive horse is so disciplined are its impulsive and mystic qualities able to contribute to the harmonious functioning of the charioteer.

Plato calls the activity of the impulsive horse "left-handed," but when it is brought into submission to reason the two horses are considered a rational whole. This wholeness is termed "right-handedness" (*Phaedrus* 266) and is a symbol of mind.

This right-hand, left-hand analogy may be a first hint that the different functions of the mind have a physiological connection, since the charioteer and the two winged horses is a parable of the mind embodied in the brain. It could be that Plato's identification of the irrational with left-handedness is only reflecting a cultural bias, which is universally found throughout human history, even in the Bible. However, in the *Timaeus* which intends to be a serious discourse on the nature of the universe, Plato attempts, among other things, to give an accurate description of the nature of the brain and its relation to the mind. In particular, Plato assumes a physiological basis of thinking and also associates speech with the activity of the mind (*Timaeus* 75d, e).

In spite of Plato's primitive scientific insight into the anatomy of the body, his understanding that qualities like intelligence, thinking, passion, feeling and intuition are philosophically distinct from and yet related to the body is still compelling today. The distinction among reason, feeling and willing is also a basic one which the history of philosophy since Plato has attempted to address.

Recent brain research has revived an enormous interest in this mind-body problem. Nobel Prize-winning neurophysiologists are becoming intentionally philosophical about the physiological link between the brain and the knowing mind. The incredibly complex composition of the human brain and the nervous system is being scientifically analyzed by means of sophisticated technology. The relatively short history of brain research already has revolutionary potential for understanding the human mind, according to the opinion of some outstanding scientists and philosophers. A rehearsal of some of the history of neuroscience will be helpful in assessing its relevance for understanding the nature of the mind.

The human brain is made up of over 12 billion nerve cells, called neurons. Nerve cells are self-contained and maintain their own separate biological life. They transmit information through brief, electrochemical impulses that travel along the fibers of each nerve cell. One nerve cell connects with the next nerve cell through synapses (which means "to clasp tightly together"). A chemical is released at the point where one nerve cell synapses with another nerve cell. This contact is the means by which the nerve impulse is transmitted to the next cell.

Bodily movement and sensory perception are mediated as these nerve impulses transmit coded messages to the brain. Stated figuratively, there are transmission lines and intervening relay stations between the sense organs and the brain. The nervous system thus includes sense organs to generate electrochemical impulses, neural "transmission lines" and "relay stations" to convey coded messages to the brain, and additional "lines" and "stations" to carry activating signals to the muscles or organs. A neuronal event is thus a passage of an impulse through the system of circuitry.

These electrochemical impulses pass through several relay stations along the way, finally reaching the cerebral cortex, the surface area of the cerebral hemispheres where the highest levels of consciousness are evidenced. Once the neuronal hook-up of the several areas of the cerebral cortex has been established, interpretation of the external sense stimuli can be made. Perception is thus an interpretation of the coded messages contained in neuronal events. It involves (1) the original external object received by the sense organs, (2) the transmission of this data through the nervous system, and (3) the neuronal patterns established within the circuit system of the cerebral cortex. This neuronal machinery is the *physical* basis of perception.[2] This is not to say, however, that perception can be simply equated with the *physical* neuronal machinery of the brain. We shall argue in this paper that perception is more than brain activity.

The popular image is that the brain is a single structure. However, it is actually two hemispheres linked together by several bundles of nerve fibers, called the corpus callosum. These nerve fibers put the hemispheres of the brain into immediate communication with each other. Bodily control and sensory pathways are both divided in an even manner between the two halves—except they are crossed.

Each half of the brain seems to be a mirror image of the other. Actually these hemispheres are instead asymmetrical in function. This was first documented in 1836 by an obscure French doctor, Marc Dax. At a medical conference he presented a formal paper on speech loss experienced by more than forty of his patients whose left hemisphere had been damaged. The early Greeks, such as Plato in the *Timaeus*, had already noted the relationship of speech to the brain, but it was Dax who documented that speech control was in the left hemisphere of the brain. His theory was largely ignored until 1864, when Paul Broca, a young French surgeon, proposed the idea of the cerebral dominance of the left hemisphere because of its capacity for speech. Broca's research efforts caught the attention of the whole medical community. Shortly thereafter the concept of cerebral dominance became the accepted view. Also, it should be pointed out that John Hughlings Jackson, a British neurologist, proposed in 1868 that while the left hemisphere is "the leading" side of the brain, the right hemisphere also performs a possible minor role. By the 1930's this idea of the dominant-versus-minor hemispheres of the brain was widely accepted.[3]

However, this dominant-versus-minor concept of the left/right hemispheres was to be challenged by experimental research on split-brain surgery of epileptic patients, requiring at least some modification of the classical concept of cerebral dominance. These experiments have produced an explosion of research with the intent of identifying the specific functions of each hemisphere and their implications for behavior. More specifically, research has focused on the implications of these hemispheric differences for determining the nature of learning disabilities, psychiatric illness, and differences in cognitive styles among individuals and cultures.[4]

Our interest will focus on differences in cognitive style as related to the anatomy of the brain and the philosophical implications of a divided *brain* in reference to the self-conscious *mind*, the assumption being that the brain and the mind are not identical.

I. Digital and Analogous Thinking: The Neurophysiological Basis

In the 1960's, Roger Sperry of the California Institute of Technology and his associates, Ronald Myers, Michael Gazzaniga, Jerre Levy, Joseph Bogen, and Phillip Vogel, reported history-making neurological research. Their work suggested that the hemispheres of the brain perform distinct functions of consciousness.[5] These research reports came from tests done with patients who had their corpus callosum severed (commissurotomy) because they were suffering from intractable epilepsy.

Sperry had originally experimented with laboratory animals, which prepared the way for this particular treatment of epileptic patients. The hope was that epileptic seizures could be confined to one hemisphere of the brain, thus leaving the other half to maintain control. These experiments proved highly successful with apparently little negative consequences despite the fact the two halves of the brain seemed to be "disconnected" through cutting the corpus callosum. The neurobiological literature on brain research is now voluminous (cf. the mammoth amount of laboratory research summarized extensively in *Lateralization in the Nervous System*, ed. Stevan Harnad, Robert W. Doty, Leonide Goldstein, Julian Jaynes, George Krauthamer [New York: Academic Press, 1977]). The significance of this pioneer work in brain research earned Roger Sperry a share in the 1981 Nobel Prize in Medicine/Physiology.

The division of the brain into halves had been obvious to medical researchers for many years. What has now emerged as a result of experiments with split-brain patients is that both halves of the brain may serve an important cognitive function.

The Classical Model: Left Brain Dominance?
The classical view of the cerebral hemispheres in neurology was that the left side of the brain is responsible for the higher cognitive faculties associated with speech and behavior. The ability to think abstractly, to identify objects in a deliberate fashion, to choose one's course of actions, to engage in self-reflection—these were allegedly the functions of the *superior* left hemisphere that made human beings distinct from animals. The right hemisphere was considered largely inconsequential in its functions, nonverbal (word-deaf) and unable to write (word-blind). The obvious conclusion was that the right hemisphere was retarded in its evolutionary development as compared to the highly developed cognitive abilities of the left hemisphere.[6]

Sperry now considers this classical neurological view to be one-sided. Tests with split-brain patients show that the right hemisphere is as impressive in its sphere of cognitivity as the left hemisphere. The comparison between the functions of the two hemispheres as a dominant-subordinate relationship may be misleading because each is dominant in its own right for the particular function it is designed to perform.[7] In other words, the hemispheres of the brain are not in competition with each other but are designed to function as an integrated unit. There is an interdependence between the right and left hemisphere of the brain, with each performing its own unique function and making its own contribution to the knowing process. The left hemisphere is primarily verbal, mathematical, analytical, sequential, and logical in its functioning. The right hemisphere is spatial, imagistic, synthetic, intuitive, and holistic.

The function of the right hemisphere is facial recognition, judging the difference between a whole circle and a small arc, recognizing shapes, hearing musical chords, determining block sizes and sorting them out into their own categories, perceiving wholes from an amalgamation of parts, and of thinking intuitively.[8]

Despite their differences, the two hemispheres can no longer be viewed as antagonistic but are now seen as mutually supportive.[9] When one half of the brain is damaged through a stroke or other causes, the other half continues to function independently. In the normal person, however, the two are integrated as two independent entities. The classic view of an inherent incompatibility between the analytical and the intuitive styles of thinking cannot now be maintained both on philosophical grounds and also in the light of this recent scientific research in neurophysiology.

The concept of *dominant* hemisphere as opposed to the *minor* hemisphere was originally used to indicate the relative insignificance of the right side. Sperry thus suggests dropping this set of terms, but another Nobel Prize winner and internationally known neurophysiologist, John Eccles, proposes that the concept of *dominance* for the left hemisphere is appropriate because it alone has speech function and genuine consciousness for 95 percent of the general population.[10] Research done subsequent to Sperry's earlier work indicates that some verbal contact of the left hemisphere with the right brain still remains intact even after split-brain surgery.[11] This would then explain why the right brain seems to have some speech capacity. Eccles affirms that the right brain is significant and certainly possesses greater ability than the highest anthropoids, but lacking speech it has a less significant role than the left hemisphere.[12]

Do Split-Brain Patients Have Two Minds?

There are many possible implications stemming from this recent brain research data. Sperry cautions, however, that the left/right dichotomy in cognition is "an idea with which it is very easy to run wild."[13] Also there is disagreement over just what the implications are. Some still would insist that the distinctive human quality is physiologically located in the left hemisphere, as would John Eccles. However, Sperry believes that his tests show that the right hemisphere, though largely nonverbal, is personally and socially aware and does not lack self-recognition. Also, tests indicate that the gifts and abilities are unique to the person's preference for either right or left hemispheric function of the brain. What this further means is that the standardized tests traditionally given to measure intellectual ability do not really measure the intellectual potential of persons since these tests are entirely discriminatory against the functions of the right brain. He further shows that nonverbal components are also essential aspects of knowledge.[14]

Another significant implication of tests with split-brain patients is that emotions play an important role in cognitive processing. Though the right hemisphere is more prominent in processing emotional information, emotions do not seem to be restricted to only one hemisphere of the brain, unlike other aspects of cognitive functions. Even after the corpus callosum had been severed in patients, the emotional effects felt in the right hemisphere were quickly transferred to the left hemisphere through another route, perhaps through the crossed fiber systems in the undivided brain stem. In tests given to discover the possibility of self-consciousness and social awareness of the right hemisphere, it was found that feelings generated in the right hemisphere actually assisted the verbal left hemisphere to guess what stimuli had stirred the emotions of the right hemisphere. Such tests suggest that knowing surely involved an affective component.[15]

Particularly, Sperry believed the most significant implication of this new data is that the mind cannot be reduced to neuronal activity. The mind has its own causal power independent of the causal power of neuromuscular activity of the brain. This discussion will be introduced subsequently, but for now the point is that the mind is a power that cannot be reduced to a stultifying notion of mechanical causality. Sperry insists that this recent brain research repudiates scientific materialism which had identified the mind as merely the by-product of neural processes and as lacking any causal power.[16]

What is further indicated is that intuition and emotion are powerful resources of knowing. What is also shown is that the right hemisphere is not to be downplayed, for tests show that it too can possibly comprehend and articulate simple words, though that is not its primary function. Sperry shows, in fact, that the left hemisphere *depends* on the right hemisphere to awaken and to help remind it what it subconsciously knows, and to help it to see what otherwise it would not see. There is a dimension of reality which far exceeds the rationalistic possibilities of the left hemisphere. There is a level of personal freedom exhibited by the spontaneity of the right hemisphere which shows that the mind has a kind of causality that is different from the causality of physics. A rationalistic reduction of reality to the logical and explicit can only be done with disregard for the intuitive and transcendent depths to reality. What Sperry's work suggests is that there is an element of mystery, religion, value, and depth to reality that the rationalistic tradition of the West often obscures. Sperry believes that scientific method and laboratory results now support religion and value. The idea of a value-free, fact-dominated model of science is obsolete.[17]

Plato had argued for a division of the mind on the analogy of a charioteer who directs two horses, one rational and the other intuitive. The history of this division between the rational and the mystical-intuitive was largely based on philosophical consideration. Sperry is now saying that neuroscience has confirmed the validity of this distinction through its laboratory-controlled experiments on the human brain. This epistemic difference is itself a reflection of our anatomical differences in the brain. Religion, Sperry believes, is now supported by scientific fact.

This alignment of science with religion goes against the almost unchallenged bias of our culture which assumes "peaceful coexistence" between the two, as if religion and science are altogether unrelated. Sperry's realignment of science and religion will be disputed by many, but the results of this highly acclaimed research under the careful control of sophisticated laboratory experiments with split-brain patients and its implication for religious philosophy cannot be easily dismissed.

Just what are the possible epistemological issues emerging from recent neurological evidence that the hemispheres of the brain have unique lateralized functions? First, it would be misleading to assume that there is a *literal* correspondence between the anatomy of the brain and cognitive function. Thinking and the lateralized activity of the hemispheres are clearly distinguished, yet it must be recognized that they are also interrelated. Also, future research will yet determine and modify scientific understanding of the precise function of the two hemispheres. However, some general conclusions can now be made about the lateralized functions of the cerebral hemispheres, though these conclusions are certainly subject to revision considering the enormous complexity of the human brain and the relatively recent beginnings of neurophysiology.

The right brain is holistic in operation, as seen for example in its tasks of being artistic and craftsmanship-oriented. It is the basis for the mind to recognize faces. It gives us our sense of spatial orientation. For the right side, reality is processed more diffusely; it seeks to integrate the numerous bits of incoming information all at the same time. It is the great synthesizer, whereas the left brain is more analytical and seeks to make reality more explicit. For example, most left brain persons write and draw with their right hand. After the surgical severing of the corpus callosum, split-brain patients can still write with their right hand, but have difficulty drawing. Using the left hand, they are able to draw. The right hemisphere is the basis of the spatial, relational mode of consciousness. The left hemisphere is the verbal mode of consciousness. Hence, these patients could only use simple words in response to information given to their right hemisphere.

In one type of test using a tachistoscope (a device which restricts the duration of a picture presented on a screen in front of the patient to one hemisphere only), a picture of a spoon was presented only to the right brain. The patients were allowed to feel and search with their left hand from among a number of objects and try to select a spoon (hidden from view) in order to match the picture. The patients showed remarkable accuracy in this task, but they were unable to name or describe the spoon which their left hand had selected; nor were they able to identify the picture as a spoon.[18] This experiment illustrates the nonverbal and tacit dimension involved in the knowing process. It dramatically illustrates that we know more than we can say.

What neurological evidence also shows is that when brain damage is sustained on the left side it may destroy the ability to speak; when brain damage is sustained on the right side, it may destroy spatial and holistic functions, such as the ability to recognize faces, to dress oneself, or to sing. The clinical neurological research of Joseph Bogen has especially documented the evidence that the right hemisphere of the brain is lateralized for spatial and holistic functions such as musical ability. For example, damage to the right hemisphere may prevent the ability to sing even though the patient may speak fluently.[19]

Sperry maintains that split-brain patients literally have *two minds*.[20] His tests with these patients lead him to believe that each hemisphere of the brain has its own particular function. For example, if a pencil were held in the right hand of a patient, the patient could say what it was since the right half of the body is controlled by the verbal left brain. If the pencil were hidden from view and were placed in the left hand, the patient could not say what it was since the left half of the body is controlled by the non-verbal right brain. Yet, the patient could purposely select the pencil again with his left hand when subsequently asked to pick out the same object from a variety of other objects.[21] With the corpus callosum severed, the right brain was severely restricted in communicating to the left brain messages which had been received from external stimuli. Unable to see the pencil, the left brain could only guess what the right hand held. Interestingly enough, when the left brain guessed wrong, the person's face would frown, indicating to the left brain that it had made a mistake.[22] This latter phenomenon, however, of showing signs of consciousness in the right brain may be explained on the basis of research done subsequent to Sperry's earlier tests that show even with the corpus callosum being cut the two hemispheres are still in touch through other avenues, though not at a level of explicit awareness of what each side knows.

Tests with visual experiments were also performed. Physiologically, the right side of both eyes inform the left brain, and the left side of both eyes inform the right brain. Using a special visual device, the word, "heart," was flashed onto a screen. When asked what he saw, the patient replied "art." This is the part of the word, *heart*, which the left hemisphere (the verbal side) saw. When the patient was asked to point with his left hand (controlled by the right brain) to what he saw, he pointed to "he." What the patient saw was split right down the middle between he/art.[23]

In another experiment with colors, Sperry tested the ability of the right hemisphere to speak. In this test, colors were allowed to be seen on the left side of each visual field, which information was sent exclusively to the right brain. The patient was asked to verbalize what the right brain had seen. When it guessed wrongly, the patient would frown and shake his head (such body movement is controlled by the right hemisphere). In this way, the left brain would conclude it had guessed incorrectly and consequently it would make another attempt to correct itself.[24]

In yet another laboratory test a female patient was shown a picture of a nude woman visible only to her right brain. This picture was deliberately introduced in the middle of a series of boring and uninteresting pictures. At first sight, the split-brain patient denied seeing anything. Suddenly she began to show signs of embarrassment such as squirming and blushing. Her left brain could not understand the emotional upheaval, and the woman brushed her reaction off by saying, "What a funny machine you have there, Dr. Sperry."[25]

These tests were all with split-brain patients, but more recent research has developed a special mechanical device which has been used with *normal* persons to test their right-left brain differences. These tests confirm results consistent with split-brain patients.[26]

Do Sperry's tests prove that a split-brain patient literally has two consciousnesses (or minds)? The world famous John Eccles (who was awarded the Nobel Prize in Medicine/Physiology in 1963 for his work on how nerve impulses are produced and transmitted) says NO. Eccles says none of Sperry's tests show that the right hemisphere actually has full consciousness in the normal sense of the term. Eccles writes: "The rigorous testing of the subjects who have been subjected to section of the corpus callosum has revealed that conscious experiences of the subject arise only in relationship to neural activities in the dominant hemisphere."[27] He further writes: "We can regard the minor [right] hemisphere as having a status superior to that of the non-human primate brain. It displays intelligent reactions, even after delays of many minutes, and learning responses; and it has many skills, particularly in the spatial and auditory domain that are far superior to those of the anthropoid brain, but it gives no conscious experience to the subject, being in this respect in complete contrast to the dominant hemisphere. Moreover there is no evidence that this brain has some residual consciousness of its own."[28]

Sperry, of course, believes it has consciousness but cannot express it because it lacks speech. Eccles agrees, only if we think of it resembling the brain of a non-human primate which is able to have consciousness of its environment but not an awareness of this consciousness. In other words, an animal may, like the right hemisphere, have consciousness but lacks *self-consciousness*. To be sure, Eccles stresses the superior function of the right brain to that of animals, but it lacks self-consciousness.[29]

So far as the experiment involving embarrassment over the nude picture is concerned, Eccles says subsequent testing shows that such consciousness is now accounted for because the two hemispheres continue to have some speech-related communication even though neither hemisphere can verbally name words presented only to the right hemisphere.[30]

At any rate, since the right hemisphere lacks speech (even as Sperry admits), it is not possible to test whether or not there is any genuine consciousness in the right hemisphere. Lacking this possible testing ability, Eccles says he is agnostic about any so-called consciousness.[31] The point Eccles makes is that the left hemisphere is obviously more in liaison with self-consciousness than other parts of the body. Surgical removal of the right hemisphere, while producing paralysis on the left side of the body, does not eliminate self-consciousness. Removal of other parts of the brain has serious repercussions, but does not necessarily destroy self-consciousness. The possibility of a head transplant, now no longer a mere piece of science fiction since the procedure is surgically possible in some mammals,[32] would not destroy either self-consciousness or personal identity. Removal of the left hemisphere, however, immediately destroys self-consciousness, putting one immediately into a comatose state.

Eccles also does not believe the left-brain in itself possesses full self-consciousness. No neurophysiological evidence has been presented to show that perception or consciousness can be equated with the neurological functions of the left-brain. As we shall see subsequently, he argues that conscious perception, voluntary action, and conscious memory, while all related to neuronal activity, are not physical happenings. Rather, the self-conscious mind transcends, though interfaces with, neuronal, physical happenings. Sperry agrees with this immaterialist concept of the self as distinct from the body, but like the ancient Pythagoreans he does not believe the individual self continues after the death of the brain. The self simply evaporates when its physical base is destroyed.

If Sperry makes too much of the cognitive significance of the right brain, Eccles may make too little of it. Though the right hemisphere may be lacking in the level of consciousness attainable by the left hemisphere, its capacity for intuition and synthesis seems to allow it to reach out into a dimension of reality unattainable by the left brain alone. This is an interesting contrast between Eccles and Sperry with their different assessment of the right hemisphere. Eccles believes in a personal God and Christian supernaturalism, but Sperry as a religious humanist does not believe in a personal God. What this contrast may illustrate is that if the *explicit* level of self-consciousness is the defining characteristic of personhood, then one's religious orientation will necessarily assume a personally, self conscious God. If mind or personality is not necessarily linked to an *explicit* consciousness, then one's religious orientation may easily leave out the notion of a personally self-aware God, as is typical of Eastern religions. This difference between the analytical, scientific consciousness of Western culture with its tendency toward theism or atheism and the synthetic, intuitive consciousness of Eastern culture with its tendency toward pantheistic monism seems to be the outgrowth of an inner tension in the human brain between the two cerebral hemispheres.

A Split-Brain Culture

The parabolic significance of split-brain tests for our Western culture is that we function largely as two independent minds. Like the split-brain patient who could not verbalize seeing a picture of a nude person, we experience a depth to reality, but then shunt it aside in a rationalistic, reductive manner as though it is mere feeling lacking substance.

Even as split-brain patients do, we use both modes of consciousness. We speak (left brain activity) and we move about in space (right brain activity). The two modes are intended to complement each other, not to be fragmented and split-off from each other. Even though the corpus callosum is severed in split-brain patients, they function normally because the same information reaches both hemispheres through external stimuli, even though there is reduced internal communication between the hemispheres.

The rational (explicit knowledge) and intuitive (tacit knowledge) approaches are different but complementary modes of awareness. Something vital to personal existence is missing when this relationship is severed. For example, one does not learn to swim merely through verbal instruction. This was Kant's defective view of reality. He completely isolated the analytical and logical from the synthetic and practical in his critique of reason. Hegel's criticism is appropriate when he says Kant's critique of knowing is like trying to learn how to swim before we get into the water.[33] But the truth is that we learn how to swim once we get into water. Likewise we do not know what is an accurate verbal description of reality until we have experienced (intuited) it. The temporal, sequential, verbal, and analytical are in a reciprocal relationship to the spatial, holistic, intuitive, and synthetic.

This specialized dual hemispheric function of the cerebral cortex seems to be limited to humans. What is unique about humans is not simply the verbal but also the intuitive. Humans exist "simultaneously as two semi-independent information-processing unities with different specialities."[34]

This distinction between the two modes of consciousness has long been recognized as a basis of the distinction between science and religion. The tendency is to exaggerate this distinction into a bifurcation. To maintain a proper balance is the ideal goal. Perhaps now with the new data from brain research, the need for this balance can be seen from a physiological standpoint as well as a philosophical one. What is needed is a creative and healthy marriage between these otherwise different spheres of awareness. Together these semi-independent spheres account for the apprehension of reality. Divorced, or in the total submission of one hemisphere to the domination of the other, they result in a reduced knowledge of what truly is. Only through the creative tension of the rational-analytical mode with the intuitive-synthetic mode can there be creative advances and growth in our perception of what this world of ours is all about. Even from a scientific perspective, Einstein recognized that "the really valuable thing is intuition."[35]

The bracketing out of one sphere of consciousness physiologically results in a condition known as "the neglect syndrome."[36] This condition is an excellent parabolic illustration of what characterizes the rationalistic bent of Western culture with its devaluation of the cognitive significance of intuition, feeling, and religious experience. This condition of the neglect syndrome sometimes occurs in some persons when the affective, intuitive hemisphere of the brain is split off from the rational, logical, and analytical hemisphere.

What seems to happen in this condition is that a person is altogether inattentive to one half of the space in front of him. This symptom is more likely when the right hemisphere has suffered lesions from a stroke or an accident. This inattention does not result from having suffered optic nerve damage. For persons with neglect syndrome cannot seem to see anything in their left visual field. For example, patients will shave only one side of their face, usually the right side. In eating their breakfast, they will not be able to see their coffee cup until someone points it out to them on the left side of their plate. They may leave half of their food on the left side of the plate. If they are asked to draw a clock, they may draw a circle correctly but then squeeze all the numbers into the right half of the circle. If asked to draw a picture of a person, they will draw only the right side of the body, leaving out the left arm and left leg.

Neglect syndrome is particularly present in those patients who have suffered a stroke in the posterior regions of the right hemisphere. What this does to the patient is to extinguish the left half of the visual field, unless the left half is seen alone.

An interesting feature of this neglect syndrome patient is that inattention is only at the conscious level, for the left visual field is still present to the nervous system. Why then this inattention? Is it merely psychological? Apparently this condition is the result of the lesions on the right hemisphere of the brain. The left hemisphere believes, so it would seem to lesion researchers, what it sees encompasses everything there is to see. Hence the left brain acts on the basis that nothing is wrong.

One of the interesting aspects of neglect syndrome is that it seems independent of the act of visual processing since it affects the recall of images from memory. An Italian afflicted with neglect syndrome was asked to imagine going into a well-known plaza in Rome from the north end. She was asked to describe what she could recall, having been quite familiar with the plaza before the stroke. The stroke patient described all the buildings to the West—that is, to her right side when she would enter the plaza—and completely omitted the buildings to the East. She was then asked to imagine herself entering from the South. This time the patient described the buildings on the east side of the plaza.

This medical condition of neglect syndrome is a parabolic illustration of much of the history of Western thought. We have permitted the verbal, temporal, analytical, and logical sphere of cognitive processing to restrict our vision of reality. Especially since the rise of modern philosophy and modern science, we have been largely inattentive to the realities of the unseen, the intuitive, the affective, and the feeling depths of reality. Consequently the intuitive mode of consciousness has been denigrated and subordinated to the rational mode of consciousness. What has been affirmed as truth is restricted to what is clear and distinct according to the demands of rationalistic thinking. The ideal of the knowing process is absolute clarity and certainty. If our perceptions are diffuse and ambiguous, they are rejected as muddled thinking. With this model of rationalistic knowing, the larger whole and depth of reality go unnoticed.

Computers Are Like Brains, Not Minds

The cognitive significance of the intuitive mode of consciousness has also been demonstrated through research in artificial intelligence. Much debate is presently going on in regard to the difference between the brain and the mind. Is it really possible to construct artificial intelligence that would be comparable to the working of the human mind? And are the human brain and the human mind not fundamentally different? In this respect, is not brain-power largely a neurophysiological activity, while the human mind is more than brain-power or neuronal activity? Stanley L. Jaki, a philosopher of science, in his book, *Brain, Mind, and Computers*, argues that computers can never truly be real intelligences. Those who think of the human mind as theoretically of the same stuff that computers can be composed of fail to see "the incongruity between the facts of consciousness and the tools of physics."[37]

He also points out that the great contributors and developers of the idea of computers refused to equate computers with thinking.[38] He writes:

> The future course of scientific insights and discoveries is a most difficult matter to foretell with some accuracy. At any rate, whatever may be the strength of one's prognosticating the future, it is mainly derived from one's familiarity with the past, as one's ideas about the future are but the projection of one's reading of history. As regards the problem of the thinking ability of computing machines, the historical record shows an impressive unanimity. From Pascal to Von Neumann, all great contributors to the theory and development of computers refused to attribute thinking or consciousness to them. Such a unanimity should give at least some pause to those claiming the possibility, let alone the existence of artificial minds. This is, of course, not to suggest that a list of prominent scientific names should ever be considered more authoritative than facts and demonstrations. Yet such a list should always deserve more credibility than the concerted voice of those who time and again try to give to great discoveries an interpretation wholly at variance with the views of the discoverers themselves.[39]

Jaki goes on to express the "sad aspect of scientific history" when "the voice of such interpreters often prevails in creating the 'momentary scientific consensus' as this is perceived by the general public."[40] In other words, Jaki shows that the views of the leading physicists do not mesh with the popularizers in regard to the idea of artificial intelligence. He shows, in fact, that the leading scientists who are responsible for the theory and development of computers argue for the spiritual uniqueness of the mind—that it is more than merely grey matter in motion.

This wide gap between computers and thinking has been unintentionally illustrated through the research efforts of H. A. Simon (a Nobel Prize winner) and his associates on the subject of long-term versus short-term memory. His field of interest has been largely the cognitive functioning of the mind which can be simulated with the computer.

With the development of high-speed computers in the 1950's and a new respect for the uniqueness of the mind in the light of brain research since the 1960's, psychological research turned its attention more and more to the study of mental processes. Up until World War II psychology had been dominated by behaviorism which rejected conscious experience as a basis for scientific research. With the apparent possibility now of simulating mental processes with computers, a radical shift away from behaviorism has taken place. Simon has been in the forefront of modeling cognitive processes with computers, and he has helped to redefine traditional psychological issues in terms of information processing systems.[41] At the center of his research is the attempt to simulate with computers those tasks which require complex thinking, such as playing chess. His assumption is that computers should be able to perform any task which humans do.[42] In attempting to simulate human thinking, a better understanding of mental processes and human behavior would hopefully be gained. It should be noted in this regard that the philosophical assumption behind this psychological research involving computers is a materialistic-mechanistic view of the mind.

It seems, however, that the difference between computers and human thinking has been dramatically illustrated by Simon's work despite his original intention. His hope continues to be simulated human thinking, but it seems that on both theoretical and practical grounds this hope is ill-founded. For thinking cannot be simulated by computers, except in an extremely restricted sense. What Simon's research demonstrates is that computers do not think. In fact, the term "artificial intelligence" is a misnomer, for there is a wide difference between "brain power" (or neuronal activity) which stores information and which indeed can be simulated by computers, and the ability to think in an intelligent fashion which the human mind uniquely does. Brain power and thinking are not identical.

Simon's work has focused for the most part on the difference between short-term memory (STM) and long-term memory (LTM) in an attempt to observe how complicated mental thinking functions.[43] What he discovered was that only approximately seven items can be held in short-term memory, while long-term memory contains numerous pieces of data stored in "chunks" as if they are pieced together through mnemonic devices which help to keep the data intact.[44] Imagery, feelings, connections, and associations are devices used in LTM (long-term memory) to assist in the retrieval of the information. STM (short-term memory) is the means of access to these chunks of data subconsciously stored. The more verbal and time-oriented chunks are stored by means of the hippocampus of the left cerebral hemisphere, while the imagery-visual chunks of memory are stored by means of the right hippocampus of the right hemisphere. What has emerged out of these experimental tests performed by Simon and his associates is that learning is not a rationalistic matter of accumulating facts; learning is a contextual process involving feelings, intuitions, imagery, and environmental factors rather than explicitly grasping facts supposedly best done by those with the highest I.Q. For example, testing results are better when the tests given to university students are given in the habitual classroom of instruction, as well as administered by the instructor rather than a proctor.[45] This means the context is a powerful retrieval for the "chunks" of information stored in LTM.

This point is further illustrated in tests with master chess players. Masters had remarkable ability to reconstruct a chess position after having observed it for only five seconds, but players below the level of masters possessed a noticeably deficient ability to perform this task. Yet when the same number of pieces were *randomly* placed on the board, the masters could do no better than the weaker players.[46] What these tests indicate is that knowing involves a tacit and intuitive dimension, not simply a rationalistic assessment of facts.

In his research on how the mind performs complicated problem-solving tasks, Simon's experiments have largely involved how chess players calculate moves on the chess boards. What he discovered is that masters have a remarkable LTM ability for recalling patterns learned in the past. The memory system of the brain is divided into verbal-temporal memory of the left hippocampus and the imagery-spatial memory of the right hippocampus.[47] Simon's assumption was that playing chess could be simulated in a strictly rationalistic, rote-memory fashion with a computer, but the results showed that a complicated thinking task like chess involved intuitive thinking which could not be reproduced in a rote-memory fashion. So far as patterns stored in the memory were concerned, masters apparently have over 50,000 patterns stored in LTM, whereas computers can only function with about 1300 patterns.[48] No high speed computer could begin to compete with the grandmaster of chess because of the inability of even high-speed computers to calculate the many patterns of possible chess moves and counter-moves. More is involved in a complicated task like chess than a mere memory bank of possible moves. Thinking involves "hunches" and "guesses" based on subconsciously remembered data. Computers just simply do not "think" in this distinctly human way. Thinking in the true sense of the term involves self-conscious agency. Computers lack this quality of free decision and self-determination; hence, computers cannot have "hunches" or make "guesses," except as they are programmed by computer engineers to do so in a restricted, artificial manner.

Charles Babbage is recognized as the founder of twentieth-century computers.[49] He specifically pointed out that computers cannot engage in guesswork but only in "the direct processes of calculation."[50] He further points out that a computer "is not a thinking being, but simply an automaton which acts according to the laws imposed upon it."[51] The computer thus has no ability to create or originate; it can be programmed to function in a prescribed manner; it does not think.[52] Karl Popper calls a computer "a glorified pencil."[53]

The Christian physicist, Donald MacKay, admitting at the present stage of computing technology that computers do not think, wants to leave open the possibility that conscious agency embodied in a computer may in fact be a reality in the future. He further likens the information process of a computer to the human mind and its mechanical-functioning components to the brain.[54] This seems to me to be a highly questionable analogy and obscures the spiritual uniqueness of personal agency by comparing it with the viewing screen of a computer. Of course, should such a computer be devised which embodied conscious agency, one then would have a basis for comparing persons with computing machines. MacKay doubts the technological possibilities of this new type of conscious computer, but should it be developed, he says this would be another instance of human "procreation" and thus in no way would it be in contradiction to the biblical doctrine of the sovereign, creative God.[55] Be this as it may, the point is that to speak of human agency (instead of the functions of the brain) in terms of the information systems of a computer is misleading. The basic problem of comparing persons with the flow charts of computing machines is that it suggests a rather rigid, inflexible, and puppet-like concept of human nature.

Simon also recognizes that computers at present lack the flexibility of human beings to adapt to new stimuli and new ideas and to comprehend the implications of new input in relation to old data already stored in its memory. Computers are too rigid, too rationalistic and structured in their method of processing data, and lack the depth of human long-term memory.[56] Simon, of course, hopes this limitation can be overcome.

Another related limitation of computers is that the effect of human emotion upon thinking cannot be simulated by computers. Simon particularly notes this present deficiency of computers, calling attention to the fact that little attempt in this area is even being made by technicians. He writes: "Relatively little modeling has been done of motivational and emotional processes or of their interaction with cognitive processes."[57] He further writes:

> Computer simulation continues to be restricted mainly to the modeling of cognitive processes, and there has been only a little research effort aimed at encompassing motivational and emotional processes in broader models and in exploring the relation of those processes with the cognitive.[58]

What if computers could be designed and programmed to simulate feelings? Would this make them human? One artificial intelligence critic, Joseph Weizenbaum, points out that simulating the feeling of desperation or love is not the same as *being* desperate and loving. And if a computer cannot *be* loving or desperate, it cannot understand love or desperation. Simulating and *being* are not identical.[59]

Reductionism Misinterprets Human Uniqueness

The dominant model in psychobiological research is materialistic and mechanistic. The assumption is that the human mind is only a more highly evolved brain than the rest of the animal world, lacking any genuine spiritual uniqueness. Hence so-called artificial intelligence is allegedly possible since the mind can be explained in terms of physics.

It has been a universal perception of Western philosophical thought that the distinctive feature of human beings is their capacity for thinking (reason). This uniqueness seems substantiated because of the human capacity for self-consciousness, freedom, and critical reflection. Of all the animal world only humans are truly creative (as in building fires to keep warm), experience aesthetic appreciation, worship, cry, and laugh. Recent experiments with animals (especially chimpanzees) seem to indicate they have a higher degree of intellectual ability than traditionally thought, but the gap between apes and humans is quite radical because of the distinctive human capacity for reflective rationality, indicating that humans are more than just instinctual beings.[60] Animals have a capacity for consciousness of their environment, but they are totally immersed in the relativities of nature as indicated by their lack of a consciousness of self which is able to project itself beyond the present moment. This classical model of human uniqueness, however, is largely rejected in the modern world; rather, human intelligence, while superior to animals, is capable in theory of being matched, if not surpassed, by artificial intelligence. Further, the distinction between the mind and the brain is dissolved.

This philosophical reductionism of the human mind to psychophysical activity has been strongly challenged by Roger Sperry and other neurobiological scientists engaged in split-brain research. Sperry's major contention is that the human mind (the self) is fundamentally distinct from the neuronal activity of the brain. He believes that recent brain research on the right brain/left brain functioning substantiates a depth to reality missed when cognitivity is restricted to a rationalistic analysis of facts. The mind is the transcendent unity of the neuronal events of the right and left hemispheres. Instead of polarizing left and right hemispheric functioning, "whole brain" functioning is the neurophysiological foundation of the knowing mind, and the mind is more than the functioning of the brain.

II. The Self-Conscious Mind and Brain-Mechanisms

Since the publication of Gilbert Ryles' highly influential book, *The Concept of Mind* (1949), the traditional belief that the mind is a semi-independent reality distinct from the brain has fallen into disrepute with philosophers in general. However, neurophysiologists have taken up this subject with renewed vigor. An examination of recent literature in neuroscience reveals numerous articles addressing the philosophical implications of the new developments in brain research. Ryles' classification of the traditional belief of an immortal mind as "the dogma of the ghost in the machine" is no longer being considered mere dogma. Many neuroscientists are alleging that new empirical evidence points to the idea that the mind is genuinely distinct from the brain. Neurophysiologists, while admitting it is like a machine composed of electrical-chemical activity, believe the brain is directed and controlled by an immaterial mind.

The Uniqueness of the Mind—A Naturalistic View
Roger Sperry describes the interesting chronology of this shift in neuroscience that began in the mid-1960's and continues into the present. Particularly, he shows how recent brain research has created a climate of rapprochement between science, religion, and ethics. Scientific-philosophi-

cal materialism has been seriously eroded as more and more scientists and philosophers are turning again to a new attitude toward the spiritual status of the mind.[61]

Sperry describes his position on the mind-brain relationship as monistic and interactionist. He also calls his position mentalist. Neuroscience, he maintains, has gathered sufficient evidence to show that values are located in the mind as opposed to the brain as such. Ideas, values, and beliefs are capable of interacting with the brain and effecting a causal control over the material world. What one believes, what one values, what one thinks—these are now scientifically shown to be a decisive factor in human behavior. This means personal freedom and rationally-chosen values are not myths to be discarded. Watsonian and Skinnerian behaviorism thus is scientifically untenable.[62]

For Sperry, the new scientific developments in brain research do not substantiate religious beliefs in a personal God or other supernatural realities such as life after death. Sperry regrets what he calls the "mythological, supernatural" interpretation of Eccles. Sperry believes Eccles' religious position to be a "major setback for those who see hope for the future."[63] Instead of relating to a personal God, science, according to Sperry, suggests that one can feel oneself relating "to a vast complex of moving forces, hierarchically interlocked from the subatomic through the cellular, organismic, cognitive, social, and even galactic levels, in a great pluralistic system of cosmic forces in which the higher transcend the lower and all are differentiated from, and united in, a common foundation."[64]

Sperry believes such a "grand design of nature" preserves the basic spiritual concerns of religion and enhances our ability to deal with the critical moral issues of the day—from birth control to environment pollution and ravishment of the ecosystem. This respect for the cosmic forces thus generates a basis for preserving a more human world. Since the self is now shown scientifically to be a morally responsible agent, the future of our planet is our responsibility. No longer can "today's prevailing objective, mechanistic, materialistic, behavioristic, fatalistic, reductionistic view of the notion of 'mind' be sustained," Sperry writes.[65] Monistic materialism is untenable; monistic "mentalism" is allegedly now scientifically supportable.

Sperry's type of monism allows a real distinction between brain and mind, but also it insists that their relationship is inseparable. The mind is an evolutionary emergent quality of the brain. It is "an organizational functional property of brain processing, constituted of neuronal and physiochemical activity, and embodied in, and inseparable from the active brain."[66] Sperry illustrates the mind-brain relationship with a wheel. The destination of a wheel determines the fate of its parts (atoms and molecules) despite the inclination of the individual atoms and molecules. For the individual parts of the wheel are controlled by the higher function of the whole system of the wheel.

This systems-explanation also describes for Sperry the relationship of the mind and brain. The brain is a coherent organizational entity which determines the timing and spacing of the firing patterns within its neuronal infrastructure. The systems-explanation thus assumes that any organizational entity is defined in terms of its space-time elements, not just in terms of its material components. A whole is thus more than the sum of its parts. What makes any "whole" an entity is the spacing and timing of the parts with reference to the organization of the whole.

The mind is thus considered to be the emergent reality in the evolutionary process of nature and is "over and above, and different from our brain physiology—just as we have cellular properties that are over and above and different from their molecular constituent."[67] Sperry is not entirely convincing in his argument that the immaterial mind is destroyed when the brain dies. What he argues in his analogy of the wheel does not necessarily apply to the mind. For the wheel is a material "whole" but the mind by Sperry's own insistence is not a material entity. If the mind is an immaterialistic state even if it is an emergent system of the brain, then the universal principle of systems and subsystems and their relationship to component parts in the space-time spectrum is not necessarily applicable to non-material realities. Sperry's monism is founded on an error of logically comparing two realities admittedly dissimilar in their very essence. What is true of material objects testable in a scientific manner is not *ipso facto* true of immaterial objects beyond empirical testing.

The Uniqueness of the Mind—A Neo-Augustinian View

This point is well made by Eccles. The self-conscious mind cannot be prejudged by the standards of scientific thought since it is not within the scope of natural science to quantify and measure it. Eccles writes: "Science is very successful in its limited field of problems; but the great problems, the *mysterium tremendum*, in the existence of everything we know, this is not accountable for in any scientific manner."[68]

However, Eccles believes that the testing results of the split-brain patients of Sperry and his associate infer a dualistic theory of the mind. The basic difference between Sperry's monism and Eccles' dualism is that Eccles believes the self continues its existence independent of the brain when it is destroyed. Otherwise, they both agree that the self-conscious mind is an immaterial entity whose function and reality is on a different level than the neuronal mechanism of the brain.

In addition to the testing results of split-brain patients, Eccles believes there are also other scientific data to support a dualist-interactionist theory of the mind-body relationship. It should be noted, however, that Eccles is not trying to pursue a God-of-the-gaps type of apologetics in this regard. The reality of faith does not depend upon scientific results. Rather, Eccles is maintaining that the remarkable results of brain research indirectly and unintentionally show the untenability of mechanistic and materialistic philosophy and at the same time allow for the intellectual viability of a Christian perspective. His apologetic is thus not intended to *prove* faith, but to enable faith to see its intellectual compatibility with science. In this respect, conscious perception, voluntary action, and conscious memory are cited as indications of the immaterial mind.

First, Eccles highlights the unitary character of the self-conscious mind, along with the mind's ability to focus first on one thing, and now on this, and later on some other object. This capacity for *attention* at the level of self-awareness cannot be explained on the basis of neuronal activity. However, some neurophysiologists do assert an identity between the activities of neurons and the mind, but Eccles points out that such a hypothesis is maintained without any scientific evidence. Neurophysiology can test and predict the functions and activities of the brain, but it cannot explain or predict the intentions of the self-conscious mind. This "negative" evidence suggests the possibility that the self-conscious mind remains superior to, and to some extent independent of, the body.[69]

This spiritual self-transcendence is illustrated not only by the experiments of split-brain patients, but also by the experiments of Wilder Penfield, a world famous brain surgeon whose pioneering efforts with epileptic patients have made a lasting contribution to neuroscience.[70] He was the first scientist to deal in direct observation of the human brain in fully conscious persons.[71] Penfield's surgical operation on these epileptic patients required that they be fully conscious. Their scalps were injected with a local analgesic to prevent pain and no sedative or anesthetic was given. The surface of one hemisphere of the brain was exposed wide enough for study and possible excision to cure the source of abnormality causing uncontrollable discharges of energy leading to epileptic attacks. The patients, awake and alert, were able to guide the surgeon's hand throughout the operation. The surgeon explained to the patients each step of the process and the patients reported back to the surgeon what they were experiencing.[72]

An important part of the process involved the use of a stimulating electrode to seek out the site of brain irritation. With the electrical stimulation of the interpretative areas of the cortex, the patients reported actually "re-living" the visible, audible, and feeling dimensions in exact detail of previous experiences. At the same time the patients were fully conscious of being on the operating table at the Montreal Neurological Institute, McGill University, and they were able to report to the surgeon their "flash-backs."[73] This doubling of their consciousness within a single awareness of what was happening provided for Penfield a conviction that the mind was above and superior to the function of the brain-mechanisms, since the unitary character of self-consciousness cannot otherwise be accounted for in these patients.

The first "flashback" was reported to Penfield in 1933 by a mother. As the electrode touched her interpretative cortex, she reported being suddenly aware of working in the kitchen and hearing her little boy's voice as he was playing in the back yard. She also heard the familiar neighborhood noises. Another patient reported being at a baseball game in a small town and watching a little boy crawl under the fence to get inside the ball park. Another patient reported hearing instruments playing. She hummed the melody which she heard, and the tempo was what one would have expected. Penfield restimulated her over thirty times, trying to mislead her. Each time she heard and relived the exact same experience, and her humming started each time with the chorus and on to the verse.[74] On another occasion, Penfield reports that a young South African patient lying on the operating table expressed amazement "that he was laughing with his cousins on a farm in South Africa, while he was also fully conscious of being in the operating room in Montreal."[75]

Penfield's studies with over a thousand patients have led him to the conclusion that though the contents of consciousness are dependent upon neuronal activity of the brain, awareness itself is not.[76] The brain has many semi-separable mechanisms which function automatically (as reading, writing, speaking, and dextrous skills), but these automatic functions of the mechanism of the brain are acquired through the conscious attention of the mind. The mind is the real person who walks around with his private brain-computer to use as one sees fit. What is learned and recorded in the computer-brain depends entirely upon the attention capacity of the self-conscious mind. What is ignored by the mind the brain fails to record.[77] Penfield writes:

> Because it seems to me certain that it will always be quite impossible to explain the mind on the basis of neuronal action within the brain, and because it seems to me that the mind develops and matures independently throughout an individual's life as though it were a continuing element, and because a computer (which the brain is) must be programmed and operated by an agency capable of independent understanding, I am forced to choose the proposition that our being is to be explained on the basis of two fundamental elements [mind and brain].[78]

In agreement with Eccles, the internationally-known philosopher Karl Popper, says these experiments by Penfield refute the materialistic view of the self. (Incidentally, Popper himself argues for a dualist-interactionist theory, though he is a religious agnostic).[79] Popper notes that some of the proponents of the identity theory of brain and mind "prophesy" with an air of dogmatism that future brain research will confirm their theory of the mind.[80] B. F. Skinner is one of these "prophets" who says "the physiologists of the future will tell us all that can be known about what is happening inside the behaving organism," thus scientifically verifying at that time behavioristic philosophy.[81] The developments in neuroscience seem to run counter to Skinner's expectations.

The experiments of Hans Kornhuber, a neurophysiologist at the University of Ulm, West Germany, and his associates (1974), demonstrate that the way one thinks changes the patterns of neuronal activity in the brain.[82] For example, when a subject "willed" an action (as moving a finger) uninflu- enced by any external stimuli, it was found that a measurable amount of time (eight-tenths of a second) was expended before the signal for movement was generated. What caused the action? Neuronal activities? It was the instru- mental cause of action, but thinking willed the activity. To be sure, most movement is automatic and carried out subconsciously with excellent skill. Yet, Kornhuber's scientifically-controlled experiments eliminated the nor- mal set of complex factors involved in initiating movement. His experiments reveal that simply by thinking one can will action that is not initiated by external stimuli. Eccles concludes that thinking thus seems to be something independent of the neuronal machinery of the brain.[83]

Kornhuber's success in scientifically measuring what is called "cerebral potentials" preceding voluntary movements is considered by some to be a revolutionary scientific breakthrough. Until Kornhuber's experiments, neuro- physiologists assumed that brain potential would be recorded only over the left motor cortex of the cerebral hemisphere. It is in this region that Penfield evoked right finger motion with electrical stimulation. Yet Kornhuber found that eight-tenths of a second before the finger moved, there was a bilateral potential (readiness potential) which spread over both hemispheres. This consists of a patterned impulse of neuronal discharges which develop and spread out over the cerebral cortex. Later this impulse activates the neurons in the motor areas responsible for programming movement. In this experi- ment, the motor neurons in the left cortex activate the muscles in the right finger. The surprising result of this extremely complex experiment was the gradual buildup of the readiness potential and its wide extent in the brain following the voluntary command.

One neurophysiologist, Richard M. Restak, says Kornhuber's discovery concerning readiness potential is a major breakthrough as significant in its implications as Einstein's formulation of relativity theory in physics. "In 1905, physics was radically altered, and along with it came a revolution in our understanding of the physical world. So, too, the discovery that willed action is not localizable in any particular area of the brain represents a radically new way of conceptualizing the relationship between mind and brain."[84]

Restak was himself a psychophysical identitist, equating the mind with the action of the brain, until the new developments in brain research com- pelled him to distinguish between the mind and the brain.[85] Such was the case with other neuroscientists as Penfield and Sperry, as we have pointed out.

Eccles concludes from Kornhuber's research: "Thus we can regard these experiments as providing a convincing demonstration that voluntary move- ments can be freely initiated independently of any determining influences that are entirely within the neuronal machinery of the brain."[86] The point

Eccles is making is, where does agency to act come from, if not a mind that transcends the brain? How the mind interfaces with the brain to initiate this action Eccles does not propose to know.

A further indication of the difference between the self and the brain is the time lapse between neuronal activity and the experience of the self-conscious mind. For example, in the sophisticated test of B. Libet covering a period of at least ten years since 1973, it has been shown that the self-awareness of a perceptual experience occurs only after a measurable time-lapse subsequent to the incoming impulses on the neurons of the primary sensory area of the cerebral cortex. For example, a brief electrical pulse applied to the skin of the hand is not self-consciously discerned by the subject until five-tenths of a second after the stimulation, yet the actual transmission of the stimulation reaches the cerebral cortex within fifteen-thousandths of a second, as shown by the evoked response. However, one will antedate the stimulation to the time it is actually felt in the cerebral cortex so that it is judged to have occurred earlier than one's actual perception of the stimulation.[87]

Extensive testing between sensory input and neuronal activity in the cerebral cortex in reference to self-consciousness has been carried out in recent years. That this temporal discrepancy between the neuronal events and the experience of self-consciousness conclusively proves scientifically that the self is more than neuronal machinery is more than can be said, but it does suggest the viability of such an interpretation, especially since there is no neurophysiological accounting for this delay and antedating. At any rate, this illustrates the distinction between what is merely physically felt and what is knowingly experienced. And it would seem to demonstrate that conscious perception involves more than mere passive reactions (epiphenomena) to neural events. Perception seems to be an intentional and inter-pretative function above and beyond the neuronal machinery of the brain.

Donald MacKay is not convinced from the scientific data of Kornhuber and Libet that one should infer that their tests imply a dualist theory of the mind and brain. He suggests their data could be given alternate interpretations.[88] However, Eccles believes that while their scientific experiments do not prove the independent existence of the self-conscious mind, their data indicate the viability of a dualist position more so than a non-dualist and non-interactionist point of view. The fact that other neuroscientists besides Eccles and Sperry were led to postulate the existence of an immaterial mind on the basis of the new brain research results, such as those of Wilder Penfield and Richard Restak, indicates that the concept of an immaterial mind above and beyond the reality of the brain is not arbitrarily super-imposed on the available scientific data. Persons such as Restak and Sperry had no particular religious inclination to abandon psychophysical, materialistic monism. Scientific and philosophical considerations and personal integrity seem to have brought them to their respective conclusions.

A further indication of the temporal discrepancy between neural events and conscious perception, Eccles believes, is seen in the slowing down of time as it is experienced in emergency situations. When a person encounters an emergency, the self-conscious mind arranges for what seems to be a slowing down of time in order for the best opportunity to be used for getting out of the difficulty. Eccles cites his experience in which a fast-moving truck was headed for his car on a collision course, and time seemed to slow down drastically allowing him to make the right maneuvers to avoid what seemed to be a life-threatening collision. This experience of time in slow motion cannot be explained in terms of neural activity, but rather the self-conscious mind seems to be exercising control over the neural activity of the brain.[89]

Another phenomenon of the self-conscious mind which neuronal machinery cannot explain is the ability of the mind to retrieve memories stored up in the cerebral cortex. The self-conscious mind "commands, as it were, the storage data banks in the cerebral cortex."[90] This retrieval is intentional and a self-conscious process. No neurobiologist can account for this, Eccles believes. Yet the ability of the mind to rise above and control mental events indicates an interactionism-dualism between mind and brain. Eccles writes:

> All the time when we are searching for a memory, searching for a word, searching for something from the past storage in our brains, we are searching and receiving and judging and evaluating with this conscious self. It is superior to its objects which are delivered, and it is superior in that it can accept or reject them and use them or modify them and put them into the brain storage. . . . The self conscious mind is in fact probing always into the brain in some matter to retrieve from there or to attempt to retrieve something which it wants back, some desired input from the brain. Now this must involve an immense learned performance. You have to conceive that the whole of our civilized development, of our cultural development, consists not in having a brain with all of this storage, but in having a self-conscious mind that can retrieve and know how to retrieve subtly and effectively from this storage. It has some way of playing into this immense store of memory that is in the spatio-temporal patterns of connectivity in the neural coding, and of receiving back from that—not perhaps the first time; but it has strategies and tricks of retrieval.[91]

Eccles believes that his mind-brain model is both experimentally and scientifically viable. He writes: "It can be claimed that the hypothesis belongs to science because it is based on empirical data and is objectively testable. It must be emphasized that, just as with other scientific theories of great explanatory power, the present hypothesis has to be subjected to empirical testing. However, it is claimed that it is not refuted by any existing knowledge. It can be predicted optimistically, that there will be a long period of remodelling and development, but not an irretrievable falsification."[92]

Eccles' dualism of brain and mind is also an interactionism. The two are genuinely different realities, but nonetheless interface and mutually influence each other. Eccles also believes research data indicate that the self-conscious mind is more directly linked to the brain by way of the left or dominant hemisphere. Just how the material brain and immaterial self interact is in principle inexplicable.[93] That they do in fact interface is scientifically testable. What further cannot be scientifically resolved is what happens to the self-conscious mind when all cerebral activity permanently ceases at death.[94] The question which Eccles is thus addressing is life after death. Does the mind continue its existence? This is the question which initially intrigued and motivated Eccles and caused him in part to choose neurophysiology as his life's vocation. Eccles believes in God and affirms the existence of personal immortality. Yet he acknowledges that this belief is not a neurophysiological finding, though it is not contrary to scientific findings. It is one thing to claim a scientific basis for a brain-self distinction, but testing the idea of immortality is not a possibility for neurophysiology.[95]

Toward a Holistic View of Persons:
A Neo-Calvinist view vs. a neo-Thomist view
Donald MacKay, an English neurophysiologist, has been a highly visible partner in dialogue with Eccles and Sperry. MacKay is a highly respected "evangelical" writer whose grasp of the issues and theological competence are impressive. His perspective on the relationship of science and faith shows remarkable balance. He has brought to this ongoing discussion among neuroscientists a sense of intellectual openness and critical scholarship, and he serves as an excellent model of Christian apologetics. In particular, he rejects a god-of-the-gaps apologetical approach.

The Unlike Eccles who cites scientific data as indirectly supporting (though not proving) the viability of a Christian interpretation, MacKay does not seek to demonstrate how scientific data reinforces Christian faith. His concern is to show how the mutually independent methods of science and religion coexist logically without there being any necessary conflict. In this respect, MacKay seems more intent on clarifying scientific data to show logically and conceptually how science does not pose a threat to belief.[96] MacKay, in the language of apologetics, is a fideist—that is, belief in God and in the Bible stems solely from the self-authenticating reality of faith. Eccles is an evidentialist—that is, the self-authenticating faith of the "heart" can be reconciled with the inquiring "mind" by citing objective data that intellectually reinforce one's personal religious convictions. In this respect, Eccles was a Christian believer long before he began to see that recent brain research reinforced the viability of his faith.[97] His apologetic is thus not intended to prove the existence of God, but to show the compatibility of science and faith as an aid to one's religious understanding. He acknowledges that the fundamental questions of existence cannot be answered by science and theoretical understanding, but only in faith.[98]

MacKay's contribution to the debate on the mind-brain relationship has been significant and has helped to clarify the real issues. Unfortunately, my general agreement with his Christian stance may not be evident in the light of my hopefully amicable disagreements with his position on the ontological status of the mind. But even here, I believe I agree more with him than what may be evident. I suspect that our differing perceptions on these matters are due in large part to our respective Arminian and Calvinistic positions.

MacKay argues that the objective scientific data cannot in principle be used as evidence against or for the religious.[99] Even the most rigorous mechanistic view of materialism is allegedly perfectly compatible with faith. Properly understood, MacKay says that the physical and the religious are not at all in competition with each other. Nor are they two opposing, independent entities. This is the point he makes against Eccles' dualism-interactionism. MacKay sides more with Sperry's monism, though he disagrees with Sperry's anti-supranaturalism and his interactionist language. MacKay uses the term "complementary" to describe the intrinsic relationship between the physical and the spiritual. He terms the physical the O-Story (outside perspective) and the spiritual-personal the I-Story (the inside perspective). This complementary relationship means that the physical and the personal-spiritual are not two independent entities but are mutual aspects of one reality. Nonetheless MacKay still assumes a real distinction between the physical and the personal (conscious agency). He specifically repudiates the idea that the personal is epiphenomenal (a mere by-product of the brain activity). Yet he argues that one is personal only in direct reference to one's physical embodiment.[100]

There are two basic views of the mind-body relationship in classic thought—the Platonic-Augustinian and the Aristotelian-Thomistic views. In this respect, Eccles is more Augustinian (Platonic) in viewing the body as an instrument of the soul, whereas MacKay's position is closer to the Thomistic (Aristotelian) view that the body is an essential aspect of the personal dimension. Yet there are significant differences between the Thomistic view and MacKay's.

One difference between MacKay's position and the classical Thomistic view is his terminological preference for conscious agency rather than the term *mind*. Hence MacKay intentionally avoids the use of the word *mind* as descriptive of the personal. The classical definition coming from Boethius in the sixth century is that a person is a rational individual. The "rational" refers to one's capacity for the conscious reflective activity of the mind intrinsically embodied in the physical world. Humans have the physical in common with animals, but their supranatural transcendent quality is specified by their rational-intellectual capacity. However, this emphasis upon the rational in Thomistic philosophy should not be identified with the rationalistic-intellectualistic identification of reality with mere abstract-deductive logic, typical of Cartesian rationalism. The concept of reason is much broader in meaning in traditional Christian thought (including thinking, feeling, willing, memory, etc.) than the rationalism of modern philosophy.

Another difference between MacKay and the Thomistic tradition is the latter's linking together both the concept of the immortality of the soul and the resurrection of the body. In Thomism, the human mind is not the brain, though an essential aspect of the mind. Aquinas thus agreed with the Aristotelian notion of the mind as the form of the body. That is, the mind is the larger significance of the body. The mind is not like a pilot's relationship to his ship as if the mind and body are mutually independent entities. Rather for Aquinas, the mind and body are one organism constituted by living, sensing, feeling, desiring, willing, and thinking. Aquinas had to address the obvious question whether or not the mind simply evaporated at the moment of death. His answer was NO. The soul (the mind) continues to exist in an afterlife. This answer appears to contradict his position on anthropological unity, except that Aquinas believed that one was not in the truest sense of the term a person in a bodiless state. Hence death—as Paul put it—is a humiliation. Aquinas thus argued that the immortality of the soul was a theologically incomplete idea except in reference to the biblical doctrine of the resurrection of the body. He postulated both the immortality of the soul and the resurrection of the body.[101]

A weakness of MacKay's position is that he only has a concept of "re-embodiment" of the self in another body and disallows the possibility of a bodiless state.[102] When does the resurrection occur for MacKay? Does an individual immediately receive a new body at death? Does one simply not exist during the interim between one's death and the resurrection which our Lord promised would occur at his second return? MacKay does not address this issue.

A further weakness of MacKay's approach is that while he argues for a difference and unity between the self and the body he fails to point out just how this difference and unity can be specified. He tends to play down the primary importance of the brain as the decisive physical location of the self rather than other parts of the body.[103] If Eccles makes too much of the self's connection with the brain as MacKay seems to think, MacKay makes too little of it. If the personal is defined in terms of conscious agency as MacKay does, surely then the brain is its primary expression at the physical level.

A strength of MacKay's position is his holistic emphasis upon the self and its physical body. The body is not a piece of baggage which the self has to carry around. Rather, it is an essential aspect of the personal. The biblical concept of the resurrection assumes the psychosomatic unity of our existence. In this sense, death is a humiliation and we are incomplete as persons until our selves are reconstituted in a "spiritual body" where the split between the body and the self is finally overcome. This Thomistic concept of the resurrection of the body and immortality of the soul has largely been the traditional belief of the church.

However, MacKay's insistence upon the unity of the conscious agency and our body tends to obscure the fallen state of our present situation which does involve a split between ourselves and our bodies. Death is an enemy precisely because it is the ultimate expression of the incongruity and disruption of the personal dimensions of our being. Consequently, there is in some limited sense an artificial relationship between the self and the brain, but that artificiality is not God's intention; it is a consequence of sin. Eccles is surely right to insist upon the superiority of the non-physical aspect of our existence, but MacKay is surely right to insist that the ultimate holistic nature of our existence will be achieved in the resurrection of the body. However, MacKay maintains that there is no self except in reference to a body. This can hardly be justified as biblical. The death of the body surely does not entail the extinction of the self. MacKay does not address this question adequately, though he dismisses biblical language that describes the body as a "clothing" and as a "tent" as mere metaphor. His suggestion is that whenever the Scriptures speak of the self as if it were an entity different from the body, such language ought to be understood figuratively since it allegedly contradicts the concept of the resurrection of the body.[104]

MacKay's stress upon the absolute dependency of the self upon the body puts him close to Sperry's antisupranaturalism which assumes a naturalistic systems-definition of the self, as he himself suggests.[105] As the melody of a harp ceases when the harp is destroyed, so the self ceases at death. MacKay does not draw this conclusion, but his apparent unwillingness to allow the self to exist in some measure independent of the body (however fragmented such a person might be without his body) is compatible with Sperry's non-theistic philosophy. MacKay's concept of complementarity may be in some ways a better term than Eccles' concept of interactionism, but it is not unbiblical to affirm a basic distinction between the self and the body (brain). (See Rudolf Bultmann, *Theology of the New Testament* [New York: Scribner, 1951], I, 211-219.) Indeed, it is a fundamental biblical assumption that even though the body is a vital aspect of the self, the self continues to exist after the body is returned to dust, however incomplete a bodiless self may be until its resurrection.

On the one hand, MacKay assumes that neurophysiological activity is a "correlate" of self-conscious activity. Things can be described from the "outside" or "inside" perspective without any basic contradiction or discrepancy. This point is further argued in reference to a Calvinistic view of divine predestination. Even though God decrees what reality will be, we nonetheless are free psychologically. That is, we are morally responsible agents who freely choose our destinies. Neither physical nor divined determinism contradict moral responsibility of conscious agents. MacKay writes: "The sense in which God 'determines' my future does not exclude, but rather requires that I determine it also. It thus offers no rational excuse from my responsibility for the choices by which I determine it."[106] To be sure, MacKay's logic is flawless. The conscious agent may, psychologically speaking, freely choose one's course of action even though God decrees it and the mechanistic laws of physics determine it.[107]

The typical Calvinistic logic which MacKay uses here is valid, formally speaking, but existentially speaking, this position is not persuasive. To talk about personal, moral responsibility within a mechanistically-determined world along with a deterministic view of divine sovereignty lessens the meaning of moral agency. His conceptual analysis of correlation and complementarity to describe the relationship between the mind and the body is too formalistic and abstract. The dialectic tension between the self and the brain cannot be resolved in the realm of logic. Indeed Sperry's experiments with split-brain patients reveal just how profoundly reality extends beyond the rationalistic-logical confines of left hemispheric functions.

One sympathetic interpreter of MacKay's position says that MacKay's logic seems too difficult for many to follow.[108] I think the problem is its logical abstraction which tries to postulate the compatibility of a mechanistic view of physics, theological determinism, and free moral agency. Such a rationalistic contruction may satisfy the demands of logic (left hemisphere) but not life (holistic thinking).

MacKay's attempt to harmonize these otherwise apparently contradictory notions is seen in his reference to "artificial intelligence" as a means of illustrating the relationship between the electro-chemical activity of nerve cells and conscious agency. A computer is made of electronic parts functioning according to the mechanical laws of physics, yet to explain a computer piece by piece is to miss the real significance of the computer—which is to perform certain functions, such as mathematical calculations. The mathematical calculation is distinct from the electronic mechanical functioning of a computer. Though the information-flow charts of a computer and its mechanical operation are distinct, they are different aspects of a single reality. This "dualism" is not a real dualism, but it is only a dualism of different perspectives concerning the one entity.[109] Likewise with human beings we are confronted with two different perspectives of the one person—conscious agency and brain states. The human brain is like "a great community of innumerable micro-computers."[110] This analogy of the brain as a network of interlocking microcomputers provides us with "new and more realistic categories,"[111] MacKay believes, for interpreting the relationship between the neuronal activities of the brain and conscious agency. The two levels are interdependent but not mutually disturbing which would be the case if they were two separate entities. Thus, the difference is that of function and of perspective, but not a difference of real entities. There is a correlation between consciousness and brain functioning, but not an exact equivalency. Consciousness is more than its mechanistic correlate, even as a mathematical computation is more than the computing electronic mechanical functioning. Yet both are interdependent aspects of one entity. MacKay thus defines human existence as "physically embodied personalities."[112]

MacKay sees his position as a mediating one between dualism and monism. With a dualist position he maintains there is more to our person than our physical aspect. This aspect is our spiritual make-up. With the monist he affirms that our bodily make-up is an essential aspect of our personhood. These aspects are "complementary" and "interdependent." "We are considering them as two equally real aspects of one and the same mysterious unity."[113] MacKay goes on to argue that even the most "physically-deterministic assumptions"[114] do not undermine the concept of moral responsibility. Likewise theological determinism—the view that every event in space-time is determined by God's *fiat*—does not undermine moral agency. His argument is based on a perspectivist view of explanation. From the perspective of the physical, all events are mechanistically caused. From the divine perspective, every event is decreed by *fiat*! From the standpoint of human agency, events in space-time are determined by one's free choice.[115] MacKay's argumentation for theological determinism and human freedom thus reflects the general Calvinistic view. Theologically speaking, God in His sovereignty has determined all events so that God knows the future from the standpoint of his decrees. This means that though all things are theologically determined, human choices are still free and consequently we are morally responsible agents. As we have already noted, logically it is consistent to argue that psychological freedom is compatible with theological determinism. A contradiction occurs only if determinism and freedom were to be argued for on the same level.[116] It is perhaps only natural to extend this argument of the logical compatibility between theological determinism and human freedom to include physical determinism. In spite of the apparent logical consistency among the three levels, one cannot help but feel the meaning of freedom has been trivialized.

MacKay's concept of levels as a model of explanation seems to trivialize freedom because it fails to show how the hierarchically-arranged levels are really related in a concrete manner. Only in the realm of formal, abstract logic can one maintain physical determinism, divine determinism, and human moral agency. A genuinely hierarchical arrangement allows higher and lower levels of reality that genuinely interact and alter their respective levels. For example, human agency can genuinely alter or suspend the normal activity of the physical level. MacKay's semi-deistic, non-interfering model thus restricts the idea of interaction "for links between events or entities at the same categorical level, whether mental or physical."[117]

Unless the idea of "interference" and "disturbance" is admitted as an essential feature of a hierarchical arrangement of the differing levels of reality, then such a hierarchical system is only a piece of static, abstract logic, and the notion of moral agency is compromised. To be sure, a term like disturbance suggests a negative and pejorative term, and Sperry rightly corrects MacKay's misinterpretation to show that interaction means supervening.[118]

One of the features of relativity theory is that one's perspective and place in space-time has more than epistemological significance; rather, the standpoint of the knower is really related to the object known such that the object's reality is altered by the standpoint of the knower. Hence one's perspective "interferes" with other aspects of existence. Relativity theory is both epistemologically explanatory and ontologically interacting with various dimensions at the same time. To be sure, MacKay argues for this point, but only at the level involving its own category of existence. There is no "interaction" between levels.

Consequently, when MacKay labels the hierarchical relationship between the physical and conscious agency as "complementary," it is difficult to know what is meant—if not that the two dimensions are only conceptually distinct or that they are without any ontological connection. If so, how then does his position differ either from the psychophysical identity theory or a form of deism? MacKay also criticizes Sperry's monism-interactionism because Sperry allows in actuality that conscious agency and neurophysiological activity are distinct and hence interact. That MacKay objects to the idea of interaction between the mental and physical but insists only a conceptual distinction with the two levels existing as different aspects of one entity would seem to imply that he had overcome monistic materialism only by a logical *fiat* and not in actuality. At least Sperry allows for a real difference even though his is a modified form of monism. MacKay's distinction between conscious agency and brain activity is well worked out conceptually but it lacks concrete specificity. His hierarchical relationships among the various dimensions of reality seem more imagined than real. When MacKay affirms the spiritual dimension of personhood and at the same time attacks Eccles' affirmation of the self-conscious mind as the decisive indicator of our spiritual uniqueness, it is difficult not to believe that he has trivialized the spiritual meaning of our existence. One can *argue with* Eccles that our personhood is defined primarily in terms of our spiritual makeup and that this aspect is decisively distinguished from our physical body, but at the same time one can *argue against* Eccles that the connection between the two aspects of our personhood is more intrinsic than his interactionism might suggest. However, MacKay tends to make the physical aspect an almost exact "correlate" of conscious agency—even though he denies it. Though he speaks of the spiritual function as a "higher" level than the physical, it is not in essence different from the physical. The spiritual is just a "higher-level explanation" than the "purely physical determinancy" of the central nervous system.[119] Again, the difference between the physical and the spiritual is not a real difference, but a difference of function. The spiritual compares with the information-flow system of a computer, and the physical brain activity compares with its electronic parts functioning according to the mechanistic laws of physics.[120]

MacKay further argues that just as a mathematician can set up the very same equation once programmed on a now-broken-down computer in another properly functioning computer, so God can take the information-flow system of our conscious agency and re-embody us accordingly. His point is made against Sperry's monism—that the mind dissipates upon the demise of the brain. MacKay believes the analogy of the human person with a computing machine illustrates the logical viability of life after death.[121] This inference is difficult to follow. It seems on the one hand that MacKay had made the complementarity of conscious agency and body to be incidental. MacKay writes: "We do not have to scrape together the bits of the original burnt-out computer and try to reassemble them in their original condition."[122] The computation can easily be re-embodied in another machine. Likewise, "the fate of our present embodiment is of no consequence." God can simply "re-embody" us in an "appropriate body" of his choosing.[123] Quite contrary to this, the biblical concept of the resurrection is not a re-embodiment; it is a transformation of our present bodies into a reconstituted body. The connection of ourselves and our present bodies is more intrinsic than MacKay's notion of re-embodiment allows. How this is a meaningful concept from the standpoint of physics needs to be addressed, but the continuity between our present body and our new body is a New Testament assumption. (For an excellent discussion on the resurrection of the body, see Wolfhart Pannenberg, *Jesus—God and Man*, trans. Wilkins and Priebe [Philadelphia: Westminster] p. 76.)

I do not believe that MacKay really intended this rather loose association between one's conscious agency and the particularity of one's earthly body, but his language states it. In this respect, MacKay's position comes closer to the Greek concept of the immortality of the soul (and reincarnation) than one would have suspected in the light of his insistence on the absolute, inseparable relationship between body and personhood. At any rate, Mac-Kay's concept of re-embodiment needs further clarification. God's promise is not simply to give us "a re-embodied existence," but to change our bodies into a renewed, "spiritual body" (1 Corinthians 15:44). To be sure, the biblical concept of resurrection does not mean a mere resuscitation of a dead corpse, but it does involve the concept of a transformation of our earthly bodies into a spiritual body (whatever that means!). The concept of continuity between our new and old bodies cannot be simply ignored without a loss of the meaning of personal identity.

Finally, I question the validity of MacKay's analogy of ourselves with a computer. Is conscious agency really comparable to the information-flow system of a computer? I think not. Rather, is not the information-flow system of a computer more comparable to brain activity? It is the brain which houses information, but only the mind knows it. The central nervous system is made up of innumerable individual cells even as the computer is made up of numerous pieces of electronic parts. Further, the neuronal circuitry in the brain establishes the physical basis of information, but, like the viewing screen of a computer, its data is unintelligible except in reference to a knowing mind. Further, just as the brain fails to record any information that the mind ignores (as Penfield's experiments with epileptic patients show),[124] even so the computer fails to record any information unless the programmer programs the computer accordingly. Hence the brain is like a computer; its programming comes from outside itself. "The mind directs, and the mind-mechanism [brain] executes,"[125] as Penfield puts it. Penfield further writes: "The mind seems to act independently of the brain in the same sense that a programmer acts independently to his computer, however much he may depend upon the action of that computer for certain purposes."[126]

MacKay dismisses the idea of "the little man in the head" who gathers the information displayed on the screen of the brain.[127] He postulates the existence of a central supervisory system in the brain which accounts for the unitary character of our experiences. This central unitary system is the correlate to our experience of conscious agency.[128] Even so, how can the information-flow charts of a computer be compared with the meaning of consciousness, even if a central supervisory system in the brain were a neurophysiological fact—which it is not.

Penfield's experiments with an electrode can cause patients to turn their heads and eyes, to move their limbs, to speak, and to swallow. The electrode, placed on the interpretative cortex, can summon the replay and a re-living in complete detail (including pictures, sounds, feelings, etc.) of past experiences in their lives, and while these patients report to the surgeon the "flash-backs" as if they were just happening, they are fully conscious on the operating table.[129] In spite of this extensive testing, neuroscience has no evidence that the function of the mind can be explained in reference to the function of the brain. Penfield writes: "There is no place in the cerebral cortex where electrical stimulation will cause a patient to believe or to decide."[130] To talk about a central supervisory system in the brain as a correlate to conscious agency lacks any scientific evidence, according to Penfield's experiments. The absence of just such a neurophysiological system is so remarkable that many brain scientists have been compelled to postulate the existence of an immaterial mind, even though they may not embrace a belief in an after-life.

Conclusion

What has been presented in this article is that recent brain research shows that the mind's perception of reality is dependent upon left and right cerebral hemispheric functioning. Such functioning includes both logical-sequential (digital) and affective-intuitive (analogue) dimensions. It has also been pointed out that these alternate modes of the mind have been acknowledged since the beginning of serious philosophical reflection. In this respect, their validity does not depend upon the experimental research of neuroscience, though recent developments in brain science do contribute significantly to the philosophical discussion.

What further has been argued here is that the mind is a causal agent and is more than the neuronal functioning of the brain. Evidence for this judgment has been indicated in the research of Herbert Simon whose attempts to simulate the human mind with so-called artificial intelligence have demonstrated that the mind cannot be simulated, though the behavior of the brain can. Thinking is more than a mere rationalistic analysis and storing of facts; it is being able to see beyond the obvious to a depth of reality that cannot be entirely structured and analyzed. Thinking, interpretation, feeling, willing, striving, etc., are activities of the mind whatever their physiological basis may be. The striking data supplied by Penfield's experiments with the electrical stimulation of the brain, as well as the experiments of Kornhuber and Libet, present persuasive indications that the concept of the mind is not a mere dogma. The dogmatists now appear to be the reductionists.

We began this article with a discussion of Plato's parable of the charioteer directing two horses; one was good will who had verbal skills to understand the command of reason (*Phaedrus* 253d); the other one was impulsive-intuitive feeling who was "deaf" and difficult to control (*Phaedrus* 253e). The point of the parable was to show that truth is not easy to come by. Plato's concept of dialectic was his philosophic method for achieving the unity of truth. The dialectic method is the process of the mind's reasoning from one side of truth to another side until the entire gamut of ideas and all the aspects of reality have been carefully examined. Only in this way can the ultimate dialectic unity of truth be attained. (*Republic* VII, 532a, b).

Brain research with its sophisticated anatomical analysis of the two hemispheres suggests the contemporary relevance of Plato's concept of dialectic. While there may be individual preferences for one aspect of truth as opposed to another, the dynamic unity of truth transcends personal cognitive styles. The wholeness of truth is always a precarious synthesis of the multidimensional aspects of reality. This dialect synthesis is a philosophical corollary to the neurophysiological concept of "whole brain" functioning.

Thanks to the recent research in neurophysiology and computer-based psychology, a greater appreciation for the inexhaustible depth of life can be obtained. Though the results of brain research will continue to be debated and contested, sufficient data already demonstrate that rationalistic-analytic (digital) thinking and intuitive-holistic (analogue) thinking as alternate cognitive styles have a neurophysiological basis and that these alternate modes of thinking mutually contribute to the mind's perception of reality. We have no reason to content ourselves with emotional shallowness, rational superficiality, and social isolationism. We have good reason to disbelieve materialistic reductionism and to affirm the possibility of existential and social meaningfulness grounded in transcendent reality. We have reason to believe the mind is more than mere neurophysiological activity of the brain. We have reason to believe there is a presence of truth in our world which is more than just a rationalistic-analytic grasp of scientific facts—a truth which is objective and subjective, social and personal, rational and emotional, analytical and synthetical, temporal and eternal, explicit and tacit. This dialectical unity of cognitivity is an expression of the *personal* and *spiritual* dimension of reality: philosophical materialism seems both scientifically and philosophically indefensible. For the mind does not permit itself to be explained on the basis of the activity of the brain-mechanisms. To be sure, Christian faith already assumes the spiritual uniqueness of human existence. Philosophy since the time of Plato has argued it. Now neuroscience in many instances is showing itself friendly toward the belief in the transcendent quality of human life. The significance, or insignificance, of the new developments in neuroscience for the mind-body dilemma is now being debated among scientists and philosophers. Undoubtedly philosophy of religion, theology, ethics, psychology, and educational theory stand to benefit greatly from the ongoing discussion.

Notes

[1] A. E. Taylor, *Socrates* (New York: Doubleday, 1953), pp. 13ff.

[2] Cf. Karl Popper and John Eccles, *The Self and Its Brain* (New York: Springer, 1981), pp. 225-249; John Eccles, *The Neurophysiological Basis of Mind* (Oxford: Clarendon Press, 1953); *The Understanding of the Brain*, Second edition (New York: McGraw Hill, 1977); *Facing Reality: Philosophical Adventures by a Brain Scientist* (New York: Springer, 1970).

[3] Sally P. Springer and George Deutsch, *Left Brain, Right Brain*, revised edition (New York: W. H. Freeman and Company, 1985), pp. 11-12.

[4] Ibid., p. xiii.

[5] Michael S. Gazzaniga, "The Split Brain in Man," *The Nature of Human Consciousness*, ed. Robert E. Ornstein (San Francisco: W. H. Freeman and Company, 1973), pp. 87-100; Roger Sperry, "Some Effects of Disconnecting the Central Hemispheres," *Science* 217:24 (September, 1982), pp. 1223-1226. Cf. Sally P. Springer and George Deutsch, *Left Brain, Right Brain*, for a summary of this research.

[6] Sperry, "Some Effects of Disconnecting the Central Hemispheres," *Science* 217:24 (September, 1982), p. 1223.

[7] Springer and Deutsch, pp. 45-46; Sperry, *Science* pp. 1224-1225.

[8] Joseph E. Bogen, "The Other Side of the Brain: An Appositional Mind," *The Nature of Human Consciousness*, pp. 103ff; Sperry, *Science*, p. 1224; Charles I. Berlin, "Hemispheric Asymmetry in Auditory Tasks," *Lateralization in the Nervous System*, ed. Stevan Harnad, Robert W. Doty, Leonide Goldstein, Julian Jaynes, George Krauthamer (New York: Academic Press, 1977), p. 311; Springer, "Tachistoscopic and Dichotic-Listening Investigations of Laterality in Normal Human Subjects," *Lateralization in the Nervous System*, p. 326.

[9] Sperry, *Science*, p. 1225.

[10] Karl Popper and John Eccles, *The Self and Its Brain*, pp. 315ff. Eccles and Daniel N. Robinson, *The Wonder of Being Human* (New York: The Free Press, 1984), p. 114.

[11] Springer and Deutsch, pp. 43f., 57, 59.

[12] *The Self and Its Brain*, pp. 357f.

[13] Sperry, *Science*, p. 1225.

[14] Ibid.

[15] Ibid., p. 1226; cf. Springer and Deutsch, pp. 172-174, 231-233.

[16] Sperry, *Science*, p. 1225.

[17] Cf. Sperry, *Science and Moral Priority* (New York: Columbia University Press, 1983).

[18] Gazzaniga, *The Nature of Human Consciousness*, p. 93.

[19] Joseph E. Bogen, "The Outer Side of the Brain: An Appositional Mind," *The Nature of Human Consciousness*, p. 91.

[20] *Science*, p. 1224; Gazzaniga, *The Nature of Human Consciousness*, p. 100.

[21] Gazzaniga, *The Nature of Human Consciousness*, p. 91.

[22] Robert E. Ornstein, *The Psychology of Consciousness* (San Francisco: W. H. Freeman and Company, 1972), pp. 55-56, 59.

[23] Ibid., p. 57.

[24] Ibid., p. 60.

[25] Ibid.

[26] Ibid., p. 61

[27] *The Self and Its Brain*, p. 362.

[28] Ibid., p. 368.

[29] Ibid., p. 328.

[30] Ibid., pp. 321, 357; Springer and Deutsch, p. 59.

[31] *The Self and Its Brain*, p. 328.

[32] John Eccles and Daniel N. Robinson, *The Wonder of Being Human* (New York: The Free Press, 1984), p. 29.

[33] Hegel, *History of Philosophy*, trans. E. S. Haldane (London: Kegan Paul, Trench, Trubner and Co., 1892), III, 428-429.

[34] Ornstein, p. 63.

[35] Quoted by Ornstein, p. 68.

[36] Kenneth M. Heilman and Robert T. Watson, "The Neglect Syndrome—A Unilateral Defect of the Orienting Response," *Lateralization in the Nervous System*, Chapter 16; *Right Brain, Left Brain*, pp. 159-165.

[37] Stanley L. Jaki, *Brain, Mind, and Computers* (South Bend, Indiana: Gateway Editions, 1969), p. 65.

[38] Ibid., pp. 59, 65.

[39] Ibid., p. 59.

[40] Ibid.

[41] Herbert A. Simon, "Information Processing Models of Cognition," *Annual Review of Psychology* (1979) 30:363-366.

[42] Ibid., p. 365.

[43] Herbert A. Simon, "Information Processing Models of Cognition," *Annual Review of Psychology* (Volume 20, 1979), pp. 363-396; William G. Chase and Herbert A. Simon, "Perception in Chess," *Cognitive Psychology* (1973) 4:55-81; Herbert A. Simon and Kevin Gilmartin, "A Simulation of Memory for Chess Positions," *Cognitive Psychology* (1973) 5:29-46.

[44] *Cognitive Psychology* (1973) 5:30, 76; *Cognitive Psychology* (1973) 4:64-65; *Annual Review of Psychology* (1979) 30:375-378.

[45] E. M. Abernathy, "The Effect of Changed Environmental Conditions Upon the Results of College Examinations," *Journal of Psychology* 10:293-301.

[46] *Cognitive Psychology*, 4:55-56.

[47] Karl R. Popper and John C. Eccles, *The Self and Its Brain* (New York: Springer-Verlag, 1981), p. 390.

[48] *Annual Review of Psychology* (1979) 30:368-369.

[49] Jaki, p. 43.

[50] "Sketch of the Analytical Engine Invented by Charles Babbage, Esq.," trans. Ada Augusta, Countess of Lovelace, in Richard Taylor (ed.), *Scientific Memoirs*, III (London, 1843), p. 675, cited by Jaki, p. 47).

[51] Ibid.

[52] Jaki, p. 48.

[53] *The Self and Its Brain*, p. 208.

[54] *Brains, Machines, and Persons* (Grand Rapids: Wm. Eerdmans, 1980), pp. 60-63.

[55] *Brains, Machines, and Persons*, p. 63.

[56] *Annual Review of Psychology*, p. 370.

[57] Ibid., p. 383.

[58] Ibid., p. 390.

[59] Richard M. Restak, *The Brain: The Last Frontier* (Garden City, New York: Doubleday and Company, 1979), p. 363.

[60] *The Wonder of Being Human*, pp. 13-17; D. Gareth Jones, *Our Fragile Brains* (Downers Grove, Illinois: IVP, 1981), pp. 57-62.

[61] R. W. Sperry, "Mind-Brain Interaction: Mentalism, Yes; Dualism, No." *Neuroscience* (1980), V, 195-201.

[62] Ibid., pp. 195-206; *Science and Moral Priority*, p. 15.

[63] Ibid., pp. 102-103.

[64] Ibid., pp. 24, 102-103.

[65] Ibid., pp. 29-30.

[66] Ibid., p. 99.

[67] Ibid., p. 102.

[68] *The Self and Its Brain*, p. 564.

[69] Ibid., pp. 361, 251-274.

[70] William Feidel, "Introduction," *The Mystery of the Mind*, xxiv-xxix.

[71] Ibid., p. xxviii.

[72] *The Mystery of the Mind*, pp. 12-13.

[73] Ibid., pp. 34-35.

[74] Ibid., pp. 21-22.

[75] Ibid., p. 55.

[76] Ibid.

[77] Ibid., pp. 61-74.

[78] Ibid., p. 80.

[79] *The Self and Its Brain*, p. VIII.

[80] Ibid., p. 97.

[81] *About Behaviorism* (New York: Alfred Knopf, 1974), p. 212.

[82] *The Self and Its Brain*, pp. 283-285; Richard M. Restak, *The Brain: The Last Frontier*, pp. 217-218.

[83] *The Self and Its Brain*, p. 283.

[84] Restak, p. 218.

[85] Ibid., p. 9.

[86] *The Self and Its Brain*, p. 294.

[87] Ibid., p. 257.

[88] "Selves and Brains," *Neuroscience* (1978), 3, 604.

[89] *The Self and Its Brain*, pp. 529-530.

[90] Ibid., p. 378.

[91] Ibid., pp. 488-489.

[92] Ibid., pp. 375-376.

[93] Ibid., p. 377.

[94] Ibid., p. 372.

[95] Ibid, pp. 555, 558.

[96] *Human Science and Human Dignity* (Downers Grove, Illinois, 1979), pp. 35ff.

[97] Cf. Sperry, "Mind-Brain Interaction: Mentalism, Yes; Dualism, No." *Neuroscience* (1980), 5, 196.

[98] Eccles, "Science Can't Explain 'Who Am I? Why Am I Here?'," *U.S. News and World Report* (1984), p. 80; *The Self and Its Brain*, p. 558; *The Wonder of Being Human*, pp. 172, 177.

[99] *Human Science and Human Dignity*, pp. 39-40, 115ff.

[100] Cf. MacKay, "The Interdependence of Mind and Brain," *Neuroscience* (1980), 5, 1389-1391; "Selves and Brains," *Neuroscience* (1978), 3, 599-606; *Brains, Machines, and Persons* (Grand Rapids, Michigan, 1980), 13ff.

[101] Frederic Copleston, *A History of Medieval Philosophy* (New York: Harper & Row, 1972), p. 188. Cf. Aristotle, *On the Soul*, Book III, Chapters IV-V.

[102] *Human Science and Human Dignity*, pp. 101-102.

[103] *Brains, Machines, and Persons*, p. 87.

[104] *Human Science and Human Dignity*, p. 33.

[105] MacKay, "The Interdependence of Mind and Brain," *Neuroscience* (1980), 5, 1390.

[106] *Brains, Machines, and Persons*, p. 97.

[107] Ibid., pp. 89ff.

[108] *Our Fragile Brains*, p. 269.

[109] "Selves and Brains," *Neuroscience* 3, 601.

[110] *Brains, Machines, and Persons*, p. 73.

[111] Ibid., p. 79.

[112] Ibid., p. 78.

[113] Ibid., p. 83

[114] Ibid., p. 94

[115] Ibid., pp. 89ff.

[116] Cf. Tillich, *History of Christian Thought* (New York: Simon and Schuster, 1972), p. 269.

[117] "The Interdependence of Mind and Brain," *Neuroscience* (1980), 5, 1389.

[118] Sperry, "Mind-Brain Interaction: Mentalism, Yes; Dualism, No," *Neuroscience* (1980), 5, 202.

[119] "The Independence of Mind and Brain," *Neuroscience* (1980) 5, 1389.

[120] Ibid.

[121] Ibid., pp. 1390-1391.

[122] *Brains, Machines, and Persons*, p. 101.

[123] *Human Science and Human Dignity*, p. 102.

[124] *The Mystery of the Mind*, pp. 49, 74.

[125] Ibid., p. 46.

[126] Ibid., pp. 79-80.

[127] *Brains, Machines, and Persons*, p. 76.

[128] Ibid., p. 77; "Selves and Brains," *Neuroscience* (1978), 3, 604.

[129] *The Mystery of the Mind*, p. 55.

[130] Ibid., p. 77.

AN EVANGELICAL REFORMULATION OF THE DOCTRINE OF THE IMMUTABILITY OF GOD

BRUCE A. WARE
Assistant Professor of Systematic Theology
Western Conservative Baptist Seminary

Article from *Journal of the Evangelical Theological Society*

The past twenty-five years have witnessed a number of significant restate ments of the doctrine of divine immutability in light of an increasing appreciation for God's real relatedness to the world.[1] In particular, many Roman Catholic theologians have devoted much thought to this doctrine in an attempt to answer the harsh attacks of process theology against Thomas' development of the doctrine.[2] But only recently have evangelicals entered this contemporary discussion,[3] and here their contributions, though very helpful and insightful, have only suggested general lines of the doctrine's reconstruction. The purpose of this article, then, is to offer a more thorough reformulation of the doctrine of divine immutability in a manner that holds firmly to the evangelical commitment to Scripture as the authoritative source of the self-revelation of God.

The place to begin is with a brief examination of the key Biblical texts that speak most clearly of God's immutability. We should avoid, as much as possible, reading into the text senses of change or changelessness that are foreign to Scripture's own statement. Following this, we will propose what seem to be the senses both of immutability and mutability that may properly be attributed to the God of the Bible.

I. Biblical Attestation to God's Changelessness

Throughout the history of the Church, theologians have referred to numerous Biblical texts in support of their teaching on the doctrine of divine immutability.[4] Among the references cited, three in particular have been prominent: Ps 102:25-27, Mal 3:6, and Jas 1:17.

In Ps 102:25-27 the psalmist contrasts the permanence and constancy of God even over the heavens and the earth. A. A. Anderson notes that elsewhere in the Psalms the heavens and earth are pictured as symbols of stability and permanence (e.g. 78:69; 104:5; 119:90; 148:6),[5] and thus in this psalm the writer purposely selects objects that are commonly thought of as constant and unchanging to emphasize the finality of God's changeless and ongoing existence when contrasted even with that which, above all else in the finite realm, pictures true permanence.

The phrase that is of special importance is in v 27 (MT v 28), *wĕ'attâ hû'*, translated here as "But thou art the same." The same phrase (in first person: *'ănî hû'*) occurs in Deut 32:39 and numerous times in Isaiah (41:4; 43:10; 43:13; 46:4; 48:12), and in each of these cases a more literal rendering of the Hebrew is commonly given—viz., "I am he." Here in Psalm 102 it seems clear that the pronoun hû' is used to express the uniqueness of Yahweh's constant identity and endless existence in contrast with what passes away.[6] This is also supported by the LXX (Ps 101:28) rendering of this passage and the quotation of it in Heb 1:12, both of which read *su de ho autos ei*, "But you are the same." The use of *autos* with the article expresses identity or sameness,[7] and thus the changelessness of God's very being and existence is affirmed. The clear stress of this passage is on the very self-existent being of God, which remains though all else perish. It is not, then, God's ethical expression but his actual nature that the psalmist has in mind in his attribution of self-sameness.[8]

Mal 3:6 also lays stress on the very being of God, which remains changeless. But in addition, God's ethical dealings are also portrayed as constant. In the immediately preceding context Yahweh has just told again of his coming judgment against those who have refused to follow his ways. There will be no exceptions: The sorcerers, the adulterers, the oppressors will all be judged by God's swift action. And immediately following this announcement of God's sure judgment comes the statement of v 6: "For I the Lord do not change; therefore you, O sons of Jacob, are not consumed."

The statement of God's changelessness at this point in the narrative functions in at least three different but related ways. First, the statement "I the Lord do not change" is a clear assertion that the very nature and being of God remains forever what it is. Again, as in Psalm 102, it is not the Lord's dealings or one of the Lord's attributes (e.g. faithfulness, justice) that is explicitly referred to as changeless; it is the Lord, Yahweh himself, who is said not to change.[9] Second, the statement "For I the Lord do not change" at the beginning of v 6 functions to emphasize the certainty of the foretold judgment of v 5. The intrinsic immutability of God's character is the basis for believing the truthfulness and certainty of his word. Third, the changelessness of God's character also forms the basis for the certainty of God's continued faithfulness to his covenant people Israel. His commitment to love them uniquely is inviolable because it is an expression of his very nature, which cannot change.[10] This important text serves to inform us, then, both of the intrinsic immutability of God's own nature and of the extension of his changeless character in his ethical dealings with people.

Jas 1:17 expresses also the dual truths of God's own intrinsic immutability and ethical faithfulness, but here in a different manner than was just observed in Mal 3:6. The statement of v 17 that every good and perfect gift comes from the changeless Father of lights is offered by James as the explanation of his previous assertion that God never tempts anyone (1:13-15). He warns his readers never to say, when tempted, that God has brought this temptation to them. God, says James, cannot himself be tempted and he tempts no one. Of course one may then wonder on what James' confidence is here founded. To this issue James directs his instruction of vv 16-18, which instruction centers on the immutable character of God's own nature, the God from whom comes only and always good. Martin Dibelius summarizes well the central point of Jas 1:17:

> God is without change. From this main idea one is obviously supposed to conclude that God, the giver of good things, is not capable of sending evil as well, for such change is contrary to his nature. . . . The saying, which portrays God as the giver of good things, is supposed to confirm the idea that temptations do not come from God; the stressing of his unchangeableness is obviously intended to exclude the possibility that sometimes good comes from God and sometimes evil.[11]

Again, then, two central truths about God are expressed: the former concerning God's nature, and the latter God's dealings with his creatures. First, God as "Father of lights"[12] is himself not subject to intrinsic variation (*parallagē*), and the light he gives can never be shadowed or darkened or in any way altered (*tropēs aposkiasma*). Second, because God is himself changeless and because God is changelessly good, one may be confident that every gift from his hand is wholly good. God's own nature is exempt from change, and hence his relations with humans express only and precisely who he is.

II. Senses of Immutability Proper to the God of the Bible

With this examination of Scripture's own attestation to God's changelessness in mind, we wish now to delineate distinct senses in which the unchangeableness of God should rightly be understood. In distinguishing these senses of the immutability proper to God the endeavor is being made to express faithfully what God has told us of himself, neither overstating nor understating his self-disclosure on this point, since serious problems can result if either imbalance is accepted. Opposition should be registered here to calling God's resistance to change that of "absolute immutability," for this not only violates what shall later be argued are valid senses to conceive of God's ability to change, but it also blurs certain distinctions that are called for by Scripture in relation to his inability to change. There is equal opposition, however, to such treatments of God's changelessness (e.g. as in process theism) that relegate his immutability fundamentally to his immutable and essential changeability. God's self-revelation must be the sole guide in thinking on this or any other issue relating to who God is, and clearly the Scriptures say something quite different about God's incapacity to change than is said of the God of process thought.[13]

1. *Ontological immutability.* First, the God of the Bible is unchangeable in the supreme excellence of his intrinsic nature. This may be called God's "ontological immutability"—that is, the changelessness of God's eternal and self-sufficient being. This sense of God's ontological immutability is the primary and most fundamental sense in which the Scriptures speak of God's constant self-sameness. It is a first-order conception under which any other sense of divine immutability is dependent. As we noted when examining the classical Scriptural texts relating to God's changelessness, the Biblical writers affirmed that God himself is unchangeable, that who he is as God is ever the same. And clearly when consideration is given to the broader self-revelation of God, that he is altogether complete in the fullness of every excellence, a better understanding may be achieved of why it is only proper for the writers of Scripture to acknowledge and affirm the impossibility of change in the intrinsic nature of God.

God is the one and only eternally self-existent being, whose very life encompasses the fullness of all value, worth, virtue, goodness, holiness, power, knowledge, and all other perfection. The God testified to in Scripture is the source of all lesser reality (Acts 17:25; Rom 11:36), he is the giver of every good and perfect gift (Jas 1:17), and as such he must necessarily contain within himself all such excellence since there is no other source but God for these good bestowments. The thought that God might in some way gain value from finite beings is completely foreign to Biblical thinking. God is debtor to no one. Instead he is the sole source and giver of all good, so that even when a virtue given to and mediated by his creatures is offered back to him, one must acknowledge that ultimately God alone is the eternal possessor of all that is excellent.

In this regard, affirmation is here made of the long tradition of Church theologians who have stressed that it is impossible for God to change for better or for worse.[14] Either course of change is precluded by his being eternally self-sufficient. God cannot gain any value, since he eternally encompasses all such value in his own intrinsic being. And God certainly does not lose any value in his creation of lesser reality, since all that is shared with others *ad extra* is always his own and in the end returns to him (Rom 11:36). Scripture's affirmation that God does not change refers fundamentally, then, to his ontological immutability, to the changelessness of who he ever is as God.

We may also note briefly the vast difference between this sense of ontological immutability here being proposed and the sense of the immutability predicated of God's abstract nature in process theism. In process thought, though God's eternal existence is affirmed, yet some form of reality other than God must also eternally exist in order for God to exist. No particular universe need exist, but some universe or other is necessary for God to be.[15] And further, the actual make-up or content of God's concrete reality is dependent largely on the experiences of all the entities of the universe, for the concrete nature of God is the bringing together of all the value prehended from the universe at large.[16] That God "is," then, is immutable, though his being depends absolutely on the eternal existence of reality other than his own. And that God's concrete essence prehends always the totality of the experiences of the world is immutable, though the actual make-up of who God is in reality is dependent in large part on the input of others into his nature.

The God of the Bible is ontologically unchangeable in quite a different sense. God is immutable not only with regard to the fact of his eternal existence but also in the very content or make-up of his eternal essence, independent of the world. He does not depend for his existence on anything external to him. The Scriptures present God alone as eternally existing when nothing else was, and they reveal him as the originator of all temporal reality. Furthermore this eternal existence of God is not conceived as empty or void until it is given form by something outside it. To the contrary, God's existence forever encompasses all perfection, and hence this true and living God, as revealed in Scripture, is not dependent in the least on anything external to himself for any quality or value or perfection. Indeed all such qualities are his alone, and their manifestation in the contingent world reveals not the intrinsic worth of finite reality, which worth can then be added to the nature of God, but rather it expresses the free grace of God to share what is his alone with that which stands before him only as its humble recipient. The line of dependence between God and the world is asymmetrical. God exists in the fullness of his own intrinsic perfection from all eternity, and his creation of a temporal and contingent reality *ex nihilo* only expresses *ad extra* what is intrinsic to the very nature of God. Whatever value or goodness we have as finite creatures we owe completely to our gracious Giver, from whom and through whom and to whom are all things (Rom 11:36). Thus in affirming God's ontological immutabilty the true and living God is attributed with the changelessness of his own independent existence, essence, and attributes, which qualities of being have ever been his alone and to which no further quality or value can possibly be added.

2. *Ethical immutability.* The God of the Bible is also unchangeable in his unconditional promises and moral obligations to which he has freely pledged himself. This may be called God's "ethical immutability," the faithfulness and reliability of God by which he is true to his word and unfailing in accomplishing what he has promised. The divine ethical immutability is secondary and derivative in nature in that it presupposes (1) God's ontologi-

cal changelessness, (2) the existence of a contingent and temporal moral order, and (3) the free decision of God to pledge himself to his creatures in certain ways that accord with his intrinsic nature. As such, then, God's ethical immutability is a second-order type of changelessness. It involves the free commitment of God in relation to his moral creatures to act in certain freely-determined ways and carry out certain freely-determined promises. These commitments and promises to which God pledges himself are not intrinsic to his immutable divine nature as such, in that it is possible for them never to have been made. Were God not to have created a moral order, or were he not to have pledged himself in the ways he has, these commitments and promises would not be. But God has created and has so pledged himself, and these pledges, rather than being intrinsic to his very nature and hence necessary, are instead freely self-imposed and self-determined. God's ethical immutability, then, is the expression in time of God's eternal intrinsic nature both of the ways in which he freely chooses to pledge himself and of his utter reliability and faithfulness in accomplishing all he has promised.

Now while God's promises and commitments are not necessary strictly speaking, it is equally important to stress that they are nevertheless faithful expressions of God's nature and character. Stated differently, although God's ethical commitments to his creatures are not determined by his divine being, they fully accord with and truly express that same eternal nature.

Certain of the Church's earliest theologians expressed the importance of understanding God's faithfulness to his promise as rooted in his immutable nature,[17] and here their insight on this important point is followed. One may be confident that God will act as he has said he will act precisely because God's ethical commitments are the natural yet free expressions of his unchanging intrinsic nature. As the apostle Paul says, "If we are faithless, he remains faithful—for he cannot deny himself" (2 Tim 2:13). Thus it seems mistaken to understand the divine immutability, as it sometimes is, solely in terms of God's faithfulness to his promise.[18] The examination of Mal 3:6 and Jas 1:17 above has shown that in Biblical thought God's ethical consistency is based on his unchanging nature. The ethical activity of God is only consistent and reliable if it is rooted in the very nature and character of a God who does not change.

Consideration should be given here to one other important point that can best be seen if we look briefly at Isaac Dorner's significant contribution to the modern discussion of divine immutability.[19] Dorner stressed, and rightly so, that our conception of the immutability proper to God must account for rather than conflict with God's vitality. The God of the Bible is actively involved in the affairs of the world, and hence the sense of immutability proper to this living and active God, says Dorner, is the immutability of his ethical nature. For Dorner, God constantly changes in his affairs with people as he encounters new happenings and responds to changing situations, but God's changes always express rather than deny his unchangeable moral nature.

There is partial truth to what Dorner advocates. As shall be discussed in more detail below,[20] God does change his stated activities in certain cases but always in ways that express his ethical nature. The problem with Dorner's view, however, is that he bases the ethical consistency or faithfulness of God strictly on God's unchanging ethical nature (e.g. that God is always loving, holy, just) rather than on a more complete sense of the fullness and supreme excellence of God's immutable being. While it is true that Scripture grounds the faithfulness of God's word in his own ethical character, the fulfillment of his word may depend on more than God's changeless ethical nature. It may depend as well on God's immutable power, or knowledge, or wisdom—i.e., facets of the nature of God that are not part of his moral nature, properly speaking. Especially when one observes the magnitude of what God has promised, one sees that God's faithfulness to his word requires that he be ontologically immutable in the full sense described above and not only ethically consistent.

Take for example the promise of God to Abraham that through his seed all the families of the earth would be blessed (Gen 12:1-3; Gal 3:14-22). Here is a promise of enormous magnitude, especially in view of its fulfillment from the vantage point of the cross and the NT. In making this covenant with Abraham, God was committing himself to the fulfillment of a task that required everything from his sovereign control over history to his limitless power over sin and death along with the infinite wisdom needed to plan and accomplish what he here promised. Thus while it is no doubt true that the faithfulness of God to fulfill this promise depended in part on his being a God who does not lie and who seeks to accomplish what is right (i.e., on his ethical immutability), in addition the fulfillment of this promise required also that God have the knowledge and wisdom and power and authority and sovereignty necessary to do in fact what he promised he would do. Furthermore it is essential that God have these attributes without fail so that his word could be accomplished no matter the opposition or obstacles it would face. The certainty with which the Scriptural writers affirm God's faithfulness to his promise presupposes not only his immutable moral nature, which assures us of his unfailing intent to do as he pledged, but also a fuller sense of his complete ontological immutability guaranteeing the limitless resources necessary to accomplish precisely that to which he freely committed himself.

III. Senses of Mutability Proper to the God of the Bible

Having stressed what may now be called God's "onto-ethical immutability"—viz., the changelessness of his nature and word as just discussed—consideration must now be given to the ways in which the self-revelation of God also describes certain changes that take place as God involves himself intimately with his creation. In what has thus far been said, an endeavor has been made to delimit the senses of changelessness appropriately elicited from God's self-disclosure rather than upholding a blanket sense of absolute divine immutability. Surely the Bible speaks meaningfully of God's immutability in the manner discussed above. But just as surely the Bible speaks about the active, intimate and concerned involvement of God with his creation, an involvement that includes innumerable changes both on the part of God and on the part of his creatures. To these senses of mutability proper to the living God we now turn.

1. *Relational mutability.* The Scriptures affirm one predominant sense of God's changeability under which specific manifestations of it are evident, and this may be called God's "relational mutability." From the creation of Adam and Eve to the consummation of history, God is involved in pursuing, establishing and developing relationships with those whom he has made. After humankind rebelled against God, the dominant purpose of God with regard to his fallen human creatures has been to restore his personal relationship with them, which he intended from the beginning.

That God changes in his relationship with others is abundantly clear from Scripture, and therefore this relational mutability of God is upheld while at the same time it is denied that such relational changes in any way threaten or endanger the immutability of his intrinsic nature or freely spoken word. In fact, when rightly understood the relational changes that occur through God's interaction with his creatures, so far from conflicting with his immutable character, actually express it.

Anselm observed long ago that one's essence need not change as a result of changing relationships with others. He argued that though another person is born, to whom one now has numerous relations which can develop or cease and all of which were formerly nonexistent, this can occur without causing any necessary changes in one's own person.[21] This point is vital for our present discussion. God freely involves himself within the spatio-temporal structure in which we humans live, and he does so not as a mere passive observer. God's involvement in history is pervasive and comprehensive. His activity extends from his ordering of the vast universe (Ps 103:19; Dan 5:35) to his concern over one sparrow that falls (Matt 10:29). And at the heart of his involvement in history is his constant endeavor to be properly related again with those who turned from him.

As one reads Scripture one cannot but notice the abundance of occasions where God changed in his attitude and relationship with his creatures. Psalm 78, for example, recalls some major events in the history of Israel, highlighting especially the continual changes both in Israel's loyalties to God and in God's attitudes toward his people. A pattern seems evident—viz., that first God would promise to shower blessings upon Israel if she would obey, and just when God began to bless, Israel would rebel, incurring instead God's wrath and judgment. Israel would then repent and God would forgive and once again bless her until she again rebelled, bringing God's judgment on herself—and so the pattern continued. The same stress on God's changing attitude toward people is found in the NT. Paul, for example, describes the results of justification in terms of our having "peace with God" (Rom 5:1) in the place of God's former attitude of "condemnation" (8:1).

In light of the Scriptural evidence that God indeed changes in relationship with his creatures, it follows next to relate this facet of God's self-disclosure to what has already been discussed regarding his onto-ethical immutability. Three comments are in order. First, while the Scriptures are replete with accounts of God's changed relationships (e.g., from one of wrath to mercy or vice versa), these changes of relationship neither entail nor involve incidentally changes in God's intrinsic nature. Certainly one cannot imagine from a Biblical perspective that such changes could be the result, for example, of a change in God from goodness to malevolence. Even when God displays his fiercest wrath on human sin, the Scriptural writers never allow us to think that this occurs because God has succumbed to the forces of evil. What is said here of God's goodness could be said of all his attributes. God's power is not diminished nor is his holiness compromised when he forgives and withholds his wrath though at first he threatened to judge. God's justice is not abandoned nor is his righteous standard relaxed when God acts to redeem what he formerly held under condemnation. Though God changes in his relations to his creatures, God remains precisely who he ever was, is and shall be.

Even more important is the second point—viz., that God's changes of relationship actually express rather than deny his immutable nature and word. Indebtedness for this insight is here expressed especially to Isaac Dorner and Karl Barth.[22] As they have explained, because God's intrinsic moral nature is unchangeable it must always and without fail express itself in ways appropriate to the moral state of any given human situation. Thus when the human moral state changes (e.g. from rebellion to repentance) the immutable divine nature must now reflect itself in ways that are appropriate to this new situation. Hence changes in God's attitudes and actions are naturally brought about as God consistently applies the standards and requirements of his constant moral nature in ways that correspond to the moral changes continually undergone by his creatures.

Barth was right, then, to speak of a "holy mutability of God"[23] whereby God is understood to change in his attitudes, conduct and relationships with humans in ways that both accord with his changeless intrinsic moral nature and properly confront the human moral situation. Whereas humans are involved in unholy changes by which they violate God's immutable moral standards, God's changeability is always and only holy in that it upholds God's intrinsic moral requirements while at the same time it alters God's relationship in ways that are appropriate to the human moral state of the moment.

A third point follows from this discussion. A good number of theologians throughout the history of the Church had denied of God any change whatever because they conceived of change as always and only for either the better or the worse.[24] That there might be some sort of change that involved no such qualitative increase or decrease was not always given due consideration. But the relational mutability of God as has been presented here is of just such a sort. God is made neither better nor worse by his relational changes. He neither increases nor decreases in excellence since he is, as already stated, the fullness of all excellence. Indeed God cannot change for the better or the worse, but he can change in some sense nonetheless. He changes from anger to mercy, from blessing to cursing, from rejection to acceptance. Each of these changes is real in God, though no such change affects in the slightest the unchangeable supremacy of his intrinsic nature. God's relational mutability only expresses in time and in personal relationship the changelessness of his intrinsic nature and free word.

2. *The question of God's repentance.* One of the most common questions raised in the minds of readers of the Scriptures in relation to the notion of God's changelessness concerns the numerous instances in which God is said to "repent" or "change his mind" regarding an action he had done (e.g. Gen 6:6-7; 1 Sam 15:11, 35) or a promise (e.g. Jer 18:10) or threat (18:8; 26:13) he had formerly made.[25] The question is a serious one because there seems, at least *prima facie*, to be a basis here for attributing a sense of change to God that is not relational only but that is also fundamental or essential within God himself. How should one understand assertions of the divine repentance in a manner that is faithful to God's full self-revelation? Do these repentance texts conflict with the onto-ethical immutability of God advocated above? A number of points need to be made in dealing with the issue.

First, the theologians of the Church have regularly treated all such assertions of God's change of mind or repentance as anthropomorphisms.[26] That is, such statements are understood not as literal assertions about God but as human and metaphorical ways of expressing certain truths that extend beyond human experience. God, then, does not actually repent, but the Scriptural writers use this and other similar terms to express the change in his action toward his people—e.g., he formerly threatened judgment but now he blesses. A natural human way of expressing such a change of action is with a term such as "repentance" or "change of mind," for human repentance or change of mind is indeed often accompanied with such changes in action. The Scriptural writers use such terms from ordinary human experience, then, to describe the radical change that often occurs in God's attitude and action toward his people, while not intending to depict God as having had a literal change of mind.

Second, the Church theologians who have proposed that we understand the divine repentance as anthropomorphic were not arbitrary in this interpretation, and though more will be said later in support of their view, here argument shall be offered for their fundamental correctness. That there are anthropomorphisms in Scripture is not genuinely disputed by most readers of the Bible. The clearest examples of anthropomorphic language concern the ascription to God of various bodily parts (e.g. ears, Ps 31:2; mouth, 33:6; eyes, Isa 1:15; hands, 41:10; heart, Gen 6:6; and even wings, Ps 57:1).[27] It has been almost universally agreed upon among Christian interpreters that these references to physical members are not to be taken literally but refer to attitudes, attributes, or activities of God. So the question is not whether there are anthropomorphisms in Scripture but rather which assertions in fact are anthropomorphic and which are literally descriptive of God.

The Church theologians supported their anthropomorphic interpretation of the divine repentance by analyzing the conditions that are sufficient to produce a change of mind and then noted that none of these conditions can obtain in God. Calvin's treatment of the divine repentance[28] illustrates this well. He proposed that a change of mind can occur when any one of three conditions is present (or any combination thereof): when one is "ignorant of what is going to happen, or cannot escape it, or hastily and rashly rushes into a decision of which he immediately has to repent."[29] Essentially, then, a true change of mind can occur when one learns something of which one was ignorant, or when one lacks the power to do as first planned, or when one gains a fresh insight or a new perspective on a situation leading to a reconsideration of one's former intent. But how can it rightly be said of the God of the Bible that he lacks either knowledge, power, or wisdom? Clearly it cannot. God's knowledge is boundless (Ps 147:5; Isa 40:13-14; Rom 11:33-34), his wisdom is flawless (Job 38-39; Ps 104:24; Jer 51:15; 1 Tim 1:17), and his power is inexhaustible (Num 11:34; Deut 3:24; Ps 115:3). Thus, it is here affirmed with the long tradition of Church history that since the conditions involved in a true change of mind cannot be present in God, the Scriptural assertions of God's repentance may best be understood as anthropomorphic expressions for his changed action.

Third, it seems that more can be said in support of the traditional interpretation, and this by means of refining the notion of anthropomorphism. Since the question here is whether the repentance assertions are anthropomorphic in nature, it would be helpful to establish a criterion to guide in determining where it is legitimate to understand the language of Scripture as anthropomorphic on this and other such issues. May I suggest here that such a criterion is implicit in much of the traditional handling of the divine repentance, and it is this: A given ascription to God may rightly be understood as anthropomorphic when Scripture clearly presents God as transcending the very human or finite features it elsewhere attributes to him. To take the clearest example of anthropomorphism earlier discussed—that of the ascription to God of bodily parts—it seems clear that the fundamental reason why one may feel confident in understanding these physical ascriptions in a nonliteral way is that elsewhere God's self-revelation discloses that God is not confined physically (1 Kgs 8:27), nor can he be seen (1 John 4:12), but he is in fact spirit (John 4:24). That is, Scripture clearly presents God (*qua* Spirit) as transcending the finite physical features it elsewhere attributes to him. It seems justifiable, then, to take these physical descriptions as anthropomorphic.

Now in regard to the issue of the divine repentance, it seems that one may apply this criterion to further support what the Church theologians have consistently affirmed. Though there are numerous references in Scripture to God's repentance, there are also a few important texts that deny of him any such change of mind. Num 23:19 contrasts God with humanity specifically on this issue. Whereas humans may change their minds on what they have said, the Balaam oracle proclaims:

> God is not a man, that he should lie,
>   or a son of man, that he should repent.
> Has he said, and will he not do it?
>   Or has he spoken, and will he not fulfill it?

Likewise 1 Sam 15:29 (significantly, within the context in which it is said that God regretted making Saul king—15:11, 35) records Samuel's words that "the Glory of Israel will not lie or repent; for he is not a man that he should repent." In addition Ps 110:4; Jer 4:28; 20:16; Ezek 24:14; Zech 8:14; Rom 11:29 each speaks of the unchangeableness of God's decision in particular instances. It seems, then, that there is additional warrant for understanding these repentance texts as anthropomorphic, for they ascribe to God certain features that Scripture itself elsewhere says are of a finite human quality and hence are transcended by God.

Last, an endeavor should be made to express more clearly just what these repentance passages mean since it has been proposed that they should not rightly be taken as literal statements of God's change of mind. In general it seems best to understand God's repentance as his changed mode of action and attitude in response to a changed human situation. In other words, these passages refer fundamentally to God's relational mutability as discussed above. The Church theologians expressed a point that modern interpreters continue to stress[30]—viz., that God's threat to judge certain people for their sins often comes through the prophet with an explicit or implicit condition attached: If the people repent of their sin, God will withhold the judgment that he so forcefully said would come. Passages that contain this condition explicitly seem less problematic. For example, Jer 26:13 proclaims that if the people of Judah turn from their sin and obey the Lord, God will "repent of the evil he has pronounced." In such a case the consistency of God's ethical immutability is upheld and expressed through his appropriate response to the human moral situation. God acts in ways that correspond to the moral state in question, and when the moral state changes in obedience to his word his action accordingly changes.

There are other passages, however—such as Jonah 3:9-10—that state no such condition, and here it may seem that God did indeed change his mind about how he would act toward the people. The message God gave Jonah to preach, as revealed in chap. 3, is strictly unilateral and absolute: "Yet forty days, and Ninevah shall be overthrown!" (3:4). And though the Ninevites had no explicit assurance that God would withhold this calamity, they fasted and repented in the hope that God's judgment would be abated (3:5-9). But when God saw that they turned from their wickedness, he accordingly withheld his foretold judgment. It seems best, then, to understand the unilateral pronouncement of God through Jonah as containing an implicit condition, for God acts always and only in accord with his moral nature, and when people turn from their sins he in turn adjusts his course of action in ways that express his unchanged intrinsic nature in his relational interactions.

Therefore God does not change his mind, as do humans. He never lacks the knowledge, wisdom, or power that would lead him to reconsider what he has said. His pronouncement of judgment, then, when in the end it is not carried out, is shown to have come with the gracious condition that where there is true repentance he will gladly pardon and forgive. God is slow to anger and eager to forgive (Ps 103:8; Joel 2:13; Jonah 4:2), and the passages telling of God's repentance proclaim, above all this, truth about the true and living God.

3. *Changeable emotions in God.* The doctrine of the divine impassibility has been a subject of considerable discussion and dispute since the days of early Greek philosophy.[31] The term "impassibility" has been used in two quite different senses. The first and most fundamental sense refers to God's freedom from external influence on his nature and will. God cannot be aroused from without so as to be forced to act, as it were, against his better judgment or will.[32] Regarding this sense of "impassible," no hesitation whatever is here felt in affirming its correctness. God as the all-sufficient and all-powerful Creator of everything certainly conditions all else while he himself remains completely unconditioned in his intrinsic being and will. The second sense refers to the lack of any negative emotions (or emotions in general) in God. In post-Reformation orthodoxy, for example, God was conceived by some theologians to be good in every respect so that he experienced only an undefiled sense of joy and blessedness but never any real sense of anger or wrath.[33] Much recent thinking has been done on the question of whether there are changeable emotions in God,[34] and it seems only appropriate to address this issue briefly since the Scriptures are replete with references to various divine passions.

The early Church theologians were divided on the issue of whether God had changeable emotions. Arnobius and Augustine, on one side, argued that passions indicate disturbances and weakness and hence are not properly found in God.[35] But thinkers such as Tertullian, Novatian and Lactantius, on the other side, proposed that whereas God is exempt from corruptible emotions as would harm his nature, he experiences true and varying emotions in a manner appropriate to his perfect divine being.[36] The issue is reduced, then, to whether the emotions ascribed to God in the Bible are literally true of him or whether they are mere anthropomorphic expressions.

On this issue of emotions and anthropomorphism, two comments will be made. First, by utilizing the criterion developed above for genuine anthropomorphic expression, it seems here that there is no basis for calling such emotions mere anthropomorphisms. The Scriptures offer abundant references to various emotions in God. He is said to be angry (Num 12:9; Josh 7:1; Isa 42:25), wrathful (2 Kgs 22:13; Ps 110:5; Jer 10:10), jealous (Exod 20:5; Josh 24:19; Zech 1:14), compassionate and merciful (Ps 103:8; 145:8; Jer 3:12), patient and long-suffering (Exod 34:6; Num 14:8; 2 Pet 3:9)—just to name a few. But in all of Scripture's references to emotions as these relate to God, there does not appear to be any instance in which it is said that in reality God transcends these emotional qualities. There seems to be no clear direction, then, as there was with regard to the question of the divine repentance, for taking the ascriptions of divine emotions in any way other than at face value.

Second, it appears that the fundamental reason why theologians of the past have felt constrained to deny the real existence of emotions in God is that they conceived of emotions as a form of weakness, a limitation, a disturbance to one's inner life that resulted often in mishap or poor judgment. But as Heschel insists, "the Bible [does not] share the view that passions are disturbances or weaknesses of the soul, and much less the premise that passion itself is evil, that passion as such is incompatible [sic] with right thinking or right living."[37]

While it is undeniably true that emotions may sometimes overrule one's best judgment and lead one into actions that one later regrets as foolish, it does not follow that emotions are necessarily of this bent. Emotions have as much potential for good as for ill in that they can also stir one up toward holiness or compassion or faithfulness. Therefore if emotions are thought of as the gifts of God that lead to misconduct only when used improperly, then it seems evident that emotions can rightly have a place in God.

The abundance of Scriptural evidence of God's expression of emotion and a more positive understanding of their nature lead to the conclusion that the true and living God is, among other things, a genuinely emotional being. Heschel suggests that instead of thinking of the emotions ascribed to God as anthropomorphic, we should rather consider our own human experience of proper emotions as theomorphic,[38] as part of what it is to be created by God in his image. The God of the Bible is personal, and while no change can ever occur to the supreme excellence of his intrinsic perfection, he has freely chosen to relate with us, his creatures. His relational changeableness includes, then, his experience of variable emotions as he interacts with us at every level and expresses himself in ways that accord both with his unchangeable character and our changeable states.

IV. Conclusion

In the endeavor to take seriously the self-revelation of God in this discussion of the divine immutability, the goal here has been to form our conceptions of change or changelessness in relation to God as much as possible from the Scriptural text. As a result, God has been presented as one who is both independent and self-sufficient and hence immutable in respect to his supreme self-existence, while also relational and self-involving and thus changeable in his comprehensive interaction with his creatures.

We have been privileged here to gain a glimpse into the nature and workings of God through our focused attention on one facet of his character. As has been seen, God stands outside all lesser reality while he also freely chooses to stand within it. His changeless character is made manifest precisely within the changing world he formed. In a word, then, this study has endeavored to show that the God of the Bible, who is ever unchangeable in himself, willingly changes in his relational involvement to which he gives himself fully. He who eternally "is," is both with us and for us.

Notes

[1] God's "real relatedness" stands in contrast to his "relation of reason." Much of classical theology so stressed God's absolute immutability that his relationship to the contingent and changing world could only be conceived, if at all, as a relation of reason—i.e., a relation that is not real in God but obtains only insofar as God knows from all eternity that creatures will be really related to him. See e.g. Thomas Aquinas, *Summa Theologiae*, I A. 13, 7. For contemporary affirmations of God's real relatedness to the world after wrestling with the traditional denial of this doctrine see esp. W. E. Stokes, "Is God Really Related to this World?", *Proceedings of the American Catholic Philosophical Association* 39 (1965) 145-151; W. J. Hill, "Does the World Make a Difference to God?", *Thomist* 38 (1974) 146-164; W. N. Clarke, *The Philosophic Approach to God: A Neo-Thomistic Perspective* (Winston-Salem: Wake Forest University, 1979) esp. 90-98.

[2] A helpful article here is B. L. Whitney, "Divine Immutabilty in Process Philosophy and Contemporary Thomism," *Horizons* 7 (1980) 49-68. For additional discussion of the process doctrines of divine mutability and immutability along with contemporary responses see B. A. Ware, "An Evangelical Reexamination of the Doctrine of the Immutability of God" (doctoral dissertation; Pasadena: Fuller Theological Seminary, 1984), chaps. 6 and 7; "An Exposition and Critique of the Process Doctrines of Divine Mutability and Immutability," *WTJ* 47 (1985) 175-196.

[3] See e.g. D. G. Bloesch, *Essentials of Evangelical Theology* (San Francisco: Harper, 1978), 1. 27-28; C. F. H. Henry, *God, Revelation and Authority: God Who Stands and Stays*, part 1 (Waco: Word, 1982), 5. 286-306; S. T. Davis, *Logic and the Nature of God* (Grand Rapids: Eerdmans, 1983) 41-51; R. H. Nash, *The Concept of God* (Grand Rapids: Zondervan, 1983) 99-105.

[4] Most often, the immutability of God's essence and attributes is said to be supported by Exod. 3:14; Num 23:19; Ps 90:2; 102:25-27; Mal 3:6; Rom 1:22-23; 1 Tim 1:17; Heb 1:10-12; Jas 1:17. The immutability of God's knowledge and decree is seen in Num 23:19; 1 Sam 15:29; Job 42:2; Ps 33:11; 110:4; 147:5; Prov 19:21; Isa 14:24; 43:13; 46:8-11; Mal 3:6; Luke 21:33; Rom 9:11, 18; 11:29; Eph 1:11; Heb 4:13; 6:17-18; Jas 1:17.

[5] A. A. Anderson, *The Book of Psalms* (NCB; Grand Rapids: Eerdmans, 1972), 2. 711.

[6] On the function of the pronoun hû' in Ps 102:27 see F. Delitzsch, *Biblical Commentary on the Psalms* (Grand Rapids: Eerdmans, 1949), 3. 117; Anderson, *Psalms*, 2. 711; BDB 216.

[7] See BDF, sec. 288; A. T. Robertson, *A Grammar of the Greek New Testament in the Light of Historical Research* (Nashville: Broadman, 1934) 687.

[8] The *JPSV* translation of Ps 102:28 reads: "But Thou art the selfsame,/ And Thy years shall have no end."

[9] The Hebrew *lo' šānîtî* (Qal perfect) is translated in the LXX as *ouk ēlloiōmai* (perfect middle indicative of *alloioō*). The use of the Greek perfect especially highlights the ongoing permanence of Yahweh's changelessness.

[10] J. Baldwin (*Haggai, Zechariah, Malachi* [London: InterVarsity, 1972] 245) comments concerning Mal 3:6: "There is utter consistency in God's dealings with men. He who once loved Jacob (1:2) did not cease to love his sons, though they continued to take after their father and were cheats and supplanters (Gn 27:36; *cf.* Mal 3:5)."

[11] M. Dibelius, *James* (Hermeneia; Philadelphia: Fortress, 1976) 102-103. For good discussions of this passage see also J. B. Adamson, *The Epistle of James* (NICNT; Grand Rapids: Eerdmans, 1976); P. H. Davids, *The Epistle of James: A Commentary on the Greek Text* (Grand Rapids: Eerdmans, 1982).

[12] See esp. Davids, *Epistle* 87-88.

[13] For a sustained critique of process theism from an evangelical scholar well-acquainted with process thought see R. G. Gruenler, *The Inexhaustible God: Biblical Faith and the Challenge of Process Theism* (Grand Rapids: Baker, 1983). See also Ware, "Exposition," esp. 191-196, (see footnote 2).

[14] See e.g. Gregory of Nyssa, *Letter to Eustathia, Ambrosia, and Basilissa*, in *Nicene and Post-Nicene Fathers*, 2, V; Athanasius, *Against the Arians*, 2.10, in *Nicene and Post-Nicene Fathers*, 2, IV; Bonaventure, *Opera Omnia*, 11 vol. (vol. 1-4 ed. Bernardinus a Portu Romantino; Colegii a St. Bonaventura, 1882-1902), I, Sent. Lib. I, dist. VIII, part 1, art. II, q. I, 4; Thomas Aquinas, *Summa Theologiae*, I A., q. 9. 1-2; F. Turretin, *Institutio Theologiae Elencticae* (4 vol.; New York: Robert Carter, 1847), Loc. 3, Q. XI, 4.

[15] See e.g. C. Hartshorne, *The Divine Relativity: A Social Conception of God* (New Haven: Yale University, 1948) 88-89; *Man's Vision of God and the Logic of Theism* (Hamden: Archon, 1941) 108.

[16] God's "supreme relativity," his apprehension of all the value from the whole universe, is a constant theme in Hartshorne's *Divine Relativity*; see e.g. pp. 11, 21, 22, 44, 60, 80, 82, 88, 94.

[17] See e.g. Clement of Alexandria, *Stromata*, 5.14, in *Ante-Nicene Fathers*; Athanasius, *Against the Arians*, 2.14.10. On the connection between God's ontological and ethical immutability in Athanasius see esp. E. P. Meijering, *Orthodoxy and Platonism in Athanasius: Synthesis or Antithesis* (Leiden: Brill, 1968) 124-125.

[18] Hartshorne proposed that we understand the immutability of God as presented in Scripture as ethical only (*Man's Vision* 112; *Divine Relativity* 22-24). I Dorner also emphasized above all the immutability of God's ethical nature ("Über die richtige Fassung des dogmatischen Begriffs der Unveränderlichkeit Gottes," *Jahrbucher für deutsche Theologie*, 1856-58, now in Dorner, *Gesammelte Schriften* [Berlin: Wilhelm Hertz, 1883] 188-377).

[19] The pertinent section of Dorner's "Unveränderlichkeit Gottes" may be found in translation in *God and Incarnation in Mid-Nineteenth Century German Theology* (ed. C. Welch; New York: Oxford University, 1965) 115-180.

[20] See esp. the forthcoming discussion on the senses of mutability proper to God, later in this article.

[21] Anselm, *Monologium*, in *Anselm of Canterbury* (ed. J. Hopkins and H. Richardson; London: SCM, 1974), 1. ch. 25: "For it is true that I am neither taller nor shorter than, equal nor similar to, a man who will be born after the present year. But after he is born, I will surely be able to have and to lose all of these relations to him—according as he will grow or change in various of his qualities—without any change in myself."

[22] See Dorner in Welch, ed., *God and Incarnation* 145-165; K. Barth, *Church Dogmatics* (ed. G. W. Bromiley and T. F. Torrance; Edinburgh; T. & T. Clark, 1956-75), II/1. 496.

[23] Barth, *Church Dogmatics*, II/1. 496.

[24] See n. 14 above.

[25] The "repentance" of God is spoken of often in the OT but only once in the NT, and this reference (Heb 7:21) is a quotation from one of the OT denials of God's change of mind (Ps 110:4). The Hebrew verb in this regard is always nḥm (used in the Niphal, Piel, Pual and Hithpael), "to be sorry, repentant, comforted." It is used of God thirty-five times, twenty-eight of which are positive (i.e., God may or does repent) and seven negative (i.e., God does not or cannot repent). The positive usages: Gen 6:6, 7; Exod 32:12, 14; Deut 32:36; Judg 2:18; 1 Sam 15:11, 35; 2 Sam 24:16; 1 Chr 21:15; Ps 90:13; 106:45; 135:14; Jer 15:6; 18:8, 10; 26:3, 13, 19; 42:10; Hos 13:14; Joel 2:13, 14; Amos 7:3, 6; Jonah 3:9, 10; 4:2. The negative usages: Num 23:19; 1 Sam 15:29; Ps 110:4 (cf. Heb 7:21); Jer 4:28; 20:16; Ezek 24:14; Zech 8:14.

[26] See e.g. M. Luther's comments on Gen 6:6 and Joel 2:13; J. Calvin, *Institutes of the Christian Religion* (ed. J. T. McNeill; Philadelphia: Westminster, 1960), 1.17.12-14; A. Polanus, *The Substance of Christian Religion* (London: By R. F. for John Oxenbridge) 10-11; S. Charnock, *The Existence and Attributes of God* (Minneapolis: Klock & Klock, 1977 [1797]) 125; Turretin, *Institutio*, Loc. 3, Q. XI, 11.

[27] Cf. E. Jacob, *Theology of the Old Testament* (New York: Harper, 1958) 39-42.

[28] Calvin, *Institutes* 1.17.12.

[29] Ibid.

[30] See e.g. H. H. Rowley, "The Nature of God," in *The Faith of Israel* (London: SCM, 1956) 67; W. Eichrodt, *Theology of the Old Testament* (Philadelphia: Westminster, 1961-67), 1. 210-217, 266; A. J. Heschel, *The Prophets* (New York: Harper, 1962), 2. 11, 66.

[31] See e.g. J. K. Mozley, *The Impassibility of God: A Survey of Christian Thought* (Cambridge: Cambridge University, 1926); B. R. Brasnett, *The Suffering of the Impassible God* (London: SPCK, 1928); T. E. Pollard, "The Impassibility of God," *SJT* 8 (1955) 353-364; and esp. the recent superb study, R. E. Creel, *Divine Impassibility: An Essay in Philosophical Theology* (Cambridge: Cambridge University, 1986).

[32] J. Moltmann *(The Crucified God: The Cross of Christ as the Foundation and Criticism of Christian Theology* [New York: Harper, 1974] 229) expresses this idea when he states that "God is under no constraint from that which is not of God." See also G. L. Prestige, *God in Patristic Thought* (2d ed.; London: SPCK, 1952) 6-7: "Just as God is supreme in power and wisdom, so is He morally supreme, incapable of being diverted or overborne by forces and passions such as commonly hold sway in the creation and among mankind. The word chosen to express this moral transcendence is 'impassible' *(apathēs)*. . . . Impassibility then implies perfect moral freedom, and is a supernatural endowment properly belonging to God alone."

[33] See e.g. Charnock, *Existence* 125; B. Pictet, *Christian Theology* (Philadelphia: Presbyterian Board of Publication, 1845) 87; J. Wollebius, *Compendium Theologiae Christianae* (1626), 1. 1.

[34] See e.g. J. Y. Lee, *God Suffers For Us: A Systematic Inquiry Into A Concept of Divine Passibility* (The Hague: Martinus Hijhoff, 1974); Heschel, *Prophets* 2; G. Wondra, "The Pathos of God," *Reformed Review* 18 (1964) 28-35; K. J. Woolcombe, "The Pain of God," *SJT* 20 (1967) 129-148; L. J. Kuyper, "The Suffering and the Repentance of God," *SJT* 22 (1969) 257-277; W. McWilliams, "Divine Suffering in Contemporary Theology," *SJT* 33 (1980) 35-53; *The Passion of God* (Macon: Mercer University, 1985); Creel, *Divine Impassibility*, ch. 7: "Divine Impassibility in Feeling."

[35] Arnobius, *Case Against the Pagans* 1.18, in *Ancient Christian Writers*, vol. 7 and 8 (Westminster: Newman, 1949); Augustine, *On the Trinity* 13.16, in *Nicene and Post-Nicene Fathers*, I, III; *Enchiridion*, 33, in *Nicene and Post-Nicene Fathers*, I, III.

[36] Tertullian, *Against Marcion* 2.16, in *Ante-Nicene Fathers*, III; Novatian, *The Trinity* 5, in *The Fathers of the Church*, vol. 67 (Washington: Catholic University of America, 1974); Lactantius, *The Wrath of God* 1-5, 13-16, in *Lactantius: The Minor Works* (Washington: Catholic University of America, 1965). See also J. R. Hallman, "The Mutability of God: Tertullian to Lactantius," *TS* 42 (1981) 373-393.

[37] Heschel, *Prophets* 2. 37-38.

[38] Ibid., pp. 37-40, 50-52.

ETHICS/SPIRITUAL LIFE

Klaus Bockmuehl, area editor

ETHICS/SPIRITUAL LIFE

KLAUS BOCKMUEHL
Professor of Theology and Ethics
Regent College

Introduction

Probably last year's most debated single piece on personal ethics or "issues" in ethics is the papal "Instruction on Respect for Human Life in Its Origin and on the Dignity of Procreation." As was to be expected, the Instruction has met with considerable secular dissension, as well as some fierce evangelical criticism (e.g., in *Christianity Today*, June 12, 1987). This took issue especially with the Roman Catholic doctrine of the two-fold purpose of marriage, namely, conjugal union and procreation, calling it "antiquated." However, that critical standard would immediately disqualify not only much of theological endeavor in general, but also several articles in this area of *The Best in Theology* (for instance, John Mason's investigation of O.T. models of assistance for the poor), if they try to look to the past in order to learn for the present. It may also fail to perceive that in the field of human action and ethics the flow of time does not command an exclusive relevance; many deeds and attitudes from the past are repeatable any day. In this particular case, the conjunction of conjugal union and procreation is not even an outdated, but an ongoing biological fact, whether we manipulate it or not. One might, however, join evangelicals questioning the Roman Catholic rejection of homologous artificial insemination (where the husband is the donor of sperm). The Instruction's argument here is not as convincing as in the rest of the document; perhaps it is too impressed by the ideal of the "proper perfection" of an action, not allowing in this case for the traditional distinction between perfect and "middle" acts that are not as yet sinful.

The Instruction has been selected not only for its material contributions, e.g., the strong emphasis on respect for the human embryo and the firm support for the family (the social unit much embattled by secularism), but also for the format of its ethical reasoning, which covers the anthropological groundwork of ethics as well as the oft-debated question of legislation of ethics.

In the field of social ethics, Professor John Mason's article, "Biblical Teaching and Assisting the Poor," gives a good summary of the somewhat scattered material on provisions for the poor in the Old Testament. Again, one might feel uncomfortable with the author's seemingly unhistorical approach that brings together texts from very different periods, but his primary purpose clearly is to present us with a typology of action for possible application today, not with a piece of historical research. One important topic unearthed is the question of the duty and the right to work. In addition, with his emphasis on the extended family as the primary agent responsible for sustaining an impoverished member, the author has, as it were, re-established one of the basic principles of Roman Catholic social ethics, i.e., the principle of subsidiarity, which calls on the smaller social unit to render support to its needy members before the respective larger unit can be implicated—the same principle which, according to 1 Tim. 5:4,16, the apostle Paul brought to bear on the problem of relief of widows in the early church. It might indeed also be the most reasonable course of action for the political community today.

The relationship of state and church, or of law and religion, is a problem of political ethics that occupies many minds today. Professor Berman's article, "Religion and Law: The First Amendment in Historical Perspective," presents a convincing interpretation of the Amendment's phrase, "establishment of religion," and at the same time helps us become more literate in the overall issues implied in the present debate. The article ends with the call for a new "public philosophy," the dangerous lack of which has recently been highlighted by Richard John Neuhaus' book *The Naked Public Square.*

In their article "The Professions and the Common Good: Vocations/ Professions/Career" (not reproduced here), professors Robert Bellah and William Sullivan, who in their highly creditable and much discussed book *Habits of the Heart* of 1985 pursued the same problem, are now giving us a first application of such a "common philosophy" in a sphere where personal and political ethics meet.[1]

Concerning the sub-section of Spiritual Life, it was a surprise to see how little, if anything, had been published on prayer during the last year. In 1986/87, the *New Oxford Review* has given its readers the benefit of an extended series of extracts from the spiritual journal of Fr. Henri Nouwen who has emerged as one of the prominent writers on spirituality in our time. As our collection of essays is directed more to the theological approach, we refrain from reprinting these primary spiritual texts and instead offer one of a pair of articles on "Re-thinking the Mystical." Due to the unmistakable present fallowness of the field, these articles are again of a more introductory nature.

Author Hugh Feiss, O.S.B., will perhaps allow that "nature, self, and the other" are not the only locales of the presence of God; indeed, an evangelical would hold that they pale beside the Christian's fellowship with Christ, the "Christ mysticism" of the apostle Paul (Gal. 2:20), which was highlighted by Albert Schweitzer. With wisdom and insight, however, Feiss points to the necessity of recovering the best of mystical theology, showing, among other things, that there is no substantive contradiction between mysticism and ministry, e.g., the practice of good works.

Protestants will be interested to learn that much of their inherited bias against mysticism stems from the nineteenth century. Since then, though, one has learned to distinguish fundamentally between the Dionysian tradition of the mysticism of being (teaching the soul's fusion with God and the deification of man), and the mystical fellowship of the believer with Christ, as in St. Bernard, Gerson, and Tauler, who matched love with a sustained humility of the soul before God. It may be time for us to learn again from *them*.

Notes

[1] *Religion and Intellectual Life* 4 (Spring 1987): 7-20.

About the Area Editor

Klaus Bockmuehl (Th.D., University of Basle) is professor of theology and ethics at Regent College (Vancouver, B.C.). A citizen of the Federal Republic of Germany, he is an ordained minister in the Evangelical Church of the Rhineland. His most recent books are *Living by the Gospel* (1986), *The Challenge of Marxism: A Christian Response* (IVP, 1980; Helmers and Howard, 1986), and *Evangelicals and Social Ethics* (1979).

INSTRUCTION
ON RESPECT FOR HUMAN LIFE
IN ITS ORIGIN AND ON THE DIGNITY OF
PROCREATION:
REPLIES TO CERTAIN QUESTIONS OF THE DAY

CONGREGATION FOR THE DOCTRINE OF THE FAITH

Vatican City 1987

FOREWARD: The Congregation for the Doctrine of the Faith has been approached by various Episcopal Conferences or individual Bishops, by theologians, doctors and scientists, concerning biomedical techniques which make it possible to intervene in the initial phase of the life of a human being and in the very processes of procreation and their conformity with the principles of Catholic morality. The present Instruction, which is the result of wide consultation and in particular of a careful evaluation of the declarations made by Episcopates, does not intend to repeat all the Church's teaching on the dignity of human life as it originates and on procreation, but to offer, in the light of the previous teaching of the Magisterium, some specific replies to the main questions being asked in this regard.

The exposition is arranged as follows: an introduction *will recall the fundamental principles, of an anthropological and moral character, which are necessary for a proper evaluation of the problems and for working out replies to those questions; the* first part *will have as its subject respect for the human being from the first moment of his or her existence; the* second part *will deal with the moral questions raised by technical interventions on human procreation; the* third part *will offer some orientations on the relationships between moral law and civil law in terms of the respect due to human embryos and foetuses* and as regards the legitimacy of techniques of artificial procreation.*

---

* The terms "zygote", "pre-embryo", "embryo" and "foetus" can indicate in the vocabulary of biology successive stages of the development of a human being. The present Instruction makes free use of these terms, attributing to them an identical ethical relevance, in order to designate the result (whether visible or not) of human generation, from the first moment of its existence until birth. The reason for this usage is clarified by the text (cf I, 1).

INTRODUCTION

1.
BIOMEDICAL RESEARCH AND THE TEACHING
OF THE CHURCH

The gift of life which God the Creator and Father has entrusted to man calls him to appreciate the inestimable value of what he has been given and to take responsibility for it: this fundamental principle must be placed at the centre of one's reflection in order to clarify and solve the moral problems raised by artificial interventions on life as it originates and on the processes of procreation.

Thanks to the progress of the biological and medical sciences, man has at his disposal ever more effective therapeutic resources; but he can also acquire new powers, with unforeseeable consequences, over human life at its very beginning and in its first stages. Various procedures now make it possible to intervene not only in order to assist but also to dominate the processes of procreation. These techniques can enable man to "take in hand his own destiny", but they also expose him "to the temptation to go beyond the limits of a reasonable dominion over nature".[1] They might constitute progress in the service of man, but they also involve serious risks. Many people are therefore expressing an urgent appeal that in interventions on procreation the values and rights of the human person be safeguarded. Requests for clarification and guidance are coming not only from the faithful but also with those who recognize the Church as "an expert in humanity"[2] with a mission to serve the "civilization of love"[3] and of life.

The Church's Magisterium does not intervene on the basis of a particular competence in the area of the experimental sciences; but having taken account of the data of research and technology, it intends to put forward, by virtue of its evangelical mission and apostolic duty, the moral teaching corresponding to the dignity of the person and to his or her integral vocation. It intends to do so by expounding the criteria of moral judgment as regards the applications of scientific research and technology, especially in relation to human life and its beginnings. These criteria are the respect, defence and promotion of man, his "primary and fundamental right" to life,[4] his dignity as a person who is endowed with a spiritual soul and with moral responsibility[5] and who is called to beatific communion with God.

The Church's intervention in this field is inspired also by the love which she owes to man, helping him to recognize and respect his rights and duties. This love draws from the fount of Christ's love: as she contemplates the mystery of the Incarnate Word, the Church also comes to understand the "mystery of man";[6] by proclaiming the Gospel of salvation, she reveals to man his dignity and invites him to discover fully the truth of his own being. Thus the Church once more puts forward the divine law in order to accomplish the work of truth and liberation.

For it is out of goodness—in order to indicate the path of life—that God gives human beings his commandments and the grace to observe them: and it is likewise out of goodness—in order to help them persevere along the same path—that God always offers to everyone his forgiveness. Christ has compassion on our weaknesses: he is our Creator and Redeemer. May his spirit open men's hearts to the gift of God's peace and to an understanding of his precepts.

2.
SCIENCE AND TECHNOLOGY
AT THE SERVICE OF THE HUMAN PERSON

God created man in his own image and likeness: "male and female he created them" (Gen. 1:27), entrusting to them the task of "having dominion over the earth" (Gen. 1:28). Basic scientific research and applied research constitute a significant expression of this dominion of man over creation. Science and technology are valuable resources for man when placed at his service and when they promote his integral development for the benefit of all; but they cannot of themselves show the meaning of existence and of human progress. Being ordered to man, who initiates and develops them, they draw from the person and his moral values the indication of their purpose and the awareness of their limits.

It would on the one hand be illusory to claim that scientific research and its applications are morally neutral; on the other hand one cannot derive criteria for guidance from mere technical efficiency, from research's possible usefulness to some at the expense of others, or, worse still, from prevailing ideologies. Thus science and technology require, for their own intrinsic meaning, an unconditional respect for the fundamental criteria of the moral law: that is to say, they must be at the service of the human person, of his inalienable rights and his true and integral good according to the design and will of God.[7]

The rapid development of technological discoveries gives greater urgency to this need to respect the criteria just mentioned: science without conscience can only lead to man's ruin. "Our era needs such wisdom more than bygone ages if the discoveries made by man are to be further humanized. For the future of the world stands in peril unless wiser people are forthcoming".[8]

3.
ANTHROPOLOGY AND PROCEDURES
IN THE BIOMEDICAL FIELD

Which moral criteria must be applied in order to clarify the problems posed today in the field of biomedicine? The answer to this question presupposes a proper idea of the nature of the human person in his bodily dimension.

For it is only in keeping with his true nature that the human person can achieve self-realization as a "unified totality":[9] and this nature is at the same time corporal and spiritual. By virtue of its substantial union with a spiritual soul, the human body cannot be considered as a mere complex of tissues, organs and functions, nor can it be evaluated in the same way as the body of animals; rather it is a constitutive part of the person who manifests and expresses himself through it.

The natural moral law expresses and lays down the purposes, rights and duties which are based upon the bodily and spiritual nature of the human person. Therefore this law cannot be thought of as simply a set of norms on the biological level; rather it must be defined as the rational order whereby man is called by the Creator to direct and regulate his life and actions and in particular to make use of his own body.[10]

A first consequence can be deduced from these principles: an intervention on the human body affects not only the tissues, the organs and their functions but also involves the person himself on different levels. It involves, therefore, perhaps in an implicit but nonetheless real way, a moral significance and responsibility. Pope John Paul II forcefully reaffirmed this to the World Medical Association when he said: "Each human person, in his absolutely unique singularity, is constituted not only by his spirit, but by his body as well. Thus, in the body and through the body, one touches the person himself in his concrete reality. To respect the dignity of man consequently amounts to safeguarding this identity of the man 'corpore et anima unus', as the Second Vatican Council says (Gaudium et Spes, 14, par. 1). It is on the basis of this anthropological vision that one is to find the fundamental criteria for decision-making in the case of procedures which are not strictly therapeutic, as, for example, those aimed at the improvement of the human biological condition".[11]

Applied biology and medicine work together for the integral good of human life when they come to the aid of a person stricken by illness and infirmity and when they respect his or her dignity as a creature of God. No biologist or doctor can reasonably claim, by virtue of his scientific competence, to be able to decide on people's origin and destiny. This norm must be applied in a particular way in the field of sexuality and procreation, in which man and woman actualize the fundamental values of love and life.

God, who is love and life, has inscribed in man and woman the vocation to share in a special way in his mystery of personal communion and in his work as Creator and Father.[12] For this reason marriage possesses specific goods and values in its union and in procreation which cannot be likened to those existing in lower forms of life. Such values and meanings are of the personal order and determine from the moral point of view the meaning and limits of artificial interventions on procreation and on the origin of human life. These interventions are not to be rejected on the grounds that they are artificial. As such, they bear witness to the possibilities of the art of medicine.

But they must be given a moral evaluation in reference to the dignity of the human person, who is called to realize his vocation from God to the gift of love and the gift of life.

4.
FUNDAMENTAL CRITERIA FOR A MORAL JUDGMENT

The fundamental values connected with the techniques of artificial human procreation are two: the life of the human being called into existence and the special nature of the transmission of human life in marriage. The moral judgment on such methods of artificial procreation must therefore be formulated in reference to these values.

Physical life, with which the course of human life in the world begins, certainly does not itself contain the whole of a person's value, nor does it represent the supreme good of man who is called to eternal life. However it does constitute in a certain way the "fundamental" value of life, precisely because upon this physical life all the other values of the person are based and developed.[13] The inviolability of the innocent human being's right to life "from the moment of conception until death"[14] is a sign and requirement of the very inviolability of the person to whom the Creator has given the gift of life.

By comparison with the transmission of other forms of life in the universe, the transmission of human life has a special character of its own, which derives from the special nature of the human person. "The transmission of human life is entrusted by nature to a personal and conscious act and as such is subject to the all-holy laws of God: immutable and inviolable laws which must be recognized and observed. For this reason one cannot use means and follow methods which could be licit in the transmission of the life of plants and animals".[15]

Advances in technology have now made it possible to procreate apart from sexual relations through the meeting *in vitro* of the germ-cells previously taken from the man and the woman. But what is technically possible is not for that very reason morally admissible. Rational reflection on the fundamental values of life and of human procreation is therefore indispensable for formulating a moral evaluation of such technological interventions of a human being from the first stages of his development.

5.
TEACHINGS OF THE MAGISTERIUM

On its part, the Magisterium of the Church offers to human reason in this field too the light of Revelation: the doctrine concerning man taught by the Magisterium contains many elements which throw light on the problems being faced here.

From the moment of conception, the life of every human being is to be respected in an absolute way because man is the only creature on earth that God has "wished for himself"[16] and the spiritual soul of each man is "immediately created" by God;[17] his whole being bears the image of the Creator. Human life is sacred because from its beginning it involves "the creative action of God"[18] and it remains forever in a special relationship with the Creator, who is its sole end.[19] God alone is the Lord of life from its beginning until its end: no one can, in any circumstance, claim for himself the right to destroy directly an innocent human being.[20]

Human procreation requires on the part of the spouses responsible collaboration with the fruitful love of God;[21] the gift of human life must be actualized in marriage through the specific and exclusive acts of husband and wife, in accordance with the laws inscribed in their persons and in their union.[22]

I
RESPECT FOR HUMAN EMBRYOS

Careful reflection on this teaching of the Magisterium and on the evidence of reason, as mentioned above, enables us to respond to the numerous moral problems posed by technical interventions upon the human being in the first phases of his life and upon the processes of his conception.

1. WHAT RESPECT IS DUE TO THE HUMAN EMBRYO, TAKING INTO ACCOUNT HIS NATURE AND IDENTITY?

The human being must be respected—as a person—from the very first instant of his existence.

The implementation of procedures of artificial fertilization has made possible various interventions upon embryos and human foetuses. The aims pursued are of various kinds: diagnostic and therapeutic, scientific and commercial. From all of this, serious problems arise. Can one speak of a right to experimentation upon human embryos for the purpose of scientific research? What norms or laws should be worked out with regard to this matter? The response to these problems presupposes a detailed reflection on the nature and specific identity—the word "status" is used—of the human embryo itself.

At the Second Vatican Council, the Church for her part presented once again to modern man her constant and certain doctrine according to which: "Life once conceived, must be protected with the utmost care; abortion and infanticide are abominable crimes".[23] More recently, the *Charter of the Rights of the Family*, published by the Holy See, confirmed that "Human life must be absolutely respected and protected from the moment of conception".[24]

This Congregation is aware of the current debates concerning the beginning of human life, concerning the individuality of the human being and concerning the identity of the human person. The Congregation recalls the teachings found in the *Declaration on Procured Abortion*: "From the time that the ovum is fertilized, a new life is begun which is neither that of the father nor of the mother; it is rather the life of a new human being with his own growth. It would never be made human if it were not human already. To this perpetual evidence . . . modern genetic science brings valuable confirmation. It has demonstrated that, from the first instant, the programme is fixed as to what this living being will be: a man, this individual-man with his characteristic aspects already well determined. Right from fertilization is begun the adventure of a human life, and each of its great capacities requires time . . . to find its place and to be in a position to act".[25] This teaching remains valid and is further confirmed, if confirmation were needed, by recent findings of human biological science which recognize that in the zygote* resulting from fertilization the biological identity of a new human individual is already constituted.

Certainly no experimental datum can be in itself sufficient to bring us to the recognition of a spiritual soul; nevertheless, the conclusions of science regarding the human embryo provide a valuable indication for discerning by the use of reason a personal presence at the moment of this first appearance of a human life; how could a human individual not be a human person? The Magisterium has not expressly committed itself to an affirmation of a philosophical nature, but it constantly reaffirms the moral condemnation of any kind of procured abortion. This teaching has not been changed and is unchangeable.[26]

Thus the fruit of human generation, from the first moment of its existence, that is to say from the moment the zygote has formed, demands the unconditional respect that is morally due to the human being in his bodily and spiritual totality. The human being is to be respected and treated as a person from the moment of conception; and therefore from that same moment his rights as a person must be recognized, among which in the first place is the inviolable right of every innocent human being to life.

This doctrinal reminder provides the fundamental criterion for the solution of the various problems posed by the development of the biomedical sciences in this field: since the embryo must be treated as a person, it must also be defended in its integrity, tended and cared for, to the extent possible, in the same way as any other human being as far as medical assistance is concerned.

2. Is PRENATAL DIAGNOSIS MORALLY LICIT?

If prenatal diagnosis respects the life and integrity of the embryo and the human foetus and is directed towards its safeguarding or healing as an individual, then the answer is affirmative.

---

* The zygote is the cell produced when the nuclei of the two gametes have fused.

For prenatal diagnosis makes it possible to know the condition of the embryo and of the foetus when still in the mother's womb. It permits, or makes it possible to anticipate earlier and more effectively, certain therapeutic, medical or surgical procedures.

Such diagnosis is permissible, with the consent of the parents after they have been adequately informed, if the methods employed safeguard the life and integrity of the embryo and the mother, without subjecting them to disproportionate risks.[27] But this diagnosis is gravely opposed to the moral law when it is done with the thought of possibly inducing an abortion depending upon the results: a diagnosis which shows the existence or malformation or a hereditary illness must not be the equivalent of a death-sentence. Thus a woman would be committing a gravely illicit act if she were to request such a diagnosis with the deliberate intention of having an abortion should the results confirm the existence of a malformation or abnormality. The spouse or relatives or anyone else would similarly be acting in a manner contrary to the moral law if they were to counsel or impose such a diagnostic procedure on the expectant mother with the same intention of possibly proceeding to an abortion. So too the specialist would be guilty of illicit collaboration if, in conducting the diagnosis and in communicating its results, he were deliberately to contribute to establishing or favouring a link between prenatal diagnosis and abortion.

In conclusion, any directive or programme of the civil and health authorities or of scientific organizations which in any way were to favour a link between prenatal diagnosis and abortion, or which were to go as far as directly to induce expectant mothers to submit to prenatal diagnosis planned for the purpose of eliminating foetuses which are affected by malformations or which are carriers of hereditary illness, is to be condemned as a violation of the unborn child's right to life and as an abuse of the prior rights and duties of the spouses.

3. ARE THERAPEUTIC PROCEDURES CARRIED OUT ON THE HUMAN EMBRYO LICIT?

As with all medical interventions on patients, *one must uphold as licit procedures carried out on the human embryo which respect the life and integrity of the embryo and do not involve disproportionate risks for it but are directed towards its healing, the improvement of its condition of health, or its individual survival.*

Whatever the type of medical, surgical or other therapy, the free and informed consent of the parents is required, according to the deontological rules followed in the case of children. The application of this moral principle may call for delicate and particular precautions in the case of embryonic or foetal life.

The legitimacy and criteria of such procedures have been clearly stated by Pope John Paul II: "A strictly therapeutic intervention whose explicit objective is the healing of various maladies such as those stemming from chromosomal defects will, in principle, be considered desirable, provided it is directed to the true promotion of the personal well-being of the individual without doing harm to his integrity or worsening his conditions of life. Such an intervention would indeed fall within the logic of the Christian moral tradition".[28]

4. How is one to evaluate morally research and experimentation* on human embryos and foetuses?

Medical research must refrain from operations on live embryos, unless there is a moral certainty of not causing harm to the life or integrity of the unborn child and the mother, and on condition that the parents have given their free and informed consent to the procedure. It follows that all research, even when limited to the simple observation of the embryo, would become illicit were it to involve risk to the embryo's physical integrity or life by reason of the methods used or the effects induced.

As regards experimentation, and presupposing the general distinction between experimentation for purposes which are not directly therapeutic and experimentation which is clearly therapeutic for the subject himself, in the case in point one must also distinguish between experimentation carried out on embryos which are still alive and experimentation carried out on embryos which are dead. *If the embryos are living, whether viable or not, they must be respected just like any other human person; experimentation on embryos which is not directly therapeutic is illicit.*[29]

No objective, even though noble in itself, such as a foreseeable advantage to science, to other human beings or to society, can in any way justify experimentation on living human embryos or foetuses, whether viable or not, either inside or outside the mother's womb. The informed consent ordinarily required for clinical experimentation on adults cannot be granted by the parents, who may not freely dispose of the physical integrity or life of the unborn child. Moreover, experimentation on embryos and foetuses always involves risk, and indeed in most cases it involves the certain expectation of harm to their physical integrity or even their death.

To use human embryos or foetuses as the object or instrument of experi-

---

* Since the terms "research" and "experimentation" are often used equivalently and ambiguously, it is deemed necessary to specify the exact meaning given them in this document.

1) By *research* is meant any inductive-deductive process which aims at promoting the systematic observation of a given phenomenon in the human field or at verifying a hypothesis arising from previous observations.

2) By *experimentation* is meant any research in which the human being (in the various stages of his existence: embryo, foetus, child or adult) represents the object through which or upon which one intends to verify the effect, at present unknown or not sufficiently known, of a given treatment (e.g. pharmacological, teratogenic, surgical, etc.).

mentation constitutes a crime against their dignity as human beings having a right to the same respect that is due to the child already born and to every human person.

The *Charter of the Rights of the Family* published by the Holy See affirms: "Respect for the dignity of the human being excludes all experimental manipulation or exploitation of the human embryo".[30] The practice of keeping alive human embryos *in vivo* or *in vitro* for experimental or commercial purposes is totally opposed to human dignity.

In the case of experimentation that is clearly therapeutic, namely, when it is a matter of experimental forms of therapy used for the benefit of the embryo itself in a final attempt to save its life, and in the absence of other reliable forms of therapy, recourse to drugs or procedures not yet fully tested can be licit.[31]

The corpses of human embryos and foetuses, whether they have been deliberately aborted or not, must be respected just as the remains of other human beings. In particular, they cannot be subjected to mutilation or to autopsies if their death has not yet been verified and without the consent of the parents or of the mother. Furthermore, the moral requirements must be safeguarded that there be no complicity in deliberate abortion and that the risk of scandal be avoided. Also, in the case of dead foetuses, as for the corpses of adult persons, all commercial trafficking must be considered illicit and should be prohibited.

5. How is one to evaluate morally the use for research purposes of embryos obtained by fertilization 'in vitro'?

Human embryos obtained *in vitro* are human beings and subjects with rights: their dignity and right to life must be respected from the first moment of their existence. *It is immoral to produce human embryos destined to be exploited as disposable "biological material".*

In the usual practice of *in vitro* fertilization, not all of the embryos are transferred to the woman's body; some are destroyed. Just as the Church condemns induced abortion, so she also forbids acts against the life of these human beings. *It is a duty to condemn the particular gravity of the voluntary destruction of human embryos obtained 'in vitro' for the sole purpose of research, either by means of artificial insemination or by means of "twin fission".* By acting in this way the researcher usurps the place of God; and, even though he may be unaware of this, he sets himself up as the master of the destiny of others inasmuch as he arbitrarily chooses whom he will allow to live and whom he will send to death and kills defenceless human beings.

Methods of observation or experimentation which damage or impose grave and disporportionate risks upon embryos obtained *in vitro* are morally illicit for the same reasons. Every human being is to be respected for himself, and cannot be reduced in worth to a pure and simple instrument for the advantage of others. *It is therefore not in conformity with the moral law deliberately to expose to death human embryos obtained 'in vitro'.* In consequence of the fact that they have been produced *in vitro*, those embryos which are not transferred into the body of the mother and are called "spare" are exposed to an absurd fate, with no possibility of their being offered safe means of survival which can be licitly pursued.

6. WHAT JUDGMENT SHOULD BE MADE ON OTHER PROCEDURES OF MANIPULATING EMBRYOS CONNECTED WITH THE "TECHNIQUES OF HUMAN REPRODUCTION"?

Techniques of fertilization *in vitro* can open the way to other forms of biological and genetic manipulation of human embryos, such as attempts or plans for fertilization between human and animal gametes and the gestation of human embryos in the uterus of animals, or the hypothesis or project of constructing artificial uteruses for the human embryo. *These procedures are contrary to the human dignity proper to the embryo, and at the same time they are contrary to the right of every person to be conceived and to be born within marriage and from marriage.*[32] *Also, attempts or hypotheses for obtaining a human being without any connection with sexuality through "twin fission", cloning or parthenogenesis are to be considered contrary to the moral law, since they are in opposition to the dignity both of human procreation and of the conjugal union.*

The freezing of embryos, even when carried out in order to preserve the life of an embryo—cryopreservation—*constitutes an offence against the respect due to human beings* by exposing them to grave risks of death or harm to their physical integrity and depriving them, at least temporarily, of maternal shelter and gestation, thus placing them in a situation in which further offences and manipulation are possible.

Certain attempts to influence chromosomic or genetic inheritance are not therapeutic but are aimed at producing human beings selected according to sex or other predetermined qualities. These manipulations are contrary to the personal dignity of the human being and his or her integrity and identity. Therefore in no way can they be justified on the grounds of possible beneficial consequences for future humanity.[33] Every person must be respected for himself: in this consists the dignity and right of every human being from his or her beginning.

II
INTERVENTIONS UPON HUMAN PROCREATION

By "artificial procreation" or "artificial fertilization" are understood here the different technical procedures directed towards obtaining a human conception in a manner other than the sexual union of man and woman. This

Instruction deals with fertilization of an ovum in a test-tube (*in vitro* fertilization) and artificial insemination through transfer into the woman's genital tracts of previously collected sperm.

A preliminary point for the moral evaluation of such technical procedures is constituted by the consideration of the circumstances and consequences which those procedures involve in relation to the respect due the human embryo. Development of the practice of *in vitro* fertilization has required innumerable fertilizations and destructions of human embryos. Even today, the usual practice presupposes a hyper-ovulation on the part of the woman: a number of ova are withdrawn, fertilized and then cultivated *in vitro* for some days. Usually not all are transferred into the genital tracts of the woman; some embryos, generally called "spare", are destroyed or frozen. On occasion, some of the implanted embryos are sacrificed for various eugenic, economic or psychological reasons. Such deliberate destruction of human beings or their utilization for different purposes to the detriment of their integrity and life is contrary to the doctrine on procured abortion already recalled.

The connection between *in vitro* fertilization and the voluntary destruction of human embryos occurs too often. This is significant: through these procedures, with apparently contrary purposes, life and death are subjected to the decision of man, who thus sets himself up as the giver of life and death by decree. This dynamic of violence and domination may remain unnoticed by those very individuals who, in wishing to utilize this procedure, become subject to it themselves. The facts recorded and the cold logic which links them must be taken into consideration for a moral judgment on IVF and ET (*in vitro* fertilization and embryo transfer): the abortion-mentality which has made this procedure possible thus leads, whether one wants it or not, to man's domination over the life and death of his fellow human beings and can lead to a system of radical eugenics.

Nevertheless, such abuses do not exempt one from a further and thorough ethical study of the techniques of artificial procreation considered in themselves, abstracting as far as possible from the destruction of embryos produced *in vitro*.

The present Instruction will therefore take into consideration in the first place the problems posed by heterologous artificial fertilization (II, 1-3),*

---

* By the term *heterologous artificial fertilization* or *procreation*, the Instruction means techniques used to obtain a human conception artificially by the use of gametes coming from at least one donor other than the spouses who are joined in marriage. Such techniques can be of two types:

a) *Heterologous IVF and ET*: the technique used to obtain a human conception through the meeting *in vitro* of gametes taken from at least one donor other than the two spouses joined in marriage.

b) *Heterologous artificial insemination*: the technique used to obtain a human conception through the transfer into the genital tracts of the woman of the sperm previously collected from a donor other than the husband.

and subsequently those linked with homologous artificial fertilization (II, 4-6).**

Before formulating an ethical judgment on each of these procedures, the principles and values which determine the moral evaluation of each of them will be considered.

A

HETEROLOGOUS ARTIFICIAL FERTILIZATION

1. WHY MUST HUMAN PROCREATION TAKE PLACE IN MARRIAGE?

Every human being is always to be accepted as a gift and blessing of God. However, from the moral point of view a truly responsible procreation vis-à-vis the unborn child must be the fruit of marriage.

For human procreation has specific characteristics by virtue of the personal dignity of the parents and of the children: the procreation of a new person, whereby the man and the woman collaborate with the power of the Creator, must be the fruit and the sign of the mutual self-giving of the spouses, of their love and of their fidelity.[34] *The fidelity of the spouses in the unity of marriage involves reciprocal respect of their right to become a father and a mother only through each other.*

The child has the right to be conceived, carried in the womb, brought into the world and brought up within marriage; it is through the secure and recognized relationship to his own parents that the child can discover his own identity and achieve his own proper human development.

The parents find in their child a confirmation and completion of their reciprocal self-giving: the child is the living image of their love, the permanent sign of their conjugal union, the living and indissoluble concrete expression of their paternity and maternity.[35]

By reason of the vocation and social responsibilities of the person, the good of the children and of the parents contributes to the good of civil society; the vitality and stability of society require that children come into the world within a family and that the family be firmly based on marriage.

The tradition of the Church and anthropological reflection recognize in marriage and in its indissoluble unity the only setting worthy of truly responsible procreation.

** By *artificial homologous fertilization or procreation*, the Instruction means the technique used to obtain a human conception using the gametes of the two spouses joined in marriage. Homologous artificial fertilization can be carried out by two different methods:

a) Homologous IVF and ET: the technique used to obtain a human conception through the meeting *in vitro* of the gametes of the spouses joined in marriage.

b) Homologous artificial insemination: the technique used to obtain a human conception through the transfer into the genital tracts of a married woman of the sperm previously collected from her husband.

2. DOES HETEROLOGOUS ARTIFICIAL FERTILIZATION CONFORM TO THE DIGNITY OF THE COUPLE AND TO THE TRUTH OF MARRIAGE?

Through IVF and ET and heterologous artificial insemination, human conception is achieved through the fusion of gametes of at least one donor other than the spouses who are united in marriage. *Heterologous artificial fertilization is contrary to the unity of marriage, to the dignity of the spouses, to the vocation proper to parents, and to the child's right to be conceived and brought into the world in marriage and from marriage.*[36]

Respect for the unity of marriage and for conjugal fidelity demands that the child be conceived in marriage; the bond existing between husband and wife accords the spouses, in an objective and inalienable manner, the exclusive right to become father and mother solely through each other.[37] Recourse to the gametes of a third person, in order to have sperm or ovum available, constitutes a violation of the reciprocal commitment of the spouses and a grave lack in regard to that essential property of marriage which is its unity.

Heterologous artificial fertilization violates the rights of the child; it deprives him of his filial relationship with his parental origins and can hinder the maturing of his personal identity. Furthermore, it offends the common vocation of the spouses who are called to fatherhood and motherhood: it objectively deprives conjugal fruitfulness of its unity and integrity; it brings about and manifests a rupture between genetic parenthood, gestational parenthood and responsibility for upbringing. Such damage to the personal relationships within the family has repercussions on civil society: what threatens the unity and stability of the family is a source of dissension, disorder and injustice in the whole of social life.

These reasons lead to a negative moral judgment concerning heterologous artificial fertilization: consequently fertilization of a married woman with the sperm of a donor different from her husband and fertilization with the husband's sperm of an ovum not coming from his wife are morally illicit. Furthermore, the artificial fertilization of a woman who is unmarried or a widow, whoever the donor may be, cannot be morally justified.

The desire to have a child and the love between spouses who long to obviate a sterility which cannot be overcome in any other way constitute understandable motivations; but subjectively good intentions do not render heterologous artificial fertilization conformable to the objective and inalienable properties of marriage or respectful of the rights of the child and of the spouses.

3. IS "SURROGATE"* MOTHERHOOD MORALLY LICIT?

No, for the same reasons which lead one to reject heterologous artificial fertilization: for it is contrary to the unity of marriage and to the dignity of the procreation of the human person.

Surrogate motherhood represents an objective failure to meet the obligations of maternal love, of conjugal fidelity and of responsible motherhood; it offends the dignity and the right of the child to be conceived, carried in the womb, brought into the world and brought up by his own parents; it sets up, to the detriment of families, a division between the physical, psychological and moral elements which constitute those families.

B
HOMOLOGOUS ARTIFICIAL FERTILIZATION

Since heterologous artificial fertilization has been declared unacceptable, the question arises of how to evaluate morally the process of homologous artificial fertilization: IVF and ET and artificial insemination between husband and wife. First a question of principle must be clarified.

4. WHAT CONNECTION IS REQUIRED FROM THE MORAL POINT OF VIEW BETWEEN PROCREATION AND THE CONJUGAL ACT?

a) The Church's teaching on marriage and human procreation affirms the "inseparable connection, willed by God and unable to be broken by man on his own initiative, between the two meanings of the conjugal act: the unitive meaning and the procreative meaning. Indeed, by its intimate structure, the conjugal act, while most closely uniting husband and wife, capacitates them for the generation of new lives, according to laws inscribed in the very being of man and of woman".[38] This principle, which is based upon the nature of marriage and the intimate connection of the goods of marriage, has well-known consequences on the level of responsible fatherhood and motherhood. "By safeguarding both these essential aspects, the unitive and the procreative, the conjugal act preserves in its fullness the sense of true mutual love and its ordination towards man's exalted vocation to parenthood".[39]

The same doctrine concerning the link between the meanings of the conjugal act and between the goods of marriage throws light on the moral problem of homologous artificial fertilization, since "it is never permitted to separate these different aspects to such a degree as positively to exclude

---

* By "surrogate mother" the Instruction means:

a) the woman who carries in pregnancy an embryo implanted in her uterus and who is genetically a stanger to the embryo because it has been obtained through the union of the gametes of "donors". She carries the pregnancy with a pledge to surrender the baby once it is born to the party who commissioned or made the agreement for the pregnancy.

b) the woman who carries in pregnancy an embryo to whose procreation she has contributed the donation of her own ovum, fertilized through insemination with the sperm of a man other than her husband. She carries the pregnancy with a pledge to surrender the child once it is born to the party who commissioned or made the agreement for the pregnancy.

either the procreative intention or the conjugal relation".[40]

Contraception deliberately deprives the conjugal act of its openness to procreation and in this way brings about a voluntary dissociation of the ends of marriage. Homologous artificial fertilization, in seeking a procreation which is not the fruit of a specific act of conjugal union, objectively effects an analogous separation between the goods and the meanings of marriage.

Thus, *fertilization is licitly sought when it is the result of a "conjugal act which is per se suitable for the generation of children to which marriage is ordered by its nature and by which the spouses become one flesh".*[41] *But from the moral point of view procreation is deprived of its proper perfection when it is not desired as the fruit of the conjugal act, that is to say of the specific act of the spouses' union.*

b) The moral value of the intimate link between the goods of marriage and between the meanings of the conjugal act is based upon the unity of the human being, a unity involving body and spiritual soul.[42] Spouses mutually express their personal love in the "language of the body", which clearly involves both "spousal meanings" and parental ones.[43] The conjugal act by which the couple mutually express their self-gift at the same time expresses openness to the gift of life. It is an act that is inseparably corporal and spiritual. It is in their bodies and through their bodies that the spouses consummate their marriage and are able to become father and mother. In order to respect the language of their bodies and their natural generosity, the conjugal union must take place with respect for its openness to procreation; and the procreation of a person must be the fruit and the result of married love. The origin of the human being thus follows from a procreation that is "linked to the union, not only biological but also spiritual, of the parents, made one by the bond of marriage".[44] Fertilization achieved outside the bodies of the couple remains by this very fact deprived of the meanings and the values which are expressed in the language of the body and in the union of human persons.

c) Only respect for the link between the meanings of the conjugal act and respect for the unity of the human being make possible procreation in conformity with the dignity of the person. In his unique and irrepeatable origin, the child must be respected and recognized as equal in personal dignity to those who give him life. The human person must be accepted in his parents' act of union and love; the generation of a child must therefore be the fruit of that mutual giving[45] which is realized in the conjugal act wherein the spouses cooperate as servants and not as masters in the work of the Creator who is Love.[46]

In reality, the origin of a human person is the result of an act of giving. The one conceived must be the fruit of his parents' love. He cannot be desired or conceived as the product of an intervention of medical or biological techniques; that would be equivalent to reducing him to an object of scientific technology. No one may subject the coming of a child into the world to conditions of technical efficiency which are to be evaluated according to standards of control and dominion.

The moral relevance of the link between the meanings of the conjugal act and between the goods of marriage, as well as the unity of the human being and the dignity of his origin, demand that the procreation of a human person be brought about as the fruit of the conjugal act specific to the love between spouses. The link between procreation and the conjugal act is thus shown to be of great importance on the anthropological and moral planes, and it throws light on the positions of the Magisterium with regard to homologous artificial fertilization.

5. Is HOMOLOGOUS 'IN VITRO' FERTILIZATION MORALLY LICIT?

The answer to this question is strictly dependent on the principles just mentioned. Certainly one cannot ignore the legitimate aspirations of sterile couples. For some, recourse to homologous IVF and ET appears to be the only way of fulfilling their sincere desire for a child. The question is asked whether the totality of conjugal life in such situations is not sufficient to ensure the dignity proper to human procreation. It is acknowledged that IVF and ET certainly cannot supply for the absence of sexual relations[47] and cannot be preferred to the specific acts of conjugal union, given the risks involved for the child and the difficulties of the procedure. But it is asked whether, when there is no other way of overcoming the sterility which is a source of suffering, homologous *in vitro* fertilization may not constitute an aid, if not a form of therapy, whereby its moral licitness could be admitted.

The desire for a child—or at the very least an openness to the transmission of life—is a necessary prerequisite from the moral point of view for responsible human procreation. But this good intention is not sufficient for making a positive moral evaluation of *in vitro* fertilization between spouses. The process of IVF and ET must be judged in itself and cannot borrow its definitive moral quality from the totality of conjugal life of which it becomes part nor from the conjugal acts which may precede or follow it.[48]

It has already been recalled that, in the circumstances in which it is regularly practised, IVF and ET involves the destruction of human beings, which is something contrary to the doctrine on the illicitness of abortion previously mentioned.[49] But even in a situation in which every precaution were taken to avoid the death of human embryos, homologous IVF and ET dissociates from the conjugal act the actions which are directed to human fertilization. For this reason the very nature of homologous IVF and ET also must be taken into account, even abstracting from the link with procured abortion.

Homologous IVF and ET is brought about outside the bodies of the couple through actions of third parties whose competence and technical activity determine the success of the procedure. Such fertilization entrusts the life and identity of the embryo into the power of doctors and biologists and establishes the domination of technology over the origin and destiny of the human person. Such a relationship of domination is in itself contrary to the dignity and equality that must be common to parents and children.

Conception *in vitro* is the result of the technical action which presides over fertilization. *Such fertilization is neither in fact achieved nor positively willed as the expression and fruit of a specific act of the conjugal union. In homologous IVF and ET, therefore, even if it considered in the context of 'de facto' existing sexual relations, the generation of the human person is objectively deprived of its proper perfection: namely, that of being the result and fruit of a conjugal act* in which the spouses can become "cooperators with God for giving life to a new person".[50]

These reasons enable us to understand why the act of conjugal love is considered in the teaching of the Church as the only setting worthy of human procreation. For the same reasons the so-called "simple case", i.e. a homologous IVF and ET procedure that is free of any compromise with the abortive practice of destroying embryos and with masturbation, remains a technique which is morally illicit because it deprives human procreation of the dignity which is proper and connatural to it.

Certainly, homologous IVF and ET fertilization is not marked by all that ethical negativity found in extra-conjugal procreation; the family and marriage continue to constitute the setting for the birth and upbringing of the children. Nevertheless, in conformity with the traditional doctrine relating to the goods of marriage and the dignity of the person, *the Church remains opposed from the moral point of view to homologous 'in vitro' fertilization. Such fertilization is in itself illicit and in opposition to the dignity of procreation and of the conjugal union, even when everything is done to avoid the death of the human embryo.*

Although the manner in which human conception is achieved with IVF and ET cannot be approved, every child which comes into the world must in any case be accepted as a living gift of the divine Goodness and must be brought up with love.

6. How is homologous artificial insemination to be evaluated from the moral point of view?

Homologous artificial insemination within marriage cannot be admitted except for those cases in which the technical means is not a substitute for the conjugal act but serves to facilitate and to help so that the act attains its natural purpose.

The teaching of the Magisterium on this point has already been stated.[51] This teaching is not just an expression of particular historical circumstances but is based on the Church's doctrine concerning the connection between the conjugal union and procreation and on a consideration of the personal nature of the conjugal act and of human procreation. "In its natural structure, the conjugal act is a personal action, a simultaneous and immediate cooperation on the part of the husband and wife, which by the very nature of the agents and the proper nature of the act is the expression of the mutual gift which, according to the words of Scripture, brings about union 'in one flesh' ".[52] Thus moral conscience "does not necessarily proscribe the use of certain artificial means destined solely either to the facilitating of the natural act or to ensuring that the natural act normally performed achieves its proper end".[53] If the technical means facilitates the conjugal act or helps it to reach its natural objective, it can be morally acceptable. If, on the other hand, the procedure were to replace the conjugal act, it is morally illicit.

Artificial insemination as a substitute for the conjugal act is prohibited by reason of the voluntarily achieved dissociation of the two meanings of the conjugal act. Masturbation, through which the sperm is normally obtained, is another sign of this dissociation: even when it is done for the purpose of procreation, the act remains deprived of its unitive meaning: "It lacks the sexual relationship called for by the moral order, namely the relationship which realizes 'the full sense of mutual self-giving and human procreation in the context of true love' ".[54]

7. WHAT MORAL CRITERION CAN BE PROPOSED WITH REGARD TO MEDICAL INTERVENTION IN HUMAN PROCREATION?

The medical act must be evaluated not only with reference to its technical dimension but also and above all in relation to its goal which is the good of persons and their bodily and psychological health. The moral criteria for medical intervention in procreation are deduced from the dignity of human persons, of their sexuality and of their origin.

Medicine which seeks to be ordered to the integral good of the person must respect the specifically human values of sexuality.[55] *The doctor is at the service of persons and of human procreation. He does not have the authority to dispose of them or to decide their fate.* A medical intervention respects the dignity of persons when it seeks to assist the conjugal act either in order to facilitate its performance or in order to enable it to achieve its objective once it has been normally performed.[56]

On the other hand, it sometimes happens that a medical procedure technologically replaces the conjugal act in order to obtain a procreation which is neither its result nor its fruit. In this case the medical act is not, as it should be, at the service of conjugal union but rather appropriates to itself the procreative function and thus contradicts the dignity and the inalienable rights of the spouses and of the child to be born.

The humanization of medicine, which is insisted upon today by everyone, requires respect for the integral dignity of the human person first of all in the act and at the moment in which the spouses transmit life to a new person.

It is only logical therefore to address an urgent appeal to Catholic doctors and scientists that they bear exemplary witness to the respect due to the human embryo and to the dignity of procreation. The medical and nursing staff of Catholic hospitals and clinics are in a special way urged to do justice to the moral obligations which they have assumed, frequently also, as part of their contract. Those who are in charge of Catholic hospitals and clinics and who are often Religious will take special care to safeguard and promote a diligent observance of the moral norms recalled in the present Instruction.

8. THE SUFFERING CAUSED BY INFERTILITY IN MARRIAGE

The suffering of spouses who cannot have children or who are afraid of bringing a handicapped child into the world is a suffering that everyone must understand and properly evaluate.

On the part of the spouses, the desire for a child is natural: it expresses the vocation to fatherhood and motherhood inscribed in conjugal love. This desire can be even stronger if the couple is affected by sterility which appears incurable. Nevertheless, marriage does not confer upon the spouses the right to have a child, but only the right to perform those natural acts which are *per se* ordered to procreation.[57]

A true and proper right to a child would be contrary to the child's dignity and nature. The child is not an object to which one has a right, nor can he be considered as an object of ownership: rather, a child is a gift, "the supreme gift"[58] *and the most gratuitous gift of marriage, and is a living testimony of the mutual giving of his parents. For this reason, the child has the right, as already mentioned, to be the fruit of the specific act of the conjugal love of his parents; and he also has the right to be respected as a person from the moment of his conception.*

Nevertheless, whatever its cause or prognosis, sterility is certainly a difficult trial. The community of believers is called to shed light upon and support the suffering of those who are unable to fulfill their legitimate aspiration to motherhood and fatherhood. Spouses who find themselves in this sad situation are called to find in it an opportunity for sharing in a particular way in the Lord's Cross, the source of spiritual fruitfulness. Sterile couples must not forget that "even when procreation is not possible, conjugal life does not for this reason lose its value. Physical sterility in fact can be for spouses the occasion for other important services to the life of the human person, for example, adoption, various forms of educational work, and assistance to other families and to poor or handicapped children".[59]

Many researchers are engaged in the fight against sterility. While fully safeguarding the dignity of human procreation, some have achieved results which previously seemed unattainable. Scientists therefore are to be encouraged to continue their research with the aim of preventing the causes of sterility and of being able to remedy them so that sterile couples will be able to procreate in full respect for their own personal dignity and that of the child to be born.

III.
MORAL AND CIVIL LAW

THE VALUES AND MORAL OBLIGATIONS
THAT CIVIL LEGISLATION
MUST RESPECT AND SANCTION IN THIS MATTER

The inviolable right to life of every innocent human individual and the rights of the family and of the institution of marriage constitute fundamental moral values, because they concern the natural condition and integral vocation of the human person; at the same time they are constitutive elements of civil society and its order.

For this reason the new technological possibilities which have opened up in the field of biomedicine require the intervention of the political authorities and of the legislator, since an uncontrolled application of such techniques could lead to unforeseeable and damaging consequences for civil society. Recourse to the conscience of each individual and to the self-regulation of researchers cannot be sufficient for ensuring respect for personal rights and public order. If the legislator responsible for the common good were not watchful, he could be deprived of his prerogatives by researchers claiming to govern humanity in the name of the biological discoveries and the alleged "improvement" processes which they would draw from those discoveries. "Eugenism" and forms of discrimination between human beings could come to be legitimized: this would constitute an act of violence and a serious offense to the equality, dignity and fundamental rights of the human person.

The intervention of the public authority must be inspired by the rational principles which regulate the relationships between civil law and moral law. The task of the civil law is to ensure the common good of people through the recognition of and the defence of fundamental rights and through the promotion of peace and of public morality.[60] In no sphere of life can the civil law take the place of conscience or dictate norms concerning things which are outside its competence. It must sometimes tolerate, for the sake of public order, things which it cannot forbid without a greater evil resulting. However, the inalienable rights of the person must be recognized and respected by civil society and the political authority. These human rights depend neither on single individuals nor on parents; nor do they represent a concession made by society and the State: they pertain to human nature and are inherent in the person by virtue of the creative act from which the person took his or her origin.

Among such fundamental rights one should mention in this regard: a) every human being's right to life and physical integrity from the moment of conception until death; b) the rights of the family and of marriage as an institution and, in this area, the child's right to be conceived, brought into the world and brought up by his parents. To each of these two themes it is necessary here to give some further consideration.

In various States certain laws have authorized the direct suppression of innocents: the moment a positive law deprives a category of human beings of the protection which civil legislation must accord them, the State is denying the equality of all before the law. When the State does not place its power at the service of the rights of each citizen, and in particular of the more vulnerable, the very foundations of a State based on law are undermined. The political authority consequently cannot give approval to the calling of human beings into existence through procedures which would expose them to those very grave risks noted previously. The possible recognition by positive law and the political authorities of techniques of artificial transmission of life and the experimentation connected with it would widen the breach already opened by the legalization of abortion.

As a consequence of the respect and protection which must be ensured for the unborn child from the moment of his conception, the law must provide appropriate penal sanctions for every deliberate violation of the child's rights. The law cannot tolerate—indeed it must expressly forbid—that human beings, even at the embryonic stage, should be treated as objects of experimentation, be mutilated or destroyed with the excuse that they are superfluous or incapable of developing normally.

The political authority is bound to guarantee to the institution of the family, upon which society is based, the juridical protection to which it has a right. From the very fact that it is at the service of people, the political authority must also be at the service of the family. Civil law cannot grant approval to techniques of artificial procreation which, for the benefit of third parties (doctors, biologists, economic or government powers), take away what is a right inherent in the relationship between spouses; and therefore civil law cannot legalize the donation of gametes between persons who are not legitimately united in marriage.

Legislation must also prohibit, by virtue of the support which is due to the family, embryo banks, post mortem insemination and "surrogate motherhood".

It is part of the duty of the public authority to ensure that the civil law is regulated according to the fundamental norms of the moral law in matters concerning human rights, human life and the institution of the family. Politicians must commit themselves, through their interventions upon public opinion, to securing in society the widest possible consensus on such essential points and to consolidating this consensus wherever it risks being weakened or is in danger of collapse.

In many countries, the legalization of abortion and juridical tolerance of unmarried couples makes it more difficult to secure respect for the fundamental rights recalled by this Instruction. It is to be hoped that States will not become responsible for aggravating these socially damaging situations of injustice. It is rather to be hoped that nations and States will realize all the cultural, ideological and political implications connected with the techniques of artificial procreation and will find the wisdom and courage necessary for issuing laws which are more just and more respectful of human life and the institution of the family.

The civil legislation of many states confers an undue legitimation upon certain practices in the eyes of many today; it is seen to be incapable of guaranteeing that morality which is in conformity with the natural exigencies of the human person and with the "unwritten laws" etched by the Creator upon the human heart. All men of good will must commit themselves, particularly within their professional field and in the exercise of their civil rights, to ensuring the reform of morally unacceptable civil laws and the correction of illicit practices. In addition, "conscientious objection" vis-à-vis such laws must be supported and recognized. A movement of passive resistance to the legitimation of practices contrary to human life and dignity is beginning to make an ever sharper impression upon the moral conscience of many, especially among specialists in the biomedical sciences.

CONCLUSION

The spread of technologies of intervention in the processes of human procreation raises very serious moral problems in relation to the respect due to the human being from the moment of conception, to the dignity of the person, of his or her sexuality, and of the transmission of life.

With this Instruction the Congregation for the Doctrine of the Faith, in fulfilling its responsibility to promote and defend the Church's teaching in so serious a matter, addresses a new and heartfelt invitation to all those who, by reason of their role and their commitment, can exercise a positive influence and ensure that, in the family and in society, due respect is accorded to life and love. It addresses this invitation to those responsible for the formation of consciences and of public opinion, to scientists and medical professionals, to jurists and politicians. It hopes that all will understand the incompatibility between recognition of the dignity of the human person and contempt for life and love, between faith in the living God and the claim to decide arbitrarily the origin and fate of a human being.

In particular, the Congregation for the Doctrine of the Faith addresses an invitation with confidence and encouragement to theologians, and above all to moralists, that they study more deeply and make ever more accessible to the faithful the contents of the teaching of the Church's Magisterium in the light of a valid anthropology in the matter of sexuality and marriage and in the context of the necessary interdisciplinary approach. Thus they will make it possible to understand ever more clearly the reasons for and the validity of this teaching. By defending man against the excesses of his own power, the Church of God reminds him of the reasons for his true nobility; only in this way can the possibility of living and loving with that dignity and liberty which derive from respect for the truth be ensured for the men and women of tomorrow. The precise indications which are offered in the present Instruction therefore are not meant to halt the effort of reflection but rather to give it a renewed impulse in unrenounceable fidelity to the teaching of the Church.

In the light of the truth about the gift of human life and in the light of the moral principles which flow from that truth, everyone is invited to act in the area of responsibility proper to each and, like the good Samaritan, to recognize as a neighbour even the littlest among the children of men (Cf. Luke 10:29-37). Here Christ's words find a new and particular echo: "What you do to one of the least of my brethren, you do unto me" (Matt. 25:40).

During an audience granted to the undersigned Prefect after the plenary session of the Congregation for the Doctrine of the Faith, the Supreme Pontiff, John Paul II, approved this Instruction and ordered it to be published.

Given at Rome, from the Congregation for the Doctrine of the Faith, February 22, 1987, the Feast of the Chair of St. Peter, the Apostle.

Joseph Card. Ratzinger, Prefect

Alberto Bovone, Titular Archbishop of Caesarea in Numidia, Secretary

Notes

[1] POPE JOHN PAUL II, *Discourse to those taking part in the 81st Congress of the Italian Society of Internal Medicine and the 82nd Congress of the Italian Society of General Surgery*, 27 October 1980: *AAS* 72 (1980) 1126.

[2] POPE PAUL VI, *Discourse to the General Assembly of the United Nations Organization*, 4 October 1965: *AAS* 57 (1965) 878; Encyclical *Populorum Progressio*, 13: *AAS* 59 (1967) 263.

[3] POPE PAUL VI, *Homily during the Mass closing the Holy Year*, 25 December 1975: *AAS* 68 (1976) 145; POPE JOHN PAUL II, Encyclical *Dives in Misericordia*, 30: *AAS* 72 (1980) 1224.

[4] POPE JOHN PAUL II, *Discourse to those taking part in the 35th General Assembly of the World Medical Association*, 29 October 1983: *AAS* 76 (1984) 390.

[5] Cf. Declaration *Dignitatis Humanae*, 2.

[6] Pastoral Constitution *Gaudium et Spes*, 22; POPE JOHN PAUL II, Encyclical *Redemptor Hominis*, 8: *AAS* 71 (1979) 270-272.

[7] Cf. Pastoral Constitution *Gaudium et Spes*, 35.

[8] Pastoral Constitution *Gaudium et Spes*, 15; cf. also POPE PAUL VI, Encyclical *Populorum Progressio*, 20: *AAS* 59 (1967) 267; POPE JOHN PAUL II, Encyclical *Redemptor Hominis*, 15: *AAS* 71 (1979) 286-289; Apostolic Exhortation *Familiaris Consortio*, 8: *AAS* 74 (1982) 89.

[9] POPE JOHN PAUL II, Apostolic Exhortation *Familiaris Consortio*, 11: *AAS* 74 (1982) 92.

[10] Cf. POPE PAUL VI, Encyclical *Humanae Vitae*, 10: *AAS* 60 (1968) 487-488.

[11] POPE JOHN PAUL II, *Discourse to the members of the 35th General Assembly of the World Medical Association*, 29 October 1983: *AAS* 76 (1984) 393.

[12] Cf. POPE JOHN PAUL II, Apostolic Exhortation *Familiaris Consortio*, 11: *AAS* 74 (1982) 91-92; cf. also Pastoral Constitution *Gaudium et Spes*, 50.

[13] SACRED CONGREGATION FOR THE DOCTRINE OF THE FAITH, *Declaration on Procured Abortion*, 9, *AAS* 66 (1974) 736-737.

[14] POPE JOHN PAUL II, *Discourse to those taking part in the 35th General Assembly of the World Medical Association*, 29 October 1983: *AAS* 76 (1984) 390.

[15] POPE JOHN XXIII, Encyclical *Mater et Magistra*, III: *AAS* 53 (1961) 447.

[16] Pastoral Constitution *Gaudium et Spes*, 24.

[17] Cf. POPE PIUS XII, Encyclical *Humani Generis:* *AAS* 42 (1950) 575; POPE PAUL VI, *Professio Fidei:* *AAS* 60 (1968) 436.

[18] POPE JOHN XXIII, Encyclical *Mater et Magistra*, III: *AAS* 53 (1961) 447; cf. POPE JOHN PAUL II, *Discourse to priests participating in a seminar on "Responsible Procreation"*, 17 September 1983, *Insegnamenti di Giovanni Paolo II*, VI, 2 (1983) 562: "At the origin of each human person there is a creative act of God: no man comes into existence by chance; he is always the result of the creative love of God".

[19] Cf. Pastoral Constitution *Gaudium et Spes*, 24.

[20] Cf. POPE PIUS XII, *Discourse to the Saint Luke Medical-Biological Union*, 12 November 1944: *Discorsi e Radiomessaggi* VI (1944-1945) 191-192.

[21] Cf. Pastoral Constitution *Gaudium et Spes*, 50.

[22] Cf. Pastoral Constitution *Gaudium et Spes*, 51: "When it is a question of harmonizing married love with the responsible transmission of life, the moral character of one's behaviour does not depend only on the good intention and the evaluation of the motives: the objective criteria must be used, criteria drawn from the nature of the human person and human acts, criteria which respect the total meaning of mutual self-giving and human procreation in the context of true love".

[23] Pastoral Constitution *Gaudium et Spes*, 51.

[24] HOLY SEE, *Charter of the Rights of the Family*, 4: *L'Osservatore Romano*, 25 November 1983.

[25] SACRED CONGREGATION FOR THE DOCTRINE OF THE FAITH, *Declaration on Procured Abortion*, 12-13: *AAS* 66 (1974) 738.

[26] Cf. POPE PAUL VI, *Discourse to participants in the Twenty-third National Congress of Italian Catholic Jurists*, 9 December 1972: *AAS* 64 (1972) 777.

[27] The obligation to avoid disproportionate risks involves an authentic respect for human beings and the uprightness of therapeutic intentions. It implies that the doctor "above all . . . must carefully evaluate the possible negative consequences which the necessary use of a particular exploratory technique may have upon the unborn child and avoid recourse to diagnostic procedures which do not offer sufficient guarantees of their honest purpose and substantial harmlessness. And if, as often happens in human choices, a degree of risk must be undertaken, he will take care to assure that it is justified by a truly urgent need for the diagnosis and by the importance of the results that can be achieved by it for the benefit of the unborn child himself" (POPE JOHN PAUL II, *Discourse to Participants in the Pro-Life Movement Congress*, 3 December 1982: *Insegnamenti di Giovanni Paolo II*, V, 3 [1982] 1512). This clarification concerning "proportionate risk" is also to be kept in mind in the following sections of the present Instruction, whenever this term appears.

[28] POPE JOHN PAUL II, *Discourse to the Participants in the 35th General Assembly of the World Medical Association*, 29 October 1983: *AAS* 76 (1984) 392.

[29] Cf. POPE JOHN PAUL II, *Address to a Meeting of the Pontifical Academy of Sciences*, 23 October 1982: *AAS* 75 (1983) 37: "I condemn, in the most explicit and formal way, experimental manipulations of the human embryo, since the human being, from conception to death, cannot be exploited for any purpose whatsoever".

[30] HOLY SEE, *Charter of the Rights of the Family*, 4b: *L'Osservatore Romano*, 25 November 1983.

[31] Cf. POPE JOHN PAUL II, *Address to the Participants in the Convention of the Pro-Life Movement*, 3 December 1982: *Insegnamenti di Giovanni Paolo II*, V, 3 (1982) 1511: "Any form of experimentation on the foetus that may damage its integrity or worsen its condition is unacceptable, except

in the case of a final effort to save it from death". Sacred Congregation for the Doctrine of the Faith, *Declaration on Euthanasia*, 4: *AAS* 72 (1980) 550: "In the absence of other sufficient remedies, it is permitted, with the patient's consent, to have recourse to the means provided by the most advanced medical techniques, even if these means are still at the experimental stage and are not without a certain risk".

[32] No one, before coming into existence, can claim a subjective right to begin to exist; nevertheless, it is legitimate to affirm the right of the child to have a fully human origin through conception in conformity with the personal nature of the human being. Life is a gift that must be bestowed in a manner worthy both of the subject receiving it and of the subjects transmitting it. This statement is to be borne in mind also for what will be explained concerning artificial human procreation.

[33] Cf. Pope John Paul II, *Discourse to those taking part in the 35th General Assembly of the World Medical Association*, 29 October 1983: *AAS* 76 (1984) 391.

[34] Cf. Pastoral Constitution on the Church in the Modern World, *Gaudium et Spes*, 50.

[35] Cf. Pope John Paul II, Apostolic Exhortation *Familiaris Consortio*, 14: *AAS* 74 (1982) 96.

[36] Cf. Pope Pius XII, *Discourse to those taking part in the 4th International Congress of Catholic Doctors*, 29 September 1949: *AAS* 41 (1949) 559. According to the plan of the Creator, "A man leaves his father and his mother and cleaves to his wife, and they become one flesh" (Gen. 2:24). The unity of marriage, bound to the order of creation, is a truth accessible to natural reason. The Church's Tradition and Magisterium frequently make reference to the Book of Genesis, both directly and through the passages of the New Testament that refer to it: Matt: 19:4-6; Mk. 10:5-8; Eph. 5:31. Cf. Athenagoras, *Legatio pro christianis*, 33: *PG* 6, 965-967; St Chrysostom, *In Matthaeum homiliae*, LXII, 19, 1: *PG* 58 597; St Leo the Great, *Epist. ad Rusticum*, 4: *PL* 54, 1204; Innocent III, Epist. *Gaudemus in Domino: DS* 778; Council of Lyons II, *IV Session: DS* 860; Council of Trent, *XXIV Session: DS* 1798, 1802; Pope Leo XIII, Encyclical *Arcanum Divinae Sapientiae: AAS* 12 (1879/80) 388-391; Pope Pius XI, Encyclical *Casti Connubii: AAS* 22 (1930) 546-547; Second Vatican Council, *Gaudium et Spes*, 48; Pope John Paul II, Apostolic Exhortation *Familiaris Consortio*, 19: *AAS* 74 (1982) 101-102; *Code of Canon Law*, Can. 1056.

[37] Cf. Pope Pius XII, *Discourse to those taking part in the 4th International Congress of Catholic Doctors*, 29 September 1949: *AAS* 41 (1949) 560; *Discourse to those taking part in the Congress of the Italian Catholic Union of Midwives*, 29 October 1951: *AAS* 43 (1951) 850; *Code of Canon Law*, Can. 1134.

[38] Pope Paul VI, Encyclical Letter *Humanae Vitae*, 12: *AAS* 60 (1968) 488-489.

[39] *Loc. cit., ibid.*, 489.

[40] Pope Pius XII, *Discourse to those taking part in the Second Naples World Congress on Fertility and Human Sterility*, 19 May 1956: *AAS* 48 (1956) 470.

[41] *Code of Canon Law*, Can. 1061. According to this Canon, the conjugal act is that by which the marriage is consummated if the couple "have performed (it) between themselves in a human manner".

[42] Cf. Pastoral Constitution *Gaudium et Spes*, 14.

[43] Cf. Pope John Paul II, *General Audience on 16 January 1980: Insegnamenti di Giovanni Paolo II*, III, 1 (1980) 148-152.

[44] Pope John Paul II, *Discourse to those taking part in the 35th General Assembly of the World Medical Association*, 29 October 1983: *AAS* 76 (1984) 393.

[45] Cf. Pastoral Constitution *Gaudium et Spes*, 51.

[46] Cf. Pastoral Constitution *Gaudium et Spes*, 50.

[47] Cf. Pope Pius XII, *Discourse to those taking part in the 4th International Congress of Catholic Doctors*, 29 September 1949: *AAS* 41 (1949) 560: "It would be erroneous . . . to think that the possibility of resorting to this means (artificial fertilization) might render valid a marriage between persons unable to contract it because of the *impedimentum impotentiae*".

[48] A similar question was dealt with by Pope Paul VI, Encyclical *Humanae Vitae*, 14: *AAS* 60 (1968) 490-491.

[49] Cf. *supra*: I, 1ff.

[50] POPE PAUL II, Apostolic Exhortation *Familiaris Consortio*, 14: *AAS* 74 (1982) 96.

[51] Cf. *Response to the Holy Office*, 17 March 1897: *DS* 3323; POPE PIUS XII, *Discourse to those taking part in the 4th International Congress of Catholic Doctors*, 29 September 1949: *AAS* 41 (1949) 560; *Discourse to the Italian Catholic Union of Midwives*, 29 October 1951: *AAS* 43 (1951) 850; *Discourse to those taking part in the Second Naples World Congress on Fertility and Human Sterility*, 19 May 1956: *AAS* 48 (1956) 471-473; *Discourse to those taking part in the 7th International Congress of the International Society of Haematology*, 12 September 1958: *AAS* 50 (1958) 733; POPE JOHN XXIII, Encyclical *Mater et Magistra*, III: *AAS* 53 (1961) 447.

[52] POPE PIUS XII, *Discourse to the Italian Catholic Union of Midwives*, 29 October 1951: *AAS* 43 (1951) 850.

[53] POPE PIUS XII, *Discourse to those taking part in the 4th International Congress of Catholic Doctors*, 29 September 1949: *AAS* 41 (1949) 560.

[54] SACRED CONGREGATION FOR THE DOCTRINE OF THE FAITH, *Declaration on Certain Questions Concerning Sexual Ethics*, 9: *AAS* 68 (1976) 86, which quotes the Pastoral Constitution *Gaudium et Spes*, 51. Cf. *Decree of the Holy Office*, 2 August 1929: *AAS* 21 (1929) 490; POPE PIUS XII, *Discourse to those taking part in the 26th Congress of the Italian Society of Urology*, 8 October 1953: *AAS* 45 (1953) 678.

[55] Cf. POPE JOHN XXIII, Encyclical *Mater et Magistra*, III: *AAS* 53 (1961) 447.

[56] Cf. POPE PIUS XII, *Discourse to those taking part in the 4th International Congress of Catholic Doctors*, 29 September 1949: *AAS* 41 (1949), 560.

[57] Cf. POPE PIUS XII, *Discourse to those taking part in the Second Naples World Congress on Fertility and Human Sterility*, 19 May 1956: *AAS* 48 (1956) 471-473.

[58] Pastoral Constitution *Gaudium et Spes*, 50.

[59] POPE JOHN PAUL II, Apostolic Exhortation *Familiaris Consortio*, 14: *AAS* 74 (1982) 97.

[60] Cf. Declaration *Dignitatis Humanae*, 7.

BIBLICAL TEACHING AND ASSISTING THE POOR

JOHN D. MASON
Professor of Economics, Gordon College

Article from *Transformation*

Introduction

From the very beginning of recorded history, societies have struggled with the same problem: how to assist the poor.[1] In the competition among economic systems and ideologies over the centuries, the most critical question asked of any society has been whether it was able to resolve effectively the 'problem' of its poorer citizens. Indeed, it is primarily this issue that Karl Marx attacked in the nineteenth century; and it has fuelled the search for a better alternative to capitalism in the period since.

In the economically undeveloped societies of today, assisting the poor quite properly involves two things: establishing the foundations for sustained economic growth; and designing redistribution policies, to protect citizens in case of income loss—or other conditions which attack their continued economic viability. The economically developed societies have felt a greater freedom to concern themselves more aggressively with redistribution policies (the 'welfare state'). In these societies, however, it has not been easy to design a set of programmes that successfully helps the poor become economically viable and independent; and some observers have argued that such societies are no more free of a concern for economic growth, in their efforts to assist the poor, than the more economically undeveloped societies.

In this essay I want to draw biblical conclusions which are more directly relevant to 'welfare state' type redistribution policies than to the foundational structures necessary for economic growth. This relative stress should not be seen however as underemphasizing in any way the fundamental importance of economic growth in an overall programme to assist the poor. The great challenge facing societies today is to maintain a delicate balance between policies that encourage effort and risk-taking—and thus result in more economic growth—and policies that offer protection to citizens from the arbitrary adversities of life.

In order to achieve this delicate balance, we need technical information about the incentive properties of programmes and taxes, and how behaviour responds to these. How can unemployment assistance be structured so as not to subsidize excessive idleness? Are there sufficient job opportunities for those who are unemployed, as well as for those who would like to better their station? Do universal children's allowances offer a more effective and efficient means of preventing poverty than assistance provided once poverty has been experienced? Is the rising incidence of out-of-wedlock teenage pregnancy a result in part of the structure of assistance programmes? A number of other questions along these lines could be posed.

But better technical information alone is insufficient. Whether a particular society is a democracy (whereby the electorate must to some extent approve the redistribution programmes), or a more totalitarian setting (in which the citizens can frustrate policy by their lack of cooperation—true also of democracies), attention must be paid to the shared sense of moral obligation held by the broader citizenry. Should unemployed citizens be allowed to remain idle for extended periods if adequate jobs exist? Is the existence of unwed pregnancy that results in public assistance an acceptable phenomenon? When assistance programmes are not consonant with the shared sense of moral obligation within society, intractable problems will inevitably result.

Effective assistance of the poor, then, means that societies must pay more attention *both* to matters of programme design *and* to the shared sense of moral obligation held by the majority of citizens. This latter issue is my primary concern here. More particularly, I intend to search the roots of a major tradition affecting moral obligation today, the Scriptures of the Judeo-Christian ethic.

I draw my biblical material almost entirely from the Pentateuch, working from the conviction that Yahweh provided to early Israel sensitivities and structures to help that society assist its poorer citizens effectively; and that the later prophetic material, as well as the New Testament, builds upon this earlier foundation rather than replaces it—calling upon individual Jews and Christians, as well as entire societies, to conform themselves to the sensitivities embedded within the pentateuchal provisions.[2]

First we will consider the socio-economic context of early Israel, as well as the basic provisions for assisting the poor that characterized this early society. Then I propose to examine the standard for assistance in early Israel, as well as the crucial issue of the *legal status* of the provisions for assisting the poor—whether the provisions were nothing more than *voluntary* moral obligations for non-poor members of society, or whether they were *legally enforceable laws* binding upon the community. Several biblical implications for contemporary societies will be developed at that point.

My major conclusions are these: Reciprocal obligations existed between the poorer members of society, in need of assistance, and the larger community (and particularly the more well-to-do citizens). Those receiving assistance were obligated to the community to work when possible, even in the actual receiving of assistance (e.g. gleanings) and to live modestly; idleness was condemned strongly. The community was responsible to assist all those who were poor due to arbitrary circumstances—including the able-bodied as well as the dependent. Though both able-bodied and dependent members of society were to receive assistance, the form of assistance for each was different, with provisions for the dependent taking more the form of charity.

The standard for assistance was specified as *sufficiency for need*, a level that would prevent impoverishment from having harmful long-term consequences. As Yahweh had been compassionate with Israel in delivering her from slavery to a land flowing with milk and honey, so the provisions for those individuals and families impoverished due to arbitrary adversity should be characterized by compassion. The general character of these provisions can be described as 'compassionate stewardship'.

Socio-Economic Setting of Early Israel

There is considerable socio-economic distance between an economically undeveloped, largely agrarian economy, built around extended family and clan obligations and an early Middle Eastern cultural setting on one hand, and the economically developed societies of the twentieth century on the other hand.[3] It is unlikely therefore that the actual institutions for assisting the poor in early Israel could be transported unchanged to the twentieth century to serve the same ends! And so we need to look instead at the *intentions* or *sensitivities* that characterized the earlier institutions, so that changed institutions today might be able to capture these same intentions. This requires a careful understanding of the broader socio-economic setting of early Israel, and not just a listing of the provisions, so that the intentions of the provisions can be understood more carefully.

The pentateuchal narratives and legislation give us a picture of a subsistence economy, primitive in economic terms, based on agriculture.[4] Productive property (primarily land) was held privately by extended-family units; but these property rights were attenuated by specific obligations to the community. For example, normal productive activity on a piece of land was to cease one year out of seven, and the resulting natural growth was to be available to the owners *and* other members of the community. Furthermore, any one piece of land was not to be alienated more than fifty years from the extended-family of original ownership (Lev. 25).

As we have noted, the basic social unit was the extended family (*beth'ab* or 'house of the father') consisting of a father/elder, mother, unmarried children, married sons with their wives and children, any servants, and possibly a few sojourners (or aliens): all of which could amount to fifty members (if not fifty fighting men—1 Sam. 8:12) but also could be quite small (e.g. Naomi and Ruth).

Of almost comparable social importance was a larger unit, the *mishpahah*, or what Gottwald calls a 'protective association of extended families'.[5] The most likely development of a *mishpahah* would be the aging of an extended family, as each of the sons becomes the head of his own *beth'ab*, with grandchildren and (less frequently) great-grandchildren. The members of different *beth'avoth* would be brothers at the patriarch level and cousins of different degrees at the lower levels.[6]

Israelites married within the *mishpahah*, members of a *mishpahah* could exact retribution or redeem a member sold into slavery, and local justice was performed by the elders of the *beth'avoth* within a *mishpahah* (elders at the gate). DeGeus writes, 'The *mishpahah* was the principal form of organization and social grouping in ancient Israel, and . . . for landowning Israelites it practically coincided with the town.'[7] A *mishpahah* could consist of twenty to fifty *beth'avoth*[8] and thus would possibly comprise a small village or extended neighbourhood of a larger town. (For the purposes of this paper, the social units beyond the *beth'ab* and *mishpahah*—the tribe and federation of tribes—are of less importance and will not be considered.)

Though the larger share of the output no doubt was consumed by the *beth'ab* producing it, the existence of laws regulating market activity (Lev. 19:35-36) attest to some exchange of goods and services.[9] Furthermore there must have been sufficient labourers seeking employment (most likely the sojourners mentioned so often in the texts, as well as citizens who either had free time from their own land or more likely had sold their land in order to pay debts), since we find provisions governing this relationship (Lev. 19:13, Dt. 24:14-15). Finally, laws are given to regulate interest rates and repayment schedules of loans (Ex. 22:24-25, Dt. 15:1-11), which means that there must have been some sort of capital market (and probably specie) as well as some surplus beyond subsistence.[10] From the complaints of the prophets during the first millennium B.C., we know that by their times numerous market transactions for labour as well as goods and services were occurring—and that the stipulated provisions regarding these were not being honoured.

Israel, then, was primarily a land-based subsistence economy, with a fringe of market-based earnings and growing commercial and capital markets. To this account we must add two more things: *inheritance practices* and *transfer obligations* of the larger community for care of the Levites and poorer members of society. For, inevitably, some would do better than others. In such a combination of subsistence and market-based sources of income, an inevitable element of chance in the economic outcomes would eventually develop.

Substantial variation in income would occur due to varying weather conditions and other natural events (insect, disease, and predator damage). In addition, sickness and injury would be frequent enough to hinder productive activity. (However, the existence of a larger *beth'ab* as the productive unit would mitigate the harmful effect of this class of difficulties.)

The particular Hebrew words describing 'poor' persons in early Israelite society—primarily *'ebyon* and *'ani*, but also *dal*—imply that the primary reason for different economic outcomes in early Israel was not that some people lacked ambition. Impoverishment would be associated in most cases with adverse circumstances.[11] It is easy to imagine a hard-working *beth'ab* quite arbitrarily falling victim to (for example) insect damage that would seriously diminish the yield, and thus impoverish the family, if some sort of community assistance were not forthcoming. It would be difficult for an individual or family to exercise a strong preference for idleness; the combination of subsistence conditions, close social relations, and the general impetus of the Mosaic legislation (which, as we will see, required work from anyone who could work), together would serve as a deterrent.

One additional background characteristic of early Israel must be considered: her implicit administrative or political structure. At the lowest level 'administrative oversight' resided with the elder of the *beth'ab*. In Dt. 16:9-17, the elder is charged to make sure that the widows, orphans, and sojourners of his area were invited to share in the various feasts. The father/elder was to exercise administrative oversight over those for whom he reasonably could be considered responsible. Job argues as much in several of his defences, noting how he cared for the weaker/poorer individuals for whom he felt responsible (Job 31:16ff.). Another example was Judah's right to consign Tamar to death or to spare her life for her adultery (Gen. 38).[12]

The next level of administrative/political oversight was the gathering of the elders of the *beth'avoth* making up a *mishpahah* (the elders at the gate). Today this gathering would most likely be called a judicial body, but for the small rural communities of early Israel, administrative and judicial functions were not divided. Before Israel had a king this gathering represented the primary form of primitive state.[13] Boaz came to the elders at the gate to request a ruling with regard to his right to marry Ruth (Rt. 4:1ff.); it was here that the widow would appeal if her brother-in-law failed to marry her and provide an offspring in order to take possession of her deceased husband's patrimony (Dt. 25:5-10); it was here that Job sat to consider the cases of the poor and needy (Job 29:7-17).[14]

With the advent of the monarchy, there developed more permanent state functions beyond the local level—though the extent of these should not be exaggerated, given the relatively poor state of mobility and communication. A system of courts was established to which appeals could be made, including appeal ultimately to the king.[15] Various public works were undertaken, including defence installations in several strategically-located cities in addition to the more famous temple and palace construction in Jerusalem. A standing army was established which, along with the various public works, necessitated a system of taxes.[16]

And so a more hierarchical and national governing order emerged with the monarchy. But the responsibility of this larger state did not change. Those responsible for national policy were to exercise 'administrative oversight' according to the Law of Yahweh, just as the elders in the local communities did. The king was admonished to read the Law daily, and to conduct himself modestly just as any other citizen (Dt. 17:16-20). Such limitations upon the power of the monarch represented a sharp break from the situation in surrounding nations of that era (and, unfortunately, did not characterize Israel's own history under a monarch).

Community Assistance to the Poor

With this background, it is now possible to consider the nature of the community's normative response, when families and individuals found themselves in difficult economic circumstances. The following specific provisions provide most of the biblical content for the programmes observed below and will be discussed in a number of different contexts:

1. A zero-interest loan will be available, and if the principal has not been repaid by the end of six years the balance will be forgiven (Ex. 22:25, Lev. 25:35-38, Dt. 15:1-11);

2. Israelites committed to slavery for debt-repayment are to be released at the end of six years (assuming the debt has not been fully repaid before then, so that release comes sooner—Lev. 25:47-53) (Ex. 21:1-11, Lev. 25:39-43, Dt. 15:12-18);

3. An Israelite forced to sell his land for debt-repayment, if the debt has not been repaid by the end of forty-eight years, will have the balance of the debt forgiven and the land returned, to him or his successors (Lev. 25:8-34);

4. Each field is to be left fallow every seventh year with the natural growth available for the poor (Ex. 23:10-11, Lev. 25:1-7);

5. The gleanings and corners of fields are to be left for the poor, and especially the widows, orphans, and sojourners (Lev. 19:9-10, 23:22, Dt. 24:19-21);

6. The third-year tithe will be available for the widows, orphans and sojourners, in addition to the Levites (Dt. 14:28-29, 26:12).

In addition to these specific provisions the more well-to-do members of society were admonished generally to care for the poor and needy, in ways such as sharing feast days with widows, orphans, and sojourners (Dt. 16:11-14). This is seen clearly in pentateuchal passages like Ex. 22:21-24, Dt. 15:11, and 24:10-15; it is affirmed throughout the Old Testament in passages referring to the 'poor and needy' (*'ebyon* and *'ani*) such as Job 29:11ff., Ps. 72, and Jer. 22:16; it is implicit in God's whole treatment of Israel, rescuing them from slavery in Egypt and providing them a land with wells they did not dig and vineyards they did not plant, even when because of their disobedience they were undeserving (Dt. 6:10-13, 8:7 to 9:6)—a description not particularly applicable to the poor in the passages considered above. Indeed this general admonition is a major part of the obligatory 'administrative oversight' that the elders (and higher administrative/political officials) were to exercise.

In understanding these provisions, it will be helpful to use a distinction that has been made for centuries in English and American welfare practice: that between the *able-bodied* and *dependent*. 'Able-bodied' Israelites were members of economically viable (propertied) extended-families (*beth'a-voth*), which typically would have contained several able workers as well as some aged and possibly some disabled members. The 'dependent' poor in Israel then would include members of economically weak *beth'avoth* (those with only disabled or sick workers), needy individuals who were not part of a larger *beth'ab* (particularly widows with child-care and domestic responsibilities, such as Ruth and Naomi), and the sojourners. Sojourner families were likely to include able-bodied workers, but their lack of citizenship and property at least early in Israel's history would have left them unable to find much economic opportunity, and hence vulnerable to poverty.

Provisions for the Able-Bodied[17]

The zero-interest loan was probably a short-term business loan without collateral to the able-bodied land owner, similar to what is still practised in numerous farm communities today. The pentateuchal provision, however, contains a clear element of *grace* in the zero-interest provision, as well as the seventh-year forgiveness of the unpaid balance;[18] it is a 'compassionate loan'. A *beth'ab* facing difficult circumstances, either because of a poor previous harvest or complications with the current year's crops, would need outside assistance. If family members could not find suitable employment outside their farm, assuming they had the time to spare, then a loan would be necessary.

It seems rather unlikely that such a loan would be available to anyone other than an economically viable (propertied) *beth'ab*, since otherwise there would be little means to raise the money to repay it.[19] The most likely source of the loan would be a more well-to-do *beth'ab* of the same *mishpahah*, particularly in an isolated village which might be comprised entirely of the member families of the *mishpahah*.[20] The most likely source of the loan would be a brother of the elder of the adversely affected *beth'ab*, and if that were not possible then an uncle on the father's side (Num. 27:9-11). If the closer relatives were not able or willing to make the loan, then the appeal would be to the wider membership of the *mishpahah*—and ultimately outside the *mishpahah*. Ideally a more well-to-do elder would initiate the loan proceedings, which would fulfill the highest intentions of the Law (Job 31:16 perhaps); but it seems more likely that the disadvantaged elder would have to initiate the proceedings himself.

Let us assume that the loan obligation would run at most six full years from the point of initiation, after which any unpaid principal would be forgiven.[21] What would most probably happen would be repayment after several years; only rarely would any balance remain unpaid beyond six years—and even then it would be a small amount (assuming the family did not experience repeated bouts of adverse circumstances). If this reconstruction is correct, there would have been few cases of forgiven unpaid balances, and rather small amounts in these few cases. Such a situation would not call for any special attention or comment in biblical or extra-biblical documents. In other words, the absence of written evidence attesting to the practice of loan forgiveness—which has caused some observers to conclude that these provisions were more sacral and symbolic than real (and possibly composed at a much later date than 1200-1000 B.C., in order to express a normative ideal)—may tell very little about whether these provisions ever *were* honoured in practice. Indeed, they could have been practised for years with little attention paid them.

During the loan period members of the indebted *beth'ab* would have to work extra hours and enjoy less income than otherwise. The community (and more particularly, the *beth'ab* making the loan) would bear the cost of the missing interest and loss of the use of the loaned surplus—money that otherwise could have been stored or used in exchange for items the loaning *beth'ab* would have liked. The indebted *beth'ab* bears the cost of loan repayment, though without a heavy interest obligation, and with the comfort (?) that if difficult circumstances were to persist, the unpaid balance ultimately would be forgiven.

Welfare-related *gift*-giving is found in numerous primitive economic settings.[22] Why then did early Israel use a *loan* provision, rather than the inter-personal gift-giving found elsewhere—or even a community-administered welfare system similar to that in contemporary societies? The loan provision is far more complex than reciprocal gift-giving. Moreover, the implied work obligation which always is a part of community-administered welfare assistance would be rather easy to monitor in that socio-economic setting. Why then the loan? The Scriptures are silent, and we can only speculate. But we do have the advantage of hindsight in having witnessed the inadequacy of contemporary, community-administered welfare programmes that do not involve loans.

To grasp this more clearly, consider for purposes of illustration the community-based assistance programmes in the United States, which provide grants (cash, food vouchers, access to medical assistance) for certain categories of individuals deemed unable to earn sufficient income (typically women with childcare responsibilities and no man present). Liberal observers argue that this approach tends to 'stigmatize' recipients, drawing inappropriate attention to them (e.g. by requiring them to produce food vouchers at special check-out counters), as well as to humiliate them by repeatedly forcing the revelation of personal information in order to qualify for assistance. The obvious remedy is to make qualification for assistance less humiliating, and in the provision of assistance to insulate recipients from broader community awareness of precisely who is 'on welfare'. Conservative observers react by arguing that U.S. welfare programmes, being too readily available, create unhealthy dependency upon them, and that 'stigmatization' is necessary in order to shame the recipients off welfare.

In the context of this debate, then, the biblical institution of a compassionate loan provides assistance to the able-bodied without *either* unnecessarily stigmatizing them *or* creating conditions ripe for excessive dependency upon the assistance programmes. A loan recognizes that the weaker family unit remains a productive component of the community which can, with time and some reduced consumption, very probably take care of its economic responsibilities. Use of a loan protects against the development of excessive dependency upon assistance. A loan requires less community concern to monitor; the loan obligation serves as a pressure to work harder rather than to shirk.[23]

The compassionate aspects of the loan indicate the community's acknowledgement that the weaker family had little control over its difficulties, and that the community is willing to assist. In other words, a compassionate loan is good for the social-psychological health of the adversely affected *beth'ab*, as well as for economic efficiency within the community—even though it appears initially to be harsher treatment than a more charitable alternative.

If adverse conditions became particularly severe or persisted over a number of years, the affected *beth'ab* would be unable to repay the initial loan and most probably be forced to incur further indebtedness. The ideal resolution, in terms of the spirit of biblical legislation, would be an *additional* compassionate loan, again without any collateral. This might be difficult to arrange, however, for at least two reasons. On the one hand, more well-to-do *beth'avoth* would be less willing to make such loans, fearing nonrepayment of the entire principal by the end of the sixth year (Dt. 15:7-9). On the other hand, the adversely affected *beth'ab* would feel reluctant to approach others repeatedly. Some other provisions would seem to be necessary.

The alternative which overcomes both of the difficulties just noted is a loan with collateral, backed either by the land of the *beth'ab* (very much like a contemporary mortgage) or by placing some member or members of the *beth'ab* into bond-slavery. It is unclear in Scripture which of these would have been pursued first. The modern sentiment against slavery and our familiarity with mortgages as commonplace would suggest bond-slavery to be the last resort.[24] This may not have been the case, however, given the virtually sacred importance of maintaining one's patrimony, as well as the fact that slavery took a benevolent form, similar to indentured servitude in the early years of the European experience in America. In fact—as we shall see—it seems likely that bond-slavery may have been the initial and most frequent alternative.[25]

As with the compassionate loan, the major share of secured loans would most probably have been repaid prior to reaching the debt-forgiveness period. The bond-slavery case appears to fit the compassionate loan provision exactly.[26] There is no provision regarding repayment of a loan secured by land collateral. But a provision *is* given to regulate forced sale of one's land—which would occur if a secured loan could not be arranged, or if repayment of a land-secured loan were not possible and foreclosure took place. Since the forgiveness period governing repurchase of one's land is so much longer than the seventh year release controlling bond-slavery, bond-slavery may have been the more frequent recourse. If the adversely affected *beth'ab* were reasonably large, it may well have been able to spare at least one member who would be obligated to work for another *beth'ab* until the loan obligation were repaid—but no longer than six years.

And so I am arguing that the compassionate loan without collateral was the primary (ideally the only) provision necessary for the able-bodied, propertied Israelites who were placed in difficult economic circumstances. The 'secured' loan was a contingent or secondary provision, necessary because of hard-heartedness by more well-to-do members, or the weaker family's reluctance to approach others for a compassionate loan. The language used in Scripture about the two types of provisions suggests that the compassionate (unsecured) loan tends to be associated more with *apodictic* ('thou shalt') commands, whereas the loans secured either by one's land or one's body are associated more with *casuistic* ('if this occurs, then . . .') construction. This supports my proposition that the Israelites were *ordered* to make compassionate loans, but *if* slavery or potential alienation of one's patrimony occurred then contingent provisions would regulate such arrangements.[27]

The Hebrew term used at Dt. 15:1-10 to describe the disadvantaged (male?) Israelite is *'ebyon*; at Lev. 25:35-37 a male Israelite is mentioned, though the term used there is *muk* (to become poor). In both cases it is presumed that the reference is to the elder of a *beth'ab*. Because the compassionate loan seems to be associated exclusively with the term *'ebyon* (see endnote 23 above) it is tempting to conclude that this particular word for 'poor' refers primarily (only?) to an economically viable *beth'ab*. Thus the companion term *'ani*, which some students interpret as synonymous with *'ebyon*, would in fact describe all *other* individuals or families who were poor and deserving of assistance. This distinction then may well represent that between the *able-bodied* and the *dependent*. Such a distinction would help to explain why the two words are used together so often.

If this interpretation holds then the fallow-year provision, whereby the natural growth of a field left idle every seventh year becomes available to the poor, is a provision for the able-bodied because the term used at Ex. 23:10-11 is *'ebyon*.[28] That seems plausible. For unlike the provisions for gleanings, which are made available to the dependent poor (as we shall see later), harvesting the natural growth may well be more demanding and thus require the efforts of able-bodied (male?) workers. Moreover, the fallow-year is symbolic of God's larger provisions for Israel, both in the wilderness as well as in the provision of a nation with vineyards planted by others. This last point suggests that *any* Israelite should have access to the land in the fallow year, and not just the able-bodied; though free access to gleanings would not be available for the able-bodied, the fallow-year provision would be—and thus the use of *'ebyon* at Ex. 23:10-11.

Provisions for the Dependent

Treatment of the provisions for the dependent poor need not consume nearly so much space. Every society has recognized the importance of assisting those who, for whatever reasons (childcare responsibilities, disablement, age), cannot realistically be expected to work for remuneration in order to subsist. The dependent poor would include widows and orphans who were not part of a larger *beth'ab*, the sojourners (*ger*), who frequently would own no property and belong to no protective Israelite *beth'ab*, and thus would be without solid means to assure sufficient income; and possibly also some *beth'avoth* with disabled or sick members, to the extent that they would not be able to carry out productive activity. Provisions for the dependent members of the community are charitable for the most part (though with work expectations, where this would be possible), in contrast to the loan provision applicable to the able-bodied.

Apart from general admonitions to the larger community to care for the widows, orphans, and sojourners (such as Ex. 22:21-24 and Dt. 16:11, 14) two explicit provisions apply to these individuals too: the right to glean, and to harvest corners of the fields; and access (with the Levites) to the third-year tithe. The third-year tithe is restricted only to widows, orphans, and sojourners; the right to the gleanings is granted to the widows, orphans, and sojourners (Lev. 19:10, 23:22, Dt. 24:19-21), and also to the poor called *'ani* (Lev. 19:9-10, 23:22)—which again raises the question of precisely who the *'ani* are in distinction to the *'ebyon* and other poor groups. The resolution suggested here, that the *'ani* describes the poor who deserve assistance and who are not part of an economically viable *beth'ab* (the *'ebyon*), would then include the widows, orphans, and sojourners but also would extend beyond them.

The Lev. 19:9-10 and 23:22 passages seem to refer to grain fields. The Dt. 24:19-21 passage explicitly mentions grain, olives, and the vineyard (similar to the fallow-year provision of Ex. 23:11). The grain harvest was conducted from April through June, with barley preceding wheat; the grape harvest ran through the summer months to October; the olive harvest took place in late October and November. In other words there was a fairly continuous annual flow of gleanings from mid-spring through late fall for the dependent poor who were able to go to the fields and gather them. This provision is a form of pure charity. No payment from the recipient of the gleanings is expected, even though much effort has been expended by the owner and any employees and servants to plant, trim, and prepare the crops for harvesting, and then to cut the grain and beat the olive trees, allowing the gleaners simply to pick up the fruit from the ground. At the same time, however, there clearly is a work expectation for the gleaners (who must work behind the reapers), and they would have had to come to the fields most days at the appropriate times (which demands punctuality and discipline). And so this provision can be considered qualified charity.

The third-year tithe provision represents pure charity and probably was restricted to those who could not be expected to conduct the effort necessary for gleaning; or perhaps it was available for the dependent when the gleanings were not sufficient or available. The Dt. 14:28 passage appears to instruct the land-owners to deposit the third-year tithe in the town, which suggests centralized administration.[29] If it is assumed that different *beth'a-voth* supplying the tithe were on separate tithe cycles, which is the most economically plausible rendering—and consistent with assumptions above regarding the sabbatical year (consisting of the seven years subsequent to a compassionate loan or initiation of bond-slavery)—then there would be an amount available every year for relief of this type.

Remembering the debate over contemporary welfare systems, such as that in the U.S., we have to ask: were the disadvantaged Israelites shamed or stigmatized in any way? Certainly the spirit of the legislation is that this should *not* have been so—we gather this from the frequent motive clauses associated with such provisions, whereby God would intervene in cases of improper treatment of the poor (e.g. Ex. 22:22-23). But the reality may well have been different. Boaz instructed his servants not to molest Ruth as she gleaned in his fields (Rt. 2:9, 16), which suggests that gleaners were susceptible to less-than-desirable treatment by the reapers. Able-bodied males that ventured into the fields to glean may have been submitted to verbal abuse, if no more. This could explain why the provisions restricted them to the fallow-year fields, if the reconstruction proposed here is correct. Community members would have been aware of who was receiving community assistance, in the close living conditions of that time. This awareness, however, should not have been used destructively. After all, God had delivered these people out of slavery and brought them into a land flowing with milk and honey, undeserving though they were.

Standard for Assistance

Differing scholars, seeking insight for contemporary society in the Bible, have discerned sharply variant general standards. Some have argued that the appropriate standard is *whatever outcome natural processes* (such as the market) *generate*, modified only by private charity, because there are no explicit biblical commands to redistribute income. Others have discerned a standard of *virtual equality of economic outcome*, drawing from passages such as Ex. 16:18, Ezek. 47:14, and 2 Cor. 8:13. What I want to do here is to keep in mind the actual assistance provisions we have just looked at, and inquire into the standard that most probably governed their administration. For example, when able-bodied *beth'avoth* (extended families) requested loans, what would the allowed size of the loan be? When dependent members actually did request part of the third-year tithe, what amount of assistance would be meted out?

The answer to this question about standards will come from two sources: first, the specific passages attached to the assistance provisions, and second, a more general inference from Yahweh's treatment of Israel. The answer is 'sufficiency for need', but with a fairly liberal interpretation of need, aiming in the direction of economic equality.

At Dt. 15:8 the law requires a more well-to-do member of the community to loan the poorer brother 'sufficiency for his needs'. At Lev. 25:35, speaking to similar circumstances, the standard is a level of support similar to that which would be provided to a stranger or sojourner: a standard at least meeting, if not exceeding, that required for subsistence. At Dt. 14:29, recipients from the third-year tithe were to be given an amount of food sufficient to satisfy them. Quite clearly, then, the passages immediately connected with the provisions for low-income assistance suggest 'sufficiency for need'.[30]

But this does not fully answer the question we asked, since both 'sufficiency' and 'need' are such elastic notions. Unless we qualify it further, our specification has ruled out only *insufficiency* at one end and *equality* at the other. (Of course, in an extreme case when the entire community lacked economic means, sufficiency for needs would *mean* economic equality— which may have been the situation at Ex. 16:18.) We need also to take into account the socio-economic setting of Israel, as well as the broader relationship of Israel to Yahweh.

As we saw earlier, the poorer members of society would be neither idlers nor sluggards, but as hard-working as other members of the community. This reality suggests a more liberal interpretation of sufficiency. Furthermore, the basic *nature* of the low-income provisions—as we saw—would protect against shirking. And so the interpretation of sufficiency could be more liberal without encouraging opportunistic behaviour. Clearly, the spirit of the legislation (see especially Lev. 25:36-38) entails such an interpretation.

Passages such as Ex. 22:21, Lev. 25:38, and Dt. 24:18, 22 deal with legal stipulations regarding poorer individuals; and each carries the argument further in support of an expansive interpretation of sufficiency, because *each describes the fundamental nature of Yahweh's relationship with Israel*. He rescued them from slavery in Egypt; he continued to nurture them in the wilderness and eventually delivered them into their own land. In other words, since Yahweh had been so liberal with them, they also should be liberal in their dealings with poorer members of the community. The phrase 'compassionate stewardship' seems an apt description of what was required.

Gottwald's treatment of the *mishpahah* reinforces the conclusion drawn here. One of the salient functions of the *mishpahah* is 'to protect the socio-economic integrity of *beth'avoth* threatened with diminution or extinction'. The *mishpahah*

> did not intersect with and impinge upon the family . . . but it heightened and brought to prominence the centrality of the family. . . . Instead of qualifying the power and importance of the family, as a clan would necessarily do, the protective association of families maximized and guarded the integrity and viability of the member families.[31]

If there were such a concern for the socio-economic integrity of the *beth'ab*, it makes it more plausible that the standard would be 'liberal sufficiency for needs'. It also suggests that action would be taken *prior* to impoverishment, as far as possible, and would not simply be reaction to an established situation of impoverishment. The biblical standard is, wherever possible, the *prevention* of dangerously low income rather than relief in the midst of it.

A lot of modern work in Christian social ethics tends to view *economic equality* as the norm, and so further comment may be helpful. The narratives describe the land as being divided into roughly equal shares when Israel entered Palestine (Num. 26:52-56), but it is doubtful if these shares would have been equal in productive capacity. Which means that eventually they would yield unequal economic outcomes. Indeed, the jubilee provision of Lev. 25 both recognizes this and seeks to correct for it—even if only every forty-nine years. The broader historical record of Israel from the time of Abraham to the settlement in Palestine presents us with a picture of differing economic fortunes but does not condemn the *fact* of the differences as such.

An appeal to the remainder of Scripture only reinforces this conclusion. It is clear that a few passages, such as 1 Sam. 30:21-25 (assuming the practice had applicability beyond a military setting), Ezek. 47:14, and 2 Cor. 8:13, present a standard of economic equality. But there is a much larger body of material that allows for some economic inequality and gives no sharp condemnation of it, when this could have been expected (especially in the teachings of Jesus, who was so sharp in his condemnation of other existing practices). This leads to the conclusion that Yahweh is less concerned about *economic equality* than about an *egalitarian bias* in the midst of economic inequality (and especially so in cases where members of society experience arbitrary adversity).

Let us summarize the essence of an appropriate standard. Assistance to the poor was intended to maintain each family unit as an economically viable and contributing component of the community; so that the family would have the confidence that if it worked as it should, and otherwise remained a faithful member of the community, then the community would not allow economic difficulties to debilitate the family so that it could not continue to be viable and contributing. Birch epitomizes this standard gracefully and efficiently: 'The entire social order was structured in a way that attempted to prevent those in need from being permanently locked into their poverty.'[32] The important element of this standard—liberal sufficiency for need—is the *confidence* or *hope* that the family unit would have: a confidence that should free them to develop and use their talents to the long-term benefit of the family and the community.

Legal Status of the Provisions

But if one purpose of our exploration is to inform contemporary social policy, we need to investigate still further. We must ask: what was the legal status of these provisions? Some observers have claimed that they were merely moral obligations, to be fulfilled by the voluntary response of those who were more well-to-do, and have argued that income redistribution was not an obligation of the Israelite community in the biblical narratives. This issue lies at the heart of much current debate, both among those who claim the Bible as normative and among those who do not.

Was it possible for the more well-to-do *beth'avoth* to be forced by the community to make zero-interest loans? Or to forgive the unpaid balance of these loans in the sabbatical year? Could farmers be required to allow dependent members of society to glean? Could bondslaves appeal to the community if they were not released at the end of six years; and could citizens be mandated to contribute to the community-administered welfare storehouse?

Let us first consider the arguments for treating these provisions as moral obligations only. Loewenstamm argues that 'the very formulation of these laws raises the doubt as to their actual implementation, or whether they were regarded as moral precepts. . . . It does not grant the poor a legal right, but merely approaches the rich with a religio-ethical appeal.'[33] Similarly, Phillips argues:[34]

> In contrast to the formal corpus of Ex. 21:12-22:7 (Mt. 22:16), with its specifications of precise legal offences and appropriate sanctions to be enforced through the courts, the laws of humaneness and righteousness are not, in a technical sense, laws at all, for they envisage no legal action for their breach and specify no penalties. Rather, they are addressed directly to the recipient and envisage unquestioning obedience. Their basis is an appeal to his sense of moral responsibility for those who are not in a position to protect themselves and to his sense of justice.

A motive clause has been attached to a number of these provisions (Ex. 22:23-24, Dt. 15:9, 24:15), which states that if the more well-to-do members of the community fail to obey these laws, then the poorer Israelite can appeal to Yahweh. Some have attributed the existence of such motive clauses to the legal unenforceability of social laws, which make an extra moral urging necessary.[35] It also has been suggested that since there is no specific legal relief attached to the low-income provisions, they must have been primarily moral (and philanthropic).[36] In the case of texts like Ps. 72:1-4, 12-13 and Jer. 22:16, passages which charge the king to protect the rights of the poor and needy, it has been argued that the admonition is simply for the king to act privately as an example for others, and that these passages are not grounds for the monarch to act with the power of the state to redistribute income or resources by force.

Reasonable as these arguments seem, and important as it is not to extend the reach and implications of biblical law too freely, it is possible to arrive at a different conclusion: that the provisions could and would have been enforced legally—at least on a number of occasions. Consider for example the compassionate loan, the institution deemed most likely to have had only voluntary significance. Suppose that a loan had been effected and that either regular payments had not been made, or the seventh-year payment had not been paid. The creditor would then become responsible to investigate the situation sufficiently either to seek repayment or to be satisfied that his charity was required. If he sought repayment, the issue most probably would have been brought before the elders at the gate, who then would decide the merits of the complaint. Since the low-income provisions are clearly a part of the law it is presumed the elders would have given them serious consideration. If the indebted *beth'ab* was found to have worked the expected amount and lived simply (in order to repay the loan), and was still unable to repay it, the elders would no doubt have admonished the creditor strongly, or possibly have offered to help share the burden of non-repayment—or both. If, on the other hand, the indebted *beth'ab* had been sluggish or consumed at too high a level, the elders no doubt would have ordered repayment in some way—perhaps by requiring collateral in the form of labour or land. It would seem that passages such as Job 29:12, 16 and 31:13, 16-21 fit situations very much like this (see also Prov. 22:22 and Amos 2:6, where the poor are found at the gate).

The less likely case is that the disadvantaged party would initiate legal proceedings, either protesting the failure of a more well-to-do *beth'ab* to make a compassionate loan in the first place, or protesting about the creditor's attempts to force repayment once the loan was made. Possibly the institution of the 'hue and cry' could have been used in such cases;[37] possibly a non-indebted friend of the disadvantaged *beth'ab* would act as an advocate before the elders (e.g. 2 Kgs. 8:1-6).

If the situation of Ruth 2:9, 15, where Boaz instructed his harvesters not to trouble Ruth, reflects a frequent hazard gleaners had to face, it suggests that the gleaning provision for dependent Israelites was subject to little legal oversight. On the other hand, the fact that the third-year tithe was gathered in a central place and then dispensed to those in need seems clearly to require a community-administered operation, for which the elders would have had to establish proper criteria as to who should receive assistance and how much. Infringements upon these criteria would most probably have been cause for some form of legal redress.

What of the third-year tithe? The question is whether Israelites would have been forced to deliver their portions to the community. The biblical record does not offer direct evidence of this, but inferential evidence can be found in Talmudic material.

> The directors [of the town charitable fund] had the right to force contribution . . . by anyone who could afford at all to give charity and had lived in the community for a period not less than one month (*Baba Batra* 8a). The amount of the contributions to be paid by one was estimated by the board of directors. If one refused to pay the full amount assessed, they levied an attachment to his property (*Baba Batra* 8b).[38]

At several places in the Old Testament reference is made to the 'rights' or 'cause' of the poor: Ex. 23:6, Dt. 24:17, 27:19, Job 36:6, Ps. 140:12, Prov. 29:7, 31:9, Eccl. 5:8 (by clear implication), Is. 10:2, Jer. 5:28, 22:16. These words have unmistakable legal significance[39] and obviously include the types of provisions which have been examined above. They refer both to the *'ebyon* and the *'ani* which means (you will remember) that legal rights adhere to both the able-bodied and the dependent.[40]

In his article on 'The Rights of the Underprivileged', Patrick argues that the Mosaic provisions dealing with the under-privileged grew out of actual legal proceedings and court rulings, with the result that here 'we have real law governing precisely defined legal relationships.'[41] Daube understands the biblical social legislation in a similar way: to have grown out of earlier practices, even before the exodus. He argues that the earlier practices tended to favour more well-to-do *beth'avoth* that could afford to redeem poorer relatives. But in the Mosaic legislation the state intervenes on behalf of the poor (he cites Ps. 72:14).[42]

Putting all these arguments together, it seems likely that the Israelite provisions for assisting the poor would have been *legally enforceable* forms of income distribution in a number of cases. The clear fact is that the provisions for the impoverished were part of the Mosaic legislation, as much as other laws such as those dealing with murder and theft. Since nothing in the text allows us to consider them as different, they must be presumed to have been legally enforceable.

Conclusion

Early Israel, then, possessed a reasonably sophisticated set of assistance programmes[43] characterized by 'compassionate stewardship'—a *stewardly* concern for efficient administration of her scarce resources. This explains the use of a loan for the able-bodied poor and work expectations for those dependent poor who could work. It also explains the legal obligation upon wealthier members of the community to assist in such a way as to prevent poverty from becoming so debilitating that the affected individual or family could no longer contribute meaningfully and productively to society (and thus become a liability). The community was to make a *compassionate* response, in recognition of the arbitrary nature of economic adversity (for otherwise hardworking individuals and families). This explains the zero-interest loan with a seventh-year cancellation of any unpaid principal, and a standard of assistance that could be described as 'liberal sufficiency for need', as the main provisions for the able-bodied poor.

So far we have not paid much attention to the jubilee provision (Lev. 25), whereby no piece of land was to be alienated from its original extended family owners for longer than fifty years.

The long term period involved[44] carries this particular provision beyond the pale of short-run assistance to impoverished members of the community, which is our concern here. The jubilee institution can be viewed, therefore, as having more to do with the necessary conditions for maintaining a social environment that was both just and conducive to economic growth. Most probably this institution was designed to accomplish two things. First, it appears to be concerned with the dangers of concentrated productive property; and so it may have something to teach us today about competition policy or inheritance laws, but not about low income assistance.

Second, the jubilee institution assured each extended family unit of a privately-owned productive base—but every 48th year, or about every second generation. The relevance of this function to our policies today, in a nonagrarian economy, would most probably involve the provision of a sound 'human capital' base (i.e. a good education) for each citizen, as the best way to maintain a secure, privately-owned productive base.

This second function draws attention once again to the importance of the community exercising protective 'administrative oversight' so as to prevent the existence of impoverishment. As we have already seen, the provisions for the poor carry reciprocal obligations. The poor are expected to work where possible in the receipt of any community assistance, and the community is expected to offer compassionate assistance. Implicit in the work-expectation facing the poor is the reasonable expectation that suitable work can be found. And so a part of the protective administrative oversight that the elders of a community were to exercise was probably the responsibility of guaranteeing that sufficient work existed for the poorer members; Mt. 20:1-16 may well be a good example of this.

A programme of protective administrative oversight—of the elders properly governing their community—has wider implications than the subject area of this essay. These implications today would embrace the proper management of the economy so as to maintain low levels of unemployment and inflation, as well as keeping conditions ripe for economic growth. They would also include a programme for educating the members of the community so that arbitrary and adverse economic circumstances would not be as devastating.[45]

An important biblical theme that has been touched on only indirectly in this paper is the *general concern for work*—and like several other tangential themes raised here it cannot be treated in adequate detail. Work has both positive and negative roles attached to it in Scripture. Positively, work can be creative and provide meaning, as well as the needed material substance, to life. God worked in creation (so much that he rested) and Jesus spent the greater part of his earthly existence in manual work. Negatively, work can be demeaning and non-creative. Even the most rewarding work is to cease at least one day of each week; and certain types of work (e.g. work which creates idols, or a harsh form of slavery, or terribly demeaning work when this is the labourer's only option) are not to be allowed.[46]

If the elders of the community were to govern the community to assure opportunities for work (and hence economic growth), they were also responsible to make sure that no members of the community were idlers. That is, a concern for assuring sufficient work in the community is also a concern to prevent any poorer members from shirking.

Contemporary Implications

Having explored the likely structure of assistance to the poor in early Israel, and having uncovered the intentions that characterize these biblical provisions, we can then examine assistance provisions for the poor in contemporary societies, in order to discern whether they embody the same sensitivities.

To draw specific policy implications would require application to one national setting, and then an extensive discussion of the history and structure of that setting. This cannot be done here. Instead we will explore several general emphases of the biblical provisions, using the framework of poverty assistance in the United States for occasional examples. These emphases are: the importance of reinforcing the extended family as a private economic base to protect against poverty; the use of a compassionate loan in providing public assistance; reasonable work expectations for assistance recipients, with reciprocal obligations upon managers of the economy to assure sufficient work opportunities; liberal standards of provision; the attempt to minimize the shaming or stigmatizing of those who are poor due to arbitrary adversity.

Assuming that there is a general public framework of laws (for example, competition policy) and the provision for certain public goods (such as, and especially, a sound education for each citizen), it is fundamentally important next to stress the necessity of a *private* economic base for each family and individual, and to seek to maintain this base as much as possible. It is undesirable that people should actively rely upon public provision of income beyond the benefits generated by the general (public) framework, even though it may be necessary (as we have seen) to counter certain adverse circumstances. To be 'on the dole' or 'on welfare' or 'drawing unemployment' inevitably marks out those involved in ways that are demeaning, and will probably have adverse behavioural effects upon the recipients when received for long periods—regardless of how much compassion goes into the design and administration of these programmes.

Scripture attests to all this, and addresses the issue in two foundational ways: practically emphasizing the importance of extended families, and then explicitly granting these families private property. It will not do to argue that the Scripture merely accepts the typical social reality in the ancient Near East of the extended family and makes this normative. In those days, the typical 'political' reality involved militarily strong and often arbitrary central power; and yet the ideal of the scriptural call was for no king or standing army (1 Sam. 8 and 12), and what some have described as a radical democracy;[47] and were these people to select a king, he should limit his power (Dt. 17:14ff.). The typical 'economic' reality of that day found a great deal of productive property concentrated in the hands of the religious and state authorities, and yet Scripture decrees that the Levites were to be severely limited in their ownership of productive property (Lev. 25:32-24, Num. 18:20, 35:1-8). The extended family, however, was embraced and reinforced, as clearly a very effective institution for the protection against impoverishment among individual members of the family; it offered a setting in which the proper degree of compassion and responsibility could be administered more effectively than through extra-familial institutions. It must be noted that implicit in the affirmation of the *extended* family is an equally strong (if not greater) commitment to the importance of the *nuclear* family.

Privately-held property, whether for personal or productive use, offers generally more potential for creativity and personal freedom, and promises generally more efficient use of productive resources. These lessons have been and are being learned by twentieth century nations such as China and the USSR, who having nationalized virtually all property are now feeling their way back to greater degrees of private ownership and control in order to encourage individual effort and realize greater efficiency and productivity. Though certain constraints upon the use of private ownership are necessary, and find expression in Scripture, the clear biblical bias is for *private* assignment over *public* assignment.[48] In addition to the personal freedom and creativity encouraged (desirable ends in themselves), private assignment generally enhances the potential for greater economic growth; economic growth in turn supplies more and better jobs, and thus becomes the means by which most nuclear and extended families can provide for themselves without outside assistance.

Public policy should therefore be consciously designed to reinforce the social and economic health of the extended family. Obviously the cohesion and healthy functioning of the extended family depends upon *far more* than various adjustments in public policy—indeed, in a sense public policy in the twentieth century has been running to keep up with family changes—but there are a number of steps which could be taken to provide incentives to maintain the stability of nuclear and extended families. As an example, within the U.S.A. the state of Wisconsin recently has required the parents to bear part of the support when a young, unwed daughter with a child applies for public assistance. Similarly there has developed in the U.S. almost universal support for searching out absent fathers and requiring them to contribute to the support of their children.

A number of other initiatives of this type could be contemplated. For example should the young, unwed daughter with child be allowed (as a general rule) to live separately from her parents and receive public assistance? Might there be ways to encourage children (perhaps by tax inducements) to care for aged or infirm parents more than they do at present? In the wake of the development of the western welfare states since the 1930s, such measures have a ring of toughness to them. So did the Apostle Paul's admonition to grandchildren in Ephesus (1 Tim. 5). But the toughness is designed to maintain the basic building block of a society. Social welfare agencies at their best remain bureaucracies, lacking in the potential to express sacrificial love. A society needs a base of healthy families, and social policy must help preserve them even when it requires seemingly tough rules.

The use of a compassionate loan for able-bodied families and individuals has rarely been considered for the public sector, although it has been used frequently to various degrees in private dealings. The public alternative for intact families has typically been some form of unemployment assistance for periods of foregone earnings, and cash or in-kind assistance (children's allowances, welfare, and so on) for employed but low-income families. Several nations have been wondering whether some of the unemployed have remained on assistance for excessive periods, and if so whether this is a result of too few jobs or too easy administration of assistance. At least one observer has recommended a form of compassionate loan as an alternative to unemployment insurance in the U.S., making a portion of the benefits a low-interest loan for the first six months of unemployment (to be repaid once work is resumed); if the period of unemployment extended beyond six months then the assistance would change to grant that would not have to be repaid.[49]

We need add little here to what we have already said about the reciprocal obligations upon the poor and those responsible for administrative oversight in the economy. As the elders of an early Israelite community may have found work repairing walls or water supplies when there was insufficient work in the private sector, so contemporary 'elders' are obligated to assure adequate work opportunity. This is a task of great complexity in the modern, interdependent economies of the world today, involving attention to such issues as international trade policy and domestic monetary policy as well as whether and how to create specialized retraining programmes or work opportunities. We cannot realistically treat it adequately in a few paragraphs here. As the able-bodied had to repay loans and the employable but dependent poor had to glean in the fields of early Israel, so the employable poor today should be expected to work in the process of receiving assistance. Such a general admonition does not answer the difficult practical questions of whether those drawing unemployment assistance should be required to take 'just any job'; or at what age of their children single mothers should be required to take employment outside the home; but it does echo the biblical emphasis upon reasonable work expectations.[50]

If work opportunities were available, and if realistic and rigorous work expectations were implemented systematically in the administration of public assistance, then the standards for assistance could be raised to levels providing liberal sufficiency for needs, without courting the danger of attracting numerous applicants for assistance. As with each of the implications being examined here, there are a host of technical issues which would have to be addressed before we could begin formulating actual policy. A basic one is whether we should be offering cash assistance as opposed to in-kind help. In early Israel the able-bodied were eligible both for compassionate loans (cash) and access to the fallow-year fields (in-kind); the dependent were confined primarily to in-kind assistance (gleanings, and access to a portion of the third-year tithe—which in early Israel most likely would have been foodstuffs, but at a later date could have been cash). Clearly the biblical account is not troubled by in-kind assistance. One presumes that 'liberal sufficiency for needs' would have meant different levels in early Israel, depending upon average consumption standards of a local area; in the difficult setting of the wilderness a daily quotient of manna and quail (the same thing day after day!) was liberal sufficiency. In other words, there may well be room in a large, regionally diversified society today for local economic variations rather than a national standard; although the standard remains 'liberal sufficiency' for needs.

From the little evidence we have (Ruth 2:9, and hints gleaned from the prophetic complaints about mistreatment of the poor) we can presume that the poor in early Israel were shamed and stigmatized. At least for those poor who were the 'ebyon and 'ani—deserving of assistance because they were victims of arbitrary adversity, this was wrong and should be addressed by the elders (Job 29 and 31, Ps. 72). Policing it today would be no easier than in early Israel. Children can be excessively cruel in their treatment of peers who are different, and thus need parental correction; in just the same way the elders and laws of a society must exhibit vigilance in addressing the inevitable reality of shaming and stigmatizing. Where the structure of assistance programmes can protect against this, for example by creating as much physical privacy as possible for citizens applying for help, protection should be given.

The contemporary policy implications come as a package. If there are liberal standards for assistance, without adequate work opportunities or work requirements and practical reinforcement of the family, there will be dangers of excessive and irresponsible reliance upon public aid. If there are work requirements without work opportunities or liberal financial assistance, the situation will only invite bureaucratic abuse, as assistance providers bend the rules in order to reflect some compassion. These contemporary realities attest once again to the socio-economic plausibility and completeness of the biblical framework. Our obligation before the awesome God of all creation, who is also the loving God who desires a personal relationship with each one of us, is to be faithful and complete in our attention to Scripture, and not to pick and choose among his provisions, imposing our own criteria for what is worthwhile and not his.

Finally, we neglect at our peril the fundamental importance of maintaining a viable private socio-economic base. Public assistance is necessary in a world constrained by selfish behaviour; private charity never has been sufficient. But public assistance is a secondary provision, and works best when it builds upon a healthy private sector of families, churches, and business enterprises which are providing the values, virtues, jobs, and intra- and extra-family assistance that are foundational to the health of any society.

Notes

[1] See F. Fensham, 'Widow, Orphan, and the Poor in Ancient Near Eastern Legal and Wisdom Literature', *Jnl. of Near Eastern Stud.* 21:129-39 (April, 1962).

[2] A rather substantial set of theological presumptions is embedded within this project that cannot be discussed here. I see myself arguing the point made well by C. Wright: 'That is, we assume that if God gave Israel certain specific institutions and laws, they were based on principles which have universal validity. That does not mean that Christians will try to impose by law in a secular state provisions lifted directly from the law of Moses. It does mean that they will work to bring their society nearer to conformity with the principles underlying the concrete laws of Old Testament society, because they perceive the same God to be both Redeemer and law-giver of Israel, and also Creator and Ruler of contemporary mankind.' [*An Eye for an Eye: The Place of Old Testament Ethics Today* (Downers Grove, IL: InterVarsity Press, 1982)], p. 162, published in U.K. as *Living as the People of God.* See also: J. Goldingay, *Approaches to Old Testament Interpretation* (Downers Grove, IL: InterVarsity Press, 1981); J. Barton, 'Approaches to Ethics in the Old Testament' in J. Rogerson (ed.), *Beginning Old Testament Study* (Philadelphia: Westminster Press, 1982), pp. 113-30.

[3] On the social and economic background of early Israel see especially: C. H. J. DeGeus, *Tribes of Israel* (Amsterdam: Van Gorcum, 1976), which is organized around testing Noth's

amphictyony thesis and provides a great deal of very helpful socio-economic information in doing so; N. Gottwald, *Tribes of Yahweh* (Maryknoll, NY: Orbis Books, 1979), which sets out to be a sociological analysis of early Israel; and the now standard R. DeVaux, *Ancient Israel* (New York: McGraw-Hill, 1965).

[4] Gottwald decribes early Israel as ' . . . an egalitarian, extended-family, segmentary tribal society with an agricultural-pastoral economic base.' Gottwald, *op. cit.* (note 3 above), p. 389. In contrast to more traditional accounts of early Israel as pastoral nomads—because they had come in to a settled state in Palestine from wandering through the regions to the south and east of their new country—Gottwald considers them transhumant pastoralists (p. 294), reflecting his thesis that the origin of Israel was not from external invasion but internal revolt against Canaanite overlords. If the biblical account is to be believed (and this paper is so inclined) the Israelites would have brought with them into Palestine a most recent history of pastoral nomadism, but a much longer history before that from Egypt of settled agriculture and small crafts (Ex. 1:11-14 notes they were subjected to construction labour and all kinds of labour in the field).

[5] Gottwald, *op. cit.* (note 3 above), ch. 28.

[6] In addition to (and based in part on) the sources listed in note 3 above, see L. Stager, 'The Archaeology of the Family in Ancient Israel', *BASOR* 260:1-36 (Nov. 1985), for a very helpful and brief review of the evidence on the likely everyday life and realities in early Israel.

[7] DeGeus, *op. cit.* (note 3 above), p. 144.

[8] Wolff gives the number twenty and Gottwald fifty. See: H. Wolff, *Anthropology of the Old Testament* (Philadelphia: Fortress Press, 1976), p. 215; Gottwald, *op. cit.* (note 3 above), p. 267ff.

[9] Israel was located on the main trading route between Egypt and nations to the north and east, so it is not at all unusual that market activity beyond subsistence farming developed quite early in her history. Archaeological findings from ancient Jericho, a city existing several millennia prior to settled Israel it is believed, offers suggestions of trading activities with other cities of Asia Minor and areas to the north and east. On the other hand DeVaux notes that extensive commercial activity developed late in Israel's history in Palestine with early commerce being local in nature only. See DeVaux, *op. cit.* (note 3 above), pp. 78-79.

[10] It is known from extra-biblical material that Mesopotamia and Egypt had rather elaborate economic arrangements for centuries prior to the settlement of Israel. Assuming Abraham and his entourage brought with them knowledge from Mesopotamia of the arrangements there, and that Moses was schooled in similar arrangements in Egypt, then it seems quite likely that at least the rudiments of a more complex economy were in place awaiting economic growth and the specialization (and thus market activity) this allows.

[11] These Hebrew words (*'ebyon, 'ani, dal*) clearly represent citizens who were deserving of community compassion, according to the texts. The Old Testament does speak of those who were poor due to laziness, with most English translations speaking of 'sluggards' or 'idlers' (main Hebrew word is *atsel*, but see also *remiyyah*); these terms are found primarily in the Proverbs and not in the narratives dealing with the first several centuries of the settled Israelite nation.

[12] Christ's parable of the workers called to the fields at various hours of the day (Mt. 20:1-16) speaks forcefully to this issue. The landowner (elder?) took compassion upon men desirous of work (v. 7), allowing them to enter his field, and then paid each man the standard (subsistence) wage—sufficient to support the worker and his family for that day.

[13] Occasional state-like functions were exercised beyond the local community. Entire tribes were enlisted on occasion, typically under the leadership of one of the 'judges' to engage in military actions. The various judges, in addition to their military duties, also spoke for Yahweh and thereby served a central unifying function which transcended the local community. But for most of the routine state-like functions the local community was indeed the most important administrative/political setting.

[14] Considerable evidence exists to substantiate the administrative and judicial roles played by the community of elders. See particularly: H. Boecker, *Law & the Administration of Justice in the Old Testament & Ancient East* (Minneapolis: Augsburg Publishing House, 1980); K. Whitelam, *The Just King: Monarchical Judicial Authority in Ancient Israel*, JSOT Supp. Series 12 (Sheffield:

JSOT Press, Dept. of Biblical Studies, Univ. of Sheffield, 1979), especially, Ch. 2 'The Administration of Justice in Pre-Monarchical Israel'; R. Wilson, 'Enforcing the Covenant: The Mechanism of Judicial Authority in Early Israel', in H. Huffman, *et al.* (eds.), *The Quest for the Kingdom of God: Studies in Honor of George E. Mendenhall* (Winona Lake, IN: Eisenbrauns, 1983), pp. 59-75.

    Though most biblical and extra-biblical mention of the gathered elders refers to judicial-type functions, it is clear there would have been other functions as well. Local communities would have engaged in the construction of such public works as cisterns and walls and gates, and hence the elders would have been responsible for the proper administration of these works.

[15] See R. Wilson, 'Israel's Judicial System in the Pre-exilic Period', *Jewish Quart. Rev.* LXXIV:229-48 (Oct. 1983), and his argument that whatever centralized legal system was developed most assuredly would have been weak. The power of the monarch and his reforms probably lacked much influence beyond his own tribe at most.

[16] See especially R. DeVaux, *op. cit.* (note 3 above), as well as M. Lind, 'The Concept of Political Power in Ancient Israel', *Annual of the Swed. Theol. Inst.* 7:4-24 (1968-69).

[17] R. North's *Sociology of the Biblical Jubilee* (Rome: Pontifical Biblical Institute, 1954) has been helpful in stimulating this attempt to give the biblical material as plausible a socio-economic rendering as possible. In no way however should North's work be implicated in the precise conclusions being drawn here.

[18] There has been considerable debate over whether the seventh (sabbatical) year was a universal year for all fields and loans, which would tend to give the provision far more sacral and therefore symbolic importance, or whether it applied to each field and loan separately (e.g. each loan having a seven year repayment period regardless of when it was initiated). North, *ibid.*, concludes that the only plausible conclusion is a separate treatment for each transaction (p. 115ff.). Childs agrees that this seems the most realistic conclusion; see B. Childs *Exodus* (Philadelphia: Westminster Press, 1974), p. 482.

[19] Of the three citations for this practice, Lev. 25:35-37 and Dt. 15:1-11 seem to fit the case suggested here quite well; Ex. 22:25 appears to be more general, inclusive of any case of borrowing to meet economic need, and not specifically tied to the practice posited here. At Dt. 24:10-13, with reference to a man, and at Dt. 24:17b, with reference to a widow, loans were made with clothing as collateral; it appears the practice here resembles 'pawn shop' type loans rather than what appears to be the more substantial commercial loans referred to at Lev. 25:35-37 and Dt. 15:1-10.

[20] Gottwald, *op. cit.* (note 3 above) notes that the *mishpahah* would stand as co-signers with the disadvantaged elder, which suggests the loan would have been made by someone outside the *mishpahah* (p. 264); although later (p. 292) he notes that the most likely source of such assistance would come from within the *mishpahah*, unless a local famine or other occurrence were to impoverish an entire area.

[21] North argues (*op. cit.*, note 17 above) that only the seventh year installment was to be forgiven, rather than the total remaining balance (p. 183ff.). No doubt he perceives the latter as too radical to be true. It is possible to demur however. Short-term business or consumption loans today do not stretch beyond several years at most, and this would seem to be even more true in a setting with an undeveloped capital market and shortened life-expectancy—the situation in early Israel; thus if any unpaid balance remained beyond six years under normal circumstances it would have been rather small.

[22] See R. Posner, 'A Theory of Primitive Society, with Special Reference to Law' *Jnl. of Law & Econs.* XXIII:1-53 (April, 1980), p. 10ff.

[23] The necessity to discern between those poor who are idlers and those who are hurt arbitrarily is not lifted entirely from the community by use of a compassionate loan. If a creditor were to observe shirking and then complain to the elders at the gate about insufficient repayment, the community would then have to decide whether the weaker *beth'ab* were really an *'ebyon* (or *'ani* or *dal*), or instead an *atsel* (sluggard). See note 11 above.

[24] Wenham argues as much *re* Lev. 25:39; see G. Wenham, *The Book of Leviticus* (Grand Rapids: Eerdmans Publishing Co., 1979), p. 322.

[25] As with the compassionate loan it is presumed that the first appeal would be to one's actual

brothers, then to an uncle, and only then to other members of the *mishpahah*. If a secured loan were secured from a *beth'ab* other than one's close relatives, these relatives were supposed to join the indebted *beth'ab* in seeking to redeem a bond-slave (Lev. 25:47ff.).

[26] The Lev. 25:39-43 passage dealing with this situation mentions the jubilee year as the year of forgiveness, whereas the Ex. 21:1-11 and Dt. 15:12-18 passages both list the sabbatical year. Longevity considerations clearly would seem to give a bias to the more frequently mentioned shorter period.

[27] The apodictic-casuistic distinction was suggested by Albrecht Alt [*Essays in Old Testament History & Religion* (London: Basil Blackwell, 1966)] as the means by which to differentiate between truly Yahwistic commands and laws borrowed from surrounding Canaanite societies. More recent scholarship has questioned various elements of Alt's analysis rather severely. The application of the two-fold categorization proposed here is not that of Alt's, for both forms are presumed to be Yahwistic.

[28] See S. Kaufman, 'A Reconstruction of the Social Welfare Systems of Ancient Israel' [in W. Barrick & J. Spencer (eds.), *In the Shelter of Elyon*, JSOT Supp. Series 31 (Sheffield, England: JSOT Press, 1984), pp. 277-86], and his argument that a '7th' year fallow cycle probably was unlikely. Using evidence from similar societies, he suggests that fields would lie fallow far more frequently than every seventh year, and thus the '7th' year provision simply was a protection.

[29] Talmudic provisions give more detail of this type of provision, involving charity wardens or overseers. See: M. Katz, *Protection of the Weak in the Talmud* (New York: Columbia Univ. Press, 1925); A. Levine, *Free Enterprise & Jewish Law: Aspects of Jewish Business Ethics* (New York: KTAV Publishing House, Inc., Yeshiva Univ. Press, 1980), especially Ch. 9 'The Role of Government in the Free Enterprise Economy'.

[30] Passages taken from other parts of Scripture which also deal with provisions for poorer community members suggest standards ranging from sufficiency for needs to complete economic equality. At Ex. 16:18 the manna was supplied daily in amounts sufficient for the needs of the day. In the Acts 2:42-47 and 4:32-35 passages describing the early Christian community in Jerusalem the standard appears to be sufficiency for need (2:45, 4:35). Luke 3:10-11, regarding clothing and food provisions, can be seen as either sufficiency or economic equality. At 1 Jn. 3:17 the implication is sufficiency for need. 2 Cor. 8:13-14 states clearly that the end result over time should be economic equality.

[31] N. Gottwald, *Tribes of Yahweh* (Maryknoll, NY: Orbis Books, 1979), pp. 315-16.

[32] B. Birch, *What Does the Lord Require? The Old Testament Call to Social Obedience* (Philadelphia: Westminster Press, 1985), p. 61. My use of this quote may be other than Birch intended, for he elsewhere writes: 'Equal access to community resources according to need formed the cornerstone for an economics of equality which is spelled out in radical terms during Israel's early life as a covenant community' (*ibid.* pp. 57-8)—a standard I cannot accept, as noted.

[33] S. Loewenstamm, 'Law' in B. Mazar (ed.), *The World History of the Jewish People, v. III Judges* (New Brunswick, NJ: Rutgers Univ. Press, 1971), pp. 246-47. On the other hand, he notes: 'The legal aspect is more evident in laws that deal with the poor as a class and assure them of some sustenance, such as the laws of gleanings, the overlooked sheaf and the poor man's tithe (Lev. 19:10, 23:22, Dt. 21)' (p. 247).

[34] A. Phillips, 'Prophecy & Law' in R. Coggins, *et al.* (eds.), *Israel's Prophetic Tradition: Essays in Honour of Peter R. Ackroyd* (New York: Cambridge Univ. Press, 1982), pp. 217-32, p. 222.

[35] 'In general, the motive clauses cited above are attached to unenforceable rather than policeable laws.' R. Uitti, 'Israel's Underprivileged and Gemser's Motive Clause', *Society of Biblical Literature, 1975 Seminar Papers*, v. 1 (Chicago: Palmer House, 1975), pp. 7-13. Uitti also notes that the use of motive clauses with regard to the underprivileged is but a small fraction of the total use of the motive clause. He does not conclude that the presence of the motive clause therefore means such provisions are legally unenforceable, but only the suggestion that they may be difficult to enforce.

[36] See H. Gilmer, *The If-You Form in Israelite Law* (Missoula, Montana, Scholars Press, 1975), and his argument that provisions of the type considered here (humanitarian if-you forms) 'are

not laws in the strictly juridical sense, for they do not describe a case subject to legal action (what is), nor do they prescribe penalties (what shall be)' (p. 46). One wonders what the legal action or penalty would be other than an order by the elders to 'loan the money' or 'forgive the unpaid balance'. In the recorded case of a breach of the levirate law (Dt. 25:5-10), a perhaps not too dissimilar situation from the one being considered here, the relief is simply legal embarrassment. In his paper on the levirate provision, Davies speaks of 'no punishment save that of the indignity of being exposed to public humiliation' and 'a measure of social opprobrium'. See E. Davies, 'Inheritance Rights and the Hebrew Levirate Marriage, Part 2', *Vetus Test.* XXXI:257-68 (July, 1981), pp. 261-2.

[37] See H. Boecker, *Law & the Administration of Justice in the Old Testament & Ancient East* (Minneapolis: Augsburg Publishing House, 1980), pp. 49ff.

[38] M. Katz, *Protection of the Weak in the Talmud* (NY: Columbia Univ. Press, 1975), p. 81. A. R. Brooks [*Support for the Poor in the Mishnaic Law of Agriculture: Tractate Peah* (Chico, Calif.: Scholar's Press, 1983)] notes: 'Each householder must designate an amount of food proportionate to his own wealth. . . . The effect of the tax, then, is to narrow the gap between the richest and the poorest Israelite' (p. 41). See also I. Twersky, 'Some Aspects of the Jewish Attitude toward the Welfare State', in *Studies in Jewish Law & Philosophy* (NY: KTAV Publishing House, 1982).

[39] Two Hebrew words are used for 'rights' or 'cause': the predominant word is *mishpat*, which is used elsewhere to refer to the laws and judgments of God; at Ps. 140:12 (with *mishpat*), Prov. 29:7, 31:9, and Jer. 22:16 the word is *din* and means most likely 'righteous judgment' or 'legal claim' (*TDOT* v. III, pp. 190-91; *TWOT* v. II, pp. 752-55, 947-49).

[40] With regard to Ps. 72:2 (judge the poor with *mishpat*) and Jer. 22:16 (he pled the *din* of the poor and needy)—passages which, as noted above, some interpret to mean the king's private actions only—the use of such clear legal language suggests either that the king was to intercede (as a community elder) in a legal action to uphold the 'rights' of the poor, or that he was to use the power of his office to affect the rights of the poor. At 1 Chr. 18:14 one reads: 'So David reigned over all Israel; and he administered justice [*mishpat*] and righteousness [*tsedaqah*] for all his people' (NASB). The clear implication here is that David would have made sure that any poor and needy known to him would have had their *legal* rights upheld.

[41] D. Patrick, 'The Rights of the Underprivileged', *Society of Biblical Literature: 1975 Seminar Papers*, v. 1 (Chicago: Palmer House, 1975), pp. 1-6, p. 2. His subsequent book [*Old Testament Law* (Atlanta: John Knox Press, 1985)] may have qualified this assessment, for he writes there: 'Most of Deuteronomy's slave provisions are idealistic and would have brought the institution to an end if enforced. The Jubilee Year in the Holiness Code is thoroughly utopian. Such idealistic and utopian rulings would not have made their way into the lawbooks if the lawbooks were designed for practical application in judicial cases' (p. 199).

[42] D. Daube, *Studies in Biblical Law* (New York: Cambridge Univ. Press, 1947), p. 45. Daube further concludes that the legal attempt was rather utopian ['No Hebrew government was high-minded and strong enough to put poor people with no connections in the positions enjoyed by the members of wealthy clans' (p. 46)] and that this explains the use of motive clauses whereby the poor can appeal to God and he completes the legal requirement.

[43] In contrast to an earlier work in this genre by N. Soss, 'Old Testament Law and Economic Society', *Jrnl. of Hist. of Ideas* XXXIV:323-44 (July-Sept. 1973), who concludes that these provisions and others not here considered must be seen as utopian and thus not practical and actually used. In fairness to Soss, he gives each provision its most literal meaning, such as a universal sabbatical year (and hence fallow year), whereas this paper has attempted to give a more plausible socio-economic rendering to such institutions. S. Kaufman, 'A Reconstruction of the Social Welfare System of Ancient Israel' [in W. Barrick & J. Spencer (eds.), *In the Shelter of Elyon*, JSOT Supp. Series #31 (Sheffield, England: JSOT Press, 1984)], argues a position closer to that developed here.

[44] Similar to the assessment of the compassionate loan provision, it is presumed that if this institution existed in the early years of Israel's occupation of Palestine (and thus had actual economic and not just sacral or symbolic content), most occasions of forced sale would have

been settled by repurchase sometime before the 49th year, and only a few cases would necessitate any forgiveness of the unpaid portion of the debt (or re-purchase price): and in the few cases involved the amount of money would have been small. That is, there would be little occasion for much historical comment on the actual practice of jubilee, to the extent that the institution was being honoured properly.

[45] A representative sample of the U.S. population, which has been tracked carefully for over fifteen years, gives rises to the following observation: 'After differences in current income, savings, and all other variables were controlled, those with college degrees experienced one less undesirable event, on average, than those with an eighth-grade education. . . . Apparently something about the skills acquired in school or possibly about the other characteristics of those who completed more schooling (e.g. perseverance or I.Q.) makes better-educated people more successful at avoiding undesirable life events.' G. Duncan, *et al., Years of Poverty, Years of Plenty; The Changing Economic Fortunes of American Workers & Families* (Ann Arbor: Institute for Social Research, Univ. of Michigan, 1984), pp. 26-27.

[46] The most comprehensive work on this theme is G. Agrell, *Work, Toil and Sustenance* (Lund: Verbum, Haken Ohlssons Forlag, 1976): which, unfortunately, does not ask the question being asked here, of whether the community has an obligation to assure sufficient work for its members. See in this regard also W. Brueggeman, *The Land* (Philadelphia: Fortress Press, 1977).

[47] See: M. Lind, 'The Concept of Political Power in Ancient Israel', *Annual of the Swed. Theol. Inst.* 7:4-24 (1968-69). J. Milgrom, 'Priestly Terminology & the Political & Social Structures of Pre-Monarchic Israel', *Jewish Quart. Rev.* LXIX:65-81 (Oct. 1978); J. McKenzie, 'The Sack of Israel' in H. Huffman, *et al.* (eds.), *Quest for the Kingdom of God* (Winona Lake, IN: Eisenbrauns, 1983), pp. 25-34.

[48] The productive property of Canaan was divided among the Israelites to extended families. Clearly Yahweh was the ultimate owner of the property and held them accountable for its proper use (Lev. 25, esp. v. 23, and the general instruction throughout Scripture treating us as stewards), but granting this he then allows private oversight of property. There would have existed pockets of publicly-assigned property, such as the walls, gates, and cisterns of the various communities, so that the argument for private assignment is not an absolute one. As the elders exercised oversight over the public property, so they would have exercised oversight over the proper use of private properties.

[49] See M. Feldstein, 'Unemployment Insurance: Time for Reform', *Harvard Busn. Rev.* 53:51-61 (March-April 1975).

[50] Of the various works published recently in the United States calling for work expectations, the one I find catches best the scriptural concern for proper stewardship and compassion is L. Mead, *Beyond Entitlement: The Social Obligations of Citizenship* (NY: Free Press, 1986).

RELIGION AND LAW:
THE FIRST AMENDMENT IN HISTORICAL PERSPECTIVE

HAROLD J. BERMAN
Woodruff Professor of Law, Emory University

Article from *CLS Quarterly* (Christian Legal Society)

The First Amendment: *Congress shall make no law respecting an establishment of religion, or prohibiting the free exercise thereof; or abridging the freedom of speech, or of the press; or the right of the people peaceably to assemble, and to petition the Government for a redress of grievances.*

The interrelationship of church and state is not only a political-legal matter. It is also a religious matter. Analysis of it should begin, in my view, with a consideration of the interaction between our religious belief, in the broad sense of our concern for the ultimate meaning and purpose of life, and faith in and commitment to two things: transcendent values, on the one hand, and the legal process, on the other, in the broad sense of the process of allocating rights and duties and thereby resolving conflicts and creating channels of cooperation. It is in the context of the interaction of religion and law, the interaction of our sense of the holy and our sense of the just—it is in that more *general* context that the more *specific* question arises of the proper relation between religious and political *institutions*.

Just as the topic "Church and State" is a part of the larger topic "Religion and Law," so the topic "First Amendment" is a part of the larger topic "Church and State." Indeed, the religion clauses of the First Amendment had only a small impact on church-state relations during the entire history of the United States prior to 1940—since prior to that time (as is universally acknowledged) those clauses applied only to the Federal Government. *"Congress,"* the Amendment said, "shall pass no law respecting an establishment of religion or prohibiting the free exercise thereof." The several states remained free to—and to a considerable extent did—continue to support religion and to restrict its exercise. It was only in the 1940s that the Supreme Court of the United States held for the first time that the religion clauses of the First Amendment, by implicit incorporation into the Fourteenth, are applicable also to the states.

To speak, then, of the history of the First Amendment, and of the intent of the Framers—as courts and writers continually insist that we must do if we are to understand what the Constitution requires in the sphere of "Church and State"—is to run up against the plain facts that the First Amendment left the protection of religious liberty at the state level to the states themselves and that the Framers expressed no intent concerning how the states should exercise their responsibilities in the matter. As Justice Story wrote in 1833, in commenting on the First Amendment, "[T]he whole power over the subject of religion is left exclusively to the State governments, to be acted upon according to their own sense of justice and the State Constitutions."

To take a religious, and not only a legal, view of the relation between religion and law, and to ask how not only the Founding Fathers but also the authors of the state constitutions understood the relation between church and state, is to raise—but not necessarily to answer—sharp questions concerning the understanding of the First Amendment which has come to prevail in America in the twentieth century.

Prior to World War I, the United States thought of itself as a Christian country, and more particularly as a Protestant Christian country; since then it has ceased to do so. James Madison's conception of the religion clauses of the First Amendment, of which he was the principal draftsman, was based in part on his belief in a divine covenant between God and man; in the twentieth century the interpretation of those clauses has been based on a political, and not on a religious, concept. Some now argue that we should return to the religious and legal values and beliefs of the eighteenth and nineteenth centuries. Yet to repudiate the past two generations of our history in an effort to return to the generations that preceded them cannot be justified in the name of history. Indeed, the strength of a historical argument, in the American legal tradition, depends on the concept of history as an ongoing process rather than as something that stopped at some particular date in the past.

By the same token, however, we cannot understand our ongoing history—where we are heading—without reference to where we have come from. In the American legal tradition the question "whither" cannot be divorced from the question "whence." Some argue that the record of the past is simply used—and distorted—by partisans of one side or the other. Yet it is important that that record be examined as dispassionately as possible, if only to see whether it might not lead in a direction different from that espoused by either side.

Not only partisans of a "wall-of-separation" theory of the First Amendment but also partisans of a theory of "accommodation" between church and state should be somewhat discomfited by the fact that, in the early part of the nineteenth century many states enacted laws that had the effect of making Christianity the official religion of the state. One may find state constitutional and statutory provisions declaring it to be "the duty of all men to worship the Supreme Being, the great Creator and Preserver of the Universe"; regulating membership in Christian denominations; imposing fines for failure to attend worship services on the Lord's day; requiring elected officials to swear that they "believe the Christian religion, and have a firm persuasion of its truth"; and establishing public education for the purpose of promoting "religion, morality, and knowledge."

In New York in 1811 the highest state court upheld an indictment for blasphemous utterances against Christ. Speaking for the court, Chief Justice Kent stated that "we are a christian people, and the morality of the country is deeply ingrafted upon christianity. . . . " The New York State Convention of 1821 endorsed the decision in that case, declaring that the court was right in holding that the Christian religion is the law of the land and to be preferred over all other religions. These statements were confirmed in an 1861 New York case in which the court said:

> Religious tolerance is entirely consistent with a recognized religion. Christianity may be conceded to be the established religion, to the qualified extent mentioned, while perfect civil and political equality, with freedom of conscience and religious preference, is secured to individuals of every other creed and profession.

Similarly, in Pennsylvania in 1822 a man was convicted of blasphemy for saying that "the Holy Scriptures were a mere fable" and that "they contained a great many lies." The Supreme Court of Pennsylvania, in affirming the conviction, stated:

> Christianity, general Christianity, is and always has been a part of the common law of Pennsylvania . . . not Christianity founded on any particular religious tenets; not Christianity with an established church, and tithes and spiritual courts; but Christianity with liberty of conscience to all men.

On the same grounds, laws restricting commercial activities on Sundays were upheld by courts of many states. In one such case, Judge Scott, speaking for the Supreme Court of Missouri, stated:

> Those who question the constitutionality of our Sunday laws, seem to imagine that the [Missouri] constitution is to be regarded as an instrument framed for a state composed of strangers collected from all quarters of the globe, each with a religion of his own, bound by no previous social ties, nor sympathizing in any common reminiscences of the past; . . . [S]uch is not the mode by which our organic law is to be interpreted. We must regard the people for whom it was ordained. It appears to have been made by Christian men. The constitution, on its face, shows that the Christian religion was the religion of its framers.

Similar judicial statements may be found in other states in similar cases, involving blasphemy, violations of Sunday laws, and other religious offenses—notwithstanding the fact that the constitutions of virtually all the states contained provisions proclaiming religious liberty.

In addition, states did not hesitate to require the teaching of the Christian religion in prisons, reformatories, orphanages, homes for soldiers, and asylums. State colleges and universities, as well as elementary and secondary schools, required the reading of the Bible and singing of hymns and saying of prayer.

In 1890 the Supreme Court of Illinois considered the case of a student at the University of Illinois who had been expelled because of his refusal to attend daily chapel exercises. He contended that the chapel requirement violated a provision of the Illinois Constitution stating that "[n]o person shall be required to attend or support any ministry or place of worship against his consent." The Court held that so long as the rules of chapel attendance were reasonable, permitting excuse on grounds of religious or other conscientious objections, the University had a right to impose the requirement, and the student could not escape it on the mere ground that he considered it unlawful. There is nothing in the Illinois Constitution, the court said, that prevents state colleges and other institutions of learning from adopting "all reasonable regulations for the inculcation of moral and religious principles in those attending them."

With regard to religious exercises and religious education in elementary and secondary schools, the courts of many states went so far as to uphold regulations requiring attendance, on pain of expulsion, regardless of religious objections. The Supreme Court of Maine states:

> The right of one sect to interdict or expurgate would place all schools in subordination to the sect interdicting or expurgating.
> If the claim is that the sect of which the child is a member has a right of interdiction [in fact she was a Roman Catholic who objected to the reading of the Protestant version of the Bible as part of a general course of instruction], and that any book is to be banished because under the ban of her church, then the preference is practically given to such church, and the very mischief complained of, is inflicted on others.

Thus far I have recounted instances of government support of religion and government restrictions upon the free exercise of religion at the state level, under state Constitutions, during the period prior to World War I. If we turn to our national experience at the federal level, we find a situation which, despite limitations on the power of Congress, was similar in its basic conception. It was generally assumed that America is a Christian country, and more particularly, a Protestant Christian country, and that the First Amendment was intended to reinforce Christianity by giving all denominations equality before the law and by permitting no government interference with the religious beliefs of any person. The notion of a "wall of separation," which would prevent any government aid to religion, was alien to the realities of American constitutional law in the late eighteenth and nineteenth centuries. As Joseph Story wrote of the First Amendment in 1833:

> Probably at the time of the adoption of the Constitution, and of the [First Amendment], the general if not the universal sentiment in America was, that

Christianity ought to receive encouragement from the State so far as was not incompatible with the private rights of conscience and the freedom of religious worship. An attempt to level all religions, and to make it a matter of state policy to hold all in utter indifference, would have created universal disapprobation, if not universal indignation. . . .

The real object of the [First] [A]mendment was not to countenance, much less to advance, Mahometanism, or Judaism, or infidelity, by prostrating Christianity; but to exclude all rivalry among Christian sects, and to prevent any national ecclesiastical establishment which should give to a hierarchy the exclusive patronage of the national government. It thus cut off the means of religious persecution (the vice and pest of former ages), and of the subversion of the rights of conscience in matters of religion, which had been trampled upon almost from the days of the Apostles to the present age . . . [footnotes omitted].

From the Constitutional Convention itself, in which Benjamin Franklin proposed that the delegates should resort to common prayer to break through an impasse in its deliberations; from the explicitly religious Presidential Proclamations of Washington, Adams, and Madison; from the designation of chaplains for the Army and Navy and for the U.S. Congress itself; from the Northwest Ordinance of 1787 with its provisions for religious education; from federal support of Christian education of Indians, including Jefferson's own treaty with the Kaskasia Indians providing for a salary to be paid by the United States Government for a Catholic priest and for United States funding of the erection of a Catholic Church (the Kaskasia Indians having been converted to Roman Catholicism); from exemption of religious activities from federal taxation; and from a host of other similar circumstances—it must be concluded that the Establishment clause of the First Amendment, drafted not by the Deist Jefferson, but by the Protestant Christian James Madison, was not intended to prevent any government aid to religion but was intended rather to prevent the establishment of a national religion.

But Jefferson, too, though against *organized* religion, believed firmly in "nature's God," "the Creator," the "Supreme Judge of the world"—all terms to be found in the Declaration of Independence. In a Thanksgiving Proclamation issued in 1797 when he was Governor of Virginia, Jefferson appointed "a day of public and solemn thanksgiving and prayer to Almighty God, earnestly recommending to all the good people of this commonwealth, to set apart the said day for those purposes, and that the several ministers of religion to meet their respective societies thereon . . . and generally to perform the sacred duties of their function, proper for the occasion." Jefferson also believed that all religions share a common morality which is essential to the welfare of any society, and that, more specifically, America needed religion to give it the necessary inner strength to survive. The First Amendment, Jefferson said, was an "experiment," designed to test whether religion could flourish in America without government support. He was confident that it could, and that its ability to do so was essential to the maintenance of peace and order.

In contrast to Jefferson, Madison derived the principle of religious liberty not primarily from its political utility in a pluralist society but also, and more immediately, from God's own will. In attacking legislation proposed in the 1780s in the state of Virginia, which would have levied taxes to contribute (among other things) to the salaries of ministers, Madison stated that it is God who forbids the establishment of religion; that God wants men to worship Him freely, and not by coercion; and that this divine requirement transcends all political considerations. The covenant between God and man, Madison said, requires free exercise of religion, and that covenant takes precedence—"both in order of time and degree of obligation"—over the social contract. This statement of Madison makes implicit reference to the Lutheran doctrine of Two Kingdoms—the heavenly kingdom of grace and the earthly kingdom of law—as well as to the Calvinist doctrine of two covenants, one between God and man, the other between government and people. For Madison, the nonbeliever was in effect a third-party beneficiary of the divine convenant.

To stress the importance of Christian concepts and values in the final achievement of religious freedom in America is not to minimize the importance of Enlightenment concepts of rationalism and individualism. It was the combination of the two—Christian faith, strongly influenced by Calvinist theology, and Deist skepticism, with its strong anti-clerical tendency—that eventually prevailed. The religion clauses of the First Amendment owe at least as much to Jonathan Edwards as to Thomas Jefferson. The struggle of the various sects—especially the Baptists, the Quakers, and the Congregationalists—against repression by one denomination or another was also a decisive factor in bringing about what may be called a Christian pluralism. Madison supplemented his theological argument with an ecclesiastical one: that the "multiplicity of sects, which pervades America, . . . is the best and only security for religious belief in any society." This position was not grounded solely in pragmatism; it was grounded also, and primarily, in principles: the principle that religion itself—religious belief—depends for its validity on the freedom to disbelieve.

In uncovering the religious roots of our constitutional guarantees of religious freedom, we also uncover the religious basis of American public discourse in general prior to the 1930s. In 1835, de Tocqueville wrote: "[T]here is no country in the world where the Christian religion retains a greater influence over the souls of men than in America. . . . " "Religion," he wrote, "is the first of their political principles." In 1888, James Bryce wrote that "the influence of Christianity seems to be, if we look not merely to the numbers but also the intelligence of the persons influenced, greater and more widespread in the United States than in any part of western Continental Europe, and probably as great as in England."

Prior to World War I, and into the 1920s, America professed itself to be a

Christian country. Even two generations ago, if one had asked Americans where our Constitution—or, indeed, our whole concept of law—came from, on what it was ultimately based, the overwhelming majority would have said, "the Ten Commandments," or "the Bible," or perhaps "the law of God." John Adams' conception that our law is rooted in a common religious tradition was shared not only by the Protestant descendants of the English settlers on this continent, and their black slaves, but also by tens of millions of immigrants from Western and Southern and Eastern Europe, a large proportion of whom were Roman Catholics and Jews. Indeed, throughout the entire nineteenth and into the early twentieth century, America studied its law chiefly from Blackstone, who wrote that "[the] law of nature . . . dictated by God himself . . . is binding . . . in all countries and at all times; no human laws are of any validity if contrary to this; and such of them as are valid derive all their force, and all their authority, mediately or immediately, from this original."

Within the past two generations the public philosophy of America has shifted radically from a religious to a secular theory of law, from a moral to a political or instrumental theory, and from a communitarian to an individualistic theory. Law is now generally considered—at least in public discourse— to be essentially a pragmatic device for accomplishing specific political, economic, and social objectives. Its tasks are thought to be finite, material, impersonal—to get things done, to make people act in certain ways. Rarely, if ever, does one hear it said that law is a reflection of an objective justice or of the ultimate meaning or purpose of life. Usually it is thought to reflect, at best, the community's sense of what is useful.

Likewise, it is only in the last two generations that the concept of religion as something wholly private and wholly psychological, as contrasted with the earlier concept of religion as something public, something partly psychological but also partly social and historical, indeed, partly legal, has come to dominate our discourse.

These contemporary views of law and religion find support in the Enlightenment philosophy of the late eighteenth century, with its emphasis on rationalism and individualism, and its attempt to divorce law and morality from religious faith—the sense of the just from the sense of the holy. It is no accident that in recent decades our courts and writers have so often cited Thomas Jefferson, America's leading apostle of the Enlightenment, when they interpret the religion clauses of the First Amendment in such a way as to separate entirely the sphere of government from the sphere of belief.

In reacting against these contemporary views, Justice Rehnquist, relying on recent scholarly research, has presented an account of the origins of the religion clauses of the First Amendment that is similar, in some respects, to the one I have presented here. He has attached to the historical record a very different significance, however, from that which I would endorse. He would turn the clock back to the founding period. He contends, in effect, that since the religion clauses were not originally intended to be applied to the states, therefore they should be restricted—as they were until the 1940s—to *federal* legislative, executive, and judicial action involving religion. Justice Rehnquist contends, further, that *if* the religion clauses are to be applied to *state* legislative, executive, and judicial action, then they should be interpreted to mean what they were understood to mean in 1791: more especially, "establishment" should be understood to mean not state "aid" to religion but rather state endorsement of a religious creed.

There are at least two strong objections to that solution. First it would be a sign not of respect but of disrespect to constitutional history for the courts to overrule the precedents of the past 45 years in favor of precedents of a more distant past. Our constitutional history is an ongoing history. It is a living tradition, not a mere historicism. Jaroslav Pelikan has defined tradition as the living faith of the dead, traditional*ism* as the dead faith of the living. It is an example of traditional*ism*, not tradition—of historic*ism*, not a belief in history—to try to restore the original understanding of the First Amendment.

Second, the religious context of the First Amendment as originally understood—and as understood at least until World War I—no longer exists, and the public philosophy generated in that context no longer exists. Today we are groping for a new public philosophy—one that will build on the past but will not be bound by the past. Such a public philosophy must be grounded in something more than the practical need to maintain peace among warring factions. It must look beyond our pluralism to the common convictions that underlie our pluralism. It must come to grips with the fact that freedom of belief—which includes freedom of disbelief—rests, in the last analysis, on the foundation of belief, not on the foundation of skepticism. That is what John Adams meant when he said that the Constitution, with its guarantee of freedom to believe or disbelieve, "was made only for a moral and religious people. It will be wholly inadequate to any other." It is not to be regarded as an instrument framed (in Judge Scott's words) for a society "composed of strangers . . . each with a religion of his own, bound by no previous social ties, nor sympathizing in any common reminiscences of the past."

At the same time—and here I speak in the spirit more of the last two generations than of the first century and a half of our history as a nation—our public philosophy must also come to grips with the deep conflict in our society between orthodox religious belief-systems and widespread indifference or opposition to such belief-systems. We have in the past sought to resolve this conflict largely by trying to sweep it under the rug. We have pretended that all belief, both religious and nonreligious, is the private affair of each individual. Public figures and others who participate in shaping public opinion have for the most part been unwilling to express publicly— that is, outside their own like-minded groups—their deepest convictions concerning religious questions. When they have done so, they have been attacked as overstepping the bounds of public discourse. This has inhibited the articulation of a public philosophy grounded in our fundamental beliefs concerning human nature, human destiny, and the sources and limits of human knowledge.

Especially with regard to debate concerning the religion clauses of the First Amendment, there should be open discussion of the significance of its historical roots in the combination of Christian and Deist beliefs. Such a discussion might lead to a new understanding of those clauses. More particularly, a reconstruction of Madison's conception that religious freedom can be secure only if it is undergirded by religious faith, could lead to a reinterpretation of the relationship between the establishment clause and the free-exercise clause. Such a reinterpretation would permit government support of any or all belief-systems, whether religious or irreligious, so long as such support does not discriminate among belief-systems (and therefore does not constitute an establishment) and so long as it is noncoercive (and therefore does not restrict free exercise).

RETHINKING THE MYSTICAL:
A ROMAN CATHOLIC PERSPECTIVE

HUGH FEISS, O.S.B.
Professor of Theology and Humanities
Mt. Angel Seminary

Article from *Word & World*

These thoughts emerge from Oregon, one of the least churched states in the union, where in recent years the only newsworthy events of a mystical flavor have been the rise and fall of the Bhagwan Shree Rasneesh. The author is a Benedictine monk, a seminary professor, a specialist in medieval spirituality. The understanding of mysticism operative in what follows draws heavily on the medieval catholic tradition and aims to reflect the tolerant eclecticism which has characterized Benedictine spirituality at its best. There are four questions to be addressed: What is mysticism? Is it desirable? Is it reviving? What would aid its revival?

I. What Is Mysticism?

Mysticism is difficult to define, as are faith and the love of God which are its essential elements. For this discussion a two-pronged, encompassing definition seems useful, if inelegant: Christian existence qualifies as mystical when it is characterized by a God-given, intense, and abiding sense of the presence of God (even in his silence and inscrutability) or when it regularly includes the wordless prayer of contemplation which comes as a divine gift after prayerful words become superfluous. Whether either of these states is possible without the other is doubtful; it is even more doubtful that one can abide in the mystical without having struggled with some success to eliminate deliberate, sinful acts from one's life. It is certain that the mystical is pure gift; if and when it comes, it is experienced as God's grace.

The first member of the definition just given described mysticism as an intense and abiding sense of the presence of God.[1] There are three main areas of human experience where Christians have found God present: nature, self, the other. Aristotle and Kant thought the starry skies above were pointers to God's existence. For the mystics the heavens declare the glory of God; and so do the earth, the trees, the grass, the seas seen from the top of Skellig Michael, and perhaps the recluse's pet cat. For the mystic:

The world is charged with the grandeur of God.

There lives the dearest freshness deep down things;
And though the last lights off the black West went
    Oh, morning, at the brown brink eastward, springs—
Because the Holy Ghost over the bent
    World broods with warm breast and with ah!
        bright wings.[2]

The Latin Middle Ages agreed with St. Augustine that the conscious self is the image and likeness of God. For Augustine and his medieval disciples there was tension between this conviction and the sacramental sense of the world, since they regularly urged that the Christian should withdraw from outward dispersal among created things to unified inwardness. However, there seems to be no inherent contradiction between awareness of God in nature and a sense of his image within oneself. The self images God in its freedom, in the boundless range of the imagination, in its capacities to know and love. Likeness to God may be obscured by the unlikeness of sin, but the image of God is ineffaceable. So to know oneself is to recognize a dignity bestowed by God's creative generosity and restored by Christ's redeeming grace. The other side of self-knowledge, which seems to have received increasing emphasis in later spirituality, is recognition of one's sinfulness and need for God's mercy.

The third locus of God's presence is one's neighbor, or more accurately, the bonds that relate Christians with each other. In the suffering Christ, divine compassion wore a human face, and wherever the power of the cross is operative, compassionate love unites the sisters and brothers of Christ in communities which range from the nuclear family (and friendship, an example not very frequently discussed in Christian authors) to the human family.

Today it seems to be difficult to find the presence of God in nature and the self. By itself nature is thought of as the field for a bloody struggle for survival; in relation to human society nature appears as an amorphous material element to be transmuted into shopping malls and mortgages. Air and light pollutions make the starry skies almost invisible. The self is no more sacred: the image and likeness of God has dissolved into the id and the ego, and of late the latter threatens to become an all-absorbing interest. Perhaps for late twentieth-century Christians it is the sacrament of the other which holds the most promise of the presence of God. However, if it is in life together that contemporary Christians are to become aware of God, what sort of communities are there or should there be for enlivening their sensitivity to God's loving presence?

The other part of the description of mysticism spoke of a Christian existence which regularly includes the wordless contemplation which comes as a divine gift after prayerful words become superfluous. Medieval writers spoke of the lifeline of Christian living as though it were woven of six strands: reading, meditation, prayer, action, contemplation and teaching.[3]

One reads slowly with purity of heart and the help of the Spirit the books written by the hand of God, above all the Scriptures. Reading leads to pondering the meaning of God's Word. Such meditation makes one conscious of God's mercy and one's own misery, and this awareness evokes prayers of thanksgiving and contrition, as well as pleas for help. Sooner or later, more or less often, meditation conscientiously practiced begins to simplify. The many tasks of the life of faith fuse in the fire of love. In prayer the Christian becomes content to be with the Triune God in expectation, silence, and dazzling darkness. What God might do next is unpredictable and ineffable: absence and visitation, suffering and consolation, darkness and light, desolation and union—these are all possibilities.[4]

Just as the awareness of God's presence doesn't seem to be thriving in contemporary society, so too the age does not seem to be conducive to contemplative prayer. If normally the life of prayer grows slowly as the Word of God sinks roots into the well-tilled soil of reading and meditation, then the prospects for contemplation do not seem very good. Whether this is a loss for the churches is the next question to be considered.

II. Is It Desirable?

There are many reasons to be suspicious of mysticism. Mysticism is usually associated with visions and raptures.[5] The definition just expounded purposely does not include such extraordinary and perplexing phenomena. St. Theresa of Avila, who experienced many such phenomena, is ample authority for not including them in our definition. That such secondary phenomena have become identified with mysticism is neither inevitable nor acceptable. Whatever the significance of visions and levitations and trances, they are not essential to mystical experience.

Second, one might ask whether mysticism does not involve a Pelagian and/or Neoplatonic effort to reach God on God's level.[6] It is perfectly possible that a Christian might be seduced into such an effort, but Christian mystics are usually very careful to warn against it. They affirm in the strongest terms that every aspect or phase of Christian life is dependent upon grace. When one crosses the threshold of contemplation, every further step depends entirely on extraordinary gifts of the Spirit which blows where it wills. Thus, for example, the word "grace" occurs more than ninety times in the short *Cloud of Unknowing*. In chapter 67 the author says to the one who experiences contemplative prayer: "Certainly you are above yourself, because you succeeded in reaching by grace what you could not achieve by nature. And that is that you are united with God, in spirit, in love, and harmony of wills."[7]

Clearly connected with the foregoing is the question of whether mystical experience purports to take one beyond the realm of faith, so that sight

somehow replaces belief; private vision, church doctrine. In fact, it is traditional Christian teaching that mystical awareness is a flowering of faith.
Moreover, there is not inbuilt conflict between church doctrine and mystical
awareness. Richard of St. Victor, St. Bernard, and the author of *The Cloud*,
were all men of unimpeachable orthodoxy, and St. Theresa was fully justified
in laughing when the Inquisition had scruples about her doctrine.

Fourth, one may object that mysticism draws people away from the
sacramental life of the church. It is certainly true that some periods of fervent
mysticism (e.g., the fourteenth century) were not times of liturgical vitality.
It also seems likely that contemplative prayer and vigorous hymn singing are
difficult to sustain simultaneously. Yet a sense of God's abiding presence in
nature, self, and community is as essential to liturgy as it is to contemplation.
Further, the prayer of most of the great mystics was nourished by the liturgy;
similarly there is every reason to think that experiences of intense mystical
union with God enhanced their appreciation and celebration of the church's
sacraments.

Fifth, it may be objected that mysticism creates an elite in the church, a
cadre of adepts who are put on a higher plane than the rest of the baptized.
This is certainly possible. Mystical gifts are not unmixed blessings to their
recipients; they bring with them temptations to pride. Hence, it is traditional
to point out that mysticism is not sanctity. The heart of sanctity is love, and
there is no reason to think that progress in charity and progress in mystical
experience are entirely equivalent.

Sixth, can the church afford the luxury of contemplation in a world in
which millions are starving for food and millions are hungering for the bread
of life? Unfortunately, there has been a sort of spirituality which cultivates
the wilting roses of one's spiritual garden in unholy oblivion of the world
around one, but this is not inherent in mysticism. St. Bernard and St. Theresa
urged their followers to avoid the world, but in fact they themselves were
deeply involved in the struggles of their times.

Who, in fact, can be a liberator? Only Christ, the Christ who preached
and who spent nights in prayer, who died on the cross in public view and
prayed in private with his disciples in Gethsemane, who healed bodies and
prayed for crucified thieves. If the church does not join him in prayer before
the Father, in the breaking of the bread, in recitation of the Psalms, there is no
chance the church will experience the transforming power of his resurrection. The church aims to slake humanity's thirst for God. It cannot do so if its
own wells run dry.

Of course, no Christian vocation fully expresses all the facets of Christian existence. The anchorite and the missionary, the executive and the
sailor, all have their own gifts from the Lord. It is a besetting temptation for
Christians to elevate their own call and their own talents into the standard for
all the baptized, instead of delighting in the variety of the Spirit's gifts.

Seventh, it may be objected that mysticism is a monastic preoccupation, something which usually is possible only for those who live in the seclusion of the cloister. It is true that cloistered life can facilitate living in God's presence and enhance fidelity to prayer. In fact, one of the main services of monasteries to the wider church has been the witness they give to silence, simplicity, the use of artistic reminders of God's presence, and a regular routine of prayer, all of which are conducive to mystical experience. If these are not found in other Christian communities, perhaps those communities should alter their lifestyles. On the other hand, monastics—especially in edifying writings designed to serve as internal reinforcement for other monastics—have made claims for the efficacy and superiority of their "contemplative" way of life which are excessive and unfounded, and which may have discouraged Christians of other vocations from developing a serious prayer life.

III. Is It Reviving?

The argument thus far has been that mysticism as defined here is a positive, even an indispensable, element in the church's life. What is its state in the church today? It is very difficult to say. There is much more data available about the intimate sexual practices of contemporary people than about their prayer. What statistical data is available from polls suggests that people pray and read the Bible more than one would have thought. One may assume that where many people pray consciously, some people are mystics.

On the other hand, Louis Dupre, an astute scholar of religion, is pessimistic:

> Never has there been more talk about "religious experience" than today. Yet actual experiences are few and mostly of low intensity. "Mysticism" has become a common term in current language. Yet religious immediacy has rarely been less available. Our existence has become so secularized that the act of faith once supported by a wealth of communal and private experiences must now almost totally dispense with direct evidence and be satisfied with the will to believe.[8]

Nevertheless, scholarly studies of mysticism are burgeoning. One reason this is so is that there is a growing distrust of one of the more questionable legacies of the Enlightenment: "the denial of cognitive value to spiritual experiences" and the concomitant "atrophy of Christian transcendental experiences."[9] In spite of all the obstacles which contemporary American culture puts in the way, there is a widespread interest in techniques and forms of prayer. It is difficult to estimate how deep this mystical interest is; it is impossible to determine whether the status of mysticism among Christians is greater or less than it was in the sixteenth century, or the thirteenth, or the first. What seems likely is that the current interest in prayer and mysticism is a call of the Spirit to deepen and explore the rich Christian tradition of prayer and the possibilities suggested by the mystical traditions of non-Christian religions.

IV. What Would Aid Its Revival?

If, as I have suggested, mysticism is a genuine part of the Christian tradition and there is an awakening interest in mystical prayer among Christians today, how might the churches respond?

First of all, ordained clergy need to be educated in the theology and practice of mystical prayer. It is at least as important that seminary students be initiated into the theology and practice of the spiritual life as that they be instructed in clinical pastoral methods. A minimum preparation for ministry should include courses in spirituality, practice in prayer, and ongoing individual spiritual direction. Moreover, Christian tradition has rightly not restricted the ministry of spiritual guidance to ordained clergy. Hence, others who wish to practice this ministry should receive a solid theological and spiritual training.

Second, some steps need to be taken to bridge the gaps between theology, spirituality, and social action. Here North Americans may have something to learn from liberation theology. There is also something to be learned from theologians like Augustine, Hugh of St. Victor, St. Bonaventure, and Luther for whom biblical studies, systematics, and spirituality formed a seamless whole. Good mysticism is no substitute for good theology, but it may be wondered if good theology is possible apart from intense personal and shared prayer. Somehow hard thinking and hard praying need to spring up together from the same ground of faith.

Third, it is crucial that the Christian churches know and assimilate the riches of the Christian spiritual tradition. There is a vast spiritual heritage stemming from the Scriptures, through the Fathers, medieval spiritual authors, and the writings of the Reformation era to our own times. This heritage varies in quality and applicability, but it can teach contemporary Christians a great deal and free them from the provincialisms of late twentieth century mentalities. Without deep immersion in the classics of Christian spirituality, contemporary Christians will have to reinvent the spiritual wheel, a difficult and dangerous task. These classics need to be read prayerfully as well as critically, so that they are not simply mined to support current manias.

Fourth, the connections between self-discipline and mysticism need to be appreciated. "Asceticism" is almost a dirty word in our theology and our culture. Culturally, though, asceticism of a sort is enjoying a modest revival in the fitness movement. Theologically, it is time to stop equating asceticism with Manicheanism and works-righteousness. That asceticism might be seen in a better light is indicated in a passage in the *Rule of St. Benedict*. After an expansive list of "tools of good works," most of which are drawn from the Bible, comes the admonition: "Place your hope in God alone. If you notice something good in yourself, give credit to God, not to yourself, but be certain that the evil you commit is always your own and yours to acknowledge."[10] Christian tradition has been well-nigh unanimous in seeing virtuous living as a necessary precondition for mysticism. The foundation for contemplative prayer and for living in God's presence is faith. Although prayer techniques have their place, they will profit only those who have given their hearts to God. It is difficult to give one's heart to God in the midst of racket and hectic activity; it is impossible to do so in the midst of self-indulgence, narcissism, and *divertissement*. On the other hand, the techniques for meditation and prayer which are enjoying some popularity now can themselves force Christians to evaluate their lifestyles and discipline their spirits. In the very effort to quench their thirst for prayer some Christians are discovering the disciplines of silence, simplicity, and compassion.

More generally, there are many ways in which human beings relate to the world; for example, contemplation sees, hears, and touches the world to perceive how beings are individually and as forming wholes (and, if the contemplation is religious, the contemplated world becomes the sacrament of God's presence); art extends and images creation in particular objects; science strives to understand beings in relation to universal laws; technology adjusts, arranges and uses the beings of the world for their benefit and for that of humanity; gratitude receives beings as gifts and celebrates the divine generosity from which they spring. Mysticism will not flourish if contemporary people do not have the capacity to perceive the world—nature, themselves, their communities—contemplatively and gratefully. Doing needs to be nourished in seeing and loving, doctrine in love. When and if this happens, mysticism does not need reconsideration; it is simply the flowing of faith. No one saw this better than Therese of Lisieux:

> In the evening of this life, I shall appear before you with empty hands, for I do not ask You, Lord, to count my works. All our justice is stained in Your eyes. I wish, then, to be clothed with Your own Justice and to receive from Your Love the eternal possession of Yourself. I want no other Throne, no other crown but You, my Beloved.[11]

Notes

[1] A classic statement of this sense of God's presence is Br. Lawrence, *The Practice of the Presence of God*, trans. John J. Delaney (Garden City: Doubleday, 1977). Not unrelated is the truism: "The interior life is not a question of seeing extraordinary things but rather of seeing ordinary things with the eyes of God" (Thomas Green, *When the Well Runs Dry* [Notre Dame: Ave Maria, 1979] 151).

[2] Gerard Manley Hopkins, "God's Grandeur," *The Poems of Gerard Manley Hopkins*, ed. Robert Bridges (Oxford: Oxford University, 1933) 26.

[3] Guigo II, *The Ladder of Monks*, trans. Edmund College and James Walsh (Kalamazoo: Cistercian Publications, 1981); Walter Hilton, "Letter to a Hermit," *Way* 6 (1965) 230-241.

[4] The spiritual journey toward contemplation has been described countless times. Three recent and very competent summaries are Jan-Hendrik Walgrave, "Prayer and Mysticism," *Communio* 12 (1985) 276-292; Aelred Squire, *Asking the Fathers* (Wilton, CT: Morehouse-Barlow, 1976); and Louis Dupre, *The Deeper Life* (New York: Crossroad, 1981).

[5] For example, Richard Kieckhefer, *Unquiet Souls* (Chicago: University of Chicago, 1984) 151: "The term 'mysticism,' more familiar in modern scholarly parlance than it would have been to the mystics themselves, can mean various things. For present purposes it may be taken as covering two closely linked phenomena: ecstatic experiences (raptures), in which a person's consciousness of the spatio-temporal order is temporarily lost or diminished; and extraordinary glimpses of spiritual or otherwise hidden realities (revelations) whether communicable or ineffable."

[6] Martin E. Marty, "Interestingness and the Imagination," *Word & World* 5 (1985) 234-235.

[7] *The Cloud of Unknowing*, trans. Clifton Wolters (Baltimore: Penguin, 1978) 37-38, 141.

[8] Louis Dupre, "Christian Spirituality Confronts the Modern World," *Communio* 12 (1985) 334.

[9] Eric Voegelin, *From Enlightenment to Revolution*, ed. John H. Hallowell (Durham: Duke University, 1975) 3.

[10] *RB 1980. The Rule of St. Benedict*, ed. Timothy Fry (Collegeville, MN: Liturgical Press, 1981) 183.

[11] *The Story of a Soul. The Autobiography of St. Therese of Lisieux*, trans. John Clarke (Washington, DC: ICS, 1975) 276.

PRACTICAL THEOLOGY: PASTORAL PSYCHOLOGY AND COUNSELING

David G. Benner, area editor

PASTORAL PSYCHOLOGY AND COUNSELING

DAVID G. BENNER
Professor of Psychology
Wheaton College

Introduction

The two articles included in this section provide a brief sample of what is being presented in journals exploring the relationship between psychology and Christian faith and ministry. The first is theoretical, dealing with the experience of God, while the second deals with an issue of increasing practical importance for the pastoral counselor, clergy malpractice.

In the first selection, Ralph Underwood of Austin Presbyterian Theological Seminary examines the question of how and why it is that at times we experience the presence of God while at other times he seems far from us. The psychological perspective is that of object relations theory, a theoretical development within psychoanalysis that focuses on the study of our internal representations of people and our relationships with them. In contrast to orthodox psychoanalysis, which emphasizes instinctual gratification in its explanation of human motivation, object relations theory emphasizes the primacy of our need for interpersonal relationships. Building on this assumption, the theory then examines the way we form internal representations of ourselves and others and the way these inner images shape human development and experience. Underwood's application of this most important contemporary theory to the experience of God is a continuation of work being carried on by a number of other scholars in the field of the psychology of religion. A more extensive treatment of the matter is presented in John McDargh's *Psychoanalytic Object Relations Theory and the Study of Religion* (University Press of America, 1983), a book that will serve as an excellent follow up for further reading.

The second selection, co-authored by a pastoral counselor and an attorney, is a succinct and helpful summary of practical advice for the pastoral counselor who wishes to avoid malpractice suits. The well publicized 1980 *Nally* v. *Grace Community Church of the Valley* lawsuit has done more to raise consciousness over the possibility of clergy malpractice than any other single event. Even the 1985 dismissal of this first and most important suit has not settled all the questions or anxieties it raised. The authors of this second article present a careful discussion of the central element of any malpractice suit, the standards of care, and follow this with advice about the need for consultation or hospitalization, the management of violent clients, the maintenance of confidentiality, handling termination, and several other areas of special concern. An excellent source for follow-up reading on this topic is *Clergy Malpractice* by Malony, Needham, and Southard (The Westminster Press, 1986).

Selecting these two articles from the many good ones appearing in the past year was not only difficult but necessarily somewhat arbitrary. A few of the others I would have liked to include are "An Integrated Approach to Pastoral Counseling" by Del Myra Carter (*Journal of Psychology and Theology, 14* [2], 146-154); "Christian Reflection on Stress Management" by James Beck (*Journal of Psychology and Theology, 14* [1], 22-28); "The Psychology of Self-Esteem: Promise or Peril?" by Richard Erickson (*Pastoral Psychology, 35* [3], 163-171); and "A Biblical Approach to Anger Management Training" by Chase Stafford (*Journal of Psychology and Christianity, 5* [4], 5-11).

About the Area Editor

David G. Benner (M.A., York University; Ph.D., York University) is professor of psychology at Wheaton College Graduate School. He is an associate editor of *The Journal of Psychology and Christianity*, a consulting editor of *The Journal of Psychology and Theology*, and is secretary of the board of directors of The Christian Association for Psychological Studies. He is editor of *Baker Encyclopedia of Psychology* (1985), *Psychology and Religion* (1987), and *Psychotherapy in Christian Perspective* (1988) and is the author of *Psychotherapy and the Spiritual Quest* (1988). In addition he serves as series editor for two current series of books exploring the relationship between psychology and Christian faith. Dr. Benner is a licensed clinical psychologist in practice in the metropolitan Chicago area where he also serves as clinical director for The Institute for Eating Disorders, Ltd.

AVOIDING MALPRACTICE SUITS
IN PASTORAL COUNSELING

THOMAS E. and MELINDA L. DENHAM
Thomas Denham is a pastoral counselor in Columbus, Ga.
Melinda Denham is an attorney at law in Birmingham, Ala.

Article from *Pastoral Psychology*

ABSTRACT: This article advises caution for ministers engaged in pastoral counseling and describes the necessary elements of a successful malpractice suit. Areas of special concern for the counselor are reviewed and guidelines for professional conduct and self-protection are outlined.

The Current Scene

Pastoral counseling is coming of age and in this day of litigation consciousness the pastoral counselor will do well to begin anticipating the scrutiny and accountability for professional conduct that other service providers have had to contend with for years. The very idea of legal issues in pastoral counseling was almost empty and meaningless twenty-five years ago; no one would have thought of initiating legal action against pastors for their conduct in the ministry. Today pastoral counselors are receiving increasing attention as responsible professionals who are liable for their actions and quality of care, not only spiritually and ecclesiastically but legally as well. It is the naïve minister who depends upon pastoral identity to provide absolution if questions of competence and proper conduct are raised. The 1980s may or may not see a successful malpractice suit brought against an ordained minister for bad pastoral counseling, but the number of disputes actually brought to trial will very likely be on the rise. Whether successful or not, involvement in litigation is an expensive proposition both financially and in terms of one's reputation.

In pastoral counseling centers around the country, more and more attention is being devoted to legal concerns. Pastoral counselors are beginning to look beyond the guidelines offered by their code of ethics and ministerial identity for a source of greater security in relationships with clients. Malpractice insurance is being discussed and purchased, not only by counseling specialists but also by pastoral generalists. The American Association of Pastoral Counselors decided in 1985 to include professional liability insurance as a membership benefit which automatically covers all certified members and Pastoral Counselors-in-Training. Contracts specifying the exact nature of pastoral counselor/client relationships are being negotiated and signed. Ministers fearful of being taken to court are searching for protection from the litigation to which they are seeing therapists of other professions exposed. The Legal Concerns Committee of the AAPC reflects current apprehensions and has advised members to seek greater legal security through defining identity more clearly and following policies and procedures that are congruent with that identity more consistently.[1] The anxiety being manifested is quite realistic and deserves a thoughtful response.

The Standard of Care

In matters of legal accountability, performance of a profession's standard of conduct or care is the relevant issue from the perspective of the courts. Failure to perform according to standards is considered negligence for which the specific term malpractice is used when a recognized profession is involved. Nowadays, law suits charging malpractice are commonly filed against physicians, attorneys, and accountants. *Mal* is a prefix meaning bad, wrong, or fraudulent. *Practice* is a verbal noun referring to the activity of a profession, occupation, or vocation. Malpractice means, therefore, professional misconduct or unreasonable lack of skill in carrying out one's work.

To recover from a malpractice suit, a client-plaintiff must prove four elements:

1. that the profession has a standard of conduct or care;
2. that the professional owed him or her a duty to conform to that particular standard of care;
3. that the professional breached his or her duty;
4. and that the client suffered damages consequently.

If one of these four elements is missing, a suit cannot be brought successfully against a defendant.

That pastoral counseling is a profession in and of itself is a question which is integral to proving that persons who provide this service have a standard of conduct or care which they owe to clients. The existence of the American Association of Pastoral Counselors, a professional organization which has certification requirements, a mandatory ethical code, and specific training standards, helps establish that pastoral counseling is a profession. The fact that in pastoral counseling there is a service for which a fee can be charged, and that it can be claimed on some insurance policies furthers the case. There is little question now that pastoral counseling is a distinct and involved profession; and as pastoral counseling acquires a broader reputation and acquires more clients, the question becomes more and more settled.

Once it is established that pastoral counseling is a profession separate and different from other professions, it has a standard of care. What the courts call a standard of care, pastoral counselors would call professional ethics or conduct. The Code of Ethics adopted by the American Association of Pastoral Counselors is the most likely source to which the courts would appeal as the minimal standard of care for which all pastoral counselors are responsible. Because of the dominance of the AAPC, even pastoral counselors not formally associated with the organization would very likely be held accountable to AAPC standards. Pastors in the local parish who describe or represent any of their work as pastoral counseling invite being held accountable to AAPC standards. Therefore, all ministers who do counseling should become familiar with the Code of Ethics of the American Association of Pastoral Counselors.

A published code of ethics is not the only source of a standard of care for which pastoral counselors may be held accountable. Community expectations regarding ministers and persons who do counseling would apply. Also, testimony from other pastoral counselors regarding what is common practice in the profession contributes to the court's view of the standard of care.

The point at which a professional owes a duty to a person is ambiguous. Any client clearly in a counseling relationship is owed a duty even if there is no charge or payment received for services rendered. On the other hand, a pastoral counselor is not responsible for performance of a professional standard of care with persons in a casual or social relationship. If, however, the pastoral counselor is viewed as a professional in the social setting, he or she may be held liable for actions if a person begins to depend upon him or her. Whether or not a particular person may be considered a client and hence deserving of professional treatment is a matter a jury could be called upon to decide.

A pastoral counselor breaches the duty to a client when he or she practices contrary to the standard of care. This issue is discussed in further detail in the next section.

An important point to remember is that unless the client has actually suffered damage, there is no case in the eyes of the law even if it may be proven that the pastoral counselor failed to perform as he or she ought to have according to the standard of care of the profession. Damages may be broadly defined, however, as including the physical, financial, or emotional and mental.

Areas of Special Concern

A pastoral counselor could become vulnerable to a lawsuit with failure to perform adequately in regards to the standards laid out in any section of the Code of Ethics of the AAPC, but there are some areas which have a greater potential for trouble than others. These are areas of special concern in regard to which therapists of other professions have faced difficulty. These areas of special concern include: sexuality and the counselor/client relationship, need for consultation or commitment to a hospital, radical or unusual methods of treatment, potential physical violence, counselor availability when needed, timeliness of referrals or termination of treatment, conflict of interest, and confidentiality. Pastoral counselors could well anticipate these as the areas in which malpractice suits may be filed.

Sexuality and the Counselor/Client Relationship

A counselor must never have sexual relations with a client. The counselor has no adequate defense in this case if a suit is brought by the client or the client's spouse. In *Horak* v. *Biris*, a certified social worker who advertised himself as a counselor for marital problems, was held liable for engaging in a sexual relationship with the wife of a couple who had come to him for treatment. The court recognized the sexual involvement of the counselor with the wife as malpractice for which the husband could recover damages.[2]

Sexual relations even after a formal termination or referral are unwise and dangerous. The demarcation between client and former-client can be sorely contested for years. Also, actual physical relations are not the extent of sexuality; and any intimacy with a hint of gender and attraction should be carefully scrutinized and delicately handled. A pastoral counselor must not allow the expression of natural and inherent sexuality to mislead a client with false hopes or fears. J. Brownfain warned, "It seems fair to state that the greatest number of actions are brought by women who lead lives of very quiet desperation, who form close attachments to their therapist, who feel rejected or spurned when they discover that relations are maintained on a formal and professional level, and who then react with allegations of sexual improprieties."[3] The pastoral counselor is advised to "Abstain from all appearance of evil" (1 Thessalonians 5:22).

Need for Consultation or Commitment to a Hospital

A pastoral counselor is responsible for recognizing the needs on the part of clients for consultation with other professionals. If a client is in need of medication, as in the case of a man suffering sleeplessness due to an anxious condition, his pastoral counselor has a duty to refer him to a physician, preferably a psychiatrist, for an evaluation. The pastoral counselor may provide all of the psychotherapeutic treatment required; but if a drug intervention is necessary, someone else must be called in to assist. If the management of a particular case requires the safety and structure of hospitalization, the pastoral counselor again has a responsibility to make appropriate recommendation and referral to the client to bring this about. In Merchants *National Bank and Trust Company* v. *United States*, the court awarded a murdered woman's estate $200,000 in damages for the negligence and malpractice committed when the staff of a Veterans Administration Hospital failed to assess properly their patient's homicidal tendencies and keep him confined to the hospital.[4]

The Apostle Paul said, "The eye cannot say to the hand, 'I have no need of you,' nor again the head to the feet, 'I have no need of you' " (1 Corinthians 12:21). Just as no part of the body can do without all of the other parts, so the pastoral counselor cannot do without the expertise and assistance of other members of the healing professions. Pastoral counselors cannot help everyone and can offer only partial help in many cases.

Radical or Unusual Methods of Treatment

The problem with radical or unusual methods of treatment is their unsubstantiated validity and potential for effectiveness. Methods of treatment for a particular malady do not have to be in accordance with majority opinion; but whenever a deviation from the norm is used, it is open to challenge. Depending on how unusual the form of treatment is, the pastoral counselor risks being sued for money invested in therapy or time spent or both when the counselor departs from commonly accepted practice. Without questioning the validity or effectiveness of a technique, it should be noted that a legal challenge to a counselor's treatment plan may be quite costly even if it is not sustained. The pastoral counselor would do well to consider that many persons associate ministry with tradition and established practice. The Apostle Paul outlined orthodoxy for Timothy and then affirmed, "If anyone teaches otherwise and does not agree . . . he is puffed up with conceit, he knows nothing; he has a morbid craving for controversy and for disputes about words" (1 Timothy 6:3-4). Now Paul and his disciples may not always be correct but their expectations are a force to reckon with.

Potential Physical Violence

The pastoral counselor has responsibilities in this area regarding both what happens with and to clients within the counseling center and outside in the community. Legal terminology relevant to this issue includes assault and battery. Assault is the fear of being harmed or violated. Battery is the harm or violation itself. Any time in therapy a client feels fear of bodily injury or is in fact injured the therapist may be liable. A pastoral counselor is vulnerable to assault charges if he or she practices a fight therapy where pounding with pillows is used to release hostility or tension. If, in the course of such a session, a client becomes frightened of being hurt, he or she may sue the therapist for assault. If one client becomes violent and harms or badly scares another during a group session, the pastoral counselor may be held liable. The pastoral counselor must be potent enough to offer a safe and secure environment in which to struggle with therapeutic issues.

Outside of the counseling center the pastoral counselor has a responsibility to warn others of danger that may be discovered in a session with a client. In *Tarasoff* v. *Regents of University of California*, a psychotherapist was held responsible for the death of a man when the psychotherapist's client killed him after telling the therapist he meant to do so.[5] Legal accountability seems dependent, in this matter, upon the therapist:

1. learning that the client may harm someone;
2. knowing who that someone is;
3. believing that in fact the client will carry out the threat;
4. and failing to provide adequate warnings.

The pastoral counselor has a special responsibility to report danger when the client is a minor. Child Abuse Laws in Alabama, for example, specifically waive any privileged communications status; and everyone from whom an abused child seeks aid is required to report the possibility of abuse to the police or the Department of Pensions and Securities. The theological dimension of the pastoral counselor's responsibility to manage potential physical violence is related to the Church's historic role in providing sanctuary to persons in danger. The Lord said to Moses, "You shall select cities to be cities of refuge for you . . . for the people of Israel, and for the stranger and for the sojourner among them, that anyone who kills any person without intent may flee there" (Numbers 35:9-15).

Counselor Availability When Needed

The responsibility which a pastoral counselor bears for being available to any given client for crisis intervention depends upon what the client has been told by the counselor or the counseling center regarding accessibility and coverage. If it is made clear to a client that the counselor is available only during scheduled appointments then there is no problem. If the pastoral counselor mentions to a client that if anything "happens" he or she may be reached through the secretary, then this must be possible. Vacations, sabbaticals, illness, and other time commitments are not excusable limitations on access unless specified to the client. The counselor is liable primarily and the counseling center secondarily when clients cannot get the attention they have been promised.

A counselor who gives a home phone number to a client and advises the client to call after hours if needed, has a responsibility to provide care to the same standard of competency as what is offered during office hours. An inebriated pastoral counselor contacted by a client on Saturday night at a country club party has a duty to function to professional standards of care in any therapeutic interaction which the counselor permits. It is important for the pastoral counselor to represent availability accurately. "A good name is to be chosen rather than great riches, and favor is better than silver or gold" (Proverbs 22:1). If a pastoral counselor dies, the center or organization with whom he or she was associated is responsible for referring the counselor's clients for further treatment.

Timeliness of Referrals or Termination of Treatment
Landau v. *Werner*, an English case, "enunciates a duty by a psychiatrist to terminate or release his patient when his lengthy and costly treatment has not borne fruit."[6] Although pastoral counselors do not promise that their clients will get well, there are times when and relationships where no progress can be made. In these cases, it is imperative to refer the client to another counselor or to terminate treatment. The time and money of all clients is valuable, and they must not be kept in therapy while the therapist blindly waits for a breakthrough, practices technique, or keeps occupied. On the other hand, the pastoral counselor may be liable if termination takes place too soon and the clients suffer a recurrence or set back. The pastoral counselor does well to heed the prayer of theologian Reinhold Niebuhr: "Lord, grant me the serenity to accept the things I cannot change: the courage to change the things I can: and the wisdom to know the difference."

Conflict of Interest
A pastoral counselor is responsible for being able to relate wholeheartedly and without division of loyalties to his or her clients. Conflict of interest occurs when the pastoral counselor has two duties which conflict. Several common situations are breeding grounds for conflict of interest. Marriages in which the couple have sought counseling but which end in divorce are a prime example. Pastoral counselors who attempt to keep both spouses in individual counseling after a divorce, compromise their loyalty to both and are in a conflict of interest. The counselor who has administrative or supervisory responsibilities for a client is in a situation of conflict of interest. This may occur when a student sees a therapist within the same training center. Hospital chaplains who take on hospital staff members as clients may easily find themselves in a conflict of interest, especially if the staff member works on the same clinical assignment as the chaplain. It is the responsibility of the pastoral counselor to anticipate conflicts and take steps to avoid them. The Wise Man of Proverbs asks, "Can a man carry fire in his bosom and his clothes not be burned?" (Proverbs 6:27). Maintaining two duties toward the same person, even when they do not yet seem at odds, is a dangerous practice. "A prudent man sees danger and hides himself" (Proverbs 22:3). This is a word of wisdom for the pastoral counselor.

Confidentiality
The Code of Professional Ethics of the American Association of Pastoral Counselors says:

> Pastoral counselors respect the integrity and protect the welfare of persons or groups with whom they are working, and have an obligation to safeguard information about them that has been obtained in the course of the counseling process.[7]

This involves keeping in professional confidence the identity of present and past clients, the nature and extent of their problems, the content of their discussions, and the information gained from them which might result in changes in their business or social status if it were made known to others. Professional confidence includes consultation with one's professional colleagues, but this should generally be understood to include only discussions within ordinary supervisory or clinical environs in the absence of a written release.

Clergy Privileged Communication Statutes vary in their usefulness to the pastoral counselor. These statutes vary radically from state to state and some states do not even have them. In some states, how closely a pastoral counselor is related to a local church makes a difference in how the statutes are applied. Pastoral counselors may also be covered by the same laws which protect psychotherapist/client relationships. A state by state review would be necessary to adequately reckon with the conditions under which pastoral counselors work across the country. In the federal courts, however, for a conversation between a person and a minister to be considered privileged and inviolable communication, a number of conditions seem to be necessary:

1. the communication must be penitential in character;
2. the communication must be made by the client;
3. the continued confidentiality of the communication must benefit the client;
4. the communication must be made in the course of the discipline of the church;
5. and the communication must be made in private.

The Clergy Privileged Communication Statutes are generally oriented toward protection of clients and not counselors. They are generally not relevant in the defense of malpractice suits against pastoral counselors.

How to Protect Yourself in Clinical Practice

The point of considering legal issues in pastoral counseling is to avoid malpractice and to reduce vulnerability to law suits. Careful attention to the following guidelines may mean the difference between winning and losing a case should it come to trial and may prevent many matters from being litigated.

1. Never have sexual relations with a client or "former" client. When sexual issues arise in a relationship, clarify them frankly and honestly. Initiate a written "no-sex contract." Such a contract might be useful in the event that sexual issues are strong. Keep careful written records detailing relation-

ship dynamics and possible misunderstandings on the part of the client. Records are a most important protection. Notes in your files made prior to being confronted with charges of misconduct are an invaluable support to your testimony.

2. Whenever consultation with another professional is recommended to a client, record it in the client's file. In the event that the recommendation is ignored and the client suffers harm, you should have documentation to protect you from charges of negligence. Use consultation generously. It is almost always useful to the client and to you in some way.

3. Whenever treatment is conducted by unusual means, seek consultation. Careful notes explaining the rationale of a particular course of therapy are important in the event of a challenge.

4. To defuse potentially frightening situations in which physical aggressiveness or shouting may be involved, let careful explanation precede the activity. Expressions of hostility and anger should be carefully managed to insure that physical violence does not erupt. Call frequent time-outs in order to focus on the process rather than the content of what is being said in sessions. Reaffirm in sessions that violence is not acceptable and then document it. This is especially wise in volatile situations. Notify intended victims and the police if you become aware of a dangerous threat. Note this in your files. You should tell your client when you are going to do this as a gesture to confidentiality laws. Report abuse of a minor to the authorities immediately. Do not wait for an adolescent child to take initiative or seek shelter. You are responsible to the State in this matter. In Alabama the consequences of not reporting child abuse is six months in prison and a fine of $500.

5. Do not promise any more availability to clients than you plan to be able to provide day after day. If you want to be available outside of regular sessions, offer a disclaimer such as "If you can reach me and I am able to talk with you. . . . " Records should be kept up to date and available to another professional person covering for you in the event of your absence.

6. Emphasize to clients a realistic estimate of the amount of time treatment may take. Be generous. Say six months to two years or longer if the issues warrant it. Keep up-to-date notes on diagnosis and treatment plans to provide support in the event of questions about length of treatment. Make termination of treatment a joint decision with the client. If you believe that termination is sought prematurely by your client, say so and document it in your records. Terminate clearly but leave the door unlocked for your client to come back. When discontinuing sessions, add a sentence like, "If something happens, call me." Do not throw your records away for three to seven years, depending on the statute of limitations in your state, even if you do not plan to see a particular client again after termination. Your records are an essential part of your defense in the event of a lawsuit.

7. Do not accept clients with whom a conflict of interest exists. This sounds simple, but so often it is ignored. If there is the possibility of a conflict

of interest, evaluate the situation before developing a therapeutic relationship. The pastoral counselor is responsible for anticipating and avoiding
conflicts of interest. If a conflict arises in the course of a relationship, take
steps to disarm it. Conflict of interest is a serious enough issue to demand
that a client be referred to another therapist if no other resolution is possible.

8. Secure a written release whenever a client is tape recorded or information will be shared with others. Make it clear to clients that inviolable
privileged communication may not be granted to the pastoral counselor as a
member of the clergy in the event of discussions regarding a felony. The
pastoral counselor may be subpoened to testify on the same basis as other
therapists. There are some protections of all therapeutic relationships, but
they are not unassailable.

9. Don't practice without professional liability insurance. Information
about providers offering coverage may be secured from the American Association of Pastoral Counselors, 9508A Lee Highway, Fairfax, Virginia 22031.
The American Professional Agency, 95 Broadway, Amityville, New York
11701 has accepted applications from AAPC members.

10. Consult with an attorney regarding clinical issues annually. Due to
the variety in state laws this is the surest way to be accurately informed. Such
an experience may be just the encouragement you need to keep doing what
you already know to do.

Conclusion

Disputes between pastoral counselors and clients are more likely to wind up
in court today than ever before. All pastoral counselors are more than likely
accountable for the standard of care published by the AAPC. Certain areas of
counseling practice deserve more careful attention than others when seeking to avoid malpractice suits. Maintaining professional behavior at all times
and consistently keeping notes on the progress of therapy are the key elements for protecting oneself in clinical practice.

Notes

[1] *AAPC Newsletter*, Summer 1985, *23*, (3), 9.

[2] See *Horak* v. *Biris*, 474 NE2d 13 (Ill. App. 1985).

[3] Brownfain, J., "The APA Professional Liability Insurance Program," *American Psychologist*,
1971, *26*, 651.

[4] See *Merchants National Bank and Trust Company* v. *United States*, 272 F. Supp. 409 (1967).

[5] See *Tarasoff* v. *Regents of University of California*, 131 Cal. Rptr. 14, 551 P2d 334 (1976).

[6] Cited in B. E. Bernstein, "A Potential Peril of Pastoral Care: Malpractice," *Journal of Religion
and Health*, 1980, *19*, (1), 54, as *Landau* v. *Werner*, Q. B. March 1, 1961, 105 S01, J. 257 (A.B. 1961),
aff'd Sol.J. 1008 (CA 1961).

[7] *AAPC Handbook*, 1982 edition, 9508a Lee Highway, Fairfax, VA 22031, p. 28.

THE PRESENCE AND ABSENCE OF GOD
IN OBJECT RELATIONAL AND
THEOLOGICAL PERSPECTIVES

RALPH L. UNDERWOOD
Professor of Pastoral Care
Austin Presbyterian Theological Seminary

Article from *Journal of Psychology and Theology*

ABSTRACT: In its examination of early personal development, psycho-analytic object relations theory contributes to an understanding of the presence of God in human experience. This contribution is analyzed with reference to the object relational explanations of creativity, person or object centered motivation, and reality experienced as otherness. From the perspective of early human development, object relations theory helps to clarify and confirm Terrien's (1978) interpretation of the presence of God as elusive. Implications of object relations theory for pastoral and clinical practice are briefly noted.

The purpose of this study is to elucidate aspects of the presence and absence of God as experienced primarily in personal life. Attention to the presence and absence of God motif, I believe, is significant for the work of pastors, pastoral counselors, and psychotherapists as they endeavor to be responsive to people's religious experiences and concerns.

The resources in this study are psychological and theological. In particular, object relations theory, a development from within the psychoanalytic tradition and in some respects perhaps beyond that tradition, is a resource for analysis of the origins of personal experiences of the presence and absence of God. Kernberg (1976) defines object relations theory as "the psychoanalytic study of the nature and origins of interpersonal relations, and of the nature and origins of intrapsychic structures deriving from, fixating, modifying and reactivating past internalized relations with others in the context of present interpersonal relationships" (p. 56). Orthodox psychoanalysis emphasizes instinctual gratification in its account of human motives, including its explanation of people's emotional attachments to others. Object relations theory holds that a person's interest in others is primary, not secondary, to drive discharge or instinctual gratification. From a psychological viewpoint, others and one's own self are represented by "objects," or mental images and concepts of self and other.

Does this shift in perspective aid our understanding of the human experience of the divine presence and absence? Terrien (1978) argues that the divine presence is the motif which most nearly pervades the canon, giving it definition, and that the divine presence consistently is portrayed as elusive. Can an object relations explanation of the origin of religious experience, then, help us to understand this divine presence, including its elusiveness? The major contribution of the object relations perspective, I shall argue, is that it helps us understand how it is that the elusiveness of this presence in human experience does not detract from an experienced sense of its reality. This is not to say that this psychodynamic explanation is adequate, even as a psychological account. The theological perspective developed here suggests that object relations theory would complement and enrich its account through an examination of the role of auditory experiences in the infant-parent relationship.

To pursue these ideas, I shall concentrate on Terrien's (1978) account of the Psalms and on the works of Winnicott (1971) and Rizzuto (1979) in object relations theory. This approach precludes inquiry into conflicts between the object relations theorists and their more orthodox colleagues in psychoanalysis, or the differences among the object relations theorists themselves. (For an excellent interpretation with critique of this literature, see Eagle, 1984; see also Greenberg & Mitchell, 1983.) Instead I shall try to identify the contributions of Winnicott and Rizzuto to our understanding of the presence and absence of God, and suggest some limits of their theory. Finally, I shall comment briefly on practical implications of the analysis put forth in this study.

Origins of a Personal Representation of God

First, it is essential to understand how object relations theory accounts for the origin of a personal image or concept of God. Rizzuto (1979) holds that virtually all persons in the Western world have a personal, mental representation of God, which may be used for belief or unbelief. She is uncertain whether this is true for persons in Eastern cultures. To be sure, the mental representation of God of which she speaks is not necessarily positive or in harmony with a person's own self-image.

How does this mental representation of God originate in the life of the individual? The following is an extremely abbreviated account of what is elaborated in the writings of Winnicott (1971) and Rizzuto (1979). Before a child is born, parents use their own representations of God and preformed representations of the child to form a "mythology" of the child's origin and destiny. That is, the child already is imagined, however unconsciously, to have particular qualities and potentials that will help give meaning to the parents' life and the family history, and that sustain hope for the future.

Though this mythology is communicated to the child in various ways over time, the primary focus for Winnicott and Rizzuto is on the mother's mirroring of the child to the child in eye contact. The object relations account does not limit itself literally to mirroring through eye contact, for all sensual modalities may be involved. Still, eye contact is the central focus and it functions as the key metaphor for this complex process. In beholding the mother's face as the mother responds to the child, infants discover what they themselves look like, at least to their mother. This reflection of oneself by the other provides children with an integrated experience of themselves and is the first core experience used by the infants later on to form their representation of God. The infants are beginning a process of organizing life into inner and outer worlds, and they go on to discover and create a representation of the primary caring person as not identical to but other than themselves. They have begun the process of experiencing themselves as individuals in relation to other persons. The child's representations of self and mother are aggrandized and swept into the larger stream of family interaction and into an ongoing process of recreating the family's mythology about the child. For object relations theory this process involves a complex period of transition, a movement from symbiosis to individuation and from global experiencing to an organized mental life centered in consciousness of self and others. For the purpose of healthy individuation, this transition from global experiencing to an encounter of self and other must be accompanied by fairly supportive, consistent, playful nonretaliatory attentiveness by the primary caring person.

Also during this transitional time, according to Winnicott (1971) and Rizzuto (1979), infants usually select an object which comes to represent the primary care giver or a part of this person. A teddy bear or a particular blanket are common examples. This transitional object reminds infants of the absent parent and has an aura of living presence. Like the parent, the object is a playful companion and a source of nurture.

According to Rizzuto (1979), as children develop they create several kinds of images and representations, including imaginary companions— some good and some bad, and most just playful. Among these is some image or mental representation of God, and at least initially this representation of God is based largely on their experience and memory of the primary caring person. Conscious thinking about God typically begins at age two or three. This representative of God is synthesized from representations of the primary parental figure. Though some people never seem to modify or elaborate their infantile image of God to any great extent, many do—and do so throughout life—as they interact with whatever faith is present in their family or origin, with any larger community of faith to which they are exposed, and with culture. Even so, according to Rizzuto, an element of our infantile experience of parents and our related understandings of God stay with us as a hidden layer of our personality.

Origin as Creative Process

Given this brief description of how our mental representation of God begins to be formed, according to object relations theory, several inferences can be elucidated in order to draw out the significance of this theory for theological reflection. John McDargh's (1983) work prepares the way for this application of object relations theory to the human experience of divine presence and absence.

First, in contrast to orthodox psychoanalysis, this origin of a personal concept of God is no longer understood primarily as a process of defense against anxiety. It is interpreted psychologically as a creative process. This does not mean that the origin of faith in God is unrelated to anxieties and need for defense. It means rather that this origin can be explained in large measure by reference to genuinely creative responses to life.

Winnicott (1971) emphasized creativity in this formula: "We create the objects we find" (p. 5). For Winnicott, such a "transitional" object is both a part of the environment of the individual and a creation by the infant. A transitional object is not simply a hallucination nor is it a projection of a wish, as classical psychoanalysis suggests. Rizzuto (1979) puts the matter this way: "God is neither magic (internal control) nor mother (outside control)" (pp. 179-180). Both Winnicott and Rizzuto emphasize this transcendence of the need to alleviate anxiety. As Rizzuto says, "In the mysterious and indescribable experience of eye contact, two human beings respond to each other beyond the boundaries of need satisfaction" (p. 184).

For these authors, the process of forming transitional objects is a creative one in that playful fantasy enters into one's response to primary personal objects. Furthermore, the formation of transitional objects is creative in terms of outcome, for the creation of a transitional environment provides the safety children need in order to explore their widening world with initiative and free responsiveness. Such spontaneity is not limited to infants. It is important to envision this creativity of the infant as the beginning of a lifelong process, to see some element of continuity between this origin and the most developed forms of human creativity. Accordingly, Winnicott (1971) sees—in the infant's creation of a world that blends the inner and the outer—the beginnings of play, culture, religion and scientific discovery.

Creative responses to one's environment do not simply reproduce outer reality in detail as a replica inside the mind. This becomes clear with regard to consciousness, in the course of human development, as one's concepts undergo continual revision. Thus reality has an elusive quality about it, and so does our experience of the presence of God. If we equate our representations of God with the reality of God we terminate the creative process. At the same time, the elusiveness inherent in creative response differs from the uncertain contact with reality that is characteristic of defensive striving.

Thus, with respect to the thesis of this study, emphasis on creative formation of a God image is consistent with Terrien's (1978) emphasis on the presence of God as being elusive. It is interesting, in light of Winnicott's (1971) and Rizzuto's (1979) concepts of mirroring, that the Psalms are replete with the image of God's face in connection with the divine presence and absence. The following are a few examples:

How long wilt thou hide thy face from me? (Psalm 13:1)

Thou has said, "Seek ye my face." My heart says to thee, "Thy face, Lord, do I seek." Hide not thy face from me. (Psalm 27:8-9)

Let thy face shine on thy servant; save me in thy steadfast love! (Psalm 31:16)

The fact, however, that the divine presence is elusive does not imply it is illusory or lacking in reality. Can object relations theory help us to discern how the elusive presence of God is experienced as intensely real? One aspect of this theory, closely related to the affirmation of creative process in the mental life of the infant, will be explored in this context.

The Centrality of Personal Relations

Object relations theory places an emphasis on the centrality of personal relations, or object relations, compared to wish fulfillment or pleasure as a basis on which to account for human behavior and conflicts. Fairbairn (1952) sets forth the thesis that libido is essentially object-seeking in contrast to the position that libido is pleasure-seeking. In this affirmation, object relations theorists depart from a view of humans as being more narcissistic than social in their basic make up. According to object relations theory people need and seek primary, personal relationships for their own sake, though they entail both pleasure and frustration. Similarly, this approach can envision that people seek a relationship with God for its own sake in contrast to the view that people project an image of God which will gratify their wishes. Theologians also like to think that the reality and qualities of God's relationship to persons and to humankind matters to people more than pleasures derived from beliefs.

Furthermore, object relations theorists proffer here a model which is compatible with the theological understanding of God as one who evokes a bond between God and person, a bond which shapes that person in such a fashion that the person's integrity is tied to this relation to God. In Rizzuto's (1979) account, for example, God is the only object who has total knowledge of the self as perceived by the person. When one's God knows and loves all that a person is, one's sense of self is grounded. In this model God may be conceived as the sort of reality that is capable of evoking full and complete affection as a personal response.

In object relations theory, then, bonding with the parent and the primary relationships in the family have central importance, and this bonding is a model for the origin of the child's sense of relatedness to God. This world of origins is a world of intense reality and strong, interpersonal ties of loyalty. The reality that matters is not known objectively or in a detached manner. In fact, love and gratitude for persons who care and simply are present undergirds both the desire to do good and an early sense of obligation.

Rizzuto (1979) believes that when infants sense that they do not fulfill the family's mythological expectations and so are not confirmed in relation to the primary caring person, they are conflicted about their own being, and the formation of a negative relationship to God is one result. Boszormenyi-Nagy and Spark (1984) analyze how deep loyalties span family generations, often creating systematically sustained problems in self concept and behavior. I suggest that we think of such phenomena as being related to a false sense of human faultedness. I speak speculatively here, but for primary relationships which basically are sound and affirming as well as for inadequate primary relationships, there remains the reality of a kind of guilt. For example, Winnicott (1971) believes that the infant's bond to the mother and gratefulness make possible experiences of feeling indebted to others. Thus there can be a sense of shortcoming that is not the mere consequence of inappropriate family images and expectations. Accordingly, one can expect that children who have a positive God representation may experience the absence of a good God as part of the experience of guilt. If so, then there is some correspondence of this early experience with the Psalms wherein, according to Terrien (1978), expressions of the experience of the absence of God usually are confessions of guilt. A matured form of the experience of guilt has the psalmist praying both for God's absence and presence: "Hide thy face from my sins . . ." (Psalm 51:9); "Cast me not away from thy presence . . ." (Psalm 51:11).

In relation to infants' anxieties, God is experienced as Comforter, and this early experience may begin the journey to knowledge of God as Governor; in relation to their creative playfulness, God is experienced as Companion, and this early experience may begin the journey to knowledge of God as Creator. Also it may be that, in relation to a guilt emerging earlier in children's development that Freud posited, children experience God as Restorer, a forerunner of knowledge of God as Redeemer. It should not be surprising, then, that in the Psalms images of a face-to-face primary relationship are linked to an understanding of righteousness, for at least in part righteousness is right relationship: ". . . I shall behold thy face in righteousness. . . ." (Psalm 17:15). Even though elusive, the presence of God is experienced as very real, according to the line of thought generated by Winnicott (1971) and

Rizzuto (1979), for it has qualities of a deep, personal relationship which evokes ultimate loyalty.

Absence and the Experienced Reality of God

In addition, the context of primary relations introduces a new element: the role of frustration in our sense of reality. Frustration plays a key role in the discovery of the reality of the primary care giver and the ensuing differentiation between reality and wish. In relation to the mother, Winnicott (1971) describes how the infant requires a reliable relationship in which frustration is initially minimized. The mother's initial hyperadaptation to the infant and its needs is vigorous yet cannot be sustained for very long. The initial, strong adaptation gives the child the illusion that an external reality corresponds to the infant's own capacities to create. Step by step the mother's preoccupation with the infant diminishes and she expects the infant to endure frustrations, including the frustration of her absence. In effect this process disillusions the infant, who begins to learn to adapt to reality and experiences reality as other than his or her own wishes and ideas. There may be a bond, including some sense of sameness or similarity, in personal relations. There is also a sense of otherness, which contributes to our experience of the genuineness and reality of an interpersonal relationship.

Thus, a child's understanding of reality advances through experiences like the parent's absence. Children and adults discover also something of God's reality through an absence that communicates otherness. Though commonplace, it is telling that people speak about an experience of the absence of God. I suggest that such experience is essential to an authentic sense of the reality of God. The simple reason is that if we experience God as always present and always attending to our well-being, then we have no basis, at least in terms of our experiences, for distinguishing God from fantasy or wish fulfillment. Certainly a number of religions, Christianity not the least among them, teach that God is present everywhere and always. My point, however, is that this belief is not based on a subjective experiencing of God as always present, and if it were we would have no abiding confidence in the veracity of our claim, for such an experience is not distinguishable from fantasy. This observation about the experience of God's absence is no proof of God's existence, but it does disclose how important this experience of absence is psychologically for a sense of God's reality. Accordingly, people say they believe that God is always present, even though at times and for extended periods in their lives they experience the absence of God. The elusiveness of God is essential to human confidence in God's reality. Without that elusiveness the distinction between reality and wish would be eroded. Object relations theory helps us to see how far back this encounter with reality as otherness goes.

Still, when Rizzuto (1979) or others speak of positive and negative representations of God, it would be a mistake to equate these as such with the presence and absence of God. It would be helpful to hear more from these professional friends of children—and the child in all of us—about children's experiences of the absence of a good God. Is it not the case that when various psalms refer to the absence of God they are affirming God's goodness as well as God's reality?

The Elusive Locus

Finally, the elusive reality of God may be examined in light of the way in which Rizzuto (1979) and Winnicott (1971) posit the infant's transition from symbiosis to individuation as the personal beginning point for encounter with a world that is neither purely psychological nor simply material. According to Rizzuto, as first experienced by the infant, the reality of God cannot be located simply in either inside or outside worlds. God is located rather in a transitional world, a transitional space, for God is encountered when outside and inside are not yet differentiated. What is freshly lived by infants has to be recreated, in ritual for example, by adults who have become overly accustomed to modern exaggerations of outer and inner realities. Children make transitions between waking and sleeping, between dreaming and fact-finding, and retain some sense of their experiences as parts of a whole cloth. The child's God is elusive, immanent yet transcendent, in that this God is not an actor under the direction of personal consciousness.

Given Winnicott's (1971) emphasis on creativity in infant development, it is not surprising that he deciphers in transitional object phenomena the origins of culture and religion. In modern thinking, objects exist either in time-space or in the psyche, but Winnicott posits three areas: the inner, psychic world; the exterior world of which the individual is a part; and an intermediate world, the realm of culture. Since transitional objects are part of the environment yet are created to a significant extent by the infant's cognitive and emotional response, Winnicott speaks of an intermediate realm, a "potential space" between subject and object (p. 149). This is the locus of play and culture. Winnicott believes that the infant has intense experiences "in the potential space between the subjective object and the object objectively perceived, between me-extensions and the not me" (p. 100). Once stabilized, transitional objects blend subjective and objective meanings.

The very awkwardness of Winnicott's (1971) metaphor of a third kind of space, a "space" which is transitional—that is, has a kind of temporality about it—testifies to the elusiveness of God's whereabouts. The spacial emphasis derives from the way in which visual images and thinking styles dominate in both Winnicott and Rizzuto (1979), though more in Winnicott than in Rizzuto. At least Rizzuto gives a place to the world of sound when she speaks of ". . . the ineffable experience of seeing oneself in their eyes, while they say one's name and give names to body parts . . ." (p. 187). There is little acknowledgement of, let alone attention to, oral communication in Winnicott. This does not mean that the process of mirroring is reducible to eye contact between infant and mother. Neither Winnicott nor Rizzuto conceptualize in such a literal fashion. Still, the visual mode is the controlling metaphor in their explanation of the child's discovery of self and other.

In Terrien's (1978) interpretation of the divine presence one finds another route to acknowledging God's elusiveness. Terrien's analysis discloses how the dominance of the visual gives way to the auditory in Scripture's testimony to the divine presence. In the end, people do not know God in visual representations. They hear the divine call, but hearing does not permit exact fixing of location. There is no need to establish a correspondence between this historical development of a theological concept and individual development, such that the auditory comes to replace the dominance of the visual in both realms of discourse. Nonetheless, the significance of oral communication in the canon can serve as an occasion to reexamine the object relations analysis of the formation of self and other representations.

Could it be, then, that the auditory not only supplements the visual but also enables and enhances the power of the visual in the infant's emergence into the world of primary relationships? For example, as children make sounds, they hear what others hear and, with the beginnings of a capacity to organize reality into inner and outer, may have an awareness of the responsive sound being similar to what they hear themselves emit; that is, an imitation. Perhaps this awareness sets the stage for an awareness that facial expressions of the mother are similar to what the mother sees when beholding her child, a mirroring. If this is so, then the mirroring process seems a bit more plausible and less mystical as an account of self-discovery.

In any case, I confess my suspicion, a "benevolent" one I hope, that the dominance of the visual does not always serve adequately the psychoanalytic explanation of the origin of the God representation. Even so, the focus on the visual translated into a third realm, transitional space, where human creativity continues to draw its strength, does highlight the elusiveness of any locus for the divine. The human representation of God is not simply a creation within the human psyche where wish prevails, nor is it located where persons can presume to endow their understanding with an objectivity that precedes or successfully evades personal involvement. In theological terms neither Feuerbach nor Barth will suffice in light of this type of psychodynamic explanation. Psychologically, even in its beginnings the self is a complicated phenomenon, for the self discovers its sociality in its isolation.

Implications

Several implications with a practical dimension can now be identified in order to highlight particular areas for further inquiry. The first has to do with the question of how to characterize psychotherapy, pastoral counseling, and related practices which endeavor to help persons and touch on the religious dimension of the self. A fruitful way to interpret these practices, it seems to me, is to understand them to be a tutoring in the religious and ethical imagination, which basically is what Paul Pruyser (1974) advocates. The imagination spawns both truth and lies as well as health and illness. For example, the "Magnificat" notes that God "has scattered the proud in the imagination of their hearts" (Luke 1:51). Accordingly, the imagination may require a tutoring in order to be directed toward creative truth. It certainly does not need to be daunted, driven underground, or stamped out; but affirmative guidance and direction may help to rescue a person's imagination from private license and from unproductive distortions.

This model of pastoral counseling and related disciplines raises further questions. Suppose one takes object relations theorists seriously when they attest to an "intermediate world" between external and internal worlds or realities. One is then led, it seems to me, to posit a third kind of mental process, correlative to primary and secondary processes. If there is a "third" world to which persons belong, then it seems reasonable to speak of a third mental system. Primary process is private and wedded to wish fulfillment. Secondary process is public, or capable of being made public, and is integrally related to adaptation in the space-time world of human affairs. Tertiary process transcends or cuts across these two, synthesizing them to enhance a world of shared, vital meaning. In order to understand this process, one examines human experiences where both intellectual and affective functioning are fully engaged. I do not mean here any and all passing emotions, however intense, but those affections that reflect a "binding" in analogy to the bonding process of a self to a primary object. Often such self-shaping loyalties are being enhanced or reworked when one's mind and affect are focused together on images, a familiar phenomenon in pastoral and secular psychotherapy. Likewise, prayer (Underwood, 1985) and poetry may be occasions when affect and cognition are synthesized in such a fashion that enduring transformation of spirit and behavior is a possible result.

Finally, an implication of this exploration of object relations theory in relation to the presence of God motif is that for our time the focus of pastoral ministry, and related forms of personal help, will be on the problems of self/other relations as the context in which the meaning of life can be affirmed. In particular, the significant question pertains to those meaningful relations that undergird the morally creative life, and primary among these is the divine/human relationship.

Summary

The elusiveness of God as experienced in personal lives has been examined in terms of the presence and absence of God. Object relations theory helps us to understand psychologically how essential is the elusive quality of the divine for any genuine sense of discovery, any authentic account of the divine as constitutive of the self, any encounter with the divine as real, and any grasp of the divine as unconfined by simple location. At selected points the object relations account of the beginnings of mental representations of God has been compared to more reflective representations of God in the Psalms, which have lost none of the elusiveness of the divine as apprehended in the sung faith of people gathered and dispersed over time and place. Perhaps it is possible to advance such a tenuous juxtaposition of two perspectives on the motif of divine elusiveness by interpretation of the practices of psychological therapists, and pastoral counselors, as they encounter religious apperceptions and reflect on a religious dimension in their work.

Works Cited

Barth, K. (1975). *Church dogmatics*. Edinburgh: T. &. T. Clark.

Boszormenyi-Nagy, I., & Spark, G. (1984). *Invisible loyalties: Reciprocity in intergenerational family therapy*. New York: Brunner/Mazel. (Original work published 1973)

Eagle, M. (1984). *Recent developments in psychoanalysis: A critical evaluation*. New York: McGraw-Hill.

Fairbairn, W. (1952). *Psychoanalytic studies of the personality*. London: Routledge and Kegan Paul, Ltd.

Feuerbach, L. (1957). *The essence of Christianity*. New York: Harper. (Original work published 1854)

Greenberg, J., & Mitchell, S. (1983). *Object relations in psychoanalytic theory*. Cambridge, MA: Howard University Press.

Kernberg, O. (1976). *Object relations theory and clinical psychoanalysis*. New York: Aronson.

McDargh, J. (1983). *Psychoanalytic object relations theory and the study of religion*. Lanham, MD: University Press of America.

Pruyser, P. (1974). *Between belief and unbelief*. New York: Harper & Row.

Rizzuto, A-M. (1979). *The birth of the living God: A psychoanalytic study*. Chicago: University of Chicago.

Terrien, S. (1978). *The elusive presence: Toward a new biblical theology*. New York: Harper & Row.

Underwood, R. (1975). The presence of God in pastoral care ministry. *Austin Seminary Bulletin*. *101*, 5-14.

Winnicott, D. (1971). *Playing and reality*. New York: Basic Books.

PRACTICAL THEOLOGY: MISSIONS

C. Peter Wagner, area editor

MISSIONS

C. PETER WAGNER
McGavran Professor of Church Growth
Fuller Seminary School of World Mission

Introduction

The development of missiology as an academic discipline over the last fifteen years has been remarkable. As late as the early seventies, missions professors were searching every nook and cranny for competent textbooks and materials for scholarly readers. Seminary curricula contained scant offerings in the field, at times taught as a sideline by professors who specialized in other disciplines. Graduate degrees in missions were a curiosity. Some theologians patronizingly looked at missions studies as barely a notch above Sunday school.

No longer. Several seminaries have faculties of four or five or more missions specialists. One boasts a faculty of twelve full time missiologists. Masters degrees in missions abound. Many schools are offering the Doctor of Ministry in Missions, the Doctor of Missiology, and a few the Ph.D. in Intercultural Studies, in Missiology, or in cognate disciplines. A major problem for contemporary professors of mission is to decide which of the excellent books available *not* to include as required reading. The formation of the American Society of Missiology in 1973 gave the field a substantial academic boost. The Association of Professors of Mission and the Association of Evangelical Professors of Mission provide forums for cross-fertilization of ideas.

Four journals in the field have a broad appeal to North American missiologists. The *International Review of Mission* is published by the Division of World Mission and Evangelism of the World Council of Churches in Geneva. Its offerings largely reflect the thinking of the more liberal wing of Christianity, although an evangelical voice advocating the necessity of conversion is occasionally heard. On the right side of the spectrum is *Evangelical Missions Quarterly*, published by the Evangelical Missions Information Service, a joint project of the Interdenominational Foreign Mission Association and the Evangelical Foreign Missions Association. Their editorial emphasis is geared to the field missionary, but articles with somewhat of an academic flavor appear from time to time. *Missiology: an International Review* is the journal of the American Society of Missiology, which by design encourages a balance of contributions from ecumenical Protestant, evangelical Protestant and Roman Catholic scholars. The *International Bulletin of Missionary Research,* published by the Overseas Ministries Study Center of New Haven, Connecticut, is designed to serve the same constituency as *Missiology*. It is from these four journals that most of the selections for this series will appear, although articles from more specialized periodicals such as *Global Church Growth*, *Urban Mission*, and others may appear from time to time.

In order to bring as broad a consensus as possible to the selections, I have elected to form an editorial committee of 13 evangelical colleagues. They include Norman E. Allison of Toccoa Falls College School of World Mission, J. Ronald Blue of Dallas Theological Seminary, Harvie M. Conn of Westminster Theological Seminary, Ralph R. Covell of Denver Theological Seminary, John D. Ellenberger of Alliance Theological Seminary, Samuel Escobar of Eastern Baptist Theological Seminary, David J. Hesselgrave of Trinity Evangelical Divinity School, Donald Hohensee of Western Evangelical Seminary, Grant McClung, Jr. of the Church of God (Cleveland) School of Theology, Marvin K. Mayers of the Biola School of Intercultural Studies, Kenneth B. Mulholland of Columbia Bible Seminary, Timothy M. Warner of Trinity Evangelical Divinity School, and Warren Webster of the Conservative Baptist Foreign Mission Society. I am grateful for their willingness to participate in this project on an ongoing basis.

The first article we have selected this time represents the fulfillment of a vision of many missionaries for decades—a movement for sending out cross-cultural missionaries by the churches of the Third World. Larry D. Pate and Lawrence E. Keyes, both of Overseas Crusades, are recognized as top researchers and practitioners in this field. "Emerging Missions in a Global Church"[1] will bring you up to date on the background, the current status, and the major issues involved in analyzing and stimulating this new development.

The other selection comes from a seminal thinker among contemporary missiologists, Paul G. Hiebert of the Fuller Seminary School of World Mission. While Pate and Keyes deal with a practical side of missiology, Hiebert wrestles with epistemology. His article, "Critical Contextualization,"[2] breaks important ground in an area which, for some time now, has hovered near the top of the agenda of most missiologists. When Christianity breaks into a different culture, how much of that culture may be absorbed into the life of the new church, and how much of it must be rejected because of obviously demonic dimensions which are incompatible with biblical Christianity? The faculties of at least two seminaries, Trinity and Fuller, each have plans for the publication of a major volume on the subject in the near future. These, and any other serious looks at contextualization, will from now on have to deal with the issues Hiebert raises. An abridged version appears here.

Any of the honorable mention articles could easily have been chosen to appear. Indeed, at least one would have been included by some member or other of the editorial committee. They fall into six high-priority areas of current missionary thinking:

1. *The future.* As the twentieth century draws to a close, a good bit of attention is being paid to where we are heading. In the past year no fewer than six significant articles have appeared on the subject. David Barrett and Tom Sine both addressed a Chicago World Mission Institute held in 1986 by the Lutheran School of Theology. *Missiology* published Barrett's "Getting Ready for Mission in the 1990s: What Should We Be Doing to Prepare?"[3] and Sine's "Shifting Mission into the Future Tense."[4] Howard A. Snyder and Daniel V. Runyon identify and explain the ten major trends affecting the church today: from regional churches to World Church, from scattered growth to broad revival, from Communist China to Christian China, from institutional tradition to Kingdom theology, from clergy/laity to community of ministers, from male leadership to male/female partnership, from secularization to religious relativism, from nuclear family to family diversity, from church/state separation to Christian political activism, and from safe planet to threatened planet.[5] Wilbert R. Shenk reflects on eight clues relating to "The Future of Mission."[6] Among other things, he feels that we are currently standing between two eras of mission due to the burgeoning strength of non-Western churches. Finally, in the 13th edition of the MARC *Mission Handbook* both Robert T. Coote and the MARC editorial staff provide extensive overviews of where we have been and where we are likely to go.[7]

2. *Urbanization.* Viv Grigg's "Sorry! The Frontier Moved," helpfully brings to our attention that one of today's massive but woefully neglected challenges for evangelistic missions is the "greatest migration in history, the migration of Third World rural peasants to great mega-cities."[8] And Raymond J. Bakke summarizes some of what he has been learning in his extensive research on more than 70 world-class cities in "The Challenge of World Urbanization to Mission Strategy: Perspectives on Demographic Realities."[9]

3. *Women.* An enlightening piece on the role of women in mission strategy development comes from Ruth Tucker entitled "Female Mission Strategists."[10]

4. *Prayer.* I foresee an increasing emphasis on practical dimensions of prayer in world evangelization in the years to come. One of the leaders in this new movement is David Bryant of InterVarsity Missions; he presents a forceful challenge in the article "Prayer movements signal new light for the nations."[11]

5. *The homogeneous unit principle.* Few missiological issues have been debated with more vigor in recent years than Donald McGavran's homogeneous unit principle. Donald Hohensee continues the dialogue with "HU Revisited: A Wesleyan Looks at the Homogeneous Unit Principle."[12]

6. *Pentecostalism.* One of the great areas of neglect among evangelical missiologists has been a study of the dynamics of the fastest growing religious movement in the world: the Pentecostal/charismatic movement. A keen young Pentecostal scholar, Grant McClung, helps fill in some of the gaps in

"Explosion, Motivation, and Consolidation: The Historical Anatomy of the Pentecostal Missionary Movement."[13]

Notes

[1] Larry D. Pate with Lawrence E. Keyes. "Emerging Missions in a Global Church." *International Bulletin of Missionary Research* 10 (No. 4, 1986): 156-161.

[2] Paul G. Hiebert. "Critical Contextualization." *International Bulletin of Missionary Research* 11 (No. 3, 1987): 104-112.

[3] David Barrett. "Getting Ready for Mission in the 1990s: What Should We Be Doing to Prepare?" *Missiology: An International Review* XV (No. 1, 1987): 3-14.

[4] Tom Sine. "Shifting Mission into the Future Tense." *Missiology: An International Review* XV (No. 1, 1987): 15-23.

[5] Howard A. Snyder and Daniel V. Runyon. "Ten Major Trends Facing the Church." *International Bulletin of Missionary Research* 11 (No. 2, 1987): 67-70.

[6] Wilbert R. Shenk. "The Future of Mission." *International Review of Mission* LXXVI (No. 301, 1987): 59-63.

[7] Robert T. Coote. "Taking Aim on 2000 AD," and MARC editorial staff, "Christianity in the World: an Overview." *Mission Handbook*, 13th Edition, Monrovia: MARC, 1986.

[8] Viv Grigg. "Sorry! The Frontier Moved." *Urban Mission* 4 (No. 4, 1987): 12-25.

[9] Raymond J. Bakke. "The Challenge of World Urbanization to Mission Strategy: Perspectives on Demographic Realities." *Urban Mission* 4 (No. 2, 1986): 6-17.

[10] Ruth Tucker. "Female Mission Strategists: An Historical and Contemporary Perspective." *Missiology: An International Review* XV (No. 1, 1987): 73-89.

[11] David Bryant. "Prayer movements signal new light for the nations." *Evangelical Missions Quarterly* 23 (No. 2, 1987): 118-127.

[12] Donald Hohensee. "HU Revisited: A Wesleyan Looks at the Homogeneous Unit Principle." *The Preacher's Magazine* 61 (No. 4, 1986): 19-23.

[13] Grant McClung. "Explosion, Motivation, and Consolidation: The Historical Anatomy of the Pentecostal Missionary Movement." *Missiology: An International Review* XIV (No. 2, 1986): 159-172.

About the Area Editor

C. Peter Wagner (M.Div. Fuller Theological Seminary; Th.M. Princeton Theological Seminary; M.A. Fuller School of World Mission; Ph.D. University of Southern California) is the Donald A. McGavran Professor of Church Growth at the Fuller Theological Seminary School of World Mission. Previous to joining that faculty in 1971, he served as a missionary to Bolivia for 16 years. He is a charter member of the Lausanne Committee for World Evangelization, currently serving as President of the North American branch. Wagner teaches an adult Sunday School class in Lake Avenue Congregational Church, Pasadena, California. He is the author of 28 books on missions and church growth. Among the latest are *Spiritual Power and Church Growth* (Creation House, 1986), and *Strategies for Church Growth* (Regal, 1987). He has also edited *Church Growth: State of the Art* (Tyndale, 1986), and *Signs and Wonders Today* (Creation House, 1987).

EMERGING MISSIONS IN A GLOBAL CHURCH

LARRY D. PATE with LAWRENCE E. KEYES
Dr. Pate is Coordinator of Emerging Missions, Overseas Crusades
Dr. Keyes is President of Overseas Crusades

Article from *International Bulletin of Missionary Research*

> How beautiful on the mountains
>   are the feet of those who bring good news,
> who proclaim peace,
>   who bring good tidings,
> who proclaim salvation [Isa. 52:7, NIV].

It is becoming clear to most missiologists who look across the mountain ranges of the future that the "feet of those who bring good news" are rapidly changing color. New streams of brown, black, yellow, and red feet are joining with the white to proclaim the salvation message. The gospel no longer masquerades as a white person's good news about a white, Western imperialistic God. It is Koreans-to-Nepal, Singaporeans-to-Nigeria, Brazilians-to-North Africa good news! More and more, the news is spreading *from* every people *to* every people.

While it is difficult to track the growth of non-Western missions with precision, it can safely be said that there are over 20,000 non-Western missionaries today. Keyes' research indicated that the growth rate for non-Western missions from 1972 to 1982 was 448 percent.[1] Our current research, which is incomplete at this point, indicates decadal rates of growth exceeding 300 percent in various parts of the non-Western world. If the decadal growth rate averages only as much as 225 percent for the next fourteen years, there will be more than 100,000 non-Western missionaries by the year 2000.

This leads to some serious questions. Exactly what is "emerging missions?" What is the nature and scope of the work of emerging missions? What are their strengths and weaknesses? What are their greatest challenges? How will they impact the work of Western mission agencies? How can Western agencies best relate to the emerging missions?

Emerging Missions: A Descriptive Summary

"Third-world missions," "non-Western missions," "emerging missions" are labels commonly attached to the phenomenon under consideration. No label seems entirely appropriate. "Third world" is primarily a political and economic term carrying a connotation of "third rate." "Non-Western" focuses on Asia and Africa, and to some degree excludes Latin Americans, who consider themselves as "Western" as North Americans. New missions are emerging in Western, first-world countries as well as in non-Western, third-world countries.

Even the connotation that emerging missions is only a recent phenomenon is not accurate. When the renowned Scottish missionary Alexander Duff landed in Calcutta (1830),

> . . . eight Tahitian missionaries were preaching the same Christ among heathen villagers on the Samoa Islands. Five years later the first European missionary arrived to find 2,000 native Christians meeting in small groups in 65 villages. It is rather surprising to realize that those islanders were missionaries ten years before David Livingstone landed in Africa; before Hudson Taylor was ever born. Since then, over 1,000 Pacific Islanders have gone out as missionaries to add a remarkable record to the history of Christian expansion.[2]

In 1833, the Karens of Burma, led by Ko-Thah-Byu, began their missionary outreach that led to the founding of the Bassein Home Mission Society (1850). They worked among a number of tribes in Burma and Thailand. In 1843 Jamaican Joseph Merrick set sail for the Cameroon coast to work among the Isubu people.

These early nineteenth-century non-Western missions predate 96 percent of today's North American sending agencies. Emerging missions is not a totally new phenomenon. On the other hand, it has developed rapidly during the last 25 years. A study conducted in 1961 identified 48 non-Western mission agencies sending at least 217 missionaries.[3] A 1972 study confirmed 203 agencies sending 3,404 missionaries.[4] The latest complete study (1980) revealed 368 agencies sending 13,000 missionaries, and projected 15,249 missionaries by the end of 1981.[5] Only in the sense of its recent rapid growth can the non-Western missions movement truly be labeled "emerging missions."

In spite of the limitations, it seems best to emphasize the term "emerging missions" above the others. "Emerging missions" is the term denoting the existing and newly forming missionary sending organizations among non-Western Christians, primarily located in Latin America, Africa, Asia, and Oceania. These mission agencies may be little more than the missions committee of a single local church, or they may be denominational or interdenominational organizations representing hundreds of workers. Though usually found in non-Western countries, they can also be formed by emigrant communities in Western countries.

The emerging missions are cross-cultural mission societies. Some people have observed the number of Koreans coming to the United States to work among Korean emigrants, or they have observed Latin missionaries working among Latinos in the United States or Europe, and therefore concluded that almost all work by the emerging missions is diaspora evangelism focused upon evangelizing their own people who live outside their homeland. That is simply not the case. The vast majority of non-Western missionaries are crossing distinct cultural boundaries. Indian missionaries are reaching tribal groups in India. Brazilian and Mexican missionaries are targeting Muslims in North Africa.[6] Filipino missionaries are going to the Indians of Peru.[7] The Koreans are considered by many to be the most ethnocentric in their missionary sending. Yet, if the missionaries sent by one single Korean church are not included in the total, even the Koreans are sending more than half their missionaries to non-Korean cultures.[8] It is true that some non-Western churches have failed to make a clear distinction between missions and extension evangelism (as have some Western churches). But when we speak of the emerging-missions movement, we are speaking of societies that, by and large, have clearly made that distinction and are engaged in true cross-cultural missionary activity.

The emerging missions are indigenous. At least 75 percent of the emerging missions and a similar percentage of non-Western missionaries represent indigenous agencies that send their own missionaries completely independent of Western agencies.[9] Fully 91 percent of the total budget of the emerging missions comes from the non-Western world.[10] Present Western support of the emerging missions represents a mere trickle of Western mission funds. Existing Western agencies are increasingly being internationalized. There are a few parts of the world, notably Singapore and Malaysia, where the dominant missionary models are those of international agencies such as Overseas Missionary Fellowship and Youth With a Mission. Most of the missionaries from those two countries enter service through such an international agency. Non-Westerners are joining such agencies in record numbers. But they prefer their own indigenous agencies, and they are joining the emerging missions at a much greater rate. India, for instance, had an estimated 2,277 missionaries in 1980,[11] but grew to at least 4,162 by the end of 1984.[12] Virtually all of them are serving in Indian mission agencies, not international ones.

The emerging missions and Western missions need each other. The emerging missions are not automatically more successful than their Western counterparts. They are aware of their need to develop better training programs, support bases, organizational structures and strategies, and increase their overall fruitfulness. Though they know they can evangelize some peoples more effectively than Western missionaries, they do not view themselves as superior to Western missionaries, or as the heirs apparent to the worldwide missionary enterprise. The majority of the emerging missions recognize that they are in the early stages of their missionary movements. As long as there is no hint of paternalistic control included with the help being offered, they welcome Western assistance for developing their effectiveness.[13]

For both theological and practical reasons, the Western church must not come to view the emerging-missions movement as deliverance from its own missionary responsibility. The teachings of Christ and the book of Acts demonstrate that the nature of the church is missionary to the core. History demonstrates that the strength and viability of any segment of the church is proportional to the strength and viability of its missionary structures.[14] To capitulate to the rising tide of anti-Western sentiment in the world, or to the increasing difficulty of obtaining visas for Western missionaries, in favor of supporting the emerging missions would be a mistake capable of ultimately destroying a primary source of vitality in the Western churches. The Western church must maintain and seek to increase its own missionary endeavors.

Ralph Winter has done more than any other individual to point toward a coming new age of pioneer missions, which he calls the "third era" of missions. He points out that there are some 16,000 "unreached peoples," or cultures without a significant gospel witness, of which 15,000 are classified "frontier missions." By definition these latter are specific cultural blocs of people who do not have one viable witnessing church among the people of their own culture.[15] It has been estimated that it will require 200,000 new missionaries to evangelize the unreached peoples in this generation. The challenge of this new kind of "frontier missions" must be accepted by the church worldwide. This will require the combined resources, expertise, and cooperative efforts of both the existing Western agencies and the emerging missions.

Major Issues Confronting the Emerging Missions

In our hopeful welcoming of the emerging missions into the mainstream of the missionary enterprise, we must not assume that their efforts will automatically be blessed more than ours, or that they do not face as numerous and formidable barriers as do Western agencies. It is just as hard for an Asian to enter India, a Brazilian to enter Morocco, a Japanese to enter Bangladesh as it is for a North American. Historical and cultural prejudices will hinder the Japanese in the Philippines or the Taiwanese in Indonesia as much as the United States missionary in Mexico. We must welcome our non-Western missionary colleagues not as the divine answer to all the obstacles we face, but as co-laborers who are experiencing similar frustrations in their efforts to fulfill the Great Commission.

In working with the emerging missions, we have identified five primary forces that apparently need to combine in sufficient strength in order to make the churches of a given country capable of producing effective and fruitful missionary activity. Each country needs: (1) a sufficient number of pastors and church leaders who have a vision to evangelize the lost of other cultures; (2) organizational structures, both denominational and interdenominational, that assume responsibility for effectively managing the missionary enterprise; (3) adequate missionary training programs; (4) adequate information to plan effective missionary strategy; and (5) ability to over-come the problems related to raising financial support and maintaining missionaries on the field.

Within a given country, extreme weakness in any of these five areas will greatly hinder the missionary effectiveness of that country's church as a whole. For instance, most Latin American churches have been historically lacking in the first element listed above. The church leaders have been more interested in extension evangelism than cross-cultural evangelism. While this has greatly contributed to laudable church growth in many Latin coun-tries, it has also helped bring the churches of Latin America to a point where they represent 25 percent of the non-Western church, but only 7 percent of the non-Western missionary force. Fortunately, the Latin churches are rapidly beginning to pick up the banner of missions. In country after country, leaders are gathering for missions consultations. Several national missions congresses have taken place, such as the First Venezuelan Missions Con-gress, which convened October 15-19, 1985, and a congress held in Guate-mala in February 1986. Perhaps greatest in impact will be the Congreso Misionero Ibero-Americano (COMIBAM 87) scheduled for November 23-29, 1987, in São Paulo, Brazil. With a goal of bringing together 3,000 mission leaders, missionaries, pastors, youth leaders, and missiologists, the con-gress intends to awaken the Latin churches of twenty-three countries to the challenge of fulfilling their missionary responsibility.

It is common to find severe weaknesses, in one or more of the five elements listed above, in non-Western countries. The churches of Malaysia and Singapore are lacking mostly in elements 2 and 4—lack of organizational structures and inadequate information for making effective strategies. The emerging missions of Nigeria suffer from a shortage of effective training programs and from government financial restrictions (elements 3 and 5).

The list could be continued, with strengths and weaknesses varying from country to country. Each area of deficiency in each country should suggest possible ways Western agencies can assist the emerging missions. There is no doubt that Western help can be valuable, but it must be rendered in a manner that will encourage the autochthonous development of the emerging missions.

Partnership

Western church and mission leaders are searching for effective ways to relate to this growing emerging-missions movement. As ideas are expressed and patterns emerge, "partnership" has become the watchword. Coopera-tion in field ministry is becoming increasingly valuable as workers from varied backgrounds combine their missionary strengths to focus on evangel-ism among peoples of diverse cultures.

The type of partnerships desired do not resemble the old "comity" agreements of Western agencies, where participants simply agreed to work separately without infringing on the other's territory. Neither do they resemble the colonial "older church/younger church" agreements of a generation ago, where one partner is dominant. What is preferred are mission-to-mission agreements, with each partner contributing what it can give most effectively while sharing equal autonomy in accomplishing the task.

Such terminology is not meant to imply organizational union. Non-Western agencies usually prefer task-focused cooperation rather than structural amalgamation. Paul Hiebert, professor of anthropology at the School of World Mission, Fuller Theological Seminary, states: "The future of missions is based in the formation of international networks rather than 'multinational organizations.' Networks build up people, not programmes; they stress partnership and servanthood, not hierarchy; they help to build up the local church, not undermine it."[16] If these preferences and distinctions are kept in mind, the Western agencies will find an open door to partnership with the emerging missions.

Many examples could be cited illustrating the various types of "international networks" or partnership agreements. One cooperative project involves the Canadian Baptist Overseas Missions Board (CBOMB), and the formation of a joint mission to the yet unevangelized Somali peoples of the Northeastern Province in Kenya. Harold W. Turner, director of the Study Center for New Religious Movements in Primal Societies at Selly Oak Colleges, Birmingham, England, writes, "This new joint operation is itself of considerable significance, and it is not known in the missions world."[17]

In 1967 an independent church group of Kikuyu peoples in Kenya, called the African Christian Church and Schools (ACC&S), sent a representative to the CBOMB. Perry V. Allaby, associate secretary of CBOMB, reports the results of that meeting.

> They wanted to know if we as a mission board would be interested in sending missionaries to Kenya to help them in certain specific areas, such as pastoral leadership training, the training of church officers, help in youth work and in women's work. Our board responded favorably, and as a result, a contingent of missionaries was sent to Kenya to work with the ACC&S and under their direction. We called this contingent of missionaries a "task force" since the missionaries were going to Kenya to do certain specific tasks, and would remain for only a limited period of time, actually ten years. The task force began in 1970 and was terminated in 1980.[18]

Up to 1980, the relationship was a "mission-church" partnership. However, one of the results of the ten-year agreement was the establishment of a new partner relationship with the ACC&S. It developed into a mission-mission agreement. Perry Allaby continues:

> We called this project *Joint Pioneer Outreach*—*joint*, because it is a cooperative effort with both Canadian Baptist and Kikuyus of the ACC&S contribut-

ing money and personnel; *pioneer*, because it is a project aimed at reaching a people (the Somalis) among whom little or no Christian work has hitherto been done; and *outreach*, because it is the ultimate objective to meet the deepest needs of these people, spiritual as well as physical.[19]

This Joint Pioneer Outreach agreement is a twenty-five-year venture, consisting of a missionary force, half Canadian and half Kenyan, with mutual funding. The overall administrative supervision is through ACC&S, which also appoints the director. This arrangement assures the development and strength of the missionary arm of the ACC&S, and also encourages the ministry to be contextual within the Northeastern Province of Kenya.

Similar partnership between Western and non-Western churches and mission societies is found on all continents of the world. Without either party being dominated by the other, both groups represent a particular contribution toward a recognized objective. Through careful planning and understanding, missionary cooperation of this caliber can greatly strengthen the effectiveness of mission work. For example, both Calvary Ministries and Worldwide Evangelization Crusade International experienced mutual benefit by deciding to work together in a survey trip to discern how best to evangelize the country of Guinea. They decided on a joint evangelism partnership as well. Mutual benefit also resulted from the development of a working agreement in India among the Christian Association, the Zoram Baptist Mission, and the Conservative Baptist Foreign Mission Society. These three mission agencies, along with the Church Growth Missionary Movement, focused on the joint task of evangelizing the Korku people in Central India. A final illustration is the daily missionary outreach into China through radio, which is a result of a three-way partnership among the evangelical churches in Hong Kong (which provide funding), the Far East Broadcasting Company (which produces and broadcasts the programs), and Overseas Crusades (which serves as sponsor and fund-raiser). Partnerships between Western and non-Western mission agencies are increasingly a necessary ingredient in the implementation of the missionary mandate.

Crucial Issues for Western Agencies

The *Evangelical Missions Quarterly*, in its twentieth-anniversary edition, invited Evangelical Foreign Missions Association Executive Director Wade Coggins and Interdenominational Foreign Mission Association Executive Director Edwin L. (Jack) Frizen, Jr., to identify the most significant trend in missions during the last twenty years. "My choice," said Frizen, "is the renewed focus on unreached people groups and penetrating the frontiers still remaining." While also identifying the unreached-people movement as a second choice, Coggins pointed to "the rise of mission agencies and missionaries in Africa, Asia and Latin America" as the most significant trend.[20]

It is significant that Frizen and Coggins identify emerging missions and unreached peoples as the most significant trends in missions today. It is highly possible that the emerging missions will prove to be the greatest single force for evangelizing unreached people. Western agencies have worked to establish the existing national churches, and have long-term-ministry commitments to continue their work with them. At least 90 percent of new recruits to Western agencies are sent to replace retiring missionaries or to establish ministries connected to the national churches that have already been established. By contrast, the emerging missions do not have an agenda connected with national churches that they have already established. They are more free to target unreached peoples, concentrating their efforts in pioneer mission activity.

There have been three principal responses to the rise of emerging missions on the part of the Western agencies. The first is a benign but distant neglect. While some agencies applaud the emerging-missions movement, they make little effort to establish working relationships with any member groups. The fruits of such benign neglect are becoming increasingly more evident around the world.

Different regions of one Brazilian denomination sent five missionaries to work in La Paz, Bolivia, a few years ago. But each worked independently of the others and of the European and North American foreign missionaries of that same denomination. They also worked independently of the denominational structure within Bolivia, establishing churches that were "daughter" churches of the sending churches in Brazil. Being directly amenable to the sending churches, the word "Brazilian" even appeared in the names of some of the churches. The Bolivian denominational leaders eventually convinced the Brazilian sending churches to withdraw their missionaries. What a different story that could have been if that denomination had already established some basic standards of international cooperation (and missionary training)! Benign neglect means that such circumstances, with variations, are destined to arise many times among many groups.

The sheer size and rate of growth of the emerging-missions movement will make benign neglect an increasingly less tenable response in years to come. The emerging-missions movement is growing at a rate more than five times that of Western missions, and it promises to change the nature of the world missionary enterprise. Benign neglect means that many emerging missions will be forced to repeat many of the mistakes the Western agencies have made in the last 200 years. Could it be that many Western agencies have succumbed to an inordinate fear of paternalizing the emerging-missions movement, with benign neglect being the result? Is it really necessary to neglect the emerging missions in order to ensure their indigeneity? Would it not be better humbly to admit our mistakes and seek ways to prevent their repetition among the emerging missions? Is it not possible to establish partner relationships that allow both partners enough autonomy to learn from each other and still increase their effectiveness by working together? The emerging missions should not be forced to learn everything through their own experience, repeating many Western mistakes. They should have the opportunity to learn from both the successes and the failures of Western missions, so they can go on beyond what the West has been able to do.

Internationalization

Another Western response to the rising interest in missions in non-Western countries is to internationalize existing Western agencies. Overseas Missionary Fellowship, Overseas Crusades, SIM International, Youth With a Mission, and Latin America Mission are among those that have strong goals toward recruiting non-Westerners as part of their ministry teams. Space cannot be given here for a full debate on the pros and cons of internationalization, but a few generalizations are in order.

Credibility is a key element in the motivation of those agencies that have internationalized. An internationalized team more adequately reflects the supracultural character of the gospel. Unfortunately, it is also a two-edged sword, which usually slices the credibility of the non-Western team member down to a fraction of what it would be if the member were sent out by an emerging mission. Meaning is perception! Too often, non-Westerners on the international teams are simply perceived as paid Western agents, causing the value of the message to be diminished in the mind of the recipient.

The negative impact is often not confined to the non-Western team member. The growth of missionary vision in the member's sending church may also be negatively affected. Depending upon the manner of recruitment, degree of Western support, and amount of dependence upon the missionary's sending church, internationalized missions may discourage the development of indigenous support-structures and mission auxiliaries within the sending church. Internationalized agencies can inadvertently perpetuate the notion that only the rich Western churches can afford to engage in missionary activity. If a non-Westerner serving with an international team must raise three times the average salary of the pastors in the person's own country in order to serve on an international team, it has a strong negative impact on the sending church's long-term interest in missions.

Generally speaking, internationalization seems to be most effective in interdenominational missions that have established nurture or service roles as their primary activity. Its most effective expressions are in relief and development work, while it tends to be least effective when engaged in church-planting efforts.[21] It is more difficult to plant churches when the missionaries are adjusting not only to the host culture, but to each other as well. Due to the nationalistic character of autonomous national churches around the world, and because existing internationalized teams have established few church-planting models, internationalization is not seen as a viable option among most denominational missions.

A Call for Task-Oriented Partnerships

"Mission partnerships created merely for the sake of demonstrating unity are superfluous and can easily siphon off valuable energies away from evangelism and pioneer missions," says Donald McGavran.[22] We agree that the Great Commission is task-oriented and that the task of reaching every people with a viable witness must take precedence. However, every missionary is not a pioneer and every missionary task is not evangelism. Researching the harvest fields, organizing good strategies, building support structures, training effective missionaries—these are also important elements that comprise the task. These are the very areas where the emerging missions need the greatest amount of assistance as is described above. Unified efforts that help respective partners accomplish those tasks more effectively must be encouraged. Here are some examples in the areas mentioned of how partnerships between Western and non-Western agencies can be effective:

Research
The ten agencies comprising the Nigerian Evangelical Missions Association (NEMA) have approved a project to survey every city, town, and village of Nigeria to determine the needs for church extension and for cross-cultural missionary activity among unreached-people groups. This one-year project could greatly benefit from partnerships with Western agencies, both in the training of research personnel and in the funding of the project.

Organization and Strategy Development
Many denominations in some parts of the non-Western world have sufficient funding and personnel available, but do not have organizational structures or a strategy to initiate missionary activity. Their Western denominational counterparts could seek ways to encourage and assist in the formation of such structure and strategy, taking care not to assume a paternal role in the process.

Motivation of Pastors and Leaders
On a larger scale, Western agencies can become partners in funding national, regional, and international meetings that focus on missions, such as COMIBAM 87 Latin America. On a personal level, individual Western missionaries should include more teaching and preaching on the missionary mandate of the church.

Training

Many theological schools founded by Western missions are beginning to include missions curricula, but consideration should be given toward establishing separate missionary training schools. Met Castillo, director of the Asian Center for Missionary Education (ACME) says: " . . . the nature of the curricula of existing theological schools in Asia explains their inadequacy in preparing cross-cultural missionaries. . . . Designed to train pastors and deaconesses, they have kept their trust faithfully. . . . This type of school, however, is far from being equipped to train missionary candidates."[23] The Nigerian Evangelical Missions Association agrees with that assessment. Though there are eleven well-acclaimed seminaries in Nigeria, NEMA sees a need to establish a separate interdenominational missionary training school. Western agencies can become valuable partners in establishing such schools. Even better, Western agencies could assist in the preparation of national missionary teachers in those countries where there has been a sufficient history of successful missionary activity, such as Nigeria and Brazil.

When there is a legitimate missionary task to be accomplished, and prospective partners in that task can both be more productive than if they worked alone, it indicates a need for partnership. Partnerships that allow participating agencies to draw on the strengths of each other in order to perform specific tasks is the need of the hour. In addition to the kinds of partnerships and examples suggested above, it is possible to form partnerships to evangelize specific groups of people. The Council of Baptist Churches in Northeast India, the Mizoram Presbyterian Synod, and the Khasi Jaintia Presbyterian Synod have united to form the Department of Mission and Evangelism of the Karbi Anglong Joint Christian Committee. One of their purposes is to evangelize the Karbi Anglong and other ethnic groups in northern India. In their first seven years of operation (1975-82), their fifty-two missionaries and field evangelists claimed 2,651 conversions.[24] Investigating the possibilities for establishing task-oriented partnerships to accomplish a variety of goals should be part of the agenda of both the Western agencies and the emerging missions.

Missions: Circa 2000

In a world of megatrends and explosive technological growth, it is dangerous to attempt accurate predictions five years into the future, much less fourteen. In the world of missions, the only thing more dangerous is not to make the attempt.

If present trends continue to the year 2000, there will be 6.135 billion people on this planet, 81.4 percent of them living in the non-Western countries.[25] Fifty percent of the total will live in an urban environment, but 75 percent of the world's sixty largest cities (over 5 million) will be in the non-Western countries.[26] Some of the largest classes of missionary candidates will be trained in Korea, Nigeria, India, and Brazil. There will likely be well over 1,000 non-Western mission agencies, and one of every two Protestant missionaries will be from the emerging missions of non-Western countries.[27]

To envision the future necessitates an attempt to prepare for it. In making the attempt, one may wish to consider the following questions.

1. As interchurch communication and cooperation increase in a shrinking Christian global community, theological and methodological barriers between various groups will likely be lowered. There will be a greater desire to cooperate with other groups to accomplish specific tasks (i.e., Bible translation, area evangelistic meetings, aid and development programs, etc.). To what degree and in what areas of missionary endeavor will a focus on task allow increased cooperation among groups of varying theological persuasion?

2. As non-Western theological and missiological education increasingly gains a global acceptance, will Western mission societies send a portion of their candidates to non-Western institutions for training and orientation?

3. As international cooperation increases of necessity, what new structural paradigms will emerge? Will multiethnic, task-oriented associations emerge? Will such partnerships be nationally, regionally, or internationally constituted? Will their structures vary by region or by continent? Will they primarily be denominational or interdenominational in nature?

4. Since many missiologists and missionaries are focusing increasing efforts toward the evangelization of many unreached ethnic and cultural subgroupings, is there a need for an international-frontiers comity agreement whereby groups who cannot work in cooperation among a specific people-group will voluntarily work among separate ones?

5. As non-Western missiology begins to develop its own theologies of mission, methodological emphases, and theoretical agenda, to what degree will Western missiology become internationalized?

6. As non-Western missionaries become increasingly more visible and recognized as representing effective ministries, Western churches will increasingly desire to support them. Many Western agencies, to varying degrees, have traditionally discouraged support for foreign nationals. Should this also be true for foreign national missionaries? If the Western societies continue their disapproval, what will be the reaction of the Western churches? What kind of new international structures would emerge? If the Western agencies do encourage their churches to help non-Western missionaries, what new patterns of missionary support would emerge internationally?

7. Missionary leaders are increasingly recognizing the need for regional and international networks of centers for missiological research. Taking advantage of research projects already initiated, what steps can be taken

toward initiating such networks? Is it desirable to coordinate, fund, collect, and disseminate information through one international and interdenominational research organization, giving equal informational access to all participating agencies? Would mission organizations be willing to write "R&D" into their annual budgets to underwrite such a venture?

8. What will be the structural composition of those Western and emerging missions that become internationalized in the future? Will a centralized, corporate, or multinational structure, so characteristic of many existing Western agencies, predominate? Or will new patterns of decentralized, locally controlled, truly international structures be developed? What linkages form the basis for developing partnerships? What are the logical steps leading to partnership?

These questions do not have easy answers. But it is an observable fact that the kind of vision that overcomes the Gates of Hell does not come without struggle. It is the struggle that captures the spirit and clarifies the vision. It very well may be that our struggle to find answers will make a big difference in whether the many-colored feet on the mountaintops of the future are wandering aimlessly or are bearing a powerful message which is really good news—*from* every people *to* every people!

Notes

[1] Lawrence E. Keyes, *The Last Age of Missions* (Pasadena, Calif.: William Carey Library, 1983), p. 65.

[2] Ibid., p. 95.

[3] Clara E. Orr, "Missionaries for the Younger Churches," *Occasional Bulletin of the Missionary Research Library*, January 1962, pp. 1-10.

[4] James Wong, et al., *Missions from the Third World* (Singapore: Church Growth Study Center, 1973), pp. 15-17.

[5] Keyes, *Last Age*, p. 65.

[6] "Projecto Magreb" is recruiting Mexicans and Brazilians for a long-term mission to Morocco and North Africa.

[7] The Philippine Mission Association has entered into partnership with SIM International to send Filipino missionaries to Latin America.

[8] The Yoido Gospel Church of Seoul, Korea, fields 167 of the 410 Korean missionaries, but 166 of them are doing diaspora work.

[9] Keyes, *Last Age*, p. 78.

[10] Ibid., p. 82.

[11] Ibid., p. 64.

[12] Larry D. Pate, "Indian Missions Continue Rapid Growth," *Bridging Peoples*, April 1985, p. 1.

[13] Keyes, *Last Age*, pp. 86-87.

[14] Ralph D. Winter, "Churches Need Missions because Modalities Need Sodalities," *Evangelical Missions Quarterly 7* (1971): 193-200.

[15] Ralph D. Winter, "Missions Today: A Look at the Future," in John E. Kyle, ed., *The Unfinished Task* (Ventura, Calif.: Regal Books, 1984), p. 74.

[16] Paul Hiebert, quoted in the *Haggai News*, Haggai Institute, (Singapore), March-April 1983.

[17] In a personal letter to Lawrence E. Keyes, dated May 24, 1983.

[18] In a personal letter to Lawrence E. Keyes, dated July 7, 1983.

[19] Ibid.

[20] *Evangelical Missions Quarterly* 20, no. 2 (April 1984): 127; 122.

[21] Donald A. McGavran, "Seoul, Lausanne and Africasian Missionary Societies" in Martin Nelson, ed., *Readings in Third World Missions* (Pasadena, Calif.: William Carey Library, 1978), p. 182.

[22] From personal interview with Donald McGavran by Larry Pate on Sept. 24, 1985.

[23] Keyes, *Last Age*, p. 113.

[24] Lawrence E. Keyes, "Emerging Missions in Partnership," an unpublished paper, (1985), p. 10.

[25] Source: World Population Data Sheet of the Population Reference Bureau, (1985), Washington, D.C.

[26] Source: State of the World Population, Population Reference Bureau, Washington, D.C. (1978 and 1980).

[27] These are conservative estimates based on less than the current rates of growth.

CRITICAL CONTEXTUALIZATION

PAUL G. HIEBERT
Professor of Mission Anthropology and South Asian Studies
School of World Mission
Fuller Theological Seminary

Article from *International Bulletin of Missionary Research*

A great deal has been written on contextualization in the past few years (see bibliographies of Bevans 1985, Gitari 1982, Haleblian 1983, and Lind 1982). I shall not summarize this literature or trace its development. Rather, I wish to propose a model, made up of three "ideal types" in the Weberian sense, which we can use to examine the ways in which Protestant missionaries have handled the problem over the past 100 years. This is not a history of events, but an analysis of how missionaries dealt with the awareness of cultural pluralism that swept the West following the age of exploration.

I shall limit myself to the narrow question of how the missionaries responded to the traditional beliefs and practices of new converts—in other words, to the "old" culture. Missionaries do not enter cultural vacuums. The people to whom they go are members of ongoing societies and cultures. The people raise food and build houses. They marry their young and bury their dead. They pray to their gods and propitiate their spirits. How did—and how should—missionaries who bring a new gospel respond to the old one?

The data will be drawn from the Indian scene, which has a long history of debates on the subject and with which I am most familiar. I believe, however, that the model is applicable to many other parts of the world.

The Era of Noncontextualization

Roughly from 1800 to 1950 most Protestant missionaries in India, and later in Africa, rejected the beliefs and practices of the people they served as "pagan." John Pobee writes: " . . . to the present time all the historical churches by and large implemented the doctrine of the *tabula rasa*, i.e. the missionary doctrine that there is nothing in the non-Christian culture on which the Christian missionary can build and, therefore, every aspect of the traditional non-Christian culture had to be destroyed before Christianity could be built up" (1978:146). Consequently, the gospel was seen by the people as a foreign gospel. To become Christian one had to accept not only Christianity but also Western cultural ways.

In view of the earlier willingness to use traditional cultural forms, what had changed? Why this growing rejection of existing cultures?

Rise of Colonialism

One reason was the emergence of colonialism with its belief in the superiority of Western cultures. The expansion of the East India Trading Company in India came at a time when the Mogul and Vijayanagar empires were decadent and collapsing. By default it became not only the economic but also the political master of much of India. The process was completed in 1858 when, because of the Indian Mutiny, the British government made India its star colony.

Colonialism proved to the West its cultural superiority. Western civilization had triumphed. It was the task, therefore, of the West to bring the benefits of this civilization to the world. Old medical systems were seen as witchcraft and hocus-pocus, and had to be stamped out. Old governments were seen as feudalistic and had to be replaced by modern, national governments. The result was "direct" rule in which the British sought to replace the Indian governmental structures from the top to the bottom.

For Christians, the parallel was the superiority of the gospel. Paganism had to be rooted out. Many missionaries, in fact, equated the two. Christianity, civilization and, later, commerce (the three Cs) went hand in hand. Western civilization was spreading around the world, and it was assumed that people would become both Christian and "modern." There was no need, therefore, to study old cultures or to take them seriously. They were on the way out.

The Theory of Cultural Evolution

A second reason for the rejection of non-Western cultures was the emergence of the theory of cultural evolution. If the political solution to the awareness of cultural pluralism created by the age of exploration was colonialism, the intellectual solution was evolutionism. Westerners could ignore other cultures by labeling them "primitive," "animistic," and "uncivilized." In fact, anthropologists until 1915 spoke of "culture," not of "cultures." They saw all cultures as different stages of development of the same thing; some were more advanced and others more primitive.

Christians argued with secular biologists over biological evolution, but cultural evolution was another matter. While biological evolution challenged the fundamental Christian tenet of the uniqueness and divine nature of human beings, cultural evolution was simply another updating (along with Marxism) of the Christian medieval paradigm that sought meaning in a universal history of humankind. Both sought meaning in diachronic (historical) rather than synchronic (structural) paradigms. Both saw history as directional—with an origin, a progression or regression, and a culmination of an ideal state whether through redemption or development. There was argument over the causes of historical progression, but not over the fact that history was going somewhere.

Given this historical paradigm, noncontextualization made sense. Why contextualize the gospel in other cultures when they are in the process of dying out? It is only a matter of time before all people are civilized. What is important, therefore, is to bring the gospel along with civilization.

The Triumph of Science

A third factor leading to the rejection of other cultures was the triumph of science. When William Carey went to India, he was much impressed by its cultural sophistication. Certainly in the fifteenth to eighteenth centuries there was nothing in Europe comparable to the sophistication and technological advancement of the Mogul empire.

The rise of science changed all this. By the end of the nineteenth century, Western technology had conquered the world, and science had made giant strides in conquering nature. Faith in the final triumph of science was widespread.

Underlying this optimism was a positivist (or, to use Ian Barbour's term, "naïve realist") epistemology (cf. Hiebert 1985a and 1985b). This held that a careful examination of experience can lead us to the discovery of the "laws of nature," which upon further examination can be proved to be "true." Scientific knowledge was seen as objective (uncontaminated by the subjectivity of the scientist), cumulative, and true in an ultimate sense. In contrast to this, the knowledge of other cultures was thought to be subjective, piecemeal, and false.

The same epistemological foundations were widespread among many conservative Christians, including most missionaries. Only here, theology replaced science, and revelation replaced experience. Carefully crafted, theology could be totally objective and absolutely true. In light of this, other religions were seen as highly subjective and totally false. Consequently, Christians did not need to take other religions seriously, just as scientists refused to take other belief systems about nature seriously. The task of the missionary was to transmit his or her theology into new cultures unchanged.

Intellectual Consequences of "Noncontextualization"

Colonialism demonstrated the superiority of Western civilization, evolutionism legitimized this in terms of history, and science and Christianity provided the intellectual foundations on which the whole was built. It is not surprising, therefore, that the period from 1800 to 1950 was anticontextual in its approach.

This stance was essentially monocultural and monoreligious. Truth was seen as supracultural. Everything had to be seen from the perspective of Western civilization and Christianity, which had shown themselves to be technologically, historically, and intellectually superior to other cultures;

and so those cultures could be discounted as "uncivilized." The missionary's culture was "good," "advanced," and "normative." Other cultures were "bad," "backward," and "distorted." Christianity was true, other religions were false.

In missions this had two consequences. First, Christianity was perceived in other cultures as a foreign religion identified with Western culture. Christian converts were expected to adopt Western ways. This cultural foreignness was a great barrier in the spread of the gospel.

The second consequence was more subtle. Old beliefs and customs did not die out. Because they were not consciously dealt with, they went underground. Young converts knew they dare not tell the missionary about their old ways lest they incur his or her anger. So these ways became part of the new Christians' hidden culture. Public marriage ceremonies were held in the church, and then the people returned to their homes to celebrate the wedding in private. Amulets were hidden under shirts, and Christians did not admit to Christian doctors that they were also going to the village shaman. In India caste differences were denied in public, although Christians privately continued to marry their children along caste lines.

In the long run, this uneasy coexistence of public Christianity and private "paganism" has led to syncretism. Non-Christian beliefs and practices have infiltrated the church from below. In India caste is becoming public in the church and destroying it with political strife and lawsuits. In Latin America, spiritism taught by nannies to upper-class children is becoming public and respectable in Kardicism and Umbanda.

From a Christian point of view this monocultural point of view has its good sides. First, it affirmed the oneness of humanity and of human history. Second, it took history and culture change seriously. Third, it affirmed absolutes and universals, both in human cultures and in the gospel. It was concerned with preserving the uniqueness of the gospel and avoiding the syncretism that might result from the incorporation of non-Christian beliefs and practices in the church.

But this view also had its bad sides. It was reductionist and acultural—it did not take other cultures and religions seriously. It was ethnocentric— it judged other cultures and religions by its own standards and found them wanting, while assuming that its own ways were right. And in the end it hindered the missionary task. The foreignness of the gospel was a barrier to evangelism, and syncretism was not prevented. Far too often the missionaries ended as policemen enforcing what they believed to be Christian practices on the people.

The Case for Contextualization

The picture began to change by the end of the nineteenth century. Colonial rule was expanding, but already the seeds of its destruction had been planted.

These were to bear fruit in the recognition that other cultures had to be understood and appreciated in terms of their own worldviews, and in a revolution that would call into question the nature and supremacy of science itself.

Postcolonialism

By 1900 three important forces were at work that would bring about the destruction of colonialism and its intellectual foundations. The first of these was the growing cry against colonialism voiced in the West. As Conrad Reining points out (1970), by 1833 the Defense of the Natives League had been formed to oppose colonial oppression. This was a loose coalition of humanists of various stripes, of evangelical Christians led by Wilberforce, and of other fruits of the Wesleyan revivals. Shortly thereafter Henry Venn and Rufus Anderson articulated in the "three-self" formula the need for churches to be organizationally independent. Discussions about the contextualization of the gospel message in local cultural forms began soon afterward. Many missions continued to exercise authority, to use translated hymns, and to impose Western forms of church polity, but some encouraged the autonomy of young churches, the use of local music, and the adoption of indigenous forms of church organization. It took, however, more than 100 years before the fourth self—self-theologizing—was raised.

The second force undermining colonialism was the very success of the colonial endeavor. In India the aim of colonialism was to bring "civilization" to the land. It is not surprising, then, that by the twentieth century there was a growing number of highly educated Indian leaders with a nationalist vision. By 1930 they had organized into an effective movement for independence. Culturally they bought into the ideas of the benevolent nation-state based on democratic principles, the British understanding of law, the modern science, health, and education. But socially they wanted the rights that British law affirmed to be enforced by Indians, not foreigners. It is not surprising, therefore, that the first area in which the Indian churches sought autonomy was self-rule.

Ironically, the third force weakening Western dominance was the introduction of "indirect rule." In India the British totally replaced the existing governmental structures from the village level to the national government. The expense of this, however, was prohibitive. Consequently, when they expanded their empire in Africa, they needed a less costly way of administering the colonies. The answer was indirect rule, in which British administrators provided the overarching government under which indigenous tribal political structures continued to function in tribal matters. But indirect rule required that British administrators know something about the political, economic, and social structures of the people they ruled. Consequently, early anthropological research in Africa, often funded by the government, focused on indigenous forms of social organization.

Phenomenology, Structural Functionalism, Linguistics, and New Anthropology

The combination of British structural functionalism, with its emphasis on the social organization of tribes, and of the American interest in languages and cultures as cognitive maps led to the school of thought known as ethno-science, or new anthropology. This theory, like those from which it was derived, emphasized the differences between cultures and the ways in which they see reality. Each culture was seen as an autonomous paradigm with a worldview of its own. In the end, all three schools of thought were forced to acknowledge the cultural relativism that was the logical outcome of their theories. Obviously, if we take all cultures seriously and emphasize their differences, no one of them can be used to judge the others. Where, then, are moral and cultural absolutes?

Postmodern Science

Not only was belief in Western cultural superiority called into question, but the certainty and absolute nature of science itself was under attack. By the mid-twentieth century, the charge was led by the social scientists who began to apply their theories to analyzing science itself. Psychologists began to examine the subjective nature of all human knowledge; sociologists showed that science was a community affair, influenced by normal social dynamics; anthropologists placed science into its larger cultural and worldview context; and historians of science showed that our textbook understanding of the nature of science was misplaced. Michael Polanyi's writings and T. S. Kuhn's *The Structure of Scientific Revolutions* (1962) drew these strands together in their theory that science was not a lineal, cumulative progression of objective knowledge, but a series of subjective, competing paradigms. Old positivist science had received a mortal blow. But where would postpositivist science find its new epistemological foundations?

For phenomenologists, including many psychologists, sociologists, and anthropologists, and for Kuhn himself, the answer was "instrumentalism." Since we could no longer show that one theory or paradigm or culture was better than another, we could no longer speak of absolutes or truth. At best, we could appeal to pragmatism. Any paradigm was adequate so long as it solved the problems humans faced.

Implications for Contextualization

In such an intellectual milieu, it is not surprising that missionaries and missiologists placed a great deal of emphasis on contextualization, not only of the church in local social structures, but also of the gospel and theology in local cultural forms.

First, on the positive side, this approach avoided the foreignness of a gospel dressed in Western clothes that had characterized the era of noncontextualization. The gospel message had to be communicated in ways the people understood. It avoided the ethnocentrism of a monocultural approach by taking cultural differences seriously, and by affirming the good in all cultures. And it affirmed the right of Christians in every country not only to be institutionally but also cognitively free from Western domination. The right of every church to develop its own theology began to be recognized.

Embracing an uncritical contextualization, however, had its problems. Obviously the denial of absolutes and of "truth" itself runs counter to the core Christian claims about the truth of the gospel and the uniqueness of Christ. Moreover, if the gospel is contextualized, what are the checks against biblical and theological distortion? Where are the absolutes?

Second, as Mary Douglas points out (1970), the separation between form and meaning implicit in these theories blinds us to the nature of most tribal and peasant societies in which form and meaning are inextricably linked. For example, names and shadows are tied to a person's identity, and religious rites are performances, not simply the communication of messages.

A third problem has to do with the emphasis that contextualization places on the accurate communication of meaning, often to the point of ignoring the emotive and volitional dimensions of the gospel. We are in danger of reducing the gospel to a set of disembodied beliefs that can be individually appropriated, forgetting that it has to do with discipleship, with the church as the body of Christ, and with the kingdom of God on earth. Here Charles Kraft's call (1979) for a "dynamic-equivalent" response to the gospel message is a healthy reminder that in the Bible "to believe" is not simply to give mental assent to something; it is to act upon it in life.

A fourth area of concern is the ahistorical nature of most discussions on contextualization. Contemporary cultural contexts are taken seriously, but historical contexts are largely ignored. In each culture Christians face new questions for which they must find biblical answers. But in many things, particularly in developing their biblical and systematic theologies (and all Christians develop these implicitly or explicitly as diachronic and synchronic paradigms of Christian truth), they can learn much from church history. Exegesis and hermeneutics are not the rights of individuals but of the church as an exegetical and hermeneutical community. And that community includes not only the saints within our cultural context, and even the saints outside our culture, but also the saints down through history. To become a Christian is to become a part of a new history, and that history must be learned.

A fifth area of concern is that uncritical contexualization, at least in its more extreme forms, provides us with no means for working toward the unity of churches in different cultures. Instrumentalism is built on the belief that different cultures and paradigms are incommensurable—there is no basis for mutual understanding. Each can be understood only in its own terms. But if this is so, there can be no real communication between Christians in different cultures, no comparison between their theologies, and no common foundations of faith. At best Christianity is made up of a great many isolated churches. For any one of these to claim that its theology is normative is ethnocentric. There may be some common ground in our common human experiences, but that is limited and certainly not enough to provide the basis for developing a common theology. The best we can do, then, is to affirm pluralism and to forget unity.

Sixth, uncritical contextualization has a weak view of sin. It tends to affirm human social organizations and cultures as essentially good. Sin is confined largely to personal evil. But social systems and cultures are human creations and are marked by sin. This is clear in Scriptures in which more than 75 percent of the time terms such as *archē* and *archōn* (organizational power), *exousia* (authority), *dynamis* (power), and *thronos* (thrones) refer to human institutions (Wink 1984). There is a need, therefore, to take a stand against corporate evil as well as individual sin.

Finally, a call for contextualization without an equal call for preserving the gospel without compromise opens the door to syncretism. William Willimon points out (1986: 26): "[T]he persistent problem is not how to keep the church from withdrawing from the world but how to keep the world from subverting the church. In each age the church succumbs to that Constantinian notion that we can get a handle on the way the world is run." There is an offense in the foreignness of the culture we bring along with the gospel, which must be eliminated. But there is the offense of the gospel itself, which we dare not weaken. The gospel must be contextualized, but it also must remain prophetic—standing in judgment on what is evil in all cultures as well as in all persons.

Critical Contextualization

Where do we go from here? We cannot go back to noncontextualization with its ethnocentrism and cultural foreignness. Nor can we stay in more extreme forms of contextualization with their relativism and syncretism.

Theoretical Complementarity
In anthropology the move is away from relativism and purely emic approaches to complementary theories and metacultural grids. Complementarity is rooted in a critical realist epistemology. In this, human knowledge is seen not as a photograph of reality but, rather, as a map or blueprint that gives us real but partial understandings of reality (Coulson 1955). Just as we need several blueprints to get a mental picture of what a house is like, so we need several complementary theories to show us the nature of reality. In anthropology there is a growing number of scholars who use more than one theory or paradigm, depending upon the questions being asked and the

reality being examined. For example, emic and etic models are seen as complementing each other.

There appears, also, to be a growing affirmation that anthropology can provide us with metacultural grids by which we can compare cultures and translate between them. Certainly anthropology has its roots in Western culture, and it is deeply molded by Western presuppositions. But in its analysis of, and dialogue with, other cultures it has begun to free itself of some of its theoretical ethnocentrism.

Beyond Postmodern Science

As Huston Smith point out (1982), we are moving beyond postmodern science and its instrumentalism and relativism. In his chapter on "The Death and Rebirth of Metaphysics" Smith argues that a "comprehensive vision, an overview of some sort, remains a human requirement; reflective creatures cannot retain the sense of direction life requires without it" (1982: 16). The epistemological foundation now emerging is critical realism (Barbour 1974; Hiebert 1985a) that affirms both the objective and the subjective nature of knowledge. We see through a glass darkly, but we do see.

In critical realism, theories are limited in the information they convey, but that information may be shown to be true by means of reality testing. In other words, theories are not totally subjective, relative, and arbitrary. Moreover, theories, like maps, may be complementary. Consequently, contradictions between them must be taken seriously. Finally, in critical realism, theories and paradigms are not incommensurable. As Larry Laudin (1977) and D. R. Hofstadter (1980) point out, metatheoretical models can be developed to compare them and to translate meaning from one to the other.

Critical Contextualization

What does all this have to say to the question of contextualization? Specifically, what does one do with traditional cultural beliefs and practices? Here I am indebted to Jacob Loewen (1975) and the work of John Geertz, who developed a method of contextualization among the Wanana of Panama that is applicable in other cultural contexts.

Exegesis of the Culture

The first step in critical contextualization is to study the local culture phenomenologically. Here the local church leaders and the missionary lead the congregation in *uncritically* gathering and analyzing the traditional beliefs and customs associated with some question at hand. For example, in asking how Christians should bury their dead, the people begin by analyzing their traditional rites: first by describing each song, dance, recitation, and rite that makes up their old ceremony; and then by discussing its meaning and function within the overall ritual. The purpose here is to understand the old ways, not to judge them. If at this point the missionary shows any criticism of the customary beliefs and practices, the people will not talk about them for fear of being condemned. We shall only drive the old ways underground.

Exegesis of the Scripture and the Hermeneutical Bridge

In the second step, the pastor or missionary leads the church in a study of the Scriptures related to the question at hand. In the example we are considering, the leader uses the occasion to teach the Christian beliefs about death and resurrection. Here the pastor or missionary plays a major role, for this is the area of his or her expertise.

The leader must also have a metacultural framework that enables him or her to translate the biblical message into the cognitive, affective, and evaluative dimensions of another culture. This step is crucial, for if the people do not clearly grasp the biblical message as originally intended, they will have a distorted view of the gospel. This is where the pastor or missionary, along with theology, anthropology, and linguistics, has the most to offer in an understanding of biblical truth and in making it known in other cultures. While the people must be involved in the study of Scripture so that they grow in their own abilities to discern truth, the leader must have the metacultural grids that enable him or her to move between cultures. Without this, biblical meanings will often be forced to fit the local cultural categories. The result is a distortion of the message.

Critical response

The third step is for the people corporately to evaluate critically their own past customs in the light of their new biblical understandings, and to make decisions regarding their response to their new-found truths. The gospel is not simply information to be communicated. It is a message to which people must respond. Moreover, it is not enough that the leaders be convinced about changes that may be needed. Leaders may share their personal convictions and point out the consequences of various decisions, but they must allow the people to make the final decision in evaluating their past customs. If the leaders make the decisions, they must enforce these decisions. In the end, the people themselves will enforce decisions arrived at corporately, and there will be little likelihood that the customs they reject will go underground.

To involve the people in evaluating their own culture in light of new truth draws upon their strength. They know their old culture better than the missionary, and are in a better position to critique it, once they have biblical instruction. Moreover, to involve them is to help them to grow spiritually by teaching them discernment and by helping them to learn to apply scriptural teachings to their own lives. It also puts into practice the priesthood of believers within a hermeneutical community.

A congregation may respond to old beliefs and practices in several ways.

Many past beliefs and practices they will keep, for these are not unbiblical. Western Christians, for example, see no problem in eating hamburgers, singing secular songs such as "Home on the Range," wearing business suits, or driving cars. In many areas of their lives, Christians are no different from their non-Christian neighbors. In keeping these practices they reaffirm their own cultural identity and heritage.

Other customs will be explicitly rejected by the congregation as unbecoming for Christians. The reasons for such rejection may not be apparent to those outside who often see little difference between the songs and rites the people reject and those they retain. But the people know the deep, hidden meanings and associations of their old customs. On the other hand, at some points the missionary may need to raise questions that the people have overlooked, for they may fail to see clearly their own cultural assumptions.

Sometimes the people will choose to modify old practices by giving them explicit Christian meanings. For example, Charles Wesley used the melodies of popular bar songs, but gave them Christian words. Similarly, the early Christians used the style of worship found in Jewish synagogues, and modified it to fit their beliefs.

At points the Christians may substitute symbols and rites borrowed from another culture for those in their own that they reject. For example, the people may choose to adopt elements of the funeral practices of the missionary rather than to retain their own. Such functional substitutes are generally effective, for they minimize the cultural dislocation created by simply removing an old custom.

Sometimes the church may adopt rites drawn from its Christian heritage. In becoming Christians they enter into a second new history. The addition of such rituals as baptism and the Lord's Supper not only provides converts with ways to express their new faith, but also symbolizes their ties to the historical and international church.

Finally, the people may create new symbols and rituals to communicate Christian beliefs in forms that are indigenous to their own culture.

New Contextualized Practices

Having led the people to analyze their old customs in the light of biblical teaching, the pastor or missionary must help them to arrange the practices they have chosen into a new ritual that expresses the Christian meaning of the event. Such a ritual will be Christian, for it explicitly seeks to express biblical teaching. It will also be contextual, for the church has created it, using forms the people understand within their own culture.

Checks Against Syncretism

What checks do we have to assure us that critical contextualization will not lead us astray? We must recognize that contextualization itself is an ongoing process. On the one hand, the world in which people live is constantly changing, raising new questions that need to be addressed. On the other, our understandings of the gospel and its application to our lives is partial. Through continued study and spiritual growth, we should, however, come to a greater understanding of the truth.

First, critical contextualization takes the Bible seriously as the rule of faith and life. Contextualized practices, like contextualized theologies, must be biblically based. This may seem obvious, but we must constantly remind ourselves that the standards against which all practices are measured is biblical revelation.

Second, this approach recognizes the work of the Holy Spirit in the lives of all believers open to God's leading.

Third, the church is acting as a hermeneutical community (cf. Kraus 1979). The priesthood of believers is not a license for theological lone-rangerism. We need each other to see our sins, for we more readily see the sins of others than our own. Similarly, we see the ways others misinterpret Scriptures before we see our own misinterpretations. Along the same line, we need Christians from other cultures, for they often see how our cultural biases have distorted our interpretations of the Scriptures. This corporate nature of the church as a community of interpretation extends not only to the church in every culture, but also to the church in all ages. To say that exegesis and hermeneutics are corporate processes does not (as some sociologists of knowledge, such as Karl Mannheim and Richter, suggest) reduce them to social determinism.

Fourth, there is a growing discussion among evangelical theologians from different cultures and, one hopes, a growing consensus on essential theological points. Just as one can often see the sins of others better than they do themselves, so also theologians can often detect the cultural biases of theologians from other cultures better than the latter do themselves. Out of the exercise of the priesthood of believers within an international hermeneutical community should come a growing understanding, if not agreement, on key theological issues that can help us test the contextualization of cultural practices as well as theologies.

Critical contextualization does not operate from a monocultural perspective. Nor is it premised upon the pluralism of incommensurable cultures. It seeks to find metacultural and metatheological frameworks that enable people in one culture to understand messages and ritual practices from another culture with a minimum of distortion. It is based on a critical realist epistemology that sees all human knowledge as a combination of objective and subjective elements, and as partial but increasingly closer approximations of truth. It takes both historical and cultural contexts seriously. And it sees the relationship between form and meaning in symbols such as words and rituals, ranging all the way from an equation of the two to simply arbitrary associations between them. Finally, it sees contextualization as an ongoing process in which the church must constantly engage itself, a process that can lead us to a better understanding of what the Lordship of Christ and the kingdom of God on earth are about.

Works Cited

Barbour, Ian G.
1974 *Myths, Models and Paradigms*. New York: Harper & Row.

Berger, Peter L.
1970 *The Sacred Canopy*. Garden City, N.Y.: Doubleday.
1974 *Pyramids of Sacrifice: Political Ethics and Social Change*. New York: Basic Books.

Berger, Peter L., and T. Luckmann.
1966 *The Social Construction of Reality*. Garden City, N.Y.: Doubleday.

Bevans, Stephen.
1985 "Models of Contextual Theology." *Missiology* 13:185-202.

Bidney, David.
1967 *Theoretical Anthropology*. 2nd edn. New York: Schocken Books.

Butterfield, H.
1949 *The Origins of Modern Science*. London: Bell & Sons.

Coulson, C. A.
1955 *Science and Christian Belief*. London: Fontana Books.

Douglas, Mary.
1970 *Natural Symbols*. New York: Random House.

Gitari, David.
1982 "The Claims of Jesus in the African Context." *International Review of Mission* 71:12-19.

Haleblian, Krikor.
1983 "The Problem of Contextualization." *Missiology* 11:95-111.

Hiebert, Paul G.
1985a "Epistemological Foundations for Science and Theology." *TSF Bulletin*. March-April, pp. 5-10.
1985b "The Missiological Implications of an Epistemological Shift." *TSF Bulletin*, May-June, pp. 12-18.

Hofstadter, D. R.
1980 *Godel, Escher, Bach*. New York: Vintage Books.

Kraft, Charles.
1979 *Christianity in Culture*. Maryknoll, N.Y.: Orbis Books.

Kraus, C. Norman.
1979 *The Authentic Witness*. Grand Rapids, Mich.: Wm. B. Eerdmans.

Kuhn, T. S.
1962   *The Structure of Scientific Revolution.* Chicago: Univ. of Chicago Press.

Laudin, Larry.
1977   *Progress and Its Problems.* Berkeley: Univ. of California Press.

Lind, Millard C.
1982   "Refocusing Theological Education to Mission: The Old Testament and Contextualization." *Missiology,* 10:141-60.

Loewen, Jacob A.
1975   *Culture and Human Values.* Pasadena, Calif.: William Carey Library.

Nida, E. A., and W. D. Reyburn.
1981   *Meaning across Cultures.* Maryknoll, N.Y.: Orbis Books.

Northrop, F. S. C.
1952   *The Taming of the Nations.* New York: Macmillan.

Pobee, John.
1978   "The Church in West Africa," in Charles Taber, ed., *The Church in Africa.* Pasadena, Calif.: William Carey Library.

Raven, C. E.
1953   *Science and Religion.* Cambridge, England: Cambridge Univ. Press.

Reining, Conrad.
1970   "A Lost Period of Applied Anthropology," in J. A. Clifton, ed., *Applied Anthropology.* Boston: Houghton Mifflin.

Schilling, Harold K.
1973   *The New Consciousness in Science and Religion.* London: SCM Press.

Simon, Francis.
1951   *The Neglect of Science.* Oxford: Basil Blackwell.

Smith, Huston.
1982   *Beyond the Post-Modern Mind.* New York: Crossroad Publishing Co.

Whitehead, Alfred North.
1926   *Science and the Modern World.* Cambridge, England: Cambridge Univ. Press.

Willimon, William.
1986   "A Crisis of Identity." *Sojourners* 15 (May): 24-28.

Wink, Walter.
1984   *Naming the Powers.* Philadelphia: Fortress Press.

Yamamori, T., and C. R. Taber (eds.).
1975   *Christopaganism or Indigenous Christianity?* Pasadena, Calif.: William Carey Library.

PRACTICAL THEOLOGY: HOMILETICS

Haddon W. Robinson, area editor

HOMILETICS

HADDON W. ROBINSON
President, Denver Seminary

Introduction

Seminary graduates who remember homiletics as three points and a poem ought to see it now. Topical preaching, deductive sermons, and three point outlines are out. Storytelling, inductive sermons, and sermon plots are now in vogue.

Most new volumes on preaching attack the old homiletic as irrelevant and increasingly out of sync with modern audiences. That explains part of the appeal of the new homiletic. In many congregations sermons substitute for Sominex tablets on Sunday morning, and preachers look for novel approaches that will keep them from talking in other people's sleep. Sometimes, without considering the theological implications of new methodologies, ministers change sermon forms as often as the networks change prime time programs.

More charitably, communication theories have shaped a new homiletic that appreciates the dynamic inter-relatedness of the various parts of the sermon. Sermons, at their best, should not be hammered together like a doghouse, but instead must possess the movement and flow of a well-designed building, each part complementing the others.

Communication experts bring precision and refinement to what skilled preachers have done intuitively. But they also challenge old ways of thinking about preaching. As a communicator who has a message from the Bible to deliver, the preacher must ask, "What should be done to communicate this truth in terms and forms my audience understands?" In the new homiletic, this sermon no longer takes a prescribed form derived from Greco-Roman rhetoric. Instead the message determines the sermon's shape much like the development of lively conversation.

Thomas Long reflects human communication theory in his article "Pawn to King Four: Sermon Introductions and Communication Design." His article's importance concerns his approach. He asks the question, "What is the communicative purpose of the introduction?"—a different question than those usually raised about introductions in traditional homiletics texts.

Biblical scholars, with their emphasis on genre, structure, and literary and linguistic analysis of the text, have also affected every area of homiletics—exegesis, hermeneutics, language, form, and even delivery. To preach the Scriptures properly, they argue, we must not only reflect the concepts of a passage, but also its form. Back in 1964, Amos Wilder, in his important but little noticed work *The Language of the Gospel* (New York: Harper & Row), warned against drawing sharp distinctions between the message and its literary form. Like a suit and its cloth, the two cannot be easily separated. "General principles of rhetoric and public address," he argued, "may be helpful in mastering the art of oral communication, but they are subservient to the basic kind of rhetoric used in the Bible. Because the biblical rhetoric is wedded in form to its content, the fabric or texture of the sermon, as well as its content, will be determined by its biblical roots" (p. 10). Wilder, by implication, raised a hard question. Does a sermon have its own prescribed form, or is a sermon defined only by its content and its purpose? In the new homiletic both the form and the content of the passage shape the sermon. Formerly preachers turned to the Scriptures as a source of objective propositions, but because of a rigid idea of the shape sermons were to take, ignored most of the metaphors and poetic images. They used biblical narratives and stories merely as illustrations for abstract concepts.

Modern approaches to preaching, while not rejecting the understandings of classical rhetoric, are not bound by it. In freeing the sermon from its rigid schema, they have actually brought exposition and innovation together. The biblical witness presented through parables, poems, hymns, apocalyptic visions, narratives, and letters now influences the sermon not only in its message, but in its development.

One of the most significant volumes written this year, David Buttrick's *Homiletic: Moves and Structures*, rejects the rationalistic approach to sermon construction. In his magnum opus, Buttrick, professor of homiletics and worship at Vanderbilt Divinity School, discards the make-up of a sermon as "points" and prefers to speak of "moves" since "points" point at concepts abstract and removed from life. Language, he argues, is best described by motion.

Buttrick devotes several chapters to words and how they work, and to the importance of metaphor and image not only for interpreting the Bible, but for presenting the sermon. In Buttrick's hands, working out a sermon from the biblical material is closer to plotting a play than outlining a lecture. *Homiletic*, though technical and theoretical, functions as a helpful entrée for the thoughtful pastor into new spheres of scholarship and thought that can influence preaching.

For ministers interested in the different options that have emerged for preaching, Richard Eslinger offers an introduction to five major models in *A New Hearing: Living Options in Homiletic Method* (Nashville: Abingdon Press). His five: Charles Rice and the storytelling method; Henry Mitchell and black narrative preaching; Eugene Lowry and the narrative/inductive method; Fred Craddock and the inductive method; and David Buttrick's phenomenological method. With each option, Eslinger offers both a description and a critique of the method plus a sermon illustrating the method at work. All five of these homileticians place great emphasis on metaphor, image, and storytelling.

The reading of sermons in which stories tell the Story sometimes gives the uneasy impression that modern preaching explores experience without interpreting it. Nonetheless, we preach in a day when Garrison Keillor put Lake Wobegon on the map of our minds, and we represent Jesus who told corking good stories to storm the defenses of his listeners. Preachers true to life and to the Bible, therefore, will not ignore storytelling. Harold Freeman, professor of preaching at Southwestern Baptist Theological Seminary, in his book *Variety in Biblical Preaching* (Waco: Word), offers specific advice on how to bring innovation to expository preaching. Particularly helpful is his section on narrative literature and the narrative sermon. The sermon as story even gets a tip of the hat in a more traditional volume, *The Preacher and His Preaching* (Phillipsburg, New Jersey: Presbyterian and Reformed Publishing House), a text for the preacher in the Reformed tradition, edited by Samuel T. Logan, Jr. Jay Adams, in his contribution, underlines the importance of storytelling and appealing to the senses of the listener, and then shows how to do it.

Swearing allegience to the Bible does not do away with creativity, but it demands that imagination be tied to the text in the same way that interpretation must relate to exegesis. That is the problem the new homiletic creates and tries to solve.

About the Area Editor

Haddon W. Robinson (Th.M., Dallas Theological Seminary; M.A., Southern Methodist University; Ph.D., University of Illinois) has been president of Denver Seminary since 1979. He was ordained in 1955 by the Conservative Baptist Association. He was professor of homiletics at Dallas Theological Seminary from 1970-79. He is co-editor (with Duane Litfin) of *Recent Homiletical Thought* (1983), and author of *Biblical Preaching* (1980).

PAWN TO KING FOUR:
SERMON INTRODUCTIONS AND
COMMUNICATIONAL DESIGN

THOMAS G. LONG
Associate Professor of Preaching and Worship
Princeton Theological Seminary

Article from *Reformed Review*

One of the many recent advances in contemporary homiletical theory has involved the acknowledgement of the inter-relatedness of the various aspects of sermon development. It is no longer thought sufficient to divide the process of sermon construction into separate "stages," such as "exegesis," "theological analysis," "outlining," "illustrating the sermon," "delivery," and so on. We discuss these aspects, of course, but only in the full awareness that, when all is said and done, they are not, in fact, discrete, but rather interpenetrating realities, and that each has much to do with all of the others.

How the preacher encounters and understands the biblical text, at one end of the process, for example, already bears (or should bear) upon delivery at the other end. For instance, a biblical text that achieves its impact through irony or poetic imagery calls for something more than a flat-footed, schoolmaster's delivery. A text that embraces a confident and ringing affirmation of the gospel calls the preacher, not to deliver a book report on the text, but rather to embody the text's assurance (or at least an involved response to the text's boldness) in his sermon. In one sense there is nothing new about all this. Good preachers have known for a long time that tugging at any single thread in the sermonic fabric causes the whole cloth to gather. What is new is that the concept of the inter-relatedness of the elements in the process of sermon development has moved from intuitive practice to the level of theory. That biblical scholars themselves are now doing such things as looking for "literary patterns" and "rhetorical cues" in texts only brings confirmation, theoretical precision, and methodological refinement to what preachers have long been doing by the seat of their pants and the hems of their skirts.

Sermon Unity: A New Perspective

This grasp of the inter-relatedness of the various portions of the process of sermon development has also transferred to the sermon itself. Sermons are now viewed as dynamic organisms, in which each part affects—and is affected by—all the others. This makes it inadequate to think, for example, of "finding an illustration to plug into a sermon," as if sermons were like chandeliers into which pieces, like bulbs, could be inserted and replaced at will. A change in one part of a sermon affects the whole.

This view of sermonic unity is not new, either. Sermons have never been seen, except in some exceedingly scholastic homiletics texts, as consisting of a set of ideas or units strung together, sharing a common theme, but otherwise disconnected. There has always been at least some awareness that the various facets of the sermon work together in some common act of communication. There is fairly good evidence that even the synogogue sermons of the first century, which almost surely were the models for early Christian preaching, were constructed according to a rather sophisticated theme that involved the interlacing of the Torah and Prophetic readings toward the goal of demonstrating what the one had to say about the other. This afforded no little opportunity for the best of the rabbinnical orators to show off, flaunting their creative skills and dazzling the hearers with the many layers at which the law and the prophets could be seen to speak to each other.

What is new in recent homiletics is the degree of theoretical precision that is beginning to be brought to bear upon the task of understanding how one portion of the sermon serves, and is served by, the others. Sermons are now seen to be "systems of communication," a ghastly phrase to be sure, but a helpful analytical abstraction nonetheless. Nowadays, when a teacher of preaching tells a student that a certain kind of "illustration" is needed at such and such a point in the sermon, this advice does not have to be made on the basis of some mechanical pattern of sermon design (e.g., "each 'point' should have an illustration") or on some pseudo-psychological understanding of communication (e.g., "the congregation needs a 'break' between points"). It can be made out of a larger vision of the communicational work of the whole sermon and how it is that each aspect of the sermon picks up a piece of that total task.

Introductions: A Test Case

One place we can see the impact of this revisioning of the sermon is in the way contemporary homileticians discuss the traditional topic of sermon structure, or "outlines." Some of them find the word "outline" to be hope-lessly mired in pedantic and deductive conceptions and refuse to use it at all, preferring a more fluid notion, like "plot" or "shape." Even when the term "outline" is retained, though, it is clear that the focus of the discussion has changed. The older preaching texts tended to discuss outlining as the way the *content* of the sermon was arranged. The newer texts make the shift from content to *communication*. A sermon outline, plot, shape, or whatever term is used, is not merely a description of the way the sermon's content is arrayed. It is a description of the process of communication between preacher and hearers. Sermons are designed in specific patterns not merely because the content assumes a certain form (e.g., "There are four claims this text makes about faith . . ."), but because of the ways people listen. The main question is not, "How can this material be divided?," but rather, "How can people best hear this material?"

An examination of the role of sermon beginnings, or "introductions," can serve as a revealing test case of this newer integrative approach to preaching theory. An "introduction" is not simply the way the content of the sermon begins. It is also the way in which a certain phase of the communication between preacher and hearer begins. We need, then, to ask about the role beginnings play in the whole process of sermon communication.

Sermon Introduction In Recent Homiletics

When George Buttrick said that preachers should prepare a sermon introduction that is "brief, interesting, and raises the issue,"[1] he said everything—and nothing. Properly exegeted, Buttrick's rule perhaps says all that can or should be said on the subject. The problem, however, is that considerable exegesis is needed to appreciate the value of the rule, and Buttrick's dictum has often been employed in a clumsy manner. If Buttrick is merely giving a three-fold check list, then the first item ("brevity") is misidentified, the second ("interesting") is obvious, and the third ("raises the issue") is biased toward an overly cognitive approach to preaching. Good sermon introductions usually *are* brief, but this is not because brevity is a self-contained virtue. Introductions are *doing* something in and for the whole sermon that can, in most cases, be done best when they are brief, but it is this communicational action which must be named, not the by-product of brevity. If being "uninteresting" is the alternative, then introductions surely ought to be "interesting," but so should "middles" and "conclusions." What needs to be specified is the particular kind of interest that introductions have as their task to arouse. To say that introductions should "raise the issue" of the sermon comes closer to the kind of specificity needed, as long as "the issue" is not misconstrued to read "state the thesis" or some similar language of ideational abstraction.

In his recent book *Fundamentals of Preaching*, John Killinger borrows Buttrick's formula (translated as "brief, arresting, and conductive") and adds a virtue to the list: memorable.[2] This is an interesting addition, mainly because Killinger may be on to more than he is aware. What Killinger really wants to say, I think, is not that sermon *introductions* ought to be memorable, but that *sermons* themselves ought to be memorable and that introductions can contribute to that characteristic. In other words, introductions are evaluated on the basis of their contributions to the sermon as a whole, rather than in isolation from the other aspects of the sermon.

Grady Davis, whose *Design for Preaching* served as a standard homiletics textbook for many years, also followed Buttrick in regard to introductions, but advanced the discussion by doing so in a far more sophisticated and complex manner than most. Davis conceived of a sermon on the model of a sentence. Each sermon consists of a subject (what the sermon is about) and a predicate (the one main thing which the sermon says about the subject). The predicate is further divided into a series of assertions, two to six claims that develop the subject and form the logical flow, or continuity, of the sermon. Davis elaborates this basic "design" in four ways. First, he identifies three possible functions, or purposes, of a sermon: proclamation, teaching, and therapy. Second, he names five different organic forms, or organizing principles, for sermons: a subject discussed, a thesis supported, a message illumined, a question propounded, and a story told. Third, he specifies four types of sermon continuity, or flow: deductive, inductive, logical, and chronological. Finally, he suggests three tenses, or modes, of preaching: imperative, conditional, and indicative.

Taken seriously, of course, Davis' scheme is an immensely complex model of preaching, and the usefulness of some of his categories justly deserves challenge. It would take more space than we have here to elaborate upon and criticize Davis' schema, and that is not our main concern. The crucial point is that Davis was among the first to discern the organic communicational unity of sermons and to attempt to mold homiletical practice around that theoretical vision. When he gets around to introductions, he remains faithful to his theory, maintaining that "the introduction should be thought of as the first two minutes of a twenty- to twenty-five minute experience by the people of the sermon's thought."[3] In other words, the introduction is the first in a series of communicational moves, each linked to the others, one phase in a comprehensive experience of listening. Davis knows that the introduction is a piece of the sermon fabric not to be considered apart from the whole garment. It sets the stage for the complete sermon and, as such, establishes limits on the style, tone, form, and purpose of the rest of the sermonic communication.[4]

The next real advance in understanding the role and communicative value of sermon introductions comes from human communication science, as brokered into the homiletical field by J. Randall Nichols in his *Building the Word*. Nichols maintains that the purpose of an introduction is

> . . . to establish between preacher and hearers a "contract for communication," a shared agreement that in the message to follow we will be talking about certain things in certain ways, trying to get certain points of understanding or action, and each contributing this or that to the unfolding process.[5]

Now, at first glance, this appears to be a nice restatement of Davis. In the introduction we talk about certain things (the subject) in certain ways (the organic form), to get certain points of understanding (the assertions), and so on. But what sets Nichols' view apart is the crucial distinction he makes between "communication," *per se* and "meta-communication," or communication *about* communication. Nichols is aware, of course, that introductions have communicational value in that they have "some informational relationship to the 'body' of the message," but that is not what concerns him. His interest, and his contribution, is the realization that introductions serve a meta-communicational purpose, that is, they serve as the basis of an agreement between the preacher and the hearers "about how we will handle and what we will make of the message content which is to come." As such, the introduction to the sermon is analogous to the "contract" made between a pastoral counselor and the counselee "to work toward certain goals and in certain ways between care giver and receiver."

What we have in Nichols, then, is a genuine innovation in homiletical theory: a thoroughgoing analysis of sermon introductions done from a communicational vantage point. Nichols has his eye on the listening process, on what happens between the preacher and the hearer. This view of the introduction allows Nichols to dismiss two of Buttrick's time-worn criteria as misplaced categories. "The communication question to ask," claims Nichols, "is 'When has the contract been set?' rather than 'How long should the introduction be?' " So much for brevity. Nichols has gone beneath the superficial quality to discern the communicational dynamic. As for the demand that the introduction be "interesting," Nichols states the following:

> Time after time we have heard that the purpose of an introduction is to "get people's attention." Now really, when was the last time anyone saw a preacher step into the pulpit at sermon time and *not* have everyone's attention. . . . We do not need to 'get it,' but we surely do need to *use* it by establishing a contract for communication.[6]

Nichols acknowledges—and addresses—two potential objections to his view of introductions. First, there is the objection that clearly setting out the contract of the sermon will spoil those sermons built around a discovery process of communication. Revealing everything in the beginning would, in effect, ruin the surprise. This would be a disappointment not only for the preacher, but, more important, for the hearers as well, who relish such experiences. Nichols answers that this objection misses the communication/meta-communication distinction. The introduction can contract with the hearers to join with the preacher in a thinking-through process toward an as-yet-undisclosed point. Thus, the contract is clear while, at the same time, the surprise remains intact.

The second objection addressed by Nichols is an aesthetic one, namely that the business of setting a contract inevitably involves the kind of technical, cards-on-the-table language that could mar a poetic and lyrical sermon. Nichols concedes that this is on occasion true (though not as often as would-be homiletical poets think). He suggests that these rare occasions can be handled by announcements about the nature of the sermon in the bulletin, elsewhere in the service of worship, or as a preface to the sermon itself.

Nichols' main point seems to be that listening to sermons is demanding work and that hearers have the need and right to know what they are in for. The introduction recognizes and respects the work of the listener by stating the nature of the task and inviting the hearer to accept his or her end of the cooperative task of co-creating the communication event of preaching.

A Critique

Nichols' work is clearly the most advanced statement to date on the nature of sermon introductions. A sermon is not primarily a literary product; it is essentially an act of proclamation. Whatever literary and aesthetic merits a sermon may possess, they must be subordinated to the larger concern that the sermon communicate something to those who hear. By introducing communicational concepts into the discussion, Nichols has refashioned the agenda in a helpful way and cleared the homiletical landscape of much clutter. Any further advance in understanding what a sermon introduction should be must begin by considering Nichols' position.

Without taking away from Nichols' contributions, which are significant, I want to raise two objections to his view on the way toward making what I hope will be a constructive proposal regarding the role sermon introductions play in sermons:

1. I will begin by conceding the main point: introductions *do* involve what Nichols calls "meta-communication" in that they signal to the hearer certain cues about the communication event that is to follow. Meta-communication, however, is not a characteristic of introductions alone, but rather occurs throughout the sermon. What conventional homiletics has called "transitions" are often particularly high in meta-communicational content. It is not strictly accurate, then, to suggest that the introduction is *the* place in the sermon where meta-communication occurs. What does happen there might best be termed "introductory meta-communication," which, in a way, sends us back around to our original question: What can be said about the special role of introductions?

2. Nichols recognizes that meta-communication can be "sometimes overt and sometimes implicit," but he clearly pushes toward the more explicit variety, complaining that "we probably err in introductions more on the side of subtlety than overdirection." One is left with the impression that there are two almost discrete *classes* of statements: communicational ones,

which involve certain kinds of information, and meta-communicational ones, which are directions or proposals for how the first class of statements shall be handled. Nichols knows that introductions contain examples of the first class of statements, but these do not attract his interest much. It is the seond class of statements that is really important in an introduction, since a cluster of such statements can serve as the contractual agreement for the communicational tasks of preacher and listener throughout the sermon. This not only deprives us of Nichols' wisdom about what introductions ought to be in terms of communication content, but it also obscures the fact that meta-communication is most often a simultaneous, and not a separate, activity in human communication. I do not need (or want) formal instruction in meta-communication to know that "Dearly Beloved, we are gathered here in the presence of God . . . " is a piece of information that has to be handled differently from "Did ya' hear the one about the sailor and the parrot?" These statements, like most human utterances, contain their own meta-communicational cues.

The point here is not that meta-communication ought to go on; it *does* go on whether we want it to or not. Part of Nichols' argument and contribution is that preachers need to become aware of this process and, to some degree, control it. Agreed, but I would insist that, most of the time, effective meta-communication occurs not by stepping aside and uttering several examples from a special class of meta-communicative statements, but rather by recognizing and regulating the meta-communicational overtones inherent in ordinary communication.

Sermon Introductions: A Proposal

So, what can we say about sermon introductions that would employ the insight of communication theory while at the same time avoiding some of the problems of Nichols' approach? I want to make six observations about sermon introductions. More observations need to be made before this can come close to a complete *theory* of introductions, but perhaps the bare outlines of a theory can already be seen here:

1. If there is anything that should have been made clear by the above discussion it is that it is not appropriate to speak about sermon introductions in isolation from their placement in the overall network of sermonic communication. An introduction gets the conversation going between the preacher and the hearers, and it already anticipates where that conversation will move. The way in which a sermon begins governs, to some degree, how that sermon can develop and how it can end.

2. This means that all homiletical descriptions of "good" introductions that are based upon the identification of self-contained virtues (such as

"brevity" or "memorability") can be dismissed. Introductions cannot be "good" in and of themselves, but only in reference to the effectiveness of their role in the whole sermon.

3. This also means that introductions function as the first "step" in the sermon journey toward a "destination." The term "destination" can be defined in communicational terms as a certain form of psychological awareness that is present in the hearer at the end of the sermon and that the sermon played an important role in creating. It can be further described with reference to the familiar triad, knowing-being-doing. The preacher hopes that at the end of a sermon the hearers will know some things they did not previously know, feel some things they did not previously feel, be ready to act in certain new ways, or some combination of these. There is, in other words, a certain psychic distance to be traveled, and the sermon is a kind of guided journey from "here" to "there." The introduction must, of course, begin "here," but it must also anticipate "there."

4. An introduction begins "here" when it raises, implicitly or explicitly, some issue, problem, question, need, or situation that is recognized and construed to be important by the hearer. This is not to say, a la Fosdick, that introductions are condemned to the presentation of "life situations." Indeed, the introduction may be a description of Assyrian cultic practices, but it must include signals to the hearer about why listening to this material is pertinent and worthwhile and at least some hint about how this material will be valuable to the sermon event as a whole. Listening to a sermon is active, not passive, and part of the activity of listeners involves their continual attempt to answer two questions: Where does this material fit in the overall "logic" of the message, and what does this material have to do with me? Introductions don't have to spell out the answers to those questions, but if they ignore them completely, they do so at great peril.

Introductions are also "here" when they guide the hearer through the first step of the sermon journey in the way in which *these* listeners can take that step. This involves strategy . . . and pastoral sensitivity. To begin a sermon with a detailed background exegesis of a biblical text may make perfectly good sense with one congregation, and yet be communicational suicide with another.

5. Introductions anticipate the "there" of the sermon when they help to shape in the hearer's mind a more or less accurate impression of where the sermon will go. Nichols is also helpful in describing how this works:

> When a message begins, a kind of mental search mission starts in the mind of the hearers. From their vast internal computer of stored experience comes a set of meanings, images, and previous understandings to which the unfamiliar incoming message is referred for translation, so to speak. That is the "story," like the accompaniment roll of a player piano, or a film clip backing up the commentary of the evening television news. As soon as that happens, which as a rule takes something like a billionth of a second,

communication has become essentially a receiver phenomenon. The meaning of the message is not "transmitted," as we sometimes mistakenly say; it is, so to speak, "transgenerated" in the awareness of the hearer, reassembled in the context of his or her own story.[7]

Since hearers listen faster than speakers speak, they are "running ahead," anticipating where the message is going, deciding if, in fact, they wish to go there. The introduction provides clues—both of the communicational and meta-communicational variety—about this journey. Indeed, implicit in each introduction is more of a "covenant" than a contract: a promise made in the context of trust that, when this sermon is done, we will have arrived together in a more or less agreed upon place. I keep saying "more or less" because I want to protect the value of unpredictability and surprise in communication. If the hearer is always able to guess exactly where the preacher is going, then boredom sets in. If the preacher is always arriving at some spot different from that predicted by the hearer, then the preacher is viewed as idiosyncratic and, thus, communicationally untrustworthy. Nobody wants the weekly experience of checking his or her luggage in the sermon introduction to Miami, only to arrive in Denver. Occasionally, it's an adventure; weekly, it's a hassle.

In order to see how this process of listener anticipation works, consider the following sermon introduction:

> The story of Noah and his ark is not something we grown-ups take very seriously. We tend to regard it as a story for children, and we have our children making replicas of the ark in Sunday school. But it is a very strange thing, really, that we should regard this as a children's story (which is to say a fairy tale), because it is a dark and frightening story. Furthermore, it is a story about ourselves and our world—a story that is quite modern.[8]

Now a hearer listening to this sermon introduction is moving ahead of the preacher, guessing where this sermon will be going, deciding whether to accompany the preacher on this particular journey. In this case, the listeners would have every reason to guess that, when this sermon is concluded, the preacher will have helped them to take the Noah story more seriously by a) exposing its "dark and frightening" side and b) connecting it meaningfully to the real issues of their personal and social lives. In fact, in this introduction the preacher has made a "covenant" with the hearers to do just that. If the preacher fails to do those things, then the communicational covenant is broken. If, sermon after sermon, the preacher breaks covenant with the hearers, the implicit and necessary trust between them is damaged.

Is the above introduction a *good* one? The answer must be a tentative "yes." It does begin "here" by naming an issue in the hearers' lives (i.e., their current understanding of the Noah story), and it does anticipate "there" (i.e., by promising to expose a new and important understanding of that story). So far, so good. We cannot yet say, though, that this is an effective introduction, because this assessment must be made in light of the *whole* sermon. Was the covenant fulfilled? Was the inquisitive, exploratory tone set by the introduction maintained throughout the sermon? In short, an introduction is effective only when it plays a consistent and satisfactory role in the total network of the sermon's communication.

6. One thing implied in the above analysis of the example introduction is that introductions have certain "tonal" qualities (what Nichols would call implicit meta-communication) that are important clues for the hearers about the nature of the overall sermon and, in fact, should be consistent with the rest of the sermon. An introduction that raises the theodicy problem in intellectual terms promises a sermon in which preacher and hearer grapple with the issues. To spend the rest of the sermon sloshing around in emotional stories and tearful examples would be, among other infractions, a betrayal of the covenant established in and through the introduction.

It is clear that the understanding of the sermon as an integrated communicational event cannot be confined to a discussion of introductions. It has clear implications for every aspect of the sermon—illustrations, transitions, conclusions, and all the rest. All of the parts of the sermon work together as a system, creating a unified event in the experience of the listeners. Viewed this way, the task of creating the sermon becomes admittedly more complex, more demanding pastorally, and more subject to local and congregational criteria than to "universal" literary canons. But this perspective also rescues the sermon from the arena of written discourse, where it has learned much, but to which it finally does not belong, and brings it home again to the world or oral communication.

Works Cited

Barron, Vance, *Sermons for the Celebration of the Christian Year*, Nashville: Abingdon Press, 1977.

Craddock, Fred B., *As One Without Authority*, Nashville: Abingdon Press, 1978.

Davis, H. Grady, *Designs for Preaching*, Philadelphia: Fortress Press, 1958.

Edwards, O. C., Jr., *Elements of Homiletic*, New York: Pueblo Publishing Company, 1982.

Killinger, John, *Fundamentals of Preaching*, Philadelphia: Fortress Press, 1985.

Lowry, Eugene L., *The Homiletical Plot. The Sermon as Narrative Art*, Atlanta: John Knox Press, 1980.

Nichols, J. Randall, *Building the Word: The Dynamics of Communication and Preaching*, San Francisco: Harper and Row, 1980.

Notes

[1] Buttrick as quoted in O. C. Edwards, Jr., *Elements of Homiletic*, p. 74. Buttrick varied his rule from time to time, occasionally adding a fourth element: appropriateness to the particular sermon (see Grady Davis, *Design for Preaching*, p. 189).

[2] John Killinger, *Fundamentals of Preaching*, p. 83.

[3] H. Grady Davis, *Design for Preaching*, p. 188.

[4] We do not have to look very far to see the impact of Davis' theory on such modern homileticians as Craddock and Lowry, both of whom have built entire theories (whether they knew it or acknowledged it or not) on a single aspect of Davis' design (for Craddock, inductive logic, and for Lowry, narrative continuity). See Fred B. Craddock, *As one Without Authority* and Eugene Lowry, *The Homiletical Plot*.

[5] J. Randall Nichols, *Building the Word*, p. 101.

[6] Nichols, pp. 102-3.

[7] Nichols, pp. 69-70.

[8] Vance Barron, "To Keep Hope Alive," in *Sermons for the Celebration of the Christian Year*, p. 14.

PREACHING BETWEEN THE LINES

RICHARD C. WHITE
Professor of Homiletics
Lexington Theological Seminary

Article from *The Christian Ministry*

You've heard it as often as I have. Whenever the Gospel lesson is "Suffer the little children to come unto me, and forbid them not" (Mark 10:13-16), the preacher explains that Jesus was encouraging adults to cultivate childlike qualities (not childish ones; those are bad) in order to "receive the kingdom of God like a child."

The sermon highlights a few of these childlike characteristics (usually three). Children are "honest, trusting, and innocent" or "unspoiled, natural, and loving" or "candid, receptive, and obedient." There are many variations on the theme, but the sermon is the same.

I tired of this teaching long ago, after hearing this sermon for the tenth time. But I also began to suspect that something more serious was wrong with it when I realized that a number of quite different virtues were being extolled based on the text. I doubted that Jesus could have meant all those things.

A few minutes in the library revealed more than 40 such childlike attributes that had been cited in sermons on this text. And some of them seemed to me not very admirable. For instance, Alexander Maclaren included dependence, simplicity and docility as the "very emotions which Christianity requires" (*Expositions of Holy Scripture* [Hodder & Stoughton, n.d.], p. 72). I certainly wouldn't preach a sermon urging people to be dependent, simple and docile. Was Maclaren wrong? Or am I? Were other past pulpiteers wrong in making similar interpretations? And if they were, are not contemporary preachers subject to the same error—with this and other texts?

Most preachers do not purposely misinterpret their texts; they simply assume too much about them. Many pastors err in developing sermon ideas from common sense or popular piety rather than from the text. In this example, the preacher's fertile imagination and acculturation dictate a whole catalogue of virtues personified by the ideal child. But does the text really imply these?

Look at the reasoning process supporting the sermon: The preacher infers that Jesus didn't spell out what he meant by his reference to children because he didn't have to—he assumed that everyone knew. Thus the preacher must specify those childlike qualities for us in the sermon. Wanting not to repeat what others have said, he or she chooses some other childlike virtues that adults would do well to emulate.

The preacher is partially correct at this point—the congregation will acknowledge the suggested character traits as virtues to be cultivated (at least in the current time and place). The preacher is also right in thinking that Jesus didn't describe what he implied about children because he assumed that his hearers understood the implication of the analogy.

However, there is a flaw in this reasoning process. What everybody believed in first-century Palestine is *not* what everyone believes now—at least not on this subject. Their assumptions reflected *their* culture, not ours or Maclaren's. Jesus was not suggesting that children have virtues that adults should copy. Rather, Jesus was assuming that everyone knew children were "trivial," "weak" and "poor," "have no standing" and "come empty-handed like a beggar," as Hugh Anderson points out in *The Gospel of Mark* ([Oliphants, 1976], p. 246).

Anderson urges us not to see children as behavior models, but to see them as Jesus' contemporaries did: weak, insignificant and unimportant, like the other nobodies of this world to whom he consistently promised the Kingdom. The ancient world never praised children or considered them exemplary. Anderson points out that instruction to "cultivate . . . childlike qualities that earn the right of entry (or prepare us for the Kingdom) . . . runs counter to Jesus' teaching that the Kingdom is God's gracious gift."

And, of course, we know that's true; all through the Gospels Jesus says that the meek, lowly and poor inherit the kingdom. He tells the virtuous leaders of Israel that tax collectors and sinners will enter the kingdom before they do. We preach this from other texts; why is it so often missed in this passage?

It is not just a case of ignoring commentaries. The modern, seminary-trained preacher may very well be anxious for scholarly help—when the need for it arises. However, the need isn't always evident. The preacher might conclude that because there are no textual problems, difficult words, obscure references, or synoptic discrepancies, the meaning that leaps out to today's reader is Jesus' meaning. But changes in language and culture can mislead the unwary exegete.

This same kind of quick, unfounded assumption is also frequently made about other texts. For example, some sermons use the text about the woman caught in adultery (John 7:53-8:11) to tell us that the Lord forgives penitent sinners (which, of course, is true). But the preacher hasn't read the text carefully enough to see that it doesn't mention penitence or forgiveness. And the preacher may not have read the footnote that indicates that many early manuscripts did not even include the passage. Could it be that ancient Christians doubted its authenticity *because* they saw no penitence or forgiveness, and because the Lord seemed to have dismissed a flagrant sinner without punishment?

The problem with this sermon's exposition of the text isn't that cultural assumptions have changed since ancient times, but that the preacher has read a conclusion into the text, perhaps because of hearing other sermons say that the woman was "saved," or simply because popular piety expects Jesus to save every sinner he meets. At any rate, the preacher hasn't carefully read the text, or heeded the warning raised by the footnotes.

The sermon I hope never to hear again (but doubtless will) is any sermon in which the preacher assumes too much about the lesson, fails to study it carefully, and thereby misses much of its content by simply applying some supposedly related popular piety. The sermon I hope to hear more often uses "suffer the little children . . . " to challenge my affluence and status by explaining that Jesus is saying that it is nobodies and outsiders who enter the kingdom. I also hope to hear the sermon that helps me wrestle with *why* Jesus released the accused woman who hadn't repented—or any sermon in which the preacher seriously wrestles with the text and avoids the conventional piety I've heard often enough to question. After all, don't we all know that children are mischievous, selfish, and gullible, as well as trusting, honest and receptive?

PRACTICAL THEOLOGY: CHRISTIAN EDUCATION

Kenneth O. Gangel, area editor

CHRISTIAN EDUCATION

KENNETH O. GANGEL
Professor and Chairman of the Christian Education Department
Dallas Theological Seminary

Introduction

Issues, issues, issues! Political; moral; ethical; religious; educational! The church's practitioners have many more questions than answers. Are issues solved from the top down or from the bottom up? Are systematicians and philosophers eagerly providing a flood of solutions, or must those answers be sucked out of the knowing ones by the doing ones?

To illustrate from the field of medical ethics, do evangelical philosophers and theologians cheerfully initiate research on the current crises, or must Christian doctors and their harried pastors scream at the library, trying to get attention focused on something "that will preach?"

Happily, the clamor for answers in the fields of practical theology and Christian education may finally be calling forth the kind of article showing that someone really does live in the study carrels. At times those answers come from expected sources; at times we are surprised at the tables from which the crumbs fall.

I have not limited my search for "The Best in Christian Education" to predictable sources. In the 1987 edition of *The Best in Theology* I started the final countdown with the top 20 articles, but this year I was forced to start with the top 30. In doing this I found myself rejecting even from that large sampling several articles that another reviewer, turned theologically or philosophically in a slightly different direction, might have taken all the way to the top ten or even the final five.

The search has unveiled so much of value that I have described it in detail and also named those top 30 articles in a forthcoming issue of *Christian Education Journal*.

The following choices are, I believe, the five best articles in Christian education (and tangential issues of practical theology) that appeared approximately between July, 1986, and July, 1987.

They deal with issues. I have looked for articles on contemporary matters that take a sufficiently fresh and broad approach to produce better informed and equipped soldiers in the trenches.

Pastoral leadership remains a major issue for evangelicals. The world's largest Protestant denomination, the Southern Baptist Convention, finds itself mired in the struggle with the rest of us. Some churches wrestle with the imperial pastorate, others with the imperial board. But central to both problems is a biblical understanding of the foundations of leadership among the people of God.

The entire spring 1987 issue of the *Southwestern Journal of Theology* is devoted to the topic of ministerial authority. From that issue I have chosen the lead article by Franklin M. Segler (condensed here). From 30 years of pastoral ministry he gives us "Theological Foundations For Ministry." Of course, his references slant toward Nashville, but he is right when he says, "Leadership impacts upon the education of the *laos* of God in every area of kingdom work, in the religious education of 'unprofessional' ministers and in the higher education of 'unprofessional' ministers." And he is right to remind us of A. H. Strong's warning of over 70 years ago: "The natural tendency of every minister is to usurp authority and to become a bishop. He has in him an undeveloped pope. . . . The remedy for such arrogance lies in the constant recognition of Christ as the only Lord." Bleeding, board-beaten pastors (and there are plenty of them around) will find small comfort in Segler's work, but that makes his contribution no less important.

A further article of interest, recommended for further reading, deals with church administration and appears in the *Ashland Theological Journal*— "Motivational Components of Theory Z Management: An Integrative Review of Research and Implications for the Church" by M. E. Drushal (Spring 1987). Operating on the sound axiom that administration is a single science, Drushal reviews the traditional motivation theories of the industrial psychologists (Maslow, Herzberg, and McGregor) and then focuses nearly half the article on the potential of Theory Z (Ouchi, 1981) and its implications for the church. She concludes, "One can only speculate what might emerge if churches adopted a participative management philosophy. Perhaps, as Walton (1985) suggests, the organizational pyramid might be flattened with the result being more workers and fewer spectators in the church decision-making process." Hear, hear!

Recommended but not printed are three selections, very different from each other and yet all "issue" articles. One concerns the role of religion in the American public school system. Many have approached the subject politically, while others seek legal solutions. James E. Wood, Jr., writing in the *Journal of Church and State*, argues the issue philosophically by analyzing what has come to be called the religion of "secular humanism." Fundamentalists and right-wing politicians will chafe at Wood's approach and, to be sure, his concerns are hardly in line with biblicism. Nevertheless, the article takes a balanced approach to a genuine problem within a pluralistic society and complains that "much of the opposition to public school textbooks has been perpetrated by those who seek to Christianize the public schools, to make them more responsive to their sectarian religious views." Wood calls for public education to offer students textbooks that will show respect "for all religious beliefs" and pay "greater attention to the role of religion in the history of man and civilization." Readers must keep in mind that Wood approaches the elephant from only one side—this is a snapshot, not a video. The solution of Christian influence on the local level, the development and maintenance of sound Christian elementary and secondary schools, and the potential of home schooling are not the educational epithalamiums of this article.

We now move to *Concordia Theological Quarterly*, and the theology and polity of the Missouri Synod. Here we find a controversial article by Klemet Preus titled "Contemporary Christian Music: An Evaluation." You say you don't think contemporary Christian music is a hot button issue in the late '80s? To draw this conclusion one must be either retired, childless, or deaf. Preus aims his Lutheran arrow directly at the abecedarian theology of contemporary Christian music. Along the way he scans its offerings in five areas: the predicament of humanity, Jesus, coming to faith, the nature of faith, and the Christian life. He finds a heavy dose of emotion serving as veneer for synergism, cheap grace, and in some cases, slovenly constructed drivel.

Preus weakens his article at the conclusion by drawing lines, not between solid evangelical theology based on historic orthodoxy and what passes for theology in contemporary Christian music, but between what Lutherans would approve and what Baptists would approve. True, probably few Baptists would "implore God to bestow upon the airwaves music which promotes a sacramental theology," but certainly every genuine evangelical would want to "petition the Almighty to grace Christian bookstores with albums which give all glory to the Holy Spirit and the new birth," and "beseech our God to bless the top ten Christian songs with lyrics which present the vicarious atonement of Jesus." Preus criticizes Christian kitsch and I agree; but his conclusion drops the credibility of the article from an A- to a B+. Nevertheless, this issue must be dealt with and few other treatments even approach his thoroughness and clarity.

Associate professor and department chairman in Christian Education, James E. Plueddemann (Wheaton College) offers an article entitled "Metaphors in Christian Education" published in the Autumn, 1986, issue of *Christian Education Journal* (Volume VII, Number 1). His issue? The big picture; the broad battlefield; the massive mural impacted by this function and ministry we call "Christian Education." Plueddemann writes, "No task is more important than the task of Christian education. Yet, because the battle is a supernatural struggle between good and evil, few tasks are as difficult or have such a discouraging history. Certainly few tasks are as exciting as the task of renewal in Christian education." What will bring about renewal? According to Plueddemann, "understanding assumptions and values which underlie the reality of Christian teaching."

He proceeds then to offer his readers five metaphors of a teacher, one of a student and one of teachers and students together. A teacher, he tells us, is a salesperson, medical doctor, assembly line worker, farmer, and soccer coach; a student is a wildflower; and teachers and students together are pilgrims. It must be said that Plueddemann does not find the metaphors equally helpful and, indeed, finds each inadequate until he comes to the interdependent role of teachers and students as pilgrims, concerning which he writes, "The pilgrim metaphor helps us to understand the need for active integration between knowledge and experience, between the process and the destination. The metaphor helps us to see the teacher, Scripture, methods and curriculum from a fresh perspective."

About the Area Editor

Kenneth O. Gangel (M.Div., Grace Theological Seminary; M.A., Fuller Theological Seminary; S.T.M., Concordia Theological Seminary; Ph.D., University of Missouri at Kansas City) is professor and chairman of the Department of Christian Education at Dallas Theological Seminary. He is an ordained minister in the Christian and Missionary Alliance. He edited *Toward a Harmony of Faith and Learning* (1983), and has written *Unwrap Your Spiritual Gifts* (1983); and *Christian Education: Its History and Philosophy*, co-authored with Warren Benson (1982).

THEOLOGICAL FOUNDATIONS FOR MINISTRY

FRANKLIN M. SEGLER
Former Professor of Pastoral Ministries
Southwestern Baptist Theological Seminary

Article from *Southwestern Journal of Theology*

We live in a power-conscious world in which the concept of power is often distorted and perverted. This era of nuclear power and Star Wars tends to encourage a Rambo-like image of leadership. Many even seem to visualize a Rambo Christ whose mission is to destroy his enemies with a literal physical warfare.

These distortions of the biblical meaning of power and authority tend to affect leadership style in business, politics, and other institutions of society, including the church.

We want to believe that the church of our Lord is above such attitudes and practices. However, Christians are not free of the temptation to use power from self-seeking motives. The great sin of religion may be its presumption that our inherited traditions immunize us from the weaknesses and temptations of society in general.

We ministers/leaders are especially vulnerable to such temptations. The Baptist pastor-theologian A. H. Strong was aware of this in the latter part of the nineteenth century. He warned, "The natural tendency of every minister is to usurp authority and to become a bishop. He has in him an undeveloped pope. . . . The remedy for such arrogance lies in the constant recognition of Christ as the only Lord."[1]

A consultant to major business foundations and leading universities makes a general appeal for "servant-leadership."[2] He states, "We are becoming a nation dominated by large institutions—churches, businesses, governments, labor unions, universities."[3] He urged students to get inside these institutions, become a force for good, and lead them into better performance for the public good. He wrote:

> The *"servant-first"* will make sure that other persons' highest priority needs are being served. Do those being served grow as persons? Do they, while being served, become healthier, wiser, freer, more autonomous, more likely themselves to become servants?[4]

The Meaning of Ministry

Undoubtedly the phrase *"ministerial authority"* is an *oxymoron*, the combination of two ideas or terms that are incongruous or contradictory, such as

429

"sharp-foolish" or "humble-arrogant."[5] In ordinary language an oxymoron appears to be a self-contradiction.

Perhaps a better combination of terms such as "minister-leader" or "servant-leader" would be acceptable if properly understood. Such expressions are known as *paradoxical*, rather than oxymoronic. Paradoxical terms and ideas are found throughout the Bible and other literature. This indicates the inadequacy of language to express ultimate reality. Our theological language is full of paradox. For example, Jesus is spoken of as "God-man" and God as "immanent-transcendent." Such paradoxical terms must be kept in tension, so that, for example, "leadership" does not overshadow "servanthood."

The purpose of this article is to explore some of the biblical and theological foundations for understanding Christian leadership in the church and denomination, and, it is hoped, appeal to us all to examine our attitudes and style of leadership, to the end that we may together build up the whole body, the church, and thus bring honor to Christ who alone is our Servant-Leader.

The Meaning of Authority
Leadership is not synonomous with authority. "In a leadership relation the person is basic; in an authority relation the person is merely a symbol."[6] In biblical truth a person can never be considered a mere symbol.

Leadership encourages and inspires followship. Authority demands obedience. "Leadership is a species of influence; authority is a function of power."[7]

Supreme authority is vested in God alone. Every constituted authority is subordinate to this primary rule.[8] A rational person's obedience to God does not mean renouncing free agency. God respects the human will. True liberty and conformity to God's law are complementary. "Only when the unique Lordship of God (Christ) is acknowledged can man find the proper authority for life or death."[9]

There is a *pattern of authority* which all Christians must share in the church's ministry: the living Word, Christ; the written word, the Bible; the Holy Spirit as teacher and guide; the intellect or reason of the individual person enlightened by study and education; and the church as a fellowship of believers who find unity under the guidance of the Bible and the Holy Spirit.[10]

The early church learned that power can create or destroy. The power that demands ascendancy or control over other persons destroys. "It destroys relationships; it destroys trust; it destroys dialogue; it destroys integrity."[11]

Our limited understanding of ultimate truth may lead us to a faulty definition or conclusion concerning the meaning of authority in the use of power. The divine function of moral law is to bring us into obedience, but when it becomes an end in itself, the "demonic perversion called legalism rears its ugly head. These rules and regulations become rival gods holding us captive and demanding our total allegiance."[12] The thing that is meant to lead us to God does just the opposite.

Biblical Models for Ministry

The idea of "servant" is central in the divine economy of God's purpose to redeem his people. *Israel as a people* is called to be God's servant. They are to represent God to the world in his redemptive purpose.

The word "servant" ('*bd*) in the Old Testament properly means slave or bondservant (cf. N.T. *doulos*). In general the term implies a covenant relationship, an emotional bond that unites the two parties to a covenant of "steadfast love," "lovingkindness," or "mercy" (e.g. Psalm 103:4).[13] The servant is bound to his God Yahweh for life, even to the point of suffering and giving up his life for his Lord.

Moses is probably the outstanding Old Testament model of the servant-leader. In him we see how God dealt with his people on the human and on the divine level. God took Moses the man and made of him a "servant-leader" for his people.[14]

Moses was the essence of humanity. He had human limitations and emotions. He sometimes failed and at other times knew moments of triumph, enjoying the accolades of the multitudes. In it all he accepted his humanity and remained a humble servant of God.

Perhaps there is no more important Old Testament passage regarding the *Servant-Redeemer-Leader* than the servant poems in Isaiah. (See Isa. 42:1-4; 49:1-6; 50:4-9; 52:13-53:12.)

The closing poem (52:13-53:12) characterizes the "suffering servant of the Lord." The emphasis there is not on the prestige or power of the servant, but on his sacrificial and self-giving love. The suffering servant gives himself willingly, with no thought of gain for himself, but for the redemption of his people. He is acting under the purpose and order of Jehovah.[15]

In this passage the servant is one who fulfills his divine mission and is exalted in triumph by Jehovah.

> The suffering and triumph of the Servant has been called the highest rank in Old Testament revelation and the heart of the Old Testament. The author's primary concern is with the amazing triumph over suffering in fulfillment of God's purpose of redemption.[16]

Jesus' Teachings

The New Testament presents *Jesus* as the fulfillment of the *Suffering Servant.* Jesus interpreted his entire ministry in light of the role of Suffering Servant.[17]

In the teaching of his disciples Jesus emphasized serving as the fundamental quality of ministry. He pointed to himself as the *model* and *example*.[18] "I am among you as one who serves" (Lk. 22:27). Greatness in the ministry is accounted not in outward rank, but in proportion to service. Only for service is there promise of great reward.[19] (See Matt. 20:25-28; Mk. 10:42-

45; Lk. 22:24-27). "If anyone serves me, he must follow me . . . ; if anyone serves me, the Father will honor him" (John 12:26).

Following the Transfiguration, the disciples were living in the afterglow of a mountaintop spiritual experience. To their shame, they saw *visions of grandeur* and *places of honor* for themselves, rather than preparation for service. They were soon asking for the privilege of position with him in the Kingdom. Jesus set a child in their midst as an example of humility and simplicity of trust. He emphasized, "Whoever humbles himself like this child is the greatest in the kingdom of heaven" (Matt. 18:1-5).

Jesus warned his disciples not to model their ministry on the ministry of the Pharisees, who loved to be called Rabbi (Matt. 23:7). "This pride of status was an ever present temptation and failing among students of the Law."[20] Jesus expected them as his servants to follow the model of ministry which he provided.

The acid test of ministry is that of willing, humble service. Jesus asked his ambitious disciples, "Are you able to drink the cup I drink?" (Mk. 10:38). He then warned, " . . . the rulers of the Gentiles lord it over them . . . and exercise authority over them. Not so with you. . . . Whoever wants to be first must be slave of all. For even the Son of Man did not come to be served, but to serve, and to give his life a ransom for many" (Mk. 10:42-45).

Paul's Teachings

Among the human servant-leaders in the New Testament story, perhaps the Apostle Paul is the outstanding model. Although he never presents himself as an example personally, he does challenge, "Follow me as I follow the example of Christ" (1 Cor. 11:1).

Paul's favorite designation or description of himself as a minister of Christ is the term "servant" (slave or bond-servant: *doulos*). He is sold out to Christ; he belongs to Christ, body and soul. (See Rom. 1:1; Titus 1:1, for example.) Paul used another term ("under-rower," *huperetes*) designating himself as a servant of Christ. Under-rowers were lowly slaves aiding the ship's captain in any service needed. Paul and his fellow ministers were "servants of Christ entrusted with the secret things of God" (2 Cor. 4:1).

Why should the ministers take the *servant role*? "Because God does so. . . . God ministers in love to win man's response."[21] God chose Israel as a servant people. God came to minister in his Son. God continues to minister through his church. God gave gifts to all his people so that they might minister to one another. God called servant-leaders to equip and perfect his ministering people. Therefore, all Christians should resist "clericalism" wherever it appears.[22]

Paul exhorted church leaders "to prepare God's people for works of service (ministry, *diakonias*)" (Eph. 4:12). Leaders are charged to "perfect" (repair, prepare) for works of service (ministry), to the end that the church may be built up, unified, and perfected (led to maturity), in Christ.[23]

A Theology of Personhood

A columnist recently commented that the most amusing and humbling fact about man is that he can have an encyclopedic grasp of any subject he tackles and still possess little knowledge of himself. This is true regarding every person, even sincere committed Christians. We need a clear picture of the meaning of persons.[24]

Meaning of Persons

Paul was genuinely redeemed and sought to live in close communion with Christ through the Holy Spirit. However, he *refused to absolutize human knowledge*. He warned the early Christians against the gnostic philosophy which unduly exalted human knowledge. The knowledge of God in Christ supersedes the so-called wisdom (*gnosis*) of the gnostic cults. Paul came not to proclaim "words of wisdom," but simply to preach "Christ crucified" (1 Cor. 1:17-2:12).[25]

Modern ministers often tend to idolize rationalistic creeds, after the pattern of the gnostics, going beyond the bounds of the knowledge of faith in Christ revealed in the gospel (*kerygma*).[26]

Even in his misery Paul believed he could be victorious in the ministry of Christ. In answer to his own cry, "Who can save me from this deadly lower nature?" he declared, "Thank God, there is deliverance through Jesus Christ our Lord" (Rom. 7:24, 25). The great apostle also appealed to the real humanity of Jesus as the model and hope for our real humanity. (See Phil. 2:5-13.)

Encounter of Persons: "In-Christ" Experience

Paul's conversion was a life-transforming experience, clarifying all that he experienced from that time onward in his life and ministry. All his values were transformed, and this changed his purposes and objective. Conversion is more than an emotional experience. "Christian faith allies itself with reality, an active synthesis of fact and meaning."[27]

Redemption is an *incarnational encounter* with God in Christ. The incarnation meant not only that God took on flesh, but that human nature was raised to share in the life of God. "Redemption in Christ aims to remove all subterfuge, artificiality, fictitiousness, and counterfeit attempts at selfhood in order that . . . the genuine human existence to which we have been called might be brought into focus."[28]

When Paul said, "It is no longer I that lives," he did not relinquish his individuality or his responsibility for his decisions and actions. When we accept our real selves as forgiven and redeemed, we must accept responsibility for our choices as human selves in a real world. Acceptance of the salvation of our souls involves the acceptance of our bodies, our minds, our total humanity, including our strengths and our weaknesses.

The Christian servant is *a responsible self*, and responsibility requires honest interpretation of our responses and accountability for our actions.[29]

Divine immanence does not destroy or impair the distinctness of the human personality. Paul did not proclaim the end of *personal identity*. "I live, yet not I, but Christ lives in me" is immediately followed by the testimony, "The life I now live I live by the faith of the Son of God" (Gal. 2:20). "Christian experience does not depersonalize men and reduce them to a monotonous uniformity: it heightens every individual power they have."[30]

Incarnational ministry must be a servant ministry. It partakes of Christ's ministry, because the believer is a "new creature in Christ Jesus" (2 Cor. 5:17). A clear distinction is preserved between the individual and Christ. "Paul is never found saying, 'Christ is I, and I am Christ.' "[31]

Paul's theology grew out of his "in-Christ" experience. In this *Person-with-person Christ-experience* lies the key to understanding Paul's life and ministry and his writings that follow.[32] Because Paul belonged to Christ, his ministry belonged to Christ. His motives must be "the mind of Christ."

Ministers and other church leaders are often tempted to claim God's knowledge and power as their own. They confuse their own wills (what they desire) and the will of God. Pruyser writes, "Knowledge of God is always approximate and full of distortions. . . . The divine purpose is never completely known by mortals, and because of this they find themselves making guesses about it."[33] Sometimes they turn out to be "wild" guesses.

And all Christian servants are still subject to sin. Seward Hiltner reminded his fellow ministers, that unless the Christian acknowledges some ambiguity, "seeing through a glass darkly," either his sin is rejected with bigotry, or it is embraced without humility, and the consequence is zealotry. In either instance there is no growth toward maturity.[34] He further wrote, "In many respects, . . . the capacity to tolerate ambiguity is a kind of final mark of mental health."[35]

Formation for Ministry

A call to ministry is a call to preparation for ministry. All servant leaders are *first learners*. Jesus said, "If anyone would be my disciple (learner), let him deny himself, take up his cross (shared suffering, servanthood) and keep on following me" (Matt. 18:24). British theologian P. T. Forsyth once described the views of a fellow theologian as resembling "a bad photograph: overexposed and underdeveloped." All serious ministers need thorough training if they are to be good leaders of God's people.

Faith Commitment

Formation for ministry is based first of all on a *relationship to God*. The ultimate quest is Person-with-person relationship to Christ. A believer does not simply have faith in the truths uttered by him; he must have faith in him as a Person, as the living Word of truth. Our Lord declared, "I am the way, the truth, and the life. No one comes to the Father but by me' (John 14:6).

Growth Through Training

Formation for ministry involves commitment to a program of training that is well-rounded and thorough. A minister must have a holistic view of himself: physically, intellectually, emotionally, relationally, and spiritually.[36] It is unworthy and indefensible that any of us should be suspicious or envious of higher education.

A minister (servant/leader) in our modern society needs preparation not only for personal living but also for "professional" leadership. In a society where moral disintegration threatens life, there is danger that people will seek authority wherever they can find it. Theologian Don Browning warns, "This is the kind of social environment out of which dictators emerge."[37] Christian ministers who are thoroughly prepared in spirit and in "professional" leadership will not so easily be tempted to step into the gap and become authoritarian.

Competence is not synonomous with authority. Neither is charisma. Nor are they necessarily related to servant leadership. The humblest servant with limited competence may be the leader with the greatest influence.

Spiritual formation also demands commitment to truth that is more than mere tradition. A living tradition may be authoritative, but it must never become authoritarian in the sense that it demands acceptance without question. Tradition is never honored as an idol or an end in itself, but only as it points to him who is the Truth.[38]

The formation and practice of the Christian life must be learned through a commitment to discipline. He who would become mature enough to be a servant-leader must develop a method for spiritual discipline. Douglas Steere declared that the "authority" of an apostle or a saint does not come by reason of any inherited characteristics "either in physique, intelligence, will, emotion, psychological type, or abnormal faculty of mystical apprehension."[39] Authenticity of leadership does not spring from one's nature, cleverness, or the richness of one's fantasy life, but from "the character and ground of his being—ordered and simplified, so that the power and authority of God makes itself felt through him."[40]

There is a sense in which a minister needs "professional" training. Just as a scientist or a doctor or a business executive needs training in certain skills in order to be of genuine service to his fellow man, a minister needs specific skills for effective ministry. However, this training does not mean power for the minister. "He who stoops to wash the feet of his friends is powerless. His training and formation are meant to enable him to face his own weakness without fear and make it available to others. It is exactly that creative weakness that gives the ministry its momentum."[41]

Growth Through Fellowship

Along with a life of personal self-discipline, the minister's formation requires also the *guidance of fellow Christians*. Myron Madden reminded us that we cannot accept the painful contradictions and limitations within ourselves alone. The growing minister needs a "fellowship of other pilgrims who accept their contradictions and his, to become a 'means of grace,' to bring a blessing."[42]

In addition to private devotions, a minister in training needs the experience of a worshiping congregation. Besides the fellowship of a local church at worship, a college or seminary should be a worshiping community. In fact, the first discipline of a seminary education should be a study and *experience in worship*, because that is where the student is in his pilgrimage.[43] The "living experience of worship" is the beginning point of theology and life. Worship aids in the "mysterious process" of self-surrender and participation in the life of God.[44]

Worship, theology, and *life* are all involved in formation for ministry. When one's worship and theology are unified, one's ethical and moral commitment can be validated. He can then treat fellow human beings with love and respect.

The Nature of the Church and Servant Leadership

The church is nothing less than "the body of Christ, the organism to which he gives spiritual life."[45] As Christ is the Suffering Servant, so the church becomes the servant of society. The church shares in his ministry of binding up wounds, of suffering service, of healing. Bonhoeffer wrote from prison, "The Church is the church only when it exists for others. . . . The church must share in the secular problems of ordinary human life, not dominating, but helping and serving."[46]

Avery Dulles writes that the *servant ecclesiology* "seeks to give the church a new relevance, a new vitality, a new modernity, and a new sense of mission."[47] We must acknowledge limited understanding of the church. At the heart of the church we find mystery. In Christ are "unsearchable riches" (Eph. 3:8); in Christ dwells the whole fullness of God (Col. 3:9); and this fullness is disclosed only to those whose hearts are open to the Spirit who is from God (1 Cor. 2:12). Its life pertains to the mystery of Christ, and he is dynamically at work in the church through his Spirit.

The New Testament presents the church first as a *fellowship of persons* in Christ (*koinonia*), and, second, as a functioning institution (*ecclesia*), sharing this fellowship of Christ with all who believe. Paul wrote, "We are members of one another . . . because we are members of his body" (Eph. 4:25).[48]

The church is also God's people in history, his *church as institution* created, called out, and commissioned to be a servant people in the here and now. It is a visible, functioning organization of redeemed human beings dedicated to "flesh out" the gospel of love.

Let the church never yield to the temptation to become a hierarchical structure in society, attempting to wield authority, but always remain a servant people representing Christ and witnessing to him as Suffering Servant who died for all people.

The New Testament presents the church as a *priesthood of believers.* Jesus asked Peter, "What about you? Who do you say that I am?" Simon Peter answered, "You are the Christ, the Son of the living God" (Matt. 16:15-16). Each individual believes for himself and is his own priest before God.

Later Peter was to write, "You are a chosen people, a royal priesthood, a holy nation, a people belonging to God" (1 Pet. 2:9). The community as a whole was a priesthood, a people (*laos*) of God.

The priesthood of the believer means *individual privilege:* access to God, acceptance of forgiveness, reconciliation to God, and fellowship (*koinonia*) with the people of God. Along with the privilege goes *individual responsibility:* to offer spiritual sacrifices to God, to do good, and to live in fellowship (peace) with God's people.[49]

The priesthood of believers does not mean extreme or independent individualism, which is born of an inadequate view of Christian piety. Such individualism tends to be egocentric and insensitive to the rights of other persons. All members of the body are *mutually dependent*; they need one another. Reinhold Niebuhr warns, "Private religious experience may be a capricious 'wish-fulfillment'. It requires the discipline of the community of believers."[50]

A servant-leader who served as a pastor for many years wrote, "The church . . . with its intensely dominant and active minister and a passively supporting laity is not God's people in the world."[51] He continued, "Lay people must become the ministry of the church in the world. It is yours!"[52]

All of life is sacred, and all work is sacred with God. The Bible knows no distinction between the "sacred" and the "secular." Since every Christian is a priest, every Christian is also a minister. "The primary responsibility for God's ministry in the world rests upon the shoulders of the lay person, and not upon the shoulders of the clergy."[53]

All of God's people (laos) *are called of God:* to salvation in Christ, to a Christian life-style, and to Christian ministry. As Martin Luther declared, every person is called to serve God in his everyday work (vocation).[54]

"Lay" ministers, along with "professional" ministers, must take responsibility for their own beliefs, decisions, and actions in the ministry of their church. "Authority" for ministry rests with all the body of Christ. Mutual trust and mutual love are the basis for authentic ministry in the church and denomination.

Every Christian is a layman (a member among members) and also a minister among ministers. All are gifted individually and variously. The gifts and forms of ministry vary, but the ministry is essentially the same in relation to our model Jesus Christ.

In Ephesians 4:11 Paul speaks of God's spiritual gifts to all of his people. Some are *designated as leaders and equippers*, to the end that all the saints may be equipped or trained for the work of the ministry, so that the whole body may be built up in unity, in knowledge, and in maturity. "Unless the members have a full knowledge of Christ, they are at the mercy of those who practice deceit and cleverness in the context of error."[55]

In the New Testament church the leader was a *servant-leader*. Leadership was based on spiritual giftedness to render service, not on authority or "lordship." Wayne Oates wrote:

> The office of pastor is not "self-contained" or individualistic. Rather, it is a *symbolic office*, a representative of God, a reminder of Jesus Christ, an instrument of the Holy Spirit, and an emissary of a particular church.[56]

The priesthood of believers prohibits a priestly monopoly of God's grace by the "clergy." "On all fundamental matters the minister is only another 'believer' of the same rank with 'ministers' in the pews."[57] Herschel Hobbs recently wrote, "A New Testament Church is not a pastor-police state in which only the *pastor* has a 'hotline' to God's throne."[58]

Leadership in the church is essential. It is a position granted and given by the congregation of believers. It is a leadership of influence, based upon maturity in Christian character and practice. It neither asks nor needs any hierarchy of control or authority. Christlikeness in spirit and service inspire confidence and cooperation.

Like all other ministries in the church, leadership is to be a *shared ministry*, shared by "lay" ministers and "professional" ministers, within the congregation as a whole and within the church staff. Leadership and followship intertwine. Everyone is part leader, part follower. "Some servants are appointed to lead, to the end that all servants may become healthier, wiser, freer, more autonomous, and therefore, better servants who at times also are called upon to lead."[59]

Both leading and following require of all a common purpose and a clear definition of obligations. In such a fellowship, trust and cooperation are developed—a demonstration of faith at work. The church is the chief nurturer of servant-leaders in society. The aim of the church is not merely to enlist its laymen in its own services. The aim is "to put theological competents in the service of the world!"[60]

The classic New Testament passage on the task of pastors and other church leaders is found in Paul's challenge in Ephesians 4:11-12: "God gave some leaders . . . to prepare God's people for works of service, so that the body of Christ may be built up until we all reach unity in the faith . . . and become mature . . . in the fullness of Christ."

A servant-leader who has served as pastor-missionary-professor warns the church not to place the minister on a pedestal. Ministers are often tempted to believe that, because they are dealing with the "holy," that they themselves are therefore "holy." They tend to develop a "walk on water" syndrome. Because the people expect them to be miracle-workers, they try to live up to these expectations. Bratcher writes, "Ministers are not miracle-workers—they cannot walk on water, but they can learn to swim."[61]

In any church or denomination, the spin-off from this kind of institutionalism is *authoritarianism*. When this happens, ethical or doctrinal principles are enforced by prescription rather than by the power of the gospel, and the "resources of the church are drained off into the support of human prestige rather than the care for human need."[62]

The church of the New Testament recognized the need for designated or "professional" leaders. Jesus called and trained some to serve as apostles and in various other forms of leadership. Their calling does not differ in essence from the calling of "lay" leaders. It differs only in function or in the form of ministry. It was not a matter of position or power or authority, but of practical functioning of the entire body. It is always a servant-ministry.

The "clergy" or "professional" is not the *esse* (being, essence) of the church, but is intended to function as the *bene esse* (well being) of the church. The church is stronger and more effective because of the designated or appointed ministry, provided they are truly servant-leaders rather than authority-leaders.[63] The New Testament calls for the priestly ministry of all believers and for the priestly ministry of designated leaders.

It is not a question of power or authority, but of the practical functioning of the entire body. The pastor or other designated leader is a "representative" person within the church, and all members are equally under the authority of Christ. Christ is the only true Shepherd. Leaders are his "under-shepherds," servants of the flock.

The pastor or any other minister, including lay ministers, is given spiritual "authority" to serve under Christ. That is, an ambassador of Christ is under Christ's commission and authority. The implication is that other members of the body are commanded to support and follow the leadership of a given minister-leader. The servant spirit will be recognized and authenticated by the church. Every part of the body has need of every part of the body as they mutually carry out their assigned functions. Every member is part leader and part follower. (See 1 Cor. 12:17-30; Eph. 4:1-13.)

Implications of Servant Leadership for Mission

Leadership style affects every area of Christian mission—worship, preaching, education, polity, citizenship, and personal relationships. God calls for servant-ministers to lead his people in the fulfillment of their mission.

We are not competent to claim anything for ourselves, but our competence comes from God. Paul said, "He has made us competent as ministers of a new convenant—not of the letter, but of the Spirit; for the letter kills, but the Spirit gives life" (2 Cor. 3:5-6).

Servant leadership enables, persuades, encourages, and unites God's people (*laos*) to fulfill the mission to which he has called them. *Authority leadership* deceives, intimidates, denigrates, and divides God's people, thus hindering the free and willing ministry their giftedness could make possible.

In Worship

Worship, doctrine, and life are woven into a unified pattern for the church. Worship is the point of concentration at which the whole of the Christian life comes to focus. The church's entire existence is gathered up in the praise of God. From the experience of worship, the people depart with a "renewed vision of the value patterns of God's kingdom, by the more effective practice of which they intend to glorify God in their whole life."[64]

God requires genuine worship. True worshipers come to him in humble spirit, and they center upon truth and reality in their rituals (acts) of worship. Jesus declared that "God wants people to worship him in spirit and in truth." (See John 4:21-24.)

Worship is the dynamic that enables the church to be the church. "A service of worship is a deliberate and disciplined adventure in reality. In church, if anywhere, we are under moral bonds to be real."[65]

The Old Testament word *leitourgia*, from which we get our "liturgy" (our forms and procedures), literally means the "work" (plans and actions) which all the members do in their efforts to renew their experience with God. The New Testament church as a "holy priesthood" implies that every member is to offer "spiritual sacrifices to God." (See 1 Pet. 2:5; Rev. 1:6.)

The leader in worship, as a priest among priests, is designated to so plan and lead worship as to assist his fellow worshipers in their work (*leitourgia*) of worship. Paul instructed, "When you come together . . . with a hymn or a word of instruction, or a revelation, or an interpretation . . . all of these must be done for the strengthening of the church . . . worship should be done in a fitting and orderly way." (See 1 Cor. 14:26-40.)

Kierkegaard reminded his fellow worshipers that, when they come together for worship, the congregation are the performers, the leaders (ministers) are the prompters, and God is the audience and judge.[66]

The authority leader in worship is often tempted to try to usurp power that belongs only to God. With an "aura" of "charisma," he may seek to center attention upon himself with the result that God is ignored or obscured. The transcendence of God is thus minimized and his truth trivialized.

The servant leader leads the congregation to unite in praise and prayer to God. They pray "our Father" as equals, each as a priest for himself, and as priests on behalf of one another.

In Preaching

Preaching is the declaration of God's "Good News" of redemption in Christ. As Jesus stood to preach in the synagogue at Nazareth, he declared, "The Spirit of the Lord is upon me, because he has anointed me to preach good news to the poor . . . to proclaim release to the captives and recovery of sight to the blind, to set at liberty the oppressed, and to proclaim the acceptable year of the Lord" (Lk. 4:18).

In our preaching our words must remain completely human. "We must not try to appear more intelligent, more profound, more lucid, more decisive, more pious, more affectionate or more cultured than we really are. . . . To try to 'transubstantiate' our speech, in order to make it worthy of the Lord, both falsifies us and compromises the word of God."[67]

The sermon is an act of the church, not merely of the preacher. God's message was revealed and entrusted to the church. The preacher must proclaim the word on behalf of the congregation and not as if he is the only one who knows the truth. The church proclaims the gospel through her commissioned representatives. True proclamation depends primarily on the willingness of the congregation to hear and not on the preacher's eagerness to be heard.

The authority leader is under constant temptation to self-aggrandizement and the use of power in the pulpit. He thinks of himself as God's "prophet," "spokesman," "ambassador"! He can easily be deceived into thinking that his own word is the authority, that it is infallible. His use of pious and even ecstatic language, in order to exert power by means of emotional persuasion, may belie or undercut the word of God he is supposed to proclaim and exemplify. "Piety slips easily into piosity, which is a pretense at virtuousness and an exaggerated show of piousness."[68]

In preaching, the "medium" (spokesman) is not the message (*kerygma*). However, the medium should be a worthy transmitter; the less static and the less clouded the medium, the clearer the message.

The servant leader seeks to preach the whole gospel with a view of eliciting a free and thoughtful response on the part of the hearers. He seeks to enlighten, edify, and build up individuals and the body as a whole, to the end that they also may be models in life and ministry. John Claypool asks, "Why do we preach?" He answers, "Not to get something for ourselves, out of need-love, but to give something of ourselves in gift-love. . . . And we do it by making available as witnesses what we have learned from our own woundedness for the woundedness of others."[69]

In Polity and Administration

Church organizations and programs, at the local or worldwide level, are merely means that help shape polity and procedure in the work of God's kingdom. "Organization and polity are powerless. They are tools in the hands of God's servants."[70] Motivation and power for serving God and people are gifts of his Spirit to be used by his servant people.

In many instances, bureaucracy, whether in religion or government, tends to grow unnoticed until it becomes a threat to leadership and followship. It always constitutes a potential threat to democracy. "Against the idea of validity of the sovereign voice of the people, it represents the testimony of the expert. Up against experts, mere people are dilettantes."[71]

As presiding officer in church, association, state, or general convention, the authority leader is inclined to claim and exert power that is not rightfully his. Even sincere leaders may function out of limited understanding, prejudice, or emotional stress.

Authority leaders are inclined to instruct members of their churches on how to vote, thus violating the priesthood of believers and the democratic polity of church and denomination.

The authority leader may be unfair to those who oppose his views, thus limiting free and open discussion. Intimidation is sometimes used for the purpose of suppression. There is always the danger that those in power may become the persecutors instead of the persecuted. The inclination is to deride the "enemy" and to gloat over one's own "victory."

Leaders who think "more highly of themselves than they ought to think" may be tempted to claim always to know the "perfect will of God," thus deceiving themselves and others. Such a person is a questionable leader. If Paul perceived only "through a glass darkly," it is not likely that we will always see clearly. No individual or group can possess all knowledge. Diversity, within the limits of biblical truth, is essential for unity of spirit.

Authoritarianism, whether based on the extremism of egocentric personalities or on misguided and unfounded legalism, leads to disunity among God's people and makes it difficult, if not impossible, for the cooperative mission of Christ to be effective.

Christ is always working with *human agency*, and it remains human agency even under the best of circumstances. The fallibility, shortsightedness, and perversity of human nature is always present and must be considered.

Servant leadership is based first of all on Christian integrity. Lloyd Elder sees certain qualities of leadership essential for the successful functioning of denominational cooperation.

The servant leader shows a *team spirit* in mutual trust, respect, and participation; aids in the *tranformation of persons*, recognizing the potential in others and encouraging their moral and spiritual growth; possesses the *moral and ethical capacity* to function at authentic Christian levels of relationship; has *power to envision*, to dream dreams of higher purposes and accomplishments; *assumes responsibility* for trust building and inspiring cooperation of others for the sake of the renewal and growth of God's kingdom work.[72]

In Religious and Higher Education

Leadership impacts upon the education of the *laos* of God in every area of kingdom work, in the religious education of "unprofessional" ministers and in the higher education of "unprofessional" ministers. Christ gave high priority to the intellectual discipline of his followers.

Authoritarian leadership presumes to possess sufficient knowledge to properly indoctrinate followers in the essentials of the faith. This is deemed necessary for unquestioned followship.

The authority leader fears areas of knowledge that are not understood or that cannot be controlled. Historically such leaders have been especially suspicious of "higher education" among the "clergy." They have, therefore, sought to enforce uniformity of belief by discouraging research and wide reading in areas other than those which they have approved.

Those who build a creed on a selected teaching of the Bible or on a narrow segment of Christian theology become defensive about testing the belief by the wider expanse of truth. This often results in the attempt to suppress teachings which threaten the fixed doctrine. Such authoritarian views of education may result in the molding of creedal clones as ministers for our churches.

The servant leader, believing that man never discovers all of God's truth, seeks to promote freedom of thought and research. This allows for diversity of belief (within the bounds of revealed truth), an essential element of the priesthood of believers.

In Personhood and Personal Relationships

Leadership style affects most seriously and first of all personhood and personal relations. It can aid or hinder the growth and usefulness of the individual, both in leadership and in followship.

God's servant is called to have the mind of Christ, to cultivate the same attitudes he had toward the Father, toward himself, toward his fellow human beings, and toward his ministry of calling. (See Phil. 2:5-13; Rom. 12:1-2.)

The authority leader forfeits the high privilege of emulating Christ because of self-serving motives. What seems to be self-serving often becomes self-defeating.

Furthermore, the authority leader is often insensitive to his fellow Christians, especially when their views are different. Presuming one's self to be on the Lord's side, the other person becomes an "outsider" or even "the enemy." The opinions and feelings of the opponent are not deemed worthy of consideration. Too often "the little ones" are offended and hindered in their faith and growth in Christ.

Such a leader is blind to his own faults and limitations. He looks for the speck in the other person's eye while ignoring the beam in his own eye. Thus the growth of the leader and the would-be follower are both hindered, and both are losers. Furthermore, the fellowship of God's people is broken.

The servant leader considers right practice as important as right teaching. Right thinking and right living are one.[73] Such a leader believes that free diversity will cultivate more unity than forced conformity.

The servant leader is an authentic leader because of influence by example, because he acts out of genuine faith. The servant leader is one whose mind never stops growing, or examining, or loving.

"Servant-leaders often stand as a kind of saving remnant of those who care for both persons and institutions."[74] They constantly examine the assumptions they live by. Thus, their leadership by example sustains trust and inspires followership. The servant leader seeks to exemplify Christ and to "keep on pursuing things that make for peace and our mutual upbuilding" (Rom. 14:19, Williams).

Conclusion

Let us as servant-leaders and servant-followers, all ministers of Christ, pray and work for his kingdom to come and his will to be done on earth as it is in heaven, beginning in the church.

In our desire to understand and follow the teachings of God's Word and the prompting of God's Spirit, let us be guided by a "theology of the cross" rather than a "theology of glory."[75] Let us learn to serve out of weakness, rather than out of personal strength. Paul acknowledged, "When I am weak, then I am strong" (2 Cor. 12:7-10).

Notes

[1] *Systematic Theology* (Philadelphia: Judson Press, 1906), p. 882.

[2] Robert K. Greenleaf, *Servant Leadership: A Journey into the Nature of Legitimate Power and Greatness* (New York: Paulist Press, 1977).

[3] Ibid., p. 1.

[4] Ibid., pp. 13-14.

[5] *Webster's New International Dictionary of the English Language*, 2nd Edition Unabridged (Springfield, Mass.: G. C. Merriam and Co., 1952), p. 1747.

[6] Robert Bierstedt, "The Problem of Authority," *The Study of Leadership*, vol. 1, U.S. Military Academy (West Point), Office of Psychology of Leadership, AY1972-73, pp. 13-15.

[7] Ibid., pp. 13-16.

[8] Carl F. H. Henry, ed., *Baker's Dictionary of Christian Ethics* (Grand Rapids: Baker Book House, 1973), p. 47.

[9] Ibid., p. 48. See also P. T. Forsyth, *The Principle of Authority* (London: 1912, Reprint, Haperville, Ill., Allenson, 1952).

[10] Bernard Ramm, *The Pattern of Authority* (Grand Rapids, Mich.: Wm. B. Eerdmans Publishing Co., 1957).

[11] Richard J. Foster, *Money, Sex and Power* (San Francisco: Harper & Row, 1985), p. 175.

[12] Ibid., p. 187.

[13] George A. Buttrick, ed., *The Interpreter's Dictionary of the Bible* (New York: Abingdon Press, 1962), p. 292.

[14] J. Kenneth Eakins, "Moses," *Review and Expositor*, vol. 74, no. 4, Fall, 1977, p. 468.

[15] Franz Delitzsch, *Commentary on Isaiah*, vol. 2, ed. Robertson Nicoll (New York: Funk & Wagnalls, n.d.), p. 301.

[16] *The Broadman Bible Commentary*, vol. 5 (Nashville: Broadman Press, 1971), p. 341.

[17] Frank Stagg, *New Testament Theology* (Nashville: Broadman Press, 1962), pp. 51ff.

[18] *Interpreter's Dictionary of the Bible*, vol. 3, p. 366.

[19] Ibid., p. 386.

[20] Maston, p. 49.

[21] Paul M. Miller, *Servant of God's Servants: The Work of a Christian Minister* (Scottdale, Penn.: Herald Press, 1964), p. 9.

[22] Ibid., p. 34.

[23] A. T. Robertson, *Word Pictures in the New Testament*, vol. 4 (New York: Harper & Bros., 1931), p. 537.

[24] Paul Tournier, *The Meaning of Persons* (New York: Harper & Bros., 1957).

[25] James Moffatt, *The Moffatt N.T. Commentary, The First Epistle of Paul to the Corinthians* (New York: Harper & Bros., n.d.), pp. 13-32.

[26] Kenneth Hamilton, *To Turn From Idols* (Grand Rapids: Wm. B. Eerdmans Publishing Co., 1973), pp. 14-15.

[27] Andre Godin, *The Psychological Dynamics of Religious Experience* (Birmingham, Ala: Religious Education Press, 1985).

[28] Wayne Oates, *Christ and Selfhood* (New York: Associates Press, 1961), p. 249.

[29] H. Richard Niebuhr, *The Responsible Self* (New York: Harper & Bros., 1963) Wayne Oates, "Qualities of Leadership," *Southwestern Journal of Theology*, this issue.

[30] James S. Stewart, *A Man in Christ, The Vital Elements of Paul's Religion* (New York: Harper & Bros., n.d.), p. 167.

[31] Wayne Oates, op. cit., p. 128.

[32] Franklin M. Segler, "Paul's Christian Experience the Basis of His Theology" (Th.D. thesis, Southwestern Baptist Theological Seminary, 1945).

[33] Paul W. Pruyser, *A Dynamic Psychology of Religion* (New York: Harper & Row, 1968), p. 8.

[34] Seward Hiltner, *Preface to Pastoral Theology* (New York: Abingdon, 1958), p. 180.

[35] Seward Hiltner, *Ferment in the Ministry* (Nashville: Abingdon, 1958), p. 35.

[36] Gary L. Harbaugh, *Pastor as Person: Maintaining Personal Integrity in the Choices and Challenges of Ministry* (Minneapolis: Augsburg, 1984). See also *Formation for Christian Ministry*, ed. Anne Davis and Wade Rowatt, Jr. (Louisville: Review and Expositor, Pub., 1981).

[37] Don Browning, *The Moral Context of Pastoral Care* (Philadelphia: Westminster, 1976), p. 129.

[38] Kenneth Hamilton, p. 144.

[39] Douglas V. Steere, *On Beginning From Within* (New York: Harper & Bros., 1943), p. 35.

[40] Ibid., p. 36.

[41] Henri J. M. Nouwen, *Creative Ministry* (Garden City, New York: Doubleday & Co., 1978), p. 113.

[42] Myron Madden, *The Power to Bless* (Nashville: Abingdon, 1970), pp. 84ff.

[43] Geoffrey Wainwright, *Doxology: The Praise of God in Worship, Doctrine, and Life* (New York: Oxford University Press, 1980), p. 2.

[44] Ibid., p. 12.

[45] A. H. Strong, p. 882.

[46] Dietrich Bonhoeffer, *Letters From Prison* (New York: Macmillan, 1967), pp. 203-4.

[47] Avery Dulles, *Models of the Church* (Garden City, New York: Doubleday & Co., 1974), pp. 8-9.

[48] Franklin M. Segler, *A Theology of Church and Ministry* (Nashville: Broadman Press, 1960), pp 3ff.

[49] Naylor, op. cit.

[50] Op. cit., p. 228.

[51] Carlyle Marney, *Priests to Each Other* (Valley Forge, Penn.: Judson Press, 1974), p. 14.

[52] Ibid.

[53] Findley B. Edge, *The Doctrine of the Laity* (Nashville: Convention Press, 1985), p. 45.

[54] Franklin M. Segler, *The Christian Layman* (Nashville: Broadman Press, 1964), pp. 35ff.

[55] A. T. Robertson, *Word Pictures in the New Testament*, vol. 4, (New York: Harper & Bros., 1931), p. 538.

[56] Wayne Oates, *The Christian Pastor* (Philadelphia: Westminster Press, 1951), pp. 26ff.

[57] James Hastings Nichols, *A Short Primer for Protestants* (New York: Association Press, 1957), p. 76.

[58] Herschel H. Hobbs, *Studying Adult Life and Work Lessons, April, May, June 1986* (Nashville: Convention Press, 1985), p. 115.

[59] Greenleaf, op. cit., pp. 240ff.

[60] Marney, p. 14.

[61] Edward B. Bratcher, *The Walk on Water Syndrome* (Waco, Texas: Word Books, 1984), p. 11.

[62] Oswald J. Hoffmann, "Laity," in *Baker's Dictionary of Christian Ethics*, ed. Carl F. H. Henry (Grand Rapids: Baker Book House, 1973), p. 377.

[63] William B. Oglesby, Jr., "Lay Pastoral Care Revisited," *The Journal of Pastoral Care*, vol. 40, no. 2, (June 1986), p. 119.

[64] Wainwright, p. 8.

[65] Willard L. Sperry, *Reality in Worship* (New York: Macmillan Co., 1925), p. 206.

[66] Soren Kierkegaard, *Purity of Heart: Is to Will One Thing* (New York: Harper & Bros., 1938), pp. 163-64.

[67] Jean-Jacques Von Allmen, *Preaching and Congregation* (Richmond: John Knox Press, 1962), pp. 13-14.

[68] Paul W. Pruyser, *A Dynamic Psychology of Religion*, p. 127.

[69] John R. Claypool, *The Preaching Event* (Waco: Word Publishers, 1980), p. 136.

[70] James L. Sullivan, *Baptist Polity As I See It* (Nashville: Broadman Press, 1983), p. 230.

[71] James B. McKee, "The Formal Organization," *The Study of Leadership*, vol. 2, U.S. Military Academy, pp. 22-26.

[72] Lloyd Elder, *Blueprints* (Nashville: Broadman Press, 1984), pp. 120-6.

[73] Walter B. Shurden, *Not a Silent People* (Nashville: Broadman Press, 1972), p. 101.

[74] Greenleaf, p. 329.

[75] Martin Luther, "Heidelberg Disputation" (1518), art. 21, trans. Harold J. Grimm, in *Luther's Works*, vol. 31: *Career of the Reformer,* no. 1 (Philadelphia: Muhlenberg Press, 1957), p. 53.

ABOUT THE AUTHORS

HAROLD J. BERMAN (B.A., Dartmouth; M.A., LL.B., Yale University) is Woodruff Professor of Law at Emory University. He is also James Barr Ames Professor of Law Emeritus at Harvard University, where he taught from 1948 to 1985. He is co-founder and member of the editorial board of *Journal of Law and Religion*. Among his books are *Law and Revolution: The Formation of the Western Legal Tradition* (1983), and *The Interaction of Law and Religion* (1974).

CRAIG L. BLOMBERG (B.A., Augustana College [Ill.]); M.A., Trinity Evangelical Divinity School; Ph.D., University of Aberdeen) is assistant professor of New Testament, Denver Seminary. He was ordained by the Southern Baptist Convention. He is author of *The Historical Reliability of the Gospels* (IVP, 1987). With David Wenham he is co-editor of *Gospel Perspectives, Vol. 6: The Miracles of Jesus* (JSOT Press, 1986).

MELINDA LAWRENCE DENHAM (B.S., Mississippi College; J.D., Mississippi College of Law) is attorney at law with Gordon, Silberman, Wiggins, and Childs, P.C., in Birmingham, Ala. She writes a Legal Concerns column for Alabama Association for Marriage and Family Therapy *News Letter*.

THOMAS E. DENHAM (B.A., Mississippi College; M.Div., Southern Baptist Theological Seminary; Certificate, Pastoral Care, University of Mississippi Medical Center; Certificate, Pastoral Counseling, Baptist Medical Centers [Birmingham, Ala.]) is coordinator and pastoral counselor, Baptist Medical Centers of Birmingham, serving at the Pastoral Counseling Center in Forestdale and in Prattville. He has been ordained by the Southern Baptist Convention and is assistant editor of *Journal of Religion and Aging*.

HUGH FEISS, O.S.B.(B.A., M.A., M.Div., Mount Angel Seminary; S.T.L., Ph.L., Catholic University of America; S.T.D., Anselmianum [Rome]; M.A., University of Iowa) is professor of theology and humanities, Mount Angel Seminary (St. Benedict, Ore.), and director, Mount Angel Abbey Library. He has been ordained by the Roman Catholic Church, and is a specialist in Hugh and Richard of St. Victor (12th century), and in medieval spirituality. He is co-author of *Mount of Communion, Mount Angel Abbey (1882-1982)* (1982). He is also translator and editor of *The Life of Marie d'Oignies. Supplement by Thomas de Camtempre* (1987).

GARY B. FERNGREN (Ph.D., University of British Columbia) is professor of history at Oregon State University. He has published extensively on the social history of medicine and the history of medical ethics, including chap-

447

ters (co-authored with Darrel W. Amundsen) in *Health/Medicine and the Faith Traditions*, ed. Martin Marty and Kenneth L. Vaux (1982).

GARY A. HERION (B.A., University of North Carolina; Ph.D., University of Michigan [ancient and biblical studies]) is adjunct assistant professor, Program on Studies in Religion, University of Michigan. He is affiliated with the Evangelical Lutheran Church of America.

PAUL G. HIEBERT (B.A., Tabor College; M.A., Mennonite Brethren Biblical Seminary; M.A., University of Minnesota [anthropology]) is professor of mission anthropology and South Asian studies, School of World Mission, Fuller Theological Seminary. He has been ordained by the Mennonite Brethren Church of North America. After having grown up in India as the child of missionaries, he later became a missionary there (1960-66), and was Fulbright Professor at Osmania University. Recent books include *Case Studies in Missions* (Baker, 1987) with Frances Hiebert, and *Anthropological Insights for Missionaries* (Baker, 1985).

LAWRENCE E. KEYES (M.Div., Talbot Theological Seminary; D.Miss., Fuller Theological Seminary) is president of Overseas Crusades, Inc. He has been ordained by the Conservative Christian Congregational Church and served as a missionary in Brazil for eleven years with Overseas Crusades. He is a member of the board of Evangelical Foreign Missions Association. He has written *The Last Age of Missions* (William Carey Library, 1981).

THOMAS G. LONG (B.A., Erskine College; M.Div., Erskine Theological Seminary; Ph.D., Princeton Theological Seminary) is Francis Landy Patton Associate Professor of Preaching and Worship, Princeton Theological Seminary. He is a minister in the Presbyterian Church (USA). He has written *Shepherds and Bathrobes* (1987) and *God's Family at the Table* (1981). He is co-editor, *Journal for Preachers*, general preaching editor, *Homiletic*, and is on the editorial council of *Theology Today*.

TREMPER LONGMAN III (B.A., Ohio Wesleyan University; M.Div., Westminster Theological Seminary; M. Phil., Ph.D., Yale University) is associate professor of Old Testament, Westminster Theological Seminary. He is a member of the Orthodox Presbyterian Church. His books include *Literary Approaches to Biblical Interpretation* (Zondervan, 1987). He has published articles in *Biblica* and the *Revue d'Assyriologique*, among others. *How to Read the Psalms* is forthcoming from IVP.

JOHN D. MASON (B.A., Kalamazoo College [economics]; Ph.D., Michigan State University [economics]) is professor of economics and chairman of the economics and business department at Gordon College. He was a board member and sometime president of Emmanuel Gospel Center (Boston) for about fifteen years.

DONN F. MORGAN (B.A., Oberlin College; B.D., Yale Divinity School; M.A., Ph.D., Claremont Graduate School) is professor of Old Testament and dean of academic affairs at Church Divinity School of the Pacific. He is affiliated with the Episcopal Church. Books include *Wisdom in the Old Testament Traditions* (John Knox, 1981), and he is co-editor of *Ras Shamra Parallels* (1972).

MARVIN R. O'CONNELL (Ph.D., University of Notre Dame [history]) is professor of history at Notre Dame. He is ordained in the Roman Catholic Church. He has written books on the Counter Reformation, Religion in Elizabethan England, and the Oxford Movement, as well as a novel. He also edited a 10-volume *History of the Church* for teenagers. His biography of John Ireland is forthcoming.

LARRY D. PATE (B.S., Bethany Bible College [pastoral theology]; M.A., Assemblies of God Theological Seminary [missiology]) is coordinator of emerging missions, International Ministry Team, Overseas Crusades. He is pursuing a D.Miss. degree at Fuller Theological Seminary and has been ordained by the Assemblies of God. 1974-80 he was a missionary to Bangladesh. Recent books include *Misionologia: Nuestro Cometido Transcultural* (Miami, Editorial Vida, 1987), and *Starting New Churches* (International Correspondence Institute, Brussels, 1984). He also edited *Baibel Bishoe Nirdeshika* (AOG Press, Calcutta, 1980); this is a topical concordance in Bengali.

FRANKLIN M. SEGLER (B.A., Oklahoma Baptist University; Th.M., Th.D., Southwestern Baptist Theological Seminary; post-graduate study at Union Theological Seminary, Boston University School of Theology, Harvard Divinity School, and Andover Newton Theological School) is professor of Pastoral Ministry, Emeritus, at Southwestern Baptist Theological Seminary. He is an ordained Baptist minister. Some of his books are: *Alive and Past 65* (Broadman, 1975); *Your Emotion and Your Faith* (Broadman, 1970); and *Christian Worship: Its Theology and Practice* (Broadman, 1967).

RALPH L. UNDERWOOD (B.A., Bluffton College; B.D., Asbury Theological Seminary; Ph.D., University of Chicago) is professor of pastoral care, Austin Presbyterian Theological Seminary, and is an ordained United Methodist. His most recent book is *Empathy and Confrontation in Pastoral Care* (Fortress, 1985).

BRUCE A. WARE (B.A., Whitworth College; M.Div., Th.M., Western Seminary; M.A., University of Washington [philosophy]; Ph.D., Fuller Theological Seminary), is assistant professor of systematic theology, Western Seminary (Portland). He is affiliated with the Conservative Baptist Association. He has been involved in summer short-term missions to Madagascar and to Australia/ New Zealand.

RICHARD C. WHITE (A.B., Transylvania University; B.D., College of the Bible [now Lexington Theological Seminary], Ph.D., University of Kentucky) is professor of homiletics, Lexington Theological Seminary. He has been ordained by the Disciples of Christ. His most recent book is *Biblical Preaching* (CBP Press, 1988).

LAURENCE W. WOOD (B.A., Asbury College; B.D., Asbury Theological Seminary; Th.M., Christian Theological Seminary; Ph.D., University of Edinburgh) is professor of systematic theology, Asbury Theological Seminary. He is an ordained elder in the United Methodist Church. He has written *Pentecostal Grace* (Francis Asbury, 1980) and various scholarly reviews, and has contributed to *The Beacon Dictionary of Theology* and *A Celebration of Ministry*. He is editor of *Asbury Theological Journal*.

N. THOMAS WRIGHT (B.A. [philosophy and ancient history], B.A. [theology] and D.Phil. [Pauline theology], Oxford University), is university lecturer in New Testament, Oxford University, and Fellow, tutor in theology, and chaplain, Worcester College, Oxford University. He is a citizen of the United Kingdom and is an ordained priest in the Church of England. His most recent book is *Colossians and Philemon* (Tyndale, U.K./Eerdmans, U.S.A., 1987). A forthcoming book, written with Stephen Neill, is *The Interpretation of the New Testament 1861-1986* (Oxford). He has also edited *The Glory of Christ in the New Testament* (Oxford, forthcoming).

ACKNOWLEDGMENTS

Harold J. Berman. "Religion and Law: The First Amendment in Historical Perspective." *CLS Quarterly* (Spring 1987): 6-12. Reprinted by permission of the author. This article originally appeared, with footnotes, in *Emory Law Journal* 35 (Fall 1986): 1-17.

Craig L. Blomberg. "Synoptic Studies: Some Recent Methodological Developments and Debates." *Themelios* 12 (January 1987): 38-46. Reprinted by permission. *Themelios* is an international journal for theological students, expounding and defending the historic Christian faith. It is published three times a year by the Theological Students Fellowship, a constituent part of the Universities and Colleges Christian Fellowship, and the International Fellowship of Evangelical Students. It seeks to address itself to questions being faced by the theological students in their studies and to help readers to think out a clear and biblical faith. It may be ordered from UCCF, 38 De Montfort Street, Leicester, LE1 7GP, England.

Thomas E. and Melinda L. Denham. "Avoiding Malpractice Suits in Pastoral Counseling." *Pastoral Psychology* (Winter 1986): 83-93. Reprinted by permission of the publisher, Human Sciences Press.

Hugh Feiss, O.S.B. "Rethinking the Mystical: A Roman Catholic Perspective." *Word & World* 7 (Spring 1987): 141-47. Reprinted by permission.

Gary B. Ferngren. "Caring and Curing: The Roman Catholic Tradition Since 1545." Chapter 18 in the book *Caring and Curing: Health and Medicine in the Western Religious Traditions* (New York: Macmillan, 1986), Ronald L. Numbers and Darrel W. Amundsen, editors. Reprinted by permission.

Gary A. Herion. "The Impact of Modern and Social Science Assumptions on the Reconstruction of Israelite History." *Journal for the Study of the Old Testament* 34 (1986): 3-33. Reprinted by permission.

Paul G. Hiebert. "Critical Contextualization." Copyright 11/3 (1987): 104-112, by *International Bulletin of Missionary Research*, New Haven, CT. Reprinted by permission.

"Instruction on Respect for Human Life in Its Origin and on the Dignity of Procreation." Prepared by Congregation for the Doctrine of the Faith. Joseph Cardinal Ratzinger, Prefect; Alberto Bovone, Titular Archbishop of Caesarea in Numidia, Secretary. 1987. Used by permission.

Thomas G. Long. "Pawn to King Four: Sermon Introductions and Communicational Design." *Reformed Review* 40/1 (Autumn 1986): 27-35. Reprinted by permission.

Tremper Longman III. "The Literary Approach to the Study of the Old Testament: Promise and Pitfalls." *JETS* 28 (December 1985; appeared September 1986): 385-98. Reprinted by permission.

John D. Mason. "Biblical Teaching and Assisting the Poor." *Transformation* 4 (April/June 1987): 1-14. Reprinted by permission.

Donn F. Morgan. "Canon and Criticism: Method or Madness?" *Anglican Theological Review* 68/2 (1986): 83-94. Reprinted by permission.

Marvin R. O'Connell. "Caring and Curing: The Roman Catholic Tradition Since 1545." Chapter 4 in the book *Caring and Curing: Health and Medicine in the Western Religious Traditions* (New York: Macmillan, 1986), Ronald L. Numbers and Darrel W. Amundsen, editors. Reprinted by permission.

Larry D. Pate with Lawrence E. Keyes. "Emerging Missions in a Global Church." *International Bulletin of Missionary Research* 10/4 (1986): 156-61. Reprinted by permission.

Franklin M. Segler. "Theological Foundations for Ministry." *Southwestern Journal of Theology* 29/2 (Spring 1987): 5-18. Condensed and used by permission of the author and publisher.

Ralph L. Underwood. "The Presence and Absence of God in Object Relational and Theological Perspectives." *Journal of Psychology and Theology* 14/4 (1986): 298-305. Reprinted by permission.

Bruce A. Ware. "An Evangelical Reformulation of the Doctrine of the Immutability of God." *Journal of the Evangelical Theological Society* 29 (1986): 431-46. Reprinted by permission.

Richard C. White. "Preaching Between the Lines." *The Christian Ministry* (September 1986): 14-15. Reprinted by permission.

Laurence W. Wood. "Recent Brain Research and the Mind-Body Dilemma." This article first appeared in the *Asbury Theological Journal* 41/1 (Spring 1986): 37-78. Used by permission.

N. T. Wright. "ἁρπαγμός and the Meaning of Philippians 2:5-11." *Journal of Theological Studies* 37 (October 1986): 321-52. Reprinted by permission.